Ubuntu® Linux®
Bible

William von Hagen

BICENTENNIAL
1807
WILEY
2007
BICENTENNIAL

Wiley Publishing, Inc.

Ubuntu® Linux® Bible

Published by
Wiley Publishing, Inc.
10475 Crosspoint Boulevard
Indianapolis, IN 46256
www.wiley.com

Copyright © 2007 by Wiley Publishing, Inc., Indianapolis, Indiana

Published simultaneously in Canada

ISBN-13: 978-0-470-03899-4
ISBN-10: 0-470-03899-3

Manufactured in the United States of America

10 9 8 7 6 5 4 3

1B/RU/RS/QW/IN

To Dorothy, for more than words can say . . .

Quidquid latine dictum sit, altum sonatur.

About the Author

William von Hagen (Bill) has been a Unix system administrator for over twenty years, and a Linux fanatic since the early 1990s. He has worked as a Linux product manager, systems programmer, system administrator, writer, application developer, drummer, and content manager. Bill has written or co-written books on such topics as Linux Server Hacks, Linux Filesystems, SUSE Linux, Red Hat Linux, GCC, SGML, Mac OS X, and Hacking the TiVo. He has also written numerous articles on Linux, embedded computing, Mac OS X, Unix, and various Open Source topics. An avid computer collector specializing in workstations, he owns more than 200 computer systems but is not compulsive at all. You can reach him at vonhagen@vonhagen.org.

Credits

Executive Editor
Carol Long

Senior Development Editor
Tom Dinse

Copy Editor
Mildred Sanchez

Editorial Manager
Mary Beth Wakefield

Production Manager
Tim Tate

Vice President and Executive Group Publisher
Richard Swadley

Vice President and Executive Publisher
Joseph B. Wikert

Project Coordinator
Erin Smith

Graphics and Production Specialists
Claudia Bell
Carrie A. Foster
Barbara Moore
Rashell Smith

Quality Control Technician
David Faust

Proofreading and Indexing
Richard T. Evans, Techbooks

Anniversary Logo Design
Richard Pacifico

Contents at a Glance

Part IV: Configuring Servers on Ubuntu

Contents

Part II: Ubuntu for Desktop Users

Contents

Contents

Contents

Acknowledgments

Nothing I have ever written would have been possible without the love, support, and infinite patience of Dorothy Fisher, my wife and best friend. Dorth believed in me on day one, removed several thousand commas from my earliest writing, and has accepted "I can't do that now—come back in fifteen minutes or six hours" as an excuse more times than anyone should ever be expected to. I am similarly lucky to have great friends like Jeff "Sunshine" Kaminski, Dr. Joe O'Lear, Jim Morgan, and Kim Walter in my life. I heard once that a good friend will come and bail you out of jail, but a true friend will be sitting in jail with you saying, "Man! That was fun!" Luckily, we haven't had to test that, but I'm sure we'd all look great in orange.

I would also like to thank Carol Long, Tom Dinse, Kit Kemper, and others at Wiley who enabled me to do this book and supported me during its creation. All errors are mine alone, but this would be a much weaker book without your contributions. I quite literally wouldn't have been able to do it without you.

Finally, this book wouldn't even exist without people like Linus Torvalds, Mark Shuttleworth, the Ubuntu folks in general, the Debian Project, Richard Stallman, the FSF, and the millions of contributors to the cornucopia that is GNU/Linux.

Introduction

A Linux distribution is basically the sum of the things that you need to run Linux on your computer. There are many different Linux distributions, each with their own target audience, set of features, administrative tools, and fan club, the latter of which is more properly known as a user community. Putting aside the downright fanatics, most of the members of the user community for any Linux distribution are people who just happen to find themselves using a distribution for one reason or another. These reasons range from what they've heard from friends, what CD or DVD came with a Linux magazine that they bought, to what Linux book they happened to buy.

Ubuntu Linux is the most exciting Linux distribution in years. Ironically, while Ubuntu itself is indeed new, it also comes with a respectable Linux pedigree. Ubuntu has direct roots in one of the oldest and best-known Linux distributions available, the Debian GNU/Linux distribution. The folks who initially created and supported Ubuntu, Canonical Ltd., started out as Debian fans who wanted a faster-moving, more up-to-date distribution than Debian provided. So, in the spirit of Linux and the Open Source movement, they made their own distribution, Ubuntu Linux, by incorporating the best of Debian, other Linux distributions and open source applications, and added their own special sauce.

Ubuntu means "humanity to others." For the people who use and bring you Ubuntu Linux, this is not just a name with touchy-feely overtones. The special sauce in Ubuntu is a social and business commitment to Ubuntu users everywhere. Ubuntu releases occur regularly, every six months, and support and updates for any Ubuntu release are available for a minimum of eighteen months after that. More about that it in the first chapter, where you'll read more about Ubuntu, its philosophy, its community, and why the sum of those makes Ubuntu different than any other Linux distribution.

In a nutshell, Ubuntu is a Linux distribution for people. While reading this book, you'll see that there are plenty of excellent technical reasons for using Ubuntu, even if you're a hard-core Linux propeller head. However, that's not the point of Ubuntu—Ubuntu is for people who want to use their computers and need a solid software foundation for doing so. Whether your focus is on writing code or surfing the Web, sending and receiving electronic mail, working with your digital photographs, watching DVDs, listening to music, and so on, Ubuntu offers the software that you need to do what you want to do.

Like any Linux distribution, you can freely download and install Ubuntu, but it gets even better. This book includes a CD of the latest Ubuntu Desktop CD at the time this book was published, but new versions may be available by the time you buy the book. If you don't have access to a CD burner, need a version of Ubuntu for a non-x86 system, or simply don't have the time, the Ubuntu folks will send you CDs that you can either use to install or test-drive Ubuntu on your current computer system. That's more than free—it's revolutionary! Downloadable copies of Linux distributions are nothing new, but sending people physical CDs if they need them shows that Ubuntu Linux is more than just another Linux distribution—the Ubuntu folks are Linux devotees on a mission. And you and I are the lucky winners.

Who Should Read This Book

If you're reading this in a bookstore and are unsure about which Linux distribution to get started with, or whether to use Linux at all, this book is for you. Ubuntu is a complete, visually friendly, and community-oriented distribution that makes it easy for you to get started using Linux. Ubuntu is designed to be a distribution for users, but as you'll see throughout this book, you can do anything that you want with it, from running your desktop to running servers and network services for the enterprise, thanks to the inherent power of Linux. Ubuntu comes with a tremendous selection of up-to-date software, and plenty more is quickly downloaded and installed thanks to its easy-to-use administrative tools. Ubuntu is frequently updated, and there is no such thing as a Linux virus or "accidentally-installed spyware." Linux is inherently secure.

Ubuntu's rich user community is a big win for new and existing Ubuntu users. There are places to ask questions and actually get answers. People seem to want to help. The Ubuntu forums and mailing lists are a live, constant demonstration of the philosophical and social aspects of Ubuntu, which are discussed in Chapter 1. In a nutshell, every Linux distribution has fans, devotees, forums, and mailing lists, but Ubuntu's are the most exciting, usable, and useful that I've ever seen in my years of using Linux. You can feel the excitement. Ubuntu brings the promise of Internationalization alive—you can get versions of Ubuntu for many languages and character sets, and more are actively on the way.

If you're already using Ubuntu, this book should be equally useful to you because it explains how to use the standard applications provided with Ubuntu, how to do common system configuration and system administration tasks, and so on. If you're already using Ubuntu on your desktop and do more with it, this book clearly explains how to install common servers for file-sharing, electronic mail handling, Web servers, and much more.

How This Book Is Organized

Ubuntu Linux Bible is organized into four parts.

Part I: Getting Started with Ubuntu Linux

The first part of this book provides background information about Ubuntu Linux, including instructions on installing it on your machine or simply taking it for a test drive from a Live CD. Chapter 1 introduces Ubuntu, the Ubuntu philosophy, and explores the Ubuntu community and the various Web sites where you can get information and assistance in using and configuring Ubuntu (if you need help NOW, rather than simply reading this book). Chapter 1 also discusses some of the main reasons why Ubuntu is the right Linux distribution to use, and compares its capabilities against several other popular Linux distributions. Chapter 2 explains how to install Ubuntu as your only operating system or as an alternate operating system on an existing computer system if you can't live without whatever you're already using. Chapter 3 explains how to experiment with Ubuntu even if you don't have a computer system or disk space to spare, thanks to the freely downloadable Ubuntu Live distribution, which boots on any modern PC but doesn't require any changes to that system.

Part II: Ubuntu for Desktop Users

Part II explores the rich set of applications that are available for Ubuntu and explains how to use them to accomplish the kinds of things that people use modern personal computers for—reading and sending e-mail; surfing the Web; creating documents and spreadsheets; playing games; and playing and managing audio CDs, online music files, and DVD movies. Chapters 4, 5, and 6 provide a basic discussion of Linux and Unix fundamentals if you are curious about using a command line, give you an overview of the graphical user interface provided by Ubuntu, and generally explain how things are organized on your Ubuntu system.

Chapters 7 through 14 are task-oriented discussions of common tasks, such as editing files, reading and sending mail, surfing the Web, printing things, working with multimedia, spreadsheets, presentations, and so on. Chapters 15 and 16 discuss how to share and transfer files with other computer systems that are on your local network or anywhere on the Internet. Chapter 17 focuses on how to connect your Ubuntu system to your PDA and share and synchronize information. This part concludes with Chapter 18's discussion of application development on Ubuntu, highlighting standard GNU/Linux development tools such as compilers, automatic build tools, graphical Integrated Development Environments, and source code control systems. All of which are free, of course.

Part III: Ubuntu for System Administrators

Anyone who sets up their computer to connect to the network, enable users to log in, and so on is an official junior system administrator as far as I'm concerned. This part explains how to do all of the system administration tasks that any home user will want to do, but also explores all of the system administration tasks that you or any other administrator will need to do when using Ubuntu in a business setting. This section explains what actually happens when your Ubuntu system boots, introduces how Linux systems help you protect your personal files and directories, and discusses ways of backing up and restoring files. Chapter 19 discusses the Linux boot process in detail to help you incorporate new procedures into the boot process and make it easier for you to diagnose problems if they occur. Chapter 20 tells you how to keep your system up-to-date and how to locate and install new software. Chapter 21 discusses standard (users and groups) and advanced (ACLs) security on your Ubuntu system, in terms of both protecting files from unauthorized access and maximizing file sharing. Chapter 22 discusses how to back up your existing system so that you can safeguard your important projects and easily restore accidentally deleted files. Chapter 23 explains how to add new hardware to your Ubuntu system if you run out of space, need faster graphics, or need anything to upgrade your machine. Chapter 24 discusses network security and how to protect yourself from crackers and other local or network vandals. This part concludes with Chapter 25, which explains how to use Ubuntu on laptops, other wireless systems, and with common wireless devices such as keyboards, mice, and even headphones.

Part IV: Configuring Servers on Ubuntu

Part IV discusses how to set up servers that provide basic network and Internet services on any network that you're connected to. Separate chapters discuss how to set up a Web server, select and configure a mail server, use your Ubuntu system as a centralized print server, provide basic file-sharing and print services to Microsoft Windows systems on your network, and set up servers such as DNS, DHCP, and NFS.

Conventions Used in This Book

Many different organizational and typographical features throughout this book are designed to help you get the most of the information.

Whenever the authors want to bring something important to your attention the information will appear in a Caution, Note, Tip, or Warning.

CAUTION This information is important and is set off in a separate paragraph with a special icon. Cautions provide information about things to watch out for, whether simply inconvenient or potentially hazardous to your data or systems.

NOTE   Notes provide additional, ancillary information that is helpful, but somewhat outside of the current presentation of information.

TIP   Tips generally are used to provide information that can make your work easier—special short-cuts or methods for doing something easier than the norm.

WARNING   The information Warnings provide advise you about the serious consequences of performing the procedure or activity described—whether to you, to your data, or to your hardware or software.

Getting an Ubuntu CD-ROM

Most books have a section in the Preface called "About the Companion CD-ROM(s)," and I don't want to disappoint you. This book includes a copy of the latest and greatest Ubuntu Desktop CD that was available when this book was published. This Ubuntu Desktop CD lets you experiment with Ubuntu Linux on an existing system (without changing anything) or use a simple graphical installer to install Ubuntu Linux permanently on a Pentium-class personal computer system. I'll discuss test-driving and installing Ubuntu Linux using this CD in more detail in Chapter 2. Other Ubuntu Linux CDs are available for different Desktop platforms (PowerPC, 64-bit PC, and SPARC) and for special purposes, such as installing servers, installing Ubuntu in alternate or OEM (Original Equipment Manufacturer) modes, and more—getting and installing these is discussed in Chapters 2 and 3.

As discussed in Chapter 1, new versions of Ubuntu are released every six months, so if a new version is available by the time you read this, you can always either download that from the Ubuntu Web site or request an official copy by going to https://shipit.ubuntu.com/, creating an account, and providing your surface address and wish list. The latest Ubuntu distribution will be winging its way to your house or apartment, but this book will still be quite useful to you.

Of course, if you have a CD burner and you don't want to wait, you can always download an image of the latest Ubuntu Desktop, Server, or Alternate releases from one of the Web sites listed at www.ubuntu linux.org/download/. If you already know what you're doing with Linux and want to run Ubuntu with KDE (go figure), see www.kubuntu.org. Similarly, if you already know what you're doing with Linux and want to squeeze the most out of your hardware by using the lightweight Xfce desktop with Ubuntu, see www.xubuntu.org. These alternate versions of the Ubuntu Project are discussed in Chapter 1.

Part I

Getting Started with Ubuntu Linux

Chapter 1

The Ubuntu Linux Project

Personal computers and their operating systems have come a long way since the late 1970s, when the first home computer hit the market. At that time, you could only toggle in a program by flipping switches on the front of the machine, and the machine could then run that program and only that program until you manually loaded another, at which time the first program was kicked off the system. Today's personal computers provide powerful graphics and a rich user interface that makes it easy to select and run a wide variety of software concurrently.

The first home computer users were a community of interested people who just wanted to do something with these early machines. They formed computer clubs and published newsletters to share their interests and knowledge — and often the software that they wrote for and used on their machines. Sensing opportunities and a growing market, thousands of computer companies sprang up to write and sell specific applications for the computer systems of the day. This software ranged from applications such as word processors, spreadsheets, and games to operating systems that made it easier to manage, load, and execute different programs.

Though the power and capabilities of today's personal computers is light-years beyond the capabilities of those early machines, the idea of writing software and freely sharing it with others never went away. Though it never got much press because nobody was making money from it, free software (and often its source code) has continued to be available from computer clubs, bulletin boards systems, and computer networks such as today's Internet. The free software movement finally blossomed with three seminal events:

- the creation of the GNU Project (www.gnu.org) by Richard Stallman in 1983, a project dedicated to developing software whose source code would always be freely available
- the announcement of the Free Software Foundation (FSF) (www .fsf.org), initially dedicated to fundraising for the GNU project

■ the introduction of a free operating system project in 1991 that came to be known as Linux, by a Finnish computer software student named Linus Torvalds

The book that you hold in your hands wouldn't exist without these three events, the resulting shockwave of independence and empowerment, and the perpetuation of the community spirit throughout the computer industry that these events (and many related ones) caused. Sometimes, if you're lucky, the more things change, the more they stay the same.

The operating system and applications discussed in this book are free, and their source code is freely available. Anyone who wants to can build, install, and run them. A huge online community of users has sprung up around them, including specialized groups who create easily installed sets of this software, known as Linux distributions. This chapter explores the philosophy, community, and history behind one of the newest, and arguably the best, of these easily obtained, easily installed, and easy-to-use free software environments, known as the Ubuntu Linux distribution.

Background

The emergence of Linux, a freely available operating system, is a landmark event in modern personal computing. Today, Linux is arguably the most popular operating system in use for server environments, and is quickly gaining significant numbers of users as a personal computer operating system for home use. The following two sections provide some background on Linux if you're just considering adopting it or are unfamiliar with some standard Linux terms such as the idea of a Linux distribution. If you're already familiar with Linux and are interested in Ubuntu as your Linux distribution of choice, you can skip this section and go directly to "Introducing Ubuntu Linux."

Why Use Linux?

Presumably, you've bought this book because you want to use Linux, but if you're just reading to find out why you might want to do so, some common reasons for using Linux are the following:

■ **Powerful, modern design:** Linux was designed from the ground up to enable you to run multiple programs at the same time and to provide services that your computer and others can use. Most other desktop computer operating systems, such as Microsoft Windows, started out as small operating systems that could run only one program at a time, and they have been trying to catch up ever since.

■ **Freely available source code means no lock-in to a single vendor:** Regardless of the operating system that you're currently using, you may have encountered problems with applications or the way things worked. However, if you're using an off-the-shelf operating system from Microsoft or Apple, you can get fixes and updates only from Microsoft or Apple. Linux is open and free, so if you don't like the way that Red Hat's Linux works, how much it costs, or the type of customer support that's available, you can always switch to Novell's SUSE Linux, Mandriva Linux, or (preferably) to Ubuntu Linux.

■ **Thousands of free, powerful applications:** Need a word processor? Download and install OpenOffice Writer, AbiWord, Kwrite, or dozens of others. Need a database? Download and install MySQL, PostgreSQL, or many others. Need to create graphics or manipulate digital photographs? It doesn't get much better than GIMP (GNU Image Manipulation Program). If anything, a problem with Linux can be that you have too many choices, none of which cost money.

- **Support for standards:** Linux and Linux applications are designed to support standards, because standards are the language of free intellectual commerce. Linux applications support modern application and data formats for audio, multimedia, document formatting, spreadsheet data, and many more. Because Linux is open and free, there can be no such thing as a proprietary Linux data or application format. This not only fosters data exchange between Linux applications, but also guarantees that you'll always be able to get to your data.

- **Lower total cost of ownership:** If you want to use Linux on your desktop or throughout your business, it's free to obtain and there are legions of Linux wizards available who can help you do whatever you want with it. There are no licensing fees — if you need to pay for something, you can pay for updates and support from the vendor of your Linux distribution.

- **Stable, powerful, and virus-free:** Linux is a mature, multiuser system that is dependable, stable, has built-in security and is immune to viruses except through system administration slipups.

It used to be the case that using Linux required some amount of special knowledge, but that's basically not the case any longer. Linux distributions such as Ubuntu make Linux easy — or, more properly, they make Linux invisible. As you'll see throughout the rest of this book, Ubuntu Linux provides an easy-to-use operating system and all of the applications that you need to do almost anything. The goal of this book is to explore Ubuntu Linux, explain how to have fun and get work done with it, and to provide any special details, insights, or knowledge that you might need. Shhh! Your grandmother doesn't have to know that she's running Linux.

What Is a Linux Distribution?

If you've been curious about Linux for a while, you've probably noticed that a bewildering number of different versions of it seem to be available. Computer magazines and Linux-related Web sites discuss Red Hat Linux, SUSE Linux, the Novell Linux Desktop, Fedora Core Linux, and many other things ending in Linux, each available from a different company or organization. Understanding exactly what people mean when they say "Linux" is the key to understanding how so many different versions of the same thing can be available, but that requires a little insight into how personal computers actually work from the software point of view.

When you install an operating system such as Linux, Microsoft Windows, or Apple's Mac OS X on your computer system, you're installing some amount of software that is invisible to any regular user because it runs behind the scenes. This software handles scheduling, starting, and stopping different programs, communicating with your computer's hardware, handling communications with peripherals such as your printer, and so on. This is generally known as system software because regular users don't directly interact with it, but it needs to be present and running to provide the services that application software relies on. The core piece of this system software is usually referred to as a *kernel* because it is the central piece of the operating system and everything else builds upon the fundamental services that it provides.

By itself, a kernel isn't very interesting — people don't actually want to run a kernel, they want to run applications. These applications depend on services that are provided both by the kernel and by other system software. For example, if you want to print a file, whatever application you're using needs to create a version of your file that is formatted in a way that your printer understands, and then schedule that file for printing. Another piece of software handles sending the formatted file to the printer, making sure that the file prints correctly, and so on.

In popular usage, "Linux" is the collective name for an operating system kernel and its associated applications. In reality, Linux is technically the name of just the kernel — most of the applications that anyone uses with Linux come from other free software projects. A *Linux distribution* is the correct term for a Linux kernel, a set of applications that can run on top of it (regardless of where they come from), and a tool to install everything and configure your system. Each company or organization that provides a Linux distribution is taking advantage of the open source nature of the Linux kernel and the applications that run on top of it by putting together the "right" version of the Linux kernel with what they view as the "right" collection of core applications that anyone would want to run on top of it.

> **NOTE** Because many of the key applications that systems running the Linux kernel depend upon have their roots in the GNU project, the historically proper way of referring to a Linux distribution is as a GNU/Linux distribution. However, given the number of other projects that have made huge contributions to today's Linux distributions, this book simply refers to the term as Linux distributions, rather than as GNU/GNOME/KDE/TeX/*your-favorite-project-here*/ Linux distributions. This, in no way, minimizes the fundamental and huge contributions that the GNU projects and the FSF have made to modern computing. I'm an FSF member, and strongly suggest that you should be one, too. See www.fsf.org/associate for details. It's always a good idea to support the things that you believe in (and depend on).

Of course, getting a CD or DVD that just contained a bunch of software would be next to useless without some easy way of installing it, configuring it so that it works with your particular computer system (identifying peripherals, setting it up to communicate over your network or with your ISP, creating user accounts, and so on). Therefore, anyone who puts together a Linux distribution also provides a tool for installing and configuring the system, which is generally what runs when you boot from a Linux CD or DVD for the first time. This installation and configuration tool generally leverages a package management system that makes it easy to add or remove sets of related applications, identifying dependencies between different software components to ensure that the applications that you install will actually execute correctly.

Linux distributions are the key to understanding how Linux can be free and sold at the same time. The source code for the Linux kernel and open source applications is indeed freely available from thousands of sites on the Internet. Anyone who wants it can get it, but putting it all together in an easily installable, usable form is another thing entirely. When people sell a Linux distribution, they are basically just charging you for the media that it comes on, the time and effort that they invested in putting it all together, and (in some cases) "charging in advance" for any customer support that you might need if you encounter installation or initial configuration problems.

Developing Linux distributions and making them widely available has been critical to the adoption of Linux as an operating system because these distributions have made it possible for people to actually install and use Linux, the GNU utilities, and so on.

Introducing Ubuntu Linux

Ubuntu Linux is a Linux distribution founded in 2004 and focused on the needs of end users. Ubuntu Linux is the product of the Ubuntu project sponsored by Canonical, Ltd. (www.canonical.com), a company founded by Mark Shuttleworth, a successful South African entrepreneur, long-time Debian Linux developer, and general open source advocate. Ubuntu is a Debian-based Linux distribution (more about that later in this chapter) that uses a graphical user interface known as GNOME as its desktop environment. (GNOME is discussed in detail in Chapter 5, "Using the GNOME Desktop.") Sister projects to Ubuntu include Kubuntu, a version of Ubuntu that uses the KDE desktop environment instead of GNOME, Xubuntu, a version of Ubuntu that uses the lighter-weight Xfce desktop, and Edubuntu, a version of Ubuntu that focuses on educational applications and popularizing the use of Linux in schools.

Everything has to have a name, but what is the Ubuntu in *Ubuntu Linux*? Not too surprisingly, the Ubuntu Linux Web site puts it best:

Ubuntu is an ancient African word, meaning "humanity to others." Ubuntu also means "I am what I am because of who we all are." The Ubuntu Linux distribution brings the spirit of Ubuntu to the software world.

Although that may be a bit touchy-feely for some, it's hard to argue with success and commitment. In 2005, its first year of availability, Ubuntu Linux received awards such as the *Linux Journal*'s Reader's Choice award, *Tux Magazine*'s Reader's Choice 2005 for Favorite Linux Distribution award, Ars Technica's Best Distribution award, the UK Linux & Open Source Industry's Best Distribution award, and the Linux World Expo's Best Debian Derivative Distribution award. Not too shabby for the new distribution on the block.

Aside from its technical excellence and usability (and some good funding thanks to Mark Shuttleworth), much of the success to date of Ubuntu Linux is due to the fact that its creators and proponents are not just the traditional Linux fanatics, but are genuinely committed to creating and promoting a usable and easily managed Linux distribution for end users all over the world.

The Ubuntu Manifesto

The Ubuntu Manifesto is a mission statement phrased in the classic manifesto form much beloved of artistic and political movements. The Ubuntu Manifesto is available online in the Philosophy section of the Ubuntu Web site (`www.ubuntulinux.org/ubuntu/philosophy`). Its core ideas are the following:

- Every computer user should have the freedom to run, copy, distribute, study, share, change, and improve their software for any purpose, without paying licensing fees.
- Every computer user should be able to use their software in the language of their choice.
- Every computer user should be given every opportunity to use software, even if they work under a disability.

The first bullet is largely a clear restatement of the goals of open source software in general, but the second and third bullets are two of the big drivers for the success of Ubuntu.

Internationalization is the term for producing software that is capable of displaying all prompts, dialogs, system messages, and so on, in any user's native language and any specific character set used with that language. The term internationalization is such a mouthful that it is frequently referred to as *i18n* because the word *internationalization* consists of the letter "i" followed by 18 letters and ends with an "n." The two aspects of i18n are *translation*, ensuring that versions of operating system and application messages and text are available in other languages, and *localization*, which ensure that messages and text can be displayed in a language's native character set(s). Amusingly, localization is often referred to as *l10n*.

Linux and its applications have been focused on i18n for years, thanks to initiatives such as the Linux Internationalization Initiative (`www.li18nux.net/`, known as *Li18nux*) and the Free Standards Group's Open Internationalization Initiative (`www.openi18n.org/`). These initiatives focus on ensuring that open source applications take i18n into account when developing, maintaining, and enhancing code. Many of the structural enhancements to the last few releases of desktop environments such as GNOME and KDE have been related to making sure that these environments and their applications support different languages and character sets.

The key to successful internationalization is two-fold — not only do applications and graphical environments need to support multiple languages and character sets, but the translations of prompts, dialogs, and system messages have to be available. Ubuntu's focus on a truly usable Linux distribution for an international audience has helped it become a hub for translation and localization work in Linux (`www.ubuntulinux.org/community/participate#l10n`) and GNOME (its primary graphical environment — more about that later) through an online translation system known as Rosetta (`https://launchpad.net/rosetta`), documentation translation efforts, active mailing lists, and other resources.

> **TIP** For additional information about Linux Internationalization, see additional Web resources such as the i18nGurus' Linux Internationalization Resources page at www.i18ngurus.com/docs/984813514.html and the Linux Internationalization HOWTO, available online at sites such as http://home.no.net/david/i18n.php.

Although many of the structural enhancements to the last few releases of desktop environments such as GNOME and KDE have been related to internationalization, a great deal of work has also been done to make Linux graphical environments easier to use by people with disabilities. Ensuring that graphical applications provide keyboard or gesture shortcuts for all menu commands and dialog interaction has been a growing focus area for GNOME, KDE, and graphical application development. Ubuntu's emphasis on usability is a boon to all computer users, regardless of whether or not they have a physical disability.

> **TIP** For additional information about Linux Accessibility projects and usability awareness, see additional Web resources such as the Linux Accessibility HOWTO (www.tldp.org/HOWTO/Accessibility-HOWTO/), the Linux Developers Accessibility HOWTO (http://larswiki.atrc.utoronto.ca/wiki), and the Linux Accessibility Resource Site (http://larswiki.atrc.utoronto.ca/wiki).

Ubuntu Linux Release Schedule

Given the pace of open source software development, it's important for anyone who depends on a Linux distribution to be able to get the latest and greatest kernels and versions of software packages. Kernel and associated device driver improvements provide security fixes, facilitate the use of the latest hardware, and often provide performance improvements in the handling of existing devices and protocols. The latest versions of software packages typically provide improvements in both capabilities and usability. Because the open source community model virtually guarantees that thousands of improvements are in progress at any given moment, delivering an integrated and tested version of the latest and greatest Linux kernel and supported software packages is a complex task, but is one that is extremely important to the success and widespread adoption of any Linux distribution.

The Ubuntu folks deliver a fresh Ubuntu release every six months. These regular releases provide an up-to-date and tested kernel and a well-tested, integrated set of user software including the X Window system release from x.org, the latest stable GNOME desktop, and core Linux and GNOME applications including Ubuntu-specific applications and customizations.

A regular release schedule is something that is unique in the Linux space, and has led to a unique approach to version numbering for Ubuntu releases. Traditional software releases are numbered according to major and minor release numbers, where the major release number is essentially arbitrary and generally indicates some major upgrade in functionality. For example, in traditional release numbering, version 4.2 is the minor release of version 4 of the software that follows version 4.1. Ubuntu uses major release numbers that identify the year in which the software was released, and what appear to be the minor numbers actually represent the month in which the release was made. Therefore, version 6.06 is the Ubuntu release from the sixth month of 2006. In typical, lighthearted Linux fashion, each Ubuntu release also has a nickname. Ubuntu releases at the time that this book was written were the following:

- 4.10: Warty Warthog (October, 2004)
- 5.04: Hoary Hedgehog (April, 2005)
- 5.10: Breezy Badger (October, 2005)
- 6.06: LTS (Long Term Support): Dapper Drake (June, 2006)
- 6.10: Edgy Eft (October, 2006)

This is a refreshing approach to version numbering, especially in the open source space where software is essentially under continuous development. Not only does it make it possible for users and system administrators to predict and schedule system updates to their systems, but it also makes it easy to identify the vintage of existing, installed systems without consulting a reference text or the Web.

Ubuntu Update and Maintenance Commitments

The frequency with which a distribution is released is important to any user in order to guarantee that they have access to the latest and greatest system and application software. However, for any business that is interested in the power, cost savings, and flexibility of Linux, the period of time in which a release will be updated and maintained is even more important. Many businesses have hundreds or thousands of computer systems. Businesses with substantial infrastructure on top of deployed systems need to spend significant time testing updates and new releases before they can even think about rolling them out to all of their computer systems. Once testing is complete, the physical act of updating deployed systems takes significant time, which literally translates into money in terms of MIS and IT personnel.

By default, security updates for each Ubuntu release are issued for 18 months after the release date — after that date, existing security updates are still available, but there is no guarantee that new updates for that release will be provided. To address the longer-term requirements of commercial Ubuntu users, Mark Shuttleworth and Canonical, Ltd., the founders and sponsors of Ubuntu Linux, formed and funded the Ubuntu Foundation in mid-2005. The Ubuntu Foundation employs some of the core Ubuntu community members to help guarantee the success and continuity of the Ubuntu development and release process. One aspect of the Ubuntu Foundation is an increased commitment to maintenance and updates. Ubuntu version 6.06 was the first Ubuntu Linux release to benefit from this when the Ubuntu Foundation announced that Ubuntu version 6.06 would be supported for three years on the desktop and five years on the server, doubling the standard 18-month support commitment that is a backbone of Ubuntu. The acronym LTS, for Long Term Support, was added to its release number to highlight that fact.

Given the pace of hardware and open source software development, Ubuntu's regular release schedule and long maintenance commitment helps ensure that Ubuntu users always have stable, secure, and up-to-date versions of the software that they depend on. It also provides a firm update and support commitment that is mandatory for the successful commercial adoption of Ubuntu.

Ubuntu and the Debian Project

Debian is one of the longest-lived Linux distributions available, and is the Linux distribution that is the conceptual parent of Ubuntu Linux. Debian is pronounced Deb'-ian, with a soft e, and is a contraction of the names of the founders of the Debian Project, Debra and Ian Murdock.

The Debian Project (`www.debian.org`) was founded in 1993 and has been delivering quality GNU/Linux distributions ever since. Debian is well known for stable releases based on a huge collection of thoroughly tested and completely integrated software packages. Unfortunately, the downside of balancing testing and integration with keeping up with the pace of open source development has led to a painfully slow release history — there have literally been years between official Debian releases. To be fair, three versions of the current Debian release are always available: stable (the released version), testing (the candidate for the next release), and unstable (the development version). However, many businesses (and users) are uncomfortable with depending on something labeled *testing* or *unstable*. Providing a faster release process, focusing on specific core technologies such as the GNOME desktop interface, and providing a better structured mechanism delivering software updates and notifying users of their availability are the key reasons why the Ubuntu project was born.

Some of the key ways in which the Debian and Ubuntu Linux distributions interact are the following:

■ Ubuntu shares the software packaging format used by Debian, and also relies on the excellent and impressive technologies that were pioneered by Debian for identifying and resolving dependencies and relationships between different open source software packages.

■ Ubuntu developers feed their changes and enhancements to open source packages back to the open source community, but also provide them directly to the Debian developers responsible for that package and even record patch information directly into the Debian bug-tracking system. Bug fixes and related enhancements made by Ubuntu developers are delivered as they are made during the Ubuntu release and testing process, not in a big bang fashion once an Ubuntu release is complete. This is better for everyone.

■ The Debian and Ubuntu distributions are based on a slightly different selection of open source packages, but follow the same general organization of those packages into separate domains, as explained in Chapter 20, "Adding, Removing, and Updating Software."

The Debian and Ubuntu Linux distributions are closely linked, complementary distributions with different goals. Ubuntu would not exist without the pioneering efforts and contributions of the Debian distribution, but provides a more predictable distribution with better support channels for many users and enterprise computing environments.

Why Choose Ubuntu?

As mentioned earlier in this chapter, in any recent computer magazine, and if you've ever looked at the Linux section in your local bookstore, there are zillions of different Linux distributions. After all, it's free, so why not? Techies aside, most of the users of any Linux distribution are people who have heard that they should be using a specific Linux distribution, got a free Linux CD for some distribution in a Linux magazine that they bought, or happened to buy a book about a specific Linux distribution.

Ubuntu means "humanity to others," but the title bar on their Web pages says "Linux for People," and that's what Ubuntu is really about — a Linux distribution for people who want to get work done with a minimum of fuss and bother. Never mind that it's also a technically sophisticated Linux distribution with up-to-date software. Does it do what I want to do?

The answer is unquestionably "Yes!" However, if you're unconvinced or find yourself in a cocktail party Linux discussion, you may want more empirical data. Here are a few of the attributes of Ubuntu Linux that make it an attractive distribution to just about anyone:

■ **Regular, up-to-date releases:** The Linux kernel and the thousands of software packages that comprise the Linux user and administrative environment are constantly being updated. As discussed earlier in this chapter, providing the latest and greatest kernel and application software on a regular schedule is a fundamental principle of Ubuntu Linux.

■ **Commitment to quality:** The quality of a Linux distribution hinges on two things: how good it is in the first place, and the distributing vendor's degree of commitment to fixing problems that arise. In both cases, Ubuntu shines. Each release goes through extensive internal testing by the Ubuntu team and extensive public testing of release candidates. Once a release occurs, updates for that release are delivered for a minimum of eighteen months (as needed, of course).

■ **Community and commercial support:** Much of the support for any Linux distribution comes from its user community, and it's hard to beat the passion and commitment of the Ubuntu community.

However, just as no business can afford to depend on an operating system without a reasonable maintenance commitment, no business can afford to depend on an operating system without some chance of guaranteed support. As discussed later in this chapter, a complete spectrum of commercial and community support is readily available for Ubuntu Linux.

- **Easy retrieval and application of updates:** The previous bullets have stressed the importance of being able to keep installed Linux systems up to date. Ubuntu provides great tools that notify users when updates are available and makes them easy to obtain and install. Ubuntu's graphical Update Manager and Synaptic Package Manager tools (discussed in Chapter 20, "Adding, Removing, and Updating Software") are the best examples of such tools that I have ever used.

- **Focus on usability:** Ubuntu defines itself as "Linux for People" and provides custom graphics, window decorations, and color schemes designed to provide an attractive, usable desktop environment for real people for personal use and to get work done. Like any other Linux distribution, you can customize this extensively, even switching to any of a variety of other window managers or desktop environments that are easily retrieved and installed through the Synaptic Package Manager. Ubuntu uses the GNOME desktop environment by default, which is well known for its support of and sensitivity toward accessibility requirements such as keyboard equivalents for menus and menu commands.

- **Focus on internationalization:** For some people, it comes as a surprise that there are people living on this planet who do not speak English, and that the languages that these people speak do not use the English alphabet and character set. I wish that I were kidding. Ubuntu is extremely focused on supporting translation efforts and providing a Linux distribution that people anywhere on the planet can use in their native language, with their native character sets.

- **Active and Involved Community:** As I'll discuss in the next section, it's hard to conceive of a more active, dynamic, and involved user community than that which surrounds Ubuntu. An active and involved community translates into more places to ask questions, a better chance of getting answers, and a more friendly experience when doing so.

As you can see from this list, Ubuntu focuses on solving many of the issues that plague other Linux distributions or which make it difficult for new users to adopt Linux as their operating system of choice. Most general-purpose Linux distributions would claim that they address the same sorts of issues, but in my experience, Ubuntu is exceptional in terms of delivering on them.

Installation Requirements

As Linux distributions have moved to the 2.6 kernel and Linux is becoming more and more popular, the chances of your having hardware that is not supported by Ubuntu Linux grow less and less. This section outlines the types of systems on which Ubuntu is supported, and the general hardware requirements for a usable system.

NOTE One of the best things about Linux is the wide range of systems types on which it is supported. Most Linux distributions, including Ubuntu, will run on older systems that would probably otherwise be discarded or used as doorstops. However (and feel free to repeat this quote), software runs slower on slower hardware. When running on older systems, you will probably want to use the command-line interface or a lighter-weight graphical environment than the default GNOME (or KDE for Kubuntu) desktops. Desktops such as Xfce or window managers such as Fluxbox and IceWM are popular and powerful alternatives to GNOME and KDE. More about these in the section of Chapter 5 entitled "What's a Desktop? Graphical Environments for Linux."

Supported System Types

Ubuntu is supported on any of the following types of systems:

- i386 or compatible processors from Intel, AMD, Cyrix, and so on
- G3 or better PowerPC (PPC) Apple Macintosh system
- 64-bit AMD or EM64T processors (which include the Athlon64, Opteron, and EM64T Xeon)
- Sun UltraSPARC systems

> **NOTE** At the time that this book was written, the Ubuntu 6.06 release for the UltraSPARC architecture was still an unofficial release, though both Canonical and Sun have announced that Ubuntu will be supported on UltraSPARC processors, highlighting the T1 ("Niagara") processors used on systems such as the Sun Fire T1000 and T2000 servers.

Hardware Requirements

As with any computer software, you'll have a better experience if you install and use Ubuntu on the most powerful system that you have available, but Ubuntu will technically still run fine (though slowly) on your dusty 25 MHz i386. However, the American national slogan is eminently true here: "More is better." Taking off my Linux evangelist hat for a moment, you shouldn't really bother trying to install and run Ubuntu on a system with a processor that runs slower than 166 MHz or which has less than 96MB of memory. I use a system with exactly those characteristics for testing purposes (an old IBM ThinkPad 380XD that I just can't bear to part with), and GNOME is excruciating on that system. If you really need to run Ubuntu on such a system, see the note earlier in this section about alternate graphical environments for low-speed or low-memory systems.

The minimum hardware requirements for installing Ubuntu and having a reasonable user experience are the following:

- 700 MHz or better processor
- 256MB of memory
- CD-ROM drive
- Ethernet interface
- VGA graphics interface
- 3GB of available disk space

If your system satisfies or exceeds these, you're good to go. You can certainly install Ubuntu on slower systems or systems with less memory, but that's like putting racing slicks on a Hyundai — you're not really going to get the most out of the experience.

Time Requirements

The amount of time that it takes to install Ubuntu depends on the speed of your system, how you are configuring that system, and the type of distribution that you're installing. Installing Ubuntu on a laptop that already runs Microsoft Windows or Mac OS X and which you want to set up as a dual-boot machine may take an hour or so. Installing any version of Ubuntu on a new machine can take less than half an hour. In general, you should plan on spending an hour or two installing Ubuntu — I'm assuming that you're not going to complain if it takes less time than that.

Ubuntu CDs

The CD that is included with this book is the Ubuntu Desktop CD, which enables you to test-drive Ubuntu on an existing computer system without changing anything, and which also provides a simple, easy-to-use installer that enables you to install Ubuntu on that system permanently. Three different CDs for each fully supported platform are actually available from the Ubuntu folks. These CDs and the capabilities that they provide are the following:

- **Desktop CD:** The CD that is included with this book, this CD provides a bootable version of Ubuntu Linux that enables you to run and experiment with Ubuntu without changing anything on your existing computer system. This CD, known as a "Live CD," also includes an easy-to-use graphical installer that makes it easy for you to permanently install Ubuntu on your computer system. Finally, this CD includes versions of some popular open source software, such as Open Office, which you can install and use on a system running Microsoft Windows. For information about using this CD, see Chapter 2, "Installing Ubuntu."

> **NOTE** When running from the live CD, any work that you do, files that you create, and so on, will be lost when you reboot your computer system unless you save it to another system over the network or to removable storage such as a USB stick, removable hard drive, and so on. See the section of Chapter 2 entitled "Using Desktop CD Persistence" for information on using a USB stick or other removable media to automatically save and restore any changes that you make while running from the Ubuntu Desktop CD, or see the "Accessing Your Hard Drive from the Desktop CD" and "Copying Files to Other Machines Over a Network" sections of Chapter 2 for information about manually saving any work that you do while running from the Ubuntu Desktop CD.

- **Server Install CD:** Enables you to install versions of Ubuntu Linux targeted towards machines that are being used as servers. You can choose to install a generic server and add the server software of your choice, or you can install a LAMP (Linux, Apache, MySQL, Perl) server where the traditional packages required for a Linux Web server will be preinstalled. None of the versions of Ubuntu installed from this CD include a graphical user interface, though you can always add one subsequently. For more information about obtaining this CD and installing from it, see the section of Chapter 3 entitled "Install Options on the Server Install CD."

- **Alternate Install CD:** Enables you to install Ubuntu on systems with certain hardware characteristics, or in specialized configurations. These include creating preconfigured systems for redistribution by Original Equipment Manufacturers (OEM), upgrading existing systems without network access, and setting up automated Ubuntu installations for multiple systems. Hardware-wise, the install options on this disk enable you to install Ubuntu on systems that use Logical Volume Management (LVM), use Redundant Arrays of Inexpensive Disks (RAID), where you want to install GRUB in a location other than the Master Boot Record (MBR), or on systems with limited amounts of memory (i.e., less than 192MB of RAM). For more information about obtaining this CD and installing from it, see the section of Chapter 3 entitled "Install Options on the Alternate Install CD."

The Desktop CD included with this book is the one that most people use to install Ubuntu. However, depending on the type of system that you want to create, you may want to download and burn a copy of another installation CD. The Ubuntu Web site provides freely downloadable ISO images of all of the available Ubuntu CDs, for all supported platforms, at `http://us.releases.ubuntu.com/releases`. (ISO images are files that contain an image of a CD in International Standards Organization CD format, which you can download and then burn to a CD yourself.) Pick the directory associated with the latest release, select the appropriate ISO image, download it, and burn a copy — or you can request that the folks at Ubuntu ship you a set of CDs. To do this, go to the page at `https://shipit.ubuntu.com`, create an account by entering your e-mail address and a password, and request Ubuntu CDs for the current release.

You can even order free CDs for multiple system types at the same time. The Ship-It site is cool for getting copies of Ubuntu to turn on your friends, but is not a good personal alternative if you're into instant gratification, because shipping and delivery can take a few weeks.

Support for Ubuntu Linux

By its nature, computer software occasionally requires that you ask questions about how to use it or ask for help with resolving specific problems. This is especially true of software such as Linux, where you are installing not only a zillion applications, but also the operating system that they depend upon. The primary advantage of off-the-shelf operating systems from a single commercial source, such as Microsoft Windows and Apple's Mac OS X, is that you can presumably contact the vendor if you're having problems installing, configuring, or using it. However, in reality, just try contacting Microsoft if you're having a problem using Windows. (Let me know how that goes.) In general, books like this one provide a central resource for installation, configuration, and general "how do I..." questions, but there are always specific questions that I can't anticipate. So how do you get your questions answered or find help when you need it?

Ubuntu offers an impressive array of support opportunities, ranging from community resources to paid support from Ubuntu's sponsor company, Canonical, Ltd., and a number of other companies located all over the world. The next few sections highlight the various ways in which you can ask questions, get answers, request paid support, and even hire experts to help with custom Ubuntu programming and support tasks.

Community Support and Information

Because Linux software depends on the community development model, getting timely, free help for problems often relies on a similar community approach. This is one of the areas in which Ubuntu truly shines, hosting mailing lists, blogs, and interactive forums that are all excellent sources of up-to-date information about Ubuntu. Forums and mailing lists enable you to post specific questions and receive responses from other Ubuntu users who have already solved the issue that you're experiencing. These online resources also serve as excellent feeder sites for the Ubuntu project, helping the project identify issues and common problems that should be addressed in future Ubuntu releases.

Blogs

Blogs (from the term "We*b log*") are a popular buzzword, and it often seems as though almost anyone with a keyboard and any control over their Web site has one. The Ubuntu blog, known as Planet Ubuntu (`http://planet.ubuntulinux.org/`) is a bit different because it's not a continuous stream of consciousness from a single individual. Instead, Planet Ubuntu is a place where Ubuntu developers and community members can share various musings, insights, complaints, and successes.

If you're enough of a blog or Ubuntu fan to want to subscribe to it rather than simply visiting its Web page, Planet Ubuntu is also available in the following popular RDF (Resource Description Framework) and general markup formats:

- FOAF: Friend of a Friend, available at `http://planet.ubuntulinux.org/foafroll.xml`.
- OPML: Outline Processor Markup Language, available at `http://planet.ubuntulinux.org/opml.xml`.

- RSS: Really Simple Syndication or Rich Site Summary, depending who you ask. Planet Ubuntu feeds are available in RSS 1.0 (`http://planet.ubuntulinux.org/rss10.xml`) or RSS 2.0 (`http://planet.ubuntulinux.org/rss20.xml`) formats. You should use the appropriate format for your RSS reader.

Forums

Forums are the latest generation of what used to be known as bulletin board system, and are an attractive alternative to mailing lists if you have the time to visit the Web site that hosts them. Ubuntu's forums are hosted at `www.ubuntuforums.org/`. This site provides a huge selection of well-organized forums that you can easily search to find specific information, where you can post questions, or where you can simply chat with or see the posts of other Ubuntu users, dipping your toe into the waters of the Ubuntu community if you're not already an active member. You don't have to be a member of the forums to read them, but you do need to be a member to post there. Registration is free and easy — just go to `www.ubuntuforums.org/register.php`, and read and accept the Ubuntu Forum rules. You can then specify the user name that you want to use on the forums, enter a password, and provide your e-mail address and some minimal personal information.

The forums index page at `www.ubuntuforums.org/index.php` displays the categories into which the Ubuntu forums are organized, which are the following:

- **Beginner Community:** A forum section that hosts the Absolute Beginner Talk forum, which provides a forum where anyone can ask questions about computers, Linux, Unix, and Ubuntu. If you were ever afraid to ask a question because it might be too basic, this forum is for you!

- **Current Version Forum:** A set of forums dedicated to supporting users of the current Ubuntu and related project releases (6.06 LTS when this book was written). This forum area is divided into the following focus areas:

  - **General Support:** A set of forums for the current Ubuntu, Kubuntu, Edubuntu, or Xubuntu releases. These forums are divided into Desktop Support, 64-Bit Processor Support, Installation or Upgrade Help, and Macintosh/Apple/PPC Users, and Sun SPARC Users forums.

  - **Hardware Help:** A set of forums targeting problems with hardware not being detected or supported by Ubuntu Linux. This forum area hosts subforums on Networking, Video and Sound, Laptop Support, and Wireless Support topics.

- **Support & Resources:** A set of forums on a variety of general topics. This forum area is divided into the following focus areas:

  - **HOWTOs, Tips & Tricks:** A forum for discussing general, KDE, and GNOME customization, tips, and cool solutions.

  - **Gaming Central:** A forum for discussing playing games on Linux.

  - **Other Support Options:** A set of forums on specific areas of interest outside the normal support forums. This forum area hosts subforums on Accessibility, Repository Support, Server Talk, Programming Talk, Ubtunu Backports, the Ubuntu Users Mailing List, Security Issues, and Ubuntu Art.

  - **Third-Party Ubuntu Projects:** A set of forums on an ever-increasing collection of projects related to the Ubuntu community, but which are not sponsored by Canonical, Ubuntu, or other Ubuntu forums. At the time this book was written, these included forums on the Alacarte Menu Editor, an Ubuntu Women forum, Easy Ubuntu, the BUM Boot Up Manager, ubuntuguide.org, and an Ubuntu Podcast forum.

- **Previous Ubuntu Releases:** A forum section that hosts forums for discussing previous Ubuntu releases. Given Ubuntu's commitment to supporting and continuing to update all of its releases for a minimum of 18 months, the forums in this section can be very useful to users and businesses that are still running previous Ubuntu releases.

- **Development Discussion:** A forum section that hosts a development forum for the upcoming release of Ubuntu, and which also archives the development forums that were used to plan and discuss the current and previous Ubuntu releases.

- **Community Discussions:** A set of forums dedicated to general discussions and announcements. This forum area is divided into the following focus areas:

  - **Ubuntu Cafe:** A forum section that hosts general chat areas for Testimonials, The Fridge Discussions (see the discussion of the Fridge later in this chapter), a forum issue Resolution Center, a SPAM Jail, a Backyard forum for political and other debates, a forum for discussing Other Linux, and a Community Market area where people can advertise or request Ubuntu-related good and services.

  - **Forum Announcements:** A forum section that hosts forums for Official Ubuntu Announcements and one for Official Security Announcements.

Although other distributions have similar forum sites (such as Fedora Core's `www.fedoraforum.org` site), the Ubuntu forums embrace and reflect Ubuntu's commitment to users of the current Ubuntu release and previous Ubuntu releases that are still supported, which is truly unique.

In addition to the English-language forums discussed previously, Ubuntu forums are also available in many other languages, reflecting the commitment of Ubuntu and Ubuntu users to provide a truly international Linux distribution. These are not just translated, native character set versions of the English-language forums — in many cases, different native language sites hosts their own forums and organize those forums differently. You can find pointers to these forums on the page at `www.ubuntulinux.org/community/forums`. At the time this book was written, specialized Chinese, Dutch, Finnish, French, German, Italian, Polish, and Portuguese forum sites hosted forums in those languages, using any associated character sets. Ubuntu is truly an international effort!

IRC

Internet Relay Chat (IRC) is a popular mechanism for interactive online discussions of just about anything. The English-language Ubuntu IRC channel is named #ubuntu, available through the IRC site at irc.freenode.net. Non-English IRC channels are also available, including Chinese (#ubuntu-zh), Dutch (#ubuntu-nl), German (#ubuntu-de), Hebrew and Arabic (#ubuntu-il), Italian (#ubuntu-it), Portuguese (#ubuntu-pt), Russian (#ubuntu-ru), and Spanish (#ubuntu-es), at the time this book was written.

An IRC channel is a great, real-time mechanism for asking about current problems and getting help for resolving them online (assuming that your problem isn't related to getting online in the first place). The XChat IRC client is installed by default as a basic part of Ubuntu Linux, making it easy to connect and take advantage of IRC as a support and community resource.

Mailing Lists

Mailing lists are a great push format, meaning that questions and posts are delivered (pushed) directly to you, unlike forums, which are generally referred to as a pull format, because you have to connect to the Web site that hosts them and locate new posts and information yourself.

There are a huge number of Ubuntu mailing lists, many of which are quite specialized, and listing them all here would simply waste paper because you have to subscribe to them online in the first place. The standard Ubuntu mailing lists, as listed at www.ubuntulinux.org/community/lists, include the following:

- **Ubuntu Announcement list** (ubuntu-announce) has very few e-mails (less than one a month, usually) and will keep you up to date on new releases of Ubuntu, and significant new developments.

- **Ubuntu Development list** (ubuntu-devel) is intended for highly technical discussions and implementation details regarding current Ubuntu development.

- **Ubuntu Security Announcement list** (ubuntu-security-announce) is a read-only mailing list to which announcements of security updates to Ubuntu releases are posted. This list is extremely useful for Ubuntu system administrators or anyone who wants to make sure that they know about the latest security-related Ubuntu package updates.

- **Ubuntu User list** (ubuntu-users) is an extremely high-traffic mailing list for technical support discussions and to which Ubuntu users can post new feature requests and wish lists.

- **Ubuntu Women list** (ubuntu-women) is intended as a mailing list for all Ubuntu users, volunteers, developers, and others who wish to involve more women in the Ubuntu community.

There are many more lists, of course — these are just some of the highlights. You can find a complete, up-to-date list of available Ubuntu mailing lists at http://lists.ubuntu.com, which will take you to http://lists.ubuntu.com/mailman/listinfo. The Ubuntu mailing lists are managed using the popular MailMan mailing list management package.

> **TIP** For Usenet fans, the Ubuntu mailing lists are also available as Usenet news groups thanks to the folks at Gmane (www.gmane.org). The Ubuntu-related news groups available as news groups are listed at http://news.gmane.org/index.php?prefix=gmane.linux.ubuntu.

What's on the Fridge?

Remember how your parents would post your latest accomplishments on their refrigerator? Hopefully, they've stopped now, but the Ubuntu Web site provides a software implementation of the same concept. The Fridge (http://fridge.ubuntu.com) provides a central location where Ubuntu users can find out what's truly new in the Ubuntu community. It features summaries of upcoming Ubuntu-related events, recent information about Ubuntu on the Web and in print media, status messages from various Ubuntu teams and projects, and newsletters such as the Ubuntu Desktop News and Ubuntu Documentation News.

Documentation

Traditional software products provide printed or online documentation to help anticipate and answer users' questions. However, as both a writer and long-time computer user, I've always appreciated and evangelized for good documentation. It doesn't matter how good software or an operating system is if you can't figure out how to use it. Linux documentation is an interesting issue because most Linux distributions are freely downloadable. There are few Linux distributions that you can actually buy off the shelf at a computer retailer, and even these provide relatively little printed documentation. Given the speed at which Linux distributions evolve and the tremendous variety of hardware on which Linux can be installed, complete printed documentation is difficult to produce in a timely fashion and is even harder to maintain. Novell's SUSE Linux is famous for the quality and bulk of the printed documentation that accompanies its boxed products.

Ubuntu has a large and well-organized documentation team that is focused on producing quality, user-oriented documentation that is just as easy to use as Ubuntu itself. Ubuntu documentation is available at two primary locations:

- `http://help.ubuntu.com`: the source for all of the official documentation that has been developed by the Ubuntu documentation team
- `https://wiki.ubuntu.com/UserDocumentation`: a hierarchical collection of resources in Wiki format that makes it easy to find documentation on specific topics

Some of the most useful Ubuntu documents that are available online are the following:

- `http://help.ubuntu.com/quicktour/C/quicktour.html`: a Quick Tour document for the current release of Ubuntu that provides a great overview of many of the significant features that it provides, as well as links to additional information
- `http://help.ubuntu.com/about-ubuntu/C/index.html`: the Ubuntu FAQ (Frequently Asked Questions) document, which provides a great starting point if you are having a specific problem or looking for answers to specific questions

The Ubuntu documentation team produces quality documentation that is well-organized and adheres to a single style guide to provide the sort of consistency that you'd expect from an organized documentation effort. The home page for the Ubuntu Documentation Project is at `http://doc.ubuntu.com/`, which provides pointers to both current documents and works in progress. All communications between documentation team members is done online, using IRC and mailing lists described at `https://wiki.ubuntu.com/DocteamCommunications`. If you're interested in contributing to the Ubuntu documentation effort, a list of current and planned projects is available at `https://wiki.ubuntu.com/DocteamProjects`.

Commercial Support for Ubuntu Linux

As discussed earlier, it's especially important for companies that are planning on adopting an enterprise-wide Linux solution to have a source from which they can get guaranteed support. Though you can typically find answers to most of your questions and solutions to most problems by simply searching the Web, most CEOs and IT managers won't accept "I'm googling it" as a suitable status message when an entire business is offline or some of their employees are unproductive because of a software or operating system problem. In business situations, it's important to have specific resources that you can depend on to solve problems in a timely fashion.

Though the majority of this chapter has stressed the scope and usability of the Ubuntu community and related resources in terms of helping you solve problems, commercial support is also available for Ubuntu from a variety of sources, as described in the next two sections.

Paid Support from Canonical, Ltd.

Canonical, Ltd. the sponsor of the Ubuntu Linux Project, offers two levels of paid support for Ubuntu Linux, known as Standard support and Premium support. These support packages and their current pricing are described at `www.ubuntu.com/support/supportoptions/paidsupport`. The basic differences between the Standard and Premium support packages is the following:

- Standard support is done online and guarantees a response within two business days, with a maximum of 10 support incidents per year.
- Premium support is done both online and by phone, guarantees a response within one business day, and entitles you to 25 support incidents per year. Phone response time is guaranteed to be within 4 hours.

The software packages that Canonical supports depends on the portion of the Ubuntu software repository in which those packages are located. As described in detail in Chapter 20, "Adding, Removing, and Updating Software," the software in the Ubuntu repository is grouped into several different classes, essentially depending upon the license(s) under which a software package has been released. Ubuntu support agreements include full support for packages in the *main* class, partial support for packages in the *restricted* class, and no support for software in the *universe* and *multiverse* classes. See Chapter 20 for details on the organization of the Ubuntu repository and the differences between package classes.

Canonical also offers special rates for certifying your in-house support organization or having Canonical's support organization function as an escalation site for problems that your support organization needs additional help with.

The Ubuntu Marketplace

The Ubuntu Marketplace is a portion of the Ubuntu Web site that lists the network of companies that provide support for desktop and server systems running Ubuntu Linux. The main page for the Ubuntu marketplace is `www.ubuntu.com/support/supportoptions/marketplace`, which provides centralized access to lists of companies all over the world that support Ubuntu, organized into separate pages listing such companies in Africa, Asia, Europe, Latin America, North America, and Oceania. (A related URL is the Community Market forum at `www.ubuntuforums.org`, which was mentioned earlier, though that is much more information than the actual Ubuntu Marketplace.)

Providing a centralized clearinghouse for companies that can help you or your firm with support problems is a tremendous advantage for companies that are just moving to Linux and would like to engage with a support organization that is geographically close to your physical location.

At the time this book was written, there were no specific certification requirements to have your company listed in the Ubuntu Marketplace — you simply send mail to `mailto:marketplace@ubuntu.com` containing the information described on the page at `www.ubuntu.com/support/supportoptions/marketplace/join`.

Getting More Information About Ubuntu

Ubuntu Linux is increasing in popularity faster than any Linux distribution that I have previously encountered. Technical excellence aside, much of the credit for its increasing popularity lies in the excellent organization and breadth of coverage provided on the main Ubuntu Web site. However, let's face it — the Ubuntu Web site is largely blowing its own horn. What do other people say? Are there locations other than the mother ship where you can go for information about and help with Ubuntu?

The answer to these questions is a definite "yes!" There are a huge number of sites that provide information about Ubuntu beyond simple software reviews. In addition to the support and general Web resources listed previously in this chapter, some of my favorite Ubuntu-related sites are the following:

- DistroWatch (`http://distrowatch.com/table.php?distribution=ubuntu`) provides summary information about the contents of most Linux distributions, including Ubuntu. Their Ubuntu page provides high-level information about the contents of the various Ubuntu releases, but more importantly provides links to many Ubuntu-related Web sites, reviews of the various Ubuntu releases, and much more. If you're not already familiar with DistroWatch, theirs is an essential Linux site for finding out just about anything about any Linux distribution.

- **Ubuntu Blog** (http://ubuntu.wordpress.com/) is a blog about Ubuntu that provides a great selection of entries about general Ubuntu tasks organized into categories such as administration, office, servers, and so on. It also features links to other sites and great task-specific articles such as the greatest of instructions for getting the MythTV package working on an Ubuntu system.

- **UbuntuGuide** (http://ubuntuguide.org/) hosts an Ubuntu "Getting Started" guide that is an excellent information resource, though it may not always reflect the latest Ubuntu release. The Ubuntu Starter Guide provides a great deal of very detailed information about how to do specific tasks on Ubuntu Linux, and is well worth a look.

- **Ubuntu Women** (www.ubuntu-women.org/) provides FAQs, a wiki, a blog, mentoring programs, and much more focused on getting more women involved in Ubuntu and FLOSS (Free/Libre/Open-Source Software) in general. This is a great site with a great message and purpose, through which we all win.

- **Ubuntux** (www.ubuntux.org/) is a community of Ubuntu users that provides a variety of forums, blogs, links to recent articles about Debian and Ubuntu, and a variety of other resources designed to help users work with Ubuntu. The forums are especially nice, covering the spectrum of topics from getting started with Ubuntu to specific customization and optimization topics. Ubuntux also features forums targeted toward Ubuntu-based distributions such as Kubuntu, Edubuntu, and Ubuntu Lite, as well as a forum on the Ubuntu server distribution. The Ubuntux site also offers an RSS feed to help you keep up to date with the latest Ubuntu-related happenings.

There are many other Ubuntu-related sites on the Web, with more appearing every day. The DistroWatch site provides a good collection of Links to Ubuntu-related sites and reviews, but as with anything on the Internet, your favorite search engine is your friend and will quickly help you find hundreds of other sites to search for answers to specific questions or simply to see what others think and say about Ubuntu.

Summary

Ubuntu is the fastest growing Linux distribution in recent memory, and is one of the finest examples of the power of open source and community that I've ever seen. After providing some general information about Linux, this chapter provided an overview of the philosophy behind Ubuntu Linux and the goals of the distribution. As discussed in this chapter, much of the success of Ubuntu to date beyond its technical excellence and ease of use is rooted in a rich, fast-growing user community and a well-organized Web site that provides easy access to various Ubuntu-related resources.

Chapter 2

Installing Ubuntu

The CD included with this book, the Ubuntu 6.06 LTS Desktop CD, is an example of a Live CD, which is a bootable CD that provides a great way to experiment with a preconfigured Ubuntu installation without actually modifying your hard drive or going through the installation process. You can use live CDs as a portable Ubuntu installation that you can take with you, temporarily converting other computer systems to Ubuntu Linux systems regardless of whether the machine is currently running Microsoft Windows, Mac OS X, or another Linux distribution. Ubuntu also offers an impressive Live CD Persistence function that enables you to save work and system configuration done using the Desktop CD to removable media that you can reuse the next time you boot the Live CD. In most cases, you can also mount and access your existing disk partitions after booting from the Ubuntu Desktop CD, so that you can even do real work with Ubuntu and save it to the partitions used by your other operating system.

Ubuntu's Desktop CD takes the Live CD concept one step further by also enabling you to quickly install Ubuntu Linux using an integrated, easy-to-use installer that is available as an icon on the Desktop CD's desktop. This chapter focuses on using the Desktop CD to install Ubuntu Linux on x86 or 64-bit PC computer systems, or on PowerPC (Apple G3, G4, and G5) systems on which you don't want to preserve any existing data. On x86 and 64-bit PC systems, the Ubuntu installer can automatically reduce the size of existing Microsoft Windows partitions to free up space in which you can install Ubuntu (assuming that your existing Windows partitions aren't full, of course).

IN THIS CHAPTER

Booting the Desktop CD

Installing Ubuntu Linux

Test-driving Ubuntu Linux

Accessing existing partitions from the Desktop CD

Saving work done using the Desktop CD

Installing Windows programs from the CD

WARNING Installing Ubuntu on PowerPC (PPC) systems where you want to preserve an existing operating system in order to dual boot is explained in detail in the section of Chapter 3 entitled "Overview of Dual-Boot Systems." If you want to preserve existing data on a PPC system and do not already have 3GB of unallocated space on your system's disks, you *must* follow the instructions in this section on repartitioning your existing Mac OS X partitions before attempting to install Ubuntu. This section of Chapter 3 also provides information about manually repartitioning Microsoft Windows disks if you have multiple Windows partitions on your existing disk or if you would simply prefer to do this manually.

Even if you're comfortable working with your existing Microsoft Windows or Mac OS X system and want to keep it as is, there's still plenty of value in the Ubuntu Desktop CD. You can use the Live CD to experiment with Ubuntu Linux and the powerful open source software that it provides. The Ubuntu Desktop CD also includes Windows versions of many popular open source software packages so that you can still experiment with and take advantage of the power of your favorite open source software packages by installing them on your Windows system(s) from the Ubuntu Live CD.

If you're using a 32-bit x86 system, the Ubuntu Desktop CD provided with this book is for you. If not, this chapter explains how to get the Ubuntu Live CD that's appropriate for the system you're using, explains the extent to which you can access your existing disk partitions and files from the Ubuntu Desktop CD so that you can work with them, and explains how to preserve any work that you've done while using the Desktop CD. It concludes by discussing the open source applications for Windows that are provided on the x86 and 64-bit Ubuntu Desktop CDs and how to install them on a Microsoft Windows system.

Getting a 64-bit or PPC Desktop CD

The Ubuntu Desktop CD provided with this book will boot on any x86 PC system. If you are using a 64-bit or PPC computer system, you will need to obtain an Ubuntu Desktop CD that has been compiled and configured to work with those types of computer systems. If you have a reasonably fast Internet connection (or plenty of time) and a CD burner, the easiest way to get an Ubuntu Desktop CD is to download an ISO image. (An ISO image is a file containing an image of a CD-ROM or DVD that is in the format mandated by the International Standards Organization 9660 specification.) To download an ISO image, go to their Web page at www.ubuntu.com/download, select a mirror site in your country or one that's closest to you in general, and select the Desktop CD that is appropriate for your computer system. Save the downloaded ISO image to a file, burn that ISO image to a CD once the download completes, and you're ready to go!

If you have a slow Internet connection or do not have a CD burner, don't panic! As mentioned in the front matter for this book, the Ubuntu folks will even ship you Ubuntu CDs, though they take a few weeks because they're shipped from the Netherlands. This isn't the right solution for those of us who are into instant gratification, but it might work for you. To request that the Ubuntu folks ship you CDs, go to their Web page at https://shipit.ubuntu.com, create an account by entering your e-mail address and a password, and request one or more sets of Ubuntu CDs for the current release. You can even order free CDs for multiple system types at the same time.

Booting the Desktop CD

Booting from an Ubuntu Desktop CD is as easy as inserting the appropriate Desktop CD into your system's CD drive, restarting your system, and making sure that the system boots from the CD drive before booting from a hard disk partition. On traditional PC systems, this is done using BIOS settings, while PPC systems from Apple simply require that you hold down the letter "c" on your keyboard while starting up the computer.

TIP   If your PC boots from the hard drive even if the correct Ubuntu Desktop CD is present in your CD drive, you'll need to modify the *boot order* in your BIOS settings. The boot order is the sequence in which available devices are searched for bootable disks when your system is powered on. To do this, turn your computer on and press the key on your keyboard that gives you access to the BIOS. This is typically either the Del (Delete) or F2 key on most modern systems, but the key that you'll need to press is usually identified at the bottom left of your screen when you turn on your computer and it first starts up.

Depending on the type of BIOS your computer uses, boot order settings are usually stored in an Advanced Settings or Boot screen, which you can navigate to using the arrow keys on your keyboard. Press Return to display this screen once its name is highlighted. Once this screen displays, use the down-arrow key to navigate to the First Boot Device or CD Drive entry, and see the help messages at the right side of the screen for information about how to make your CD Drive the first boot device. You can then press the Escape key to exit this screen, and press F10 to save the new settings, exit the BIOS settings screen, and reboot.

When you boot from the Ubuntu Desktop CD, you'll initially see a screen like the one shown in Figure 2.1.

FIGURE 2.1

Boot Options from the Desktop CD

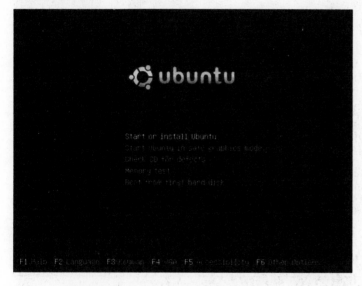

This screen enables you to select whether you want to boot from the Desktop CD, use the Desktop CD to attempt to rescue (repair) an existing system, boot from the hard disk and ignore the Ubuntu CD, or test the CD or your system's memory.

To boot Ubuntu Linux on your system, press Return or wait 30 seconds, at which point your system will automatically boot Ubuntu Linux from the Desktop CD. The standard Ubuntu Desktop displays, as shown in Figure 2.2.

Once you're running Ubuntu, you can install Ubuntu Linux as described in the next section, or you can explore Ubuntu using the menus that are available in the upper-left corner of the screen and the sample files provided in the Examples folder as described in the section of this chapter entitled "Test-Driving Ubuntu Linux." When test-driving Ubuntu, you can practice running specific applications and even experiment with installing and configuring software, as discussed in the remainder of this book.

FIGURE 2.2

The standard Ubuntu Desktop from the Desktop CD

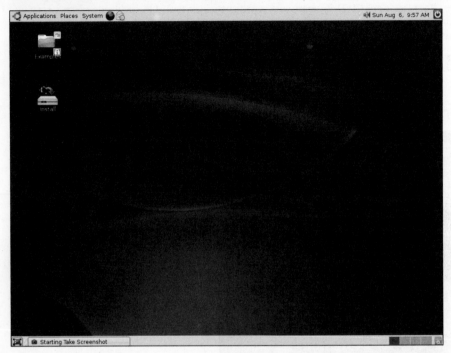

Installing Ubuntu Linux from the Desktop CD

After you have booted from the Ubuntu Desktop CD, you can use Ubuntu's graphical installer to permanently install Ubuntu on your computer system. The instructions in this section describe how to install the Desktop, or end-user, version of Ubuntu Linux from the Ubuntu Desktop CD that is included with this book. See Chapter 3, "Installing Ubuntu on Special-Purpose Systems," for information about installing other versions of Ubuntu Linux, such as the Ubuntu Server or OEM distributions, that require obtaining a different installation CD from the Ubuntu Web site. For an overview of the different Ubuntu CDs, see the section of Chapter 1 entitled "Ubuntu CDs."

WARNING The instructions in this section assume that you are installing Ubuntu Linux on a new computer system or on a computer system where you do not want to preserve any existing files, applications, and other data that are currently on its hard drive(s). If your computer system already has another operating system installed on its hard drive(s) that you want to preserve, see the section entitled "Overview of Dual-Boot Systems" in Chapter 3 and follow the instructions that pertain to the type of computer system that you are using.

You'll need to supply a few pieces of information during the installation process so that Ubuntu is correctly configured for your system, language, and geographic location. To install Ubuntu Linux from the Ubuntu Desktop CD's desktop, do the following:

1. Double-click the Install icon on the desktop shown in Figure 2.2 to begin the installation process. The dialog shown in Figure 2.3 displays, which prompts you to select the language you would like the installation process to use in subsequent dialogs and messages. You can either click Forward or press return to accept the default value of English, or use the arrow keys to scroll up and down in the list of supported languages until you find your native language.

FIGURE 2.3

Specifying the language for the installation process

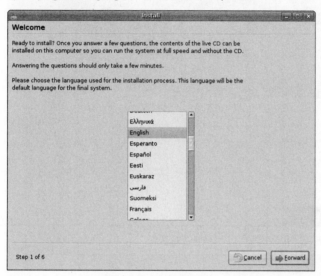

2. The dialog shown in Figure 2.4 prompts you to specify the location where you are using your computer. This value is used to further customize the language that you specified in the previous screen by using the appropriate date and time formats, numeric conventions, and currency values for your geographic location. If the city shown as the Selected City is incorrect, click the name of that city to display a drop-down menu that enables you to select a major city that is close to your geographic location and therefore is in the same time zone as you are.

3. If the time or time zone shown in the dialog in Figure 2.4 is incorrect, click Set Time to display the dialog shown in Figure 2.5. Otherwise, click Forward to proceed to the next step. If you need to change the time or time zone, click Select Time Zone to display a map that enables you to graphically select a major city near your current location. You can also use the text areas at the top of this dialog to set the correct time, or click Synchronize Now to tell the installer to contact an Internet time server to obtain the current time for the specified time zone. Click Forward to proceed.

4. The dialog shown in Figure 2.6 prompts you to specify the type of keyboard attached to your computer. The default value is based on your settings on previous screens — if this is incorrect, select your keyboard type from the full list of supported keyboard types. Click Forward to proceed.

FIGURE 2.4

Specifying your geographic location

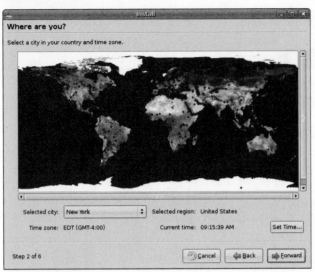

FIGURE 2.5

Setting your time zone and the current time

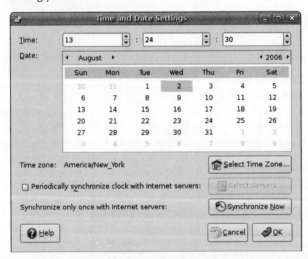

5. The dialog shown in Figure 2.7 enables you to provide personal information that will be used to create your account during the installation process. This account will have the ability to execute privileged commands on the system, as explained in the section of Chapter 4 entitled "Performing Privileged Operations in Ubuntu." After you have filled out all of the fields on this form, click Forward to proceed.

FIGURE 2.6

Specifying your keyboard type

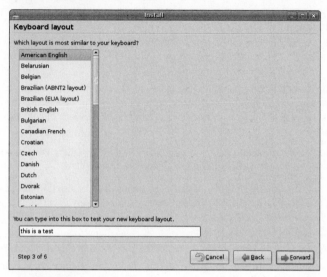

FIGURE 2.7

Specifying information about your account

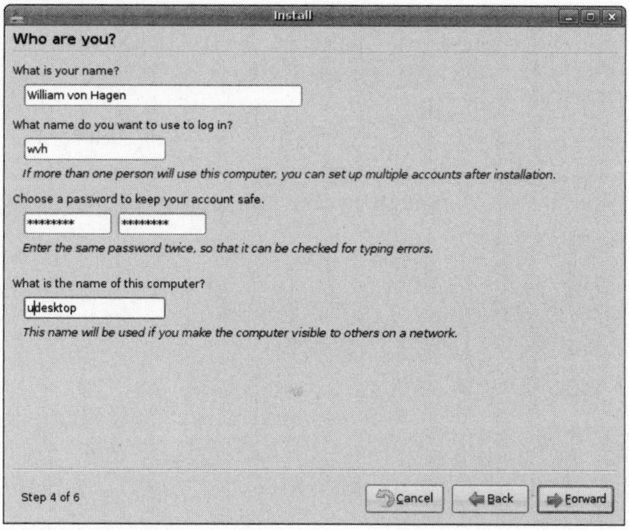

6. The dialog shown in Figure 2.8 enables you to select where you want to install Ubuntu. This dialog looks different and displays different options depending on how the disks in your system are currently configured and what partitions they already contain (if any). The option that you want to select therefore depends on the current state of your system and where you want to install Ubuntu Linux:

   ■ If you are installing Ubuntu on a new computer system or on a computer system where you do not want to preserve any existing files, applications, or other data that are currently on its hard drive(s), select the Erase entire disk option.

   ■ If you are installing Ubuntu on an x86 or 64-bit PC system on which Microsoft Windows is already installed and do not have unallocated space on your disk, select the Resize option and drag the slider at the bottom of the dialog to reflect the new size of your existing Windows partition.

   NOTE You will see the slider and Resize option only if you are installing Ubuntu on an x86 or 64-bit PC system on which Microsoft Windows is already installed.

   ■ If your system contains multiple hard drives, they will all be listed in this dialog. You should generally select the first drive listed that does not contain any data that you want to preserve. Be careful to select the correct drive!

   ■ If you have unallocated space on your disk (such as if you follow the instructions about setting up a dual-boot system in Chapter 3), select the Use the largest contiguous free space option.

   ■ If you are an experienced Linux user and want to manually specify how to partition your disk, select the Manually edit partition table and see the sidebar entitled "Manually Partitioning a Disk" for additional information about using Ubuntu's graphical disk partitioner.

   WARNING As mentioned previously, the Ubuntu Desktop installer for PPC systems cannot automatically resize your existing Mac OS X partitions, as the x86 and 64-bit Desktop CD installers can. You must be willing to either let the installer erase your existing Mac OS X installation, or you must manually resize your existing Mac OS X partition(s) before attempting to install Ubuntu Linux on a PPC system. For information on manually resizing existing Mac OS X partitions, see the section of Chapter 3 entitled "Overview of Dual-Boot Systems."

   Once you have selected the appropriate option for your system, click Forward to continue.

7. The Ubuntu desktop installer displays the screen shown in Figure 2.9, which summarizes the information that you have supplied on previous dialogs. Click Install to proceed.

FIGURE 2.8

Specifying where you want to install Ubuntu Linux

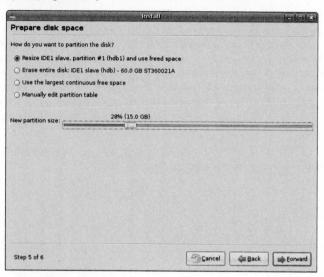

FIGURE 2.9

The summary dialog for starting the installation process

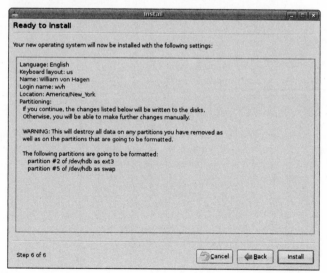

Manually Partitioning a Disk

If you are an experienced Linux user and have a specific reason to do so, you may want to manually specify how you want to divide up the space on your hard disk (or unallocated space on a dual-boot system). If you do not manually partition your disks, Ubuntu provides reasonable default values for the different partitions that it creates automatically (a swap partition whose size is a multiple of the amount of memory in your system and a single large root partition). However, you may want to further divide the disk space on your system and/or allocate it differently. For general information about disks and partitions, see the section of Chapter 4 entitled "Disks, Partitions, and Mount Points" for more information.

If you select the Manually edit partition table option on the dialog shown in Figure 2.8, the dialog shown in the following figure displays after you click Proceed.

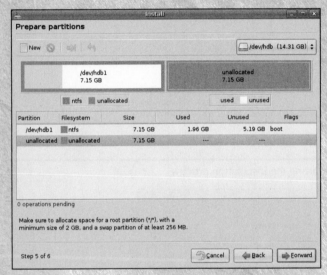

Ubuntu's manual disk partitioner

If your disk contains existing partitions and you want to delete any or all of them on your disk, select each partition that you want to delete and click Delete (the international no icon) to delete that partition. Be careful — deleting a partition permanently removes any information that it contains. Next, select the unallocated space on your disk and click New to define a new partition. The dialog shown in the following figure displays.

Specifying partition size during manual partitioning

Enter the size of the partition that you want to create, verify the type of partition that you are creating (physical or extended) and its format (usually ext3 or swap), and click Add to schedule the creation of this partition on your disk. This redisplays the dialog shown in the first figure in this sidebar, which now contains information about the partition that you just defined, as shown in the following figure, which lists several partitions that have been defined. As shown in this figure, any partitions that you define are not created immediately, but are simply scheduled for creation in a later step. The location where these partitions will be mounted is also specified in a later step.

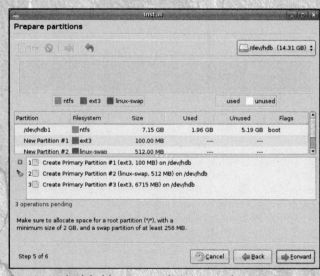

Partitions scheduled for creation during manual partitioning

continued

continued

Repeat this step for every partition that you want to create. You must create at least one swap partition, which Ubuntu will use to support virtual memory and which should be a multiple of the amount of memory in your system, and one partition to hold your Ubuntu system's root filesystem, which should be at least two gigabytes in size. Once you have defined all of the partitions that you want to create, click Forward. The partitioner displays a confirmation dialog, asking if you're sure that you want to proceed. Click Apply to proceed or click cancel to return to the partitioner to make changes. After you click Apply, the partitioner creates the specified partitions and displays the dialog shown next.

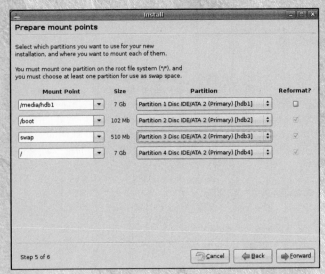

Identifying partition mount points during manual partitioning

The dialog shown in the preceding figure enables you to specify where the partitions that you have just created will be mounted so that Ubuntu Linux can be installed on them, and they are subsequently available to your system. Use the drop-down Mount Point and Partition menus to make sure that all of your partitions are listed in this dialog, that you do not reformat any existing partitions that contain data that you want to preserve, and that your swap partition is not mounted and is identified as a swap partition. Double-check the settings on this dialog before proceeding, because this step actually formats your partitions and tells your system how to use them. Once you're sure that these settings are correct, click Forward to proceed.

8. The Ubuntu installer displays several progress dialogs as it formats the partitions on your hard disk, installs Ubuntu Linux to your system, creates accounts and other system configuration information, and so on. Once the installation completes, the dialog shown in Figure 2.10 displays. To restart your system and run the version of Ubuntu Linux that you just installed, click Restart now, remove the Live CD from your system's CD drive after it is ejected during the shutdown process, and press Enter to reboot your system. Alternately, you can click Continue using the Live CD to continue experimenting with Ubuntu Linux or to save files that you may have already created. See the section entitled, "Test-Driving Ubuntu Linux," later in this chapter for information about saving any work that you may have already done when using the Desktop CD.

FIGURE 2.10

The final installation dialog

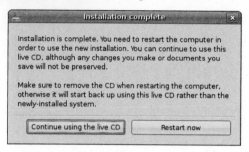

This completes the Ubuntu Desktop installation process — the next time that you boot your system (after removing the Ubuntu Desktop CD), you're ready to run Ubuntu Linux from your system's hard drive(s). Congratulations!

Booting Ubuntu Linux

If you installed Ubuntu Linux as the only operating system on a new or existing computer, you will see a quick message about "GRUB loading, please wait... Press ESC to access the menu" on the screen once the system begins to boot from the hard drive. Ubuntu Linux will boot automatically after 5 seconds, but you can press any key during this time to display the GRUB boot menu, which enables you to boot different kernels (if more than one kernel is installed), boot any available kernel in different modes, or test system memory. For more information about GRUB and its menus, see the section of Chapter 19 entitled "Using the Boot Loader."

Booting Ubuntu Linux on Dual-Boot Systems

If you installed Ubuntu Linux on a system on which another operating system is also installed, the GRUB boot loader menu displays automatically to let you select the operating system that you want to boot. By default, your dual-boot system will boot Ubuntu Linux after 30 seconds. On an x86 system, this screen looks like the one shown in Figure 2.11.

FIGURE 2.11

Selecting an operating system on a dual-boot x86 system

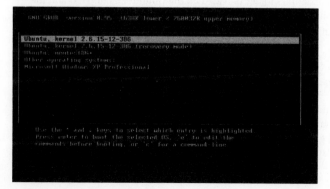

On a PPC system, you will see text messages like the following:

```
First Stage Ubuntu Bootstrap

Press: l for GNU/Linux,
       x for MacOSX,
       c for CDROM

Stage 1 Boot:


Welcome to yaboot version 1.3.13
Enter help to get some basic help information

boot:
```

On a dual-boot PPC Max OS X system, enter the letter l and press Return to boot Ubuntu Linux, or enter x to boot Mac OS X.

The First Time You Boot Ubuntu Linux

The first time that you boot Ubuntu Linux, you will want to update your system. This ensures that you have the latest and best versions of all of the standard Ubuntu software, which provides security-related fixes, bug fixes, and general enhancements. For information about updating your system, see the section of Chapter 20 entitled "Using the Ubuntu Update Manager."

Test-Driving Ubuntu Linux

Figure 2.2 shows the standard Ubuntu desktop displayed after you boot from the Ubuntu Desktop CD that is provided with this book. Though you can experiment with any of the applications that are provided on the Desktop CD, the Desktop CD also provides a folder of sample documents, graphics files, and so on, that simplifies experimenting with different types of applications by giving you some actual documents to experiment with. The Desktop CD is a complete Ubuntu system, and you can follow the instructions in any of the chapters of this book to experiment with Ubuntu without ever installing it to your hard drive. The down side of this type of experimentation is that any files that you create or software that you configure will usually be lost when you reboot your system.

This section discusses the contents of the Examples folder provided on the Ubuntu Desktop CD and the applications associated with each of the files that it contains. It also explains a variety of ways that you can save any data that you create, ranging from manually saving it to an existing filesystem or networked system to combining the Ubuntu Live CD with a specially formatted USB stick to provide a truly portable, persistent system based on the Ubuntu Desktop CD.

Exploring the Desktop CD's Examples Folder

The Ubuntu Desktop CD that is provided with this book includes a folder of sample documents, graphics files, and so on, that makes it easy for you to experiment with different Linux applications by giving you some actual files to open, edit, save, and generally play with. Double-clicking on the Examples folder on the Ubuntu Desktop CD's default desktop displays the contents of that folder in the Nautilus file browser, as shown in Figure 2.12.

FIGURE 2.12

The Desktop CD's Examples folder

The documents and other files in the Examples folder are the following:

- Experience `ubuntu.ogg`: A sample Theora video (an open source video codec) in Ogg container format. Double-clicking this item opens and plays it using the Totem video player application.

- `book-toc.html`: A table of contents for three sample chapters of the "Official Ubuntu Book" that are provided in the Examples folder's book subdirectory. Double-clicking this item opens it in the Firefox Web browser.

- `fables_01_01_aesop.spx`: A sample Speex audio file (an open source audio compression format) in Ogg container format. Double-clicking this item opens and plays it using the Totem video player application.

- `gimp-ubuntu-splash`: A sample Ubuntu splash screen in the native open source XCF format used by the GIMP imagine manipulation program. Double-clicking this item opens it in the GIMP.

- `kubuntu-leaflet.png`: A sample Kubuntu document in the Portable Network Graphics (PNG) format. Double-clicking this item opens it in the GIMP.

- `logo-Edubuntu.png`: A sample Edubuntu logo in the PNG format. Double-clicking this item opens it in the GIMP.

- `logo-Kubuntu.png`: A sample Kubuntu logo in the PNG format. Double-clicking this item opens it in the GIMP.

- `logo-Ubuntu.png`: A sample Ubuntu logo in the PNG format. Double-clicking this item opens it in the GIMP.

- `oo-about-these-files.odt`: A sample OpenOffice.org document that provides information about the files in the Examples folder. Double-clicking this item opens it in OpenOffice Writer.

- `oo-about-ubuntu-ru.rtf`: A sample Russian document in Microsoft's Rich Text Format (RTF) markup. Double-clicking this item opens it in OpenOffice Writer.

- `oo-access.odt`: A sample OpenOffice.org document that provides information about accessibility and assistive technologies in Ubuntu. Double-clicking this item opens it in OpenOffice Writer.

- `oo-cd-cover.odg`: A sample OpenOffice.org Draw file that provides a cover and tray insert for an Ubuntu CD-ROM. Double-clicking this item opens it in OpenOffice Draw.

- `oo-derivatives.doc`: A sample document in Microsoft Office/Word document format that discusses derivatives of the Ubuntu Linux distribution, such as Edubuntu, Kubuntu, and Xubuntu. Double-clicking this item opens it in OpenOffice Writer.

- `oo-maxwell.odt`: A sample OpenOffice.org document that shows the mathematical capabilities of OpenOffice.org Writer by discussing Maxwell's equations. Double-clicking this item opens it in OpenOffice Writer.

- `oo-payment-schedule.ods`: A sample OpenOffice.org spreadsheet that shows calculations and other capabilities. Double-clicking this item opens it in OpenOffice Calc.

- `oo-presenting-kubuntu.odp`: A sample OpenOffice.org presentation that discusses Kubuntu. Double-clicking this item opens it in OpenOffice Impress.

- `oo-presenting-ubuntu.odp`: A sample OpenOffice.org presentation that discusses Ubuntu. Double-clicking this item opens it in OpenOffice Impress.

- `oo-trig.xls`: A sample Microsoft Office/Excel document that shows calculations and the graphical display of results. Double-clicking this item opens it in OpenOffice Calc.

- `oo-welcome.odt`: A sample OpenOffice.org document that contains embedded graphics and provides an introduction to Ubuntu Linux. Double-clicking this item opens it in OpenOffice Writer.

- `ubuntu Sax.ogg`: A sample Vorbis (an open source audio codec) in Ogg container format. Double-clicking this item opens and plays it using the Totem video player application.

Double-clicking on these sample documents and files gives you the opportunity to experiment with the associated software package without having to start from scratch. You cannot modify these documents in place because they are loaded from the CD. To modify any of them, copy the document or file to the login directory and make it writable. For information about changing Linux file permissions, see the section of Chapter 4 entitled "Understanding Linux Permissions."

Accessing Your Hard Drive from the Desktop CD

Booting a Desktop version of Ubuntu on your Microsoft Windows or PPC Macintosh system is fun, but if you do any real work while in "Ubuntu mode," you may actually want to save it for future reuse. Both Microsoft Windows and PPC Macintosh systems use special types of filesystems to store user and system data. Because the Ubuntu Desktop CD runs from an in-memory filesystem (known as a RAM disk), the key to saving data that you've created when running Ubuntu from a Desktop CD is being able to access your existing filesystems from Ubuntu and saving your data there, or using an external persistent storage device as explained later in this chapter in the section entitled "Using Desktop CD Persistence." To access the filesystems on your local disk drives, you have to explicitly make them available (mount them) when running Ubuntu, and this requires that you use a few special utilities.

Unfortunately, as subsequent sections explain, Ubuntu cannot currently provide out-of-the-box support for writing to all of the filesystems used by Microsoft Windows because of their proprietary nature.

The next sections explore the types of filesystems used on Microsoft Windows and Apple Macintosh computer systems, how to access those filesystems, and how to copy files and data that you've created when running Ubuntu from a Desktop CD to another machine over the network if you can't access your local filesystems for one reason or another.

Accessing Microsoft Windows Partitions From the Desktop CD

At the time this book was written, most Microsoft Windows systems use either the NTFS (NT File System) or the older FAT32 (32-bit File Allocation Table) filesystems. NTFS is a proprietary and complex format, and the standard Linux device and filesystem drivers only support read-only access to NTFS partitions. In plain English, this means that you can mount and read files from the NTFS partition(s) on your Linux system, but you cannot modify files on your NTFS partitions. Even if you copy files from an NTFS partition to work on them, you cannot copy the modified files back to your NTFS partition once you're done if you are using the standard Linux NTFS drivers.

> **TIP** Though the standard Linux device drivers will eventually support writing to NTFS partitions, drivers to do this are commercially available from Paragon Software (www.ntfs-linux .com). Driver source code is included with your purchase, and Paragon provides demonstration versions that provide these drivers as loadable kernel modules for the vanilla kernels delivered with many popular desktop Linux distributions. These drivers are slow, but have worked perfectly for me. Unfortunately, at the current time, the Desktop CD does not include the compiler (gcc) necessary to build and install these temporarily while running from the Desktop CD. Your only alternatives for saving work done on a Windows system that you've booted using the Desktop CD and which has only NTFS partitions are to use a persistent storage device with your Ubuntu Desktop CD (as explained in "Using Desktop CD Persistence"), copy the files to another device (as explained in "Accessing Your Hard Drive from the Desktop CD"), or transfer modified files to another system (as explained in "Copying Files to Other Machines Over a Network"). For information about building, installing, and using special devices and filesystem drivers when running Ubuntu from a hard drive, see "Customizing the Kernel" in Chapter 18. The rest of this section explains how to use Ubuntu's Disks Manager application to mount existing partitions so that you can read (and, if possible, write to) them.

After booting from the Desktop CD, select the System ➪ Administration ➪ Disks menu item. The Disks Manager starts, displaying a list of all of the disks and other storage media available on your system. To mount a partition from your hard disk, do the following:

1. Select your system's hard drive from the list at left and click the Partitions tab to see the list of available partitions on that hard drive. Select the hard drive partition that you want to access. A screen like the one in Figure 2.13 displays.

2. Click the Change button beside the Access Path entry, and select a directory on which you want to mount the selected filesystem by clicking File System from the list at left and navigating to that directory. The directory /mnt is the standard location for mounting partitions, as shown in Figure 2.14.

FIGURE 2.13

Selecting a Windows partition in the Disks Manager

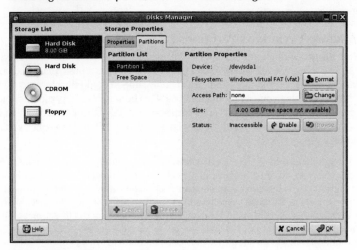

FIGURE 2.14

Selecting a mount point for your windows partition

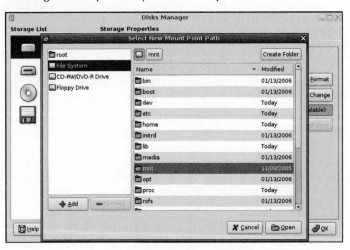

3. Click Open to select the /mnt directory. The dialog shown in Figure 2.14 closes, and the main Disks Manager dialog displays again. Click the Enable button to make your Windows partition available to your system by mounting it on the directory /mnt. The Disks Manager dialog updates to reflect the amount of free space available on the mounted partition, as shown in Figure 2.15.

FIGURE 2.15

Information about a mounted partition

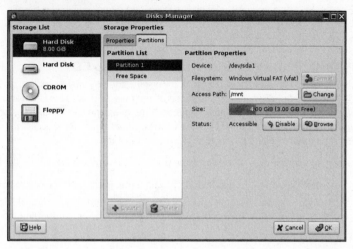

4. To verify that you can access files in the Windows partition, click Browse. The Nautilus file manager starts, displaying a list of the files available at the top level of the selected partition, as shown in Figure 2.16.

FIGURE 2.16

Browsing your mounted windows partition

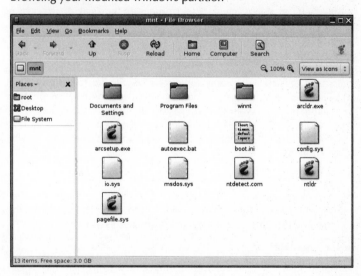

Once you've mounted a Windows partition, you can drag and drop files from it to your desktop to work with a temporary copy of your file, or work with them directly from the mounted partition if it is a FAT32 partition. If your system has only NTFS partitions and you work with temporary copies of your Windows files, you can always save them to another storage device that Ubuntu can access, or you can transfer them over the network to another machine, as explained in "Copying Files to Other Machines Over a Network" later in this chapter.

Accessing PPC Macintosh Partitions From the Desktop CD

Most modern PPC Macintosh systems use a type of filesystem known as HFS+, which the Disks Manager (discussed earlier) does not understand how to access at the present time. This is unfortunate, but not insurmountable. If you're willing to do a little command-line magic on a PPC Macintosh that you've booted from the Ubuntu Desktop CD, you can still mount your Macintosh partitions, access the files that are stored there, and even save modified files back to your Macintosh partitions.

To manually mount your Macintosh partitions using the Linux mount command, do the following:

1. Select the Applications ➪ Accessories ➪ Terminal menu item. A Linux terminal window displays.

2. Use the fdisk -1 /dev/hdc command to list the partitions that are available on your Macintosh hard drive, as in the following example (abbreviated to show only important information):

```
sudo fdisk -1 /dev/hdc
/dev/hdc
          #                   type name        ...
/dev/hdc1   Apple_partition_map Apple     ...
/dev/hdc2    Apple_Bootstrap untitled      ...
/dev/hdc3         Apple_HFS Apple_HFS_untitled  ...
/dev/hdc4   Apple_UNIX_SVR2 untitled       ...
/dev/hdc5   Apple_UNIX_SVR2 swap           ...
/dev/hdc6         Apple_Free Extra          ...
```

3. The PPC Macintosh partition is identified as an Apple_HFS partition in the second column of this output. You can mount any of these partitions on the /mnt directory by using the mount command, as in the following example, which mounts the HFS+ filesystem /dev/hdc3 on the directory /mnt:

```
sudo mount -t hfsplus /dev/hdc3 /mnt
```

Once you have mounted your HFS+ partition, you can browse the /mnt directory to see your files. Unfortunately, this filesystem can be written to only by a privileged user, so you probably want to copy any files that you want to modify to your Desktop CD desktop, modify them, and then copy them back using the sudo command. For example, the following command copies a file to the directory /mnt/Users/wvh, which is my Mac OS X home directory as seen under the directory on which I mounted my PPC Macintosh partition:

```
sudo cp Desktop/the_file_I_modified.doc /mnt/Users/wvh
```

If you follow the instructions in this section for manually mounting a partition, you should also unmount it before shutting down your Ubuntu Desktop CD session. As an example, I would use the following command to unmount the HFS+ partition that I mounted earlier in this section:

```
sudo umount /dev/hdc3
```

Using Desktop CD Persistence

Live CDs like the Ubuntu Desktop CD provide an easy way to temporarily turn any compatible computer system into an Ubuntu Linux system. However, the fact that most live CDs don't provide any sort of persistent storage for configuration data, custom applications, and so on (other than manually copying files to other local or networked storage) limits the practical usability of Live CDs to simple demonstrations, general one-time experimentation, rescuing data from crashed systems, and for general system repair and recovery efforts. Until now, that is.

The Ubuntu 6.06 Desktop CD provides a built-in mechanism for recognizing an external storage device with a special name at boot-time and using the contents of that device to restore desktop settings, application configuration files, and even installed applications. The amount of custom configuration information and installed applications that you can save and restore is only limited by the size of the external storage device that you use. The requirements for taking advantage of this capability are the following:

- The external storage device must be one that can be found by the Desktop CD kernel when it boots.
- The external storage device must contain a Linux filesystem that is supported by the Desktop CD kernel. VFAT, NTFS, and HFS+ filesystems will not work — the filesystem must be an actual Linux filesystem. Ext2 or ext3 filesystems are recommended for portability.
- The filesystem on the external storage device must have the name `casper-rw`.
- You must add the `persistent` keyword to the kernel command line when you boot from the Desktop CD.

The most common devices used for persistent storage with the Desktop CD are USB devices. USB sticks (a.k.a. *pen drives*) are extremely portable, but provide a limited amount of storage. An external USB hard drive is a better alternative if you need to install applications, related files, and other data that would exceed the amount of storage available on a USB stick.

> **TIP** If you are using an Ubuntu Desktop CD for demonstration purposes and do not need to save changes to associated data files across demos, creating a customized version of the Ubuntu Desktop CD might be a simpler approach than using an external drive for persistent storage with the Desktop CD. The Ubuntu Web site has a great set of instructions for creating your own customized version of the Ubuntu Desktop CD for the 6.06 LTS release at `https://help.ubuntu.com/community/LiveCDCustomization/6%2e06`.

Formatting and Labeling Your External Storage Device

After you attach your removable storage device to your system, boot Ubuntu from that system (or from the Desktop CD). See the section of Chapter 23 entitled "Locating, Partitioning, and Formatting New Drives" for information about how to identify and format drives on your system. If you are using a USB stick or removable hard drive, the name of that drive will be something like sda, sdb, and so on. Make sure that you do not accidentally format the wrong disk! If the USB stick or removable hard drive that you are using already contains a filesystem, mount it manually (as discussed in the section of Chapter 4 entitled "Mounting Filesystems") to verify that this is the disk that you want to format, and then umount it before proceeding to format the drive. As mentioned previously, the type of filesystem that you create on your external drive must be an actual Linux filesystem such as ext2, ext3, jfs, reiserfs, or xfs. I suggest using ext3 filesystems because they are readable from any Linux system if you want to copy additional data to the drive from some other Linux system. The ext2 filesystem might be a better choice for devices with limited amounts of storage, such as USB sticks.

TIP If you want to add data to your removable drive from another Linux system, you can do so by simply attaching the removable drive to that system, mounting it, and copying data into the appropriate locations. External storage devices used for persistent storage contain a Linux filesystem with its familiar directory structure. For example, you could copy other data files to the home directory of the Live CD's default user by copying those files to the directory `home/ubuntu` on the removable storage device, and they will appear in that user's home directory the next time that you boot your system from the Desktop CD as described in the next section.

Once the external storage device contains a suitable filesystem, you will need to label that filesystem as `casper-rw`, which is the special name that Ubuntu 6.06 uses to recognize a persistent storage device. Labeling an ext2 or ext3 filesystem is done using the `e2label` command from any Linux command line, such as a GNOME Terminal or an xterm. (Other Linux filesystems use other utilities, such as `reiser fstune` for reiserfs filesystem, `xfs_admin` for XFS filesystems, and so on.) For example, correctly labeling the ext2 filesystem on the device `/dev/sda1` would be done using the following command:

```
$ sudo e2label /dev/sda1 casper-rw
```

Once you have labeled the filesystem, you're ready to boot the Desktop CD and incorporate that device as persistent storage, as described in the next section.

Modifying Kernel Command-Line Arguments for Persistent Storage

Once you have created and labeled the filesystem on your persistent storage device as described in the previous section, attach that device to the system that you want to boot from the Ubuntu Desktop CD and reboot from the Desktop CD. When the Ubuntu splash screen displays, press the F6 key and type a space and the word **persistent** on the kernel command line that displays, as shown in Figure 2.17.

FIGURE 2.17

Adding the persistent keyword to the Desktop CD kernel command line

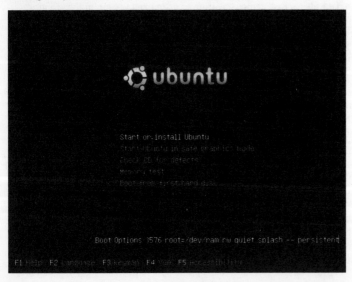

After adding this keyword, press Return to continue the Desktop CD boot process. Once the system has booted, you can change configuration settings, create new files, install applications, and so on. Any changes

that you make will be saved to your persistent storage device, and will be available the next time you boot from the Desktop CD as long as you specify the `persistent` keyword on the kernel command line, as described in this section.

Copying Files to Other Machines Over a Network

If you create or modify files while running from a Desktop CD, you may want to save those changes. If you're running from a Desktop CD but are unable to write to any of your system's hard disk partitions (as described earlier in this chapter), you can still save those files by copying them over the network to another machine.

Linux provides several ways to enable copying files to other systems over the network. Some of the most common and popular of these are the following:

- the `ftp` (file transfer protocol) utility, which establishes a connection to another machine and enables you to interactively transfer files in either direction
- the `scp` (secure copy) utility, which enables you to quickly transfer files to other machines over a secure, encrypted connection
- the System ⇨ Administration ⇨ Shared Folders menu item, which enables you to mount a shared network drive on another system to which you can copy files.

All of these are explained in detail in Chapter 15, "Connecting to Other Systems." They're summarized here so that you know that there are ways to save any work that you've done from the Ubuntu Desktop CD, even if you can't directly access the partitions on your Microsoft Windows or Apple Mac OS X systems for one reason or another.

Installing Windows Programs from the Desktop CD

The Ubuntu Desktop CD not only provides a great way to try out Ubuntu, but also provides a great way to try out some powerful and excellent open source applications on your Windows system. If you insert an i386 Ubuntu Desktop CD into the CD drive of a system that's running Microsoft Windows, you'll see a dialog like that shown in Figure 2.18.

This dialog enables you to install any of the following applications on your Windows system:

- Mozilla Firefox is a Web browser that provides a popular and secure alternative to Microsoft's Internet Explorer on Windows systems. The core capabilities provided by Firefox are easily extended using hundreds of plug-ins that are freely available over the Internet. Using Firefox is discussed in Chapter 9, "Surfing the Web with Firefox."
- Mozilla Thunderbird is an e-mail client (MUA) that provides a popular and secure mechanism for reading e-mail from POP/POP3 and IMAP mail servers.
- AbiWord is a popular word processor that is part of the GNOME office suite and provides a free, open source alternative to expensive, proprietary word processors such as Microsoft Word.
- Gaim is an open source alternative to most instant messenger software that can exchange messages in all of the formats used by popular instant messaging packages from AOL, Yahoo, and so on.
- GIMP is a popular image creation and manipulation package that provides a free, open source alternative to expensive, proprietary software packages such as Adobe Photoshop. Using GIMP is discussed in the section of Chapter 12 entitled "Using the GIMP."

To install any of these packages, click the Install now button beside its entry. A Windows installer for this software starts, as shown in Figure 2.19, where I'm installing Firefox.

Once the installation completes, these open source applications run natively on your Windows system, without the need for the Ubuntu Desktop CD. For example, Figure 2.20 shows Firefox running natively on my Windows system.

FIGURE 2.18

Open source software for Windows on the Ubuntu Desktop CD

FIGURE 2.19

Installing Firefox on Windows from the Ubuntu Desktop CD

FIGURE 2.20

Running Firefox on Windows after installation

Summary

This chapter explained how you can take Ubuntu Linux for a test drive or even permanently install Ubuntu Linux after booting from the Ubuntu Desktop CD that is appropriate for the type of personal computer that you're currently using. This book includes an Ubuntu Desktop CD for x86 systems. Though I hope that you've installed Ubuntu Linux permanently on your computer system, this chapter also discussed various ways of experimenting with Ubuntu and saving your data if you don't want to install Ubuntu on your computer yet.

Even if you're not ready to completely commit yourself to Ubuntu Linux, the Ubuntu Desktop CD enables you to sample the power of both an open source operating system (GNU/Linux) and popular open source software packages. This chapter explained how to access filesystems on your existing PC from the Desktop CD while test-driving Linux, and how to install open source software from the Desktop CD on an existing Windows system so that you can take advantage of the power of open source software on that platform.

The next chapter discusses other ways of installing Ubuntu Linux using other Ubuntu CDs, and also discusses how to install Ubuntu on more complex systems, such as systems on which you want to be able to boot Ubuntu Linux and other, preexisting operating systems.

Chapter 3

Installing Ubuntu on Special-Purpose Systems

The previous chapter discussed the graphical installer that is provided as part of the Ubuntu Desktop CD, which is the CD that is included with this book. Using this CD and its installer is the standard way of installing an Ubuntu Desktop system. However, as discussed in the section of Chapter 1 entitled "Ubuntu CDs," two other CDs are also available from the Ubuntu folks for each fully supported platform. These are the Ubuntu Server Install CD and the Ubuntu Alternate Install CD. This chapter discusses how to obtain these CDs and the installation alternatives that each of them provides, and begins with a discussion of installing Ubuntu on dual-boot systems, which are systems that can boot more than one operating system (though not at the same time). Dual-booting means that when you turn the machine on, you'll be given the choice of booting Ubuntu Linux or another operating system, such as Microsoft Windows or Mac OS X. This is the easiest path to take if you don't have a machine to dedicate to Ubuntu or if there are some critical pieces of software that you depend on which run under another operating system, and you aren't sure how to accomplish the same things using Ubuntu. Hopefully, by the end of this book, you'll feel more comfortable giving up on Windows, but it's always better to be safe than truly sorry when you can't figure out how to get your work done.

IN THIS CHAPTER

Setting up dual-boot x86 and PPC systems

Repartitioning existing disks

Getting other Ubuntu CDs

Installing Ubuntu servers

Resolving installation problems

Installing from the Alternate CD

The Ubuntu Desktop CD's graphical installer differs from the quasi-graphical, Debian-based installers used on the Server and Alternate Install CDs. Before providing a graphical installer on the Desktop CD, Ubuntu's Debian-based installer received its share of the criticism traditionally aimed at the Debian installer — "It's not fancy enough," "It looks like something from 1985," "It doesn't use all of the whizzy features of my five-dimensional, accelerated graphics card," and so on. These are all true, and for good reasons. Although it's nice to have a fancy, mouse-oriented, graphical installation program, an installer is something that you use once per system and then forget about. An installer therefore has to be rock-solid, easy-to-understand, and easy-to-use. It also has to work on any computer system from the most wretched, low-resolution VGA system to the high-end gaming systems of today, which provide stunning resolution and visual nuances that many people can't even detect. Server systems often run headless (i.e., without a graphical console), and therefore an installer that works on those types of systems is fairly important.

47

Overview of Dual-Boot Systems

As explained in the introduction to this chapter, *dual-booting* is the term used to describe a computer system that can run more than one operating system (though not at the same time). Dual-booting is an attractive option if you want to experiment with Ubuntu but still depend on applications that run on whatever existing operating system you're using. Because Ubuntu Linux is officially supported on x86 and 64-bit PC machines that often run Microsoft Windows and on PPC systems that typically run Mac OS X, this chapter explains how to install Ubuntu as a second operating system on these types of machines. The only requirement for doing this is that you have sufficient space on your computer's drives to hold both operating systems and their associated applications.

 The Ubuntu Desktop CD Installer discussed in Chapter 2 will automatically offer to resize an existing Microsoft Windows partition if one is detected on your x86 or 64-bit PC system. In most cases, you do not have to manually repartition your existing Windows partitions as explained in this chapter. The information in this section on manually repartitioning Windows partitions is provided for your convenience, just in case you want to do this yourself. If your disk contains multiple Windows partitions and you want to resize and move them to create free space, or if you would simply prefer to resize partitions yourself, "just in case," the Windows repartitioning information in this chapter will hopefully be useful to you.

Your Computer's Boot Process

To understand how dual-booting works, it's useful to have a little insight into what exactly happens when you turn on a computer system, which is known as your computer's *boot process*. When you turn on your computer system, a hardware subsystem known as the *Basic Input Output System (BIOS)* loads, explores and tests your hardware, and then reads some configuration setting from a special memory chip on your system. On x86 systems, these BIOS settings specify a variety of configuration data including the order in which your hard drive, CD-ROM, DVD, or other media are searched to find something that it can execute. (On Apple Macintosh systems, this is automatically a disk partition unless you actually specify an alternate boot device by holding down an associated key on your keyboard.)

Once your system knows where to boot from, it searches these devices and loads a master boot record from the bootable device. At this point, your system doesn't know anything about the geometry of your hard disks or other storage devices, but it can always find the first few blocks on any device to identify whether the drive is bootable. On Ubuntu Linux systems, the MBR contains the first stage of the Linux GRUB boot loader, which is loaded into memory and is executed. The first stage of the GRUB boot loader then loads a second stage installer that understands the type of filesystem used on the bootable drive.

Once the second stage boot loader is loaded into memory and executing, it reads a configuration file located on the device that contained the boot loader and displays any available options for booting the computer system. On computer systems that run only one operating system, your boot options are fairly straightforward, simply listing different ways of starting that single operating system. On systems that can boot multiple operating systems, the boot loader options list all of the available operating systems on your computer. In addition to offering multiple ways of booting each operating system, they typically also enable you to choose between operating systems.

Loading a sequence of increasingly complex programs, starting with the BIOS or boot monitor and ending with a full-blown operating system is known as *booting* your system because the system has essentially pulled itself up by its bootstraps.

TIP For more detailed information about Linux boot loaders and the Linux boot and system startup process, see the section of Chapter 19 entitled "Overview of the Ubuntu Linux Startup Process."

Configuring a System for Dual-Booting

It's quite easy to configure your system to run your choice of operating systems. This enables you to boot Microsoft Windows or Mac OS X when you need to read mail from applications that only run under those operating systems, but boot Linux when you need to do more complex tasks or want to explore the power and elegance of Ubuntu. Setting up a dual-boot system is also a great way to learn Linux if you have only one computer system and aren't willing or able to simply take the plunge and move to Linux full-time.

When you install Mac OS X or Microsoft Windows on a system with a single disk drive, these operating systems typically create only a single partition on each of your disk drives. This makes it tricky to add another operating system to that same computer system. You generally have two choices:

- Add another hard drive to that computer system and install Linux there.
- Change the existing partitions on your computer's hard drive to free up space in which you can create another partition where you can then install Linux.

The first of these is usually an option in desktop computer systems, assuming that you have room inside your machine for another drive, have sufficient funds to buy another disk drive, and are dedicated and technical enough to open up your computer and add a hard drive correctly. However, if you have sufficient free space available on your system's existing drive, the second option is cheaper, faster, and easier. This chapter focuses on installing a system with an existing operating system — installing onto a second disk is identical to installing on a single-disk system except that you must make sure that you select the correct disk to install onto.

As mentioned earlier in this chapter, you should plan on devoting a minimum of 3GB to an Ubuntu Linux installation, which gives you sufficient space in which to install the operating system, a standard set of applications, and enough room to create and store a reasonable amount of your files and other personal data. 3GB does not leave you all that much free space, but is usable — anything larger than 3GB is, of course, better because it will provide more space for you to create and store personal information and files on your Ubuntu Linux partition. Changing the existing partitions on your computer system is known as *repartitioning* your system.

> **WARNING** Several free and commercial software packages are available that make it easy to repartition existing disks. However, the first part of software is the word *soft*, which in this case means that something can go wrong. Please make sure that you back up your critical OS X or Windows data before proceeding!

Ninety-nine times out of a hundred, repartitioning an existing disk drive is completely safe and will not damage or lose any of the existing programs or data on your Windows or Mac OS X partition. However, preventing the pain associated with that one remaining time is worth the extra time that it takes to back up your important personal data before making any changes to your disk partitions. If you're tempted to skip this step and just go ahead with repartitioning, stop and think for a moment what it would be like if you lost your computer system or it was destroyed: the saved e-mail that you've exchanged with friends and family, those letters you've written, your digital photographs, your music collection, the great American novel — all gone. Are you really willing to take that chance? If so, you're braver than I am.

Repartitioning an Existing Disk

Once you've done backups of your important files and verified that the backups are readable, you can move on to actually repartitioning your disk to make room for Linux. The first step in doing this is to defragment your disk, which packs the disk space associated with all of the files and directories on your existing partition as closely together as possible. Disks become fragmented as you create and delete files — there's nothing that you can do about it except to clean things up occasionally. When you repartition your disk, you're essentially slicing off a portion of an existing partition so that you can use it for something else. You can't just remove a portion of an existing partition if it contains parts of files that you are using.

Microsoft Windows and Mac OS X Backup Software

Though this isn't a book about Microsoft Windows or Mac OS X, recommending that you back up those systems before repartitioning without providing some suggestions would be rude. Both Microsoft Windows and Mac OS X provide basic backup software for their platforms. Versions of Microsoft Windows such as Windows XP provide backup software that you can access via the Programs ➪ Accessories ➪ System Tools ➪ Backup menu item. The generic Mac Backup software is available for free via Apple's .Mac online storage subscription service (you can sign up for a free trial of the .Mac site if you don't want to permanently subscribe). Both of these packages support backups to removable media.

More sophisticated, and expensive, backup solutions are available for both platforms. For Windows systems, I've heard good things about SyncBackSE (www.2brightsparks.com), Genie-Soft Backup Manager (www.genie-soft.com), and I have used Veritas' Backup Exec (www.backupexec.com) commercially, though it's probably overkill for laptop or desktop systems. For Mac OS X systems, Lacie's Silverkeeper (www.lacie.com/silverkeeper) is a popular, free package that requires registration to download. Bombich Software's Carbon Copy Cloner (www.bombich.com/software/ccc.html) is another free package that is extremely popular.

If you have multiple types of systems, a multiplatform solution such as EMC Insignia's Retrospect (www.emcinsignia.com) will enable you to do Windows and Mac OS X backups, and will also enable you to back up Linux systems from your Mac when they are mounted via NFS or SMB. Similarly, but a bit more powerful, the Tolis Group's BRU (www.tolisgroup.com) package supports Windows, Mac OS X, and native Linux backups.

Defragmenting Microsoft Windows Systems

Windows provides a built-in defragmentation utility, which you can start by selecting the Programs ➪ Accessories ➪ System Tools ➪ Disk Defragmenter menu item. In this utility, (shown in Figure 3.1) first select the drive letter associated with the disk partition that you want to reduce in size to make room for Linux, and then click Defragment. The Disk Defragmenter will do its work and display a before and after picture of fragmentation on that partition once it completes. Running the Defragmenter once is sufficient, even if the Defragmenter reports that your disk is still somewhat fragmented.

You may wonder why Figure 3.1 shows some system files that haven't been moved closer to the beginning of the disk. The defragmenter doesn't relocate Microsoft Windows system files such as its paging file because these files are used internally by Windows and shouldn't be modified after they are created. However, they are recreated if any problems are found with them, so they will be recreated even if they are located in the part of the disk that you're going to allocate for use by Linux.

NOTE   The Linux utility that you'll use later to repartition your disk is supposed to be able to deal with fragmentation, safely moving fragmented portions of files from the part of the existing Windows partition that you'll be dedicating to Linux. However, defragmenting your disk from Windows beforehand can never hurt, so I still recommend that you defragment your disk before proceeding.

Once you've defragmented your disk, the next step in manually creating space for Linux is to repartition your disk using the tools found on the Ubuntu Desktop CD. Skip ahead to the section entitled "Repartitioning Microsoft Windows Systems Using the Ubuntu Desktop CD." Using the Ubuntu Desktop CD is discussed in detail in Chapter 2 — the "Accessing Microsoft Windows Partitions from the Desktop CD" section in this chapter focuses on how to use the Desktop CD to perform a simple repartitioning task on a system running Microsoft Windows.

FIGURE 3.1

Cleaning up a partition with the Windows Disk Defragmenter

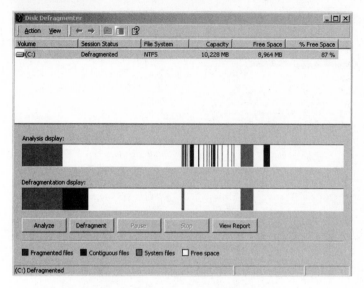

Defragmenting Mac OS X Systems

Apple's Disk Utility is an excellent tool for testing the internal consistency of your Mac OS X HFS and HFS+ partitions. Unfortunately, it does not defragment disk partitions, so third-party utilities are your only option when defragmenting or otherwise modifying Mac OS X disk partitions.

Mac OS X systems running Mac OS X 10.3 (Panther) and later that use the HFS+ journaling filesystem automatically defragment files less than 20MB in size whenever these files are updated. Mac OS X 10.3 and greater HFS+ filesystems also use a mechanism known as *Hot-File-Adaptive-Clustering* to put frequently-used files less than 10MB in size in a special portion of the filesystem, known as the *hot band*, that provides optimal performance based on the characteristics of your disk drive. Files moved to this area are defragmented as they are moved. Though it can provide substantial performance improvements, the use of Hot-File-Adaptive-Clustering complicates life for defragmentation utilities.

However, this is another situation where it's better to be safe than sorry. For PPC-based Mac OS X systems, disk utilities such as Micromat's TechTool Pro (my personal favorite, available at www.micromat.com) perform defragmentation during disk optimization.

Repartitioning Microsoft Windows Systems Using the Ubuntu Desktop CD

Now the fun begins! The Ubuntu Desktop CD includes a nice graphical utility called GNOME Partition Editor that makes it easy to resize existing partitions on a Microsoft Windows system. Most Windows filesystems today are in NT File System (NTFS) format, though some systems still use the 32-Bit File Allocation Table (FAT32) format, also known as VFAT. The GNOME Partition Editor can resize either of these types of filesystems.

To use the GNOME Partition Editor to resize an existing Microsoft Windows partition, boot from the Ubuntu Desktop CD as described in Chapter 2. When the GNOME desktop displays, select System ⇨ Administration ⇨ GNOME Partition Editor. A dialog like the one shown in Figure 3.2 displays.

FIGURE 3.2

The GNOME Partition Editor's utility's startup dialog

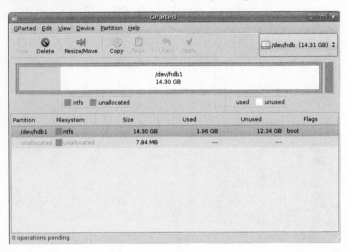

At this point, do the following:

1. Select the hard disk partition that you want to resize from the partition list at the bottom of this dialog and click the Resize/Move button in the icon toolbar above the listing of your disk's current partitioning scheme. The dialog shown in Figure 3.3 displays.

FIGURE 3.3

The Resize dialog

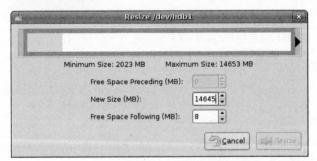

2. Left-click the arrow at the right end of the area at the top of this dialog, and drag it to the left to represent moving the end of the partition. As you drag it, you'll the see the numbers in the bottom of the dialog change to reflect the proposed new size of your partition. This isn't actually making any changes to your disk, it's just setting things up to do so, so there's no problem if you drag the end of the partition with your mouse button, let go, and then want to make additional changes. Figure 3.4 shows this dialog after I've proposed resizing my current partition so that it is evenly divided between an NTFS partition and free space into which I can install Ubuntu.

FIGURE 3.4

The Resize dialog after resizing a partition

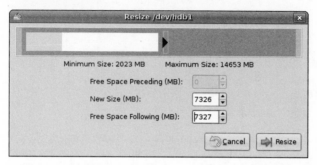

3. Click Resize to schedule this operation and close the Resize dialog. As shown in Figure 3.5, the main Partition Editor dialog displays, listing the pending resize operation at the bottom.

FIGURE 3.5

The Partition Editor showing a pending resize operation

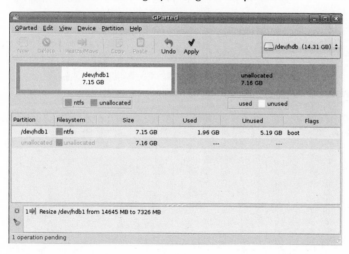

4. Click Apply. A dialog displays, asking if you're sure that you want to perform the pending operation. Click Apply. The dialog shown in Figure 3.6 displays as the resize operation is performed.

FIGURE 3.6

The Partition Editor's operation in progress dialog

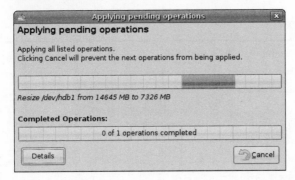

5. When the resize operation completes, an updated summary dialog displays, showing that your existing partition has been split into an NTFS partition and unallocated space in which you can now install Ubuntu Linux (see Figure 3.7). Select the GParted ⇨ Quit menu command to leave the partition editor, and select the System ⇨ Administration ⇨ Log Off menu command to terminate your live Ubuntu session. Click Restart on the pop-up dialog that displays.

FIGURE 3.7

The Partition Editor dialog after completing the resize

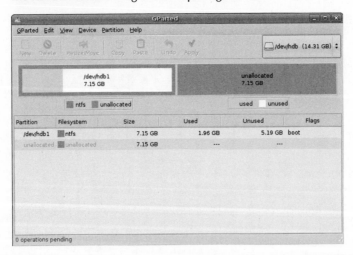

Congratulations! You've successfully resized your partition and created space for Ubuntu. To reboot your system into Microsoft Windows to double-check that your Windows installation is still fine, press the Return or Enter key on your keyboard after removing the Ubuntu Desktop CD. Once you're sure that Windows is as good as it ever was, you're ready to begin the Ubuntu installation process using a Desktop, Server, or Alternate Install CD.

NOTE The first time that you boot Windows after repartitioning a partition, Windows may notice that your disk parameters have changed, and will run its CHKDSK utility to correctly set Windows' idea of partition size and to recreate its paging file if necessary. You will see the screen shown in Figure 3.8 during the Windows startup process. Don't worry, just let Windows do its thing—Windows will simply check the disk partition, adjust its internal parameters, and then start Windows correctly.

FIGURE 3.8

Microsoft Windows checking the resized partition

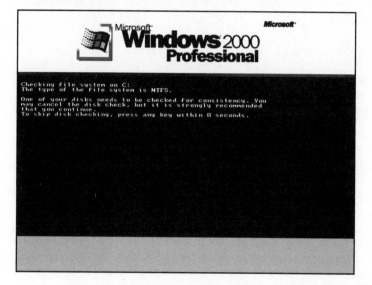

Repartitioning PPC Macintosh Systems Using the Ubuntu Desktop CD

Though it seems strange, the whizzy graphical utility for resizing partitions that was discussed in the previous section does not know how to deal with Macintosh HFS or HFS+ partitions. Not to worry—the Ubuntu Desktop CD includes a command-line utility called `parted` that can easily resize HFS or HFS+ partitions. Though it's not quite as elegant as the graphical utility discussed in the previous section, think of it as your first step into the rich set of powerful command-line tools that are available in Linux! In most cases, you won't need to use them, but when you do, it's nice to know that they're available.

Mac OS X 10.2 introduced a journaling version of the traditional Macintosh HFS filesystem. *Journaling* is a technique that improves throughput and minimizes system restart time by saving disk updates in a special part of the each partition (known as its *journal*) before writing those changes to disk. Sets of related changes are applied to partitions transactionally and are removed from the journal only when the transaction completes successfully. When your system restarts, it checks the journal for each filesystem and applies any pending changes to that filesystem, which helps ensure that your partitions are always up-to-date and also minimizes the chance that any partition could be left in an inconsistent state because of a partially-applied update.

Before resizing an HFS+ partition, you must disable journaling on the filesystem to guarantee that the filesystem is up-to-date, because this guarantees that the journal does not contain any pending updates to portions of the partition that may no longer be present after resizing. You must do this when you are

Problems with Graphical Repartitioning?

In some cases, the graphical repartitioning utility discussed in this section won't enable you to resize your existing Windows partitions. Although this is a hassle, it isn't fatal — you can manually repartition your existing partition using the command-line parted application and the techniques discussed in the next section for repartitioning PPC Apple Macintosh disks. The only difference will be in the names and numbers of your partitions. The following is a transcript of manually repartitioning a Windows disk using parted — for specific instructions, see the next section and substitute Microsoft Windows each time you see the words *PPC Macintosh, Apple Macintosh, Mac OS X,* and so on.

```
(parted) p
Disk geometry for /dev/hda: 0kB - 8590MB
Disk label type: msdos
Number  Start   End     Size    Type     File system  Flags
1       32kB    8579MB  8579MB  primary  fat32         boot, lba
(parted) resize 1 32kb 4096MB
(parted) p
Disk geometry for /dev/hda: 0kB - 8590MB
Disk label type: msdos
Number  Start   End     Size    Type     File system  Flags
1       32kB    4096MB  4096MB  primary  fat32         boot, lba
(parted) quit
```

Part of the beauty and power of Linux is that there are always multiple ways to accomplish specific tasks. The primary difference between these solutions is typically whether you want to perform a task from the command line or a graphical application you want to use to accomplish the same task.

running Mac OS X. To do this, start the Mac OS X Terminal application (Applications ➪ Terminal) and execute the following diskutil command in the terminal window:

```
$ diskutil list
/dev/disk0
   #:                     type name        size        identifier
   0: Apple_partition_scheme         *9.6 GB      disk0
   1:    Apple_partition_map          31.5 KB     disk0s1
   2:            Apple_HFS Boot        9.4 GB      disk0s3
```

As you can see from the output of this command, my active Mac OS X partition is partition 3 on /dev/disk0, which is identified as the partition /dev/disk0s3 (slice 3 of disk 0). To disable journaling on this filesystem, execute the following command:

```
$ diskutil disableJournal /dev/disk0s3
Journaling has been disabled on /dev/disk0s3
```

As you can see from the output of this command, journaling has been successfully disabled on this partition. Insert the PPC version of the Ubuntu Desktop CD, shut down your Mac OS X system, and boot from the PPC Ubuntu Desktop CD as described in Chapter 2.

Now the fun begins! Start a terminal window using the Applications ⇨ Accessories ⇨ Terminal menu command. In the terminal window, do the following:

1. Execute the `parted` command, followed by the name of the disk drive that you want to repartition. On most PCI Macs, the device name for your main hard disk will be `/dev/hdc`. You should see output like the following, concluding with the `parted` command prompt, (parted):

```
# parted /dev/hdc
GNU Parted 1.6.21 with HFS shrink patch 16
Copyright (C) 1998 - 2004 Free Software Foundation, Inc.
This program is free software, covered by the GNU General Public
License.
This program is distributed in the hope that it will be useful, but
WITHOUT ANY WARRANTY; without even the implied warranty of
MERCHANTABILITY
or FITNESS FOR A PARTICULAR PURPOSE. See the GNU General Public
License
for more details.

Using /dev/hdc
(parted)
```

2. Type the `p` (print) command to display the specified disk's current partition table, which should look something like the following:

```
(parted) p
Disk geometry for /dev/hdc: 0.000-9787.148 megabytes
Disk label type: mac
Minor    Start       End      Filesystem  Name                    Flags
1         0.000      0.031                 Apple
3       128.031   9787.140    hfs+         Apple_HFS_Untitled_1
```

3. Use the resize command to reduce the size of the HFS+ partition. This command takes three arguments: the minor number of the partition that you want to resize, the starting block for that partition, and the new ending block for that partition. Using the partition size shown in the previous item to reduce the size of my current HFS+ partition by approximately 4GB, I execute a command like the following:

```
(parted) resize 3 128.031 5600
```

4. Because HFS+ support is still experimental in many versions of `parted`, you may see a warning like the following:

```
Warning: You have an HFS+ file system that has a feature that I
haven't seen
used anywhere. Parted can theoretically handle it, but the
corresponding code
has never been tested, so this might be risky. Please e-mail me so I
can see how it works! <xilun666@libertysurf.fr>
Ignore/Cancel?
```

5. Enter the letter `i` and press return to begin resizing the disk. A continuously updating message like the following displays:

```
shrinking... NN%      (time left MM:SS)
```

6. Once resizing the partition completes, the `parted` prompt redisplays. Enter `quit` to exit parted.

Congratulations! You've successfully resized your partition and created space for Ubuntu. To reboot your system into Mac OS X to double-check that your HFS+ installation is still fine, press the Return or Enter key on your keyboard after removing the Ubuntu Desktop CD. Once you're sure that Mac OS X is fine, you're ready to begin the Ubuntu installation process using a Desktop, Server, or Alternate Install CD.

Getting a Different Install CD

Ubuntu isn't available in stores, which is fine because a CD suitable for test drives and installation is provided with this book, and other Ubuntu installation CDs are readily available over the Internet. If you have a reasonably fast Internet connection and a CD burner, the easiest way to get a different Ubuntu Install CD than the one provided in this book is to download an ISO image for that CD. (An ISO image is a file containing an image of a CD-ROM or DVD that is in the format mandated by the International Standard Organization 9660 specification.) See the section of Chapter 1 entitled "Ubuntu CDs" for more information about the Ubuntu CDs that are available other than the one provided in this book. Once you've decided which Ubuntu CD meets your needs, go to the page at www.ubuntu.com/download, select a mirror site in your country or a site that's closest to you in general, and select the Install CD that is associated with your platform and the type of system that you want to install. Save the downloaded ISO image to a file, burn that ISO image to a CD once the download completes, and you're ready to go!

If you have a slow Internet connection or do not have a CD burner, don't panic! As mentioned in the front matter for this book, the Ubuntu folks will even ship you Ubuntu CDs, though they take a few weeks because they're shipped from the Netherlands. This isn't the right solution for those of us who are into instant gratification, but it may work for you. To request that the Ubuntu folks ship you CDs, go to https://shipit.ubuntu.com, create an account by entering your e-mail address and a password, and request Ubuntu CDs for the current release. These come in an attractive two-pack that includes both the current install CD and a Desktop CD for each selected system type. You can even order free CDs for multiple system types at the same time.

Booting from a Server or Alternate Install CD

Booting from an Ubuntu Server or Alternate Install CD is as easy as inserting the appropriate CD into your system's CD drive, restarting your system, and telling the system to boot from the CD drive instead of booting from a hard disk partition. On PC systems, this is done using BIOS settings, while Mac OS X systems from Apple simply require that you hold down the letter "C" on your keyboard while starting up the computer.

TIP   If your x86 system boots from the hard drive even if the correct Ubuntu install CD is present in your CD drive, you'll need to modify the *boot order* in your BIOS settings. The boot order is the sequence in which available devices are searched for bootable disks when your system is powered on. To do this, turn your computer on and press the key on your keyboard that gives you access to the BIOS. This is typically the Del (Delete) or F2 key for most modern systems, but the key that you'll need to press is usually identified at the bottom left of your screen when you turn on your computer and it first starts up.

Depending on the type of BIOS your computer uses, boot order settings are usually stored in an Advanced Settings or Boot screen, which you can navigate to using the arrow keys on your keyboard. Press Return to display this screen once its name is highlighted. Once this screen displays, use the down-arrow key to navigate to the First Boot Device or CD Drive entry, and see the help messages at the right side of the screen for information about how to make your CD Drive the first boot device. You can then press the Escape key to exit this screen, and press F10 to save the new settings, exit the BIOS settings screen, and reboot.

Once your system begins booting from an Ubuntu Server or Alternate Install CD, you'll supply some basic information to help the installer correctly configure your system, install the correct internationalization and location software, and set up an initial user account. The next two sections discuss your install options from the Server and Alternate Install CDs, which share the same quasi-graphical installer discussed in the introduction to this chapter, and walk you through the installation process.

WARNING A bug in the installation process for any Ubuntu systems that are installed from some Ubuntu Server or Alternate Install CDs can leave your system vulnerable if you press Go Back in the final installer screen (shown in Figure 3.25) rather than Continue. Doing this sets the root password to a null string, which means that anyone can log in on your system as root without a password or use the su command to become root. If you must go back to a previous installation step, you must manually set, or preferably disable, the root password on your system. This bug may have been fixed by the time that you read this, but better safe than sorry.

Install Options on the Server Install CD

As you might guess, the Ubuntu Server Install CD is intended for use in installing Ubuntu on a system that will be used as a server. Because many server systems are rack-mounted systems that use a system console rather than a graphical monitor, Ubuntu Server installations do not include a graphical user interface such as an X Window system window manager or desktop such as GNOME. Not installing these packages by default reduces the amount of disk space required for a basic installation and reduces the amount of software that you have to keep up-to-date.

TIP You can always add a graphical interface to server systems later if you want to have a graphical interface available on your server system to support specific tools or for your general convenience. For example, you can add the xubuntu-desktop package to add the Xfce desktop system, the ubuntu-desktop package to add the complete GNOME desktop, the kubuntu-desktop package to add the complete KDE desktop, or add the xserver-xorg package, the window manager of your choice, and specific graphical tools. Adding software packages is discussed in detail in Chapter 20, "Adding, Removing, and Updating Software."

Figure 3.9 shows the menu that is displayed when you boot your system from an Ubuntu Server Install CD.

The options on the Server Install CD's boot menu are the following:

- **Install to the hard disk:** Installs a basic Ubuntu server system to your hard drive(s) using Ubuntu's quasi-graphical installer. Installing an Ubuntu server using this installer is discussed in detail in the next section, "Installing an Ubuntu Server."

- **Install a LAMP server:** Installs a basic Ubuntu LAMP (Linux, Apache, MySQL, and Perl) server system to your hard drive(s) using Ubuntu's quasi-graphical installer. Unlike the standard Ubuntu Server installation, this server installation includes all of the packages necessary to run a LAMP server. Installing an Ubuntu LAMP server uses the same installer, with the same installation screens, as is discussed in detail in the next section, "Installing an Ubuntu Server." Additional configuration and installation steps are discussed in the section entitled "Installing an Ubuntu LAMP Server."

- **Check CD for defects:** Tests the integrity of the CD that is currently inserted in your system and verifies its contents.

- **Rescue a broken system:** Prompts for a few pieces of information such as the language that you want messages to be displayed in and your geographic location, and then boots a diskless version of Ubuntu Linux that runs from the CD and which you can use to repair corrupted disks, correct or reinstall your GRUB boot loader's configuration, and so on.

FIGURE 3.9

The Boot Menu on the Ubuntu Server Install CD

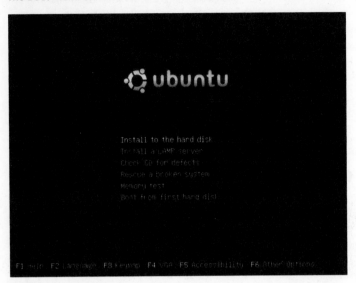

> **TIP** If you have problems entering rescue mode, booting from the Ubuntu Desktop CD included with this book provides the same capabilities as a rescue mode installation, but with a whizzy graphical interface.

- **Memory test:** Performs several memory tests to verify your system's memory and associated cache. You can press the letter "C" to display a configuration menu that enables you to run or rerun specific tests. Once you are finished testing your system's memory, press Escape to reboot your system and return to the Ubuntu Server Install CD boot menu.

- **Boot from first hard disk:** Bypasses booting from the Ubuntu Server Install CD and boots from your system's hard drive. This is the option to use if you accidentally left the Ubuntu Server Install CD in the CD drive of a system on which you did not intend to install Ubuntu or perform the available system tests.

Either the Install to hard disk or Install LAMP server boot menu options will install an Ubuntu Linux server system on your hard drive(s). The next section walks you through the process of installing an Ubuntu Server after selecting the Install to hard disk option. See the section entitled "Installing an Ubuntu LAMP Server" for details about the installation process that follows if you select the Install LAMP server option instead.

Installing an Ubuntu Server

Depending on the speed of your system and Internet connection, installing Ubuntu can take a little while. However, the wait is worth it. Insert the Ubuntu install CD in your CD drive and boot from it. Now do the following:

1. After booting from the CD, the screen shown in Figure 3.9 displays. To proceed, make sure that the Install to the hard disk entry is selected, and press Return.

2. The screen shown in Figure 3.10 displays, prompting you to select the language in which you would like system messages and dialogs to be displayed. You can either press Return to accept the

default value of English, or use the arrow keys to scroll up and down in the list of supported languages until you find your native language, and then press Return to continue.

FIGURE 3.10

Specifying your language

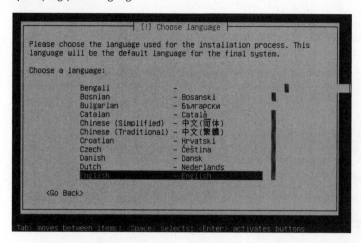

3. The screen shown in Figure 3.11 prompts you to specify the location where you are using your computer. This value is used to further customize the language that you specified in the previous screen by using the appropriate date and time formats, numeric conventions, and currency values for your geographic location.

FIGURE 3.11

Specifying your geographic location

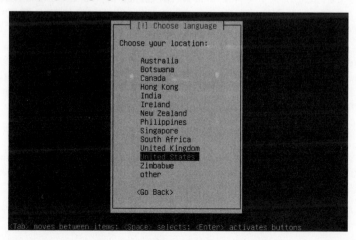

4. The screen shown in Figure 3.12 prompts you to specify the type of keyboard attached to your computer. The default value is based on your setting on the two previous screens — if this is incorrect, you can use the down-arrow to select Find your layout by pressing some keys and type a few keys to have the installer attempt to identify your keyboard type. If you are using a non-U.S. keyboard, it is often easiest to press the down-arrow twice. Press Return, and simply select your keyboard type from the full list of supported keyboard types.

Specifying your keyboard type

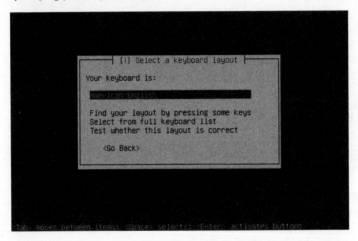

At this point, a few screens display as the Ubuntu installer looks for your CD-ROM drive, probes your system's hardware, and identifies and configures your network interface. These screens are not interactive.

TIP   If the installer has problems automatically configuring your network interface and you see an error dialog at this point, see the sidebar entitled "Resolving Installation Problems" later in this chapter for more information.

5. The screen shown in Figure 3.13 prompts you to enter a name for this machine. This is a one-word entry (without any domain name) that can be used to uniquely identify this system on your local network. If you are dual-booting, I tend to use the same name for the system whenever possible, to avoid confusing myself. If you want to accept the default name *ubuntu*, or once you've entered a name for your machine, press Return to continue.

FIGURE 3.13

Specifying a name for your Ubuntu server

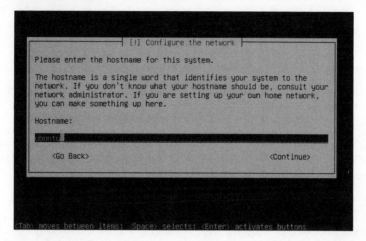

6. Next, the installer displays several informative screens as it probes and identifies your system's hard disks. The partitioning screen shown in Figure 3.14 displays once these tests have completed.

FIGURE 3.14

The standard Ubuntu Partitioner screen

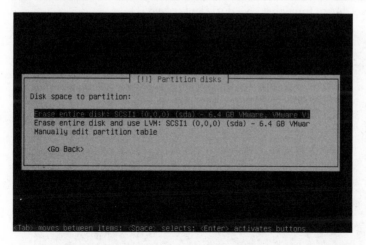

7. The partitioning screen shown in Figure 3.14 is the only potentially complex portion of the Ubuntu installation process. If you are installing Ubuntu on a system with a single disk and you want to devote that entire disk to Ubuntu, the installation screen should look much like the screen in Figure 3.14 except for differences in device names and sizes. In this case, you have three options:

   ■ Erase the entire disk and use traditional physical partitions.

   ■ Erase the entire disk and use logical volumes.

   ■ Manually specify the partition layout for your system.

   If you want to manually partition your system, see the section later in this chapter entitled "Manually Specifying Your Partition Layout," and then return here once you've finished partitioning. Otherwise, select one of the previous two options. The advantage to using logical volumes is that if you run out of space on your existing system, you can always add another disk drive and add the space that it provides to your existing logical volume. There are plenty of ways to do the same sort of thing using physical volumes, so unless you're sure that you want to use logical volumes, just press Return to accept the default value and proceed to the next step.

> **TIP**   If you are installing Ubuntu on a dual-boot x86 or 64-bit bit PC system, you will see something more like the partitioning screen in Figure 3.15. In this case, you can select the Resize option to let the installer automatically resize your disk, or you can select the Use the largest continuous free space option to install Ubuntu on the largest unused portion of your disk if you manually resized your partitions or simply have unallocated space on the disk. If you select the Resize option, a subsequent screen displays on which you must specify the size to which you want to reduce your Windows partition. This size can be expressed as an absolute size (for example, 10GB), or as a percentage of the disk (for example, 25%).

FIGURE 3.15

The Ubuntu Partitioner on a dual-boot system

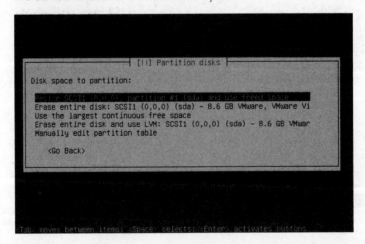

8. The Ubuntu Partitioner's summary screen displays, as shown in Figure 3.16. As the screen says, this operation cannot be undone. Double-check the displayed values. To accept the values that it displays, press the Tab key to select the Yes value on the screen, and press Return to continue. To make changes to the suggested partitioning scheme, make sure that you select the No value and press Return. You will be returned to the manual partitioning screens discussed later in this

chapter in the section entitled "Manually Specifying Your Partition Layout." In that case, please see that section of this chapter for more information, and then return to this point of the installation process.

The partitioning summary screen

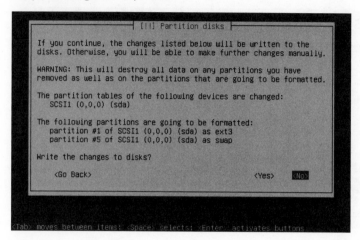

9. The screen shown in Figure 3.17 enables you to specify the default time zone in which you will be using your system. Even if you're installing on a laptop, you should enter your home time zone as a base reference — you can always change this later if you travel for an extended period of time. Use the arrow keys to select the appropriate time zone for your home location and press Return to continue.

The time zone screen

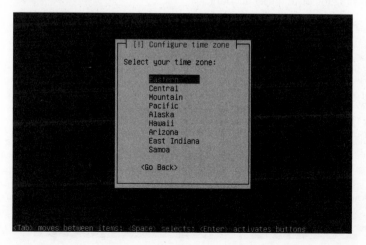

10. The screen shown in Figure 3.18 displays, asking whether the system clock on your motherboard is set to universal time (UTC) or local time. Use the Tab key to select the appropriate answer and press Return to continue.

FIGURE 3.18

The system clock configuration screen

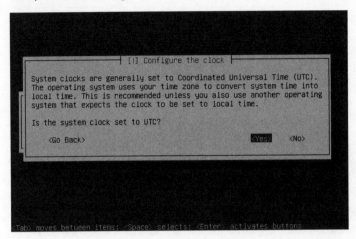

11. Next, the screen shown in Figure 3.19 displays, prompting you for the name of a user to create on your system. As discussed in Chapter 4, "Basic Linux System Concepts," Ubuntu uses a special permissions scheme to give a single user (by default) the ability to perform administrative tasks on your machine. The name of the user that you enter here will have those administrative abilities, so this should almost always be your name or the name of a generic system administration user (as shown in Figure 3.19). Enter an appropriate full name and press Return to proceed.

FIGURE 3.19

Creating the default user account

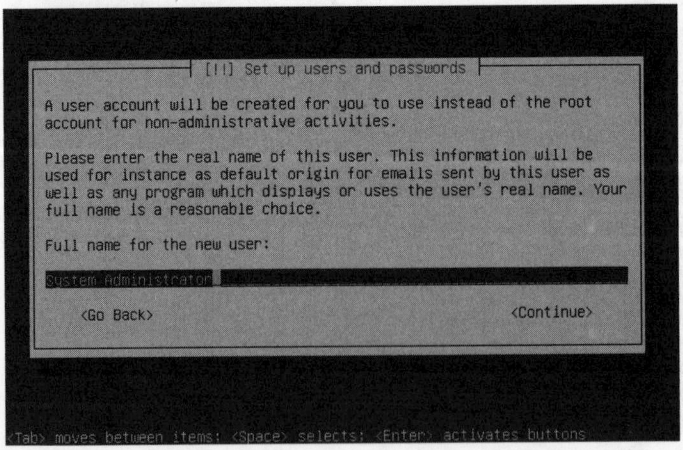

12. Next, the screen shown in Figure 3.20 displays, on which you must enter the login name for the user whose name you specified in the previous step. This screen initially displays a suggested login name based on the full name that you specified in the previous step. If you want to change this, use the Backspace key to delete the default suggestion and enter the login name that you want to use. To proceed with the default or with a custom username, press Return to continue.

FIGURE 3.20

Creating the default login name

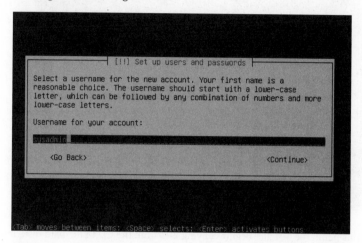

13. Next, the screen shown in Figure 3.21 displays. Enter the password for the user that you are creating, following good password rules such as using a password that contains a mixture of upper- and lowercase letters and one or more numbers, and *not* using the name or birthday of your spouse, children, or yourself. Press Return to continue.

FIGURE 3.21

Specifying a password

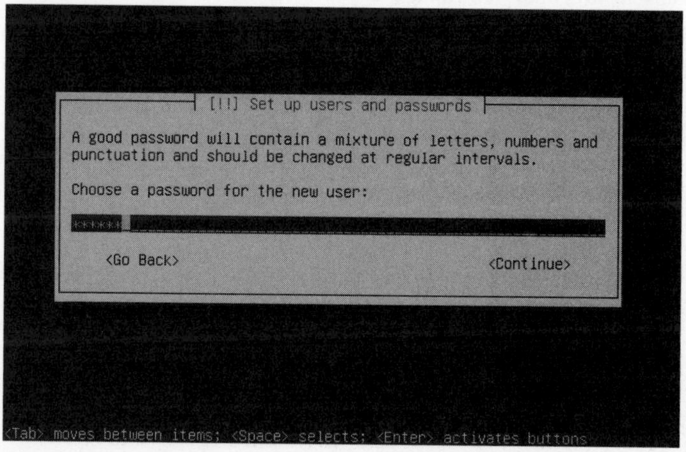

14. After entering your password for the first time, the password confirmation screen shown in Figure 3.22 displays. Enter the same password that you entered on the previous screen, and press Return to continue.

Confirming a password

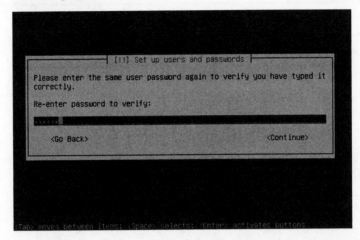

15. At this point, the installer begins copying files from the CD to the hard disk, installing those packages with the information that you have supplied. It also configures the software update system that is used to retrieve and install additional software from an Ubuntu software repository on the Internet, selecting their geographically closest repository based on the geographic location that you specified earlier. (Ubuntu software update systems such as apt-get, aptitude, and Synaptic are discussed in Chapter 20, "Adding, Removing, and Updating Software.") The installer displays several progress screens as this takes place.

TIP If you see an error message about the Ubuntu repositories during the installation process, see the sidebar entitled "Resolving Installation Problems" later in this section for more information. This is a nonfatal error, but is something that you'll want to correct.

16. If you are installing an Ubuntu Server on a dual-boot system, the screen shown in Figure 3.23 displays during the package installation process. The default location to which GRUB, the Linux boot loader used by Ubuntu, is installed is to the master boot record on the primary hard drive. To install GRUB to this location, press Return.

FIGURE 3.23

The GRUB boot loader location screen for dual-boot systems

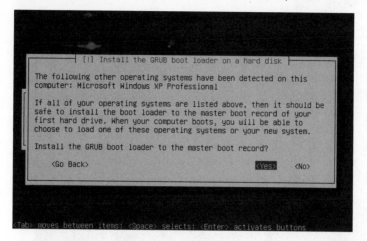

To install GRUB to a different location, use the Tab key to select No and press Return. The screen shown in Figure 3.24 displays, in which you can specify where you want to install GRUB. Enter the value where you want to install GRUB and press Return to continue.

FIGURE 3.24

The GRUB boot loader installation screen

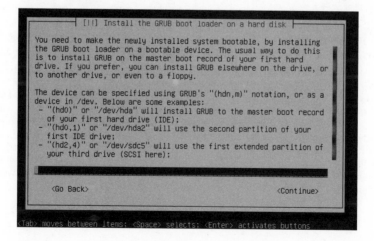

17. After some additional package configuration, the screen shown in Figure 3.25 displays.

FIGURE 3.25

The final installer screen

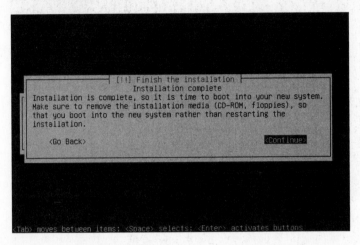

Once you see the screen in Figure 3.25, remove the install CD and press Return to reboot your computer into your newly installed Ubuntu Linux server system! Skip ahead to the section of this chapter entitled "Booting Your System for the First Time" for more information.

Resolving Installation Problems

Most of the problems that you encounter when installing any operating system, including Ubuntu Linux, are fatal. Problems encountered when reading from the installation media, accessing, partitioning, and formatting your system's hard drives, and other hardware-related problems are problems that you must resolve before you can successfully install Ubuntu Linux. However, you may encounter two fairly common problems when installing Ubuntu Linux that can easily be corrected. The first is a problem with automatic network configuration; the second is a problem accessing Ubuntu's online repositories and correctly configuring the Ubuntu software update system.

If the Ubuntu installer cannot automatically configure the network, you will see a screen stating that automatic network configuration failed and asking you if you want to manually configure the network, as shown in the following figure.

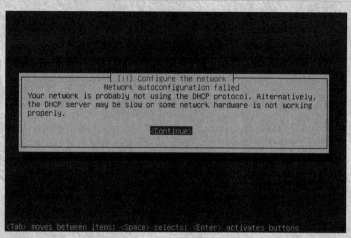

The Network autoconfiguration failed screen

Select Continue or press Return to display the screen shown in the next figure.

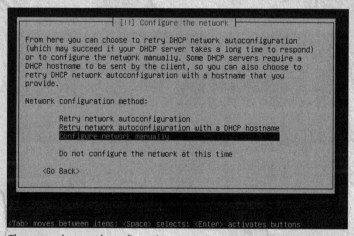

The manual network configuration screen

This screen enables you to retry automatic network configuration via DHCP broadcasts, retry automatic network configuration via DHCP by querying a specific host, configure your network manually, or skip network configuration altogether. Before doing anything else, check your network cabling to make sure that the machine you are installing Ubuntu on is correctly attached to the network, especially if your network is actually running a DHCP server.

continued

continued

You can select any of the available options, but I suggest that you select the Configure network manually option to provide your Ubuntu server with a static IP address and related networking information. In my experience, few servers have dynamic IP addresses because this makes it more challenging to contact them remotely if a problem occurs, because you aren't guaranteed to know their IP address.

If you select the Configure network manually option, the installer displays four additional network configuration screens that respectively prompt you for the server's IP address, the netmask for that IP address, the IP address of your network gateway, and the name server(s) on your network. (If you want to enter multiple name servers, separate them by a space, not a comma.) Once these screens are displayed, the system's network interface is configured, and you are returned to the installer.

Another common problem you may encounter when installing Ubuntu Linux is contacting and verifying all of the default Ubuntu Linux repositories, which are sites on the Internet that provide new and updated software packages for different Ubuntu releases. If problems occur contacting the Ubuntu repositories, a message such as the one shown in the following figure may be displayed during the installation process.

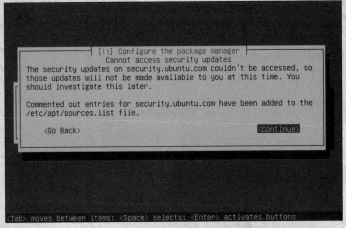

Problems contacting or verifying the Ubuntu repositories

If you see this message, you need not be concerned. This is usually a transient, network connectivity or load problem. After you reboot, you will need to uncomment the repositories that were identified in a dialog like the one shown in Figure 3.26. (Most of these problems occur contacting the security repositories.) To uncomment these, use your favorite text editor via a command like `sudo vi /etc/apt/sources.list`. Remove the hash mark at the beginning of each of the lines associated with the specified repositories, save the modified file, and execute the command `sudo apt-get update` to verify that the new repositories can be contacted successfully. See Chapter 20, "Adding, Removing, and Updating Software," for more information about the Ubuntu repositories and software update commands such as `apt-get`.

Manually Specifying Your Partition Layout

Manually specifying the layout of the partitions on your system can be useful, but is also time-consuming and requires some understanding of the Linux filesystem. Manually partitioning your system enables you to put specific directories from the Linux filesystem on their own partitions, which can improve performance, minimize the size of backups for your system (because backups are usually done on a per-filesystem or pre-directory basis), and simplify future upgrades and system reconfiguration.

NOTE　By default, the Ubuntu installer automatically creates a reasonable partitioning scheme for you, which means that it creates one large partition for user and system files and another, smaller, partition to use as swap space to support virtual memory on your Ubuntu system. This section describes an alternative to the quasi-graphical Ubuntu installer's automatic partitioning scheme. If you're reading this book linearly, you can skip over this section if you've already installed your system.

If you are installing Ubuntu for the first time or are relatively unfamiliar with Linux, I'd suggest letting the Ubuntu installer automatically partition your disk for you. Automatic partitioning will get you up and running much more quickly, and doesn't require understanding the content and use of various directories on your Linux system. As you become an Ubuntu and Linux expert, you can always subsequently back up your user account to another machine, and then reinstall Ubuntu using manual partitioning.

Common directories in the Linux filesystem that are often put into their own partitions are the following:

- `/`: The top level of the Linux filesystem. A partition must always be available through the `/` directory in order for a Linux system to boot.
- `/boot`: The directory that holds the Linux kernel and other associated system files used during the boot process.
- `/home`: The directory where user files and accounts are located.
- `/opt`: A directory where optional programs and related files are typically installed.
- `/tmp`: A directory used to hold temporary files created by user and system processes.
- `/usr`: A directory that holds applications, system files, and libraries used by the standard Linux system. On Ubuntu systems, the `/usr` directory requires approximately 1.25GB of disk space by default.
- `/usr/local`: A directory that holds applications, system files, and libraries used by a particular Linux system, but which may not be present on all Linux systems.

Most Linux systems that do not use a single partition to hold the entire filesystem create separate partitions for `/`, `/boot`, and `/home`. For more information about these directories and the structure of the Linux filesystem in general, see Chapter 4, "Basic Linux System Concepts."

Linux partitions can be grouped into two general types: swap partitions, which are used internally by the system to support virtual memory, and data partitions, in which files and other directories are located. A Linux system must have at least one area to swap to in order to function correctly — this is usually a dedicated partition, though you can also swap to a file in the filesystem if you are desperate. (See Chapter 4 for more information about partitions and virtual memory.) In this section, you will create a few basic data partitions and a single swap partition to illustrate manual partitioning — how you actually decide to partition your system is up to you.

Manually partitioning your disk involves steps like the following:

1. In the screen shown in Figure 3.14, select the Manually edit partition table option. The screen shown in Figure 3.26 displays.

FIGURE 3.26

The manually partition disks screen

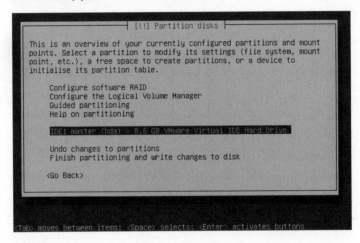

2. Use the arrow keys to select the entry representing the disk drive that you want to partition and press Return to continue. The screen shown in Figure 3.27 displays.

FIGURE 3.27

A warning screen regarding manual partitioning

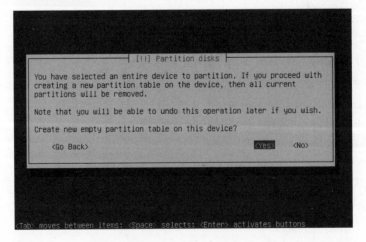

3. Use the Tab key to select Yes and press Return to continue. This creates a huge pool of free space from the selected disk, as shown in Figure 3.28 displays.

FIGURE 3.28

Selecting free disk space for partitioning

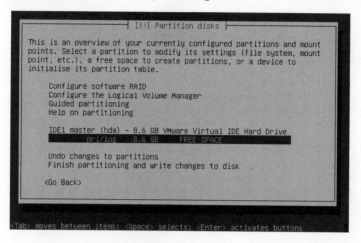

4. Use the arrow key to select the pool of available space on that disk and press Return to continue. The screen shown in Figure 3.29 displays.

FIGURE 3.29

Beginning to define a new partition

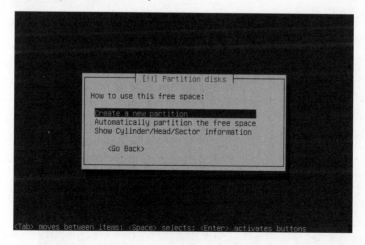

5. Select the Create a new partition entry and press Return to continue. The screen shown in Figure 3.30 displays.

FIGURE 3.30

Specifying the size of your new partition

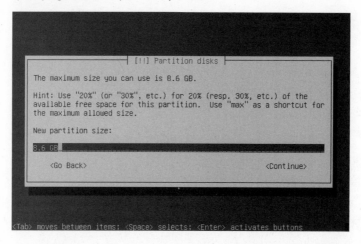

6. Enter the size that you want your new partition to have. The amount of unallocated disk space is displayed as a default value. You can specify the size of your new partition as an absolute value, such as 100MB; specify it as a percentage of the available space, such as 10%; or use the max keyword to create a partition of the maximum size available based on existing free space. After entering this value, press Return to continue. The screen shown in Figure 3.31 displays.

FIGURE 3.31

Specifying the type of your new partition

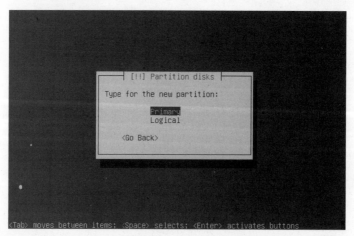

7. Select the type of partition that you want to create. Disks can contain up to four physical partitions—any partitions beyond that number must be logical partitions. Logical partitions can contain other partitions, while physical partitions are just that—physical portions of your disk drive that cannot be further subdivided. Unless you plan to create more than four partitions, use the arrow keys to ensure that the physical entry is selected, and press Return to continue. The screen shown in Figure 3.32 displays.

FIGURE 3.32

Specifying the location of your new partition

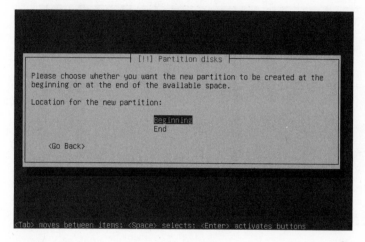

8. Unless you have a specific reason to position the new partition on a special portion of your disk, accept the default value Beginning and press Return to continue. The screen shown in Figure 3.33 displays.

FIGURE 3.33

Specifying the type and mount point of your new partition

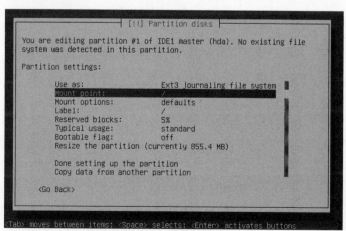

9. The *mount point* for a partition is the directory through which the contents of that partition are made available to your system. (See Chapter 4, "Basic Linux System Concepts," for more information about Linux directories and mount points.) A list of common partitions and associated mount points was given at the beginning of this section. The only mandatory filesystem and associated mount point on a Linux system is /, the root directory of the Linux filesystem. Use the arrow keys to select the Mount Point menu item, and press Return to continue. The screen shown in Figure 3.34 displays.

FIGURE 3.34

Specifying the mount point for your new partition

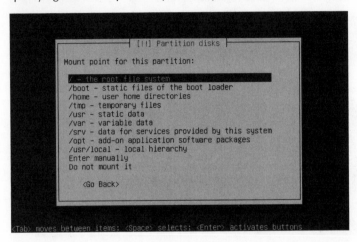

10. In this example, you'll mount your new partition at /boot, which is the directory that holds the Linux kernel and associated system files. Use the arrow keys to select the entry for /boot, and press Return to continue. The screen shown in Figure 3.35 displays.

FIGURE 3.35

Specifying the partition type

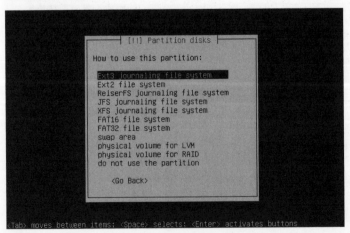

11. Linux systems support several different filesystem types. Each type of filesystem has certain characteristics that are explained in more detail in Chapter 4, "Basic Linux System Concepts." In this case, /boot is a data partition, and the Linux ext3 filesystem is the default, and most popular, format for data partitions. Press Return to continue. The screen shown in Figure 3.27 redisplays.

12. Repeat steps 3 through 11 to create additional partitions. As discussed in the previous section, filesystems that are often created on their own partitions are /boot (used in this example), /, /home, and a swap partition. Creating any other filesystem partitions follows exactly the same process as described previously. To create a swap partition, follow the same process as when creating other partitions, but select swap area from the screen shown in Figure 3.35. The size of a swap partition should be approximately the same size as the amount of memory in your computer system. Figure 3.36 shows an additional screen that displays when you define a partition as a swap area. This screen merely confirms that you are creating a swap area that does not contain a filesystem that can be used to hold data files.

 **CAUTION** If you plan to create more than four partitions, the fourth partition that you create must be an Extended partition, in which the other partitions that you want to use can then be created.

FIGURE 3.36

The details screen when creating a swap partition

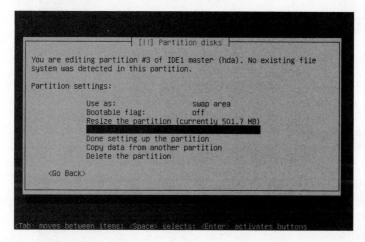

TIP To help guarantee that you do not encounter installation problems, you may want to ensure that the partition that you mount at / is at least 3GB in size. Following this rule should guarantee that your Ubuntu system will install correctly unless you have defined other partitions such as /usr with insufficient space to hold the files that are installed under that directory when it is used as a mount point.

13. Once you have allocated all of the available free space on your system to partitions, your screen should like something like the one shown in Figure 3.37.

FIGURE 3.37

The partition summary screen

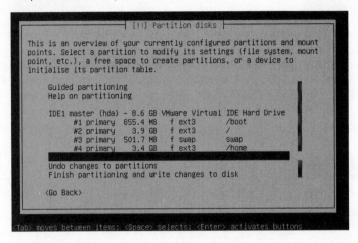

14. The screen shown in Figure 3.37 displays a summary of the partitions that you have defined for use on your system. Remember that there must be one partition mounted at / and one swap partition. To accept the values shown on this screen, use the arrow keys to select the Finish partitioning and write changes to disk option, and press Return to display the screen shown in Figure 3.38.

FIGURE 3.38

The final partition confirmation screen

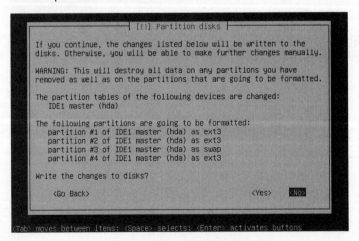

15. Because disk partitioning cannot be undone, the screen shown in Figure 3.38 requests final confirmation of your manual partitioning selections. To accept these values and continue with the installation process, use the Tab key to select Yes, and press Return to continue.

You can now return to step 9 of the Ubuntu installation process in the previous section. And congratulations — you're now at least a Linux wizard in training!

Installing an Ubuntu LAMP Server

Installing an Ubuntu LAMP Server follows exactly the same installation process as installing a generic Ubuntu server, which was described in the section entitled "Installing an Ubuntu Server" earlier in this chapter. The installation process automatically installs the Apache 2, MySQL, and Perl packages during the installation process.

After the installation completes and you log in for the first time (as described in the next section), you will probably want to fine-tune the configuration of your system. See Chapter 26, "Setting Up a Web Server," for more information on configuring Apache 2. You will probably also want to set a password for the root account on your MySQL server, which you can do with the following commands:

```
$ mysql -u root mysql
mysql> update user set Password=password('newpassword') where
user='root';
mysql> flush privileges;
mysql> quit
```

In the MySQL update command, replace the string newpassword with whatever you want your MySQL root password to be. Once you have executed these commands, you can verify that the root password has been set correctly by executing the following command and entering the new root password at the prompt:

```
$ mysql -u root mysql -p
Enter password:
```

If the password change worked correctly, you will be connected to your MySQL database.

Booting Your Server for the First Time

Once the server installation process completes, the screen shown in Figure 3.23 displays. Remove the install CD and press Return to reboot your system into your newly installed Ubuntu Linux server!

NOTE The Ubuntu boot process differs depending on whether you have installed Ubuntu as a dual-boot system or as the only operating system on your computer. Though it is highly unlikely that you would have installed an Ubuntu server on a dual-boot system, see the section of Chapter 2 entitled "Booting Ubuntu Linux on Dual-Boot Systems" for more information if that is the case.

As Ubuntu boots, you will see several text messages displayed to the screen as it probes and initializes your hardware and related system software. When the boot process is complete, you will see a command-line login screen like that shown in Figure 3.39. You can now log in using the username and password that you defined during the installation process.

Congratulations — you're running an Ubuntu Linux server! For more basic information about Linux, see Chapter 4, "Basic Linux System Concepts." If you would prefer to simply start running some of the hundreds of powerful applications provided with Ubuntu Linux, check the table of contents in this book for the type of application that interests you, and skip to the chapter of this book that discusses such applications.

FIGURE 3.39

The Ubuntu login screen

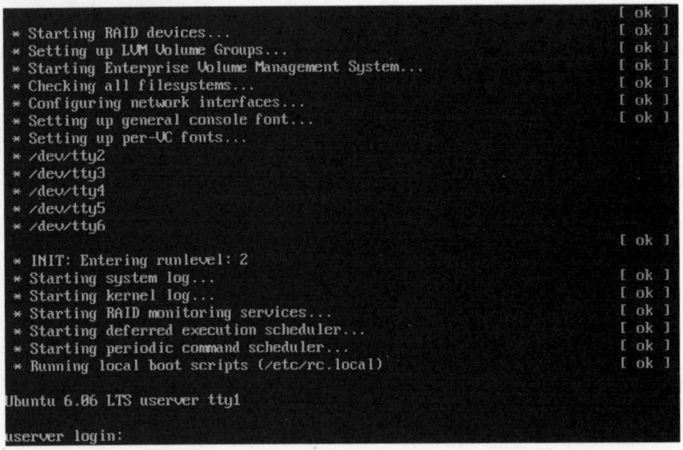

* Starting RAID devices... [ok]
* Setting up LVM Volume Groups... [ok]
* Starting Enterprise Volume Management System... [ok]
* Checking all filesystems... [ok]
* Configuring network interfaces... [ok]
* Setting up general console font... [ok]
* Setting up per-VC fonts... [ok]
* /dev/tty2
* /dev/tty3
* /dev/tty4
* /dev/tty5
* /dev/tty6
[ok]
* INIT: Entering runlevel: 2
* Starting system log... [ok]
* Starting kernel log... [ok]
* Starting RAID monitoring services... [ok]
* Starting deferred execution scheduler... [ok]
* Starting periodic command scheduler... [ok]
* Running local boot scripts (/etc/rc.local) [ok]
Ubuntu 6.06 LTS userver tty1
userver login:

Install Options on the Alternate Install CD

Figure 3.40 shows the menu that is displayed when you boot your system from an Ubuntu Alternate Install CD.

FIGURE 3.40

The boot menu on the Ubuntu Alternate Install CD

ubuntu
Install in text mode
Install in OEM mode
Install a server
Check CD for defects
Rescue a broken system
Memory test
Boot from first hard disk
F1 Help F2 Language F3 Keymap F4 VGA F5 Accessibility F6 Other Options

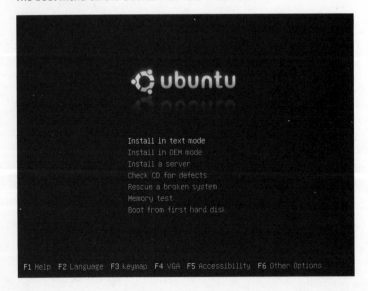

The options on the Alternate Install CD's boot menu are the following:

- **Install in text mode:** Installs a basic Ubuntu Desktop system to your hard drive(s) using Ubuntu's quasi-graphical installer. Installing an Ubuntu Desktop using this installer is discussed in detail in the next section, "Installing an Ubuntu Desktop System in Text Mode."

- **Install in OEM mode:** Installs an Ubuntu Desktop system to your hard drive(s) using Ubuntu's quasi-graphical installer. Unlike the standard Ubuntu installations, the OEM mode install enables you to define an OEM user that you can use to customize the system so that you can distribute it to end users. They then run a simple command to remove the OEM user and define a standard Ubuntu privileged user. Installing an Ubuntu OEM system is discussed in the section entitled "Installing Ubuntu Linux in OEM Mode."

- **Install a server:** Installs a basic Ubuntu server system to your hard drive(s) using Ubuntu's quasi-graphical installer. Installing an Ubuntu server using this installer is discussed in detail earlier in this chapter, in the section entitled "Installing an Ubuntu Server."

- **Check CD for defects:** Tests the integrity of the CD that is currently inserted in your system and verifies its contents.

- **Rescue a broken system:** Prompts for a few pieces of information such as the language that you want messages to be displayed in and your geographic location, and then boots a diskless version of Ubuntu Linux that runs from the CD and which you can use to repair corrupted disks, correct or reinstall your GRUB boot loader's configuration, and so on.

> **TIP** If you have problems entering rescue mode, booting from the Ubuntu Desktop CD included with this book provides the same capabilities as a rescue mode installation, but with a whizzy graphical interface.

- **Memory test:** Performs several memory tests to verify your system's memory and associated cache. You can press the letter "c" to display a configuration menu that enables you to run or rerun specific tests. Once you are finished testing your system's memory, press Escape to reboot your system and return to the Ubuntu Alternate Install CD boot menu.

- **Boot from first hard disk:** Bypasses booting from the Ubuntu Alternate Install CD and boots from your system's hard drive. This is the option to use if you accidentally left the Ubuntu Alternate Install CD in the CD drive of a system on which you did not intend to install Ubuntu or perform the available system tests.

Any of the "Install in text mode," "Install in OEM mode," or "Install a server" boot menu options will install an Ubuntu Linux system on your hard drive(s). The next sections explain each of these options and highlight the differences between the text-mode installers used by these options and the quasi-graphical installer described earlier in this chapter in the section entitled "Installing an Ubuntu Server."

Installing an Ubuntu Desktop System in Text Mode

Selecting Install in text mode from the Ubuntu Alternate Install CD's boot menu enables you to install an Ubuntu desktop system using the text-mode installer. This menu option is useful in various scenarios, such as the following:

- You are having problems getting the Ubuntu Desktop CD to boot on your system because of conflicts or problems with your graphics hardware.

- You want to install the Ubuntu Desktop system but use logical volumes rather than physical partitions to hold your filesystem(s).

- You want to install the Ubuntu Desktop system but want to install GRUB to a location other than the master boot record of your primary hard drive.

As with the other quasi-graphical Ubuntu installers, the quasi-graphical Desktop install follows the same series of prompts and steps as discussed earlier in this chapter in the section entitled "Installing an Ubuntu Server." The noninteractive package installation step installs a different set of packages to your system, including the GNOME desktop, the X Window system, and several graphical tools. The only difference between a quasi-graphical desktop install and the server install process that was discussed earlier comes at the very end of the installation process where, before ejecting the CD and suggesting that you reboot your system, the desktop installer prompts you for information about the resolution at which you want to display your desktop. This screen is shown in Figure 3.41.

FIGURE 3.41

Specifying available screen resolutions

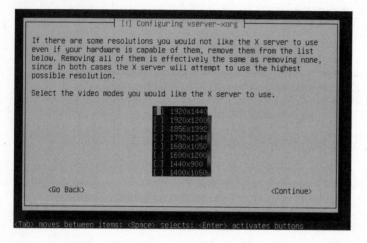

When you see this screen, select the screen resolution(s) that you want Ubuntu to use when it starts the graphical GNOME desktop environment. To enable an unselected screen resolution, use the arrow keys to select that entry and press the space bar. Pressing the space bar will also deselect a previously selected value. By default, the values 1024×768, 800×600, and 640×480 are selected, because most modern systems can display graphics at any of these resolutions. You should select higher resolutions if you're sure that your graphics card supports them — the installer displays a list of the resolutions that it believes your graphics hardware can handle based on probing the graphics card. Ubuntu will try to use the highest selected value and proceed to the next highest if an error occurs. Press Return to continue.

After this screen, the standard installation procedure continues, eventually ejecting the CD and prompting you to reboot into your new, graphical Ubuntu Desktop system.

Installing Ubuntu Linux in OEM Mode

Selecting Install in OEM mode from the Ubuntu Alternate Install CD's boot menu enables you to install an Ubuntu desktop system using the text-mode installer, but installs the system with a temporary privileged user (OEM). This enables OEMs to perform additional configuration on this system using this privileged user, installing custom software, installing additional packages, and removing packages as necessary, and then to redistribute the system to their customers. To turn this system into a standard Ubuntu Desktop installation with a customer-specific privileged user after completing its configuration, the OEM should execute the `sudo oem-prepare` command, which will delete the OEM user and will prompt the customer to enter customer-specific user and other configuration questions the next time the system boots.

As with the other quasi-graphical Ubuntu installers, the quasi-graphical OEM install follows much the same series of prompts and steps as discussed earlier in this chapter in the section entitled "Installing an Ubuntu Desktop System in Text Mode." Because an OEM system is installed with a specific privileged user (OEM), the install process does not prompt you for a username and login, but only prompts you for a password for the OEM user. Like the text-mode desktop install process, the OEM mode installer prompts you for information about the resolution at which you want to display your desktop, and then continues with the installation and configuration process.

Just before the final installation summary screen, the OEM mode installer displays a screen that summarizes how OEM mode is to be used, as shown in Figure 3.42.

FIGURE 3.42

OEM mode process summary

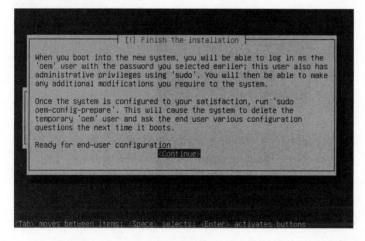

After this screen, the standard installation procedure continues, eventually ejecting the CD and prompting you to reboot into your new, graphical Ubuntu OEM mode system to complete its configuration before distribution to the OEM's customers.

Installing a Server from the Alternate Install CD

Selecting Install a server from the Ubuntu Alternate Install CD's boot menu enables you to install an Ubuntu server system using the text-mode installer from the Server Install CD, and is provided on the Alternate CD for your convenience. The installation process for installing an Ubuntu Server from the Alternate Install CD is exactly the same as installing a server from the Server Install CD, as described in the section of this chapter entitled "Installing an Ubuntu Server."

Summary

This chapter covered a lot of ground, explaining some basic concepts required to successfully install Ubuntu Linux as an alternate operating system on an existing machine or as the only operating system on a system using various specialized installation configurations via the quasi-graphical Debian installer. Topics discussed included the system boot process, repartitioning existing disks, manually partitioning your disks, and following various specialized Ubuntu installation processes. Regardless of the type of system that you installed or are using, by the end of this chapter, you have Ubuntu Linux installed and running on your computer system.

Chapter 4 discusses basic Linux concepts that may be new to you if this is the first Linux or Unix-like system that you have used. Chapters 5 and 6 discuss the basics of using Ubuntu with a graphical interface or from the command line, which are good starting points if you are already familiar with basic Linux concepts and just want to start getting your hands dirty with your Ubuntu installation.

Part II

Ubuntu for Desktop Users

Chapter 4

Basic Linux System Concepts

This chapter explains basic Linux system concepts, focusing on how data is stored and organized on all Linux systems and how the Linux operating system controls access to that data and to privileged operations. Aside from specific sections on how Ubuntu deals with and grants high-level permissions, the information in this chapter applies to any Linux system and to most other Unix-like systems.

This chapter errs on the side of caution. As impossible as it now sounds, I had never used a computer before deciding to study Computer Science at university. (I can be excused for this to some extent because this was a zillion years ago, just as personal computers were starting to become popular and long before DOS, Microsoft Windows, Apple Macintosh, and so on.) At any rate, I remember sitting in my first class while the professor said things such as, "Once you write your program, save it to a file" and thinking "What the heck is he talking about?"

This chapter therefore contains some sections, such as "Working with Files and Directories" that some might find insulting in their simplicity and exploration of basic concepts that "everybody knows," which is fine with me. Everybody who knows that stuff can skip over it, but the people who just got their Ubuntu Linux boxes at the local electronics shop or from well-meaning friends or relatives can secretly read these sections, think "Oh, I get it!" and we'll all be happier.

IN THIS CHAPTER

Understanding files and directories

Understanding disks and disk partitions

Linux filesystems

Introduction to users and groups

Privileged operations on Ubuntu systems

Working with Files and Directories

A file is nothing more than a collection of information that programs and your operating system can locate and deal with as a single unit. Files are containers for some sort of data, whether they contain a letter to your mother or parole board, a copy of one of your favorite songs (legitimate, of course), a digital photograph, or the data used by a spreadsheet to calculate the health of your personal finances. Providing the general concept of a file as a container for related data makes it easy for applications and Linux to locate and use that information. Hence the File menu that is present in most graphical applications today — this menu contains the commands that you use to open existing files, create new ones, and save changes that you have made to any file that you are working with.

Files are mandatory on a computer system — the operating system has to have a way to identify and access your data, the applications that it needs to run, any configuration files used by those applications, and so on. Similarly, when you turn it on, your computer system needs to know how to find the operating system and related configuration information that it requires to boot. However, as more and more files were required, used for different purposes and created by different users, it didn't take long for users to look for an intermediate mechanism for organizing files, which led to the introduction of directories. Directories are simply containers for groups of related files, and they can also contain directories (or subdirectories). This is what is known as a hierarchical collection of files — the location of any specific file is described by identifying the series of directories that eventually contain the file that you're looking for. The directory that all searches start with on Linux systems is known as the *root directory*, because it is the starting point for the description of how to navigate to any file that is stored locally (i.e., on your computer).

The standard analogy for files and directories is a filing cabinet — you can find any file in the filing cabinet by following a process like this: Start at the filing cabinet, open the first drawer, open the hanging file labeled Personnel, select the manila folder with your name on it, and check your healthcare enrollment form. On a computer, the process for finding the location of an analogous file might be something like this: Go to the root of the filesystem (/), go to the home directory, go to the wvh directory (my login name), and look for the file named health_enrollment.txt.

Linux systems use the "/" character to separate file and directory names, so this is often more simply expressed as, "get the file /home/wvh/health_enrollment.txt." The series of directories leading to a given file is often referred to as the "path" to that file.

Linux systems that provide a graphical user interface, such as GNOME, provide graphical ways of navigating through directories, typically by clicking on them to open them and opening a window that displays graphical icons corresponding to the files that they contain. As explained in more detail in Chapter 6, "Using Command-Line Tools," any Linux command-line environment uses a command known as cd (which stands for change directory) to navigate through a sequence of directories. You can change to each directory in a series of directories (paths) one at a time, or you can simply cd to a specific target directory. In other words, the following two sequences of commands are equivalent:

```
cd /
cd home
cd wvh
```

and

```
cd /home/wvh
```

Linux systems also provide a variety of tools to list the contents of directories and provide detailed information about specific files and directories. I explain these in detail in Chapter 6 — for now, I'll focus on describing how things are organized on a Linux system.

Standard Linux Directories

All Linux systems provide a standard set of core directories. The following directories are used to hold programs that must run when you are booting your Linux system, configuration files for those programs, libraries used by those programs, temporary files created by running programs, and so on:

- **/**: As the top-level directory of a Linux system, this directory must exist so that other directories can be located within it.

- **/bin**: A directory that holds core applications used by a Linux system.

- **/dev**: A directory that holds special files, known as device nodes, which are used to access any devices that are attached to your Linux system.

- **/etc**: A directory that holds system configuration information, contains the files that explain the sequence of applications that execute on a Linux system as part of its boot process, and stores configuration files for some of the applications that are executed by a Linux system.

- **/lib**: A directory that holds libraries of functions that can be called by other applications.

- **/proc**: A directory in which the Linux kernel tracks active processes and general status information.

- **/sbin**: A directory containing applications that are usually executed only by the superuser.

- **/sys**: A directory in which the Linux kernel tracks the status of system hardware and related hardware interfaces.

- **/tmp**: A directory that holds temporary files created by various applications on a running system.

You will find these standard directories on most Linux systems, regardless of the type of distribution or the size of the disk they are using.

Other Common Directories on Linux Systems

Depending on the number of files you've installed on your system and its layout, you will probably find several other directories on any Linux system. Some other commonly used directories on Linux systems are the following:

- **/home**: A directory that holds the subdirectories where different users store their files. For example, most (if not all) of the files owned by the user "wvh" are stored in the /home/wvh directory (or subdirectories of that directory). The directories used by individual users to store their personal files are known as their "home directories" — this name led to user directories being stored in /home, not the other way around. On older Unix and Unix-like systems, users' home directories were stored under /usr (pronounced "slash user"), but are now created under /home to simplify system upgrades.

- **/opt**: A directory typically used when installing third-party software. This directory takes its name from the idea that it contains "optional" (i.e., non-system) software that may differ across different machines.

- **/usr**: A directory hierarchy that contains files meant to be used by normal users as they use a Linux system. The directory /usr/bin contains applications that users may need to execute, /usr/lib contains libraries used by those programs, and so on.

- **/var**: A directory that holds other directories with variable content. For example, the directory /var/log contains log files for system applications and events. These log files are created while a system is running, and can grow very large over time.

As you can see, a Linux system provides a large, hierarchical collection of files and directories that are organized to simplify locating certain types of files such as executables, libraries, configuration files, system status information, and so on. Now, let's look at how Linux uses various types of storage devices to store and deliver all of this information.

Introduction to Linux Filesystems

The directories discussed in the previous section provide a standard way of organizing the files and directories required for a Linux system to boot, run standard applications, and so on. You'll note that the path to all of these directories begins with the / symbol. This doesn't necessarily mean that they're all located on the same hard drive or other storage device. Unlike Windows systems, which refer to different disk drives or disk partitions by using unique drive letters (C:, D:, and so on), or Mac OS X systems, which represent different disk drives or disk partitions as different volumes on the desktop, Linux systems provide what is known as a "single name space" for all of the storage devices and partitions that it can access.

This section discusses how Linux systems manage and access disks, what disk partitions are, and how disk partitions are integrated into the hierarchy of directories that you can access on a Linux system. The hierarchy of files and directories on a Linux machine is generally referred to as the Linux filesystem, though, as I'll discuss in the next few sections, the term filesystem is also used to refer to the way that data is organized on a specific disk partition.

Disks, Partitions, and Mount Points

The bottom line of any computer system is storing, retrieving, manipulating, and saving information. As a writer and computer systems administrator, I'm always amazed when friends who are generally computer savvy say to me, "Your laptop is so slow. Why don't you upgrade?" Frankly, if I could type faster than my primary laptop's 1.4 GHz Pentium processor could handle, I'd be posing for "Ripley's Believe It or Not!" ads or touring with the circus instead of writing books. On the other hand, if it took five minutes for me to save a chapter of whatever I'm working on or if I could never find the space to save a modified file without deleting something else, I'd drop-kick my current laptop into the river in a heartbeat and buy the newest, brightest, shiniest Linux-capable laptop available today. For what I do, being able to reliably and quickly read and write data is far more important than blazing CPU speed.

Every computer system includes some sort of storage devices such as hard disks, DVD and CD drives, CompactFlash cards, and so on, which store the operating system and your applications, and also provide some space that you can use to store the files and directories that you create. One of my favorite bits of technical writing ever is the following quote from a Hewlett-Packard manual shipped with one of their Unix (HP-UX) workstations in the mid-1980s:

"On a clear disk, you can seek forever."

In geek-speak, this means that without imposing some organization on the devices used to store your data, your operating system would have no idea where to look for specific files, directories, or anything. To store data on a disk and access that data afterward, a disk has to be prepared in such a way that your operating system and associated applications can read, write, and interact with. This preparation usually consists of two steps:

1. Dividing the disk into one or more sections that can be uniquely located by the operating system. Each section of a disk is known as a partition.

2. Formatting the partitions, referred to as "creating a filesystem," in such a way that your operating system can access each partition and create files and directories there.

Disk drives are partitioned for several reasons:

- To reduce the amount of time required to locate a specific piece of data on the drive. It simply takes less time (and less location information) to find a specific piece of data in a smaller pool of information.

- To limit the amount of data that can be lost or damaged if a disk or partition becomes corrupted.

- To speed up administrative operations such as defragmentation, consistency checking, and repair (when necessary).

- To simplify administrative operations, such as backups. It's simpler to back up partitions that will fit on a single tape or other backup media, because no operator intervention is required (such as switching tapes). Multiple partitions also enable you to install system files and applications on different partitions than where you store your user data. You can then back up the partition containing user data relatively frequently, without accidentally backing up a vast amount of relatively unchanging executables, system files, and so on.

As mentioned in the previous section, the term filesystem is often used to colloquially refer to the entire hierarchy of files and directories that make up a Linux system. In this section, I'm using filesystem in its more specific sense, which refers to the way in which a disk partition is formatted so that you can store data there and even retrieve it.

Once you format a partition and create a filesystem on it, you need to be able to make that disk partition available to your system. This is known as *mounting* that filesystem, which simply attaches that filesystem to some part of the Linux directory structure so that you can use the storage that it provides. Linux systems mount filesystems on a directory so that they become a part of the standard Linux filesystem namespace, which I'll discuss in more detail in the section on "Mounting Filesystems," later in this chapter. Any Linux directory can act as a mount point for a filesystem, and many of the standard directories discussed in the previous section are actually mount points for separate filesystems that hold the contents of those directories. The standard Linux /mnt directory generally contains special-purpose subdirectories that are used as mount points for filesystems that you are planning to use temporarily.

Local Filesystems: Standard and Journaling

Local filesystems are filesystems that are located on storage devices that are physically connected to your computer. Access to data on local filesystems is therefore fast because they are directly connected to your machine. On the other hand, local filesystems are useful only if you and any other users who need access to the data that they contain can connect to the machine on which they are located. When you need access to data that is stored in a local filesystem, connecting to the machine on which specific data is physically located generally isn't a problem in today's networked environments—you can always open an SSH (Secure Shell) or telnet connection to that machine, as long as that specific machine is up and working correctly, of course.

The most common type of filesystem used on Linux systems is the ext2 filesystem (Extended Filesystem, Version 2). I'll call this a standard filesystem because it works the way most vanilla filesystems work. When you update a file, the changes to that file are written directly to the target filesystem. If your system goes down at that exact point, your changes may or may not have been made to the target filesystem. As your system comes back up, part of its startup sequence is to check the consistency of all of its filesystems. (For information about how your system knows what filesystems it should use and check, see "Automatically Mounting Filesystems at Boot Time," later in this chapter.) The utility used to check the consistency of a standard ext2 filesystem is known as `fsck` (file system consistency check). The `fsck` utility traverses all of the data structures within a filesystem to make sure that all of the data in the filesystem is correctly associated with files and directories.

Running the `fsck` utility (known as fscking a filesystem) can take quite a bit of time on large partitions, which means that it takes longer for your system to become available to users. To help minimize system restart time by eliminating the need to run `fsck` (or by reducing the type of work that `fsck` has to do), a newer type of filesystem known as a *journaling* filesystem has been developed. In journaling filesystems, changes made to any file in the filesystem are initially written to a special part of the filesystem known as the journal (sometimes referred to as log) in the form of a transaction. The changes recorded in the journal are then applied to the filesystem asynchronously and transactionally. The record of these changes stays in the filesystem log until they have completed successfully, at which point the records associated with that transaction are removed.

Journaling filesystems improve system restart time because a filesystem can always be made consistent by playing any pending transactions against the filesystem. Therefore, running the `fsck` utility generally consists, at most, of executing any pending changes that are recorded in the filesystem log. Journaling filesystems can also improve overall filesystem performance because the filesystem doesn't have to wait until a file update completes successfully, as standard (i.e., non-journaled) filesystems do. Once changes are written to the log, normal filesystem operations can continue and the filesystem can be updated asynchronously. Because the log is usually stored in special, high-performance portion of the filesystem that uses a special format, log updates can be substantially faster than updates to the actual filesystem. Obviously, changes to any file must be completed before that file can be modified again, so it is necessary to check whether there are pending updates to a file before modifying it.

The most common journaling Linux filesystem in use today is the ext3 filesystem, which is basically the ext2 filesystem with journaling capabilities. This type of filesystem is quite popular because ext2 filesystems can be converted into ext3 filesystems with a simple change, and all filesystem repair, debugging, and analysis software written for the ext2 filesystem automatically works with the ext3 filesystem. Other popular types of journaling filesystems are ReiserFS and Reiser4 (both written by Hans Reiser and friends from namesys.com), the JFS filesystem (originally written by IBM for OS/2 and AIX, and released by IBM as an open source project, `http://jfs.sourceforge.net/`), and XFS (originally written by SGI for IRIX and released by SGI as an open source project, `http://oss.sgi.com/projects/xfs/`).

For a bit of humor, here is the man page for the `fsck` utility for the XFS journaling filesystem:

```
fsck.xfs(8)                                              fsck.xfs(8)
NAME
       fsck.xfs - do nothing, successfully


SYNOPSIS
       fsck.xfs [ ...]


DESCRIPTION
       fsck.xfs is called by the generic Linux fsck(8) program at
       startup to check and repair an XFS filesystem.  XFS  is  a
       journaling  filesystem  and  performs recovery at mount(8)
       time if necessary, so fsck.xfs simply exits  with  a  zero
       exit status.


FILES
       /etc/fstab


SEE ALSO
       fsck(8), fstab(5), xfs(5).
```

Well, that certainly cuts down on `fsck` and restart time!

Network Filesystems

Network filesystems are filesystems that are stored on remote systems (usually known as file servers) and can be mounted on your local machine just like a local filesystem. Networked filesystems provide users with the freedom to access their information from any system on which they can log in and which has access to those networked resources.

Network filesystems offer several advantages over local filesystems:

- They reduce the chance that the failure of a single machine will prevent you from accessing your data. Most networked filesystems enable you to log in on multiple machines and access your data in exactly the same way.

- They provide central locations for data that must or should be shared among all users.

- They simplify accessing existing data from faster systems. Suppose that you have written an application to test CPU and memory performance, or that your work or research depends on CPU and memory-intensive calculations. Running your application on a faster, more powerful machine is as simple as logging in on that machine and running the application from the networked filesystem.

- They provide the opportunity to centralize administrative operations such as backups.

- They promote interoperability and flexibility. You can usually access networked filesystems from systems running Linux, Microsoft Windows, Mac OS X, and so on. This makes it easy for you to use the software and hardware that is best suited to your desktop requirements and still access the same data on the networked filesystem.

A variety of networked filesystems are available for Linux. The most popular of these is NFS, the Network File System originally written by Sun Microsystems and subsequently supported on almost every other Unix-like system since the dawn of the workstation. NFS is actively supported by Apple's Mac OS X, and NFS clients (and servers) are even available for Microsoft Windows systems. The other most commonly used network filesystem is, ironically, Microsoft's SMB (Server Message Block) filesystem, which has been renamed CIFS (Common Internet File System) in an attempt to hide its proprietary roots and the fact that it had to be reverse engineered to be accessed from Linux and other Unix-like systems. SMB/CIFS is supported on Linux systems by a suite of client and server software known as Samba (www.samba.org). Samba clients enable Linux systems to mount and access SMB/CIFS filesystems exported by Microsoft Windows systems. Samba servers enable Linux systems to export their filesystems so that they can be mounted and accessed from machines running different versions of Microsoft Windows. Linux systems also support connectivity to Novell Netware filesystems through the Linux NCP — Novell Core Protocol — utilities (www.novell.com/coolsolutions/feature/15350.html) and Pre-OS X MacOS Apple filesystems via the Linux netatalk and afpfs utilities (http://netatalk.sourceforge.net/ or, historically, www.anders.com/projects/netatalk/).

Working with Partitions and Filesystems

Like Ubuntu, most Linux systems automatically identify the disks in your system and propose a reasonable partitioning scheme as part of the installation process. Similarly, when you attach a new disk to your system or add one internally, Ubuntu displays a dialog box asking if you want to configure that disk. Partitioning during the installation process is explained in Chapter 2, "Installing Ubuntu"; using graphical partitioning utilities after your system is already running is explained in detail in Chapter 23, "Adding Hardware and Attaching Peripherals."

Even after you partition and mount a disk, or you attach an existing disk that has already been partitioned and formatted, your system can't access it until you mount it somewhere. This section discusses how to temporarily mount a disk using the Linux mount command, the most popular options that are available for that command, and how to mount a specific disk as part of your system's startup process by adding it to your system's filesystem configuration file, /etc/fstab.

Mounting Filesystems

Once you've attached a disk, you can always query the filesystems that it contains by using the Linux fdisk utility's -l (list) option, as in the following example:

```
$ sudo fdisk -l

Disk /dev/sda: 250.0 GB, 250059350016 bytes
255 heads, 63 sectors/track, 30401 cylinders
Units = cylinders of 16065 * 512 = 8225280 bytes

   Device Boot      Start         End      Blocks   Id  System
/dev/sda1               1        1306    10490413+  83  Linux
/dev/sda2            1307        2090     6297480   82  Linux swap
/dev/sda3    *       2091        2122      257040   83  Linux
/dev/sda4            2123       30399   227135002+   f  W95 Ext'd (LBA)
/dev/sda5            2123        2645     4200966   83  Linux
/dev/sda6            2646        6562    31463271   83  Linux
/dev/sda7            6563       10478    31455238+  83  Linux
/dev/sda8           10479       30399   160015401   83  Linux

Disk /dev/hde: 250.0 GB, 250059350016 bytes
255 heads, 63 sectors/track, 30401 cylinders
Units = cylinders of 16065 * 512 = 8225280 bytes

   Device Boot      Start         End      Blocks   Id  System
/dev/hde1               1       30401   244196001   83  Linux

Disk /dev/hdf: 250.0 GB, 250059350016 bytes
255 heads, 63 sectors/track, 30401 cylinders
Units = cylinders of 16065 * 512 = 8225280 bytes

   Device Boot      Start         End      Blocks   Id  System
/dev/hdf1               1       30401   244196001   83  Linux
```

By default, the fdisk command lists all partitions on all disks that it can detect in your system. You can also use the fdisk command to list the partitions on a specific device, as in the following example:

```
$ sudo fdisk -l /dev/sda
Password:

Disk /dev/sda: 250.0 GB, 250059350016 bytes
255 heads, 63 sectors/track, 30401 cylinders
Units = cylinders of 16065 * 512 = 8225280 bytes

   Device Boot      Start         End      Blocks   Id  System
/dev/sda1               1        1306    10490413+  83  Linux
```

```
/dev/sda2              1307       2090      6297480     82   Linux swap
/dev/sda3      *       2091       2122       257040     83   Linux
/dev/sda4              2123      30399   227135002+      f   W95 Ext'd (LBA)
/dev/sda5              2123       2645      4200966     83   Linux
/dev/sda6              2646       6562     31463271     83   Linux
/dev/sda7              6563      10478     31455238+    83   Linux
/dev/sda8             10479      30399    160015401     83   Linux
```

Note that the primary argument to this command is the base name of the disk that you want to query, not the name of a specific partition. You can get similar information, though in a slightly less usable form, by examining the file /proc/partitions, which a running system uses to track all disks and partitions that are currently in use on your system. The contents of this file are the following on the same system from which the previous example was taken:

```
$ cat /proc/partitions
major minor  #blocks  name
    8     0  244198584 sda
    8     1   10490413 sda1
    8     2    6297480 sda2
    8     3     257040 sda3
    8     4          1 sda4
    8     5    4200966 sda5
    8     6   31463271 sda6
    8     7   31455238 sda7
    8     8  160015401 sda8
   33     0  244198584 hde
   33     1  244196001 hde1
   33    64  244198584 hdf
   33    65  244196001 hdf1
```

Once you've identified the partitions on your new disk (and presumably know which ones you want to use), mounting them using the mount command is easy. You will always need to explicitly mount filesystems that aren't listed in the file /etc/fstab (explained in more detail in the next section).

For example, the following command mounts the partition /dev/sda5 on the mount point /mnt/tmp (which must already exist):

```
$ sudo mount /dev/sda1 /mnt/tmp
```

If you're mounting a partition that contains an ext2 filesystem or a type of filesystem that your system can auto-detect, you don't need to specify the type of filesystem that the partition/device uses. If it is something non-standard, you will have to identify the type of filesystem using the mount command's -t option, followed by the name of that type of filesystem, as in the following example which mounts the XFS filesystem on /dev/sda6 on the mount point /mnt/xfs:

```
$ sudo mount -t xfs /dev/sda1 /mnt/tmp
```

The -t option actually causes the mount command to first look for a special, filesystem-specific mount command, /sbin/mount.type, where type is the name of that type of filesystem. These filesystem-specific commands are usually installed along with the other administrative utilities for different types of filesystems using the Synaptic Package Manager or apt-get, as explained in Chapter 20, "Adding, Removing, and Updating Software."

Supported types of filesystems that you can specify using the -t option are dfs, affs, autofs, coda, coherent, cramfs, devpts, efs, ext, ext2, ext3, hfs, hpfs, iso9660, jfs, minix, msdos, ncpfs, nfs, ntfs, proc, qnx4, ramfs, reiserfs, romfs, smbfs, sysv, tmpfs, udf, ufs, umsdos, usbfs, vfat, xenix, xfs, and xiafs.

Some filesystems require additional options, such as NFS filesystems, SMB/CIFS filesystems, and so on. These options are highly filesystem-specific, so I won't bore you with all of them here. Instead, I'll focus on the options for SMB/CIFS filesystems, because that is probably the most common networked filesystem that you'll want to mount. Some other mount options that are commonly used in the filesystem/mount configuration file are discussed in the next section.

When mounting a networked SMB/CIFS filesystem, you will need to specify the name of the Windows user that you want to access the filesystem as, your Windows password, and also the identity of the Linux user who should appear to own the files in the filesystem, so that you write to the remote filesystem as needed. An example of specifying these in a mount command is the following:

```
$ sudo mount -t smbfs -o username=wvh,password=mypassword,uid=wvh \
    //192.168.6.66/share /mnt/terastation
```

This command mounts the smbfs filesystem called share on the host 192.168.6.66 on the Linux directory /mnt/terastation, using the Windows username of wvh and whose password is mypassword. The mounted filesystem will appear to be owned by the user wvh, which means that I'll have the ability to write anywhere on that filesystem that isn't protected by Windows ACLs or some similar mechanism.

Automatically Mounting Filesystems at Boot Time

When your Ubuntu system boots, the boot block on your primary disk identifies the filesystem that contains the second-stage boot loader, which uses a configuration file to determine what kernels and associated boot options are available on your system. Older Linux systems used a boot loader called LiLo (Linux Loader), while Ubuntu and most other modern Linux systems use a boot loader called GRUB (Grand Unified Boot Loader).

During the boot process, the root filesystem is initially mounted read-only for standard processes so that its consistency can be verified. Once this is done, it is remounted in read-write mode, and your system verifies the existence and consistency of any other filesystems that it will be using. The list of filesystems that are available to your system is contained in the file /etc/fstab (File System Table).

Each line in the /etc/fstab file provides information about one of the filesystems that should be available to your system. To add a new filesystem so that it will always be mounted when your system boots, or to customize how your system interacts with a specific type of device, you need only add or customize an entry for that filesystem in the /etc/fstab file. A sample section of the /etc/fstab file on one of my systems looks like the following (this file will be different on your system):

```
$ cat /etc/fstab
LABEL=/      /             ext3      noatime,acl,user_xattr 1 1
/dev/sda3    /boot         ext3      acl,user_xattr         1 2
/dev/sda8    /home         ext3      noatime,acl,user_xattr 1 2
/dev/sda5    /tmp          ext3      acl,user_xattr         1 2
/dev/sda6    /usr          ext3      noatime,acl,user_xattr 1 2
/dev/sda7    /usr/local    ext3      noatime,acl,user_xattr 1 2
/dev/sda2    swap          swap      sw                     0 0
/dev/hde1    /opt2         ext3      noatime,acl,user_xattr 0 0
```

```
devpts      /dev/pts      devpts        mode=0620,gid=5     0 0
proc        /proc         proc          defaults            0 0
sysfs       /sys          sysfs         noauto              0 0
/dev/hdd    /media/cdrom0 udf,iso9660   user,noauto         0 0
/dev/fd0    /media/floppy0 auto         rw,user,noauto      0 0
```

The fields in each /etc/fstab entry (i.e., each line) are the following:

- The first field is the device or remote filesystem to be mounted. This is usually the Linux device file for the partition that is to be mounted, but can also be an entry of the form hostname:directory for networked filesystems such as NFS. ext2 and ext3 filesystems can also be identified by the name that they were assigned in the filesystem volume label when the filesystem was created. For example, the entry LABEL=/ in the example /etc/fstab file could be replaced with /dev/sda1, because that is the disk partition where my root filesystem actually lives. However, using labels is more flexible than using specific partition device files, because the device file associated with a specific partition may change if the disk containing that partition is moved to another system or if other disks are added to an existing system.

- The second field is the directory on which the specified filesystem should be mounted. For special types of partitions that should not be mounted, such as swap partitions, this field should contain the entry none.

- The third field identifies the type of filesystem. Common entries in this field are ext2 (the standard Linux local filesystem type), ext3 (the journaling version of ext2), vfat (a 32-bit Windows FAT partition), iso9660 (the standard CD-ROM filesystem), nfs (networked filesystems using Sun's NFS protocol), and swap (swap space). If a filesystem is not currently used but you want to keep an entry for it in /etc/fstab, you can put the word ignore in this field, and that filesystem will not be mounted, checked for consistency, and so on.

The types of filesystems that are compiled into your kernel are listed in the file /proc/filesystems, but this can be misleading. Your kernel usually also supports other types of filesystems, but as loadable kernel modules rather than being hardwired into the kernel. For example, the /proc/filesystems file on my system contains the following entries:

```
        ext3
nodev   sysfs
nodev   rootfs
nodev   bdev
nodev   proc
nodev   sockfs
nodev   debugfs
nodev   securityfs
nodev   pipefs
nodev   futexfs
nodev   tmpfs
nodev   inotifyfs
nodev   eventpollfs
nodev   devpts
        ext2
nodev   ramfs
nodev   hugetlbfs
        minix
        iso9660
nodev   nfs
```

```
nodev    nfs4
nodev    mqueue
nodev    rpc_pipefs
         reiserfs
nodev    usbfs
nodev    subfs
         vfat
         hfsplus
nodev    smbfs
```

Filesystems whose types are prefaced by a `nodev` entry are not associated with physical devices, but are used internally by applications and the operating system.

- The fourth field contains a comma-separated list of any options to the `mount` command that should be used when the filesystem is mounted. Many mount options are filesystem-specific, but some common ones are the following:

  - `async`: Writes to the filesystem should be done asynchronously.

  - `auto`: The filesystem should be automatically mounted when detected or when a command such as `mount -a` is executed.

  - `defaults`: The default options `-async`, `auto`, `dev`, `exec`, `nouser`, `rw`, `suid` are used.

  - `dev`: The character or block device containing the filesystem is local to the system.

  - `exec`: You can execute programs, scripts, or anything else whose permissions indicate that it is executable — from that filesystem.

  - `gid=value`: Set the group ID of the mounted filesystem to the specified numeric group ID when the filesystem is mounted.

  - `noauto`: Don't automatically mount when a filesystem is detected or when the command `mount -a` is issued. Usually used with removable media such as floppies and CD-ROMs.

  - `nouser`: You must be root to mount the filesystem — the filesystem can't be mounted by any non-root user.

  - `owner`: The ownership of the filesystem is set to the user who mounted it — usually root if the filesystem is automatically mounted by the system.

  - `ro`: Mount the filesystem read-only.

  - `rw`: Mount the filesystem read-write.

  - `suid`: Allow programs on the filesystem to change the user's user or group ID when they are executed if their permission bits indicate that they should do this. Be very careful when using this option with imported filesystems that you don't actually administer, because running a program that sets the UID to root is a common way of hacking into a system.

  - `uid=value`: Set the user ID of the mounted filesystem to the specified numeric user ID when the filesystem is mounted.

  For more information on generic options available to the `mount` command, see the man page for the `mount` command in section 8 of the online Linux manual (by using the `man 8 mount` command).

- The fifth field is used by the `dump` command, a standard Linux/Unix filesystem backup command, to identify filesystems that should be backed up when the `dump` command is executed. If the fifth field contains a '0' (or is missing), the dump command assumes that the filesystem associated with that `/etc/fstab` entry does not need to be backed up.

- The sixth field is used by the Linux/Unix filesystem consistency checker (discussed in the next section) to identify filesystems whose consistency should be verified when the system is rebooted, and the order in which the consistency of those filesystems should be checked. If the sixth field contains a '0' (or is missing), the `fsck` program assumes that the filesystem associated with that `/etc/fstab` entry does not need to be checked.

The contents of this file may seem complex at first, but over time you'll get used to creating and editing them. Many of the graphical utilities provided for manipulating disk partitions automatically create these entries for you — or you can always do what I do, which is to copy an existing, but similar, entry and then modify it as needed for the partition(s) I'm adding.

Automatically Mounting Removable Media Filesystems

Beyond the entries in your `/etc/fstab` file, Ubuntu also provides special support to simplify interacting with removable media on your system. Though discussed in more detail elsewhere in this book, it is worth mentioning this here to complete this section's overview of storage device handling on Ubuntu systems.

Ubuntu's automatic recognition of removable media is done via the gnome-volume-manager application, which is configured using the gnome-volume-properties application. You can start this configuration application by selecting Removable Drives and Media from the System menu's Preferences submenu.

Once configured, the gnome-volume-manager makes it easy for your system to automatically recognize CDs, DVDs, CompactFlash cards, and other common removable media and automatically mount them for you in appropriate mount points under your system's `/media` directory. Using and customizing the gnome-volume-manager's recognition and handling of these types of media is discussed in detail in Chapter 23, "Adding Hardware and Attaching Peripherals."

The gnome-volume-manager's support for devices that are often attached to your system while it is running extends beyond just storage devices — it includes peripherals such as printers, mice, keyboards, tablets, and so on. It also makes it easy for your system to automatically recognize consumer electronics devices such as digital cameras and personal digital assistants (PDAs) so that you can easily transfer files back and forth to the storage media that these devices use. This aspect of the gnome-volume-manager is discussed in detail in Chapter 17, "Consumer Electronics and Ubuntu."

Understanding Linux Permissions

If you're sharing your Ubuntu system with other users, it's useful to understand how Linux systems protect files and directories so that they can be accessed by only the people that you want to have access to them. Similarly, if you have installed your own Ubuntu system and are therefore responsible for taking care of it ("system administration" in geek-speak), you need to know how Ubuntu systems ensure that only specific, authorized users can perform privileged tasks. For example, it would be potentially inconvenient if random users could format disk drives, reconfigure your system's connection to networks such as the Internet, and so on. Though you'd hope that no one would do these sorts of things maliciously, it's easy enough to accidentally click OK when exploring system configuration applications, thinking perhaps that this would simply exit from the application.

Linux supports the traditional permission model used by all Unix-like systems, users and groups, with a few interesting twists that have been introduced to foster Ubuntu's goals of usability and user-friendliness. If you've used other Linux systems in the past, it's easy enough to adapt to doing things the Ubuntu way, and if you're new to Linux, you'll find the Ubuntu model for privileged commands to be quite easy to understand, configure, and use.

> **NOTE** Ubuntu provides an easy-to-use graphical application for creating and managing the users on your Ubuntu systems. This section focuses on the underlying concepts of Ubuntu permissions — using Ubuntu's graphical application for creating and managing Ubuntu users and groups is discussed in detail in Chapter 21, "Managing Users, Groups, Authentication, and Advanced Permissions."

Basic Concepts: Users and Groups

All Linux systems provide two basic administrative entities that are used to determine who has access to what files and who can perform specific, privileged operations. Each person who can log in on a Linux system does so via a user account, which consists of a name and password, and which has a specific home directory that contains that user's configuration data as well as any files that they create. The file `/etc/passwd` (known as the password file, but why type a few extra letters if you don't have to) contains a list of every user who has an account on that specific machine.

All Linux users belong to one or more groups. A *group* is an administrative entity that makes it easier for multiple users to access the same sets of files. Information about the groups that are defined on your Ubuntu system and the users that belong to those groups is stored in the file `/etc/group`, which is a text file with easy-to-understand entries. As explained later in this section, file and directory permissions can be set such that users who are a member of a specified group can read and/or write files in shared directories, which other users on the system still cannot access. This makes it easy to set up collaborative projects or to simply share information with selected other users on your systems.

> **NOTE** Most Linux systems use the local `/etc/passwd` and `/etc/group` files for authentication and group membership information, but systems that use networked authentication mechanisms can get these types of information from other systems on your network. For example, systems that use NIS, the Network Information Service that is used in many NFS-based Linux environments, can contain entries in the password and group files that tell your system to check NIS for user, group, and authentication information. Linux also supports PAMs (Pluggable Authentication Modules), which enable the system to contact networked sources of these types of information such as LDAP (Lightweight Directory Access Protocol) servers, Kerberos servers, and even Microsoft Windows authentication servers. PAMs aren't discussed here because they are very special, advanced cases, and this section is only intended as an introduction to Ubuntu and basic Linux security. NIS is discussed in Chapter 21, "Managing Users, Groups, Authentication, and Advanced Permissions. "

My entry in the `/etc/passwd` file on one of my Ubuntu systems is the following:

```
wvh:x:1000:1000:William von Hagen,,,:/home/wvh:/bin/bash
```

The fields in this entry are the following:

- My login name.
- The password field. In this case, an x means that password information is actually stored in the file `/etc/shadow`.
- My user ID, which is the numeric value associated with my login name.
- The numeric group ID of the default group of which I am a member.
- A field containing my full name and other text information such as office location and office and home phone numbers.
- My home directory.
- The application that runs when I log in, in this case a shell.

A few sample entries from the `/etc/group` file on that same system are the following:

```
adm:x:4:wvh,juser
cdrom:x:24:hal,wvh,juser
lpadmin:x:106:wvh,juser
admin:x:112:wvh,juser
wvh:x:1000:
```

Each entry in the `/etc/group` file begins with the name of the group, a password field (in these examples indicating that any group passwords are stored in the file `/etc/shadow`), the numeric identifier associated with that group, and the list of users who belong to that group.

As you can see from these examples, it is common for users to belong to multiple groups, each of which provides access to a specific resource such as files, directories, or administrative capabilities. You can list the groups that you belong to by executing the `groups` command at any Linux command-line prompt.

When you create user accounts on an Ubuntu system (including during the installation process), a default group is created for each of those users. This group is the group to which that user is a default member when he or she logs in on your system. Most applications that use group membership to indicate administrative privileges will automatically check the `/etc/group` file when they first execute. To access shared directories, you may have to change the group that you are actively a member of. You can do this using the `newrgp` command at any Linux command-line prompt.

Ubuntu systems reserve group numbers less than 1000 for administrative purposes. The different applications that use these groups, generally referred to as system groups, automatically check group memberships when they execute. There's no need to memorize the default groups used by different system applications on Ubuntu, because the administrative applications that require them typically add you to the right group. See the section entitled "Performing Privileged Operations in Ubuntu" later in this chapter, for details.

File and Directory Permissions Under Linux

This section provides an overview of how file and directory permissions are displayed and used on Linux systems. Though discussed in more detail in Chapter 6, "Using Command-Line Tools," it makes sense to introduce this topic here to illustrate how user and group identities can provide shared access to files, directories, and other resources, and how to manipulate those settings.

The easiest command to use to view the permissions on a file or directory is the Linux `ls` (list) command, which displays information about the files and directories in a specified location.

For example, the command `ls -ld /home/wvh` provides a long listing of my home directory, which includes information about the current permissions on that directory:

```
drwxr-xr-x  145 wvh wvh 7728 2006-03-05 10:54 /home/wvh
```

I'll focus on the first field, which shows the current permissions on my directory—see Chapter 6, "Using Command-Line Tools," for detailed information about all of these fields, options to the `ls` command, and the `ls` command itself.

The permissions field of `ls` output can be broken down into four sections:

- The first character, which identifies the type of object you're looking at. The most common of these are a – if the thing you're listing is a regular file, a d if it's a directory, a c if it's a device node that can be accessed as a stream of characters, or a b if it's a device node that can be accessed as a block device.
- Three sets of three characters, which represent the permissions that the owner, the group owner, and all others have on the file or directory.

The most common values for each position in the three permissions sections are r, which means that the file or directory can be read, a w, which means that the file or directory can be written to, and an x, which (for a file) means that the file can be executed or (for a directory) means that the directory can be searched for other files or directories. If any of these permissions are not set, its position is represented by a dash. In addition, the user and group execution bits can be set to an s, which means "set user or group ID upon execution" — in other words, executing that file is done as though it were being done by the owner and/or group of the specified file. This is commonly done to execute a command as though it were being executed by another, more privileged user on your system.

Default Permissions When Creating Files and Directories

A umask is the classic Unix mechanism for setting the default protections of file and directories that you create. By default, the umask is a four digit octal number that is logically ANDed with the generic file protections of octal 0666 (ironically) when you create a file or octal 0777 when you create a directory. The default umask value on most Linux distributions is 0002, meaning that any file you create is created with the octal protection mode 0664—both the owner and group can read and write any file that you create, but randoms can only read the file. Similarly, any directory that you create is created with the octal protection mode 0775—both the owner and group can create files in that directory, and anyone can list the contents of the directory and search for files in it. You find out a user's default umask setting by issuing the umask command from any Linux command-line prompt.

Most people set their umask to 0022 in their shell configuration command file (typically ~/.bashrc) to change their default file creation settings so that files can only be written by their owners (i.e., are created with an octal protection of 0644) and directories can only been written to by their owners (i.e., are created with an octal protection of 0755). The ability to define a umask is built into all Unix shells; for more information about setting or using your umask, see the online documentation for the shell that you are using (typically the bash shell, as discussed in Chapter 6, "Using Command-Line Tools").

Performing Privileged Operations in Ubuntu

Aside from your own user name and numeric ID, the most important other user name on a Linux system is the user named root, whose user ID and group ID are both 0, and who is often known as the *superuser*.

On most Linux systems, privileged operations are often done by using the su (substitute user ID) command to become the root user. However, Ubuntu does things slightly differently. Ubuntu uses the sudo (substitute user ID do) command to perform all privileged operations. The sudo command uses the text-format configuration file /etc/sudoers to determine which users can perform privileged operations as the superuser. On Ubuntu systems, any member of the admin group can perform privileged operations as the root user. You can use the sudo command on any Linux system, but you cannot use the su command on a Ubuntu system.

The difference between using the su and sudo commands is subtle but significant:

- When using the su command to perform a privileged operation, you execute the su command, supply the root user's password in response to the password prompt, which then starts a sub-shell with root privileges. You then execute whatever privileged commands you want within the context of that shell. They are all therefore executed as the superuser. When you are done, you can either exit from that shell or suspend it for subsequent reuse.

- When using the sudo command, you execute the sudo command, followed by the name and arguments to the command that you want to execute.

The su and sudo commands are not restricted to executing commands as the root user. You can become any user using the sudo command by specifying that user's name after the su command and providing that user's password in response to the password prompt. Similarly, you can use the sudo command's -u option to specify the name of the user that you want to execute a command as. As always, the su command requires that you know a specific user's password, while the sudo command only requires that you provide your password.

Let's look at a few examples to compare using these commands. An example of using the su command to display the partitions available on a disk is the following:

```
$ su
Password: <enter-root-password>
#  fdisk -l /dev/sda
[output]
# exit
$
```

To do the same thing using the sudo command, you would do the following:

```
$ sudo fdisk -l /dev/sda
Password: <enter-your-password>
[output]
$
```

On Linux systems other than Ubuntu, you could also use the su command's -c option (execute a single command) to do something similar, as in the following example:

```
$ su -c fdisk -l /dev/sda
Password: <enter-root-password>
[output]
$
```

The key difference between the su and sudo command is whether the command prompts you for the root password or your personal password. However, Ubuntu's focus on using the sudo command has a few basic advantages:

- The system is harder to attack because an attacker first has to discover the identity of a privileged user on the system before they can attempt to break in.

- Users have to remember only their personal password to perform privileged operations if they are permitted to do so. There is no need to separately set and secure the system's root password.

If you want to execute several privileged commands in a row on a Ubuntu system, you have two alternatives. First, you can execute the sudo -s command to execute a shell as the root user. Second, you can do the same thing by running the sudo /bin/bash command. In both of these cases, you have to remember to explicitly exit from the root shell once you're done running the commands that you want to execute.

Summary

This chapter covered some of the basic concepts of Linux and Ubuntu. The chapter began by introducing files and directories and explaining the directories that are commonly used on Ubuntu systems. It then discussed how Ubuntu uses disks, how it partitions them into separate filesystems, the different types of filesystems that you can use on partitions or on Ubuntu systems in general, and how to make those filesystems available for use on your system. The last few sections introduced basic Linux administrative concepts such as managing users, groups and file permissions, and executing privileged commands on the Ubuntu system. This chapter provided the basic knowledge that you'll need to understand these concepts when you encounter them elsewhere in this book.

The next chapter introduces GNOME, the graphical user interface that is installed by default with the Ubuntu desktop system. It discusses how to use the different mouse buttons to interact with GNOME and graphical applications, discusses how to use the GNOME menus to start applications, explains how to interact with panel applications (the GNOME equivalent of desk accessories), and helps you start to actually use your newly installed Ubuntu Linux system.

Chapter 5

Using the GNOME Desktop

Though many curmudgeons and long-time Unix users eschew any sort of graphical interface, let's face it — most people today want (and expect) one. The graphical environment used on Ubuntu systems, the GNOME desktop, provides a stable and usable environment for running your graphical applications and interacting with your system graphically. Most of the Linux utilities used for system administration and configuration provide graphical interfaces to simplify formerly complex tasks, and are easily accessed from one of the primary menus provided by the GNOME desktop.

This chapter begins by providing some background information on the graphical environment used on all Linux systems, such as explaining exactly what the word *desktop* means, and what graphical alternatives exist on Linux systems. The remainder of the chapter focuses on discussing the organization and use of the GNOME desktop provided on Ubuntu systems. GNOME is a powerful graphical interface with all of the features that you'd expect in a modern graphical user interface (GUI) — once you know where to find them.

What's a Desktop? Graphical Environments for Linux

Almost all of the high-resolution support for interacting with any Linux system is handled by a graphics package called the X Window system, known to its friends as X11 or simply X. The X Window system is one of the most attractive aspects of Linux and almost any operating system running on modern bitmapped graphics workstations. X is a network-aware graphics windowing system that provides a similar set of capabilities for creating and working with applications as do the graphical environments used on Microsoft Windows and Mac OS X systems. The X Window system was designed to provide a common windowing environment on multiprocessing, networked computer systems and is the industry standard windowing system for computers running different versions of Linux, any other Unix-like operating system, and even computers that are still running Compaq's VMS operating system. Versions of the X Window system are also available for all releases of Windows greater than 3.1, and for any version of Mac OS X — these run X Window system applications in the context of the native windowing systems for those platforms.

The X Window system was originally developed at the Massachusetts Institute of Technology (MIT), was under the custodianship of the Open Group (`www.opengroup.org`) for a while, and is now stewarded by the X.org Foundation (`www.x.org`). A previous implementation of the X Window System for Linux systems, known as XFree86, is no longer used on Linux systems — the official source of the X implementation for Linux systems is now X.org.

The X Window system enables you to run multiple applications on a bitmapped display screen, each of which displays its own windows, graphics, dialog boxes, and so on in one or more separately controllable windows on the screen. An X Window system window manager is an application that also runs on a bitmapped display screen, but its job is to manage the individual windows that are created and used by other applications. The window manager is the application that enables you to move windows around on the screen, and raise and lower windows; displays the window borders that enable you to move applications; displays the menus that pop up when you click on a part of the screen that is not occupied by a window; displays the window controls that enable you to minimize, maximize, and close separate windows; and so on. Popular window managers include After Step, Black Box, Fluxbox, FVWM, ICEwm, kwm, Metacity, twm, vtwm, and Window Maker. All of these provide the same types of functionality, though they differ in terms of how and where they manage minimized applications, how the window manager is configured, how applications are bound to menus and/or graphical areas on your screen, support for alternate fonts and display styles, and so on.

> **TIP**   One great feature of the X Window system is that, because it was designed to work across multiple hardware platforms, you can start X Window system client applications on one system but have them display on the bit-mapped screen of another system (assuming that this capability is not blocked by a firewall or system configuration setting). This is done by setting an environment variable called `DISPLAY`, and then starting the application that you want to display remotely. The `DISPLAY` environment variable has the following form:
>
>   `host:display.screen`
>
> `host` specifies the name or IP address of the system that you want to display the window on, and is followed by a colon. After the colon, the first number identifies the graphics *display* on which the window should be displayed, followed by a period, and the number followed by a colon, followed by the number of the physical *screen* attached to that card. In most cases, both `display` and `screen` are 0.
>
> See the section of Chapter 6 entitled "Using Environment Variables" for more information about setting environment variables. In many cases, you can also start an X Window system application on a remote screen by starting the application from the command line and specifying the `-display host:display.screen` argument.

After window managers, the next step in the evolution of the X Window system desktop experience is the desktop manager. Desktop managers, colloquially referred to simply as desktops, always run a window manager under the covers, but also provide additional capabilities such as the following:

- Drag and drop
- A file manager of some sort to simplify graphically browsing files and directories
- Easy, flexible ways to tie applications to buttons, icons, and menu items

- A centralized mechanism for configuring the appearance of your screen and the windows that it displays, generally referred to as applying a *theme*

- Support for running lightweight applications (known as *applets*) within the context of the window manager to support certain types of tasks

The most common desktops for Linux systems are GNOME (GNU Network Object Model Environment, www.gnome.org), KDE (K Development Environment, www.kde.org), ROX (rox.sourceforge.net), and XFCE (www.xfce.org). Both GNOME and KDE are rich, robust desktop environments that provide their own window managers (GNOME uses Metacity, while KDE uses kwm) and primarily differ in terms of default mouse and key bindings, menu organization, and the underlying graphical toolkit (GNOME uses a widget toolkit known as GTK, while KDE uses one called QT). Both ROX and XFCE are lightweight desktops, which means that they attempt to strike a balance between the heavy resource requirements and corresponding power of rich desktop environments such as GNOME and KDE, and the much lighter requirements but more limited capabilities of traditional window managers. You can find a great introduction to most of the X Window system window managers and desktop environments available for Linux at http://xwinman.org.

The rest of this chapter primarily focuses on GNOME, which is the desktop environment that is used on Ubuntu systems, and which starts automatically the first time you log in to an Ubuntu system. Though you can change the window manager used by GNOME, switch to KDE, or even switch your Ubuntu experience to using a window manager rather than using its default GNOME configuration, those are all advanced tasks. First things first — let's explore how things work on a standard Ubuntu system just in case your goal is getting your work done rather than tweaking your Ubuntu system. There's plenty of time in the future to trick out your graphical environment, which I'll discuss in the section entitled "Switching to a Window Manager" later in this chapter.

What About KDE on Ubuntu?

As mentioned earlier in this chapter, KDE (the K Desktop Environment) is a desktop environment that is designed to provide normal computer users with a standard, easy-to-use graphical desktop environment. KDE was initially inspired by CDE (the Common Desktop Environment), which was cooperatively designed by major Unix vendors such as IBM and Sun Microsystems and originally ran on those vendors' hardware. CDE was designed and built using the Open Group's Motif X Window system libraries, which meant that any vendor wishing to deploy CDE had to license Motif. This was unacceptable in the free, Open Source environment of Linux, so KDE was initially written to provide a free, Open Source alternative to CDE. The KDE project was originally sponsored by several Linux vendors and fans, including Caldera, Delix, O'Reilly Associates, and SUSE. Unfortunately, KDE selected a widget and windowing package called Qt to serve as its graphical underpinnings, which initially had some licensing issues. This has all been straightened out now, but the side effect of these issues was the formation of the GNOME project, which many people and Linux distribution vendors (Ubuntu, Red Hat, Yellow Dog, Mandrake, and so on) have come to prefer over KDE as their default desktop environment. For more detailed information about KDE, see the K Desktop Environment Web site at www.kde.org.

Favorite desktop environments are like opinions — everybody has one. Even those of us who have used many different window managers and desktops over the years, and are therefore reasonably agnostic, have our own favorites. To keep the many KDE fans happy, a special version of Ubuntu known as Kubuntu is available that is based on the KDE desktop. You can download Kubuntu CD images or request Kubuntu CDs just as you can Ubuntu CDs, from www.kubuntu.com. You can certainly get KDE to work fine on a standard Ubuntu system, but why not let the KDE fans in the Ubuntu community do the work for you? Similarly, the Xubuntu project provides a pre-assembled version of Ubuntu Linux that uses the light.weight XFCE desktop environment by default.

Using the Mouse

Interacting with a graphical user interface of any kind traditionally requires the use of a mouse and keyboard to control the cursor to select and move items, access menus, and enter data within applications. As you'll see throughout this book, the actions associated with the different mouse buttons do different things depending on the portion of the screen or application in which you use them. This is known as being *context sensitive*, and is one of the keys to performing many different types of actions using only three little buttons.

By default, the mouse in GNOME is configured for a right-handed user, with the different mouse buttons assigned to the following actions:

- **Left Button:** Single-clicking selects an icon, menu, menu item, or object within an application. Double-clicking on a desktop icon opens the item associated with that icon. Holding down the left button and dragging the cursor in an application or on the desktop selects multiple icons or objects within that application. Holding down the left button and dragging a selected object moves that object. These operations can be (and often are) combined. For example, in a word processor, you frequently left-click once to position the cursor, hold down the left button and drag the cursor to select a block of text, and then left-click, hold down the mouse button, and drag the selected text to a new location in your text.

- **Middle Button:** Single-clicking pastes text or objects that have been cut or copied, or moves a selected window behind other windows that are currently displayed on the screen. Clicking on a desktop icon and dragging it to a new location displays the Move menu, which enables you to move icons to new locations without actually relocating the icon until you confirm your intentions.

- **Right Button:** Displays any context-sensitive menu that is available at the current cursor position.

You can configure how reactive the mouse is, what your mouse cursor looks like, and what the various mouse buttons do using the Mouse Preferences application, which is explained later in this chapter in the section entitled "Customizing Mouse Behavior." For example, if you are not right-handed and haven't been beaten into submission so that you use the mouse with your right hand, you can configure the mouse for left-handed use (which reverses the meaning of the various buttons) using this application.

> **NOTE** If you have trouble seeing the screen or using a mouse or keyboard, don't worry — the GNOME and Ubuntu folks are sensitive to your needs. See the section entitled "Assistive Technologies for Using GNOME," later in this chapter, for more information.

GNOME Desktop Overview

Figure 5.1 shows the default GNOME desktop on an Ubuntu Linux system the first time you log in. This figure also displays a single application window as an example — you won't see that unless you explicitly select the Applications ➪ Accessories ➪ Terminal menu command, but I wanted to be able to explain the window controls that are available in any GNOME application window. The Ubuntu folks have gone through a lot of effort to create an attractive, eye-pleasing background, set of fonts, window decorations, and control buttons for any applications that you start on your Ubuntu system. These window decorations and controls are known as a *theme*, which you can easily customize yourself, as explained later in this chapter.

FIGURE 5.1

The default GNOME desktop in Ubuntu Linux

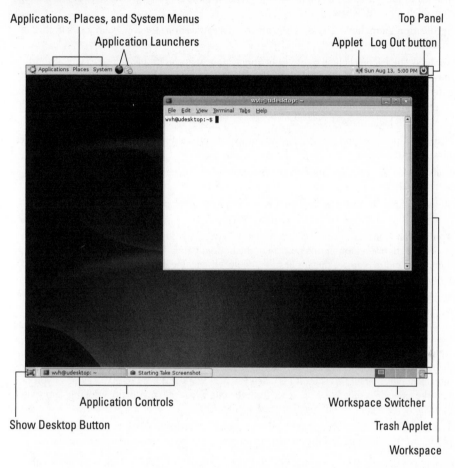

Figure 5.1 identifies the various portions of the default GNOME desktop. The following describes them in more detail:

- **Top Panel:** A panel is a special portion of your desktop, controlled by the gnome-panel application, which provides access to various ways of interacting with the desktop and launching different types of applications. GNOME can display panels along any edge of the screen, but the default GNOME configuration displays panels at the top and bottom of the screen. By default, the top panel contains the following items:
    - **Applications, Places, and System Menus:** A menu consists of a list of shortcuts to specific commands, tasks, or applications. These three menus provide easy, graphical access to applications, portions of your computer system or network locations, and system-related tasks,

111

respectively. Each of these menus is described in more detail in the next section, "Menus in GNOME." To display any of these panel menus, you simply left-click on the name of the menu, and the associated menu drops down and displays on your screen. To close the menu, simply left-click elsewhere on the screen.

- **Application Launchers:** These icons start specific applications for you when you left-click on them.

- **Applets:** These icons launch lightweight applications that run in the context of a panel and provide various capabilities. Adding and configuring applets is discussed later in this chapter in the section entitled "Customizing Panels."

- **Log Out Button:** This button quickly terminates your current login session and re-displays the GNOME login manager.

- **Workspace:** This is the portion of the screen in which applications execute and display associated windows and dialogs.

- **Bottom Panel:** This panel is displayed at the bottom of the screen and contains the following items by default:

  - **Show Desktop Button:** This button minimizes all windows and dialogs that are currently displayed on the screen, revealing the current desktop.

  - **Application Controls:** Each application that is active on your current workspace displays an associated control region in this portion of the bottom panel. Right-clicking on this control minimizes and maximizes the application, while left-clicking on this control displays a context-sensitive menu for moving and controlling that application's window(s).

  - **Workspace Switcher:** This is a special applet that enables you to manage multiple workspaces and provides a miniature display of each active workspace. Workspaces are essentially separate virtual screens that are provided by the GNOME desktop. You can run applications on different workspaces, move applications between workspaces, and so on. Multiple workspaces provide a convenient way of running different types of applications on different virtual screens without them being visible until you actually switch to the workspace where they are displayed. A common example of when this is useful is when you're at work and want to play a game — you can start the game on a different workspace from the one where you're actually working, and switch to it whenever no one is looking over your shoulder.

  - **Trash Applet:** This is a special applet that provides access to the Trash Can, which is a special portion of the GNOME desktop to which you can drag files to subsequently delete them.

As you'll see throughout the rest of this chapter, GNOME is extremely configurable — the chances are that no two users' GNOME desktops will look the same, which is completely fine. How you configure and use your computer system is up to you, and should reflect your interests and the types of things that you want to do. The job of desktops such as GNOME is to make it as easy and as comfortable as possible to accomplish whatever task you are trying to do.

GNOME Application Windows

The GNOME application window shown in Figure 5.1 provides a number of window controls that enable you to move the window around on the screen, control its size, and so on. The window manager that you are using determines the location of these controls, the number of controls displayed, and the capabilities provided by these controls. These window controls are shown in the top part of the frame around the application window in most window managers, typically known as the title bar.

The control at the far left of the title bar displays a menu of window control commands. The contents of this menu depend on the window manager that you are using. The window control menu displayed by the default window manager used by GNOME, Metacity, is shown in Figure 5.2.

The Metacity window manager's window control menu

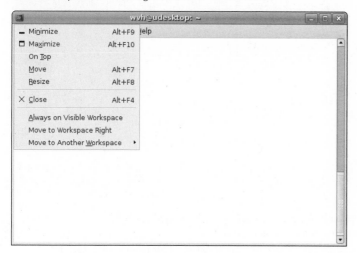

The three window controls at the right of the title bar in Figure 5.2 do the following, from left to right:

- Minimize the current window.
- Switch between a full-screen or a user-specified window size.
- Close the current window, terminating any processes that it is running.

All of these window controls are fairly standard, and are found in the window decoration and title bar layouts used by most modern window managers.

Menus in GNOME

As discussed earlier in this chapter, GNOME provides two different types of menus: menus located in a panel, which provide easy access to different applications, locations, and capabilities on your system, and context-sensitive menus that provide access to different capabilities depending on where you've activated them. This section provides a more detailed discussion of these different types of menus, how to display them, the types of actions that they provide access to, and how to customize them.

Panel Menus

Menus are displayed in the panels when you left-click on the menu name in the panel. Menus either contain entries for specific tasks or locations on your system, or contain other menus. Menus located on other menus are known as *submenus*. As an example, Figure 5.3 shows the default contents of the Application menu's Internet submenu, which I'll discuss later in this section.

FIGURE 5.3

Menus and submenus in GNOME

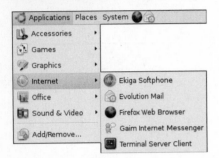

The next few sections describe the standard panel menus and their contents in more detail.

The Application Menu

The Application menu makes it easy to launch different types of GNOME applications, grouping them into submenus that display when you move the cursor over each menu entry. The Application menu provides the following groups:

- **Accessories:** Contains a general category for small, commonly-used applications such as a calculator, dictionary, text editor, and command-line terminal.

- **Games:** Contains exactly what you'd expect. Ubuntu is designed for people, so it naturally includes several games as part of its default installation. For more information about games on Ubuntu Linux, see Chapter 14, "Would You Like To Play a Game?"

- **Graphics:** Provides access to several applications for creating graphics, capturing and manipulating images off the screen or from a scanner, and a small, lightweight image viewer for previewing existing graphics files. See Chapter 12, "Working with Graphics," for more information about graphics software on Ubuntu Linux systems.

- **Internet:** Contains entries for working with the Internet, such as a Voice-Over-IP telephone system, the Evolution e-mail client (discussed in Chapter 8, "Reading and Sending Mail with Evolution"), the Firefox Web browser (discussed in Chapter 9, "Surfing the Web with Firefox"), instant messaging and IRC clients, and so on.

- **Office:** Lists the standard business applications available on your system. By default this menu includes an entry only for the Evolution e-mail client, but you can easily add entries for your favorite word processors (see Chapter 10, "Creating and Publishing Documents"), spreadsheet and presentation software (see Chapter 11, "Other Office Software: Spreadsheets and Presentations"), and any other Linux software that you use as part of your daily activities.

- **Sound and Video:** Provides easy access to audio and video applications, including applications for recording sounds, converting your (officially purchased) audio CDs to online format, playing online audio and video, and sophisticated applications for creating different types of CD, VCD, and DVDs. See Chapter 13, "Working with Multimedia," for more information about working with different types of multimedia files and mediums on Ubuntu Linux systems.

In addition, the Applications menu provides an Add/Remove Applications entry that makes it easy to add applications to the menu. As discussed later in this section, the Add/Remove Applications is seamlessly integrated with Ubuntu's package update mechanism — if you add an application that is available from the Ubuntu repositories but is not already installed on your system, the application will be seamlessly downloaded and installed as part of the menu update. Pretty cool!

The Places Menu

The Places menu provides quick access to files, directories, and storage-related activities. Selecting a location or storage device on the Places menu opens the Nautilus file manager, displaying the contents of the selected location. The Places menu also provides convenient access to storage-related actions, such as writing to a CD or DVD, connecting to a file server, and searching for or revisiting specific files and directories. For more information about the Nautilus file manager, see the section later in this chapter entitled "Introducing the Nautilus File Manager."

 The contents of the Places menu on your system will change as you add and remove external storage devices to your system, visit remote file servers, and so on.

Aside from shortcuts to specific locations on your system, the Places menu provides two submenus: Bookmarks, which lists any bookmarks to specific directories that you've created in the Nautilus file manager, and Recent Documents, which contains a list of the 10 files or desktop objects that you've most recently opened. This menu makes it easy for you to continue working on the same documents each time you log in on your Ubuntu Linux system.

The System Menu

The System menu provides access to commands for interacting with GNOME and your Ubuntu system, such as setting personal preferences for how the GNOME desktop looks and behaves, performing system administration tasks such as configuring hardware, updating your system, and configuring network services, getting help, and logging out of or shutting down your Ubuntu system.

The System menu contains the following items:

- **Preferences:** Provides access to a large number of applications that enable you to configure how you interact with GNOME, your Ubuntu system, and any networks that you have access to (such as the Internet or a home network). If you don't like the way that something works on your Ubuntu system, check the items on the Preferences menu for something that seems appropriate, start any applications that appear to be relevant, and explore a bit. The section entitled "Customizing Your Desktop," later in this chapter, explains how to perform many of the most common GNOME and Ubuntu configuration tasks using commands from this menu.

- **Administration:** Provides access to several applications that enable you to configure the software installed on your Ubuntu system, the devices attached to your Ubuntu system, the services that your system runs, and core system information such as the time, the date, the list of users who are authorized to access your system, and so on.

- **Help:** Provides different types of help for using your system. This menu provides access to the online documentation installed on your Ubuntu system, provides a shortcut to the Ubuntu documentation team's Web site on the Internet, and even provides a shortcut to the Ubuntu Marketplace (discussed in Chapter 1), where you can identify firms that may be able to help you with any tough problems or configuration issues that I may have missed in this book.

- **About GNOME:** Displays information about the specific version of GNOME that you are running, as well as general information about the many wizards who have contributed to the GNOME project in one way or another. You will probably need to provide GNOME version information if you post problem reports, questions, or if you contact any of the Ubuntu vendors in the Ubuntu Marketplace.

- **About Ubuntu:** Displays online documentation for the Ubuntu Project, which includes information about the specific version of Ubuntu Linux that you are using. As with GNOME version information, you will probably need to provide Ubuntu version information if you post problem reports, questions, or if you contact any of the Ubuntu vendors in the Ubuntu Marketplace.

- **Lock Screen:** Provides a convenient shortcut to an application that prevents unauthorized users from accessing your system from its console when you're not sitting in front of it. This application hides the current contents of the screen and requires that you enter your password in order to use the console.

- **Log Out:** Provides a convenient shortcut to an application that logs you out of the system and can optionally cleanly shut it down and turn it off for you after performing several housekeeping tasks. See Chapter 18, "Software Development on Ubuntu," for more information about how your system boots and what it does when it shuts down.

Context-Sensitive Menus

The menus discussed earlier in this chapter always display when you left-click on a specific menu heading or submenu, regardless of what else is happening on your Ubuntu Linux system. Context-sensitive menus display when you right-click on something on your Ubuntu Linux screen, but have different contents depending on what you've clicked on. Because their contents differ based on the context in which you've right-clicked, these right-click menus are referred to as context-sensitive menus. Figure 5.4 shows the context-sensitive menu that you see when you right-click on any portion of the background for your Ubuntu desktop.

FIGURE 5.4

The GNOME desktop's context-sensitive menu

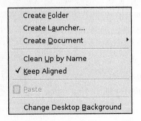

To show how application-specific these different context-sensitive menus can be, Figure 5.5 shows the context-sensitive menu that displays when you right-click within the main window for the Firefox web browser.

FIGURE 5.5

A context-sensitive menu in the Firefox Web browser

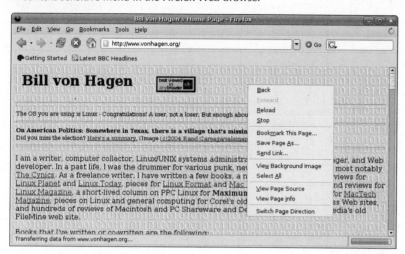

The contents of context-sensitive menus are application-specific, which means that you can't directly customize them. However, these menus can be customized by installing additional applications, applets, or (in the case of extensible applications such as Firefox or Nautilus), by installing extensions or plug-ins that add new capabilities and therefore provide associated menu items.

Customizing Menus

Ubuntu Linux provides you with two ways to customize the contents of the basic GNOME menus. The Add/Remove item at the bottom of the Applications menu makes it easy for you to add new applications to any of the preexisting sections defined on the Applications menu, and will even install those applications for you if they're not already present on your system. The Accessories menu's Alacarte Menu Editor makes it easy for you to add your own group (submenu), shortcut, or application entries to any of the standard GNOME menus, but won't install anything for you. The next two sections explain how to use these applications.

Adding Applications to the Applications Menu

Selecting the Add/Remove item at the bottom of the Applications menu displays the dialog for the gnome-app-install application, shown in Figure 5.6.

FIGURE 5.6

Adding predefined applications to your Ubuntu system

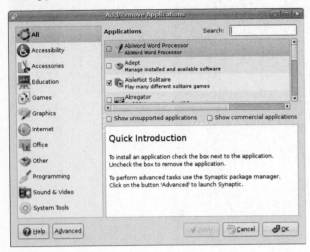

The portions of the Add/Remove Applications window are the following:

- **Software Category List:** Lists all of the predefined types of software that the Add/Remove application knows about.

- **Applications Pane:** Lists all of the applications that are available in the currently selected category.

- **Search Field:** Enables you to search for a specific application by name if you aren't sure which category it falls under.

- **Extra Applications Checkbox:** Checking this box includes applications in the Applications Window that are not officially supported by Canonical, Ltd, but are available in the user-supported *Universe* portion of the Ubuntu repositories. (For more information about Ubuntu repositories and how software is classified there, see Chapter 11, "Other Office Software: Spreadsheets and Presentations.")

- **Show Proprietary Applications Checkbox:** Similar to the Extra Applications Checkbox, checking this box includes applications in the Applications Window that have some restriction on copying, use, redistribution, or enhancement, and therefore do not fall under the Ubuntu/Debian definition of open source software. This software is available in the *Multiverse* portion of the Ubuntu repositories. (For more information about Ubuntu repositories and how software is classified there, see Chapter 11.)

- **Application Description Pane:** Displays a description of any currently selected software package.

- **Buttons:** Perform the following various actions:

  - **Help:** Displays detailed online help for the `gnome-app-install` application.

  - **Advanced:** Starts the full-blown Synaptic Package Manager application, which provides capabilities beyond those provided by the `gnome-app-install` application.

- **Apply:** Updates the Applications menu based on your selections, installing any necessary software, and returning to the `gnome-app-install` application when done.

- **Cancel:** Exits the application without making any pending changes to the Applications menu. Any changes that you've already applied using the Apply button are already done, and are not undone.

- **OK:** Makes any pending changes to the Applications menu, and then exits the application.

As an example, assume that you wanted to add the Gnumeric spreadsheet application to your Office menu. You would do the following:

1. Select the Add/Remove item from the Applications menu.

2. Select the Office category in the Software category List pane and browse the Applications pane for the `Gnumeric` application or enter **gnumeric** in the Search field and press Return.

3. Select the checkbox to the left of the Application pane entry for the Gnumeric spreadsheet.

4. Click Apply to install Gnumeric and return to the Add/Remove Applications software to install other applications later, or click OK to install only this application and exit afterward.

5. Enter your password in the Administrative privileges dialog and press Return.

The `gnome-app-install` application automatically retrieves and installs the requested software and any associated packages required to satisfy its requirements. If the software package you've requested conflicts with any existing software, a dialog displays that identifies the conflict and offers you the option to remove the conflicting package.

As mentioned previously, the Add/Remove Packages application provides a convenient and easy-to-use mechanism for installing most standard software packages. You should use the Synaptic Package Manager for more sophisticated software installation requests, but it's hard to beat the convenience of this menu item when installing commonly used and popular software packages.

Adding Items to Any Menu

The `gnome-app-install` application discussed earlier is extremely convenient if you want to add applications to the Applications menu, but isn't much use if you want to add your own menus or create custom menu entries for specific applications. To do this, you'll need to use the Applications ➪ Accessories submenu's Alacarte Menu Editor, which makes it easy for you to add almost anything (including custom submenus) to any existing GNOME menu.

As an example, suppose you wanted to create your own submenu called Favorites and begin adding entries for your favorite applications to it. To do this (using emacs as an example), do the following:

1. Select the Applications ➪ Accessories ➪ Alacarte Menu Editor to start the menu editor. This menu editor dialog consists of two primary panes—a menu catalog pane at the left and a menu contents pane at the top right that show the contents of any currently selected menu. If the Applications menu is expanded when this dialog opens and/or no menu is currently selected, select the Application entry in the menu catalog pane at the left, and click the arrow to the left of its name to collapse the listing of entries on that menu. The menu editor should look like the dialog shown in Figure 5.7.

TIP   You'll notice that the menu catalog pane lists many menus that are not currently displayed on your system. This is because they are not marked as Visible in the menu contents pane at right, as shown in Figure 5.7.

FIGURE 5.7

The Alacarte Menu Editor on your Ubuntu system

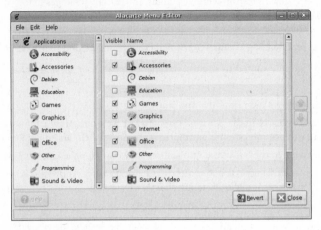

2. Select the File ⇨ New Menu command. A dialog like the one shown in Figure 5.8 displays.

FIGURE 5.8

Adding a new menu to your Ubuntu system

3. Enter the name of the new menu that you want to create (I'm using Favorites in this example), add an optional comment that will be used as the tool tip for this menu, and click OK. The new menu will be added to the Applications menu, and the Applications menu entry in the menu catalog pane will expand to show the current contents of that menu (which should be identical to the list in the menu dialog at the top right). Select the name of your new menu in the menu catalog pane. The contents of the new menu (i.e., nothing) displays in the menu contents pane at the top right, as shown in Figure 5.9.

FIGURE 5.9

The new menu to your Ubuntu system

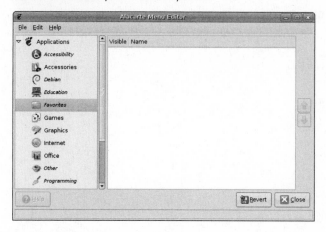

4. Select the File ➪ New Entry command. A dialog like the one shown in Figure 5.10 displays.

FIGURE 5.10

Adding a new menu entry to your Ubuntu system

5. Enter the information about your new entry (in this case the emacs text editor) and click OK. The dialog closes and the new entry on your Favorites menu displays, as shown in Figure 5.11.

TIP   If you don't know exactly where the application that you want to add is located, you can click Browse to display a browse dialog that lets you navigate to and select the application for which you want to create a new menu entry.

FIGURE 5.11

Your new menu entry in the menu editor

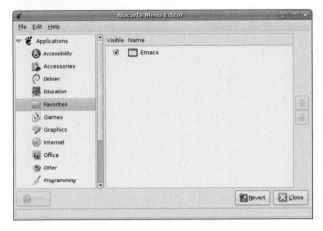

6. Select the Applications menu in the menu catalog pane at the left, and make sure that the check-box in the Visible column for your new menu is selected in the menu listing pane at the top right, as shown in Figure 5.12. This entry is required so that the menu is listed in the Applications menu once you exit from the menu editor.

FIGURE 5.12

Making sure that the new menu is visible

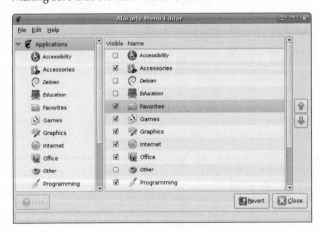

7. Click Close to exit from the Alacarte Menu Editor and add your changes to the Applications menu. The Applications menu is updated, and your new menu and entry are now available, as shown in Figure 5.13.

FIGURE 5.13

Your new entries on the GNOME Applications menu

If you decide not to save your changes, you can click the Revert button to undo your current changes, and then click Close.

The flexibility provided in the dialog shown in Figure 5.10 makes it easy for you to create menu entries for applications that you have manually compiled and installed yourself, such as in corporate or academic environments, and also to add your own favorite command-line parameters to new or existing menu entries.

TIP   You can also add menus in GNOME using the Nautilus file manager, but I find that using applications designed for editing menus is easier to understand. For information about using Nautilus to create menus and menu items, see the online GNOME Users Guide, available through the System menu's Help menu.

Customizing Your Desktop

As explained earlier in this chapter, GNOME makes it easy to customize its menus and the sections and applications that they contain. Luckily, every part of the GNOME desktop is similarly configurable. This section highlights how to do some of the most common customizations that most people do to make their systems easier to use and generally personalize them. Many other customizations are available, but discussing each one would require its own book. Let's focus on the highlights!

Customizing Mouse Behavior

One of the most common customizations that people want to do is to change how responsive the mouse is, in one way or another. Available customizations include:

- Whether the mouse is configured for left-handed or right-handed users. The latter is the default, but may not suit you if you are left-handed and use the left hand to control the mouse.

- The speed at which the cursor moves and the amount of screen real estate the mouse covers in relation to your moving the mouse

- The period of time that can elapse between two mouse clicks to consider them as a double-click (which opens the target) rather than simply two single clicks (which simply selects something). If you have difficulty double-clicking, you can increase the double-click time period.

All of these customizations are controlled by the System ➪ Preferences menu's Mouse application, which is shown in Figure 5.14.

FIGURE 5.14

The Mouse Preferences dialog

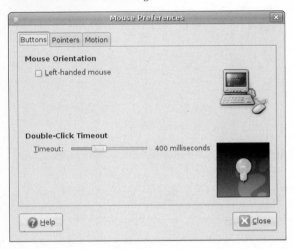

This application provides three tabs that enable you to configure different aspects of the mouse: the behavior of the buttons, things related to the cursor (known as the *mouse pointer* here), and the speed and sensitivity of mouse motion. The Buttons tab is shown in Figure 5.14. To switch between different tabs, simply select the appropriate tab in the Mouse Preferences application.

The configuration items in all of these tabs are pretty straightforward, so I won't explain each of them. However, the tab that does require some explanation is controlling the motion and sensitivity of the mouse. These options are located on the Mouse Preferences application's Motion tab, which is shown in Figure 5.15.

The entries on this tab have the following meanings:

■ **Acceleration:** This option controls how far the cursor moves on the screen in response to your moving the mouse, and is controlled by a slider. Being able to change this ratio guarantees that you don't need a mouse pad the size of your computer monitor — acceleration enables the cursor to cover larger distances as you move the mouse continuously. Slower values mean that cursor movement is closer to the actual distance that you're moving the mouse; faster values mean that the cursor moves proportionately farther distances as you continue to move the mouse — in other words, the cursor starts out moving slowly and accelerates as you continue to move the mouse. To change your settings, click and hold the button on the slider using the left mouse button and drag it to the new value that you want to use.

■ **Sensitivity:** This option determines how sensitive the cursor is to any movement of the mouse. If you have set Acceleration to be very fast, you may find that the cursor jumps when you simply touch the mouse. In this case, you could decrease the sensitivity of the mouse, while still retaining fast acceleration.

- **Drag and Drop:** This option controls the distance that the mouse must cover when you have selected a desktop object in order to consider that to mean a drag-and-drop action. For example, when double-clicking, you may find that you move the mouse slightly between the two clicks. If the drag-and-drop threshold is set very low, GNOME will interpret this as a drag-and-drop or move operation rather than a double-click operation. In this case, you would want to increase the threshold value.

Changes to your mouse preferences take effect immediately, so it's easy for you to experiment with the set of values that gives you the control and behavior that you want on your system.

FIGURE 5.15

Configuring the mouse motion

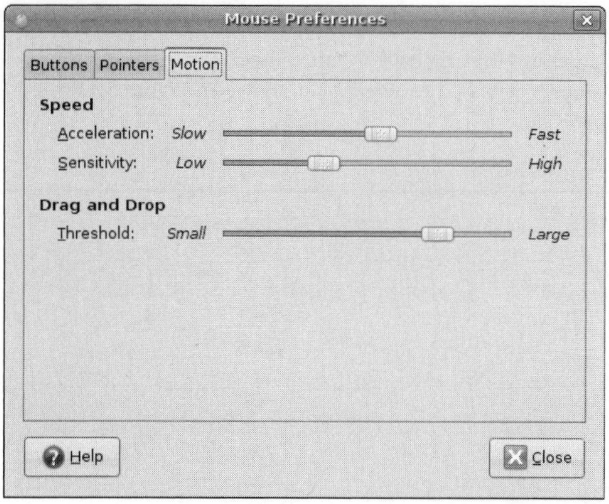

Configuring Display Resolution

When you installed Ubuntu, one of the questions you were asked was to select the display the resolutions that you want to be able to use. It's nice of the Ubuntu installer to ask this question, but display resolution is one of those things that's hard to visualize in advance — it really makes sense only when you can see what different resolutions actually look like. Consequently, even if you are using a 30-inch monitor and the sexiest video card in the universe, you may find that your Ubuntu Linux system insists on displaying everything at a resolution like 1024×768, where each of the icons on your screen is approximately the size of a grapefruit. This is probably not what you had in mind, and is certainly not the best use of your hardware. This section explains how to correct that problem by selecting a higher screen resolution. Internally, this means that your screen displays more pixels, but the visual effect is that things on the screen are both smaller and sharper. In the computer industry, this is known as "*the right thing*™."

Screen resolution in GNOME is controlled by the System ⇨ Preferences menu's Screen Resolution application, which is shown in Figure 5.16.

FIGURE 5.16

The Screen Resolution application

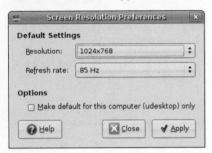

Once this application displays, you can see the list of available screen resolutions by clicking and holding the left mouse button on the current resolution value. A pop-up list displays, as shown in Figure 5.17.

FIGURE 5.17

Selecting other screen resolutions

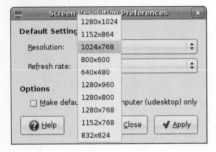

After selecting another screen resolution, click Apply to try out the new resolution. GNOME will change your screen to the new resolution and display the dialog shown in Figure 5.18, asking if you want to keep the new screen resolution or permanently switch to the new resolution.

FIGURE 5.18

Confirming screen resolution changes

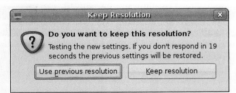

NOTE Because it's possible to select a resolution that may not actually work correctly, your screen will automatically revert to its former resolution in 20 seconds. No need to panic if your screen goes haywire for a little while!

If you're happy with the new resolution, click Keep Resolution. The dialog will close, your screen will remain at the new resolution, and it will be the default screen resolution used whenever you log in to your Ubuntu system.

If the new resolution looks odd or is simply too small for your taste, click Use previous resolution. You can then experiment with other resolutions, clicking Apply to test out any newly-selected resolution until you find one that you're happy with.

Customizing Panels

As discussed earlier in the chapter, panels are regions on your desktop that are displayed by the gnome-panel application and provide access to various ways of interacting with the desktop and launching different types of applications. The gnome-panel application can display panels along any edge of the screen, but the default Ubuntu configuration displays panels at the top and bottom of the screen.

NOTE A single instance of the gnome-panel application controls all of the panels that are displayed on your system. The fact that multiple panels are displayed on your screen does not mean that multiple copies of the gnome-panel application are running.

By default, the GNOME panels displayed at the top and bottom of your screen contain the menus, applets, and buttons listed in the "GNOME Desktop Overview" section earlier in this chapter. Not only can you configure how and where the panels are displayed on your screen and how many panels are displayed, but you can also extensively customize the contents of each. Ubuntu's default installation of GNOME comes with many other applets, buttons, and controls that you can install in the panels on your system.

Right-clicking on any existing panel displays that panel's context-sensitive menu, as shown in Figure 5.19.

FIGURE 5.19

The gnome-panel application's context-sensitive menu

Along with standard entries to display online help and get information about the version of the application, the context-sensitive menu for the gnome-panel application displays the following configuration-related entries:

- **Add to Panel:** Enables you to add a new applet, button, or other supported object to any panel that is currently displayed on your screen. See "Customizing Panel Contents," later in this section, for details on adding objects to an existing panel.

■ **Properties:** Displays a panel properties dialog that enables you to set certain properties for the currently selected panel. See "Customizing Panel Properties," later in this section, for details on the types of things that you can customize for an existing panel.

■ **Delete this Panel:** Deletes the currently selected panel from the screen and removes all information about its current configuration from the system.

■ **New Panel:** Creates a new panel on the next available edge of the screen. You can create an essentially infinite number of panels — each new panel will simply start on the next edge of your screen, adjacent to any existing panel that is already associated with that edge. I find two panels to be the right number, but you may feel differently.

The next two sections explain how to modify the properties of the existing panels on your screen, add other applets, buttons, and controls to those panels, and highlight some of the most fun and useful of these that are provided with Ubuntu Linux.

Customizing Panel Properties

Selecting the Properties entry on any panel's context-sensitive menu displays the dialog shown in Figure 5.20.

FIGURE 5.20

The gnome-panel application's Panel Properties dialog

This dialog contains two tabs: a Background tab, which enables you to control the color and transparency of the current panel or select an existing image to use for its background, and the General tab, shown in Figure 5.20, which enables you to control the location and behavior of that panel. The properties that you can configure on this tab are the following:

■ **Orientation:** Enables you to specify the edge of the screen at which the currently selected panel should display. Selecting another value immediately moves the currently selected panel to the specified edge.

 You can also move an existing panel to another edge of your screen by left-clicking on its background, holding down the left mouse button, and dragging it to the new edge.

■ **Size:** Enables you to specify the height (or width, depending on the panel's orientation) in pixels of the currently selected panel.

- **Expand:** Selecting or deselecting this toggle checkbox determines whether the panel occupies the entire edge of the screen or whether it only takes up that portion of the edge that is required to display the objects that it currently holds.

- **Autohide:** Selecting or deselecting this toggle checkbox determines whether the panel is only displayed when the cursor is moved to the edge of the screen that the currently selected panel is associated with. If this property is selected, the panel is not displayed when the cursor is located over any other portion of the screen.

- **Show hide buttons:** Selecting or deselecting this toggle checkbox determines whether buttons for collapsing or expanding the currently selected panel are displayed at each end of that panel. Selecting this checkbox also activates the Arrows on hide buttons option, which simply determines whether the icons at either end of the panel display arrows to highlight the direction in which the panel will expand or contract if they are selected.

Changes that you make to the properties of any panel take effect immediately. To close the Panel Properties dialog, click Close.

Customizing Panel Contents

Selecting Add to Panel from any panel's context-sensitive menu displays the Add to Panel dialog, as shown in Figure 5.21.

FIGURE 5.21

The Add to Panel dialog

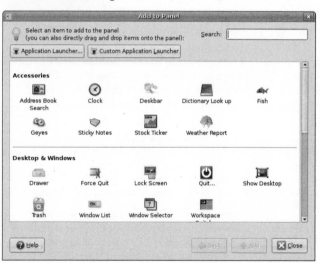

This dialog enables you to add application launchers, buttons, and common applets to any panel that is currently displayed on your screen. All of the currently available buttons and applets are displayed in this scrollable dialog. To add any of these to any panel that is currently visible on the screen, left-click on that applet, hold down the left mouse button, and drag the applet to the location on the panel where you want it to be displayed. Releasing the mouse button positions the selected applet at that location in the panel.

> **TIP** After adding any applet to any panel, you can move that applet by dragging and dropping or by right-clicking on the applet and selecting Move from its context-sensitive menu. If you use the Move option, the applet will follow the current cursor position—once you have moved the applet to its new location, left-click to position it at the new location. Applets can be moved to any other panel that is currently displayed on the screen.

The applets displayed in the Add to Panel dialog are organized into general categories such as Accessories, applets for Desktop & Windows manipulation, applets for viewing System and Hardware information, and generic utilities. Some of my personal favorite applets are the following:

- **Dictionary Look up:** Located in the Accessories section, this applet provides a quick and easy way of looking up specific words from an online dictionary server.

- **Drawer:** Located in the Desktop & Windows section, a drawer is a convenient way of adding multiple applets or buttons to a panel without consuming all available panel real estate. A drawer is essentially just an extension of a panel that can hold other panel objects. Clicking on a drawer causes it to expand, showing the panel objects that it contains, which you can then select just as if they were directly located on a panel. If you're really into applets but don't want to use too many panels, using Drawers can be a big convenience.

- **Sticky Notes:** Located in the Accessories section, this applet enables you to create and manage multiple on-screen sticky notes that are analogous to the Post-Its that festoon everyone's monitors and physical desktops nowadays.

- **System Monitor:** Located in the System & Hardware section, this applet can be configured to display graphical and associated tool tips that provide information about processor, memory, network, swap space, and hard drive usage, as well as general system load information.

- **Volume Control:** Located in the System & Hardware section, this applet provides an easy way of increasing (or occasionally decreasing) your sound card's volume. This applet is installed by default on Ubuntu systems.

- **Weather Report:** Located in the Accessories section, this applet displays information about the temperature and general weather conditions in any specified location. Because many of us don't have windows in our offices (or perhaps offices at all), this can be very handy when you're thinking about going outside. It's somewhat sad how often I have found this applet to be useful. "Oh, it's snowing outside?"

> **TIP** Each panel applet has its own configuration opportunities—for example, the Weather Report applet requires that you identify your location to be able to display accurate information about the local weather, but that information isn't really germane to any other applet. To configure any panel applet, right-click on its panel icon and select the Preferences item from the context-sensitive menu that displays. The configuration dialog for that applet displays, showing any configurable properties of that applet.

Application launchers are panel entries that execute a specific application for you. Ubuntu comes with several predefined application launchers that you can choose to add a shortcut for starting that application from any panel. To add one of these predefined application launchers, click the Application Launcher button in the Add to Panel dialog. The Application Launcher dialog displays, as shown in Figure 5.22.

To add a predefined application launcher, simply select it from this dialog's scrollable list. To return to the main Add to Panel dialog, click Back.

FIGURE 5.22

FIGURE 5.22

Adding a predefined application launcher to a panel

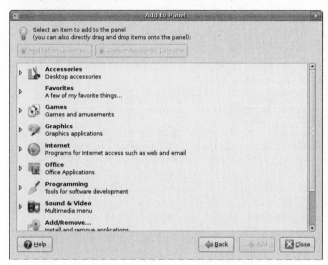

The Add to panel application also enables you to add custom application launchers that you can define yourself. This enables you to create panel entries that will launch your favorite applications with your own favorite command-line options. To define a custom application launcher, click the Custom Application Launcher button in the Add to Panel dialog. The Create Launcher dialog displays, as shown in Figure 5.23.

FIGURE 5.23

Defining a custom application launcher

The Create Launcher dialog enables you to set various characteristics of the launcher that you are defining, the application that it starts, and how that launcher displays in the panel. After providing that information, click OK to create the new launcher. By default, the new launcher is displayed in the panel from which you started the Add to Panel application.

Once you're finished customizing and fine-tuning the applets, buttons, and launchers that are displayed in your system's panels, click Close to close the Add to panel dialog and get back to work.

 To remove an applet from any of your panels, right-click on its name and select the Remove from Panel command from its context-sensitive menu.

Configuring the Screensaver

There was a time when computer monitors were quite sensitive to displaying the same characters for long periods of time. Monitors that showed the same applications in the same locations for long periods of time would end up damaging the phosphors on the inside of the monitor, which therefore displayed a ghostly outline of that application on the screen. (This was known as *screen burn* or *video burn*.) To eliminate, or at least, reduce this problem, many companies developed applications known as screensavers, which would start automatically after a computer system had been unused for a specified period of time, and would display random patterns or images on the screen, preventing the burn-in of default images.

Today's monitors are much more sophisticated than the monitors of old, and are therefore less susceptible to image burn-in. Today, screensavers are typically used because they look nice or for security purposes, so that unauthorized users can't see what is displayed on the screen of your computer while you're at lunch.

By default, your Ubuntu system comes configured to activate a random screensaver after 10 minutes of inactivity on your Ubuntu system. You can select a specific screensaver for your system to use (there are hundreds), to configure the period of time after which a screensaver is activated, or to disable the screensaver on your system entirely. All of these are done through the System ⇨ Preferences menu's Screensaver Preferences application, which is shown in Figure 5.24.

FIGURE 5.24

Configuring your system's screensaver

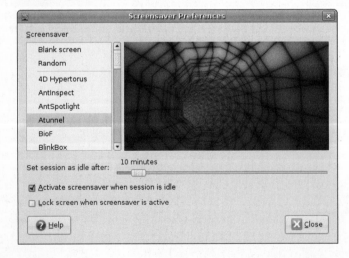

Once this dialog displays, you can explore all of the other screensavers that are available on your system by selecting them from the scrollable Screensaver pane. A preview of the appearance and behavior of the currently selected screensaver displays in the preview pane to the right of the screensaver list.

Once you've select the screensaver that you want to use, the Screensaver Preferences dialog also enables you to set some general characteristics of your system's use of that screensaver. To change the period of time after which the screensaver is activated, drag this dialog's slider to reflect the new time period. To deactivate the screensaver entirely, uncheck the Activate screensaver when session is idle checkbox.

Ordinarily, moving the mouse or pressing any key on your keyboard causes the screensaver to stop displaying its default image and reset its inactivity timer. To combine the screensaver with a dialog that requires that you provide your password to stop displaying the screensaver and regain access to your keyboard and screen, click the Lock screen when screensaver is active checkbox. You will need to supply your password to redisplay your normal desktop.

Once you are finished configuring the screensaver, click Close to terminate the Screensaver preferences application.

Changing Desktop Backgrounds

GNOME also makes it easy for you to change the background displayed on your system's desktops. The background is a solid color or image that is displayed on your screen and over which all other application windows are displayed. To do this, select the System ⇨ Preferences menu's Default Background menu entry. The Desktop Background Preferences application displays, as shown in Figure 5.25.

FIGURE 5.25

Configuring your desktop background

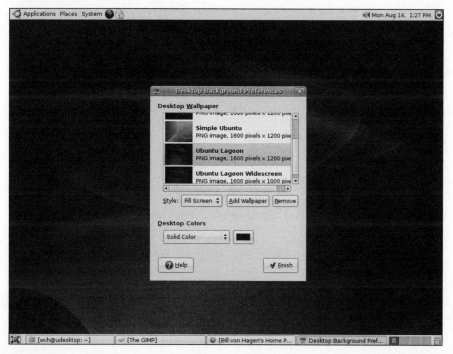

Changing the background of your desktop is one of the more common configuration tasks that anyone wants to do when personalizing their system. To customize your desktop, you can select a solid background color, select an existing graphics image from the default list given in the Desktop Wallpaper dialog, or click Add Wallpaper to navigate to the location of a specific graphics file that you may want to use as your background. (I tend to use vacation photos, myself.)

Once you've selected an image, the Style value determines how that image is used as the background. Your options are the following:

- **Centered:** The selected wallpaper is displayed in the center of your screen at its original resolution.
- **Fill Screen:** The selected wallpaper is increased in size as needed to completely fill the background of your screen. This does not preserve the aspect ratio of your original image.
- **Scaled:** The selected wallpaper is stretched to fit your screen without changing its aspect ratio.
- **Tiled:** The selected wallpaper, at its original size, is repeated multiple times across your screen as many times as needed to fill the background.
- **Zoom:** The selected wallpaper is increased in size so that it completely fills your screen. If the image is not exactly the right size, some portions of the image may be clipped so that the image completely fills the screen.

As you select different wallpaper and style options, the background changes instantly to reflect the current selections. Once you're happy with your background, click Finish to close the Desktop Background Preferences application.

Switching Themes

A theme is the term for the combination of window and dialog controls, a color scheme, and a set of icons that gives your desktop and the windows that it displays a specific look and feel. Many themes also come with a specific desktop background to complete the visual experience that their author was trying to achieve. Experimenting with different themes can be a lot of fun, and can also be extremely useful to make it easier to read window titles and generally adjust contrast on your screen.

To change or configure the theme used on your Ubuntu system, select the System ➪ Preferences menu's Theme menu item. The Theme Preferences dialog shown in Figure 5.26 displays.

Ubuntu's GNOME desktop comes with many attractive themes. By default, Ubuntu uses a theme called Human that is designed to be attractive, easy on the eyes, and easy to use. To switch to another of the themes provided with Ubuntu Linux, select it from the scrollable theme pane at left. Even though the theme pane includes preview images of each available theme, the new theme takes effect immediately so that you can see what it will actually look like. As an example, Figure 5.27 shows the Theme Preferences dialog after selecting the Mist theme. You'll have to trust me that the window decoration background is now blue, but you should be able to see the differences in font placement, highlighting, window controls, dialog button shapes, and so on.

Once you've selected the theme that you like best at the moment, click Close to close the Theme Preferences dialog. Your new theme will be used each time you log in, until you change it.

FIGURE 5.26

Specifying theme preferences

FIGURE 5.27

Selecting a different window theme

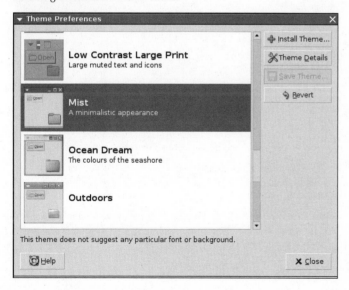

> **TIP** Though Ubuntu provides a large collection of nice themes, artistically inclined users are always creating new ones. Many excellent (or just plain interesting) themes are available at a variety of Web sites. My favorites are the GNOME Art site (`http://art.gnome.org/`), **GNOME-Look.org** (`www .gnome-look.org/`), and Freshmeat's GNOME themes section (`http://themes.freshmeat.net/ browse/58/`). A quick Web search for "GNOME themes" with your favorite search engine will turn up many more sites. To add any of these themes, simply select the Install Theme button after downloading the theme and navigate to its location on your system. The new theme is added to the scrollable themes list, and can selected like any other theme. Somewhere out there is the perfect theme for you!

Assistive Technologies for Using GNOME

If you have trouble seeing the screen or using a keyboard or mouse, the GNOME and Ubuntu folks are sensitive to your needs and offer various Assistive technologies that do things such as providing on-screen keyboard support, and supporting screen magnification and audio output from portions of the screen. These features are available through the `gok` (GNOME On-Screen Keyboard), `gnopernicus`, and `gnome-mag` applications, which are installed by default on all Ubuntu Desktop installations.

You can activate the capabilities of these packages by selecting the System ➪ Preferences ➪ Assistive Technology Support menu item, which displays the dialog shown in Figure 5.28, enabling selected items, and logging out and logging back in to activate them.

FIGURE 5.28

Enabling Assistive Technologies in GNOME

These applications aren't perfect, but are actively under development to guarantee that anyone can take advantage of the power of Ubuntu Linux. Figure 5.29 shows a sample Ubuntu Linux screen with these technologies active on a sample GNOME desktop.

> **TIP** Not all of the libraries used by GNOME's assistive technology support are loaded by packages such as `gok` and `gnome-mag` — some are already presumed to be on your system. If you see a message like the following when running a GNOME or other GTk application:

```
Failed to load module "atk-bridge": libatk-bridge.so \
     cannot open shared object file: No such file or directory
```

use the Synaptic package manager (or other software update application) to ensure that the `at-spi` package is installed.

FIGURE 5.29

The on-screen keyboard and screen magnifier in GNOME

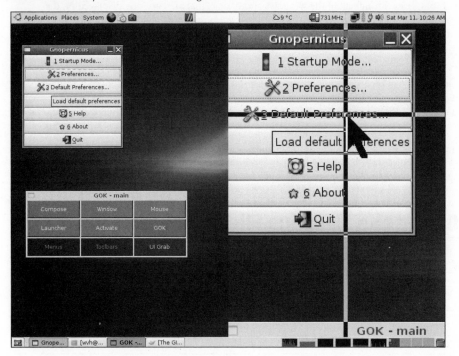

GNOME Keyboard Shortcuts

If you have problems controlling a mouse or simply prefer to keep your hands on the keyboard at all times, GNOME provides several special key sequences that enable you to perform most traditionally mouse-driven desktop activities using only the keyboard. These are commonly referred to as *keyboard shortcuts*. To activate these, press and hold down the first key in the sequence while pressing the second. The most popular keyboard shortcuts for the GNOME desktop are the following:

- **Alt+F1:** Displays the Applications menu.
- **Alt+F2:** Displays the Run Applications dialog, in which you can enter the name of a specific application that you want to execute.
- **Alt+F4:** Closes the window that is currently selected.
- **Alt+F5:** Reduces the size of the current window if it is maximized.
- **Alt+F7:** Enables you to move the window that is currently selected. After pressing this key combination, use the arrow keys to move the window to a new location and press any other key on the keyboard to complete the move operation.
- **Alt+F8:** Enables you to resize the window that is currently selected. After pressing this key combination, use the arrow keys to increase or decrease the size of the window and press any other key on the keyboard to complete the resize operation.

- **Alt+F9:** Minimizes the window that is currently selected.
- **Alt+F10:** Maximizes the window that is currently selected.
- **Alt+Tab:** Cycles through all of the windows and dialogs that are currently displayed on the screen, highlighting each in turn (known as *giving the focus* to that window) until you find the one that you're interested in.
- **Alt+Spacebar:** Displays any context-sensitive menu associated with the window that is currently selected.
- **Control+l:** When browsing for a file in any File ➪ Open dialog, displays a pop-up box in which you can type the full pathname of the directory containing the files that you are looking for, saving you many clicks if you need to drill down to a deeply-nested directory. This dialog does automatic directory-name completion as you type, and is one of my personal favorite GNOME features.

GNOME supports several other keyboard shortcuts, most of which perform standard actions within various applications. For a complete list of available keyboard shortcuts, see the GNOME Accessibility Guide, available by selecting the System ➪ Help ➪ System Documentation menu item.

Introducing the Nautilus File Manager

The Nautilus file manager, known to its friends simply as Nautilus, is a convenient application for computer users who are used to graphically displaying, examining, and moving around in files and directories on their computer systems. Nautilus is GNOME's equivalent of the Microsoft Windows Explorer or the Mac OS X Finder, and makes it similarly easy to work with and modify your files and directories. Figure 5.30 shows Nautilus exploring the contents of my home directory on one of my systems.

FIGURE 5.30

Exploring my home directory in Nautilus

As mentioned earlier in this chapter, the Places menu in the top panel on the default GNOME desktop shipped with Ubuntu systems is actually a collection of shortcuts to using Nautilus to explore different portions of your system or network. For example, I displayed my home directory in Nautilus by selecting Home Folder from the top panel's Places menu.

Basic Operations in Nautilus

Like other graphical file managers, Nautilus makes it easy to manage and manipulate files and directories. Most of the commands related to working with files and directories are located on its Edit menu, and are also accessible from the context-sensitive menu displayed when you right-click on any object in the Nautilus display pane. Figure 5.31 shows the context-sensitive menu displayed when right-clicking on one of the files with the .txt extension in my home directory.

FIGURE 5.31

A context-sensitive menu in Nautilus

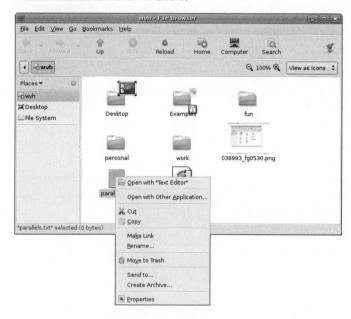

As you can see, this menu provides the standard actions that you'd expect to find in any file manager, enabling you to do the following:

- Open the file with the default application associated with that type of file.
- Open the file with other applications associated with that type of file.
- Cut or copy the file, enabling you to paste the file (or a copy of it) into another location to move or copy the file.
- Create a symbolic link to or rename the selected file.

- Delete the file by moving it to the Trash Can, which is a temporary repository for files before they are actually purged from your system.

- Send the file to a specified device or create an archive file in compressed tar format containing that file. (See Chapter 22, "Backing Up and Restoring Files," for information about Linux archive file formats.)

- Examine or modify the properties of the file, including its name, permissions, and how it is displayed in Nautilus.

Examples of Using Nautilus

The previous section described the most common operations that you can do in Nautilus; this section provides a few examples of such operations to get you started working with Nautilus if you haven't used graphical file managers before.

Exploring the Filesystem

The GNOME desktop's Places menu contains several pre-configured shortcuts to various locations on your system and on your local network. If you're lucky, the directory or network location that you want to explore will be listed there. If not, you can navigate to any location on your system in Nautilus by doing the following:

1. Open Nautilus in a predefined location by selecting it from the Places menu.

2. Drill down into subdirectories of the selected location and double-click on the icon for that folder.

3. Move up a level to the directory that contains the directory you are currently viewing and click the Up button in the Nautilus toolbar.

Moving around between different files and directories in Nautilus is easy once you get the hang of it, and will soon become second nature to you.

> **TIP** You can start Nautilus and instantly display the contents of any accessible directory by starting Nautilus from the command-line and specifying the name of that directory as an argument. For more information about using the command-line, see Chapter 6, "Using Command-Line Tools."

Copying Files or Directories

To copy a file or directory in Nautilus, do the following:

1. Navigate to the directory that contains the file or directory that you want to copy.

2. Left-click on the icon for that file or directory to select it.

3. Select the Copy command from the Edit menu or right-click on the selected icon and select Copy from the context-sensitive menu.

4. Navigate to the directory where you want to place the copy of the selected file or directory.

5. Select the Paste command from the Edit menu or right-click on the background of the current directory in Nautilus and select Paste from the context-sensitive menu.

At this point, the icons for the files and directories that you had selected for copying display in the current Nautilus window, and the copy operation is complete. Copying directories that contain many files may take a bit of time.

Don't worry about accidentally overwriting files with the same name — if the directory to which you are copying files already contains files or directories with the same names as the files or directories that you are copying, you will see a dialog like the one shown in Figure 5.32, which asks if you want to replace the existing file or directory with the same name.

FIGURE 5.32

A directory showing with duplicate file names after a copy

Selecting Multiple Files and Directories

As you work with Nautilus, you may find that you want to move or copy multiple files and directories at the same time. This is easy enough to do as long as you select all of the icons associated with those files and directories before performing a copy or cut operation. You can select multiple items in Nautilus in a variety of different ways as follows:

- To select multiple files and directory icons, hold down the Control key on your keyboard while selecting each of the icons for those files and directories.

- To select all of the files and directories that are alphabetically between two files and directories, select one icon, hold down either Shift key, and select the icon at the end of the range of files that you want to select.

- To graphically select multiple files that are next to each other in the Nautilus display windows, left-click the Nautilus background beside any of those files, hold down the left mouse button, and drag the mouse cursor to display a rectangle that contains all of the files that you want to select.

You can also combine these selection operations. For example, you could select a range of files graphically by using the Shift key and then holding down the Control key to add other files or directory icons to the current selection.

Moving Files or Directories

To move a file or Directory in Nautilus, do the following:

1. Navigate to the directory that contains the file or directory that you want to move.
2. Left-click on the icon for that file or directory to select it.
3. Select the Cut command from the Edit menu or right-click on the selected icon and select Cut from the context-sensitive menu. The icons for the selected file or directory are removed from the current Nautilus window.
4. Navigate to the directory where you want to place the selected file or directory.
5. Select the Paste command from the Edit menu or right-click on the background of the current directory in Nautilus and select Paste from the context-sensitive menu.

At this point, the icons for the files and directories that you removed from the first directory will display in the current Nautilus window, and the copy operation is complete. Copying directories that contain many files may take a bit of time.

Renaming a File or Directory

To rename a file or directory in Nautilus, do the following:

1. Navigate to the directory that contains the file or directory that you want to rename.

2. Right-click on the selected icon and select Rename from the context-sensitive menu. The name of the file will be selected in Nautilus.

3. Enter the new name of the selected file or directory and press Return. The updated name displays in Nautilus.

Creating a Directory

Creating a file is usually done by starting the application associated with that type of file and saving your work with the name of the file that you want to create. Creating directories can either be done from the command-line, as explained in Chapter 6, or quickly and easily within Nautilus.

To create a directory in Nautilus, do the following:

1. Navigate to the directory where you want to create the new directory.

2. Right-click on the background of that directory as shown in Nautilus and select Create Folder from the context-sensitive menu, or select File ➪ New Folder from the Nautilus menus. A new folder with the default name "untitled folder" displays in the Nautilus window, as shown in Figure 5.33.

FIGURE 5.33

Creating a new folder in Nautilus

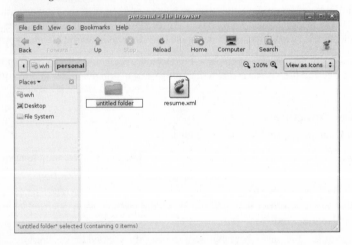

3. Note that the name of the new folder is highlighted when that folder is created. To give the new folder a specific name, you can simply type that name or rename the directory as explained in the previous section.

Getting More Information About Nautilus

Nautilus includes extensive and excellent documentation that is available by selecting Contents from its Help menu. Because it is so similar to the types of file managers used on other systems, you should find Nautilus extremely easy to use and master.

Using a Window Manager

The first section of this chapter, "What's a Desktop? Graphical Environments for Linux," discussed the differences between window managers and desktops, and hinted at the fact that more X Window system window managers are available than you could shake a stick at. Popular window managers include After Step, Black Box, enlightenment, Fluxbox, Fvwm, ICEwm, kwm, Metacity, twm, vtwm, and Window Maker, but there are many, many more.

After you experiment with GNOME for a while, you may be curious about what these window managers look like and how they work. Half the fun of a flexible computing environment such as Linux and the X11 Window system is experimenting with new software "because it's there." You might be especially interested in window managers if you are running Ubuntu on a slow system or a system with a limited amount of memory, such as many older laptops, because window managers require far less memory and other system resources than complete desktop environments such a GNOME and KDE do.

As you might hope, it is extremely easy to temporarily switch between using GNOME and a specific window manager. First, you must enable the Universe repository, as explained in Chapter 20, "Adding, Removing, and Updating Software," because that is the place where most of the window manager packages are located. Next, you have to install one or more window managers using any of the software update tools that are also discussed in Chapter 20. After installing window managers and logging out, you can start any installed window manager by clicking the Options button at the bottom left of the login window and selecting Select Session from the menu that displays. Figure 5.34 shows a sample session menu on an Ubuntu system where a few window managers (Fvwm, IceWM, and Fluxbox) have been installed.

FIGURE 5.34

The GNOME login screen's Sessions menu

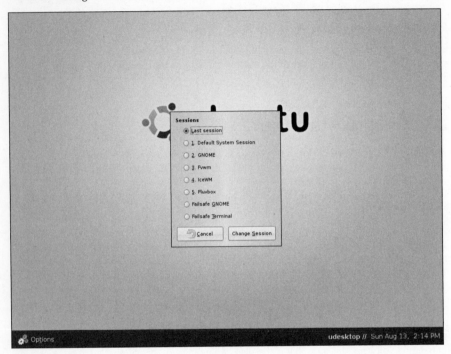

Select the radio button beside the window manager that you want to experiment with, and click Change Session to close the menu. When you log in, you will see a dialog like the one shown in Figure 5.35, asking if you want to use this window manager permanently.

FIGURE 5.35

Permanently changing your window manager in the GNOME login screen

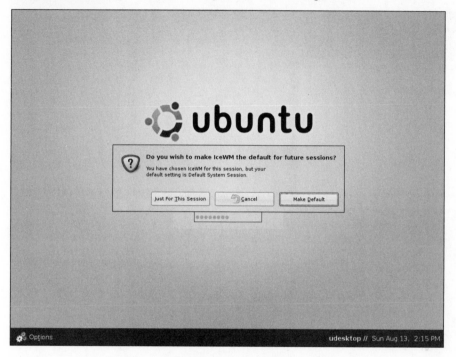

For now, select Just For This Session. If you decide that you always want to use a certain window manager, you can click Make Default here the next time you use the Sessions menu, or change it permanently by creating a special configuration file in your home directory (which I'll explain a little later in this section). After clicking Just For This Session, the command files that start the X Window system on your computer will start the selected window manager. Figure 5.36 shows the IceWm window manager running on one of my Ubuntu systems.

FIGURE 5.36

The IceWM window manager on an Ubuntu System

To permanently change to using a specified window manager, you can either use the Sessions menu shown in Figure 5.34 and the subsequent dialog shown in Figure 5.35 to make a window manager your permanent choice, or use a text editor to create a file called .xsession in your home directory, which contains a line like the following:

```
exec /usr/bin/icewm
```

Make the file executable (chmod 755 ~/.xsession), and the next time that you log in on your system, the system will automatically start the IceWM window manager (in this example) instead of the GNOME desktop. For compatibility with other ways of starting the X Window system, you should also create a symbolic link to this file called .xinitrc, also in your home directory. You would do this with a command like the following:

```
ln -s ~/.xsession ~/.xinitrc
```

Experimenting with different window managers is fun, because each represents someone's idea of how you "should" interact with a graphical system, start applications, and so on. I've been using the X Window system since version 10, and thus have burned more time than I could ever calculate in experimenting with, configuring, and customizing many of the window managers that have been written in the last 20+ years. But it's been fun.

TIP On low memory, low resource systems like older laptops, you may want to start Linux without a graphical interface — if you do this, you can always start the X Window system using a command such as `startx` or `xinit`, which will also pick up the X11 startup file and symbolic link that you just created, and will therefore start your window manager for you. See Chapter 19, "Understanding the Unix Startup and Shutdown Processes," for information about changing whether your system starts in graphical or command-line mode.

The previous instructions changed whether your Ubuntu system runs GNOME or a window manager. However, as mentioned earlier, all Linux desktop systems run a window manager under the covers. By default, GNOME runs Metacity, KDE runs kwm, and so on. If you still want to run GNOME but are interested in changing the window manager that it runs underneath, you must run another window manager that conforms to the Inter-Client Communication Conventions Manual (ICCCM) 2.0 standard (`http://en.wikipedia.org/wiki/ICCCM`) published by the X Consortium, and also to the EWMH (Extended Window Manager Hints) guidelines. The former is an official specification for how X Window system clients running on the same server should interact, while the latter is an unofficial set of extensions to ICCCM 2.0 that were defined by the FreeDesktop.org folks to specify additional window manager, window, and utility interaction mechanisms. Window managers that conform to these specifications are often simply referred to as GNOME-compliant. Some GNOME-compliant window managers are After Step, Enlightenment, Fvwm2, IceWM, Metacity, and WindowMaker. Figure 5.37 shows GNOME using the IceWM window manager.

FIGURE 5.37

GNOME running with the IceWM window manager

There are a variety of ways to change the window manager that GNOME uses, some more complex than others. The simplest, which is something of a hack, is to modify your ~/.xsession file so that it first starts the window manager that you want to use, and then starts GNOME. A sample ~/.xsession file that starts the IceWM window manager, and then starts GNOME is the following:

```
/usr/bin/icewm&
exec gnome-session
```

This is a hack because it relies on the fact that only one window manager can be active at a time. By starting IceWM before starting GNOME, the Metacity window manager cannot start, and thus GNOME continues to run using IceWM.

You should actually be able to change your window manager by simply putting a line like the following in your ~/.gnomerc file:

```
export WINDOW_MANAGER=/usr/bin/icewm
```

Unfortunately, this doesn't work for me. If you search the Web, you'll find many other suggestions, such as modifying your gconf (GNOME configuration) database (using database entries that are explicitly unsupported in the latest GNOME releases), modifying GNOME window manager startup scripts (such as gnome-wm), modifying your session control file to reference the GNOME window manager scripts, and many combinations of these. In general, I'm a fan of things that "just work," so I prefer my "solution."

Summary

This chapter introduced the graphical user interfaces used on Linux systems, focusing on the GNOME desktop that is the default user interface provided on Ubuntu Linux systems. After discussing the general organization of the GNOME desktop, the majority of the chapter focused on explaining how to customize and extend the default configuration of the GNOME desktop as installed on your Ubuntu system. Personalizing your computer system's desktop is one of the first steps to making it truly yours. GNOME provides the same types of customization and supports the same level of personalization as provided by other operating systems, such as Microsoft Windows or Mac OS X — it just doesn't cost as much.

Chapter 6 complements our exploration of the graphical power of GNOME and the X Window system by exploring the power of the Linux command line. The fact that many Linux commands are command-line oriented is one of the reasons that many hard-core Windows users disparage Linux, which is just plain silly, because Linux gives you both a powerful graphical interface *and* a powerful command-line interface. You don't have to look any further than Mac OS X, with its Unix underpinnings and Terminal window, to see just how empowering the marriage of a great GUI and a powerful set of command-line tools can be in a commercial product. Ubuntu gives you this same power, if not more, but at no cost.

Chapter 6

Using Command-Line Tools

Because Linux has its conceptual roots in the older Unix operating system, many Linux applications are designed to be executed from a command line. A command line is the traditional interface found on older computer systems that may not have used the high-resolution, graphically oriented monitors that most people expect today. In the command-line model, the system runs a program, known as a *command-line interpreter*, which does just what its name suggests. A command-line interpreter reads the commands that you type, locates the appropriate application on your system, and executes that application for you as instructed based on what you've typed. Once the command completes, the command interpreter displays a sequence of characters, known as a *prompt*, signifying that it is ready to accept another command.

Linux systems aren't addicted to the command-line approach simply out of historical interest — when a Linux system boots, it needs to be able to run several commands long before the graphical interface is available. On Linux systems, the graphical interface itself is started by a command-line utility, after which (of course), fancy graphics are available, expected, and used.

For most people, simply displaying a command-line prompt on a fancy graphical monitor powered by a multi-megabyte graphics card would be a waste of good hardware. However, Linux provides thousands of useful and extremely powerful command-line applications, so graphical user interfaces (GUIs) such as GNOME and the X Window system offer applications that display a command prompt in a separate window, giving you the best of both worlds. You can be running Open Office Writer or the GIMP in separate windows, making the most of their graphical capabilities, while you can be simultaneously displaying a command prompt in another and executing command-line utilities there.

This chapter explains the basic ideas behind command-line utilities and the commands that execute them, discusses the primary Linux command-line interpreters, explains how to access them, and explores some of the most popular utilities for running command-line utilities on your Ubuntu Linux system.

NOTE   Most of the sample command-line examples given throughout this chapter begin with the character $, which is the default prompt used by Ubuntu's default Linux command interpreter. (A prompt is the character or characters that a command interpreter displays to signify that it is waiting for you to type something.) If you're following along, you should not type this character — you'll already see it (or some more complex prompt) at the beginning of your command line.

Why Use the Command Line?

Linux provides thousands of command-line utilities that range from simple programs for creating, examining, and modifying files and file permissions to complex utilities that enable you to fine-tune the performance of your hardware and low-level operating system capabilities such as filesystems and networking. Many of these applications have graphical equivalents, especially user-level applications and system configuration utilities. For example, the System ➪ Administration menu's Networking menu item starts the graphical network-admin application, which performs the same functions as the command-line ifconfig utility. Similarly, GNOME's Nautilus file manager is roughly equivalent to a Linux command-line interpreter in general, because it enables you to examine and manipulate files and directories, execute other applications, and so on.

Using the command line isn't really an alien notion even to users of operating systems such as Microsoft Windows and Mac OS X (though it's newer to the latter). Many Windows users, especially system administrators, have always found a certain convenience in some of the command-line configuration utilities provided with Windows systems, especially those related to network configuration and status reporting such as ipconfig. The idea of a command line may be somewhat new to long-time Macintosh users, because the command line was a serious alternative to the GUI when Apple introduced its Unix-based Mac OS X operating system.

Even if you don't specifically want to use the Linux command line, there is one case in which you may have to, which is if your Ubuntu system encounters major hardware or configuration problems during the boot process. If, for example, your system finds that its root filesystem is corrupted or inaccessible during the boot process, you'll see a command-line prompt faster than you can say, "Hmmm, I wonder if that's a major problem." All Linux systems fall back to the command line when major problems are identified during the boot sequence to give you access to the command-line applications that you'll need to use in order to correct the problem and reenable the system to boot normally. The Linux boot process is a command-line process, executing the appropriate configuration utilities in the correct order, the last of which is the command that starts the X Window system and your GNOME desktop (or window manager, if you've customized things). Even if your system's filesystems are in good shape and all of your hardware and associated system software runs correctly during the boot process, configuration problems with the X Window system are a common cause of seeing a command-line prompt instead of the glorious Ubuntu login screen when you boot your system. The Ubuntu Linux boot process is described in detail in Chapter 19, "Understanding the Ubuntu Startup and Shutdown Processes."

Executing Commands from the Command Line

Applications that are designed to be executed from a Linux command line are typically referred to as command-line utilities. All command-line utilities have the same general organization — they begin with the name of the command that you want to execute, and are optionally followed by information about the way in which you want the command to behave. Anything following the name of the command that you want to execute is known as an *argument* to that command. The arguments to each command-line utility differ based on the command that you want to execute. In an interesting example of recursion, the arguments to command-line utilities are generally referred to as *options*, each of which may take an argument.

Confused? If this is all new to you, don't worry. A few examples will help clear this up, and soon you'll be as comfortable at the command line as anyone. Let's use the Linux ls command as an example, because it has more options than almost any other command and was also introduced in the section of Chapter 4 entitled "Understanding Linux Permissions."

The ls command lists information about files and directories on your Ubuntu system. The Linux ls command is an updated version of a classic Unix utility by the same name. In true Unix fashion, no one was willing to type extra characters like "i" and "t", so the command was given the faster-to-type abbreviation of ls.

When used by itself on the command line, the ls command simply displays the contents of the current directory, as in the following example:

```
$ ls
boot_services.txt   hello.c    hello.o   include_example.c
include_test
hello               hello.foo  hello.s   include_example.out
```

You can also supply the name of a specific file or directory as an argument to the ls command, as in the following examples:

```
$ ls hello
hello
```

Using the ls command to list the name of a file that you already know is spectacularly uninteresting (though it can be very useful when combined with wildcards, which are discussed later in this chapter). However, listing a directory shows the contents of that directory, as in the following example:

```
$ ls include_test
libxml2   netdev   system
```

The output from this command shows that the include_test directory itself contains three other files or directories. I happened to know that include_test was a directory — if you're not sure what types of things are in the current directory, you can use the ls command's -F option to give you this information. For example, here's the current directory as shown using the ls -F command:

```
$ ls -F
boot_services.txt   hello.c    hello.o   include_example.c
include_test/
hello*              hello.foo  hello.s   include_example.out
```

The ls command's -F option decorates the names of the objects in the current directory with an extra character to identify any object that isn't simply a text file. An asterisk following the name of an object shows that this is an executable file, while a slash ("/") following the name of an object shows that this is indeed a directory.

The ls command's -F option is very useful, but (in true Linux fashion) isn't the only way to get detailed information about each of the objects in the current directory. You can also get this sort of information using other options to the ls command. For example, one of the most commonly used options to the ls command is the -l option, which means "display output in long format." Using this option gives a variety of additional information about the objects in the current directory, as in the following example:

```
$ ls -1
total 44
-rw-r—r—  1 wvh users  783 2006.03-15 06:36 boot_services.txt
-rwxr-xr-x 1 wvh users 9249 2006.03-15 06:37 hello
-rw-r—r—  1 wvh users   60 2006.03-15 06:37 hello.c
-rw-r—r—  1 wvh users   60 2006.03-15 06:37 hello.foo
-rw-r—r—  1 wvh users 2504 2006.03-15 06:37 hello.o
-rw-r—r—  1 wvh users  857 2006.03-15 06:37 hello.s
-rw-r—r—  1 wvh users  202 2006.03-15 06:37 include_example.c
-rw-r—r—  1 wvh users  736 2006.03-15 06:37 include_example.out
drwxr-xr-x 5 wvh users 4096 2006.03-15 06:37 include_test
```

As you can see, the long option displays more complete information about the files and directories in the current directory. From left to right, this information consists of the following: current permissions, the number of hard links to that file in the Linux filesystem (more about that later in this section), the owner and group, size, the date and time at which it was last modified, and the file or directory name.

As mentioned previously, you can combine options and arguments on the same command line to refine the behavior of most command-line utilities. For example, to get a long listing of the contents of the include_test directory, you would execute the following command:

```
$ ls -1 include_test
total 0
drwxr-xr-x 2 wvh users 72 2006.03-15 06:37 libxml2
drwxr-xr-x 2 wvh users 80 2006.03-15 06:37 netdev
drwxr-xr-x 4 wvh users 96 2006.03-15 06:37 system
```

One other very popular option to the ls command is the –a option, which shows all of the objects in the current directory. By default, the ls command doesn't show objects whose names begin with a period (aka full stop). This is because all Linux directories contain two special entries that many people don't care about, but which are useful to traverse and support the hierarchical structure of a Linux filesystem. These are the ".". entry, which always refers to the current directory, and the ".." entry, which always refers to the parent of the current directory. Using the ls –a command to look at the contents of the current directory shows the following:

```
$ ls -a
.                      hello.c    include_example.c    .run_me_now
..                     hello.foo  include_example.out
boot_services.txt      hello.o    include_test
hello                  hello.s    .my_music_directory
```

You'll note that the "." and ".." entries are listed in the first column. However, you'll also note that two new files have appeared in the directory. These are the files .my_music_directory and .run_me_now, which are listed in the directory listing based on the first alphanumeric character in their names because the ls command ignores leading periods when sorting file names (unless, of course, the filename has no other characters as is the case with the ". " and ".. " entries, which therefore appear first in the listing).

TIP Because files beginning with periods aren't included in directory listings unless you use the –a option, using file names that begin with a period has become a standard convention for "hiding" those files. Files and directories whose names begin with a period are most commonly used to hold configuration information used by various Linux commands. The most common example of this type of file is the .bashrc configuration file used by the bash shell, which I'll discuss later in this chapter.

You can combine multiple single-letter options after a single leading dash, and the ls command will perform all of the specified actions. For example, let's combine the -a and -F options to look at the current directory:

```
$ ls -aF
./                      hello.c     include_example.c      .run_me_now*
../                     hello.foo   include_example.out
boot_services.txt       hello.o     include_test/
hello*                  hello.s     .my_music_directory@
```

From the output of this command, you can see that the "." and ".." entries are both directories (actually, they are hard links to the current and parent directories), and the mysterious .run_me_now file is actually an executable command. The name of the .my_music_directory file is followed by an at symbol (@). What's up with that?

I've used the term "links" in passing previously, and this is a good time to explain it. Links are essentially just pointers to other files and directories in the Linux filesystem. Linux supports two types of links: hard links, which are actual connections to an existing file or directory, and symbolic links, which contain the name of some other file or directory that you want to refer to. Because hard links are actual connections to an existing data structure, the thing that you're linking to must actually exist and must be within the same disk partition as the thing that you're hard linking to. (This is a side effect of the internal data structures used by filesystems, which are too detailed to discuss here. This whole options concept may already be making you drowsy, let alone plunging into a discussion of filesystem data structures.) Unlike hard links, because symbolic links just contain the name of something else, they can point to any file or directory on your machine. As you may now suspect, an @ symbol following the name of a file or directory indicates that this file or directory is just a symbolic link to another file or directory somewhere else on your system. Let's combine the ls command's -a and -1 options to get some detailed information about everything in the current directory:

```
$ ls -al
total 45
drwxr-xr-x   3 wvh users   400 2006.03-16 06:20 .
drwxr-xr-x  13 wvh users  1376 2006.03-16 05:38 ..
-rw-r—r—    1 wvh users   783 2006.03-15 06:36 boot_services.txt
-rwxr-xr-x   1 wvh users  9249 2006.03-15 06:37 hello
-rw-r—r—    1 wvh users    60 2006.03-15 06:37 hello.c
-rw-r—r—    1 wvh users    60 2006.03-15 06:37 hello.foo
-rw-r—r—    1 wvh users  2504 2006.03-15 06:37 hello.o
-rw-r—r—    1 wvh users   857 2006.03-15 06:37 hello.s
-rw-r—r—    1 wvh users   202 2006.03-15 06:37 include_example.c
-rw-r—r—    1 wvh users   736 2006.03-15 06:37 include_example.out
drwxr-xr-x   5 wvh users   120 2006.03-15 06:37 include_test
lrwxrwxrwx   1 wvh users    11 2006.03-16 06:20 .my_music -> /opt2/music
-rwxr-xr-x   1 wvh users   269 2006.03-16 05:47 .run_me_now
```

This actually shows you a fair amount of information about everything in this directory, especially in terms of links. Remember that the second column in a long directory listing identifies the number of hard links to each object. For example, the second column for the "." entry shows that there are three hard links to the current directory — these are the "." itself, it's entry in the parent directory, and the hard link to "." that is present in the `include_test` subdirectory because it is the parent of the `include-test` directory. The ".." entry, which is a hard link to the parent directory of the current directory, seems to be very popular because there are 13 hard links to it. This means that the parent directory of the current directory probably contains several other directories. Looking at the `.my_music`, you can see that it is indeed a symbolic link, because its name in the long listing actually shows the other object that it is a symbolic link to. In this case, the file `.my_music` is a symbolic link to a directory that happens to live on another filesystem that is mounted on the `/opt2/music` directory on my system.

All of the command-line options I've discussed up to this point have begun with a single dash. This isn't always necessarily the case for all commands and their options. Some Linux commands with their conceptual roots in ancient versions of Unix (like the `tar` command) don't even require a leading dash before a single command-line option or a single group of command-line options. This antique command-line convention is deprecated, which means that anyone who implements a command nowadays that doesn't require at least one dash before its options will be mocked and verbally abused via e-mail by the Linux and open source communities. (All Unix commands that don't require a dash before their options have also been updated so that they can also handle finding a dash before their options.) Nowadays, command-line options always begin with a dash, but in an interesting usability twist, they can also begin with two dashes. The conventions for this are that single-letter options are preceded by a single dash, while multi-letter, "whole word" options begin with two dashes. This is necessary for two reasons:

- Most command-line utilities support both styles of options: the traditional single letter options and the newer whole-word options pioneered by the folks at the Free Software Foundation.

- Because you can combine multiple, single-letter options into a single group of options (as you've seen throughout this section), unless you use two dashes to identify a whole-word option, the command that you're executing can't differentiate between the two.

To illustrate this, let's ask for help from the `ls` command:

```
$ ls -help
/bin/ls: invalid option—e
Try `/bin/ls —help' for more information.
```

Well, that was actually both illustrative and friendly. When preceded with a single dash, the `ls` command interprets each of the letters that follow as a single option, and therefore complains because no option matches the letter e in the `—help` option. Let's try that again, correctly. Running the `ls —help` command displays the following output (truncated here because this is just an example):

```
$ ls —help
Usage: /bin/ls [OPTION]... [FILE]...
List information about the FILEs (the current directory by default).
Sort entries alphabetically if none of -cftuSUX nor —sort.

 Mandatory arguments to long options are mandatory for short options
too.
  -a, —all                    do not ignore entries starting with .
  -A, —almost-all             do not list implied . and ..
[remaining output deleted]
```

Getting Information about Commands

As you can see from the final example in this section, many command-line utilities provide a −help option, which displays what is known as a usage message. A usage message is a short summary of how to use a command, summarizing available options and their meanings. Unfortunately, not all commands offer a −help option and those that do can't display all possible information about those options. As discussed in Chapter 5, the graphical user environment used on Ubuntu systems provides a huge assortment of online help that makes it easy for you to get information about how to use graphical commands. Luckily, the Ubuntu command-line environment also provides a similar amount of online help in the form of the man and info commands.

The man command is your best friend when using or simply experimenting with command-line programs. The man command displays online manual pages, formatted for your screen. In true Linux/Unix fashion, the man command paginates its output using the Linux version of the familiar Unix more command — known as less — to make it easy to scroll forward or backward in its output. Because the online reference information displayed by the man command is displayed a screen/page at a time and corresponds to the documentation you'd tradition-ally find in a printed reference manual, the documentation displayed by man is generally referred to as a *man page* or as *man pages*.

As an example of using the man command, you can type man man for additional information on the man com-mand itself. The first part of this man page looks like the following:

```
man(1)                        Manual pager utils                        man(1)


NAME
       man - an interface to the on-line reference manuals

 SYNOPSIS
       man  [-c|-w|-tZHT  device]  [-adhu7V]  [-i|-I] [-m system[,...]] [-L
       locale] [-p string] [-M path] [-P pager] [-r prompt] [-S  list]  [-e
       extension] [[section] page ...] ...
       man  -l  [-7] [-tZHT device] [-p string] [-P pager] [-r prompt] file
       ...
       man -k [apropos options] regexp ...
       man -f [whatis options] page ...


DESCRIPTION
       man is the system's manual pager. Each page argument given to man is
       normally  the   name   of  a  program, utility or function.  The manual
       page associated with each of these arguments is then found and  dis-
       played. A section, if provided, will direct man to look only in that
       section of the manual.   The default action is to search  in  all  of
       the  available  sections,  following a predefined order and to show
       only the first page found, even if page exists in several  sections.
[Additional output removed]
```

continued

155

continued

As you can see, the online man pages for Linux command provide extensive information about available options, but also provide a significant amount of general information about using the commands themselves, usually including examples.

A more modern alternative to the man command, the `info` command provides similar usage and explanatory information about Linux commands. The `info` command uses emacs to display its output and also provides more extensive and up-to-date command documentation than the traditional `man` command. The following figure shows a window displaying info on the `info` command.

The info command running in a terminal window

The `info` command was introduced by the GNU folks to provide a richer, more robust environment for displaying online help for command-line utilities. The text files that are used by the `info` command provide a very rich syntax for hyperlinking between different sections of info documentation, and the use of emacs as the application for displaying info pages provides a much more flexible environment for moving around in the info that you're looking at. The `info` command can also display traditional Linux `man` pages, so you can even examine existing man pages using `info` — the `info man` command is perhaps the best example of that sort of recursion.

The Linux `man` and `info` commands will quickly become your new best friends when you are using or simply learning about command-line utilities.

What's a Shell?

A shell is the generic name given to any Linux command-line interpreter, and comes from Unix, the conceptual parent of Linux. Unix was one of the first operating systems to introduce the idea of using a command-line interpreter that was not built into the operating system and which had no special permissions to do mysterious operating system tasks. These ideas have been preserved in every conceptual descendant of Unix and have proved handy for several reasons. The most interesting of these is that, because it is a separate, stand-alone executable, a Linux system can offer each user their choice of multiple shells, all of which can be upgraded independently from the operating system.

The original Unix shell was written by Ken Thompson, one of the two primary creators of Unix, and was extended by John Mashey, also at Bell Labs. These shells were somewhat primitive — the first shell that has the types of capabilities we have come to know and love today was the Bourne Shell, written by Stephen Bourne at Bell Labs in 1974. This shell, known to its friends as /bin/sh, is the shell that is used by default on most Unix systems, and is the conceptual parent of the /bin/bash shell (which stands for Bourne-Again Shell) that is used by default on most Linux systems today. As I'll explain in the next section, there are a variety of other shells to choose from on Linux systems. If you've come to Linux from a version of Unix that features another shell, you'll be able to feel at home pretty quickly (and perhaps even bring over and reuse your existing shell configuration files.)

> **TIP**
> One term that you will frequently hear when discussing shells, Linux, or Unix in general is the term *shell script*. A shell script is a command file containing commands that are either internal to the shell (such as those for setting variables, conditional expressions, and looping constructs) or which reference other commands on your Linux system. The ability to write very sophisticated command files is a feature of the Linux/Unix utility model, where each utility does one thing and does it well, and many different utilities can be linked together via pipes or temporary files to process each other's output.

For additional information about shells on Unix systems, see:

- www.softpanorama.org/People/Shell_giants/introduction.shtml
- www.faqs.org/faqs/unix-faq/shell/shell-differences/
- www.unix.org.ua/orelly/unix/ksh/ch01_03.htm

Available Shells for Linux Systems

A standard Ubuntu distribution installs only the standard GNU bash shell. However, other shells are available for installation through apt-get or the Synaptic Package Manager. The following shells are found on many Linux systems:

/bin/ash: The Almquist shell, a small-footprint shell that began as a clone of the SYSV R4 version of the Bourne shell. The ash shell is often used on embedded systems or during the system startup and installation process on some Linux distributions.

/bin/bash: The default, Bourne-Again shell inspired by /bin/sh and /bin/ksh. This is the default shell installed and used by all users on Ubuntu systems.

/bin/csh: If you install tcsh (see its description later in this list), a symbolic link from /bin/csh to /bin/tcsh is also created. This link is provided to support shell scripts that reference the traditional location of the C-Shell, the standard shell used on Berkeley Unix (BSD) systems and their descendants. The C-shell supports configuration commands that are reminiscent of C-language programming constructs, and was originally written by Bill Joy, later a founder of Sun Microsystems.

/bin/dash: The Debian Almquist shell, the Debian Linux distribution's version of the standard Almquist shell. If you're interested in experimenting with this shell, it is available in the standard Ubuntu repository.

continued

continued

/bin/ksh: If you install pdksh (see its description later in this list), a symbolic link from /bin/ksh to /bin/pdksh is also created. This link is provided to support shell scripts that reference the traditional location of the Korn shell, the standard shell used on later SYSV Unix systems from AT&T and their descendants

/bin/nash: Another small-footprint shell used during the startup process on many Linux systems, specifically on Red Hat and Fedora Core Linux systems

/bin/pdksh: An open source version of David Korn's Korn shell, written at AT&T and was available with the SYSV R3 (as part of the "Experimental Toolchest") and R4 (as a completely supported utility) Unix distributions. The Korn shell (and thus pdksh) is completely backward compatible with the original Bourne shell. If you're interested in experimenting with this shell, it is available in the standard Ubuntu repository.

/bin/sh: A symbolic link to /bin/bash, provided for compatibility with generic Linux and Unix shell scripts.

/bin/tcsh: The TENEX C-Shell, which is an advanced, open source version of the C-shell with command-line editing extensions that were originally introduced by the command interpreter used by DEC's TOPS-20 operating system for PDP-10 systems, which began life as BBN's TENEX (for the 10 in PDP-10) operating system and was therefore later mutated into TWENEX (for the 20 in TOPS-20) by the PDP-10 hacker community. If you're interested in experimenting with this shell, it is available in the standard Ubuntu repository.

/bin/zsh: The Z shell is a powerful, tremendously extensible shell that provides many of the capabilities of bash and ksh, and much, much more. If you're interested in experimenting with this shell, it is available in the standard Ubuntu repository.

You can use the chsh command-line command to change the default shell used by your account if you decide that you want to use a shell other than the one that is currently listed in your /etc/passwd entry. However, you can't change your login shell to any random binary — all of the programs to which you can change your shell are listed in the text file /etc/shells on your Ubuntu system. If you want to be able to set some other application as a login shell using the chsh command, you must first add it to the file /etc/shells.

Getting to a Shell

Assuming that I've hyped the value of the Linux command line sufficiently and that your Ubuntu system boots correctly in graphical mode, you're probably wondering how to start a shell so that you can experiment a bit. Ubuntu provides two applications that are the most common mechanisms for starting a shell, one that is a standard part of the X Window System distribution, and another that is a standard part of any GNOME distribution. Both of these are referred to as terminal applications, not because they imply an end to life as we know it, but because they are reminiscent of the user experience on systems without bitmapped graphical displays, when most users accessed their computer systems through terminals that couldn't do much more than display the input and output of a command interpreter.

Using the GNOME Terminal Application

The GNOME terminal application is the most common way of starting a command-line shell on a graphical Ubuntu system. To start the GNOME Terminal, select the Terminal command from the Applications ➪ Accessories menu. Figure 6.1 shows the default GNOME Terminal window.

FIGURE 6.1

The GNOME Terminal application

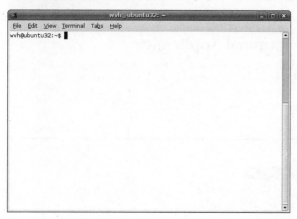

Like most GNOME applications, the GNOME Terminal provides extensive online help that is available by selecting Help ➪ Contents.

The GNOME Terminal application provides a variety of menus that make it easy to configure things like the title of a GNOME Terminal window (Terminal ➪ Set Title); configure the character set (Terminal ➪ Set Character Encoding); and configure the size, fonts, colors, and other display attributes of the GNOME Terminal window (Edit ➪ Current Profile). In my opinion, its most generally useful feature is its ability to open and manage multiple command-line sessions within a single Terminal window. To open a new tab, select the File ➪ New Tab command. A new tab displays, as shown in Figure 6.2.

FIGURE 6.2

Multiple tabs in the GNOME Terminal

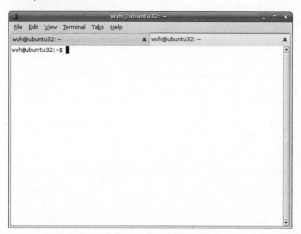

Once multiple tabs are displayed, you can move between tabs by clicking on a specific tab or by using the appropriate command from the Tabs menu. If you want to have an existing tab display in its own window, you can select the Tabs ➪ Detach Tab command. You can also start a new GNOME Terminal window by selecting the File ➪ New Terminal command.

Using the X Window System Terminal Application

Any X Window System distribution includes a lightweight terminal application known as xterm. The executable for the X Window System's terminal application, shown in Figure 6.3, is located in /usr/bin/xterm.

FIGURE 6.3

A traditional xterm

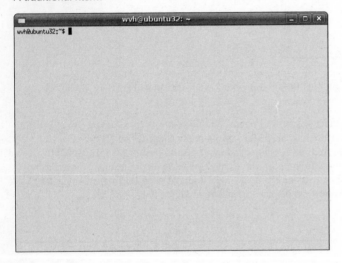

To start the xterm application, you can do any of the following:

- Add a menu item for the xterm application, as explained in "Adding Items to Any Menu" in Chapter 5, and then select that menu item.

- Create a launcher for the xterm application on your panel using the Run Application panel applet, and then select that panel applet. Adding items to a panel is explained in "Customizing Panel Contents" in Chapter 5.

- Create a desktop launcher for the xterm application by right-clicking on your desktop's background, selecting the Create Launcher command, and filling out the dialog shown in Figure 6.4. You can then start an xterm by clicking on the desktop launcher.

- Execute the xterm command directly from the GNOME Terminal, which is somewhat recursive, but eminently doable.

Many users who are new to Ubuntu by are already familiar with the xterm application find that they prefer familiar xterms to the GNOME Terminal. For complete details on all of the capabilities of the xterm application, see its man page — perhaps by starting an xterm and executing the man xterm command in that window.

FIGURE 6.4

Creating a desktop launcher for the xterm application

As a generic X Window system application rather than a GNOME or KDE application, you'll note in Figure 6.3 that an `xterm` window doesn't provide a menu or toolbar to provide easy access to configuration commands. Instead, you display `xterm`'s configuration menus by holding down the Control key on your keyboard and clicking the left, middle, or right mouse buttons on the background of the `xterm` window. Figure 6.5 shows the menu that you see when holding down the Control key and left-clicking the background of an `xterm` window.

FIGURE 6.5

An xterm's Main Options menu

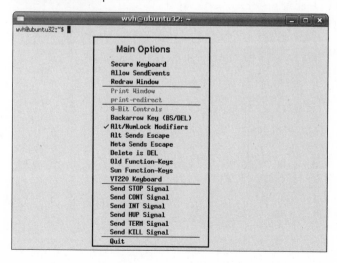

Each `xterm` configuration menu provides access to different `xterm` configuration commands:

- **Control-left-click:** The Main Options menu, which primarily enables you to send various signals and special key sequences to the selected `xterm`.

- **Control-middle-click:** The VT Options enables you to set various characteristics of the terminal emulation provided by the selected `xterm`. The name VT Options comes from the name of the default type of terminal that is emulated by an `xterm`, which is a DEC VT-100. Figure 6.6 shows the VT Options menu.

- **Control-right-click:** The Fonts menu lets you control the size of the fonts used in the selected `xterm`. Figure 6.7 shows the Fonts menu.

TIP By default, an `xterm` starts a copy of your login shell, but one of the most common ways of using the `xterm` application is to automatically start another application in the xterm window using the `xterm` command's `-e` (execute) option and specifying the name of the application that you want to start. For example, the following command starts an `xterm` that is running the `ssh` command to connect to the system `writing.vonhagen.org`:

```
$ xterm -e ssh writing.vonhagen.org
```

This command would prompt for a login password, and then give me a shell on the specified system. (For more information about connecting to remote systems, see Chapter 15, "Connecting to Other Systems.") Because xterms don't feature multiple tabs like the GNOME Terminal application (explained in the previous section), an `xterm -e` command is one of the most common ways for Ubuntu users to start a separate window that is running another nongraphical command.

FIGURE 6.6

An xterm's VT Options menu

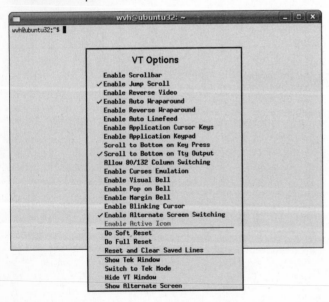

FIGURE 6.7

An xterm's Fonts menu

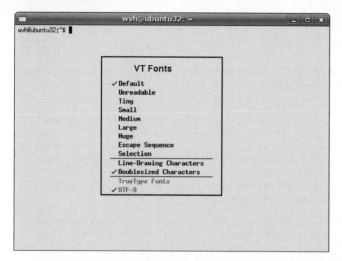

Popular Command-Line Commands

The section of this chapter that introduced command-line utilities, options, and arguments used the standard Linux `ls` command as an example. Listing files and directories is one of the most common things that you'll want to do from a shell (or, at least, will find yourself doing). However, as explained in the previous section, your Ubuntu system provides hundreds of commands. I can't go into all of them here, because that would mean that Wiley would need to put wheels on this book, but there are certainly some common tasks that you'll want to do from a shell. This section highlights some of the more common tasks you'll want to do from the command line, and concludes by discussing how to figure out which commands to use if you don't already know the cryptic name of the appropriate command-line utility.

Moving Around in the Linux Filesystem

Just as when you use a graphical user interface, you will want to organize your files and directories in some logical fashion if you're working from the command line. Once you've organized things that way, you'll need to use the `cd` (change directory) command, which does exactly what you'd expect. In hard-core Linux terms, the `cd` command changes your current working directory to be the directory that you supply as an argument. For example, to change directory into a directory named `include_test`, you'd simply execute the following command:

```
$ cd include_test
```

 If you're hanging around with hard-core Linux folks and want to fit in, you should refer to changing to another directory as *cd'ing* there.

If you don't know the name of the directory where you are currently working, that's somewhat scary, but you can use the pwd command (process working directory) to provide that information. The pwd command lists the full pathname of the directory in which the current process (in this case, your shell) is running, as in the following example:

```
$ pwd
/home/wvh/include_test
```

You can change directory to any directory on your Linux system by specifying its full pathname as the argument to the cd command, as in the following example:

```
$ cd /usr/local
$ pwd
/usr/local
```

As you can see, my shell is now working in the /usr/local directory and any other commands that I execute will be performed in that directory. As a convenience, if you execute the cd command without any arguments, the cd command automatically changes directory to your home directory, which is probably where most of your files and directories are located in the first place.

> **TIP** As you work at the command line, you may find that you often want to change to some other directory, do one or two things, and then return to the directory that you started in. When changing directories frequently, it's handy to let your shell keep track of things like "where did I come from." To save you time and mental energy, most Linux shells provide built-in commands called pushd and popd to track this for you. The pushd command changes to a specified directory, but remembers where you came from by pushing the name of the directory that you came from onto a list of previous locations known as a *stack*. Once you're done working there, you can type the popd command to return to the directory that you came from, which removes it from the stack (i.e., the list of previous working directory locations). If you're unfamiliar with the idea of a stack, the standard example of a stack is the spring-loaded plate stacks of plates that you find at a cafeteria or your favorite local buffet. Pushing something onto the stack is analogous to putting a new plate on the top of the stack of available plates. Popping something off the stack is analogous to removing the top plate from the stack, which makes the next one available.

Copying, Moving, Renaming, and Deleting Files and Directories

Copying, moving, and renaming files are some of the most common actions that any computer user performs, regardless of whether you're using the command line or working with a graphical user interface. Whether you're cloning an existing file to use the former as a starting point for new work or reorganizing your files and directories to make things easier to find, copying and moving file and directories is just as easy to do from the command line as it is from a GUI, modulo the fact that you have to type rather than point and click. In many cases, the zillions of options provided by many Linux command-line utilities give you much finer control over things than a generic graphical command ever could.

In the continuing Linux/Unix tradition of "why type more letters than necessary," the Linux command to copy files and directories is the cp command. To copy one file to another, you simply execute the cp command, followed by the name of the existing file and the name that you want to have the copy to have. For example, to copy a file named file.txt to the new file new_file.txt, you would execute the command:

```
$ cp file.txt new_file.txt
```

CAUTION Be very careful when specifying the name of the file that is the destination of a `cp` command. If a file with the same name as the file to which you are copying already exists, the `cp` command overwrites the existing file with the contents of the file that you are copying. If you're really paranoid about this, see the section later in this chapter on "Defining and Using Aliases" for information about how to permanently set up a safe version of the `cp` command.

By specifying the full pathnames of the source or destination file, the `cp` command can copy files anywhere in the Linux filesystem in which you have permission to create files. For example, to copy the file `file.txt` from my home directory to the file `newfile.txt` in the directory `/tmp` (where everyone can create files), I could execute the following command regardless of the file or directory in which I was currently working:

```
$ cp /home/wvh/file.txt /tmp/newfile.txt
```

You can also use the `cp` command to copy file to different directories by specifying the name of a directory as the target of the `cp` operation. Continuing with the previous example, if I had wanted to copy the file `file.txt` from my home directory to `/tmp`, but have the copy retain the same name as the original file, I could have done so with the following command:

```
$ cp /home/wvh/file.txt /tmp
```

This command would create the file `/tmp/file.txt` as an exact copy of `/home/wvh/file.txt`.

The `cp` command doesn't require any special options when simply copying files. However, you can also copy directories using the `cp` command, by specifying its `-r` (recursive) option. For example to copy the contents of a directory of mine called `include_test` to a new directory called backup, I would execute the following command:

```
$ cp -r include_test backup
```

After the command completed, the new backup directory would be an exact copy of the `include_test` directory. If you're from Missouri and need proof that the right thing is happening, you can add the `-v` (verbose) option to the `cp` command to list each part of the copy command. This command and its output would look like the following:

```
$ cp -rv include_test backup
`include_test' -> `backup'
`include_test/libxml2' -> `backup/libxml2'
`include_test/libxml2/xmlops.h' -> `backup/libxml2/xmlops.h'
`include_test/netdev' -> `backup/netdev'
`include_test/netdev/devname.h' -> `backup/netdev/devname.h'
`include_test/system' -> `backup/system'
`include_test/system/libxml2' -> `backup/system/libxml2'
`include_test/system/libxml2/xmlops.h' ->
`backup/system/libxml2/xmlops.h'
`include_test/system/netdev' -> `backup/system/netdev'
`include_test/system/netdev/devname.h' ->
`backup/system/netdev/devname.h'
```

As you'd hope, a recursive `cp` command also recursively copies all subdirectories and any files that they contain.

I'd mentioned earlier that specifying the name of a directory as the target when copying a file creates a file with the same name as the original in the target directory. The same is true when specifying the name of a directory as the target for a recursive cp command. This can initially be confusing if you're trying to copy a directory to a directory with a new name and a directory with that name already exists. In that case, the cp command creates a directory with the same name as your original directory as a subdirectory of the target directory.

Moving and renaming files from the command line is similarly easy. Linux systems don't actually provide a separate rename command — on a Linux system, the mv command both moves existing files and directories to a new location and also optionally renames them as part of the move operation. For example, to rename the file file.txt to the new name newfile.txt, you would do the following:

```
$ mv file.txt newfile.txt
```

The mv command follows the same conventions as the cp command in terms of specifying full pathnames and when specifying a directory as the name of the location to which you want to move a file. For example, the following command moves the file /home/wvh/file.txt to the /tmp directory, and renames it newfile.txt:

```
$ mv /home/wvh/file.txt /tmp/newfile.txt
```

If you wanted to move the file to the /tmp directory and keep its original name, you would do so with the following command:

```
$ mv /home/wvh/file.txt /tmp
```

Unlike the cp command, the mv command doesn't need any special flags when moving or renaming directories. For example, to rename the directory include_test to backup, you would do the following;

```
$ mv include_test backup
```

Like the cp command, if the backup directory already existed, the mv command would move the include_test directory into the backup directory, retaining its original name. The mv command also provides a -v (verbose) option to show you what's going on during a mv operation, but this is somewhat less exciting when just renaming a directory, as you can see from the following example:

```
$ mv -v include_test backup
`include_test' -> `backup'
```

In this case, the mv operation only needs to rename the directory. However, because of the way that Linux filesystems are created, moving directories across filesystems that live on different hard disk partitions requires that each file and subdirectory be first copied and then deleted by the mv command, as in the following example:

```
$ df . /tmp
Filesystem              1K-blocks       Used Available Use% Mounted on
/dev/sda8             160010472  117909468  42101004   74% /home
/dev/sda5               4200824     984200   3216624   24% /tmp
$ mv -v include_test /tmp/backup
`include_test' -> `/tmp/backup'
`include_test/libxml2' -> `/tmp/backup/libxml2'
`include_test/libxml2/xmlops.h' -> `/tmp/backup/libxml2/xmlops.h'
`include_test/netdev' -> `/tmp/backup/netdev'
`include_test/netdev/devname.h' -> `/tmp/backup/netdev/devname.h'
`include_test/system' -> `/tmp/backup/system'
`include_test/system/libxml2' -> `/tmp/backup/system/libxml2'
```

```
`include_test/system/libxml2/xmlops.h' ->
`/tmp/backup/system/libxml2/xmlops.h'
`include_test/system/netdev' -> `/tmp/backup/system/netdev'
`include_test/system/netdev/devname.h' ->
`/tmp/backup/system/netdev/devname.h'
`include_test/new_file' -> `/tmp/backup/new_file'
removed `include_test/libxml2/xmlops.h'
removed directory: `include_test/libxml2'
removed `include_test/netdev/devname.h'
removed directory: `include_test/netdev'
removed `include_test/system/libxml2/xmlops.h'
removed directory: `include_test/system/libxml2'
removed `include_test/system/netdev/devname.h'
removed directory: `include_test/system/netdev'
removed directory: `include_test/system'
removed `include_test/new_file'
removed directory: `include_test'
```

As you can see, much of this output is very similar to that of the cp command. In this example, I first used the df command to demonstrate that my current directory (".") and the target directory (/tmp) are actually located on different filesystems. You can see the different in the verbose output of the mv command.

Along with copying and moving files and directories, deleting files and directories is a similarly common operation. Whether you're deleting things to free up disk space for future projects, deleting backup copies of projects that you've finished, or deleting things that you don't want anyone else to see, it's quite easy to delete files from the command line. The key to doing so is the rm command, which continues the "the less typing, the better" philosophy and stands for remove.

To remove a single file on a Linux system, you simply type the rm command followed by the name of the file. For example, to delete the file file.txt, you would do the following:

```
$ rm file.txt
```

The file is gone. Like the cp command, the rm command provides a -r recursive) option to enable you to remove entire directories. For example, to permanently remove a directory named include_test, you would issue the following command:

```
$ rm -r include_test
```

TIP You can remove empty directories using the rmdir command, but I don't find that to be a common scenario. I rarely have empty directories just sitting around, because I usually create directories to store something there. I generally use the rm -r command to delete any directory, because that way I don't have to manually delete its contents first. Your mileage may vary.

If you've moved to Ubuntu from a Microsoft Windows system, you may be painfully aware that it is almost trivial to recover files that you've deleted on a Windows system. This is because deleting a file on a Windows system initially just erases the directory entry that identifies the file or folder that you're deleting. This is not the case on a Linux system. When you delete a file or directory on a Linux system, all of the disk storage associated with the file, directory, and the contents of that directory are returned to a general list of free space that is available on your system. Although deleted files and directories can still be recovered on a Linux system, it is much harder to do so and requires the assistance of someone who really knows the details of the filesystem.

The downside of this is that you can't easily recover any files that you've deleted by mistake. To help protect yourself from accidentally deleting files, see the section later in this chapter on "Defining and Using Aliases" for information about how to permanently set up a safe version of the rm command that will ask you for confirmation before it actually removes anything.

> **TIP** All of the cp, mv, and rm commands have many more options than I've covered here. To see all of the options available for any of these commands, use the man or info commands to see the online reference information for the command that you're interested in.

Changing File and Directory Permissions

Chapter 4 introduced the idea of Linux users and groups, and also provided an initial explanation of how file and directory permissions are represented when listing the contents of files and directories. You saw the same thing earlier in this chapter when exploring the ls command's -l option. Being able to set protect files so that only certain users or groups can examine or execute them is certainly handy, but it begs the question, "How do I do that?" You can easily change file and directory permissions from graphical applications such as Nautilus by right-clicking, selecting Properties, and selecting the Permissions tab, as shown in Figure 6.8. Fortunately, changing file and directory permissions from the command line is similarly easy, and may even be easier.

FIGURE 6.8

Setting permissions in Nautilus

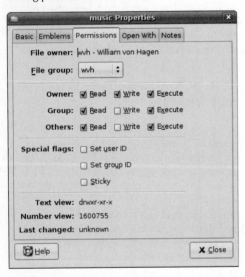

The chmod (change mode) command enables you to change any of the permissions associated with files and directories that you own. The chmod command supports two ways of setting permissions:

- Using octal values that actually represent the bits in the permission field of a file or directory.
- Using friendly letters to represent permissions for the user who owns a file or directory (u), the group with which that file or directory is associated (g), other users on the system that are not in that group (o), or all users on the system (a), and using the plus and minus signs to add or subtract permissions. This is known as changing permissions in symbolic mode.

In this section, I'll focus on the second approach because many of us may be a bit rusty working in octal, and the symbolic mode is easier to visualize and use. I'll use the file `hello.sh` as an example, which happens to be a bash command file (shell script) that simply prints the string "Hello, World!" in the shell window from which it is executed. Let's first look at its default permissions:

```
$ ls -l hello.sh
-rw-r-r-  1 wvh wvh 36 2006.03-18 16:30 hello.sh
```

As explained in detail in Chapter 4, the characters at the left portion of the `ls` command's long output describe the current file permissions. These file permissions fall into four groups: the leading dash identifies the type of object that this is (a dash means that it's just a regular file), and the remaining three groups of three characters indicate the permissions that the owner of the file (wvh) has, the groups associated with that file has (also named wvh), and the rights that all other users have to the file. In this example, we can see that I can both read and write the file, but that other members of the group wvh can only read the file, and all other users on the system can also only read the file.

Because this is a shell script, I presumably want to be able to execute it. To make the file executable by its owner (me), I would issue the following command:

```
$ chmod u+x hello.sh
```

Listing the file again, we can see that the file is now marked as being executable by its owner:

```
$ chmod u+x hello.sh
$ ls -al hello.sh
-rwxr-r-  1 wvh wvh 36 2006.03-18 16:30 hello.sh
```

If I want others in the group wvh and all other users on the system to be able execute this shell script, I could issue the following commands to make those changes and verify them:

```
$ chmod u+x hello.sh
$ ls -al hello.sh
-rwxr-xr-  1 wvh users 36 2006.03-18 16:30 hello.sh
$ chmod a+x hello.sh
$ ls -al hello.sh
-rwxr-xr-x 1 wvh users 36 2006.03-18 16:30 hello.sh
```

That's a lot of typing for a repetitive series of operations! Luckily the `chmod` command enables you to group multiple permission operations together. Suppose I wanted to remove the ability for anyone other than myself to execute this script. I could do this with the following single command:

```
$ chmod go-x hello.sh
$ ls -l hello.sh
-rwxr-r-  1 wvh users 36 2006.03-18 16:30 hello.sh
```

Note that I used o, which means anyone who is not in the group wvh, rather than a, which means all users on the system, because all users on the system would include me.

You can add or remove read and write permissions for any supported permission group using the `chmod` command and similar options. Files and permissions have the same meanings for directories as they do for file, with the exception of the executable bit, which for directories grants permission to search that directory. For example, you can create a directory that no one but you can read, but still enable people to execute programs or shell scripts that it contains by removing read permission (`r`), but making sure that search permission (`x`) is still set. People won't be able to see what's in the directory, but they can execute scripts or programs that it contains if they know their exact names.

> **TIP** On a related subject, you can use the chown (change owner) and chgrp (change group) commands to change the owner and group of a file, but that's a privileged operation that you must do using sudo, and is a relatively rare task unless you're working as a system administrator. The online reference pages for these commands explain how to run them and provide a good number of examples.

Finding Commands That Do Specific Things

The command line is a pretty friendly place to execute commands if you know what you're doing and know what command to do it with. Unfortunately, given the Linux tendency to avoid typing long command names by dropping extra characters from their names, it's often hard to figure out what command you want to use to do a specific task.

Luckily, the Linux online manual command, man, provides a truly convenient keyword search option (-k) that automatically searches for a specified keyword or phrase in the description fields of each man page. For example, supposed that you didn't know about the chmod command, and wanted to see a list of commands that has something to do with file permissions. You could look for appropriate commands using the following command:

```
$ man -k permissions
chmod (1)                  - change file access permissions
```

Note that this can be tricky, because just like a Web search, you have to look for the right phrase. However, at least the possibility is always there. You can search for single words or quoted strings to try to refine the list of commands that match what you're looking for.

If your man -k output lists a command but you can't seem to execute the command (you see the message "command not found" when you try to execute it), this means that the directory where that command is stored isn't one of the directories where you ordinarily look for commands. In that case, you can try using the whereis command to locate that command, as in the following example:

```
$ man -k "physical volume"
pvchange (8)          - change attributes of a physical volume
pvdisplay (8)         - display attributes of a physical volume
pvremove (8)          - remove a physical volume
pvs (8)               - report information about physical volumes
pvscan (8)            - scan all disks for physical volumes
vgextend (8)          - add physical volumes to a volume group

$ pvscan
bash: pvscan: command not found

$ whereis pvscan
pvscan: /sbin/pvscan /usr/share/man/man8/pvscan.8.gz
```

The whereis command tells you where the command is located (and where its documentation is found). You can then execute that command by specifying the full pathname of the executable, which in this case is /sbin/pvscan.

Working with the Bash Shell

Now that you've started a shell and learned some of the commands that you want to run from the command line, it's time to explore some of the cooler aspects of working with and configuring the bash shell. Obviously, you could simply type commands at the command prompt to your heart's content, but the bash shell provides many nice features that make it easy to use and are well worth taking advantage of. Some of these features can save a significant amount of time, typing, and typos when executing the same command over and over, when executing a group of similar commands, when typing the names of long commands, complex filenames as arguments to commands, and so on.

Using Command History

All Linux shells provide a history mechanism, which is a way of recalling and reexecuting commands that you have previously executed. To see the list of recently executed commands, you can simply type `history` at any shell prompt, which displays something like the following:

```
$ history
231  make distclean
232  ../gcc/configure —enable-threads
233  make bootstrap
234  info -f gcc.info
235  export INFOPATH=`pwd`:$INFOPATH
236  vi ~/.bashrc
237  pushd ~/new
237  ls /mnt/terastation/CDs
238  pushd /mnt/terastation/CDs
239  find . -name "T*.txt"
240  find . -name "T*.txt" -exec rm {} \;
250  rar x ../United_Empire_Loyalists.rar
[much more output deleted]
```

You'll have to trust me that this list contains a recording of a certain number of the commands that I have executed on my system, The number of commands that the history mechanism records is identified by the HISTSIZE environment variable. (The section on "Using Environment Variables" later in this chapter provides information about setting and displaying the values of environment variables.)

There are several different ways of recalling or reexecuting commands:

- using the shell's built-in `fc` command
- using the shell's mechanism for interacting with the commands that you have typed (known as the *readline library*) to scroll backward through the history list from the command-line
- using the exclamation point to identify the command that you want to display and re-execute

I generally use one of the last two mechanisms, so I'll focus on those here.

You can redisplay any recently executed command by typing the `Control-p` command at any command prompt. Each time you type `Control-p`, the shell displays the previous command in its history list. When you find the command that you want to reexecute, you can simply press Return to reexecute it or edit that command using emacs commands such as `Control-b` to move backward one character in that command,

`Control-f` to move forward in that command one character, the backspace and delete keys to delete the previous and current characters, and so on.

Obviously, if the command that you want to reexecute is far back in your command history list, scrolling back through a few hundred commands can be a bit tedious. In this case, you can use the exclamation point to identify a particular command from the history list in one of the following ways:

- **Identifying a command by its sequence number:** Each command in the history list is preceded by its sequence number in your command history. If you've displayed the history list and can see the command that you want to execute, you can reexecute a specific command by typing an exclamation mark followed by its sequence number. For example, using the history output displayed earlier in this section, the command `!236` would reexecute the `vi ~/.bashrc` command.

- **Identifying a command by name:** You can reexecute the most recently executed command that begins with a certain command name by typing an exclamation mark followed by the name of the command that you want to reexecute. For example. using the history output displayed earlier in this section, the command `!vi` would reexecute the `vi ~/.bashrc` command.

> **TIP** If you want to redisplay a previous command and edit it before reexecuting it, you can use the history mechanism's `:p` modifier to simply print the command without executing it. You can then type `control-p` to redisplay that command, edit it however you wish, and then press Return to execute the modified command.

If you've already executed several similar commands, you can narrow down the list of those shown by the history command by displaying only commands that contain a certain substring. For example, the command `history | grep vi` uses a pipe and the `grep` command to only display lines of output from the history command that contain the string "vi." (See the section "Pipes and Input and Output Redirection" later in this chapter for more information about connecting different commands in this way.)

The Bash shell's command-line history mechanism is extremely powerful, and this discussion only scratches the surface of the zillions of ways that you can save yourself typing by recalling and updating previously executed command. For all of the gory details on the shell's command-line history mechanism, use the `info bash` command to display the current online help for the bash command.

Using Command and Filename Completion

As you've seen throughout this chapter, the command line provides a very powerful, flexible mechanism for executing commands, but one of the goals of all Unix and Linux developers seems to have been to type as few characters as possible in order to execute commands. This gave us cryptic commands like `ls` and `pwd`, but has probably saved wear and tear on thousands of keyboards over the years.

This same "type as little as possible" philosophy extends to the shell in a variety of ways. One of the most useful is the use of the tab key to help the shell match and display commands and filenames. Pressing the tab key while typing the name of a command will cause the shell to expand the name of that command as uniquely as possible. For example, because I use the emacs text editor for almost all activities related to text files (see Chapter 7, "Working with Text Files on Ubuntu," for a discussion of my love affair with emacs), I type commands like "emacs `this_is_the_name_of_a_file.txt`" a few hundred times a day. In true Linux fashion, I can save myself a few characters of typing by typing "ema" on the command –line, and then pressing the Tab key. This displays the first matching command, which happens to be `emacs`, and I can then press a space and enter the name of the file that I want to edit.

But wait, there's more! The Tab key will also match and insert the names of filenames. For example, if I were indeed trying to edit a file called "`this_is_the_name_of_a_file.txt`", I could type the first few characters of its name and press the Tab key to (hopefully) match and insert the complete filename so that all I'd have to do is press return to begin editing the file. This is a more common use of the Tab key than completing the names of commands since, as we've seen throughout this chapter, the names of Linux commands tend to be short. On the other hand, they are cryptic, so if you don't remember the exact spelling of the command that you want to execute, the Tab key can often help you figure it out.

Pressing the Tab key matches as much of the name of a command or file as it can. If multiple commands or filenames match what you've typed before you press the Tab key, pressing Tab will have no effect, because the shell can't tell which of the possible commands or filenames you mean. In this case, you can press the Tab key twice (quickly) to cause the shell to list all of the available matches. You can then type the additional few characters that are required to uniquely identify the command or filename that you're actually interested in.

Using Wildcards

Another example of the "type as little as possible" philosophy is the ability of the shell to identify groups of files whose names match certain patterns. The characters used to define those patterns are known as *wildcards*, because they can match any single or multiple group of characters. The shell supports four primary types of wildcards:

- ?: (question mark) which matches any single character
- *: (asterisk) which matches any group of characters
- {string1, string2}: (curly bracket) which represents either string1 or string2
- [char1,char2,...]: (square bracket) which matches any character or range of characters inside the square brackets

These wildcards can be extremely handy when working with directories containing multiple files with similar names. Consider the following directory containing a number of audio files in different formats:

```
$ ls
d1t01.flac    d1t04.flac    d1t07.flac    d1t10.flac    d2t02.flac
d1t01.mp3     d1t04.mp3     d1t07.mp3     d1t10.mp3     d2t02.mp3
d1t01.wav     d1t04.wav     d1t07.wav     d1t10.wav     d2t02.wav
d1t02.flac    d1t05.flac    d1t08.flac    d1t11.flac    d2t03.flac
d1t02.mp3     d1t05.mp3     d1t08.mp3     d1t11.mp3     d2t03.mp3
d1t02.wav     d1t05.wav     d1t08.wav     d1t11.wav     d2t03.wav
d1t03.flac    d1t06.flac    d1t09.flac    d2t01.flac    Horslips info.txt
d1t03.mp3     d1t06.mp3     d1t09.mp3     d2t01.mp3     playlist.m3u
d1t03.wav     d1t06.wav     d1t09.wav     d2t01.wav
```

You'll note that these filenames follow a certain convention, which in this case is disc <number> track <number>.format. To list just the MP3 files in this directory that are the first track on a given disc, you could type the following:

```
$ ls d?t01.mp3
d1t01.mp3   d2t01.mp3
```

This uses the question mark to represent the disc number, which is a single digit in my sample filenames.

Similarly, to list all of the MP3 files in this directory, you could use the asterisk to represent any matching filename with the `.mp3` file extension, as in the following example:

```
$ ls *.mp3
d1t01.mp3  d1t03.mp3  d1t05.mp3  d1t07.mp3  d1t09.mp3  d1t11.mp3
d2t02.mp3
d1t02.mp3  d1t04.mp3  d1t06.mp3  d1t08.mp3  d1t10.mp3  d2t01.mp3
d2t03.mp3
```

Assume that you want to list just the files with extensions that are either `flac` or `wav`. You could do this using the curly bracket wildcard in the following command:

```
$ ls *.{flac,wav}
d1t01.flac  d1t03.wav  d1t06.flac  d1t08.wav  d1t11.flac  d2t02.wav
d1t01.wav   d1t04.flac  d1t06.wav   d1t09.flac  d1t11.wav   d2t03.flac
d1t02.flac  d1t04.wav  d1t07.flac  d1t09.wav  d2t01.flac  d2t03.wav
d1t02.wav   d1t05.flac  d1t07.wav   d1t10.flac  d2t01.wav
d1t03.flac  d1t05.wav  d1t08.flac  d1t10.wav  d2t02.flac
```

Finally, suppose that you want to list all of the seventh and eighth songs in MP3 format from the first disc in this directory. You could do this using the square bracket wildcard, as in the following example:

```
$ ls d1t0[78].mp3
d1t07.mp3  d1t08.mp3
```

You can combine any of these wildcards to identify increasingly specific sets of files. For example, the following would identify just the seventh and eighth songs from the first disk that are in `flac` and `wav` format:

```
$ ls d1t0[78].{flac,wav}
d1t07.flac  d1t07.wav  d1t08.flac  d1t08.wav
```

The bash shell provides a very powerful wildcard mechanism. Wildcards such as these are especially useful when attempting to move, copy, or delete specific groups of files.

> **TIP**   If you're used to wildcards on other types of systems, be careful, Linux wildcards may not work exactly the same way. For example, on some systems, you can type something like `ren *.txt *.foo` to rename groups of files with the `.txt` extension to files with the same base filename but with the `.foo` extension. This will not work on a Linux system because wildcards are expended before the command is executed, and the `*.foo` portion of the command line wouldn't match anything, because no files with that extension currently exist.

Pipes and Input and Output Redirection

As discussed in Chapter 1, a core element of the basic philosophy of Unix, and therefore Linux, is that utilities should do one thing and do it well. This avoids a lot of duplicate code by enabling one command to process the output produced by another command. For example, you might want to find the number of files in a directory by listing the files in a directory, and then counting the number of outlines. One easy way to do this is to write the output of the `ls` command to a temporary file, and then counting the number of lines in that temporary file using the Linux `wc -1` command. Linux makes it easy to write the output of a command to a file by using what is called output redirection, which is represented on the command line by the greater-than symbol ('>'). As an example, the following command writes the output of the `ls` command to the temporary file `/tmp/my_dir_list.txt`:

```
$ ls > /tmp/my_dir_list.txt
```

I could then count the number of lines in that file using the wc -l command, as in the following example:

```
$ wc -l /tmp/my_dir_list.txt
8
```

There are apparently eight files in my current directory. However, using a temporary file required some extra typing and also requires that you clean up after yourself. Luckily, Linux comes to the rescue again with the notion of using a special symbol, the vertical bar, to connect the output of one command to the input of another. This symbol ('|') is known as a *pipe*. You could use a pipe to avoid the temporary file and get the same results by typing a command like the following:

```
$ ls | wc -l
8
```

If you find yourself performing many command-line operations, you will find both the output redirection and pipe concepts to be very convenient. Redirecting output is an easy way of keeping track of the contents of files and directories, recording system information, and so on.

An even more interesting use of output redirection is its ability to append some amount of information to an existing file. In the previous example, using a single greater-than symbol creates a file if it doesn't exist, but overwrites the contents of that file if it already exists. You may want to append to an existing file rather than completely overwriting it, which you can easily do by using two greater-than signs rather than a single one, as in the following example:

```
$ ls > /tmp/my_dir_list.txt
$ ls >> /tmp/my_dir_list.txt
$ wc -l /tmp/my_dir_list.txt
16
```

As you can see, the temporary file now contains twice as many lines, which is what you'd expect because you wrote the same eight lines to it twice.

The Bash shell also support input redirection, which is the ability to read data from a file and use that file as input to another command. For complete information on input redirection and redirection in general, see the online help for the Bash shell. You'll find that you use output redirection and pipes much more often than input redirection, but you never know...

Introducing Job Control

Throughout this chapter, you've always executed commands at the shell prompt, and then waited for them to finish. That's fine for commands that are relatively quick, but what about command that run for a long time? The bash shell provides a nice solution for this sort of thing by enabling you to start commands but run them in what is known as the background. This enables you to type a command, indicate that it should run in the background, and that command will continue to execute even though the shell prompt is redisplayed in your current shell window. For example, suppose that you want to use the emacs text editor to edit the file myfile.txt, but also want to be able to use you current xterm or GNOME Terminal window while emacs was running in its own window on the screen. To start a command in the background, you simply follow its name with an ampersand, as in the following example:

```
$ emacs myfile.txt &
[1] 7539
```

Starting a command in the background is known in Linux-speak as starting a background job, and causes the shell to display two bits of information:

- the job number (inside square brackets)
- the process ID of the process that was started to run your command

The job number is useful because it is possible to run multiple commands in the background at the same time. The job number therefore provides a unique way of identifying any particular background command. The job number is an identifier for that background job within the context of your current shell. The process identifier is a unique identifier for that process in terms of your entire Ubuntu system.

Why care about identifying these processes? Primarily so that you can either terminate them or wake them up if something goes wrong. For example, suppose that you accidentally started a command in the background, but that command actually requires interactive input. To bring a background command back to the foreground (meaning that it is interactively running in the current shell), you can simply refer to it by using a percent symbols and its job number, as in the following example:

```
$ %1
```

This would bring the emacs command back to the foreground so that anything you typed in the shell is actively sent to the command. Suppose, however, that you've lost your emacs window on the screen and simply want to terminate the background job manually. You can do this by using the Linux `kill` command, providing the job number to identify the job that you want to terminate, as in the following example:

```
$ kill %1
```

Knowing not only the job number for a background process but its system-wide process identifier enables you to use the `kill` command to terminate a process from another shell. Because job numbers are unique to a specific shell, you can use the `kill` command to terminate a process by process ID from any shell or terminal session, as in the following example:

```
$ kill 7539
```

Being able to execute long-running commands in the background is very important in today's multiwindowed graphical environments, because you usually want to be able to continue to use your current shell while the long-running command continues on its merry way.

As always, job control is much more flexible and powerful than the introduction given here describes. For complete information on job control, use the `info` command to see the online reference information for the bash shell.

Exploring the Bash Configuration File

When you start a bash shell on your Ubuntu system, it reads a certain amount of configuration information from various text files on your system. In the order they're read, these configuration files are the following:

- `/etc/profile` (login shells only)
- `/etc/bash.bashrc` (all bash shells)
- `~/.bash_profile` (login shells only)
- `~/.bashrc` (all bash shells)

NOTE   The ~ symbol is a bash shortcut for referring to any user's home directory. ~/.bashrc is the file .bashrc in my home directory; ~juser/.bashrc is a reference to the user juser's home directory.

The first two of these are shell initialization files that are read and incorporated when any user logs in on the system (`/etc/profile`) or starts a bash shell (`/etc/bash.bashrc`). The second two are personal configuration files that are stored in each user's home directory. Like the system-wide configuration files, the `~/.bash_profile` file is read by the user's login shell, while the `~/.bashrc` file is read by any shell that the user creates, such as in an `xterm` or GNOME Terminal window. Of these, the `.bashrc` file is most important for two reasons:

- The default `~/.bash_profile` on Ubuntu systems reads it even in the context of a login shell.
- Starting a bash shell is a much more common operation than logging in. A user only logs in once, though he or she may subsequently create many different `xterms` or GNOME Terminal windows.

The `.bashrc` file enables each user to customize various aspects of the bash shell, such as where it looks for commands, the prompt that it displays, the number of commands that it remembers in your command-line history, and many more things. The `.bashrc` file enables you to create your own shortcuts to specific Linux commands if you still feel that you're having to type too many characters and even enables you to create your custom shell commands. Lines in any bash configuration file (or shell script, for that matter) that begin with the hash mark (#) are considered to be comments and are not interpreted.

> **TIP** All Linux shells provide a command language, constructs for looping, and support conditional expressions to make it easy to write shell scripts. Explaining shell programming is outside the scope of this introduction, but there are many excellent books and Web sites on that topic. Two of my favorite Web sites for this sort of information are the Linux Shell Scripting Tutorial at www.freeos.com/guides/lsst/ and the Linux Documentation project's Advanced Shell Scripting Guide at www.tldp.org/LDP/abs/html.

When a user account is created on your Ubuntu system, the default `.bashrc` and `.bash_profile` files are created by copying them from the templates with the same names that are stored in the directory `/etc/skel`. The following is the beginning of the default `.bashrc` file used for all Ubuntu user accounts:

```
# ~/.bashrc: executed by bash(1) for non-login shells.
#
# If not running interactively, don't do anything
[ -z "$PS1" ] && return
[much more text deleted]
```

The last statement in this example stops shells from reading the default `.bashrc` file if they are not running in interactive mode. It does this by using the [command to test the value of the PS1 environment variable, which defines the user's prompt, and to return to the parent shell if this variable is not set (which it would not be in the context of a shell used to run a shell script).

What's an environment variable? I'm glad you asked.

Using Environment Variables

Environment variables are variables that are defined in the context of a shell and which are read and used by applications on your system, including the shell itself. One of the most commonly used environment variables is the PATH environment variables, which contains a colon-separated list of directories that the shell searches (in order) to try to find commands. You can examine the environment variables that are defined in a shell using any of three mechanisms:

- using the shell's built-in `set` command to display all shell variables that are currently defined
- using the `printenv` command to display a list of selected (or all) environment variables that are currently defined

- using the shell's built-in `echo` command to display the value of a specific environment variable

Both the `set` and `printenv` command produce large amounts of output, so the `echo` command is most commonly used to display the value of a single environment variable, as in the following example:

```
$ echo $PATH
/home/wvh/bin:/usr/local/Adobe/Acrobat7.0/bin:/usr/local/gcc_svn/bin:\
/home/wvh/BitTorrent/src/BitTorrent:/home/wvh/cxoffice/bin:\
/usr/lib/mit/bin:/usr/lib/mit/sbin:/usr/NX/bin:/usr/local/sbin:\
/usr/local/bin:/usr/sbin:/usr/bin:/sbin:/bin:/usr/bin/X11:/usr/games:
```

 **The value of the PATH environment variable is a single string containing colon-separated directories. This example has been split across multiple lines for formatting purposes.**

When using the `echo` command to display the value of an environment variable, you must refer to the environment variable by preceding its name with a dollar sign (`$`). This tells the shell to echo the value of a variable rather than simply echoing a string, which is what would happen if you simply typed the following:

```
$ echo PATH
PATH
```

This example of the PATH environment variable has been heavily customized. The default setting for the PATH environment variable on Ubuntu systems is actually the following:

```
/usr/local/sbin:/usr/local/bin:/usr/sbin:/usr/bin:/sbin:/bin:\
/usr/bin/X11:/usr/games
```

To add a directory to the list of directories that are searched for commands, you can execute something like the following from a shell prompt:

```
$ export PATH=/usr/wvh/bin:$PATH
```

This command sets the environment variable and exports it to the general shell environment. This example adds my personal bin directory as the first element of my PATH, so that the shell looks there first for any commands that I try to execute. To make this change permanent, I would add this line to the end of my `~/.bashrc` file.

The echo command is useful for displaying the value of a single environment variable. You can also use the `printenv` command to do the same thing, as in the following example:

```
$ printenv PATH
/home/wvh/bin:/usr/local/Adobe/Acrobat7.0/bin:/usr/local/gcc_svn/bin:\
/home/wvh/BitTorrent/src/BitTorrent:/home/wvh/cxoffice/bin:\
/usr/lib/mit/bin:/usr/lib/mit/sbin:/usr/NX/bin:/usr/local/sbin:\
/usr/local/bin:/usr/sbin:/usr/bin:/sbin:/bin:/usr/bin/X11:/usr/games:
```

Because the `printenv` command is designed to display environment variables, you do not need to precede the name of the environment variable with a dollar sign.

The `printenv` and `set` commands are more commonly used to display the values of all environment variables that are currently defined. You can then search for a certain substring by piping their output to the `grep` command, as in the following example:

```
$ printenv | grep HIST
HISTCONTROL=ignoreboth
```

```
HISTFILE=/home/wvh/.bash_history
HISTFILESIZE=1000
HISTSIZE=1000
```

This sample command shows me the name and value of all environment variables that contain the string HIST, which are environment variables related to the shell's command-line history mechanism (discussed earlier in this chapter).

Defining and Using Aliases

Another interesting feature of the bash shell is its ability to enable you to define aliases for various commands. An alias is a string that the shell recognizes and expands into some other command. Some of the most common aliases used on Linux systems are aliases for the cp and rm commands that automatically execute those commands with their interactive option, which prevents you from accidentally overwriting or deleting files that you didn't want to by prompting you to confirm each operation. These aliases are defined in the following way at the bash command line (or, permanently, in your ~/.bashrc file):

```
$ alias cp="cp -i"
$ alias rm="rm -i"
```

After defining these aliases, the shell automatically replaces either the cp or rm commands with the command that it has been aliased to.

To simplify defining aliases (and to minimize the number of changes that you make to your ~/.bashrc file), the default ~/.bashrc file used on Ubuntu system contains the following entries, which are initially commented out:

```
#if [ -f ~/.bash_aliases ]; then
#    . ~/.bash_aliases
#fi
```

If uncommented by removing the leading hash marks, this clause enables you to define all of your aliases in a file called ~/.bash_aliases, which would be located in your home directory.

Summary

This chapter introduced you to the Linux command line, the terminology used when discussing Linux command-line interpreters, and the basic capabilities of the bash shell, the command-line interpreter that is used by default on Ubuntu Linux systems. It discussed how to access a shell on your Ubuntu system and some of the more common commands that most people execute within a command-line environment. It concluded with an explanation of the configuration files used by the bash shell and some of the more common items that they contain.

Hand in hand with the idea of working from a command line is the notion of working with text files, which is discussed in Chapter 7. Though many word processors store their files in special binary formats nowadays, text files are alive and well on the Internet and on Linux systems. Documents written using markup languages such as HTML, SGML, and XML are all text files and are easily created and edited in a standard text editor. Most Linux servers, including those discussed in the last few chapters of this book, are configured by setting or changing operational parameters that are stored in text-format configuration files. For these reasons and many more, learning how to use a text editor is a fundamental Linux skill.

Chapter 7

Working with Text Files on Ubuntu

Most of us are used to working with files in various application-specific formats, often identified by their file extension or a special icon on your graphical desktop. We're all familiar with the doc files produced by graphical word processors such as Microsoft Word, pdf files used by Adobe Acrobat and other PDF readers, xls files produced by spreadsheets such as Excel, fm files produced by FrameMaker, ppt files produced by PowerPoint, and so on. All of these files contain application data in a specific, often binary, format that lets the associated application make the best possible use of these files, but which often makes them hard to use with any application other than the one that created them.

At the other end of the spectrum from these application-specific files is the lowest-common-denominator file format known as text files or, to be a bit more specific, *ASCII text* files. The contents of these files consist of only the standard letters, numbers, punctuation, and symbols that you find on a computer keyboard. The nice thing about these types of files is that they are easy to read, easy to process, and easy to work with in general.

Regardless of what you use your Ubuntu Linux system for, you will almost certainly end up editing a text file one of these days. If you write code, it is almost certainly in standard ASCII text files because they provide a lowest-common-denominator format that can be processed by any compiler. If you're a writer, you may want to work with text files because you can work with them on any system, with any editor or word processor — so you can work on them just as easily on your Ubuntu Linux system as you can on your Mac OS X system.

An even more critical point is that most system-level Linux utilities use one or more files to hold their configuration and initialization information. Even though most Linux utilities can also be configured using a graphical interface, editing a text file is often faster and simpler than locating and starting the right graphical tool, finding the correct tab or panel, and so on.

This chapter begins by briefly describing the history of editors on Unix systems and the religious war over the "right" approach to editing text that still rages on in Linux/Unix circles today. It then provides detailed information about using vi and emacs, the two primary editors used on Linux systems, and tosses in an introduction to ed, a fast, simple, and minimal editor that is perfect for quick text file changes. The chapter concludes by discussing gedit, a graphical text editor provided in the GNOME environment that walks the line between pure text and graphical editing.

Introduction to Linux Text Editors

The first versions of Unix for the PPD-11 that were distributed by Bell Telephone Laboratories included a small, line-oriented text editor call ed, which was written by Ken Thompson. Various people enhanced ed, most notably George Coulouris at Queen Mary College (QMC) in the UK, who added interactive support for editing single lines as part of his em editor (editor for mortals), which he brought with him to the University of California at Berkeley (UCB) in 1976. At the same time, Ken Thompson had gone to UCB to teach for a year or so, and while there had begun working with Bill Joy and Chuck Haley on the Unix enhancements that would eventually make up the original Berkeley Standard Distribution (BSD).

Haley and Joy hacked em for a while, revising it into en and then a bunch of other names, working their way through the alphabet until the arrived at ex, which was still line-oriented. In 1976, however, Joy created vi (which stands for Visual), a screen-oriented editor that shared the ex command set, thanks to motivation provided by a number of ADM-3A terminals which were donated to UCB. The flexibility provided by vi in terms of using the entire screen thanks to the /etc/termcap (terminal capabilities) file was a huge step in divorcing detailed knowledge about the hardware from an editor, and editing under Unix has never been the same.

Around the same time, on the other side of the country, a bunch of Lisp and ITS/TOPS-20/TWENEX hackers at the MIT Artificial Intelligence (AI) Lab were enhancing an aging line editor for their PDP-10 systems known as Text Editor and Corrector (TECO). With some inspiration from graphical editing work being done at Stanford's AI Lab, Richard Stallman (later of GNU and FSF fame) and Guy Steele collected and developed a version of TECO to which users could add their own commands, and created and aggregated a set of TECO commands into a single package that provided support for screen-oriented editing using TECO. The TECO commands consisted of a set of macros (sequences of commands that execute together), so the set of macros became known as *Editing MACroS*, or more simply, *EMACS*.

This was all well and good if you happen to be using a DEC PDP-10, and emacs would be an interesting footnote were it not for the efforts of Dave Conroy, who wrote a version of emacs called MicroEmacs that ran on just about anything, and James Gosling (later of Java fame), who wrote a version of emacs for Unix systems in 1981. Unlike the EMACS macros that were their inspiration, these were actual compiled programs that ran directly on specific systems as compiled binaries. Gosling's version of emacs, cleverly named Gosling emacs or simply gosmacs, served as the original foundation for an open source version of emacs for Unix from none other than Richard Stallman, who began writing GNU emacs in 1984. For legal reasons, Stallman eventually replaced all of the Gosling emacs code in GNU emacs, and replaced Gosling's MockLisp emacs configuration language with a full-blown internal Lisp interpreter to parse configuration files and other startup data.

NOTE   Over the years, several alternative expansions of the EMACS acronym have been offered to replace the original Editing MACroS. Some of my favorites are "Escape Meta Alt Control Shift," referring to emacs' heavy dependence on the Control and Escape keys in its command set, and "Eight Megabytes and Constantly Swapping," which was funnier when 8MB was a lot of memory for a computer, and referred to its large memory requirements (for the time). Today, I think that my garage door opener has 8MB of memory.

Modal vs. Modeless Editors

As mentioned earlier in this chapter, among Linux and Unix users, there is no more entertaining or more long-running flame war than the debate over which editor is better: vi or emacs. If all of the characters expended on this topic alone had been given instead to random monkey typists, they would have indeed produced the works of Shakespeare. As a new Ubuntu fan, you'll eventually hear something about this, so this sidebar gives you a little background.

The basic difference between how you use vi and emacs boils down to the following: emacs is what is known as a *modeless editor*, which means that any standard characters that you type are always inserted into whatever you're editing (which is therefore known as *insert mode*), while vi is what is known as a *modal editor* in which insert mode is just one available mode. Both emacs and vi are extremely configurable, though vi doesn't provide an internal implementation of Lisp to "simplify" creating your own functions. On the other hand, because vi doesn't provide an internal implementation of Lisp, it is much smaller and faster to execute than emacs. Emacs is more powerful because it includes a mail client, newsgroup reader, and even a few games. On the other hand, you may just be looking for a text editor, not a one-stop-shopping computing environment.

People often complain that vi and emacs are hard for new users to learn. In my experience, it just depends where you want new users to get confused. In emacs, the chances of figuring out that you hold down the Control key, and then press a particular two-key combination to save your file and exit are pretty small. However, vi rarely does anything useful until you enter insert mode, and trying to get out of insert mode and figuring out how to save your file has brought many a Linux/Unix novice to tears.

Here's my take: I have used versions of emacs since gosmacs, and I am writing this book in emacs. My fingers work that way. However, I use vi regularly when I'm performing most system tasks and especially when I'm sitting down at someone else's machine for the first time. Why? Because vi starts more quickly than emacs, but primarily because emacs fans often extensively customize their emacs key bindings. The key sequence that justifies a paragraph on my system might post a random snapshot to the alt.binaries newsgroup if I type it on your system. Your mileage may vary.

If you're interested in more details on the history of editing text on Unix systems (and thus on Linux), some great links are the following:

- ed History (and more): www.english.uga.edu/hc/unixhistory.html (from Peter H. Salus, *A Quarter Century of UNIX*; Reading, MA: Addison-Wesley, 1994).
- George Colouris on em: www.dcs.qmul.ac.uk/~george/history/.
- Bill Joy Interview: www.cs.pdx.edu/~kirkenda/joy84.html (originally printed in the August 1984 issue of *Unix Review* magazine).
- The Lemacs/FSFmacs Schism: www.jwz.org/doc/lemacs.html.

Using vi

Because the actual source code for the "real" version of vi is owned by AT&T, vi fans have completely rewritten vi from the ground up. Two popular vi clones are available today: nvi (new vi) and vim (vi improved). The version of vi used on Linux systems is vim, but nvi is quite popular and is the default version of vi used on many open source BSD-like systems such as OpenBSD, FreeBSD, and so on. Throughout this section, I'll generally refer to vim as vi because it is indeed compatible with vi, and the package that installs vim on your Ubuntu system also installs an alias for vim called vi — and vim is, after all, just vi, *improved*. In any sections that are specific to vim and do not apply to vi in general, I'll refer to vim explicitly.

> **TIP** Although this book is an excellent source of information about using vim, so is vim itself. The default vim installation comes with an application called `vimtutor`, which starts vim with a copy of a tutorial on using vim. If you want to actually walk through many examples of using vi and get a feel for its command set, the `vimtutor` is an excellent starting point.

As discussed in the previous section, vi is a modal editor (which, if you skipped the previous section, means that the same keys do different things depending on the mode that you're in). The primary vi modes are the following:

- **Normal:** vi is in normal mode when you first start vi. In this mode you can enter all of the standard cursor movement and text deletion commands, but not enter text into the file that you are editing. This is the primary source of confusion for new vi users, because most people expect to start an editor and begin editing text.

- **Insert:** In this mode, typing the standard alphanumeric and symbol keys on your keyboard enters those characters into the file that you are editing. Insert mode is the mode that most people expect to be in when you start a text editor. The fact that once in insert mode, you need to press a special key (the Escape key) to return to command mode, is the second primary source of confusion for new vi users who find themselves trapped in insert mode.

- **Command-line:** In this mode, the cursor is positioned at the bottom line of your vi window, and you can enter a single line that is interpreted as a vi command, search request, or a request to invoke an external command on a portion of the file that you are editing (often referred to as a *filter* command).

The modal editor concept may initially seem confusing, but it makes vi a fast, extremely powerful editor. Once you learn how to get from one mode to another and work with vi for a while, you will find it to be an excellent editor. The fact that some version of vi is found on every Unix-like system makes it well worth your time to learn.

One of the coolest features of vi is the ability to preface most vi commands with a numeric argument, movement, or scoping command, which executes that single command the specified number of times, the number of times specified by the movement command that you've specified, or applies a command to a specified portion of your file. I'll provide examples of this throughout the rest of this section, as well as some of the favorite vi tips and tricks that I've accumulated over the years.

> **NOTE** All of the examples in the vi portions of this chapter show vi in an `xterm` window rather than the GNOME Terminal to emphasize that vi is a command-line application that does not provide or use menus by default. For information on graphical versions of vi that do provide and use menus, see "Graphical Versions of vi" later in this chapter.

Starting and Exiting vi

The core tasks for any application are how to start it and how to get out of it. As mentioned previously, getting out of vi the first time can be tricky because of its modal nature, but after that, it becomes second nature.

Because vi is a command-line application, you usually start it by simply typing the vi command in a GNOME Terminal or `xterm` window. You can optionally provide the name of the file that you want to edit on the command line, and vi will automatically open and display that file for you. Figure 7.1 shows vi editing the text of this chapter in an `xterm` window.

An xterm window showing the vi editor

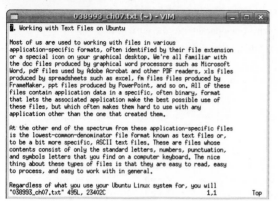

You can exit vi and return to the command prompt in several ways, but you first have to be in vi's normal mode to do so. If you are editing a file and want to return to normal mode, simply press Escape. If the key sequence ^[displays in the file that you're editing, press Escape again. You can then exit from vi in the following ways:

- To exit unconditionally without saving any changes, type the :q! or ZQ commands. The :q command is the standard quit command, which will complain if you have made changes to the current file and have not saved them. The :q! command essentially means "Yes, I really want to quit and I know what I'm doing."

- To save any changes that you've made to the current file and exit, type the :x or :wq commands. The :x command is specific to vim, while the :wq command is the traditional vi exit mechanism (it stands for "write and then quit"). You can also write any changes to the current file and exit by typing the ZZ command (no colon required).

- To specify the name of the file that you want to save your changes to, type the :w filename command, where filename is the name of the file that you want to create. If the file already exists, you will have to use the :w! filename command which, loosely translated, means "Yes, I really want to write this file and I know what I'm doing."

Inserting Text in vi

Once you've started vi, you'll certainly want to start creating the program, letter, or other document that you're working on. As mentioned in the previous section, starting vi leaves you in normal mode, where you can move the cursor and enter commands, but not actually enter text.

To begin inserting text, type the i command. This causes vi to enter insert mode. Any characters that you type will be inserted into the file that you are editing until you exit from insert mode. As a reminder, the easiest way to exit from insert mode is by pressing the Escape key on your keyboard.

Using the i command begins inserting text at the current cursor position, which can be awkward. If you want to begin adding text immediately after the current cursor position, use the a command. To begin appending text after the end of the current line, use the A command. The a and A are just specialized commands for entering insert mode at a specific point — to exit insert mode after using these commands, press the Escape key.

Moving Around in vi

The vi editor is knee-deep in cursor movement commands. The most common are the following:

- h or left-arrow: Move the cursor backward one character in the current line.
- l or right-arrow: Move the cursor forward one character in the current line.
- j or down-arrow: Move the cursor down one line, maintaining the current column position in the new line when possible.
- k or up-arrow: Move the cursor up one line, maintaining the current column position in the new line when possible.

Cursor movement commands such as h, j, k, and l may initially seem pretty strange, but remember that vi was originally designed to be used on terminals, some of which didn't have the arrow keys. Ask your grandfather.

> **TIP**   When in insert mode, the old-time vi cursor movement commands (h, j, k, and l) insert those letters rather than moving the cursor. (vi is a modal editor, remember?) However, the arrow cursor movement keys "do the right thing" when you're in insert mode — they simply move the cursor but leave you in insert mode.

As mentioned previously, you can repeat these simple cursor movement commands a specific number of times by prefacing them with a numeric argument. For example, you can move the cursor forward five letters by typing 5l, up five lines by typing 5k, and so on. This is handy, but requires that you count how far you want to move the cursor first. That's somewhat tedious when you really want to do things like move to the next word, move to the previous word, or (more commonly) go to some logical place in the current text. To simplify things, vi provides handy cursor movement commands like the following:

- b: Move backward one word.
- w: Move forward one word.
- ^: Move to the beginning of the current line.
- $: Move to the end of the current line.
- (: Move to the beginning of the current sentence.
-): Move to the end of the current sentence.
- {: Move to the beginning of the current paragraph.
- }: Move to the end of the current paragraph.
- 1G: Go to the first line in the current file.
- 0G: Go to the last line of the current file. Just pressing G in vim does the same thing, but that may not work in all versions of vi.

The last two commands are actually examples of the standard vi commands to go to a specific line, and highlight how nicely vi commands work with numeric arguments. For example, you could move to the 14th line in your file by typing the 14G command. Similarly, you could move to the end of the third paragraph from your current position by typing the 3} command.

In addition to these cursor movement commands, vi also provides several commands to enable you to scroll the screen without moving the current cursor position (unless necessary, of course). These screen movement commands are the following:

- `Control+d`: (Hold down the Control key and press the letter d.) Scroll down one screen in the current file.

- `Control+e`: (Hold down the Control key and press the letter e.) Scroll down one line in the current file.

- `Control+u`: (Hold down the Control key and press the letter u.) Scroll up one screen in the current file.

- `Control+y`: (Hold down the Control key and press the letter y.) Scroll up one line in the current file.

The `Control+d` and `Control+u` commands scroll the screen but leave the cursor at the same position on the screen (though the text underneath the cursor has changed). The `Control+e` and `Control+y` commands keep the cursor at the same position in your text until that line scrolls off the screen, at which point the current position is preserved but the text below it has changed.

Deleting and Changing Text in vi

Like most operations, there are several different commands that enable you to delete text in vi. To delete the character at the current cursor position, press the letter x. You can, of course, delete a specific number of characters by prefacing the x command with a numeric argument. For example, 14x deletes 14 characters from the current character position.

Although the x command is handy when deleting a few characters, most people think of deletion in terms like "delete the current word," "delete everything to the end of the current line," or "delete the rest of the current paragraph." To perform these sorts of action, you use the d command, followed by a cursor movement command that delimits the end of the area that should be affected by the delete operation. For example, the command dw deletes all of the text from the current cursor position to the end of the current word, d$ deletes everything from the current cursor position to the end of the current line, and d} deletes everything from current cursor position to the end of the current paragraph. If you remember, the second character of each of these commands is one of the cursor movement commands described in the previous section.

When you're editing a file, it is common to delete some text and then immediately replace it with new text. You could do that with a combination of one of the delete commands, followed by an insert or append command. To save typing, vi provides the c (change) command to do both of these things (deleting a delimited portion of your text and entering insert mode) at the same time. For example, you could use the cw command to change the text from the current cursor position to the end of the current word, the c$ command to change the text from the current cursor position to the end of the current line, and so on. When using vi's change command, you are placed in insert mode, so you must use the Escape key to return to normal mode when you're done entering text.

Cutting, Copying, and Pasting in vi

It's easy enough to cut and paste text using a graphical text editor, because a mouse-aware text editor enables you to copy and cut text with a combination of the mouse and special keyboard commands. You can, of course, do the same thing in vi, but it requires a bit more knowledge of vi internals and visualization.

Cutting text is done using the delete command (explained in the previous section), which actually just puts the text in an internal storage area (known as a buffer) from which you can subsequently paste it back in. However, the vi editor also provides the y (yank) command to copy a specified region to a buffer so that you can subsequently paste it somewhere else. Like the delete command, you can delimit the area that you want to copy by following the y command with a cursor movement command. For example, y$ copies the text from the current cursor position to the end of the line into the buffer, while y} copies all of the text from the current cursor position to the end of the paragraph into the buffer. If you copy or delete anything more than a single line, the number of lines yanked into the buffer is displayed at the bottom of your vi window. Figure 7.2 shows the message displayed by vi running in an xterm window after copying the current paragraph (which is 9 lines long) into the buffer.

FIGURE 7.2

The vi editor displaying a yank status message

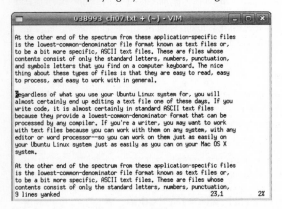

Of course, cutting or copying text isn't all that interesting without being able to paste it back in somewhere, for which vi provides the p and P commands. To paste a single line from the buffer back into your text at the current cursor position, you simply use the p command. However, if you have copied multiple lines into the buffer, you should preface the p command with the number of lines that you want to paste back in. If you didn't happen to notice how many lines you yanked and you simply want to paste all of the text that you recently copied to the buffer, you can simply use the P command to paste it all back in at once.

Searching for and Replacing Text in vi

The vi editor provides separate commands for searching forward and backward in your file. Pressing the / command, followed by the sequence of characters that you want to search for, and pressing return causes vi to search forward in the current file until (if) it locates a matching sequence of characters. Figure 7.3 shows vi running in an xterm window, getting ready to search for the string cantelope in the text. If the string is found, vi adjusts the text display window and moves the cursor forward in the file to display the line of text containing the match. If no matching string is found in the text, vi displays a status message to that effect and does not move the cursor.

The ? command is the opposite of the / command, searching backward through the current file for a specified string. Both the / and ? commands are examples of vi's command-line mode, where pressing a command positions the cursor at the bottom of the screen, waiting for subsequent information.

Searching for a string in vi

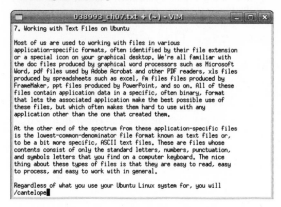

The vi editor's command-line mode also provides a convenient text substitution command to enable you to search for a string and either globally or conditionally replace it with another. This is the `:%s/foo/bar/` command, which (in this case) would search for the next instance of *foo* and replace it with *bar*. You can follow the final / with other characters to indicate whether the replacement should automatically be done globally throughout the rest of the file (`:%s/foo/bar/g`), or whether vi should ask you for confirmation before performing each substitution (`:%s/foo/bar/gc`). Figure 7.4 shows a conditional replacement of the string vi with vim. Conditional replacements of this sort are often known as query/replace operations, because they ask you for confirmation before doing each replacement.

A query/replace operation in vi

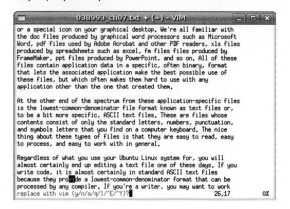

Note that the prompt at the bottom of the screen asks you to confirm (Y) or reject (N) each change, but also provides two cursor movement commands. The query/replace operation also supports the use of the Control+e (scroll down one line) and Control+y (scroll up one line) commands to make it easier for you to see the context in which you're replacing the specified text.

Undoing Changes in vi

Unless you're a much better writer and programmer than me, and therefore never make a mistake, you'll eventually find yourself making several changes to a file and then thinking, "Oh, crap — I didn't want to do that." Luckily, vi remembers all of the commands that you executed in your current editing session and enables you to undo all of them, in order, until you get your file back to the state in which you wish you'd left it in the first place. To undo the last operation you performed in vi, use the u (undo) command. Each subsequent u command undoes one previous operation. Some complex operations, such as a global search/replace operation, are remembered (and therefore undone) as a single operation, but for the most part, you can use the u command to undo each single command until you return your file to the right state.

Using Multiple Windows in vi

One of the longest running complaints about vi is that it doesn't support multiple windows. In terminal-oriented applications such as vi, multiple windows are typically just views onto multiple files in the same application at the same time, with each having its own status bar. One of the oldest and choicest bits of vi folklore is that Bill Joy had apparently been working on a multiwindowed version of vi, but that the source code got lost, and thus vi never developed multiple windows until the advent of modern versions of vi, such as vim. In Joy's own words, as quoted from an interview in the August 1984 issue of *Unix Review* magazine:

"...What actually happened was that I was in the process of adding multiwindows to vi when we installed our VAX, which would have been in December of '78. We didn't have any backups and the tape drive broke. I continued to work even without being able to do backups. And then the source code got scrunched and I didn't have a complete listing. I had almost rewritten all of the display code for windows, and that was when I gave up. After that, I went back to the previous version and just documented the code, finished the manual and closed it off. If that scrunch had not happened, vi would have multiple windows, and I might have put in some programmability — but I don't know..."

Luckily, the vim folks have solved this problem by implementing several commands that enable you to split the current window, open another file in another part of your vim window, cycle between multiple files displayed in different windows, and so on. Figure 7.5 shows vim displaying two different files in separate windows within the same vim session.

The primary command-line commands for manipulating multiple windows in vim are the following:

- :hide: Close current window (only works when multiple windows are displayed).
- :only: Close all windows except for the current one.
- :split filename: Split window horizontally and load filename in the new window.
- :sview filename: Same as split, but displays filename in read-only mode.
- :vsplit filename: Split window vertically and load filename in the new window.

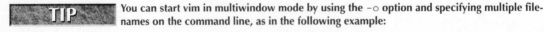

TIP   You can start vim in multiwindow mode by using the -o option and specifying multiple filenames on the command line, as in the following example:

```
$ vim -o file1.txt file2.txt file3.txt
```

FIGURE 7.5

Multiple windows in vim

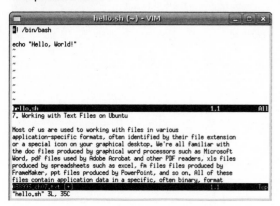

Once you've created multiple windows, you can move between and manipulate them using the following commands:

- Control+w up arrow: Move cursor up a window.
- Control+w control+w: Move cursor to another window (cycle).
- Control+w_: Maximize current window.
- Control+w=: Make all equal size.
- Control+w+: Increase window size by one line.

After a bit of experimentation (and training your fingers to use a few new commands), working with multiple windows in vim is just as easy as working with them in any other text editor.

Customizing vim

By default, vim reads three configuration files when you first start the editor. These are the following:

- The system configuration file /etc/vimrc.
- A per-user configuration file, located in each user's home directory and called .vimrc.
- The traditional per-user configuration file used by vi, located in each user's home directory and called .exrc.

It is not an error if any of these files do not exist, but together they provide a very flexible mechanism for customizing vim. Each of these files can contain any number of the following types of configuration commands:

- autocmd: Automatically execute specific commands based on the type of file that you are editing.
- iab: Define abbreviations that will be expanded into a specific sequence of characters when they are encountered as a word in the text that you are typing.
- map: Map existing vim commands to a custom key or define your own vi commands.
- set: Set a vim variable to a value.

In addition to these specific commands, vim configuration files also support a rich set of conditionals that enable you to write your own functions and execute them in different contexts.

As an example of configuring or personalizing vim, my `.vimrc` file is the following:

```
"
" wvh's .vimrc
"
" Variable Settings
"
" Don't use vi-compatibility mode
set nocompatible
" use the smart version of backspace
set backspace=2
" I don't like syntax highlighting
syntax off
" define the point at which lines wrap in vanilla mode
set wrapmargin=10
" always display row/column info
set ruler
" don't highlight all search terms, just find them
set nohls
" create backup files with a tilde extension
set backupext=~
set backup
"
" Abbreviations
"
" auto-correct a favorite typo
iab teh the
"
" special key mappings
"
" use F5 to reformat paragraphs
map <F5> !}fmt <CR>
"
" Specific settings for different types of files
"
" define some specific settings for when editing C files
au FileType c setlocal shiftwidth=4 softtabstop=4 expandtab
```

As you can see, lines that begin with a single double-quotation mark enable you to intersperse comments in your `.vimrc` file.

Unfortunately, a complete discussion of the possible contents of a `.vimrc` file would require its own book. Some excellent examples of much more complex vim configuration files are available on the Web at the following URLs:

- www.stripey.com/vim/vimrc.html
- www.cs.mcgill.ca/~navindra/editors/sven.vimrc

Graphical Versions of vi

Many people, especially those that are former users of systems such as Microsoft Windows and Mac OS X, expect applications to have a graphical user interface. This poses an interesting problem for applications such as vi and emacs, which were originally designed for use with terminals back when a mouse was just a pesky rodent. To make people feel more at home with powerful tools such as vi (and to drag them, often kicking and screaming, into the 21st century), various graphical interfaces for vi have been developed over the years. Figure 7.6 shows `gvim`, which is a version of vim to which menu support has been added.

FIGURE 7.6

GNOME vim, a graphical version of vim

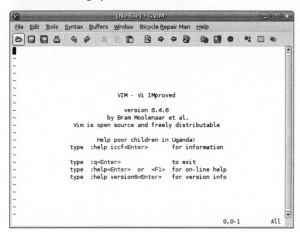

> **NOTE** GNOME vim is not installed by default on your Ubuntu system, but can easily be installed from the repository using the Synaptic Package Manager, as explained in Chapter 20, "Adding, Removing, and Updating Software."

Other graphical versions of vim are available, most notably `kvim`, which is a version of vim tailored to the KDE desktop environment. From what I hear, most of the `kvim` developers are now working on an open source project known as Yzis, which is a fast, powerful editor inspired by vim that is being written in a more modular fashion to more easily implement graphical extensions. For more information about this project, see `www.yzis.org`.

More Information About vi and vim

Because vi is one of the oldest text editors available for Unix-like systems, you can find numerous sources of information about it on the Web, including many that are specific to vim. Some of my favorites are the following:

- Vim Home Page: `www.vim.org/`
- Vi Lover's Home Page: `www.thomer.com/thomer/vi/vi.html`
- Introduction to Display Editing with vi: `http://ex-vi.sourceforge.net/viin/paper-4.html`

- An Introduction to Vim's Many Features: `www.burdell.org/articles/vim/`
- Vim Regular Expressions: `www.geocities.com/volontir/`

A simple Internet search will turn up hundreds of other sites containing tips, tricks, and configuration settings for customizing your version of vim. However, remember that one of the primary advantages of using a vi-like editor is that it can be found on any Linux-like system, and generally works the same way on all systems. If you customize your copy of vim to death and grow to depend on your customizations, you might as well be using emacs.

Using emacs

The history of emacs was described earlier in this chapter — now, let's meet our new best friend. As I mentioned earlier, I am a long-time emacs user, and find it to be "the right editor" for me. Your mileage may vary, but no one can ignore the power and flexibility of emacs. Many of the old arguments against using emacs, such as its memory requirements, simply don't matter anymore thanks to the generally increasing memory requirements of desktop systems and improvements in the type of hardware that most personal computer systems have today. As far as I'm concerned, the simple fact that emacs is a modeless editor that starts up in edit mode, enabling you to create files without having to do anything fancy, is a great argument for using emacs.

> **TIP** For some unknown reason, the emacs21 package is not installed by default on Ubuntu systems. You will have to install it using any of the software update tools discussed in Chapter 20, "Adding, Removing, and Updating Software," before you can experiment and become one with emacs. This is the first thing that I do after installing any Ubuntu system. From my point of view, a Linux system without emacs is a contradiction in terms.

By default, the version of emacs that is available for your Ubuntu system is integrated into the X Window system, and therefore automatically starts up its own window, which provides both an extensive set of menus and a graphical toolbar to simplify selecting frequently-used commands. Figure 7.7 shows an emacs window, displaying a text file that represents the beginning of this chapter.

The emacs editor can also be started in nongraphical mode, which can be handy if you simply want to do some quick editing, or if you've connected to a remote machine and don't want to enable the remote system to create windows on your screen. To start emacs in nonwindowed mode, use the `-nw` command-line option when starting emacs. Figure 7.8 shows emacs editing the same file as that shown in Figure 7.7, but in the context of an `xterm` window.

Emacs on an Ubuntu system

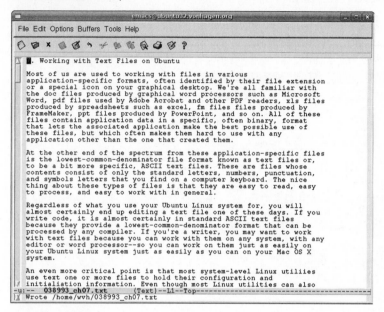

Emacs in an xterm window on an Ubuntu system

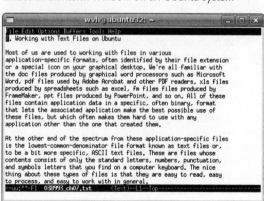

One of the best features of emacs is its customizability, which extends to its graphical display. As an example, Figure 7.9 shows emacs with the graphical customizations that I normally use, with the toolbar hidden and the scroll bar moved to the right of the emacs window.

FIGURE 7.9

Emacs showing graphical customization

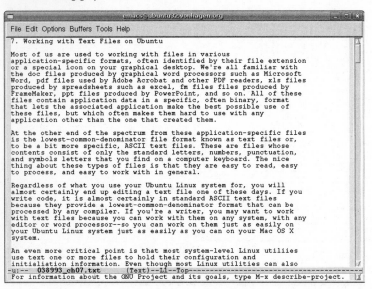

If you're a fan of graphical customization and are interested in being able to use a variety of fonts in your emacs session, another version of emacs known as XEmacs, is available. Figure 7.10 shows the default XEmacs startup window, which highlights the fact that XEmacs provides great support for multiple fonts, provides much more extensive toolbar and icon support, and even supports displaying graphical images within an XEmacs window.

XEmacs was originally the work of the folks at Lucid, Inc., but is now an open source project that is hosted at www.xemacs.org. XEmacs was originally created to provide a more graphically — and mouse-aware — version of emacs, primarily because the first release of GNU emacs to intrinsically support the mouse in a meaningful way, emacs 19, took forever to be released. Because of several legal issues that would numb my brain to discuss here, the XEmacs code has never been merged back into the official GNU emacs, and it exists as a separate entity today. Regardless, XEmacs is a fantastic version of emacs that many people find much more attractive and usable than GNU emacs, and is therefore well worth looking into. XEmacs is not officially supported by the Ubuntu folks, so to install XEmacs on your Ubuntu system, you will have to enable the multiverse repository, and then install a variety of associated packages as explained in Chapter 20, "Adding, Removing, and Updating Software."

The startup screen for XEmacs, the "other" emacs

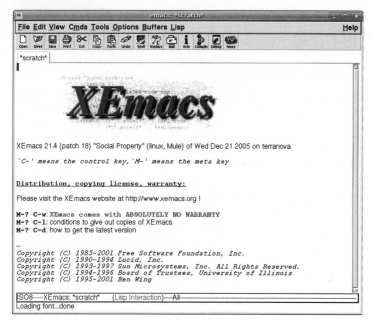

A Few Words About emacs Commands

Before telling you how to do anything in emacs, it's important to have a quick discussion of emacs commands, how they work, and how they're represented in this book.

Because emacs is a modeless editor, typing any standard keyboard character actually inserts that character into the file that you're working on. That makes perfect sense in a graphical environment where you can use menu commands to perform most emacs commands (as long as they're listed on a menu). However, because emacs predates the use of graphical environments and therefore menus, there has to be another way to issue basic emacs commands.

All available emacs commands are bound to a combination of keystrokes that use the modifier keys on your keyboard. These modifiers are keys like Ctrl (known as Control), Esc (known as Escape), and the Alt and Shift keys. If you think about how a computer works, you'll realize that these keys, when combined with the standard alphanumeric and symbol keys, change the signal that is sent to your system when one of these standard keys is sent. Using the Control, Escape, and Alt keys does exactly the same sort of thing as what happens when you press the Shift key when typing a letter or number key on your keyboard — it sends a different signal than what that key normally sends.

Emacs commands are therefore bound to key combinations that are represented as things like `Control+s`, `Esc+s`, `Alt+s`, `Control+Shift+s`, and so on. This is one of the things that the users of editors like to make fun of, because watching someone type in emacs can be quite amusing if they are executing a continuous mixture of text insertion keystrokes and emacs commands. As an example of this, one of my old office mates described my typing as looking like an "epileptic spider." Of course, the fact that I don't touch-type didn't help me any here, but his point was still both amusing and well-taken, and I am clearly still amused (but have not changed). This has something to do with how different keyboard modifier keys work.

The Control key works as a direct modifier by being held down while another key is pressed. This is usually represented as something like Control+s, which means "hold down the Control key, press the letter s, and then release the Control key." The Control key is much like the Shift key in this respect, except that there is no equivalent "Control Lock" key to confuse and irritate people.

> **TIP** A printed sequence beginning with the caret symbol (^) is often used as a shortcut when referring to the Control key. For example, ^s and Control-s are two ways of representing the same thing. This simplifies continually typing Control-s, and also prevents anyone from being confused about whether to type the - (you don't). Some books also use Control+s, Ctrl-s, or simply C-s as other shortcuts for Control-s. I'll stick with Control+s or, occasionally, ^s. Emacs can be confusing enough without drowning in a sea of duplicate representations.

On the other hand, the Escape and Alt keys work as prefix keys. To use these keys, you press and release them once, and then press another letter. These are still represented as Esc+s and Alt+s, but the keyboard interaction is very different. Commands associated with the Escape key are therefore often referred to as an *Escape sequence* to reinforce the notion that these are a sequence of key presses, not a simultaneous combination of multiple keys.

This would be pretty simple if emacs commands were limited to a single Control command, Escape sequence, and so on. However, this would limit emacs to having a hundred or so possible commands, which is hardly sufficient. Therefore, most emacs commands are combinations of Control keys, Escape sequences, Alt sequences, and the Shift key. This gives you an essentially infinite number of available commands, which can be hard to remember, leads to derogatory comments like those of my old office mate, and amuses everyone with potential key sequence descriptions like Esc+s+Control+Shift+s. However, I feel that this is a small price to pay for the power of a zillion possible commands.

> **TIP** One thing that confuses users who are familiar with text editors or word processors on other systems is that emacs does not follow the traditional conventions for things like cutting, copying, and pasting text. This is unfortunate, but the reason for this is because emacs predates these conventions, and those key sequences are already used for other things in emacs. Who would you rather tick off — thousands of emacs users who are potentially unruly in the first place, or new users who are new to emacs anyway? I thought so...

Emacs Terminology

Because GNU emacs is designed to interact with a graphical window manager, I have to use slightly different terminology to describe what you see on the screen. This section explains that terminology so that I can use it without guilt throughout the rest of this chapter.

Figure 7.11 shows two windows on an Ubuntu system, each running emacs but visiting different files. Each emacs window has its own menu bar and toolbar. The window in the foreground displays two different files, each in its own buffer. Each emacs buffer has a mode line at the bottom, which provides information about the file being viewed in that buffer and its state. At the bottom of each emacs window is a status line in which you interact with emacs, or in which emacs displays any messages displayed by a particular emacs function.

Windowing terminology for GNU emacs

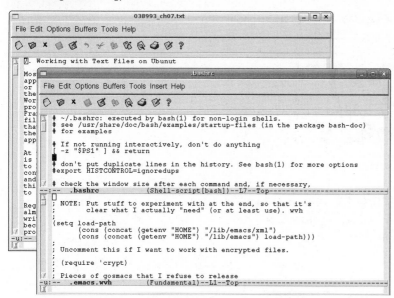

NOTE The term *window* has a different meaning in this section than the way in which I used it in the portions of this chapter that discussed vi and vim. This is because emacs is natively aware of the X Window system and therefore can display multiple windows on the screen, while vi can only divide a terminal application screen into multiple sections. In the context of emacs, a vi window is equivalent to an emacs buffer.

Starting and Exiting emacs

Like vi, to begin editing a file in emacs, you can do either of the following:

- Select the Emacs 21 (X11) command from the Applications ⇨ Accessories menu.

- In any xterm or GNOME Terminal window, simply type the command emacs filename, where filename is the name of the file that you want to edit. By default, starting emacs from a terminal window on an Ubuntu system creates a new window for the emacs application, so you will probably want to follow the name of the file that you want to edit with an ampersand to start your emacs session in the background and return control to the terminal window so that you can type additional commands there while emacs is running.

In either case, emacs will create an initial window displaying any file that you are editing, as shown in Figure 7.7. If you start emacs from the GNOME menus, emacs displays an initial welcome screen, as shown in Figure 7.12.

FIGURE 7.12

The startup screen for GNU emacs

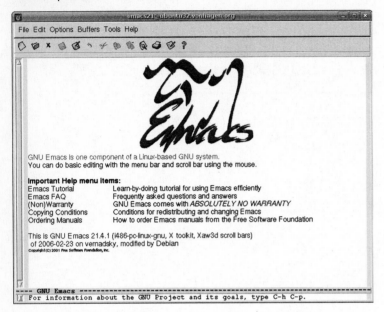

To exit emacs, you can either use the Exit Emacs command on the File menu, or use the ^x^c (as a refresher, this means to hold down the Control key and press the letter x, then press the letter c, and then release the Control key) key combination.

If you have not modified any files while working with emacs or have already saved all of the changes that you have made, emacs exits immediately. However, if you attempt to exit from emacs using menu commands and have not saved any of the changes to the file(s) that you've been editing, emacs displays the confirmation dialog shown in Figure 7.13 for each file that contains unsaved changes.

To proceed without saving your change, click No. To save your changes and proceed, click Yes. If you save your changes by selecting Yes, emacs exits immediately once those changes have been saved for each modified file that you were working on. If you click No, emacs displays yet another confirmation dialog, asking if you're really, really sure that you want to exit without saving your changes, as shown in Figure 7.14. Emacs doesn't quite beg you to save your files, but it makes every attempt to ensure that you know what you're doing and aren't accidentally exiting without saving the great American novel.

FIGURE 7.13

Changed file notification when exiting emacs graphically

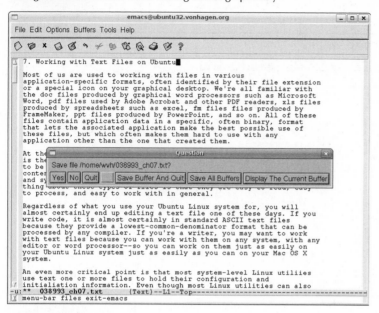

FIGURE 7.14

Final confirmation dialog when exiting emacs graphically

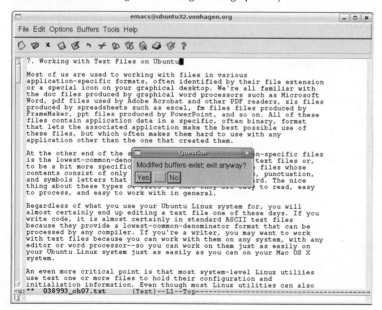

This same exchange occurs when you're attempting to exit emacs using the equivalent command (^x^c), but it occurs in the emacs message buffer, as shown in Figure 7.15.

FIGURE 7.15

Final confirmation dialog when exiting emacs using the keyboard

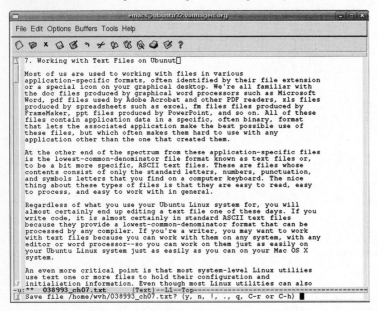

Moving Around in emacs

There are many different keys for moving the insertion cursor in emacs:

- ^a: Go to the beginning of the current line.
- ^e: Go to the end of the current line.
- ^f: Move forward one character.
- ^b: Move backward one character.
- ^p: Move to the previous line.
- ^n: Move to the next line.
- ^v: Scroll down one screen.
- Esc+b: Move backward one word.
- Esc+f: Move forward one word.
- Esc+v: Scroll up one screen.
- Esc+<: Go to the beginning of the current buffer.
- Esc+>: Go to the end of the current buffer.

These are the most common keyboard commands for moving the cursor around within the current window. When using emacs in any graphical mode, you can also scroll the screen by clicking and dragging the elevator in the scroll bar, or simply move the cursor by pointing and clicking.

For information about the commands used to switch or move between multiple buffers that are displayed on the screen, see the section later in this chapter entitled "Working with Multiple Windows and Buffers in emacs."

Cutting, Copying, and Pasting in emacs

Because emacs is aware of the X Window system and therefore supports moving the cursor using the mouse, there are two different ways to select the text that you want to copy or move:

- By positioning the cursor using the left mouse button, holding down the left mouse button, and dragging the cursor to select a portion of your text. If you move the cursor into the mode line of any emacs buffer, emacs will automatically scroll the text while continuing the selection operation.

- By setting a mark at the current cursor position by using the Control+@ or Control+space commands, and then moving the cursor to the location that delimits the end of the text that you want to cut or copy.

Once you have identified the region that you want to copy or cut, you can copy that region to an internal paste buffer by pressing Esc+w, or cut the selected text to the paste buffer by pressing Control+w. You can then move the cursor to the position where you want to paste the copied or deleted text, and press Control+y to paste the text at the new location.

 **If you simply want to cut the text from the current cursor position to the end of the current line, you can press ^k to kill that text, and then press ^y to paste it back in elsewhere.**

Searching for and Replacing Text in emacs

By default, the ^s key is bound to an incremental search mode that is extremely convenient to use. After you press ^s, the message I-Search: displays in the emacs message buffer, and as emacs searches forward in the current buffer for the text that you type there, finding the first match for whatever string you are currently typing. For example, if you are searching for the string cantelope, as you type each letter of that word, emacs searches forward for the first instance of the letter c, then the first instance of the letters ca, the first instance of the letters can, and so on. You can press ^g at any time to abort the search and return to the cursor position at which the search began. Typing any other emacs command (with the exception of ^g, that is) terminates the search and leaves the cursor at the current location in the buffer.

Working with Multiple Windows and Buffers in emacs

If you are using emacs in graphical mode, switching between buffers or windows using the mouse is pretty easy — you just left-click the mouse in the window or buffer that you want, and voila! However, if you're already working in a window that's been split into multiple buffers (or if you're using emacs in no-window mode), it's useful to know how to switch between different buffers.

To switch to another buffer that is currently displayed on your emacs screen, press the ^x^o command. This command cycles through all of the buffers that are currently displayed on your screen.

If you want to switch to another buffer regardless of whether or not it is displayed on the screen, you can press ^x+b (Control+x, and then the letter b) and enter the name of the buffer that you want to switch to at the prompt in the emacs status line.

If you don't happen to remember the name of the other file that you were working on or are using a temporary name, you can press ^x^b to list all available buffers, and then middle-click on the name of the buffer that you want to switch to.

Customizing emacs

If you've ever gone to the desk of any emacs aficionado and used emacs there, you've probably noticed that it doesn't seem to work the same way for them as it does on your system. The reason for this is that emacs is the most configurable editor in existence. Not only does emacs provide a rich configuration language for changing the commands that different keys are associated with (known as *key bindings*), but it includes a complete implementation of the Lisp programming language that makes it easy for serious emacs users to write their own commands or modify the behavior of existing ones.

Most Linux systems store all per-user emacs customization information in the file .emacs in the user's home directory. As mentioned throughout this chapter, emacs' customizability and flexibility accounts for much of its popularity. The next few sections highlight the basic types of customizations that you can make in an emacs configuration file, providing examples of each. Several excellent sites on the Web provide much more detailed information about customizing emacs, such as http://jeremy.zawodny.com/emacs/emacs-4.html and http://linuxplanet.com/linuxplanet/tutorials/3166/4/.

Changing Key Bindings

Whenever you execute an emacs command, you are actually executing a Lisp function. As explained earlier, emacs is configured to execute specific commands in response to combinations of the Control or Escape keys and the standard keys on your keyboard. These are known as key bindings because they associate (bind) a specific function with a specific key sequence. However, if you're already familiar with another editor that also used commands consisting of combinations of the Control or Escape keys and the standard keys on your keyboard, your fingers are probably used to pressing certain keys to execute certain commands. The most common customization made to emacs is therefore to change the keys to which commonly used commands are associated.

Though emacs enables you to change key bindings globally or within a specific mode, it is more common to customize a specific key binding so that it works regardless of the mode in which you are using emacs. The emacs configuration command to globally set a key binding is global-set-binding. For example, to globally set the key sequence Control+z to a function that scrolls the current buffer up one line rather than attempting to suspend emacs, you would put the following command in your ~/.emacs file:

    (global-set-key ?\C-Z? ?scroll-one-line-up)

In Lisp fashion, you must preface the name of the function that you are referring to with a single-quotation mark (not the back quote). If you're interested, the scroll-one-line-up function is provided as an example in the section entitled "Defining Your Own Functions" later in this chapter.

 When you are specifying key bindings in an emacs configuration file, the Control key is usually represented by \C- and the Escape key is usually represented by \M-.

Setting Variables

Emacs used several internal variables to control its behavior. You can modify these variables using the setq command. For example, to cause emacs to scroll more smoothly in one-line increments, you could add the following line to your ~/.emacs file:

    (setq scroll-step 1)

As another example, the default settings in emacs cause it to automatically save your files each time you have typed or modified 300 characters. To decrease this value to every 100 changes, you could add the following line to your ~/.emacs file:

```
(setq auto-save-interval 100)
```

Specifying Modes

As discussed earlier, emacs provides different key bindings and functions based on the types of files that you are using, known as *modes*. The default mode used by emacs when you start emacs without specifying the file that you want to edit is known as *fundamental mode*. You may want to customize emacs to always use a different mode by default, regardless of the name of the file. For example, to make text mode the default mode each time you start emacs, you could add the following line to your ~/.emacs file:

```
(setq default-major-mode 'text-mode)
```

As you can see from this example, the name of the default mode in emacs is defined through an emacs variable, `default-major-mode`, which in this case requires the name of an emacs function rather than a numeric value as shown in the examples in the previous section.

Each emacs mode also enables you to specify other actions whenever you use that mode. For example, to turn on auto-fill (wrapping words to the next line when you reach a certain column on your screen), you could add the following line to your ~/.emacs file:

```
(add-hook 'text-mode-hook 'turn-on-auto-fill)
```

Changing File Associations

As discussed earlier, emacs automatically enters specific modes when you open files with a specific extension, just like many GUIs do when you click on a specific type of file. You may occasionally want to have emacs automatically enter a specific mode when you open files that the specified mode is not traditionally associated with. For example, emacs automatically enters text mode when you edit files with the .txt or .text extensions. But what if you typically name text files with the .inf extension and want emacs to automatically enter text mode when entering files of that type?

The file extensions associated with different emacs modes are stored in a list consisting of extension/mode-name pairs. Therefore, to add the .inf extension to the list of extensions associated with text mode, you would simply append that extension to the list of extensions associated with text mode, as in the following example:

```
(setq auto-mode-alist
    (cons '(".inf" . text-mode) auto-mode-alist))
```

This example uses the Lisp `cons` function to append the pair .inf and `text-mode` to the list of automatic file associations, and then uses the `setq` function discussed earlier in this chapter to set the `auto-mode-alist` variable to the new, expanded list.

Defining Your Own Functions

The fact that emacs includes an internal implementation of Lisp makes it relatively easy to define your own functions and provides a practical reason for learning Lisp if you've always wanted one. Lisp functions are defined using the `defun` command, which takes a list of five values as arguments. Without turning this into a Lisp tutorial, let's just quickly look at a sample function definition and examine its components.

The following emacs Lisp code defines a simple function that scrolls the contents of the current window up some number of lines, with the default number being 1:

```
(defun scroll-one-line-up
  (&optional arg)
  "Scroll the selected window up one or N lines."
  (interactive "p")
  (scroll-up (or arg 1))
)
```

The name of the function that you are defining is the first argument to the `defun` command. The second argument is the list of arguments that are used by the function that you are defining. In this case, this list uses the `&optional` argument to state that this function can take one argument, but that the argument is optional. The third argument to the `defun` command is an informational message about the function, enclosed in double quotes. The fourth argument defines whether the function is interactive (p means true in Lisp). The fifth argument is the actual Lisp code for the function that you are defining, which in this case executes the built-in emacs scroll-up function a single time or the number of times you specified as a numeric argument to the function.

This section won't exactly make you a Lisp wizard, but just knowing that emacs includes a complete Lisp implementation can be quite empowering. As you can see from this example, defining simple functions is not all that complex. The power and flexibility of emacs provides you with the chance to add that function you've always wished for in a text editor!

Getting More Information About emacs

The emacs editor contains its own tutorials and help files: Type M+x `help` to begin. These include a "learning by doing" tutorial. There are also plenty of emacs tutorials out there, some of which are written from the beginner's point of view. The official GNU emacs manual is available from `www.gnu.org/software/emacs/manual/`. It can also be purchased in book form. There is also an emacs Wiki at `www.emacswiki.org`.

Using gedit

Now that I've discussed the favorite two classic Unix/Linux text editors and their attendant philosophies, it's worth mentioning that Ubuntu also provides text editors that you can use without a class in Unix history and pledging your undying allegiance to Richard Stallman or Bill Joy. Both the GNOME and KDE desktops provide easy-to-use graphical text editors called `gedit` and `kedit`, respectively. Figure 7.16 shows `gedit` displaying the same file used to illustrate the vi and emacs editors earlier in this chapter, namely, the text of this chapter as I was writing it.

The `gedit` editor is completely mouse- and menu-driven, and follows the standard keyboard conventions for most graphical editors. These include the following:

- `Control+c`: Copy selected text.
- `Control+n`: Open a new file.
- `Control+s`: Save the current file.
- `Control+v`: Paste copied or cut text.
- `Control+x`: Cut selected text.

FIGURE 7.16

The gedit text editor

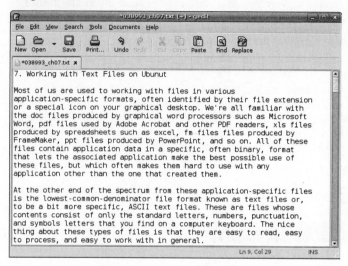

In addition to following more common keyboard conventions, gedit also provides convenient and more traditional dialogs for interacting with, moving around in, and selecting files and directories. Figure 7.17 shows the dialog displayed after selecting the File menu's Open command in gedit.

As with most GNOME applications, extensive online help for gedit is available by selecting the Help menu's Contents command.

FIGURE 7.17

Gedit's open file dialog

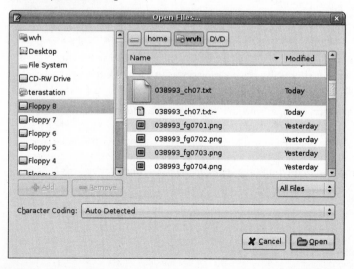

Other Text Editors for Ubuntu

Several other editors are available for Ubuntu systems. By default, the following other editors are installed by default on an Ubuntu system:

- **ed**: A simple, line-oriented editor inspired by the original Unix text editor.

- **ex**: Invokes the vim editor in line-oriented mode. When using **ex**, you can instantly switch to vim's full-screen mode by typing the keyword **visual**.

- **nano**: An enhanced clone of **pico** that is available under the GPL (unlike **pico**). One of the nicest things about **nano** and **pico** is that the bottom of any window always provides a quick summary of the most useful commands in the current context. **nano** (and **pico**) are completely unaware of the X Window system, and must be executed within an xterm or GNOME Terminal window. Figure 7.18 shows **nano** editing the text file for this chapter.

FIGURE 7.18

The nano text editor

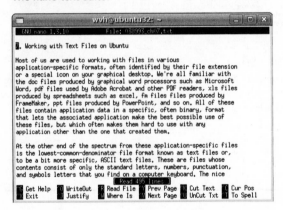

- **pico**: A simple, screen-oriented text editor that was originally introduced by the Pine mail system on Unix systems. On Ubuntu Linux systems, this is actually just a symbolic link to the **nano** editor, and thus looks exactly like the screen shown in Figure 7.18.

If you are new to Linux, two other popular editors that are not provided with Ubuntu but which you can compile or execute on your Ubuntu system are the following:

- **jedit**: A popular, cross-platform editor for programmers. For more information, see www.jedit.org/index.php.

- **THE**: The Hessling Editor, a clone of the popular IBM mainframe editor XEDIT, THE includes support for various Linux versions of the associated REXX scripting language. See www.lightlink.com/hessling or http://sourceforge.net/project/showfiles.php?group_id=29648 for more information.

If you're looking for a Linux clone of a specific editor, check the Web page at `http://texteditors.org/cgi-bin/wiki.pl?EditorIndex`. This page lists many available editors for different operating system (including Linux), and may provide information about one that meets your needs.

Summary

Your Ubuntu Linux system provides a variety of text editors that different types of users can quickly get comfortable with. If you are familiar with Linux or other Unix-like systems, Ubuntu installs vim (a vi clone), and GNU emacs is easily installed using the software update commands discussed in Chapter 20, "Adding, Removing, and Updating Software." This chapter discussed in detail how to use both vi and emacs, how to accomplish the most common tasks you'll need to do in an editor, as well as how to customize each to suit your preferences. It then provided an introduction to `gedit`, a fast graphical editor that is installed as part of the GNOME desktop environment. The chapter concluded with information about other editors that are available on your Ubuntu system, and provided suggestions for finding other editors that may be more to your liking.

Now that you have the fundamentals of using Ubuntu graphically and from the command line out of the way, and have discussed the text editors that are a basic component of Linux systems, it's time to move on to discussing some of the graphical applications that you will use on a day-to-day basis on your Ubuntu system. Chapter 8 discusses Evolution, a powerful GNOME-based e-mail and personal information management system that does a great job of sending, receiving, and organizing your e-mail.

Chapter 8

Reading and Sending Mail with Evolution

After Web browsers, e-mail is the Internet's killer application. Like Web browsers, there are many different client applications for sending and receiving e-mail, especially in the open source community. In addition (and unfortunately unlike Web browsing, which basically uses HTML everywhere) there are many different protocols used to send e-mail. Your choice of an e-mail client can therefore depend to some extent on whether it supports the protocols that your Internet Service Provider (ISP), business, or academic institution uses to send, store, and deliver e-mail.

The easiest solution to the "which protocol, which client" problem is to use a single e-mail client that speaks every modern e-mail protocol known to man. Ubuntu includes an e-mail client known as *Evolution*, which lives up to this promise. Evolution is a GNOME-based mailer that was originally developed by a company called Ximian. Oddly enough, Ximian was eventually acquired by Novell, whose SUSE Linux product is largely KDE-centric, but it's at least clear that Novell knows good software when they see it.

Evolution can receive mail from mail servers that speak all of the popular e-mail protocols including POP, IMAP, IMAP4rev1, Microsoft Exchange, Novell GroupWise, and a few that would require a Google search to figure out who uses them (and why). For outgoing mail, Evolution can communicate with any Simple Mail Transport Protocol (SMTP) server or any server that is compatible with the standard Linux/Unix sendmail application.

Beyond all this, Evolution is much more than just a multiprotocol e-mail client — it is actually more of a Personal Information Manager (PIM), of which sending and receiving e-mail is just one aspect. Evolution also provides integrated support for the following:

- managing contacts stored locally or on Lightweight Directory Access Protocol (LDAP) or Microsoft Exchange servers
- managing task lists stored locally or on a Microsoft Exchange server
- managing local calendars, Web-based calendars, or Microsoft Exchange calendars

By now, you may see something of a thread in this introduction—compatibility with Microsoft Exchange servers and the services that they provide. Like it or not, many businesses depend on Microsoft Exchange to satisfy groupware requirements such as scheduling meetings, checking and sharing coworker's calendars, and so on. The e-mail server portion of an Exchange Server is just a special type of IMAP mail server, but the calendaring and scheduling portions of Exchange are largely Microsoft-only. Evolution's support for complete interoperation with a Microsoft Exchange environment is truly impressive.

This chapter focuses on the e-mail aspects of Evolution. It explains how to configure and use evolution, starting with how to create your initial mail accounts, continuing with how to read, send, organize, and filter mail, and concluding with a discussion of the powerful virtual folders feature that is unique to Evolution. For information on Evolution's other personal information management capabilities, see the section entitled "Additional Sources of Information About Evolution" at the end of this chapter.

Starting Evolution

You can start Evolution in a variety of different ways:

- By clicking the Evolution icon in the GNOME toolbar at the top of the screen, shown in Figure 8.1. This is the easiest and most common way to start Evolution.

- By selecting Evolution browser from the Applications ⇨ Internet menu.

- By typing the `evolution` command in a GNOME Terminal or xterm window and pressing Return.

Ubuntu's GNOME desktop is also preconfigured to start Evolution for you if you click on a Uniform Resource Locater (URL) that is designed to send an e-mail message (known as a *mailto* URL) in a Web browser or other Internet-aware application.

FIGURE 8.1

The Evolution icon on your GNOME desktop

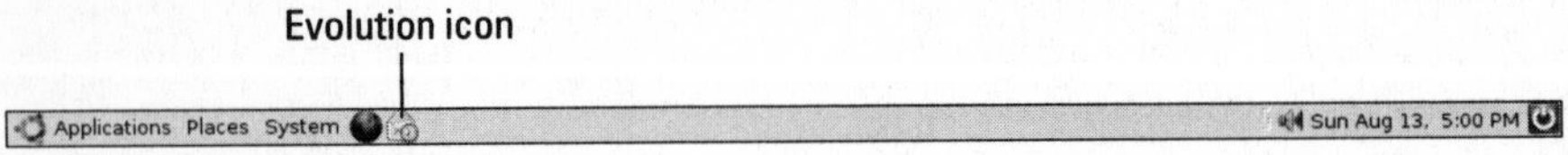

Evolution icon

| Applications Places System 🐧 🔛 | 🔊 Sun Aug 13, 5:00 PM ⏻ |

> **TIP** When starting Evolution, you might initially see a warning dialog, telling you that you are running a pre-release of the software. Whether or not you see this depends on the version of Evolution that the Ubuntu folks are shipping at the time you read this and any updates that you've installed. One of the greatest features of Ubuntu is the fact that you always get the latest and greatest software. Coupled with the fact that the Ubuntu folks and community do significant testing, this warning is safe to ignore—it's just in the code. If you see it, you can disable it in the future by selecting the Do not tell me again checkbox and clicking OK.

The next section discusses the Evolution Setup Assistant, which walks you through the process of creating your first e-mail account in Evolution.

Using the Evolution Setup Assistant

When Evolution actually starts up for the first time, the first window of the Evolution Setup Assistant, like the one shown in Figure 8.2, displays, which walks you through the process of creating your first e-mail account in Evolution.

FIGURE 8.2

The Setup Assistant when starting Evolution for the first time

A slight clarification here, just to be on the safe side — the Evolution Setup Assistant configures Evolution to send and receive e-mail for an existing e-mail account somewhere — it doesn't actually create the account. For example, even though I use my Ubuntu machines to send and receive mail, my e-mail account is actually located at the ISP that hosts my domain. The Evolution Setup Assistant lets me tell Evolution about where it should look to retrieve my incoming e-mail and the mail server through which it should send outgoing mail. In my case, the machine on which I'm running Evolution is separate from the machine through which I actually send and receive my e-mail.

NOTE   Of course, if you run your own mail server and it's running on the same machine where you're running Evolution, your Ubuntu account may well be your official e-mail account. I discuss this in more detail in Chapter 27, "Setting Up a Mail Server."

The idea of receiving e-mail can be confusing, so I generally think of this as the difference between *receiving* and *retrieving* — my actual e-mail account (at my ISP) receives my e-mail, and Evolution lets me retrieve my e-mail from there in order to read it, archive it locally or delete it, and so on. In official mailer-speak, this is the difference between a Mail Transfer Agent (MTA), a Mail Delivery Agent (MDA), and a Mail User Agent (MUA). The MDA at your ISP takes mail received by the MTA and puts it in your mailbox at your ISP. An MUA (in this case Evolution) retrieves a piece of mail from your mailbox at your ISP and displays it on your local system. (For more detailed information about these terms, see Chapter 27.)

Once you see the window in Figure 8.2, click Forward to move to the next portion of the setup process. A window like the one shown in Figure 8.3 displays.

FIGURE 8.3

Specifying your e-mail address

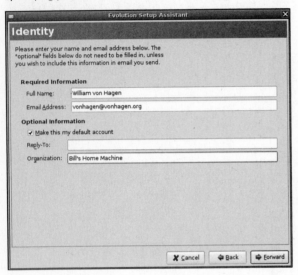

The Full Name field should already be filled out for you — Evolution grabs this information from the account from which you're running Evolution. You can change that name, of course, if you'd prefer to have the people who receive mail from you see a name that's more "clever" than your actual account name. The critical bit of information on this panel is in the E-mail Address field. This must be the e-mail address that you want to associate with this account. As mentioned previously, this is typically your e-mail address at your ISP or wherever else you get your e-mail through.

The Make this my default e-mail account checkbox is selected by default in this dialog because Evolution starts the Setup Assistant only when it detects that you are starting Evolution for the first time. Your default account is simply the one that Evolution will continue to use unless you activate another account.

If you want people who receive e-mail from this account to actually reply to another, you can specify the e-mail address of that account in the Reply-To field, but this is usually unnecessary. Similarly, if you want mail headers to announce that your mail is coming from a specific organization, you can specify the name of that organization in the Organization field. This is invisible to most recipients, but it can be handy for filtering e-mail messages (explained later in this chapter) if you use this field to uniquely identify that this mail was coming from a specific location. I typically put something like "Bill's Home Machine" in this field, so that I can tell that I actually sent a specific piece of mail from my machine at home, if necessary.

Once you've filled out this panel, click Forward to display the next panel in the Setup Assistant, shown in Figure 8.4.

FIGURE 8.4

Specifying incoming mail server (MTA) parameters

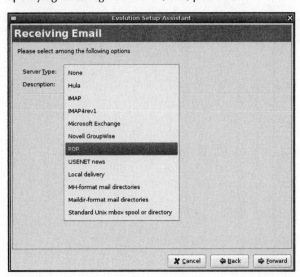

When you first see this panel, it will be largely empty and the Server Description field displays the type None. Click the Server Description field to display a list of the different types of mail servers that Evolution can talk to, and select the one that corresponds to the primary e-mail protocol supported by the mail server at the location that actually hosts your e-mail, which is typically your ISP. Most mail servers nowadays speak POP (Post Office Protocol) or a special version of POP known as POP3, which adds some extensions to the standard POP mail server capabilities. The second most popular protocol nowadays is IMAP, which also includes Microsoft Exchange mailers, because they speak a variant (of course) of IMAP.

Once you select a specific type of server, the panel changes to reflect the particular types of settings that are associated with a mail server of that type, as shown in Figure 8.5, which shows the setting for a POP mailer.

On this panel, enter the name of your mail server and your username as far as the mailer is concerned. Note that your mailer's idea of your username may not actually be the same as your login name there — many POP mailers require a username of the form *login%domain.name* to guarantee the uniqueness of usernames on mailers that support multiple domains. For example, my login at my ISP is *vonhagen*, but my POP username is *vonhagen%vonhagen.org*.

Next, specify the security settings required to log in on your mailer — whether or not to try to use a secure connection to retrieve your mail from the mail server (which I always set to Whenever Possible), and the type of authentication required to connect to the server. Evolution provides a convenient Check for Supported Types button that you can click to probe your mail server to see what type(s) of authentication it supports. In most cases, you'll use Password authentication, but this option makes it easy to check whether your mailer supports more sophisticated types of authentication such as Kerberos or GSSAPI.

You can select the Remember password checkbox to optionally specify that Evolution remembers the password to your incoming mail server, but I don't recommend that because this means that anyone who has access to your account will be able to read your mail, which may not be "the right thing."

Specifying parameters for an incoming mail server

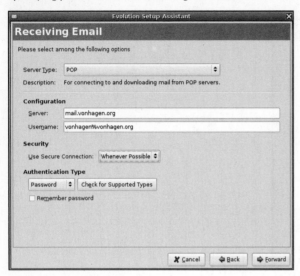

Once you're finished specifying the options for receiving and retrieving incoming mail, click Forward to proceed to the next panel. A panel like the one shown in Figure 8.6 displays.

Options for handling incoming mail from a POP server

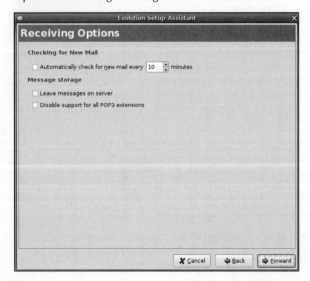

A Quick Guide to POP vs. IMAP

The key difference between the POP and IMAP e-mail protocols is where your e-mail is actually stored. POP mail clients typically download your e-mail from the POP server and store it on the machine where your mail client is running. This is extremely convenient for the operators of the mail server, because they don't have to provide huge amounts of storage for e-mail because the storage requirements for POP mailers are transient — as people read their mail, it is downloaded to the client and then usually deleted from the server. IMAP servers, on the other hand, permanently store your mail on the server and download the mail headers to your mail client only when you first check your mail. These headers include the subject line, information about the sender, the date on which the message was sent, and so on. When you select a message to be read from an IMAP server, the mail is copied to your local system, but the master copy of the message remains on the IMAP server. The storage requirements for IMAP mailers therefore tend to increase over time, as more and more people accumulate larger collections of saved e-mail.

Each of these approaches has advantages and disadvantages. POP lets you keep all of your mail on your local machine, which is handy if you want to review your existing mail when you're not connected to the net. The downside, of course, is that all of your mail lives on a single machine and it's therefore tricky to read old mail from a machine other than the one where that mail is actually stored. IMAP mailers make it easy to access your old mail from any machine, anywhere, but require a network connection to that machine in order to do so. Most IMAP clients enable you to synchronize your local mailboxes with those stored on the IMAP server, so that you can easily access old mail while traveling without requiring a network connection. However, ISPs that use IMAP hate people like me, who have huge mail archives going back ten years or so, and therefore require significant storage on an IMAP server.

Most POP mail clients, including Evolution's POP support, provide a special option called Leave mail on server. This enables you to configure multiple clients to read your POP mail, but only one of them (typically your home machine) actually downloads the mail and deletes it from the server. All POP clients remember the last message that they read, so they don't re-download all of your mail each time you check your mail — only those that they recognize as being new. This provides a nice compromise between the flexibility of IMAP and the local permanence of POP. For example, when I'm on the road, the copy of Evolution on my laptop lets me read my mail but doesn't delete it from the server — this happens only when I get back home and check mail from my primary machine. The downside of POP while traveling, of course, is that I don't have access to all of my old mail when I'm on the road but if I'm really desperate, I can always connect to my home machine and either manually look through my mailboxes or run Evolution from that machine over the net. Slow, but successful.

Panels like the one shown in Figure 8.6 let you configure the available options for how your mail client should interact with your incoming mail server. For all types of incoming mail servers, you can specify if, and how often, your mail client should automatically check for new e-mail. When configuring how Evolution interacts with an incoming POP mail server, you can also identify whether the copy of Evolution that you're configuring should remove the mail. As discussed in the sidebar "A Quick Guide to POP vs. IMAP" earlier in this chapter, POP mailers typically provide short-term storage for mail, while other types of mailers, such as IMAP, provide long-term storage for your mail. This panel also lets you configure whether Evolution should pay attention to POP3 extensions, which are site-specific extensions that the administrator of the mail server may have implemented.

Many of the options for interacting with an incoming mail server are specific to the type of server that you're connecting to. For example, Figure 8.7 shows the configuration options available when communicating with an IMAP server.

FIGURE 8.7

Options for handling incoming mail from an IMAP server

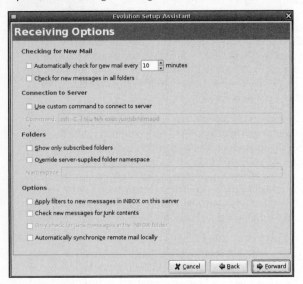

You'll notice that there are many more options for configuring Evolution's interaction with an IMAP server than with a POP server. Because IMAP servers maintain a master repository for your e-mail, Evolution's IMAP configuration panel offers options for how to connect to the server (such as through a secure tunnel), how to interact with the mail folders on the IMAP server (both your personal folder and public ones to which you may have access), whether to synchronize your local mail folder with those on the server (giving you a local copy of all of your mail), and whether mail filters and general junk mail (SPAM) processing should occur against your master mailboxes or just locally. I'll discuss mail filters and junk mail handling in the section entitled "Filtering Incoming Mail" later in this chapter. If you're configuring Evolution to interact with an IMAP server, I suggest activating both the Apply filters... and Check new messages... options for now. You can always turn them off later, and selecting these options initially will ensure that Mail Filters work as expected, and will also help get rid of some of the SPAM that plagues every e-mail user nowadays.

After you configure how Evolution interacts with your incoming mail server when you read your mail, regardless of the type of incoming mail server you're using, you need to configure how Evolution actually sends mail. Click Forward to proceed to the setup panel shown in Figure 8.8.

FIGURE 8.8

Options for sending mail

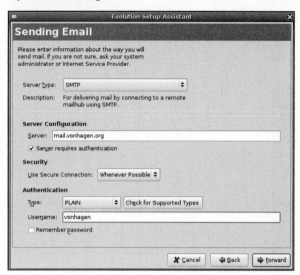

Previous configuration steps helped you configure how your system receives mail and the characteristics of your incoming mail server. The panel shown in Figure 8.8 enables you to specify the characteristics of the mail server that you use to send outgoing mail. Your incoming and outgoing mail servers may be different machines or processes because the tasks involved with sending and receiving mail are very different.

The critical piece of information on this panel is the type of your incoming mail server. Evolution supports two types of outgoing mail servers — SMTP (Simple Mail Transport Protocol), which simply means any mail server that conforms to the SMTP standard, and Sendmail, which is the most popular mail server used on Linux and other Unix-like systems and runs locally on most Ubuntu systems. Most people will want to select SMTP — if you are running your own mail server on your system (and plan to continue to do so), you can select Sendmail but if you are using an ISP for mail handling, you'll want to select SMTP. (For more information about running your own mail server, see Chapter 27, "Setting Up a Mail Server.")

If you select Sendmail, no additional configuration is required on this panel (because the server is running on the same machine as Evolution) but if you select SMTP, you'll need to specify the name of your outgoing mail server and provide information about how you authenticate to that server, if necessary. Most modern SMTP servers require authentication, so you need to check the Server requires authentication checkbox, specify that Evolution should use a secure connection whenever possible, and verify the type of authentication that your mail server supports by clicking the Check for Supported Types button, just as you did when providing similar information about your incoming mail server. As with the configuration of your incoming mail server, you can optionally specify that Evolution remembers your password to the outgoing mail server, but I don't recommend that because this means that anyone who has access to your account will be able to send mail as you, which may not be "the right thing."

Once you've correctly configured Evolution's information about your outgoing mail server, click Forward to continue with the configuration process. Don't worry—you can always change these settings later if you discover that mail isn't working correctly, as explained in the next section. The panel shown in Figure 8.9 displays.

Naming a configured e-mail account

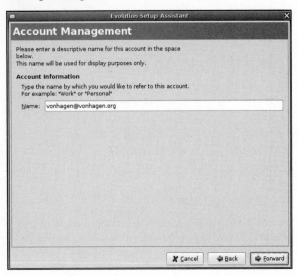

Almost there! The panel shown in Figure 8.9 simply requests a name for the e-mail account that you're configuring. This is the name that Evolution uses internally to identify this particular collection of e-mail settings, and is the name that you'll select in Evolution's Preferences dialog (discussed in the next section) if you need to update or modify the settings for this e-mail account. By default, the name of a particular collection of settings is the same as the e-mail address for that account, which is what I typically use.

After making any desired changes to the name of this e-mail account, click Forward to continue. The panel shown in Figure 8.10 displays.

This panel enables you to specify the time zone that Evolution believes that you're running in, and thus uses to set the timestamps on your outgoing mail. By default, this panel displays UTC (Universal Time Coordinated), which means that Evolution believes that your system's clock is tracking time in location-independent, universal mode. Most people will want to specify their actual local time zone here, which you do by clicking on a location that is in the time zone as yours. You do this by moving the cursor over the map and clicking on a nearby location. As you move the cursor over the map, the status line at the bottom of this panel identifies the nearest city on the map that corresponds to the current cursor position. Clicking on any part of the map causes Evolution to zoom in on the associated portion of the map, as shown in Figure 8.11.

FIGURE 8.10

Specifying your time zone

FIGURE 8.11

Zooming in on your actual location

The Timezone map may not include the city that you actually live in. For example, I live near Pittsburgh, Pennsylvania, which (for some odd reason) isn't considered a major city, so I typically choose the nearest "real" city, which is New York City. Once you've selected the nearest city to your actual location (or any city in the same time zone as yours), click Forward to proceed. The panel shown in Figure 8.12 displays.

Congratulations!

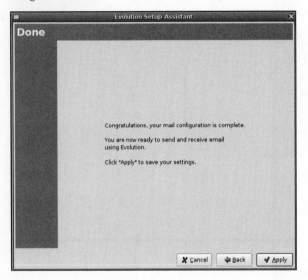

As you might gather from the panel shown in Figure 8.12, setting your time zone concludes setting up your initial mail account in Evolution. To save your settings, click Apply. Once you apply the current settings, you're ready to check your mail for the first time and begin using Evolution in general, as explained in the remainder of this chapter.

TIP
Unlike many e-mail clients, Evolution enables you to simultaneously send and receive mail for multiple e-mail accounts. Each e-mail address has an associated server (and protocol) from which to read mail and another through which to send outgoing mail. You can define other e-mail accounts using Evolution's Preferences dialog, which you can display by selecting the Preferences command from the Edit menu. One issue with Evolution's handling of multiple e-mail addresses is that all addresses for which you retrieve and store mail in Evolution share the same set of folders — each individual mail address doesn't have its own Inbox and set of folders. However, as I'll discuss later in this chapter, you can easily use mail filters or virtual folders to provide the appearance of having a per-address Inbox, which is the next best thing to having one.

Sending and Receiving Mail

Figure 8.13 shows the window that you'll see when starting Evolution (once you've gone through its Setup Wizard to create an initial account). Let's read mail!

FIGURE 8.13

The primary Evolution window

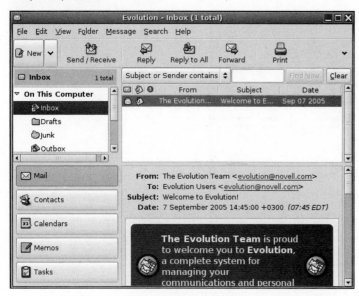

To read your mail, click Send/Receive in the Evolution toolbar. Evolution prompts you for your password, contacts the remote mail server, and begins retrieving your mail. As it retrieves your mail (and sends any outgoing mail), Evolution displays a progress dialog, as shown in Figure 8.14.

FIGURE 8.14

Evolution's e-mail progress bar

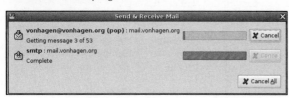

Once Evolution retrieves your incoming e-mail and sends any queued outbound mail, the progress dialog closes and Evolution updates its internal information about the state of the various mail folders on your system. To read your new mail, select your Inbox from the navigation pane at the left, and select any of the new mail messages to display that message, as shown in Figure 8.15.

Any folder shown in bold in the pane at the left is a folder that contains a message that is currently identified as being unread. You'll notice that the Evolution title bar displays the number of unread messages in your Inbox, as does the number in parentheses beside the Inbox folder in the navigation pane at the left.

FIGURE 8.15

Displaying a new message

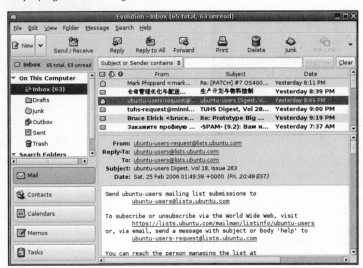

The buttons in the Evolution toolbar are your key to the most common functions in Evolution:

- **New:** Creates a new item of any of the types of items supported by evolution: mail messages, contacts, calendar items, memos, and tasks.

- **Send/Receive:** Retrieves any new mail held at your incoming mail server and sends any pending mail that you've sent.

- **Reply:** Replies to the sender of the currently-selected e-mail message.

- **Reply to All:** Replies to the sender of the current message and sends a carbon copy (CC) of the mail message to anyone else who received a copy of that sender's message.

- **Forward:** Lets you forward the current e-mail message to a new recipient.

- **Print:** Opens a dialog that enables you to print the current message on any printer that has been configured on your system. (See Chapter 23, "Adding Hardware and Attaching Peripherals," for information on configuring printers.)

- **Delete:** Marks the current message for deletion, which removes the message from the list of active messages. To actually delete messages marked for deletion, you have to select the File menu's Empty Trash command.

- **Junk:** Marks the current message as junk, reducing the chance that you'll receive similar messages in the future. For more information about junk mail handling, see "Automatically Checking for Junk Mail," later in this chapter.

- **Not Junk:** Enables you to identify a message that you had previously identified as junk as being acceptable. For more information about junk mail handling, see "Automatically Checking for Junk Mail," later in this chapter.

The down-arrow at the end of the Evolution toolbar indicates that other tool buttons are available, but that the Evolution window on my screen currently isn't wide enough to display them all. You can click on the down arrow to select these other commands (Cancel, Previous, and Next, by default) or simply resize the window to see these other tool buttons.

The buttons on the Evolution toolbar provide easy access to most of the commands that you'll ever need to work with your mail. However, Evolution is a large and powerful application with many bells, whistles, and knobs that you can turn, and deserves its own book. Luckily, Evolution also includes a great online manual that explains the ins and outs of using all of its capabilities. To access this online help, select Contents from the Evolution Help menu. Evolution's online manual displays, as shown in Figure 8.16.

FIGURE 8.16

Evolution's online help

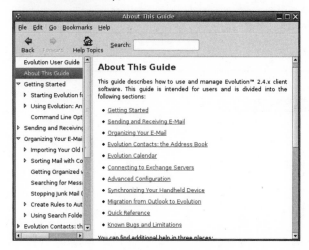

Because this is a book on Ubuntu, not Evolution, the focus of this chapter is on helping you get started with Evolution. Until a book dedicated to Evolution is published, Evolution's online help and various Evolution-related Web sites are the ultimate source of information for this e-mail client. The next few sections provide some of my favorite tips for efficiently working with and managing your e-mail in Evolution. For additional information, see the Web sites listed in "Additional Sources of Information About Evolution" later in this chapter.

Sending Mail in Evolution

You can begin composing a new message in Evolution in a variety of different ways, including:

- Clicking the New button when you are viewing e-mail.
- Pressing Control-+Shift+M on your keyboard.
- Selecting Compose new message from the Message menu.

You can reply to a message that you are currently viewing by doing any of the following:

- Clicking the Reply button, pressing Control+R on your keyboard, or selecting the Reply command from the Message menu.

- Clicking the Reply to All button. Pressing Shift+Control+R on your keyboard, or selecting the Reply to All command from the Message menu. This has the same effect as Reply if you are the sole recipient of the currently selected message.

TIP If you are currently viewing a message that was sent to a mailing list to which you are a subscriber, you can press Control+L or select the Message menu's Reply to List command to reply to the list rather than to the individual who posted that specific message. To follow the rules of good Netiquette, always trim as much of the message you're replying to as possible — especially if you're replying to a mailing list that you receive in digest form.

Selecting any of these options displays Evolution's Compose Message dialog, as shown in Figure 8.17. If you are replying to an existing message, the contents of that message are displayed in the composition window in quoted form to provide some context for your response.

FIGURE 8.17

Composing a message in Evolution

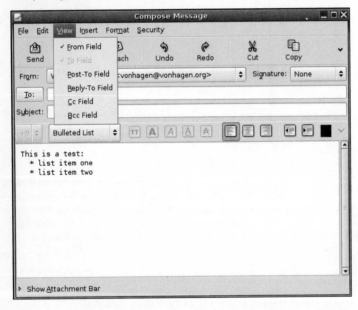

When composing e-mail, Evolution initially displays only the From and To fields in the message header to save space. In many cases, you'll want to send a copy of your mail to someone else (or perhaps to another e-mail address of yours). To display the fields of the mail header that support such additional recipients, click the View menu and select the other fields that you want to see such as CC (Carbon Copy), BCC (Blind Carbon Copy — one or more e-mail addresses that aren't listed in the mail that is actually sent to the other recipients), and so on.

Once you've finished composing your e-mail message, click Send to send the message. This queues the message to be sent, and you can continue working with your e-mail — while you're working, Evolution contacts the remote mail server in the background and sends the message as quickly as it can.

Setting Evolution Preferences for Sending and Viewing Mail

Two basic types of encodings are used when composing and receiving e-mail. One is plain text, which means that your messages display as standard text that might come out of a typewriter (if you remember what those are), with no special fonts or special formatting. The other is e-mail that is formatted as HTML, which lets you use different fonts, special characters for bullets, and so on. Many people prefer one or the other, and whether or not you can read mail delivered in HTML format is up to the e-mail client that you're using (though most can, nowadays).

NOTE Whether or not an e-mail client *can* send mail in HTML format is a different question than whether you *should* send e-mail formatted as HTML. Many people, and many specific recipients such as mailing lists, do not want to receive or will not accept e-mail formatted as HTML.

As shown in Figure 8.17, when you first compose messages in Evolution, it uses standard text format for your messages by default. If you want to switch to using HTML mail, you can do this in one of two ways:

- If you just want to send the current message in HTML format, select the HTML command from the Format menu in the window where you're composing your message. Figure 8.18 shows the same mail composition window as that in Figure 8.17, but displayed as HTML. Additional formatting buttons are active when sending an HTML message, enabling you to use different fonts, different justification formats for the paragraphs in your messages, and so on.

- If you want to send all of your mail as HTML, you must set that as your preference in Evolution's Preferences dialog.

FIGURE 8.18

A message formatted as HTML

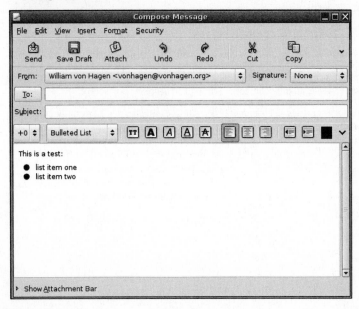

Evolution provides two Preferences panels for setting how it sends and interacts with incoming mail that is formatted as HTML. These are located on the Preferences dialog's Mail Preferences and Composer Preferences panels. To display Evolution's Preferences dialog, select the Edit menu's Preferences command.

To configure Evolution so that it always sends HTML mail, click Composer Preferences in the pane at the left. The panel shown in Figure 8.19 displays.

FIGURE 8.19

Specifying HTML as your default mail format

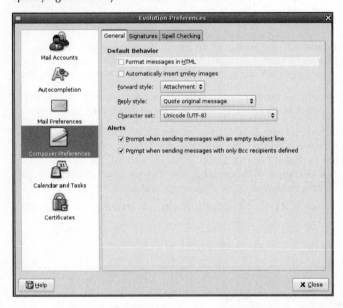

To always send HTML mail, click the checkbox beside Format messages in HTML. When you close Evolution's Preferences dialog, this will become the default format for all new messages that you create.

To set the options for how Evolution handles HTML-formatted mail that you receive, click Mail Preferences in the pane at the left and click the HTML Mail tab. The panel shown in Figure 8.20 displays.

This panel provides several options for incoming HTML mail. For example, if you are occasionally checking your personal e-mail on a machine other than your primary home machine, you may want that to be as fast as possible. In that case, you do not want to load images, because reading mail that contains images is slower than plain mail because images take some time (and network bandwidth) to download. To stop Evolution from downloading images at all, select the Never load images from the Internet radio button. If you want to download images only from people that you know (i.e., people who are in your contacts list), select the Load images in mail from contacts radio button. If you always want to load images, select the Always load images from the Internet radio button.

FIGURE 8.20

Options for displaying incoming HTML mail

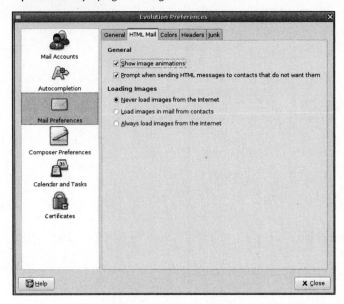

The panel shown in Figure 8.20 also provides a nice option for the benefit of those entities that do not want to receive HTML e-mail, the Prompt when sending HTML... option. This causes Evolution to display a confirmation dialog if you are sending HTML mail to a person or mailing list that identifies itself as not wanting to receive HTML e-mail.

Once you've finished setting Evolution's mail preferences, click Close to exit the Preferences dialog. Most of the preferences that you can set take effect immediately. Some may not take effect until the next time that you start Evolution.

TIP Evolution enables you to customize many other aspects of how it composes new messages, displays incoming e-mail, interacts with remote mail servers, and many more. Explaining all of these is outside the scope of this chapter, but I encourage you to explore the various panels and tabs available in Evolution's Preferences dialog to make sure that Evolution works exactly the way that you want it to.

Undeleting Mail Messages

Like files deleted on DOS and Microsoft Windows systems, e-mail messages that you delete aren't immediately purged, but are just marked for deletion when you explicitly empty the Trash or exit Evolution (if you've configured Evolution to do that).

If you accidentally delete an e-mail message and would like to get it back, you can deselect the View menu's Hide Deleted Messages option. After selecting this option, the titles for messages that are marked for deletion are shown with a line through them, as shown in Figure 8.21.

FIGURE 8.21

Showing mail messages that are marked for deletion

You can undelete any mail messages that are currently marked for deletion by selecting the message title and selecting the Edit menu's Undelete message command.

Creating and Using Mail Folders

After sending and receiving a fair amount of e-mail, your Inbox will become pretty cluttered and you'll find it hard to locate a specific message even though Evolution provides some nice options for locating specific messages above the window where your Inbox is displayed. But why search for something if you can organize things better in the first place? The list of mail folders that Evolution provides by default is always displayed in the navigation pane at the left of your mail Evolution window, but Evolution also makes it easy for you to create your own custom folders to better (and permanently) organize your mail.

Evolution creates the following folders for you during its configuration process:

- **Inbox:** The folder in which incoming mail is deposited when read from your mail server.

- **Drafts:** A folder in which you can put mail messages that you're working on but which have not yet been sent.

- **Junk:** A folder that holds messages that have been identified as junk messages by Evolution's junk-mail scanner. For more information about this folder and junk mail in general, see "Automatically Checking for Junk Mail," later in this chapter.

- **Outbox:** A temporary location where mail that you have sent is stored before it is actually sent to your outgoing mail server.

- **Sent:** A folder that, by default, holds copies of outgoing mail that you have sent, so that you have a record of their contents.

- **Trash:** A folder that contains messages slated for deletion when you explicitly empty the Trash or exit from Evolution (if you've configured your Evolution preferences to perform that action).

With the exception of your Inbox, mail folders are listed alphabetically. Your Inbox is always the top folder in Evolution's navigation pane, so that it is always easy to find.

You can create a new mail folder by doing either of the following:

- selecting New from the Folder menu
- right-clicking the folder or location in which you want to create the new folder and selecting New Folder from the pop-up menu

After performing either of these actions, a dialog like the one shown in Figure 8.22 displays.

FIGURE 8.22

Creating a new mail folder

In this dialog, you can navigate to the location where you want to create the mail folder, enter the name of the new folder, and click Create.

Creating special-purpose mail folders makes it easy to organize your mail so that your Inbox contains only a minimum number of messages — often, only new ones. Mail folder can be hierarchical — in other words, the folder can also contain other folders. For example, I typically create a Friends folder with subfolders that correspond to each of the people that I regularly communicate with. Once I've read or responded to a message, I put it in the appropriate folder. This makes it easy to review my correspondence with specific people without having to sift through many unrelated messages.

Using Search Folders

In addition to standard mail folders for organizing your mail, Evolution was the first mail client to introduce the idea of search folders for viewing related groups of mail messages. Standard mail folders actually hold mail messages — search folders are like an index or table of contents to a group of related messages that contains pointers to those message rather than the messages themselves. This makes it easy to store your messages in explicit mail folders but use virtual folders to give you alternate views of your mail folders. Search folders were known as *vfolders* or *virtual folders* in older releases of Evolution.

As an example, suppose that you subscribed to various mailing lists about different Linux distributions and types of Linux filesystems, and organized your incoming mail based on the name of the mailing list. Suppose that you also wanted to be able to examine all of the messages about a specific type of filesystem, regardless of which list they were posted on. You could always create a mail filter (as explained in the next section) to file the messages according to the mailing lists that they arrived on and copy them to a filesystem-specific folder, but that would eventually end up wasting a significant amount of space. Evolution's search folder concept to the rescue — it is easy to create a search folder that simply contains pointers to all of the matching messages without duplicating them.

Like most tasks in Evolution, there are a variety of ways to create a new search folder. These include the following:

- Right-clicking on the Search Folders item in the navigation pane and selecting the New Folder command from the pop-up menu.

- Right-clicking on the heading on any sample message that satisfies the criteria for the search folder that you want to create, selecting the Create Rule From Message submenu, and selecting any of Search Folder from Subject, Search Folder from Sender, Search Folder from Recipient, or Search Folder from Mailing List. (The last only displays if you select a message that Evolution can recognize as having been sent to a mailing list.) Each of these menu commands creates an initial search folder based on searching the specified portion of that mail message, which you can retain as is or further customize.

- Selecting the Edit menu's Search Folders command and clicking Add to create a new search folder.

- While any sample message that satisfies the criteria for the search folder that you want to create is highlighted, selecting the Message menu's Create Rule submenu, and selecting any of Search Folder from Subject, Search Folder from Sender, Search Folder from Recipients, or Search Folder from Mailing List. (The last only displays if you select a message that Evolution can recognize as having been sent to a mailing list.) Each of these menu commands creates an initial search folder based on searching the specified portion of that mail message, which you can retain as is or further customize.

Performing any of these actions displays a dialog like the one shown in Figure 8.23 that contains any initial criteria implied by the command that you selected.

Once this dialog displays, you can specify a name for the search folder and add or refine the selection criteria for the search folder in the same way that you create filter rules for incoming mail, as explained in the next section. The primary difference between search folder and filter rule creation lies in the bottom half of the dialog shown in Figures 8-23 and 8-24, which (for search folders) identifies the location(s) that the folder should search for matching messages. You can specify that only certain folders be searched by clicking add and selecting their names, or you can select With all Local Folders to include messages from any folder, or With all Local and Remote Folders to search the server-side, remote folders supported by mail protocols such as IMAP. Figure 8.24 shows a search folder that has been defined to search only a specific set of local folders.

Once you're finished fine-tuning the rule that messages must match to be included in your new search folder, click OK to close this dialog and return to Evolution. The search folder is created under the Search Folder item in Evolution's navigation pane, and contains pointers to any existing messages that match the specified criteria.

FIGURE 8.23

Creating a new search folder

FIGURE 8.24

A search rule associated with specific local folders

Filtering Incoming Mail

We all receive a significant amount of e-mail nowadays, some of which we actually want to receive. It's a sad fact of modern Internet life that all of us receive a significant amount of SPAM or junk mail. These are essentially equivalent terms for mail that we didn't ask for, but which is either broadcast to collections of randomly generated e-mail addresses or perhaps sent to us directly if we were unlucky enough to get our e-mail addresses included on one of the lists that some companies, and certainly spammers, sell to each other.

Evolution provides two sophisticated features for automatically analyzing incoming mail and performing specific actions on mail messages that match these criteria. In the case of legitimate mail, Evolution enables you to create powerful filtering rules that can automatically file incoming mail in appropriate folders. Mail filters can also discard incoming messages from known spam sites, messages that contain words that only a spammer would use, or messages that match any other criteria that you define as SPAM.

In addition to making it easy for you to create powerful filtering rules, Evolution can also be integrated with other free Linux software that uses different approaches to identify SPAM and junk mail and automatically move it to your Junk folder. You can then quickly scan your Junk folder occasionally to see if all the mail in there is indeed junk and, if so, you can easily delete it without having to read it.

The next two sections explain how to create your own filter rules and how to install the software required for junk mail processing in Evolution on Ubuntu systems.

Automatically Processing Incoming Mail

To expand on the definition of filtering given in the introduction to this section, filtering e-mail means to analyze its contents based on various criteria and to use the results of that examination to perform some action regarding that message. Message filters are typically applied to incoming messages that are stored locally — if you want to apply message filters to messages stored in remote folder (such as you Inbox on an IMAP server), you must specify that as an option when creating your account, as shown in Figure 8.7.

Like most tasks in Evolution, there are several ways to create a new mail filter. These include the following:

- Right-clicking on the heading on any sample message that satisfies the criteria for the message filter that you want to create, selecting the Create Rule From Message submenu, and selecting any of Filter on Subject, Filter on Sender, Filter on Recipients, or Filter on Mailing List. (The last only displays if you select a message that Evolution can recognize as having been sent to a mailing list.) Each of these menu commands creates an initial message filter based on the specified portion of that mail message, which you can retain as is or further customize.

- Selecting the Edit menu's Message Filters command and clicking Add to create a new message filter.

- While any sample message that satisfies the criteria for the search folder that you want to create is highlighted, selecting the Message menu's Create Rule submenu, and selecting any of Filter on Subject, Filter on Sender, Filter on Recipients, or Filter on Mailing List. (The last only displays if you select a message that Evolution can recognize as having been sent to a mailing list.) Each of these menu commands creates an initial message filter based on the specified portion of that mail message, which you can retain as is or further customize.

Performing any of these actions displays a dialog like the one shown in Figure 8.25 that contains any initial criteria implied by the command that you selected.

FIGURE 8.25

Creating or editing a message filter

When creating a message filter, the default action to perform on matching messages is to move that message to a specified folder. To identify that folder, click <click here to select a folder> and locate the target folder in the navigation dialog that displays.

Evolution provides a very sophisticated set of possible ways of matching messages in a message filter. The following are the portions of the message that you can match and the comparison operators that you can use. These correspond to the contents of the drop-down menus you see when clicking on the first two buttons when creating or editing a rule:

- You can examine the following portions of a mail message when creating a rule: Attachments, Date Received, Date Sent, Expression, Follow Up, Junk Test, Label, Match All, Message Body, Mailing List, Pipe to Program, Recipients, Regex Match, Score, Sender, Size (KB), Source Account, Specific Header, Status, and Subject.

- You can analyze those portions of an e-mail message using the following comparison operators: Contains, Does Not Contain, Does Not End With, Does Not Sound Like, Does Not Start With, Ends With, Is, Is After, Is Before, Is Greater Than, Is Less Than, Is Not, Returns Greater Than, Starts With, Sounds Like, And Starts With. Some of these operators can only be used when examining specific portions of a mail message. As an example, the "Is After" And "Is Before" operations can only be used with dates.

When creating a rule for matching a filter, you can select any of the items in the first and second columns, in any combination. Not all of the items in the second column are available for all types of match conditions — for example, options such as is greater than and is less than only apply when you are checking a match condition, such as Size, that has a numeric value.

As an example of using match conditions for filter rules, to create a rule that matches when a recipient of an e-mail message was ubuntu-users@lists.ubuntu.com, you would select Recipients from the first drop-down menu in the dialog shown in Figure 8.25, is from the second drop down rule menu in that Figure, and enter ubuntu-users@lists.ubuntu.com in the text area at the right to complete the rule.

> **TIP** When creating match rules, the most important control to set is whether a message must match only one (or more) of the specified criteria, or whether the associated operations will be performed only if the message matches all of the specified criteria. This can be the difference between a successful rule and one that doesn't work as you intended. This is controlled by the Find Items control, shown in the upper-right corner of any message filter dialog, which you can set to either If any criteria are met or If all criteria are met.

Table 8.1 shows a list of the possible operations that you can perform on messages that match any (or all) of your filter conditions.

TABLE 8.1

Actions to Perform on Matching Messages

Operation	Action
Adjust Score	Select value from 3 to –3 or enter number to add.
Assign Color	Select color.
Assign Score	Select value from 3 to –3 or enter number.
Beep	N/A.
Copy to Folder	Select folder.
Delete	N/A.
Move to Folder	Select folder.
Pipe to program	Select program.
Play Sound	Select sound file.
Run program	Select program.
Set Status	Select from Replied to, Deleted, Draft, Important, Read, and Junk.
Stop Processing	N/A.
Unset Status	Select from Replied to, Deleted, Draft, Important, Read, and Junk.

In Table 8.1, column one is the action that you want to perform, and column two enables you to specify the value for that operation. For example, if you want to move a message to a specified folder after matching a filter rule, you would select the Move to Folder operation from the first drop-down menu in the Then portion of the rule, and click <click here to select a folder> to identify the target folder for that operation.

As an example of creating the Then portion of a filter rule, I'll continue with the example of messages whose recipients match ubuntu-users@lists.ubuntu.com. Assuming that I want to move such messages to their own folder, I would click Move to Folder from the drop down menu in the first column and then navigate to the correct target folder. I could also add extra actions, such as Setting the status of the message to Read (otherwise the folder will show up in bold, indicating that it contains one or more unread messages), and conclude the rule with a Stop Processing instruction, which ensures that no other filter rules will be applied to the current message. This generally expedites messages filtering, because once a rule matches a message, no other analysis of that message is performed and Evolution moves on to checking the next message.

Automatically Checking for Junk Mail

Evolution's ability to filter e-mail messages based on criteria that you can define is powerful, but requires that you create a potentially huge number of rules to catch all of the SPAM and other junk mail that you may receive. Luckily, Evolution also supports the integration of external applications that can analyze messages and identify them as junk if that's the case. Popular examples of this sort of junk e-mail filter application are SpamAssassin (`http://spamassassin.apache.org/`) and Bogofilter (`http://bogofilter.sourceforge.net/`).

Evolution includes a plug-in for SpamAssassin, which will automatically execute the SpamAssassin program and apply it to incoming mail. Because SpamAssassin has special licensing requirements, the Ubuntu folks do not include SpamAssassin as part of a default Evolution installation. To install SpamAssassin on your system, you must manually enable the officially unsupported Universe repository and use Synaptic Package Manager or `apt-get` to install SpamAssassin to enable Evolution's default Junk mail filtering. I describe enabling different repositories and installing custom software packages in Chapter 20, "Adding, Removing, and Updating Software."

Once you have downloaded and installed SpamAssassin, check Evolution's plug-in list to make sure that SpamAssassin integration is active. To do this, select Plugins from the Edit menu to display the Plugin Manager dialog, shown in Figure 8.26.

FIGURE 8.26

Enabling the Spamassassin plug-in

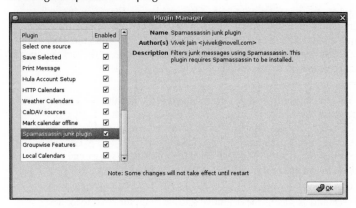

Once this dialog displays, scroll down to the SpamAssassin junk plug-in entry and make sure that it is enabled. Click OK after verifying this and enabling this plug-in, if necessary.

Once you install SpamAssassin and make sure that it is enabled, clicking the Junk button in the Evolution toolbar will identify the currently selected message as junk and will mail it to your Junk folder. Subsequent messages that you receive, which are conceptually similar to that message, will automatically be identified as junk and also moved to the Junk folder. You should check the Junk folder periodically, verify that all of the messages that it contains are actually junk mail, and delete those messages. If you see messages classified as junk that are actually valid messages, select those messages and click the Not Junk button in the Evolution toolbar to make sure that similar messages are not categorized as junk. Over time, you will see that Evolution's support for junk mail filtering does a good job of identifying SPAM and other junk mail, saving you lots of time that would otherwise be spent examining such messages for criteria that you could use to manually filter out those e-mail messages.

> **TIP**   If you are having problems installing or using SpamAssassin, make sure that Evolution's BogoFilter plug-in is not enabled on the Edit ⇨ Plugins dialog. This conflicts with SpamAssassin and can cause problems.

Additional Sources of Information About Evolution

Don't get your hopes up, Charles Darwin fans! This section discusses other sources of information about the Evolution PIM/e-mail application, not the theory of Evolution.

Because the Evolution application is generally very popular and is the default e-mail application on most GNOME-based systems (such as Ubuntu), there are a good number of Web sites that can provide you with additional information about using Evolution, as well as mailing lists that you can join to ask questions, file problem reports, and so on. Some of my favorites are the following:

- Evolution Forums (`http://nabble.com/Gnome---Evolution-f1297.html`): If you prefer to use a forum interface instead of a mailing list, Nabble provides a great collection of forums that present the various Evolution mailing lists in a user-friendly forum format. Messages posted to these forums go directly to the associated mailing list.

- Evolution IRC Channel: If you're a fan of Internet Relay Chat and have a client handy (such as the XChat-GNOME IRC client that is provided with Ubuntu), you can discuss developing and using Evolution in the #evolution channel on `irc.gimp.org`. You should lurk for a little while before broadcasting your questions, just to get a feel for the channel and to reduce your chances of being flamed if you ask "the wrong question" or one for which an answer is readily available in the documentation or elsewhere.

- Evolution Mailing Lists: You can subscribe to a general mailing list for Evolution users (known as the *evolution-list* — catchy, no?) at `http://mail.gnome.org/mailman/listinfo/evolution-list`, and you can also subscribe to a more advanced Evolution hackers list (evolution-hackers) at `http://mail.gnome.org/mailman/listinfo/evolution-hackers`. For general information about all GNOME-related mailing lists, see `http://mail.gnome.org/mailman/listinfo/`.

- Evolution Project Home Page (`http://gnome.org/projects/evolution`): This is the home page of the Evolution project, and as such is the definitive starting point for looking for additional information about Evolution, the source code for the latest version of Evolution, and so on.

- Evolution Wiki (`http://go-evolution.org/Main_Page`): This is a great site for information about the current release of Evolution and for getting insights into (or making suggestions for) the capabilities that will be present in upcoming versions of Evolution.

Any reasonable Internet search engine will display many more sites with information about Evolution, but these are the primary official conduits for Evolution information.

Summary

This chapter explained how to configure and use Evolution, a powerful e-mail client and Personal Information Manager, focusing on the e-mail aspects of Evolution. Evolution is a great e-mail client that supports all popular e-mail protocols and provides unrivaled connectivity to specific types of mail servers such as Microsoft Exchange e-mail servers.

Reading and sending e-mail is one of the most common tasks that anyone does with their personal computer nowadays. Equally common is surfing the Web, which is explained in the next chapter. To satisfy your Web surfing requirements, Ubuntu automatically installs the Firefox Web browser, the most powerful, extensible, and just plain fun Web browser available today.

Chapter 9

Surfing the Web with Firefox

Like all open source software, many Web browsers are available for installation on your Ubuntu Linux system. Desktop systems such as GNOME and KDE both have multipurpose object browsers (Nautilus and Konqueror, respectively) that can also browse Web pages and are fine for that purpose if you want to learn only one tool and use it for almost everything. However, Ubuntu installs the Mozilla project's Firefox browser as its default Web browser for a good reason — it's the best Web browser available on Linux systems (and on any other system too, IMHO). Firefox is the most popular open source browser available today, and is the only browser in the last decade or so to have actually taken market share away from Internet Explorer. Many of the innovations that Microsoft Windows users are looking forward to in upcoming releases of Internet Explorer were first introduced in Firefox and have been present for quite a few versions.

This chapter starts out with a bit of history that explains what a long strange trip it's been for Firefox, and then discusses how to start, configure, use, and customize Firefox.

A Quick History of Firefox

Firefox has what is perhaps the best possible pedigree in Web browsing history — it is the latest descendant of the original Mosaic Web browser, the original graphical Web browser for Unix systems. Mosaic was created in 1992 at the National Center for Supercomputing Applications (NCSA) at the University of Illinois at Urbana-Champaign.

> **TIP** For a quick history of the World Wide Web, see the section of Chapter 26 entitled "World Wide Web 101."

As the Internet boom unfolded around the Web and its killer application, the graphical Web browser, much of the team that developed Mosaic left the NCSA to found Mosaic Communications Corporation, including the leader of the team, Marc Andreessen. Because of issues with NCSA over the Mosaic name, Mosaic

Communications Corporation quickly became Netscape Communications Corporation, and their fledgling browser product became known as Netscape Navigator. Early versions of Netscape Navigator were available by mid-1994, with the first official release occurring near the end of the year.

In one of the incestuous twists of fate that make hi-tech history interesting, a company named Spyglass, Inc. licensed the Mosaic technology and trademarks from the University of Illinois and used it to develop their own Web browser, Spyglass Mosaic for personal computer systems running Microsoft Windows. Spyglass then eventually licensed the source code for Spyglass Mosaic to Microsoft, where it became the basis for Microsoft's Internet Explorer.

Back to the somewhat biblical history of Firefox. Netscape Navigator was merely a Web browser, and the growing legions of Internet fanatics clamored for other Net-related applications. Demand for other Net-related applications, such as mail clients and Web page composition tools, led Netscape to make Netscape Navigator a part of their new Netscape Communicator Suite.

Internet Explorer quickly began to take over the browser market from Netscape — after all, it came free straight from the mother ship on every Microsoft Windows desktop system, and its accompanying Web server product, Internet Information Server that was included for free with every Microsoft Windows server system. By 1998, Netscape Communications Corporation was essentially dead as a stand-alone entity, though it was acquired by America Online (AOL) for a surprising $4 billion.

Netscape's last gasp as a stand-alone entity was to found the open source Mozilla project, donate the Netscape Communicator source code, and create an accompanying Mozilla Organization. Both were chartered with stewarding the creation of the next-generation Internet suite for Netscape. Mozilla was the original code name for the Netscape browser throughout its creation, and an accompanying red dragon was a popular decoration at Netscape. The Mozilla project, often flamed for disorganization, eventually stabilized and modularized its code base, and continues to form the basis of a Netscape browser that is available at www .netscape.com and is still under development today.

Meanwhile, the Mozilla project began to create its own Web browser product. This browser was originally named Phoenix, and then Firebird, both of which had naming conflicts with existing applications, so the browser eventually settled on the name Firefox.

Throughout its history, Firefox has introduced features that we all take for granted nowadays, such as an integrated pop-up blocker, a customizable toolbar, a sidebar, integrated searches on the toolbar, graphical cookie management, a download manager, customizable themes, the ability to easily add external browser extensions, and tabbed browsing.

NOTE Though Firefox (and its sibling Thunderbird e-mail client) are the primary products of the Mozilla Foundation, other, related applications are still under development and available. The most interesting of these is the SeaMonkey project, a suite of Internet applications based on the original Mozilla Application Suite, the descendant of the Netscape Communicator. The SeaMonkey project includes a Web browser, an e-mail and newsgroup client, and IRC chat client, and a tool for composing HTML Web pages. SeaMonkey is available at www.mozilla.org/projects/seamonkey.

Starting Firefox

You can start Firefox manually in a variety of different ways:

- By clicking the Firefox Web Browser icon in the GNOME toolbar at the top of the screen, shown in Figure 9.1. This is the easiest and most common way to start Firefox.

- By selecting Firefox Web browser from the Applications ⇨ Internet menu.
- By typing the `firefox` command in a GNOME Terminal or xterm window and pressing return.

Ubuntu's GNOME desktop is also preconfigured to start Firefox for you if you click on a URL (Uniform Resource Locater) in an e-mail reader or another Internet-aware application.

FIGURE 9.1

The Firefox icon on your GNOME desktop

After you start Firefox for the first time, a screen such as the one shown in Figure 9.2 displays, showing the default home page, which displays a "welcome" page and provides general information about the Ubuntu release that you're running. If you've started Firefox for the first time by clicking on a URL in another application, the Web page corresponding to that URL displays.

FIGURE 9.2

Starting Firefox for the first time

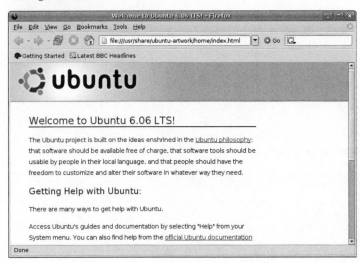

Most people configure Firefox (or any Web browser, for that matter) so that it starts up on a Web page of their choosing, referred to as your home page. I'll explain how to configure that later in this chapter — for now, let's explore the meaning and use of the different parts of any Firefox window.

The Firefox User Interface

Though most Web browsers look and work approximately the same nowadays, this section provides an overview of the different portions of a Firefox window, just in case you're lucky enough to be running Ubuntu on your first computer. If you're already comfortable with Web browsers and graphical applications in general, feel free to skip this section entirely or skip ahead to the section entitled "Special and Not-So-Special Firefox Features" to get an overview of some of the special capabilities available in Firefox that may not have been available in Web browsers that you've used previously.

Standard Parts of a Firefox Window

Figure 9.3 shows a sample Firefox screen, showing the different portions of a standard Firefox window.

FIGURE 9.3

Different portions of a Firefox window

These different areas provide the following functionality:

■ **Menus:** Displays a drop-down menu of related commands when you position the cursor over any of the items in this area and click on them.

■ **Navigation Toolbar:** Displays icons that control the Web page displayed in the main Firefox window. By default, the Navigation toolbar also provides quick access to the Google search engine.

■ **Bookmarks Toolbar:** Provides quick access to selected bookmarks that are more frequently visited than the standard bookmarks saved on the Bookmarks menu.

■ **Tabs:** Represents different Web pages that you are currently visiting. By default, this portion of the screen displays only if you are currently visiting more than one site, though this is configurable.

■ **Main Window:** Displays the contents of the Web page that you are currently visiting.

■ **Search Toolbar:** Displays commands that enable you to search for specific text in the Web page that you are currently visiting. This portion of the screen displays only if you have previously executed a Search command.

■ **Status Bar:** Provides summary information about Firefox's retrieval of the Web page that you are currently visiting. Icons at the right end of this page display status information about that page if indexing is enabled, an RSS feed is available on that page, the page is retrieved through a secure connection, and so on.

As I'll explain later in this chapter, you can configure many of these items — what they contain (Navigation Toolbar, Bookmarks Toolbar), how they look (by using custom themes), and whether they display at all (Navigation Toolbar, Bookmarks Toolbar, Status Bar).

Using the Mouse in Firefox

There's nothing different about using the mouse in Firefox than in any other graphical application except for the contents of any menus that pop up in response to a right-click. However, if you're new to graphical applications, let's review. On a standard three-button mouse, clicking (pressing and releasing) a mouse button does the following:

■ **Left Button:** Selects something. Left-clicking on a menu displays that menu and left-clicking on an item from that menu selects a command or submenu. Left-clicking on a button in the Navigation toolbar executes the command associated with that button or, in the case of the Google toolbar, positions the cursor so that you can specify what you want to search for. Left-clicking on a portion of a Web page performs any action associated with that area — following a hyperlink, displaying a larger graphic, submitting a form, and so on.

■ **Middle Button:** Depending on where you click, middle-clicking can open a hyperlink in a new tab, paste selected text into a selected text area, and so on

■ **Right Button:** Displays different menus depending on what you right-click on. These are known as *context-sensitive menus* for this reason. Figure 9.4 shows two context-sensitive menus from Firefox: The menu at the right displays if you right-click on the background of the current Web page, while the menu at the left displays if you right-click on a hyperlink in the current Web page. (By the way, you can't get both of these context menus to display at the same time as this figure might suggest.)

Context-sensitive menus such as those shown in Figure 9.4 can be customized by adding Firefox extensions that have associated menu items, as explained in the section entitled "Adding Firefox Extensions," later in this chapter. You can even customize how the mouse behaves to some extent by adding Firefox extensions that tell Firefox to perform specific actions when specific types of mouse movements occur.

FIGURE 9.4

Context-sensitive menus from Firefox

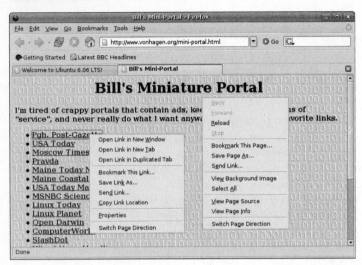

Special and Not-So-Special Firefox Features

If you're familiar with the vanilla Web browsers installed with other operating systems, such as Internet Explorer on Microsoft Windows and earlier releases of Mac OS X, Firefox provides the same capabilities as those browsers and adds a few powerful, exciting capabilities. Some of the most interesting features first added by Firefox and standard browser capabilities that aren't active by default in Firefox are the following:

- **Tabbed Browsing:** Enables you to open multiple Web pages simultaneously without creating separate windows for each. Each Web page that is currently open is represented by a separate tab, which displays above the portion of the screen that shows the current Web page. You can quickly and easily switch between these Web pages by clicking on the appropriate tab. This feature is so useful that it has been incorporated into most other modern browsers — for example, Microsoft added this capability in Internet Explorer 7, and this feature is also available in Mac OS X's Safari browser. To close a selected tab, click the red "X" icon at the top right of the Tab display area.

- **Sidebars:** Provide easy navigation through a given list of Web pages. Firefox provides two different sidebars, one displaying your bookmarks and a second that provides a list of the Web pages that you have visited recently (known as a *history* sidebar). These sidebars aren't turned on by default in Firefox, but you can easily activate whichever you prefer by selecting Bookmarks or History from the View ⇨ Sidebar menu. Figure 9.5 shows Firefox with the Bookmarks menu displayed. To close a sidebar, click the red 'X' icon at the top right of the sidebar.

- **Built-in Popup Blocking:** Prevents sites from displaying annoying pop-up windows unless you specifically authorize a site to display them (or you disable this feature entirely). Figure 9.6 shows the banner that displays when Firefox blocks a pop up. You can click the Preferences button in this banner to customize how Firefox handles popups from the current site, or in general. If this banner displays and you don't want to change anything, you can close it by clicking the red 'X' icon at the right of this banner. Customizing how Firefox handles popups is explained later in this chapter.

FIGURE 9.5

The Bookmarks Sidebar in Firefox

FIGURE 9.6

The pop-up blocking banner in Firefox

■ **Live Bookmarks:** Provide a special type of bookmark that is dynamically constructed from an RSS feed provided by a specific site. Creating live bookmarks is explained later in this chapter.

Firefox is a powerful, flexible Web browser with all of the features that you'd expect in any modern Web browser, and then some. You could easily devote an entire book to exploring each and every menu and Firefox feature, but I see the publishers of this book waving their arms frantically and saying "Not here!" So I'll agree with them, and just encourage you to explore the various Firefox menus and the hundreds of available themes and extensions (some of which are discussed later in this chapter).

Configuring Firefox

Firefox is extremely configurable, and provides enough knobs to turn that you could probably spend as much time tweaking your configuration and enhancing Firefox as you can in actually using the browser. Luckily, books such as this one and Firefox's own documentation can help make sure that you spend more time browsing than fine-tuning. Firefox provides great online help at www.mozilla.org/support/firefox/, which includes a tutorial that will walk you through its most popular configuration tasks.

Almost all of the permanently configurable aspects of Firefox are located in its Preferences dialog, which you display by selecting the Preferences item from the Edit menu. Figure 9.7 shows the Firefox Preferences panel in the version of Firefox that was current when this book was written. Yours may look slightly different, but the core contents are the same.

FIGURE 9.7

The Preferences window in Firefox

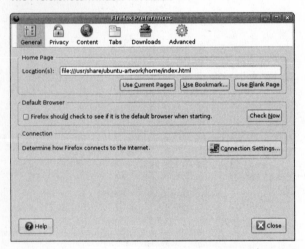

This section discusses the highlights of Firefox configuration, focusing on configuration options that you'll eventually want to know about, regardless of whether or not you want to customize them immediately.

Setting Your Home Page

Your *home page* is the Web page that displays when you first start Firefox (or any Web browser). Many people use a Web portal site of some sort, such as yahoo.com, msn.com, aol.com, or netscape.com as their home page, others use news sites that are specific to their job or interests, and others use personally created

Web pages on Internet sites that they have created or are affiliated with. Regardless of what you use, setting your home page is one of the key aspects of personalizing your use of Firefox.

To set your home page in Firefox, first display the Edit ➪ Preferences dialog. Next, click the General button at the top of the dialog to display the pane shown in Figure 9.8.

FIGURE 9.8

The General preferences pane in Firefox

The Home Page section at the top of this pane gives you four options for setting your home page:

- by explicitly typing a URL into the Location text area
- by clicking Use Current Page to use the page that is currently displayed in Firefox
- by clicking Use Bookmark, selecting one of your existing bookmarks from the dialog that displays, and clicking OK to close that dialog
- by clicking Use Blank Page to cause Firefox to start without displaying a specific page

Once you've used one of these mechanisms to select your new home page, click OK to close the Preferences dialog. The home page that you specified will be displayed the next time you start Firefox.

Controlling Popups, JavaScript, and More

Firefox provides a single Preferences pane where you can configure its support for various features of modern Web pages, and how these Web features behave when enabled. You can enable, disable, or customize the behavior of the following from a single dialog:

- **Block Pop-up Windows:** determines whether to block all remote sites from displaying pop-up windows, allow selected sites to display popups, or allow all sites to display popups on your system
- **Allow Web Sites to Install Software:** determines whether to prevent any remote site from installing software on your machine, permit selected remote sites to install software on your local machine, or allow all remote sites to install software

- **Load Images:** determines whether to load all images on any Web page, load images only from the site that actually hosts the Web page (to block ads and graphics provided by other sites), and load images from a list of sites even if loading images is prohibited

- **Enable Java:** determines whether to support Java in Firefox so that remote sites can download Java applets that will execute locally on your machine

- **Enable JavaScript:** determines whether to support JavaScript, which enables programmatic content generation and window manipulation, and (if so) determines which specific features to support

To enable, disable, or customize these content-related features, first display the Edit ➪ Preferences dialog. Next, click the Content button at the top of the dialog to display the pane shown in Figure 9.9.

FIGURE 9.9

Enabling and customizing content in Firefox

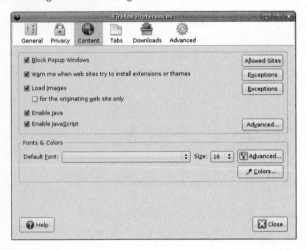

Once this pane displays, you can select the checkbox beside the feature you're interested in tuning to enable or disable that activity. For options that allow you to create lists of sites to be excluded from a specific setting, click the Allowed Sites or Exceptions button to the right of that option, and enter the names of the sites that you want to exclude from that setting. Similarly, support for JavaScript is usually enabled by default in Firefox, but the dialog that displays after clicking the Advanced Settings button gives you very fine-tuned control over the sorts of things that JavaScript-enabled Web pages can do on your system.

Once you've finished configuring these content-related features, click OK to close the Preferences dialog. Changes to some settings will not take effect until you restart Firefox, so it's always a good idea to exit from and restart Firefox after changing content settings, just in case.

Configuring Your Privacy Settings

Like the Preferences pane for Content settings, Firefox provides a single Preferences pane where you can configure various privacy settings. In the Privacy pane, different topics are organized onto separate tabs across the center of the pane. To modify a certain privacy setting, click the tab with its name, and customize the options displayed below the tab. Customizable privacy settings include the following:

- **History:** Determines the period of time (in days) for which Firefox keeps a record of the URLs for the Web sites that you've visited.

- **Saved Forms:** Determines whether or not Firefox remembers the values that you've entered when searching for things in the search toolbar or when filling out forms on the Web.

- **Passwords:** Determines whether or not Firefox stores username/password pairs that you've used to log in to different secure sites. This configuration item provides special dialogs for managing any login/password combinations that are currently saved. (More about that later in this section.)

- **Download History:** Determines when the Download Manager removes the names of files that you've downloaded from its history list. Possible values are Manually, meaning that you must remove them yourself and they are otherwise remembered forever; Upon Successful Download, meaning that they are removed when the download completes successfully; and When Firefox Exits, meaning that the list of files is cleared each time you exit Firefox.

- **Cookies:** Determines whether or not Firefox accepts cookies in general, a list of sites excluded from this policy, and, if so, how long cookies are retained. Cookies are encoded chunks of information remote Web sites can set in your browser to immediately recognize you the next time you visit. Like the Saved Passwords setting, this configuration item provides a special dialog that enables you to manage the list of cookies that are currently stored on your system.

- **Cache:** Maintains the size of the cache of recently visited Web pages on your system. Caching means to save a local copy of the HTML and graphical content of each Web page that you visit. If you revisit a given site whose content you have cached and that content has not changed, Firefox can immediately redisplay the page from its cache rather than having to retrieve it from the remote site. This provides a tremendous performance improvement, but can use up a large amount of disk space.

Most of these privacy settings are accompanied by a Clear... button that enables you to quickly erase all of the information associated with that privacy setting that is currently saved.

To enable, disable, or customize these privacy-related settings, first display the Edit ⇨ Preferences dialog. Next, click the Privacy button at the top of the dialog to display the pane shown in Figure 9.10.

FIGURE 9.10

Customizing privacy settings in Firefox

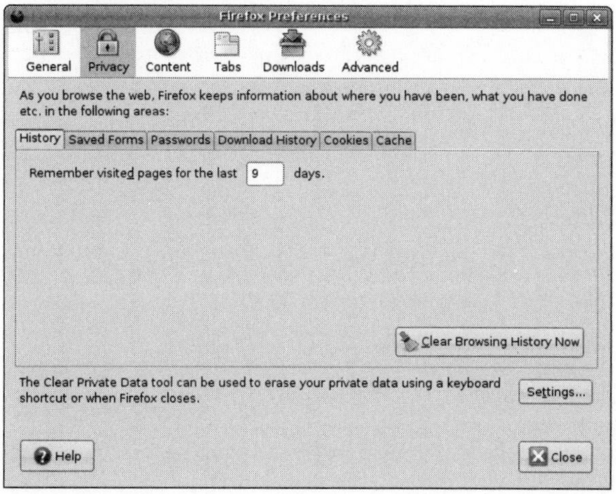

Once this dialog displays, click on the tab for the privacy-related setting that you want to customize to see what configuration options are available. For example, Figure 9.11 shows the list of available settings associated with Saved Passwords in Firefox.

FIGURE 9.11

Saved Password settings in Firefox

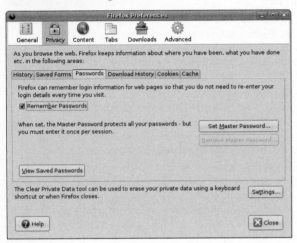

In this case, clicking the View Saved Passwords button displays the Password Manager dialog shown in Figure 9.12, which enables you to manually delete any username/password pairs that are currently saved in Firefox.

FIGURE 9.12

Managing Passwords Saved in Firefox

To remove a saved username/password pair for a specific site, highlight that entry and click Remove at the bottom of the dialog, as my wife would probably like to do with my eBay login information. Like most graphical selections, you can hold down the Control key while clicking on entries to select multiple username/password pairs, or select one item, hold down the shift key, and click another to select those two items and all of the items between those two username/password pairs. Click Close to close this dialog and return to the Privacy Settings pane when you're done.

Once you've finished configuring your privacy settings, click OK to close the Preferences dialog. Changes to some settings will not take effect until you restart Firefox, so it's always a good idea to exit from and restart Firefox after changing privacy settings, just in case.

Working with Bookmarks

In a Web browser, a bookmark is a record of the Uniform Resource Locator (URL) for a Web page that you've visited, and which you want to visit again. When you select a bookmark, Firefox goes directly to the page that it represents — no fuss, no muss.

NOTE If you're used to Internet Explorer, "bookmarks" is the more common term for what Internet Explorer calls Favorites.

Bookmarks are great things, just as they are in real books. Without a bookmark, you'd have to start searching a book at the beginning each time you picked it up. The same thing is true of bookmarks in terms of Web searches — once you've found somewhere that you want to return to on the Web, it's important to save a bookmark to that location so that you can easily return there. You certainly don't want to have to redo a complex Web search process or Web page navigation sequence any more times than you have to — which should be once, if you've bookmarked a page.

Firefox provides two primary locations in which to save bookmarks: a hierarchical collection of bookmarks that you can access by selecting the Bookmarks menu, and the Bookmarks Toolbar, which is displayed directly below the Navigation Toolbar in the main Firefox window. The Bookmarks Toolbar is designed to provide quick access to frequently visited bookmarks, while the Bookmarks menu provides access to everything. You can think of the Bookmarks Toolbar as the bestsellers section of a bookstore, while the Bookmarks menu is the entire store.

Over time, most people tend to accumulate huge collections of bookmarks, which makes managing them — and being able to find the one you want when you want it — a very critical task for continued happiness through Web surfing. Firefox includes an excellent Bookmarks Manager that simplifies both of these tasks. The next few sections explain how to create bookmarks in various ways, how to organize them using the Bookmarks Manager, different ways to back up your bookmarks and even access them from other Web browsers, and how to use an exciting feature introduced by Firefox, known as Live Bookmarks, to automatically construct dynamic menus that provide an overview of selected Web sites.

Creating Bookmarks in Firefox

Firefox provides three basic ways of creating a bookmark to the page that you're currently viewing, namely by:

- pressing Control+D on your keyboard (hold down the control key and press the letter D) when viewing that page
- right-clicking on the background of the current page and selecting the Add Bookmark command from the pop-up menu
- selecting the Add Bookmark command from the Bookmarks menu

You can also create a bookmark for a link on the page that you're viewing by right-clicking on the link and selecting the Bookmark This Page command from the pop-up menu.

Regardless of the mechanism that you use to create a bookmark, creating one causes the dialog shown in Figure 9.13 to display. The top portion of the dialog shows the name that the bookmark will have. By default, this is the text under the link or the name of the current page, but you can change it to be something more memorable if you'd like.

FIGURE 9.13

The Add Bookmark dialog in Firefox

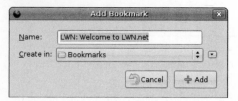

The bottom portion of this dialog represents where the bookmark will be saved. You can click on this entry to see a list of the folders that already exist in your bookmarks, or you can click the down arrow to the right of this dialog to display a browsable dialog that enables you to select a folder within those folders as shown in Figure 9.14, or click on the New Folder button to create a new folder in which to store your new bookmark.

FIGURE 9.14

Navigating folders when saving a bookmark

Once you've made any modification that you want to the name of the bookmark and selected the location where you want to store it, click Add to save the bookmark in that location. The dialog closes, and you can now easily go to that page again by selecting the bookmark.

Managing Your Bookmarks

Over time, most people tend to accumulate huge collections of bookmarks, which makes it harder and harder to find the right bookmark — which somewhat defeats the idea of bookmarks in the first place. To solve this problem, Firefox includes an excellent Bookmarks Manager that makes it easy to organize and reorganize your valuable collection of bookmarks. To display the Bookmarks Manager, select Bookmarks Manager from the Bookmarks menu. A dialog like the one shown in Figure 9.15 displays.

FIGURE 9.15

The Bookmarks Manager in Firefox

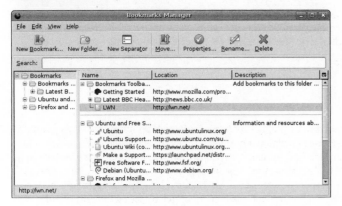

The panel at right provides a hierarchical overview of how your bookmarks are currently organized, while the panel at left provides a detailed view of the bookmarks in the folder that is currently selected. You can move bookmarks around by dragging and dropping them (left-clicking on the bookmark and dragging it to the new location) within either window or even between the two. You can create new folders, new bookmarks, or new separators (the lines that appear in your bookmarks menu) by selecting the appropriate location in either panel and doing any of the following:

- selecting the appropriate icon from the top of the Bookmarks Manager
- right-clicking and selecting the appropriate command from the pop-up menu
- selecting the appropriate command from the File menu

Any changes that you make are immediately reflected on the Firefox Bookmarks menu and Bookmark Toolbar. Once you're finished reorganizing your bookmarks, select the File menu's Close command to close the Bookmarks Manager.

Regardless of how you choose to organize your bookmarks, the one cardinal rule is to avoid having one huge list of bookmarks. You probably have specific interests, and can easily store your bookmarks in folders that represent those interests. This makes it easy to find a given bookmark, and also helps prevent you from accidentally bookmarking the same page eleven times because you couldn't find a specific bookmark when you were looking for it.

Backing Up Your Bookmarks

Because your evolving collection of bookmarks is one of the most precious things that you build up as you surf the Net, making sure that you don't accidentally lose them is critical. The Bookmarks Manager's File menu provides an Export command that enables you to save a copy of your current bookmarks in a separate file. I tend to save my bookmarks every week or two, giving them names containing the current date, like `bookmarks-27-Jan-06.html`, so that I can tell one from the other. This also makes it easy to find a specific bookmark in one of these files if you've accidentally deleted the bookmark but have some idea of the last time that you saw it.

You can also back up your bookmarks from the command line by changing directory into the directory where they are actually stored, which is usually in a directory whose name ends with default that is located in the directory ~/.mozilla/firefox in your home directory. The file `bookmarks.html` in this directory contains your current bookmarks.

Creating Live Bookmarks

Live bookmarks are one of the latest — and most useful — enhancements to Web surfing that have been introduced by the Firefox team. Live bookmarks exploit a popular Web technology called RSS, which stands for Really Simple Syndication, or Rich Site Summary, depending on who you ask. Many Web sites today use RSS to publish a summary of recent changes to their site (known as an *RSS feed*), which other sites can read and display to provide links to those changes. A live bookmark to a site is essentially a special type of bookmark that points to the RSS feed on that site, made more usable by the fact that live bookmarks display the headings in an RSS feed as menu items.

Sites that provide RSS feeds that can be used as live bookmarks in Firefox display a Live Bookmark icon at the far right of their URL in the Firefox Navigation Toolbar, as shown in Figure 9.16.

To create a live bookmark, click the Live Bookmark icon in the URL for that site. The standard Add Bookmark dialog displays, enabling you to specify where you want to create the live bookmark. The Add Bookmark dialog closes, and the live bookmark menu item displays. After a few seconds (the time it takes for Firefox to read the RSS feed and create the live bookmark) you can access the live bookmark menu like any other menu in Firefox, as shown in Figure 9.17.

> **TIP** Your Personal Toolbar is the most common location for creating live bookmarks, because they represent an up-to-date summary of a site that you're presumably very interested in.

The live bookmark shown in Figure 9.17 is for the site that is currently shown in the main browser window in the same figure. If you look closely, you'll notice that the first item on the menu is the first heading on the page in the main browser window. As the site is updated, my live bookmark menu will automatically update to reflect the changes to the site. What could be easier? Perhaps Firefox could also read each of those topics and tell me which ones I should actually care about — maybe in the next release?

FIGURE 9.16

The Live Bookmark icon for a URL in Firefox

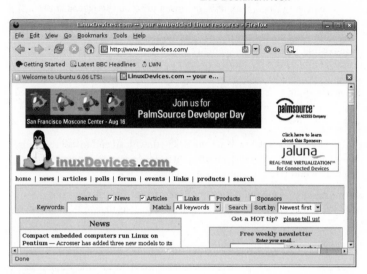

FIGURE 9.17

A live bookmark menu in Firefox

Enhancing Firefox

This chapter has stressed the power and usability of Firefox as it comes "out of the box." However, Firefox provides a final set of capabilities that make it even more interesting: You can easily add new capabilities (known as *extensions*) and new ways of displaying icons, windows, menus, and so on (known as *themes*). This section explains how to add each of these items to further customize your Web surfing. In many cases, Firefox extensions provide extra capabilities that are worthy of being separate applications — but which Firefox smoothly integrates into your existing Web surfing experience. Similarly, everyone has their own idea of meaningful icons and appealing graphical design. Firefox themes — much like the skins that you may be familiar with from popular audio applications such as WinAmp or XMMS — let you customize its appearance so that it is more attractive and quite possibly more usable for you.

Adding Firefox Extensions

Adding new extensions to Firefox is easy, because Firefox will automatically download and install them for you — but figuring out which ones you like best can be hard, because there are so many to choose from. But that's what the hours between midnight and 6 AM are for anyway, right?

To add new extensions, first select the Extensions command from the Tools menu. This displays the Extensions dialog, shown in Figure 9.18, which displays a list of all of the extensions that you've currently installed.

FIGURE 9.18

The Extensions dialog in Firefox

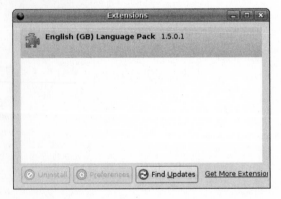

Once this dialog displays, click Get More Extensions in the lower right-hand corner to open a new Firefox window that connects to Firefox headquarters at the Mozilla project and displays a page that shows all of the extensions that are currently available, as shown in Figure 9.19.

FIGURE 9.19

Available extensions at the Mozilla mother ship

The menu at the right of the Firefox Extensions page lists a number of topics into which available extensions are organized, making it easier to find a specific extension or an extension that is related to some specific task that you want to accomplish in Firefox. Once you've located an extension that you want to install, you'll see two icons below the description of that extension, one of which displays the size of the extension, and the other which lists the versions of Firefox that this extension is designed to work with. The extension shown in Figure 9.19, Duplicate Tab, is one of my personal favorites — it adds a `Duplicate Tab` command to the pop-up menu that you see when you right-click on a tab, enabling you to clone a tab and its current content, which is handy for drilling down on a page without losing your place or having to bookmark the higher level.

You can click the Install Now link beside the install icon to automatically download and install the selected extension. This displays a dialog like the one shown in Figure 9.20, in which you click Install Now to automatically download and install the selected extension.

Once you've downloaded and installed an extension, the Extensions dialog updates as shown in Figure 9.21 to reflect the fact that the new extension is installed, but will not be active until after you restart Firefox.

TIP So many interesting extensions are available for Firefox that it's tempting to download and install a huge number of them at the same time, just to see which ones you like. I suggest that you try to control yourself and only install one or two at a time, for two reasons. First, some extensions may conflict with others, and this can cause problems with Firefox. Second, if you install too many extensions, it's hard to tell which one is responsible for which changes in Firefox. This can make it tough if you want to install the same set of extensions on multiple machines, because you may waste time installing extensions that you don't actually want or need.

FIGURE 9.20

The software installation dialog for an extension

FIGURE 9.21

The Extension dialog after installing a new extension

Once you've finished installing the extensions you're interested in, close the Firefox window that displays the extensions available from the Mozilla project, and click the close icon in the top right corner of the Extensions dialog to close that dialog. As the Extensions dialog reminded you, it's a good idea to restart Firefox at this point, both to enable your new extension(s) and to make sure that Firefox still works correctly.

After experimenting with your new capabilities in Firefox, you can always uninstall an extension that you don't like or want by selecting the Extensions command from the Tools menu, highlighting the extension in question, and clicking Uninstall.

Adding New Firefox Themes

Adding new themes to Firefox is easy, because Firefox will automatically download and install selected themes for you. Experimenting with different themes is actually somewhat easier than experimenting with extensions, as described in the previous section, because only one theme can be active at any given time.

To add new themes, first select the Themes command from the Tools menu. This displays the Themes dialog, shown in Figure 9.22, which displays a list of all of the themes that you've currently installed.

FIGURE 9.22

The Themes dialog in Firefox

Once this dialog displays, click Get More Themes in the lower right-hand corner to open a new Firefox window that connects to Firefox headquarters at the Mozilla project and displays a page that shows all of the themes that are currently available.

The process of browsing for and downloading new themes is essentially identical to the process for locating and downloading new extensions (discussed in the previous section), so I won't bore you by describing it in detail. The key difference occurs after the new theme is downloaded and installed. Because each theme provides a complete graphical makeover for Firefox, only one theme can be active at a time. To use a new theme, you must select it from the Themes dialog and click Use Theme, as shown in Figure 9.23.

After restarting Firefox, you'll notice that it uses the new icons, menu items, and other graphical aspects of the new theme. Figure 9.24 shows Firefox after downloading, installing, and switching to a very popular theme known as Noia 2.0 (eXtreme). There are obvious changes to the icons, fonts, and menus in the Personal toolbar—all of which are improvements as far as I'm concerned. Your mileage may vary.

FIGURE 9.23

Selecting a new theme in Firefox

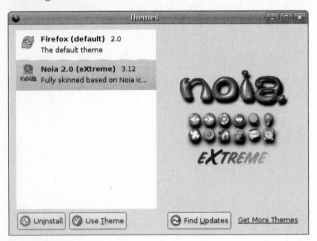

FIGURE 9.24

Using a different theme in Firefox

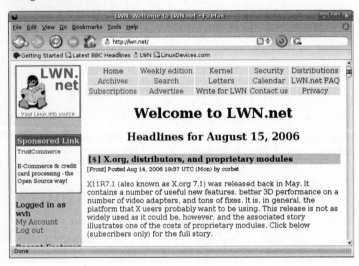

Like extensions and the Extensions dialog, you can uninstall themes from the Themes dialog by selecting them and clicking Uninstall. In general, it's not a good idea to uninstall the theme that you are currently using — use the Themes dialog to switch to another theme first, restart Firefox, and then uninstall any theme(s) that you're no longer interested in.

Summary

This chapter provided the highlights of configuring, using, and customizing Firefox, the most popular browser for Linux systems and one which is growing in popularity on other types of systems such as Microsoft Windows and Mac OS X. Firefox is the culmination of years of development and evolution in the Web browsing and open source communities. After using Firefox for a while on Ubuntu, it's certainly worth installing and using Firefox on any other computer systems that you might have to use. You'll be happier because you'll have the same browser experience no matter what system you're using, and you're certainly not going to get any complaints from the open source community in general.

The next chapter continues to explore the basic capabilities of a default Ubuntu system by discussing how to create and publish formatted documents on Ubuntu. Chapter 7 discussed how to use text editors on Ubuntu, which are fine for notes or other documents that don't require font changes, style sheets, and other fancy formatting. However, at some point, everyone wants to create fancy documents with different fonts, different font sizes, special formatting, and so on. Chapter 10, "Creating and Publishing Documents," explores the free software that is available for Ubuntu and which enables you to quickly and easily produce nicely formatted documents.

Chapter 10

Creating and Publishing Documents

Chapter 7 discussed using text editors on Linux systems, which are fine for creating documents if the document that you're creating is a shopping list, TODO list, or ransom note. For more sophisticated documents, most people nowadays expect an actual word processor, which is an application that enables you to create documents that use multiple fonts, different typefaces within a font (bold, italic, fixed, and so on); create billeted and numbered lists automatically; and provide some port for page layout using whizzy constructs such as tables, multiple columns, and so on.

This chapter explains how to do various types of word processing on your Ubuntu Linux system. It begins by discussing the various markup languages, which are text-format ways of creating formatted documents in a text editor on your Ubuntu Linux system. Though somewhat old school, markup languages are still popular, and Ubuntu supports popular, open source, markup-oriented document production systems such as TeX, and even a clone of the venerable system from bygone Unix days.

> **NOTE** If you're reading this chapter and thinking, "Where the heck does he talk about markup languages that I actually care about like HTML and XML?" I'm sorry to disappoint you. These markup languages are not discussed in detail in this book because they are more focused on Web site than document creation, and because the world is already knee-deep in books dedicated to these topics.

Next, this chapter discusses more familiar types of graphical word processors, focusing on OpenOffice.org Writer, which is the word processing component of the powerful OpenOffice.org suite of applications that are featured throughout this book. OpenOffice.org is a fantastic suite of office software, and this chapter's discussion of using OpenOffice.org Writer should make even the most dyed-in-the-wool Microsoft Word, Corel WordPerfect, or Mac OS X Nisus Writer user feel right at home.

Finally, this chapter discusses desktop publishing on Ubuntu, and highlights the excellent Scribus application. When you have to do serious, hard-core layout in your documents, a word processor is no longer the right tool because it doesn't provide enough granular control of page elements. Desktop publishing software makes it easy to create documents that contain many different page elements, routing text from one to the other as needed, and easily inserting and manipulating graphics to create documents that look exactly the way that you need them to. Scribus is a relatively, but incredibly impressive young, application. Adobe InDesign, Adobe PageMaker, and Quark XPress users, hold on to your hats, but don't worry about your wallets — Scribus is open source!

Using Document Markup Languages on Ubuntu

Long ago, when people just used terminals, word processing meant creating documents in a text editor and embedding special commands to tell some other application how to format your document for a specific target printer. The format in which these documents were created is known as a *markup language*, of which the most common example is HTML. Of course, HTML is designed to mark up documents that are targeted for use as Web pages, but the same principles apply. Creating documents in markup languages is still popular in academic and publishing circles because many institutions and journals use text files in a markup language as the lowest common denominator for submissions. This enables them to combine documents from multiple sources into a single, stylistically consistent publication without worrying about what version of Word everyone used, what fonts they'd used, and so on.

TeX (pronounced *tech*) is a typesetting program and associated markup language that is designed to produce extremely high-quality output, especially for scientific and mathematical notation. Eminent computer scientist Donald Knuth wrote TeX in 1977, largely because he needed a suitably high-quality tool for producing the three volumes of his "Art of Computer Programming" series. If it wasn't cool enough to write your own document formatting system, Knuth originally wrote TeX in a system of his own called WEB, which is a mixture of documentation and Pascal source code in a single source file. The source code is extracted from the WEB document using a program called tangle, and the formatted source code and integrated documentation is extracted (in TeX format, of course) using a program called weave. None of which matters if you just want to use TeX, but it is pretty entertaining and sounds like a recursive episode of "Computer Scientists Gone Wild" (available soon on DVD), so I thought that you might enjoy adding this tidbit to your collection of interesting but non-essential knowledge.

Many different implementations of TeX are available today, all extracted from the original `tex.web` document, converted into other languages, and some enhanced to add extra capabilities. The source code for TeX is freely available, but in order for anything based on the TeX source code to call itself TeX, it must pass a TeX formatting torture test known as TRIP. The version of TeX provided in the Ubuntu repository (as on most Linux systems nowadays) is teTeX, a complete TeX distribution for Unix-like systems that is maintained by Thomas Esser (hence the "te" in teTeX). The home page for teTeX is `www.tug.org/tetex`.

Installing TeX on Your Ubuntu System

Because TeX isn't for everybody, it isn't installed by default on an Ubuntu Linux system. To install TeX, start the Synaptic Package Manager from the System ⇨ Administration menu, and select the TeX Authoring section from the left of the Synaptic dialog. Though there are many TeX-related packages, the three critical ones are the following:

- `tetex-base`
- `tetex-bin`
- `tetex extra`

You may also want to select the `tetext-doc` package, which provides various HOWTOs and other documents about the TeX system. Figure 10.1 shows these packages selected in the Synaptic Package Manager.

Installing TeX in the Synaptic Package Manager

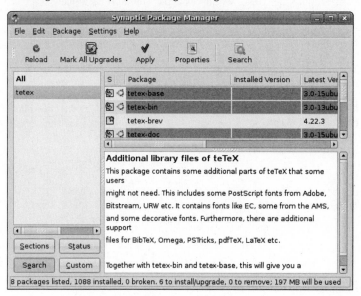

Selecting these three packages and installing them will also install a few other mandatory packages. Once these packages are installed, you're ready to begin experimenting with TeX.

See Chapter 20, "Adding, Removing, and Updating Software," for more detailed information on installing applications using the Synaptic Package Manager.

Using TeX Markup

TeX markup is quite simple. For example, the source code for a TeX document that produces formatted output that displays the string "Hello, World!" is the following:

```
Hello, World!
\bye
```

To format this document, you simply execute the `tex` command from an Ubuntu command line, supplying the name of the file as an argument. You'll see something like the following on your screen:

```
$ tex hello.tex
This is TeX, Version 3.141592 (Web2C 7.5.4)
(./hello.tex [1] )
Output written on hello.dvi (1 page, 228 bytes).
Transcript written on hello.log.
```

Processing a file using TeX produces an output file in DVI (Device Independent) format. DVI output is an intermediate binary form that only contains character positioning and font information (as well as the content of your document, of course), and must be post-processed by another program that understands how to display this file on your screen or produce output in the specific format or printer control language used by your printer.

As you can see from the sample TeX markup for the "Hello, World!" example, you don't need many TeX commands to produce simple documents. However, the key word here is simple. To produce a slightly more complex document using different fonts, centering, and different sections, your native TeX code would look something like the following:

```
\centerline{This is a Title}
\smallskip

\centerline{Bill von Hagen}
\centerline{\tt 24 March, 2006}

\bigskip

 {\narrower\noindent
This example shows some of the complexity of executing raw \TeX\
commands and is designed to illustrate how much simple this same text
would be if I were using a higher-level macro package of some
sort. Wouldn't it be nice...\par}

\bigskip

\beginsection 1. Introduction
\smallskip
This would be the text of an introduction...
\bye
```

Figure 10.2 shows a preview of the DVI file produced by processing this plain TeX document, shown in the xdvi DVI previewer.

FIGURE 10.2

Previewing output from the plain TeX example

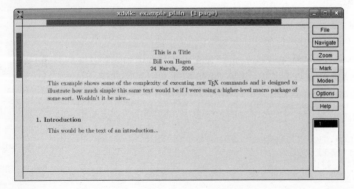

Introducing LaTeX Markup

Let's face it — regardless of how good the output looks, writing documents using the low-level TeX commands shown in the previous section would be a tremendous pain, especially the extensive use of manual formatting and spacing commands. To simplify creating documents using TeX, a variety of macro packages have been developed, the best known of which is Leslie Lamport's LaTeX macro package. These macro packages support different types of documents, such as articles, manuals, letters, and so on, and provide easy-to-remember macros for the traditional components of those types of documents. For your convenience, the LaTeX macros package and associated applications is automatically installed when you install teTeX on your Ubuntu system.

As an example of using the LaTeX article document type, the previous plain TeX code would look like the following in LaTeX:

```
\documentclass{article}
\begin{document}
\title{This is a Title}
\author{Bill von Hagen}
\date{\today}
\maketitle

\begin{abstract}
This example shows how much simpler this same document would become
when marked up using \LaTeX\ macros rather than raw \TeX\
commands, and is designed to illustrate how much simpler this same text
would be if I were using a higher-level macro package of some
sort. It sure is nice (and can also be understood by mere mortals).
\end{abstract}

\section{Introduction}
This would be the text of an introduction...
\end{document}
```

Running LaTeX produces slightly more verbose output than the previous example of running TeX. The output from processing the previous example, stored in the file `example_latex.tex`, is the following:

```
$ latex example_latex.tex
This is pdfeTeX, Version 3.141592-1.21a-2.2 (Web2C 7.5.4)
entering extended mode
(./example_latex.tex
LaTeX2e <2003/12/01>
Babel <v3.8d> and hyphenation patterns for loaded.
(/usr/share/texmf-tetex/tex/latex/base/article.cls
Document Class: article 2004/02/16 v1.4f Standard LaTeX document class
(/usr/share/texmf-tetex/tex/latex/base/size10.clo))
(./example_latex.aux)
Overfull \hbox (9.76526pt too wide) in paragraph at lines 10-14
\OT1/cmr/m/n/9 become when marked up using L[]T[]X macros rather
than raw T[]X commands
[1] (./example_latex.aux) )
(see the transcript file for additional information)
Output written on example_latex.dvi (1 page, 1164 bytes).
Transcript written on example_latex.log.
```

Note that the command to format a LaTeX document is `latex` rather than the `tex` command used earlier. The `latex` command invokes a version of TeX that has been precompiled with all of the macros, font data, and other information that LaTeX defines. Figure 10.3 shows a preview of the DVI file produced by processing this LaTeX document, shown in the xdvi DVI previewer. As you can see from the sample LaTeX input, LaTeX provides macros for logical elements such as title, date, an abstract, sections (with automatic numbering), and so on. Figure 10.3 shows that the output is essentially identical, modulo some differences in margins and page centering.

FIGURE 10.3

Previewing output from the simple LaTeX example

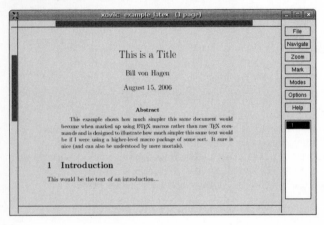

Most people who create documents using TeX actually use LaTeX nowadays for the convenience of its macros, but also because it supports the automatic creation of things such as a table of contents, lists of figures, an index, and other document constructs that are both important and useful. However, discussing the details of creating LaTeX documents is outside the scope of this book, but many other people have already done that. For suggested sources of detailed information about creating LaTeX documents and using LaTeX, see "More Information About TeX and LaTeX" later in this chapter.

Formatting and Previewing DVI Files

As mentioned previously, formatting a TeX or LaTeX document using the `tex` or `latex` commands produces a DVI file as output. You can instantly preview your DVI files using an application called xdvi, or can use DVI postprocessors to generate output that is suitable for printing on the type of printer that you are using. Figures 10.2 and 10.3 show DVI files being previewed in the xdvi application. The DVI postprocessors that produce output for various printers are the following:

- `dvilj`: Produces output suitable for a Hewlett-Packard LaserJet.
- `dvilj2p`: Produces output suitable for a Hewlett-Packard IIp LaserJet.
- `dvilj4`: Produces output suitable for a Hewlett-Packard IV LaserJet.
- `dvilj6`: Produces output suitable for a Hewlett-Packard VI LaserJet.
- `dvips`: Produces output suitable for any PostScript printer.

- `dvipdf`: Produces PDF output that you can view using Adobe Acrobat Reader, xpdf, or any other PDF viewer.

- `dvired`: Produces 2-up output suitable for any PostScript printer. (This application requires `pstops`, which must be separately installed from the `psutils` package.)

All of these applications were installed on your system as part of the basic teTeX installation described in "Installing TeX on Your Ubuntu System."

> **TIP**
>
> If you need to use TeX or LaTeX for the documents that you're working on, or are simply interested and want to experiment, some additional DVI-related utilities are available in the `dviutils` package, which you can install using the Synaptic Package Manager. The `dviselect` utility enables you to print selected pages from or organize the pages in a DVI file, while the `dviconcat` utility enables you to combine DVI files and print them 2-up (two DVI pages per printed page) to save paper or simplify review.

Using Graphical Tools to Work with TeX and LaTeX

As much of this book highlights, it's a graphical world nowadays, and Ubuntu provides all of the graphical applications that any computer user expects to find. Though command-line utilities such as TeX and LaTeX are easy to use, and the text-based format of TeX and LaTeX files makes them easy to exchange with users of many other computer systems and applications, it's hard to beat the convenience of a graphical application, especially when you're doing something such as word processing.

Luckily, the folks in the world of open source have stepped up to provide graphical solutions for creating and working with documents in LaTeX format. These are the Lyx and TeXmacs applications, both of which are available in the Ubuntu repositories. Like teTeX, these packages are not installed by default on your Ubuntu system, but are easy enough to locate and install using the Synaptic Package Manager. (See Chapter 20, "Adding, Removing, and Updating Software," for more detailed information on installing applications using the Synaptic Package Manager.) Installing Lyx adds the Lyx command to the Applications ⇨ Office menu, while you will have to execute TeXmacs by running the `texmacs` command from a command line.

If you are working with LaTeX documents, it's hard to beat the convenience of the Lyx document processor. Lyx provides a convenient graphical interface for creating and working with LaTeX documents, including conveniences such as being able to select document elements and styles from drop-down menus, reformat selected characters, paragraphs, and so on, all without having to remember the low-level LaTeX commands that perform these functions in your text.

> **NOTE**
>
> If you install Lyx and want to execute it from the command line, the actual name of the program that you need to execute to run Lyx on your Ubuntu system is `lyx-qt`, because the version of Lyx in the Ubuntu repositories uses the QT graphical library to provide the core components of its graphical user interface.

Figure 10.4 shows the same LaTeX document used as an example earlier in this section (and shown in Figure 10.3) in the Lyx document processor. You'll immediately notice that the on-screen representation of this document is almost identical to the appearance of the DVI file that was produced by formatting it using LaTeX.

Lyx actually uses its own format for creating and storing documents, known as lyx format. To work with standard LaTeX documents, you must import them into Lyx using the File menu's Import command, and can export them as standard LaTeX once you're ready to share them with you co-authors. If you compare them to any LaTeX file that you originally imported, you'll note that Lyx adds a few more detailed LaTeX formatting commands to its LaTeX output, but the LaTeX files produced by Lyx are completely normal otherwise.

FIGURE 10.4

Sample document from Figure 10.3 shown in lyx-qt

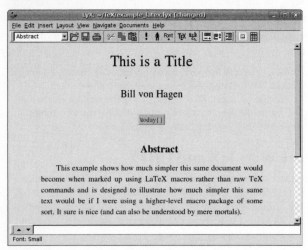

Lyx is an excellent tool, and well worth experimenting with if you are working with LaTeX documents but want the convenience of a graphical application or simply can't remember all those pesky LaTeX commands. For more information about Lyx, see its home page at www.lyx.org.

The other alternative for working with LaTeX documents in a graphical form is the TeXmacs package, which is a graphical, LaTeX-aware package that is implemented on top of GNU emacs. This enables you to use familiar emacs commands while working with your LaTeX documents in a graphical fashion. Figure 10.5 shows the same LaTeX document used as an example earlier in this chapter (and shown in Figure 10.3) in the TeXmacs document processor. You'll immediately notice that the on-screen representation of this document is almost identical to the appearance of the DVI file that was produced by formatting it using LaTeX.

After installing TeXmacs, you must execute it from a Linux command line by typing the texmacs command, or selecting the Accessories ⇨ GNU TeXmacs Editor menu command. If you execute TeXmacs from the command line, you'll see that it does a lot of initial setup and configuration, which you can ignore — and don't worry, it will be quiet the next time you run it.

TeXmacs is very convenient to use and provides several LaTeX-specific menus and icons that make it easy to apply LaTeX styles, document elements, and even select and reformat portions of your documents. Unlike Lyx, you can use TeXmacs with TeX documents as well as LaTeX documents, and it is not necessary to import your LaTeX documents — TeXmacs works directly with your existing files. For more information, see the TeXmacs home page at www.texmacs.org or consult the extensive online help that it provides.

FIGURE 10.5

Sample document from Figure 10.3 shown in TeXmacs

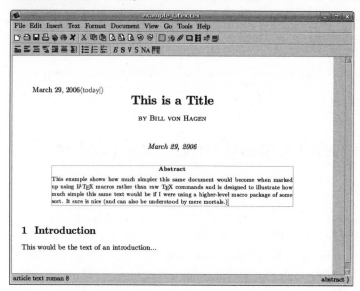

More Information About TeX and LaTeX

Because TeX and LaTeX have been used for many years on a wide variety of systems, a tremendous amount of information about using them is available on the Web. A simple Internet search will turn up more hits than you could possibly want. As a timesaver, some of my favorite sites for information about TeX and LaTeX are the following:

- Getting to grips with LaTeX (`www.andy-roberts.net/misc/latex/index.html`) is a great series of tutorials on using LaTeX from Andrew Roberts.

- Introduction to LaTeX (`www.math.uiuc.edu/~hildebr/tex/course`) is a short course prepared at the University of Illinois Department of Mathematics, and provides a nice, quick overview of TeX and LaTeX.

- Text Processing with LaTeX (`www.eng.cam.ac.uk/help/tpl/textprocessing`) is a great site at the University of Cambridge in the UK that provides many online tutorials and examples of creating a variety of documents using LaTeX.

- The teTeX HOWTO (`www.tldp.org/HOWTO/TeTeX-HOWTO.html`) was written a few years ago, but one of the nice things about stable software like TeX and LaTeX is that things don't change much. This document provides a good deal of general information about creating TeX and LaTeX documents, as well as specific information about using the teTeX TeX implementation provided on your Ubuntu Linux system.

Several books dedicated to TeX and LaTeX are available, but I've been using TeX and LaTeX since the early 1990s, so I don't have any opinions about any of them aside from the original books on the subject. No discussion of TeX and LaTeX would be complete without identifying the two seminal texts for each of these:

- *TeXbook* by Donald E. Knuth (Addison-Wesley Professional, 1984, ISBN: 0201134489)
- *LaTeX: A Document Preparation System*, 2nd Edition by Leslie Lamport (Addison-Wesley Professional, 1994, ISBN: 0201529831)

Since these two books are by the authors of the respective systems, you can certainly consider them to be definitive. Some changes have certainly been made to LaTeX since its creation by Lamport long ago, but these are still the seminal bibles of both document preparation systems.

Word Processing with OpenOffice.org Writer

OpenOffice.org (`www.openoffice.org`) is a suite of office applications including a word processor (Writer), a spreadsheet (Calc), a drawing program (Draw), software for creating presentations (Impress), and a database program called Base, which keeps tagging along after the rest of OpenOffice. This section focuses on the word processing application — other chapters in this book discuss the OpenOffice.org spreadsheet, graphics, and presentation software. But first, a word from our sponsor.

OpenOffice.org is one of the most powerful and popular open source projects on the Web — and the people who are largely responsible for its existence are the folks at Sun Microsystems! Scott McNealy, president of Sun Microsystems, has a long-standing hatred of Microsoft, so it wasn't all that surprising when Sun purchased StarDivision in 1999, the German vendor of a suite of office software called StarOffice. The purchase of StarOffice was originally seen as both a way to leverage Sun's Java offerings (because StarOffice and OpenOffice.org are both heavily dependent on Java), and to provide Sun users with an office suite that they could run natively on their Suns.

Sun then released the then current source code for StarOffice into the open source community under the terms of Sun Industry Standards Source License (SISSL). Beginning with release 2.0 of the OpenOffice.org suite, all of the source code is now available under the GNU Lesser General Public License (LGPL). Sun still markets StarOffice, which is both supported and offers some capabilities beyond those provided by OpenOffice.org — but that's moot for us, because StarOffice doesn't run on Ubuntu Linux.

Aside from its power and the absence of cost, a truly compelling reason for using OpenOffice.org Writer is its use of the new OpenDocument standard for storing and exchanging documents (`www.oasis-open.org/committees/tc_home.php?wg_abbrev=office`). Historically, all word processors used their own binary format for storing documents, which made it a hassle when switching from one word processor to another or when simply trying to exchange documents with friends or coworkers who used a different word processor. The OpenDocument standard is designed to provide a published standard for storing documents in an XML format that can instantly be used in any other word processor that supports this format. This may seem like a minor thing, but get back to me after you try to open the WordStar files for your family history, short stories, or other documents that you may have written long ago but still want to be able to use.

To save repeating the phrase "OpenOffice.org Writer" more times than necessary throughout the rest of this section, I'll typically refer to OpenOffice.org Writer simply as Writer (its name to its friends) or occasionally as `oowriter` (the name of the application that you must type to execute OpenOffice.org Writer from a command-line interface).

File Extensions for OpenOffice.org Documents

With the adoption of the OpenDocument format, OpenOffice.org Writer changed the names of its default file extensions. The following list shows the file extensions used by different OpenOffice.org versions:

- odm: OpenDocument Master Document
- odt: OpenDocument Document, OpenOffice.org 2.0 and greater
- ott: OpenDocument Document Template, OpenOffice.org 2.0 and greater
- sxw: Writer Document before OpenOffice.org 2.0
- stw: Writer Document Template before OpenOffice.org 2.0
- sxg: Writer Master Document before OpenOffice.org 2.0

The most common documents that you will see and create are those with the ODT and OTT file extensions. However, you may encounter the older SXW format when exchanging documents with long-time OpenOffice.org users. SXW files are actually very interesting, because they are actually zipped archives containing XML document files and associated metadata. You must use the Document Converter wizard to import old-format SXW OpenOffice.org files into the new OpenOffice.org OpenDocument format, as explained in "Importing Documents from other Word Processors" later in this chapter.

Installing Files for Writer

Writer is installed by default if you install Ubuntu from the Live CD, from the Alternate Install CD using the Text Mode installer, and from the Alternate installer using the OEM Mode installer. If you want to add Writer or the entire OpenOffice.org suite to a server system that has a graphical user interface, you can install them using `apt-get`, `aptitude`, or `Synaptic`, as explained in Chapter 20, "Adding, Removing, and Updating Software."

One of the things that differentiates Ubuntu Linux from other Linux distributions is its extreme dedication to the user, especially in terms of internationalization. If you are only working in a single language, the correct localization packages for your physical location are installed with your default Ubuntu installation. However, if you are installing Writer for use when creating documents in multiple languages, you may also want to search for and install the appropriate hyphenation, localization, and thesaurus packages for whatever other locales you are writing for. You can easily find these by looking for a string that represents the country code that you are looking for. For example, Figure 10.6 shows the specific German language support packages for OpenOffice.org that have been identified by searching for the string "-de" in the Synaptic Package Manager.

> **TIP** If you've already installed the localization and internationalization packages for any component of the OpenOffice.org suite, there is no need to reinstall them. Installing them once installs them as a shared resource that can be used by every component of the suite.

> **TIP** You can install complete language support for all applications (without translating the GNOME user interface itself) by installing the appropriate language support metapackage for your target locale(s) — these packages have names of the form language-support-country-code (for example, language-support-de), and include the dictionaries for the specified locale. To fully translate the GNOME interface and all internationalized applications, select the appropriate language pack. The names of the language packs are of the form language-pack-country-code. Once you've installed multiple dictionaries, and so on, you can set the default language for your document using the Tools ⇨ Options ⇨ Language Settings ⇨ Language drop-down list.

FIGURE 10.6

Sample additional language packages for the OpenOffice.org suite

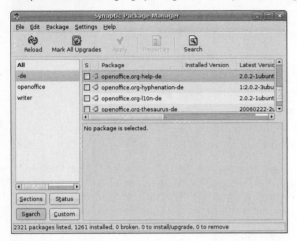

See Chapter 20, "Adding, Removing, and Updating Software," for more detailed information on installing applications using the Synaptic Package Manager and similar command-line utilities.

Taking a Quick Tour of Writer

You can start Writer from the command line by executing the `oowriter` command. More conveniently, a menu item for Writer is installed in the Applications ➪ Office menu called OpenOffice.org Word Processor. To start Writer from the menus, select this menu item. The application starts, displaying an empty document, as shown in Figure 10.7.

Writer provides excellent online help, as do all of the tools in the OpenOffice.org suite, so I won't bore you by walking you through each menu and entry that it contains. However, as a quick overview of the Writer interface, the callouts in Figure 10.7 highlight the following areas:

- **Menus:** The drop-down menus in Writer are organized much like the menus in Microsoft Word to provide a familiar user experience. Menu items with an arrow at their right edge lead to other, related submenus.

- **Toolbars:** By default, Writer displays the Standard and Formatting toolbars, which provide one-click access to specific commands when you click on the appropriate icon. You can modify the list of icons displayed on a toolbar by clicking on the control for that toolbar, located at the far right. You can display other toolbars or deactivate the default toolbar by selecting toolbars from the View ➪ Toolbars submenu.

- **Rulers:** These rulers display the horizontal and vertical location of the text insertion point in the current document. The grayed-out portions of each ruler reflect the page margins used in the current document. You can disable these rules by deselecting the View ➪ Ruler menu command.

FIGURE 10.7

Starting Writer

- **Styles and Formatting window:** Though not displayed by default, you can display this window at any time by pressing the F11 key on your keyboard. (You can press F11 again to close this window.) The Styles and Formatting window provides easy access to various sets of styles that are available for the current document, and is especially convenient if you choose not to display the formatting toolbar. The drop-down menu enables you to display specific sets of styles in this window, such as Character Styles, List Styles, and so on. You can dock this window by holding down the control key and double-clicking on the gray portion of the window heading (beside the icons), making it a part of the default Writer interface rather than a floating window. Figure 10.8 shows Writer with the Styles and Formatting window docked. You can undock a docked window by repeating this process in the docked area.

- **Context-sensitive menu:** Right-clicking on the background of any document that you are working on in Writer displays the context-sensitive menu shown in Figure 10.9. This menu provides quick access to several formatting and style-related submenus.

FIGURE 10.8

FIGURE 10.8

Docking the Styles and Formatting window

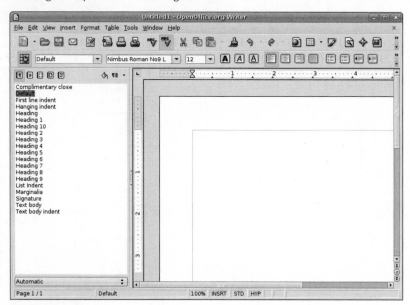

FIGURE 10.9

Writer's context-sensitive menu

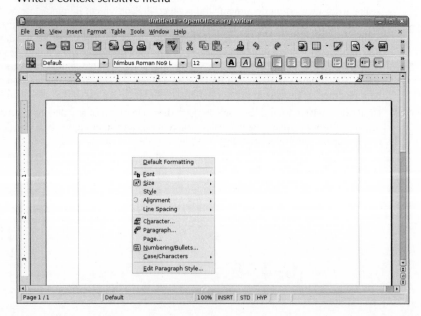

Writer provides extensive online help, available by selecting OpenOffice.org Help from the Help menu, or by pressing the F1 key on your keyboard at any time. Figure 10.10 shows the main page for Writer's help, which provides both a searchable index and a list of popular, general topics from its initial display window (at right).

FIGURE 10.10

Writer's Online Help

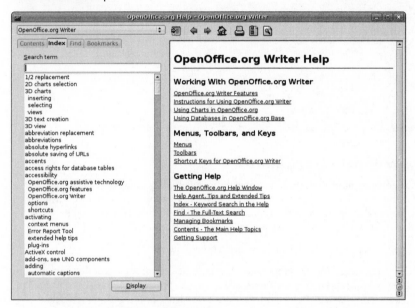

Personalizing Writer

The first thing that you'll want to do when getting started with Writer is to enter some information about yourself into its User data fields. This is primarily useful because Writer will use this information in various places when filling out fields in documents that you create using the OpenOffice.org Wizards (as explained in the next section).

Select the Tools ➪ Options menu item to display the Options dialog's User Data form, as shown in Figure 10.11. Fill out the fields in this form and Click OK to return to Writer and your document.

FIGURE 10.11

Writer's User Data form

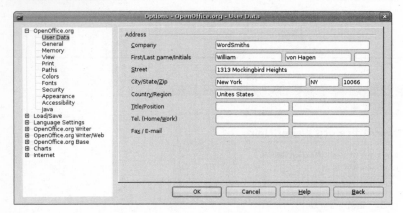

Using Wizards to Create Documents

The easiest way to create a document in Writer is to use one of the document wizards that it provides for many popular types of documents. This section provides an example of creating a letter in Writer using the Letter wizard, but the process of using any wizard is quite similar regardless of the type of document you're creating — and the goal of these wizards is to be easy to use in the first place.

To start the appropriate wizard for creating a new document, do the following:

1. Select File ➪ Wizards, and select the appropriate wizard for the type of document that you are creating. Writer provides wizards for creating letters, faxes, agenda, presentations, and Web pages. For this example, I'll select the Letter wizard. Writer creates a new letter document using its default, and displays the first Letter Wizard dialog, as shown in Figure 10.12.

2. Select the radio button for the type of letter that you want to create: business, formal personal, or personal. Each type of letter provides some default page styles and decorations, which you can select from the Page design drop-down list. The window behind the Letter Wizard shows a preview of a letter with your current selections, so that you know what you're getting into. If you look closely, you'll see that the Letter Wizard has already filled out some fields in the letter from the User Data form that was discussed in the previous section. In this example, I'll select Personal Letter. Once you've made your selections, click Next to proceed. The second Letter Wizard dialog displays, as shown in Figure 10.13.

> **TIP**   If you are creating a business letter and you are going to be printing it on your corporate letterhead, you can select the Use letterhead paper with pre-printed elements checkbox (shown in Figure 10.12). This removes any existing graphics from the letter preview, and activates the Letterhead layout step in the wizard, so that you can specify the dimensions of your letterhead stationery and thus avoid overprinting portions of it with your letter.

FIGURE 10.12

The first Letter Wizard dialog

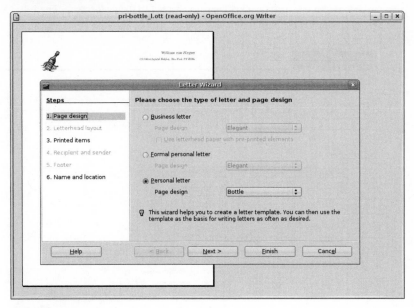

FIGURE 10.13

The second Letter Wizard dialog

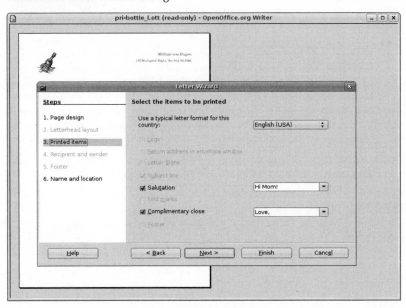

3. Select the Salutation or closing message for your letter. You can change these by selecting existing values from the drop-down menus or personalize them by selecting and replacing the default values shown for these. As you update these, the preview of your letter changes to reflect the new values. When you're done, click Next to proceed to the next screen. The Letter Wizard's third dialog displays, as shown in Figure 10.14.

FIGURE 10.14

The final Letter Wizard dialog

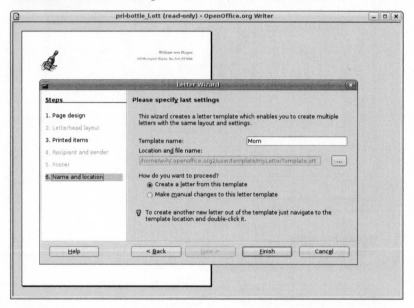

4. If you've made any changes to the default letter settings and are going to be reusing them, then final Letter Wizard dialog enables you to update the wizard's default settings or save your modifications as a new template. To update your default settings, enter a name to associate with your new settings. If you want to create a new template from these settings and continue writing your letter, click the browse button and enter a new file name for the new template. This file will still be used the next time you use the Letter Wizard, but you can easily create documents from different templates as described later in this chapter in the section entitled "Creating and Using Templates."

Once you're done, click Finish to terminate the Letter Wizard and proceed with actually writing your letter. Your new letter displays in the main Writer window, as shown in Figure 10.15.

TIP If you'd rather tweak the template further before actually using it, select the radio button beside "Make manual changes to this letter template" (shown in Figure 10.14) and click Finish. This displays the template, at which point you can add or modify styles and page formatting, as described in the next section.

FIGURE 10.15

Editing your new letter

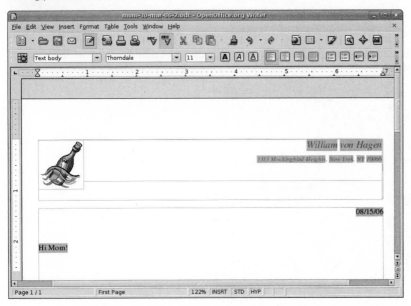

As you can see, Writer's wizards make it easy for you to create documents of certain predefined types. Writer's wizards leverage some of the predefined document templates that are provided with a default installation. If you want to create your own documents based on a template that is not supported by a wizard, Writer still makes it easy for you to define and use your own, specialized types of documents, as described later in this chapter in the section entitled "Creating and Using Templates."

Modifying Document Styles and Layout

A style is the word processing term for a set of formatting and display characteristics that are associated with a specific portion of your text, usually a paragraph. Once you're actually editing a document, you can apply any of the existing styles that have been defined for that document by selecting the name of a style from the drop-down list in the formatting window, or by selecting it from the Styles and Formatting window. To display the Styles and Formatting window, press F11. (You can always press F11 again to close the Styles and Formatting window.)

All of Writer's default document templates provide a default set of styles that enable you to format the different portions of your document. To apply a style to an existing paragraph, simply select it using the mouse and select the style that you want to apply from the drop-down list or Styles and Formatting window. I'm using the term "paragraph" here because, by default, styles are associated with any element in your document that ends with a carriage return, which technically makes it a paragraph even if it has an associated style like heading, greeting, closing, and so on.

To modify a single instance of a paragraph formatted with an existing style, position the cursor in that paragraph, right-click, and select Paragraph from the pop-up menu. This displays the dialog shown in Figure 10.16, which enables you to modify the style settings used in a single element in your document without changing them for other elements in your document that use the same style.

FIGURE 10.16

Modifying the style for a single paragraph

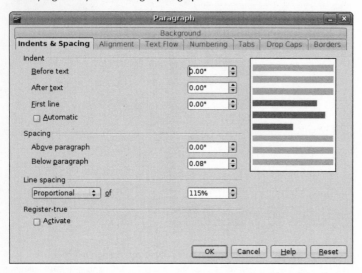

Though all OpenOffice.org documents come with a good set of default styles, everyone's tastes differ. To modify an existing style to reflect your personal tastes or corporate standards, right-click on any portion of your document that is currently formatted with that style, and select Edit Paragraph Style from the pop-up menu. A dialog like the one shown in Figure 10.17 displays.

Changing any of the settings in this dialog will change the style itself, which means that any other elements of your document that use this style will also be updated with your modified settings. You'll notice that this dialog has many more options and tabs than the simple Paragraph formatting dialog shown in Figure 10.16. This is because the dialog in Figure 10.17 enables you to modify any aspect of the style, not just the formatting of a selected element.

Changing the default styles is fine, but may be the wrong thing to do if you want to modify only a few elements in your document that use a certain style. When the default styles aren't sufficient and it's a waste of time to tweak multiple paragraphs, the right thing to do is to create a new style, based on an existing one, which has slightly different characteristics.

To create a new style based on an existing style, first make sure that the Styles and Formatting window is shown on your screen (press F11 if it is not). Next, position the cursor in a paragraph formatted with the existing style, and click the New Style from Selection icon at the far right of the Styles and Formatting window toolbar. Select New Style from Selection from the drop-down menu to display the dialog shown in Figure 10.18.

FIGURE 10.17

Modifying the values for an existing style

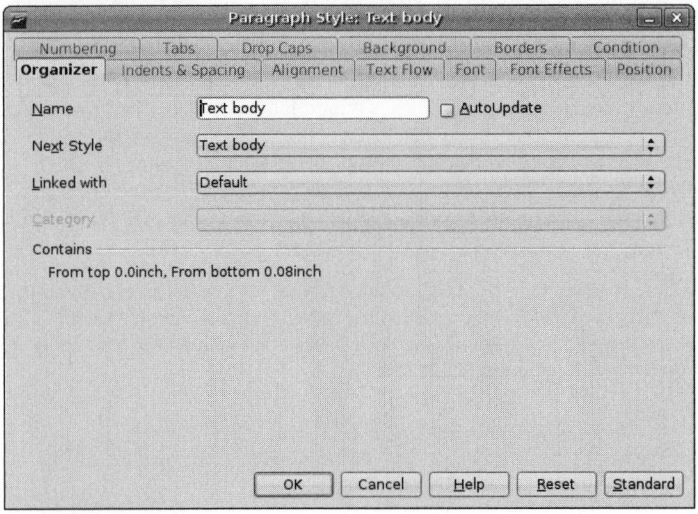

Paragraph Style: Text body

| Numbering | Tabs | Drop Caps | Background | Borders | Condition |
| **Organizer** | Indents & Spacing | Alignment | Text Flow | Font | Font Effects | Position |

Name: Text body □ AutoUpdate

Next Style: Text body

Linked with: Default

Category:

Contains
From top 0.0inch, From bottom 0.08inch

OK   Cancel   Help   Reset   Standard

FIGURE 10.18

Creating a new style from a selection

Create Style

Style name
Quote
Date
Opening
Subject

OK
Cancel

Enter the name that you want to associate with your new style, and click OK. Figure 10.18 shows me creating a style named Quote, which I use for indented quotations from other sources. Whatever value you enter, the name of your new style displays in the Styles and Formatting window, and the new style is associated with the currently selected element. You can then repeat the process for modifying an existing style, as described earlier in this section, to add the custom settings that you want to associate with your new style.

TIP You should, of course, minimize the number of new styles that you create whenever possible. For example, you may be working with corporate document standards that mandate specific formatting and styles. In this case, adding new styles may be at worst a violation of corporate policy and at best an irritation to anyone who subsequently has to work on a document that you've authored. Always make sure that it's absolutely necessary before creating a new style.

Creating and Using Templates

As mentioned earlier in this chapter, Writer comes with a good selection of default document types, known as *templates*, and provides wizards to help you use them or even create new templates based on those document types. The previous section described how to create your own styles to further fine-tune the settings that you use in your documents. This is very convenient, but only modifies the styles associated with a specific document—the template from which that document was created doesn't pick up the new styles, which makes it hard to share your stylistic insights with others. It also makes it hard for you to reuse them yourself, unless you subsequently create every new document by copying an existing document that has the new styles, and then replace its contents. At best, this is a pain in the anatomy, and at worst, it is almost completely inefficient. The right solution is to be able to easily create and manage your own document templates. You can then reuse your styles by starting new documents from your updated template, and even share your Writer wizardry with other users by simply giving them copies of your templates.

NOTE The process of creating a new template is initially the same as that for manually creating a new document (i.e., without using a wizard). The primary differences are that you don't need to add much content (only representative elements for designing new styles) and that you save the new document as a template rather than as a document. Read on!

To create a new template, do the following:

1. Select File ➪ New ➪ Templates and Documents from any Writer window to display the dialog shown in Figure 10.19.

Creating a new template

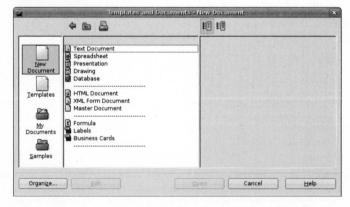

2. Select the New Document icon at the left, and select Text Document as the type of document that you're creating. Click Open to begin modifying the new document, which displays an empty document in a new Writer window. In this window, create any stylistic elements and layout settings that you want to provide through your new template. The previous section explained how to create new styles from existing ones in your documents.

3. Next, make sure that your page settings are correct for the new style. Beyond creating new styles, one common change that you will want to make in your new template is to change the default page layout by selecting Format ➪ Page, selecting the Page tab, and modifying the page size, margins, and other settings in the dialog shown in Figure 10.20.

FIGURE 10.20

Modifying page type and layout settings

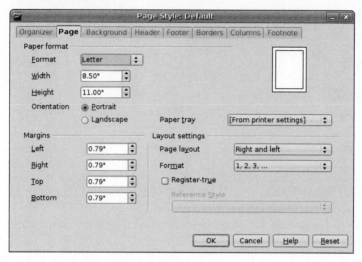

4. Once you've finished modifying your new template, you can save it as a template by selecting the File ➪ Templates ➪ Save command. A dialog like the one shown in Figure 10.21 displays.

FIGURE 10.21

Saving your new template

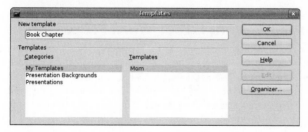

5. Enter the name for your new template and click OK. Figure 10.21 shows the creation of a new style called Book Chapter.

Congratulations, you've created a document template! Once you've created a template, you can easily create new documents based on that template by doing the following:

1. Select File ➪ New ➪ Templates and Documents to display the dialog shown in Figure 10.19.

2. To create a document from a specific template, click the Templates icon at the left and select the location where you saved the template (usually "My Templates"). You will see your templates listed in the window to the right of the icons. Figure 10.22 shows this dialog, which includes the template that I just created in the previous step.

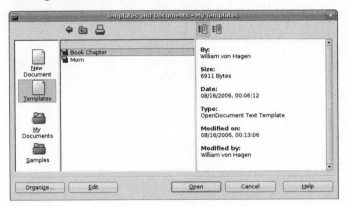

FIGURE 10.22

Creating a new document from a template

3. Select the template that you want to use and either click Open or double-click on its name to create a new document from this template.

Once you are finished editing your document, save it by using the standard File ⇨ Save As command.

Creating and using templates is a great way to standardize the documents that you or your organization is creating.

TIP Updating a template does not automatically update any documents that have been created from it. After updating a template, opening any document that was created from it will prompt you as to whether or not you want to update the document to reflect the updated template. That's usually a good idea, but it's nice that Writer is kind enough to ask you about it.

Importing Documents from Other Word Processors

Writer can open documents produced by many other word processors, especially those created by Microsoft Word, Corel WordPerfect, or documents stored in the intermediate Rich Text Format (RTF) document type. This is fine if you have only one or two documents that you want to update, but if you are moving all of your work to Ubuntu, you may find that you have hundreds of documents that you want to update to Writer format. Luckily, Writer provides a wizard for this that will not only import all of your documents, but also will import and convert any existing or attached style sheets that it detects.

To bulk import your existing Microsoft Word (or older OpenOffice.org documents), do the following:

1. Select File ⇨ Wizards ⇨ Document Converter to display the dialog shown in Figure 10.23.

2. To bulk import Microsoft Word files and style sheets, select the Microsoft Office radio button and select the Word Documents checkbox. To import existing SXW documents from StarOffice or a version of OpenOffice.org prior to 2.0, leave the StarOffice radio button selected. Click Next to proceed. The dialog shown in Figure 10.24 displays.

FIGURE 10.23

Specifying the input format when converting documents

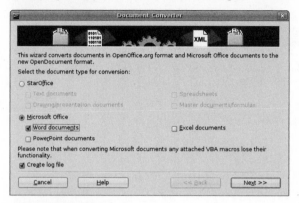

FIGURE 10.24

Specifying document and template locations when importing

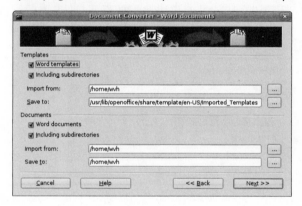

3. Specify the directories in which you want the wizard to search for the specified document types, and the locations to which converted documents should be saved. You may want to update the location to which converted templates should be saved — I typically use my home directory, and subsequently move the files around manually. Once you've checked the directory locations, click Next to proceed. A status dialog displays, summarizing the conversions that are about to take place. Click Convert to begin the conversion process. The dialog shown in Figure 10.25 displays as the conversion process progresses.

FIGURE 10.25

Monitoring the document conversion process

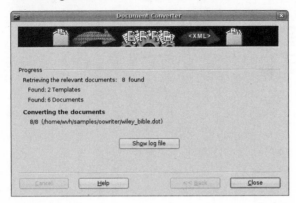

4. During the conversion process, the conversion wizard may display a character code confirmation dialog like the one shown in Figure 10.26. This generally means that the wizard encountered unknown characters in one of the documents. When the conversion process completes, the Close and Show log file buttons are activated on the dialog shown in Figure 10.25.

FIGURE 10.26

The character set conversion dialog

Congratulations—the conversion process is complete! Your converted documents and templates are ready for use in Writer. Before clicking Close, it's a good idea to click the Show log file button. As shown in Figure 10.27, the log file for the conversion process lists successful conversions, and also identifies documents that should be fine-tuned or corrected before they can be used with Writer. This is often the case with Word DOT files, which may contain macros that are not completely compatible with anything other than Microsoft's own Visual Basic.

A log file of the conversion process

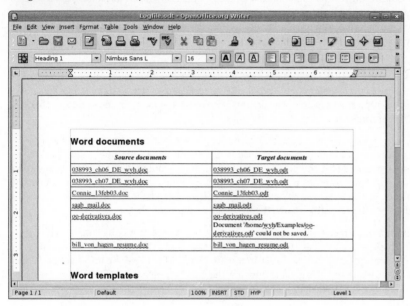

More Information About Writer

As mentioned earlier in this chapter, all OpenOffice.org applications provide complete, well-written online help. However, like most online help, this information is reference information, not HOWTO information.

If you are serious about using OpenOffice.org Writer for all of your documentation needs, the best site that I have seen on the Web for HOWTO information about using Writer is www.tutorialsforopenoffice.org. This site features great tutorials in PDF and OpenOffice.org formats, as well as links to a great selection of other sites with useful, hands-on information about using Writer. Check it out — it's well worth your time! After you become an OpenOffice.org wizard, you may want to create a tutorial of your own and contribute it to the site. One of the tutorials that they provide is an interesting example of creative recursion — it's a tutorial on using their template for creation tutorials.

Desktop Publishing with Scribus

The previous two sections of this chapter discussed how to create different types of documents on your Ubuntu system using command-line and graphical word processors. These tools provide powerful styles to standardize the appearance of repeated elements in your documents. However, when the presentation and layout of your document is just as important as its content, you need a different sort of tool. Word and text processors do just that, formatting and organizing the content in your documents, usually providing little support for actual page layout beyond controlling the page margins, size of the print area, and the number of columns of text that are displayed on each page. To do actual, detailed document layout, you need an application that combines word processing capabilities with the layout and detailed formatting capabilities required by the publishing industry — in other words, a desktop publishing package. Luckily, the open source folks ran into that problem too, and an excellent (and free) desktop publishing package for Linux, named Scribus, is easily installed on your Ubuntu system.

Scribus has been under development for a few years now, and is an open source application that is available at no cost for Linux, Apple Mac OS X (see http://aqua.scribus.net), and Microsoft Windows (see http://windows.scribus.net) systems and uses the QT graphical interface so that it looks and behaves the same way on all supported systems. The Scribus home page is www.scribus.net — check there for the latest Scribus information.

The basic concept in desktop publishing is the frame, which is conceptually similar to the idea of a paragraph in a word processing system. A frame is the key document element in desktop publishing. Desktop publishing documents are composed of many different frames, which can contain text, graphics, and so on. Dividing documents into these compositional elements makes it easy to move or resize them independently to suit changes in the document, its target layout, and so on. Text frames can be linked so that text flows from one frame to another, but they are still separately manageable document elements.

The next few sections explain how to install Scribus, how to create documents using the templates that it provides, and explain the basic steps necessary to create new documents with the detailed page layout required by your most demanding publishing work. It's not quite Quark XPress, Adobe InDesign, or Adobe PageMaker, but my old boss used to say, "It's good enough for the girls I go out with." (I never was quite sure what she meant by that, but it's a great expression.)

Installing Scribus on Ubuntu

Because not everyone needs or wants a desktop publishing package, Scribus isn't installed by default on an Ubuntu Linux system. To install Scribus, start the Synaptic Package Manager from the System ⇨ Administration menu, select Search, enter **Scribus** in the Search box that displays, and click Search. Once the search completes, as shown in Figure 10.28, right-click on the scribus package and select Mark for installation from the pop-up menu.

 **TIP**   You may also want to install the scribus-templates package, which provides some additional templates for Scribus documents, by right-clicking on its name and selecting Mark for installation.

Next, click Apply in the Synaptic toolbar to install Scribus on your system. Once the installation completes, you're ready to begin working with Scribus! Installing Scribus on your Ubuntu system installs a Scribus menu item on the Applications ⇨ Office menu that you can use to run the application.

See Chapter 20, "Adding, Removing, and Updating Software," for more detailed information on installing applications using the Synaptic Package Manager.

FIGURE 10.28

Installing Scribus in the Synaptic Package Manager

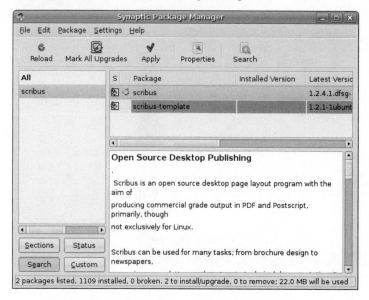

Taking a Quick Scribus Tutorial

Like OpenOffice.org Writer and most other publishing-related applications, Scribus comes complete with a few templates to get you started. When you first use a new application, it's often easiest to start with someone else's document, and then modify it to suit your purposes. Once you get the hang of using the application, you can create your own documents, as explained in the next section. This section provides a whirlwind tour of the key features of Scribus to get you comfortable with the basics.

To start Scribus, select Applications ➪ Office ➪ Scribus. Scribus takes a little bit of time to start up as it examines your system's font resources (which are critical to a detailed, layout-oriented application). Once Scribus starts, you can create a new document from one of its templates by doing the following:

1. Select the File ➪ New from Template menu command to display the dialog shown in Figure 10.29.

2. Select the template that you want to use for your new document and click OK. In this example, I'll use the Newsletter_2 template, which provides a working model for a newsletter that includes graphics. As Scribus opens the template, you may see one or more warning dialogs if the template uses fonts that are not installed on your system, as shown in Figure 10.30. For each warning dialog (if any), write down the font that was missing and click OK to substitute a similar font that is present on your system. You can subsequently use the Synaptic Package Manager to search for and load any available font packages.

FIGURE 10.29

Selecting a template as a starting point

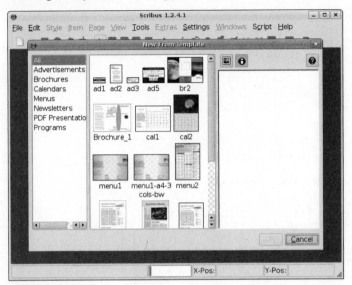

FIGURE 10.30

Font warnings when loading a template

3. Once font processing completes, a copy of the template displays in the main Scribus window, as shown in Figure 10.31.

4. Now things get interesting. To work with or simply change the text in any frame, you can select the Edit Contents of Frame button in the toolbar. After selecting this command, you can directly add or delete text in the current frame. However, for more detailed changes involving font and text changes, I tend to use the Edit Text dialog. To access this dialog, you can simply click the Edit the text with the Story Editor icon in the toolbar. I tend to access this through the context-sensitive menus rather than the toolbar, so you can also right-click on that frame to display the pop-up menu shown in Figure 10.32.

FIGURE 10.31

Scribus showing your working copy of a template

FIGURE 10.32

Editing options for frames in Scribus

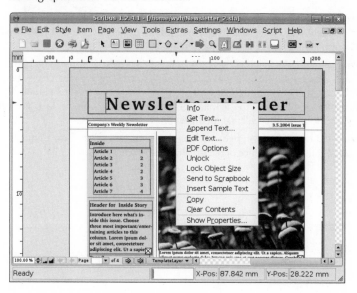

5. To view the dialog used for low-level font changes, select the Edit Text menu item. A Story Editor dialog like the one shown in Figure 10.33 displays. The Story Editor is a small word processor, encapsulated within Scribus. Using the Story Editor, you can modify, replace, or add to the text in the frame using the lower window. The controls available in the Story Editor enable you to change justification within a frame, fonts, and font characteristics.

FIGURE 10.33

Modifying the text in a frame

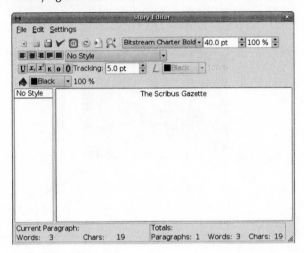

6. After modifying the frame text or its characteristics, click the green checkmark icon or select the File ➪ Update Text Frame and Exit command. An updated version of your document with the new information displays, as shown in Figure 10.34.

7. Working with graphical frames is similar but uses an external application (GIMP, which is discussed in Chapter 12, "Working with Graphics") to edit any existing image. For example, to replace the graphic shown in Figure 10.34, right-click on its frame and unlock the current frame. This enables modifications to the frame. As you're working, you can lock any frame that you're happy with to prevent accidental modification.

8. To delete the existing image, right-click on the frame and select Clear Contents. The document updates to reflect the absence of the graphic, as shown in Figure 10.35.

FIGURE 10.34

The updated version of your document

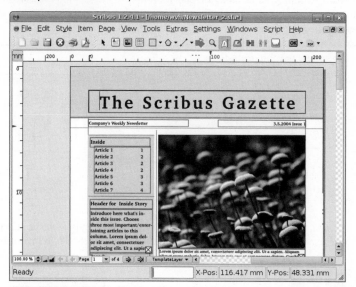

FIGURE 10.35

The newsletter after removing a graphic

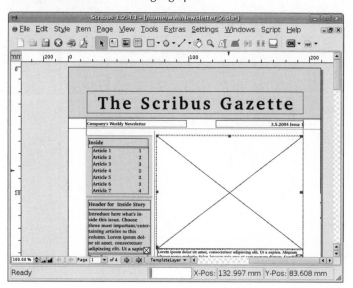

9. To select a new graphic for the frame, right-click on the frame and select the Get Frame menu command. The dialog shown in Figure 10.36 displays, enabling you to navigate to, select, and preview any existing graphic on your system.

FIGURE 10.36

Selecting a new graphic for a frame

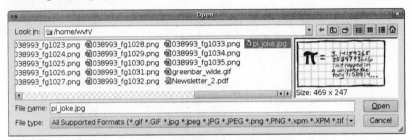

10. After selecting the new graphic, click Open to open the new graphic in the selected frame. The view of your newsletter updates to reflect the new graphic, as shown in Figure 10.37.

FIGURE 10.37

The updated document showing the new graphic

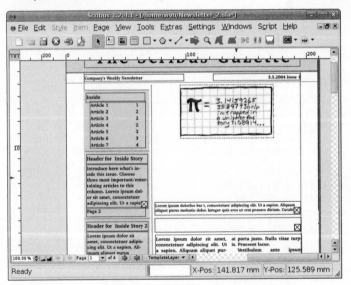

11. Because the graphic is now smaller than the original frame, right-click the graphic and select the Adjust Frame to Picture command. The original frame shrinks to match the perimeter of the actual image. You can also move an image frame by clicking and dragging.

12. The extra space available in the document is a good location for a new text frame. To add a new frame, click the Insert Text Frame icon from the toolbar (it looks like a small document) and click and drag to insert the new frame. For the purposes of this example, I'll insert some sample text into the frame by right-clicking the frame and selecting Insert Sample Text. It may seem odd to have a command that inserts random text into a frame, but this is useful when laying out a document before the final content is ready. Your document updates to reflect the new frame and its contents, as shown in Figure 10.38.

FIGURE 10.38

The updated document showing the new text frame

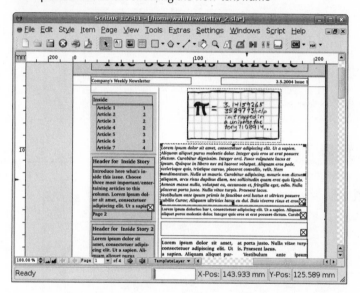

13. The final step in this quick tutorial is to link two text frames so that any text that overflows from the first goes into the second. You can link any two frames, but the frame that you are linking to must be empty. To clear the frame directly below your new frame, right-click on it and select Unlock. Then right-click again and select Edit Text. Once the Story Editor displays, select all of the existing text in the frame, delete it, and click the Update Text Frame and Exit icon. The frame is now empty, as shown in Figure 10.39.

14. Click the frame that you want to flow text from, and select the Link text Frames button in the toolbar. (It shows two text frames with an arrow beside them, and is to the right of the Edit the text with the Story Editor button. Left-click on the frame that you want to flow text to. The screen updates, flowing text from one frame to the other, as shown in Figure 10.40.

FIGURE 10.39

The updated document after emptying a text frame

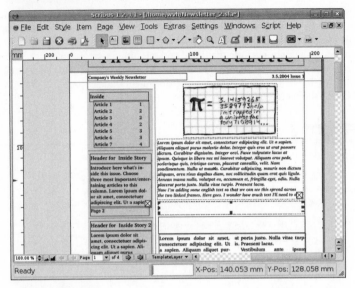

FIGURE 10.40

The updated document showing linked text frames

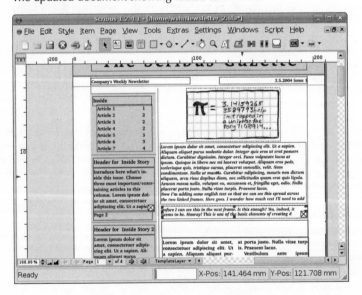

That's it for this tutorial. You can now save your document, or export it for printing by selecting the Save the current document as PDF icon (identified by the familiar PDF graphic).

Scribus is a powerful application with many features, and deserves its own book some day. This tutorial guided you through the basics of creating, modifying, and linking text frames, as well as inserting and modifying graphics. Scribus is an impressive program that is a shining example of the power of the open source model and the skill and determination of a few developers who saw a need, and filled it.

More Information About Scribus

Scribus is a relatively young application, but a significant and ever-increasing amount of information about it is already available on the Web, in various forums and in different parts of the Scribus Web site. My favorite locations for HOWTO information about Scribus are the following:

- Scribus Documentation Site (`http://docs.scribus.net/`) provides a good deal of information about setting up and using Scribus, printing, color management in Scribus documents, and so on.
- Scribus Wiki (`http://wiki.scribus.net/`) provides a great forum for discussing and documenting how to use Scribus.
- Tutorial: Getting Started with Scribus (`http://docs.scribus.net/index.php?lang=en&page=tutorials/freedomyug/scribustutorial`), though written for an older version of Scribus and thus slightly dated, is an excellent hands-on tutorial for getting started with Scribus. The sample files used in the tutorial are also available for download from this site.

Scribus is an open source project staffed by volunteers. If you become a Scribus fan and have something to contribute, I'm sure they'd be glad to hear from you.

Other Word Processors and Office Suites for Linux

This chapter focused on the most popular, open source command-line and graphical applications for word processing and page layout. There are certainly others — this is open source, after all, where anything worth doing is worth doing several times because of different perspectives on the task at hand. Some other popular word processors for Linux are the following:

- AbiWord: The AbiWord word processor is part of the GNOME Office Suite (`www.gnome.org/gnome-office`). AbiWord is a powerful and popular word processor for Linux, with excellent capabilities for importing and working with existing documents in formats such as Microsoft Word. AbiWord is available in the Ubuntu repositories, and can easily be installed on your Ubuntu system using the Synaptic Package Manager.
- Applixware: Applixware is an office suite that includes a powerful word processor, but has had an on-again, off-again relationship with Linux. Originally marked as an end-user package that was a direct competitor to StarDivision's original StarOffice Office Suite, Applixware has morphed into more of a toolkit for developing real-time and analytical applications. For more information about Applixware, see `www.vistasource.com/vs2/en/index.php`. For an article on installing Applixware on Ubuntu Linux, visit the Applixware group at `http://groups.google.com/group/Applixware` and search for Ubuntu.

- KWord: The KWord word processor is part of KOffice, the KDE Office Suite (www.koffice.org). KWord is both powerful and popular, but requires KDE. If you are interested in KWord, you might want to consider using Kubuntu, a KDE-centric Ubuntu Linux distribution, rather than the standard, GNOME-oriented Ubuntu Linux distribution. KWord is available in the Ubuntu repositories, and can easily be installed on your Ubuntu system using the Synaptic Package Manager. Doing so will install many underlying KDE components, but what's a little disk space between friends?

All of these word processors are quite easy to use and have their own circle of devotees. If you find something that you don't like about OpenOffice.org Writer, installing and experimenting with any of these is well worth your time. After all, you can't beat the price.

Summary

This chapter explained how to do several word processing tasks on your Ubuntu system. It began by discussing TeX and LaTeX, the classic, command-line formatted document processors for Linux and Unix systems, and even highlighted some of the graphical tools that are available for working with LaTeX documents. Then it covered OpenOffice.org Writer, the word processing component of the powerful OpenOffice.org office suite, and explained how to create documents and templates in Writer. Next it discussed Scribus, a powerful desktop publishing application for Linux, which provides the layout and formatting power that you need when appearance and detailed layout is just as important as content. In conclusion, some other word processing packages not discussed at length in this chapter but which are also available for Ubuntu Linux were briefly described.

The document production software packages provided with Ubuntu Linux are great, but people do not live by documents alone. Chapter 11 explains how to use other office-related software on your Ubuntu system to create other popular types of files, such as spreadsheets and presentations.

Chapter 11

Other Office Software: Spreadsheets and Presentations

The previous chapter discussed how to create documents on your Ubuntu system. Along with surfing the Web and sending and receiving e-mail, writing letters, TODO lists, and working on your novel are probably the most common personal tasks that you'll find yourself doing on your new machine. Word processing is also a fairly critical business task because, although most companies live on e-mail nowadays, there's still always the need for the occasional memo, planning document, and so on.

This chapter discusses the other office-related software that's available for your Ubuntu Linux system, namely spreadsheets and presentation software. While few people actually need to give presentations on their home computer or to their family (maybe "Next Month's Budget — What It Means To You"?), spreadsheets are a crossover task that is often as important to home users as it is to office workers. If you are working from home or using Ubuntu on a laptop for business reasons, you may need to create both spreadsheets and presentations, and Ubuntu Linux makes this easy (well, as easy as it is on any computer system).

Ubuntu Linux Desktop, OEM, or Text-Mode installations automatically install the OpenOffice.org Calc spreadsheet application as part of the OpenOffice.org suite, and the easy-to-use Synaptic Package Manager makes it easy to install other spreadsheets (such as the lighter-weight but equally powerful Gnumeric spreadsheet package. Ubuntu Linux Desktop, OEM, or Text-Mode installations also automatically install the OpenOffice.org Impress presentation application as part of the OpenOffice.org suite.

NOTE To save repeating the phrases "OpenOffice.org Calc" and "OpenOffice.org Impress" more times than necessary throughout the rest of this section, I'll typically refer to OpenOffice.org Calc simply as Calc (its name to its friends) and OpenOffice.org Impress simply as Impress.

IN THIS CHAPTER

Using spreadsheets: A tutorial

Using Gnumeric

Using OpenOffice Calc

Creating presentations with Impress

Introduction to Spreadsheets: A Quick Tutorial

This section provides background information on what a spreadsheet is, how it works, and how to use one. If you're already familiar with spreadsheets, you can skip this section. However, if you're not, this section is for you.

In paper terms, a spreadsheet is a sheet of paper divided into rows and columns. Each rectangle on the spreadsheet is referred to as a *cell*. Each row on a spreadsheet typically provides a variety of information about a specific transaction or other entity, while the columns are used to visually compare, mathematically summarize, or perform some other mathematical operation on the values for each row that appears in that column. The following is an example in text form:

```
Meal            Cost            Tax             Tip
Breakfast       5.79            0.41            1.25
Lunch           8.48            0.60            1.75
Dinner          13.23           0.93            2.75
```

This simple table reflects my meals for a (fictitious) day. The first row is a set of headings that identify the meaning of the entries in each column. Each row provides the details of each of the meals for that day. It would be easy enough to find out the total cost for my meals that day in various ways — either by adding a summary column to the end, which contains the total cost of each meal, and then adding all of the values in that column together, or by adding a new row, which contains the totals of all of that type of item for the day, and then adding all of the value in that row together. I prefer the first approach, a summary column, so let's go with that approach for the remainder of this section. There's nothing preventing you from calculating your daily totals the other way if you prefer (or doing it both ways, for that matter) — the ability of spreadsheet applications to automatically perform these calculations is one of their coolest features.

> **NOTE** From this point on, this section is a hands-on tutorial to creating a simple spreadsheet. The instructions provided in the rest of this section work exactly the same way whether you're using Gnumeric or OpenOffice.org Calc. If you want to follow along, skip ahead to the section on starting your spreadsheet of choice, and then jump back here to work through the tutorial. It may be simpler to follow along in Gnumeric because that is already installed on your Ubuntu system, but there are plenty of good reasons to install and use OpenOffice.org Calc, especially if you're going to be using some of the other tools in the OpenOffice suite, such as Writer or Impress (discussed later in this chapter). The screen shots in this tutorial show the example in Gnumeric, but they will look exactly the same in Calc, modulo differences in the menus and toolbars in Calc.

Manually performing these calculations is fine if you don't have a computer or if you're far better at math than I am, but I prefer to use the appropriate tool whenever one is available — and spreadsheets to the rescue in this case. I'd therefore start up a spreadsheet application (more about how to do that later), and enter the values from my paper table in the appropriate cells of the spreadsheet. (To enter a specific value in a cell in a spreadsheet, select that cell using the mouse and type the value.) Figure 11.1 shows the sample values after entering them into a sample spreadsheet.

Now the fun begins! To create a cell that contains the sum of selected values from each row, click the cell where you want to create the value, and enter the value =sum(. The equals sign tells the spreadsheet that you are using a function, *sum* is the name of the function that you want to perform, and the opening parenthesis identifies the fact that this will be followed by a list of the cells that you want to be involved in the function. (You can also do this using the mouse, which I'll explain later, but typing the function operator is easier for the purposes of this example.) Figure 11.2 shows the sample spreadsheet at this point.

FIGURE 11.1

Sample values in a Gnumeric spreadsheet

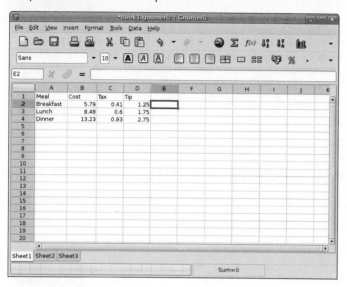

FIGURE 11.2

Beginning to define a formula

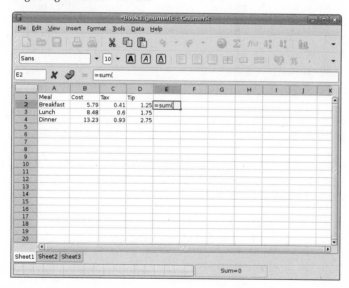

Next, identify the values that you want to summarize. This is most easily done using the mouse. To select the existing numeric values in a row, click the cell containing the cost value in the second column and hold down the left mouse button while dragging the cursor to the right to encompass the other two numeric values in that row. This is known as selecting a *range* of cells. As you select a range of cells, a dotted rectangle outlines the cells that you've selected, and the identifiers for those cells are listed following the opening parenthesis in the formula, as shown in Figure 11.3. (This is often referred to as a *selection box*.) As you can see in this figure, the cells in a spreadsheet are identified by their column and row — for example, B2 refers to the cell in column B, row 2. When represented in a formula, a range of cells is identified by referring to the first cell and the last cell in the selected range, separating their names by a colon. In this example, B2:D2 means "all cells between cell B2 and D2, including those two cells."

FIGURE 11.3

Selecting a range of cells for a formula to act on

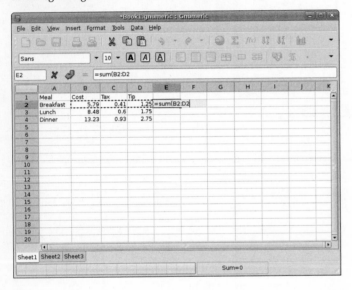

After selecting the cells for the function to act on, you terminate the function by entering a closing parenthesis, as shown in Figure 11.4.

Once you've terminated the function, press return to tell the spreadsheet that you're done with that cell, Your spreadsheet calculates the value of the function that you've entered, displays that value, and moves the cursor to the next available call, as shown in Figure 11.5. That was easy!

FIGURE 11.4

Ending the definition of a formula

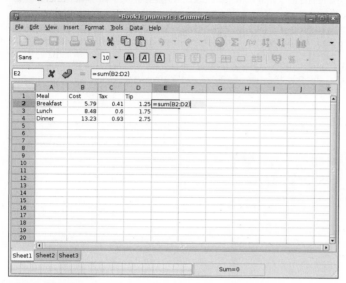

FIGURE 11.5

Displaying a calculated value

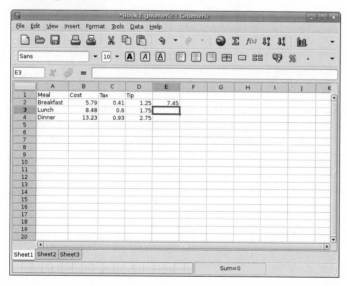

You could do the same thing in the next two rows, but there are easier ways to accomplish this that will help show some other basic spreadsheet capabilities. The easiest way to clone a calculated value to other cells in a column is to copy the contents of the first cell that contains the function and paste it into the other cells in that column. When you copy a calculated cell and paste it into multiple other cells at the same time, the spreadsheet figures out that you actually want to paste in a version of that function which applies to the rows in each column that you're pasting the function into. And people say that computer programs can't be smart!

To copy the function from the cell where you defined it, click that cell and select the Edit menu's Copy command. A dashed line appears around the selected cell, as shown in Figure 11.6.

FIGURE 11.6

Copying a cell in the spreadsheet

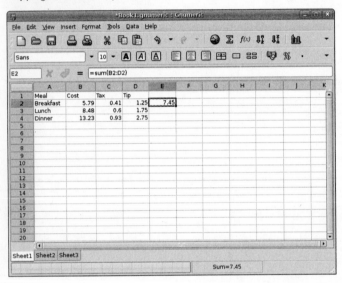

Next, select the range of cells that you want to paste that value into, in the same way that you selected a range of cells when defining your function. To do this, click the cell below the one that currently contains the formula and hold down the left mouse button while dragging the cursor down one row to encompass the same cell in the Dinner row, as shown in Figure 11.7.

Finally, select the Edit menu's Paste command to paste the function into the selected range of cells. Voila! The function is pasted into each cell and automatically calculates the right value for each row, as shown in Figure 11.8.

FIGURE 11.7

Selecting the range of cells to paste the function into

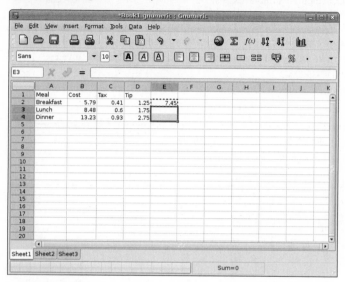

FIGURE 11.8

The updated spreadsheet with per-row calculations

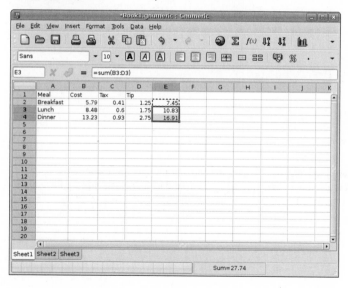

I love it when a plan comes together! The only numeric calculation that remains is to create another cell that summarizes the calculated values in the per-meal summary column. This is easy enough to do, in exactly the same way as you did before, which I'll summarize:

1. Select the cell in which you want to invoke a function.

2. Type =sum(to start defining the function.

3. Click the left mouse button, hold it down, and drag the selection box to select the three cells in the column that you're summarizing.

4. Enter the closing parenthesis to conclude the function and press return to enter it and perform the calculation.

If all went according to plan, your spreadsheet should now look like the one shown in Figure 11.9. Congratulations — you've learned the basics of working with a spreadsheet!

FIGURE 11.9

The sum of your previously calculated sums

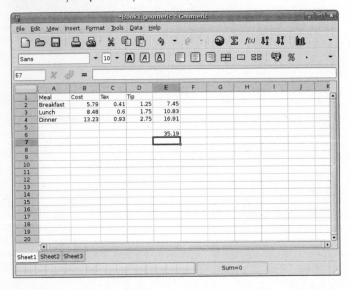

Aside from the fact that you didn't have to do any of the math in this example (hooray!), one of the coolest things about a spreadsheet containing calculated values is that you can update any of the other cells that are involved in those calculations, and the spreadsheet will automatically update itself to reflect the new value in any cells that are based on the contents of the modified cell. Try it yourself — as all good software should do, *it just works*!

Once the basic calculations are complete, you can add some labels to clarify the meaning of the values in the different fields. You already have row and column headings, but nothing explains the cell that displays the daily total. To enter text in a cell of the spreadsheet, click that cell to select it and type whatever you want. Figure 11.10 shows the sample spreadsheet after entering the value "Daily Total" in cell D6.

FIGURE 11.10

Adding a few text fields to the spreadsheet

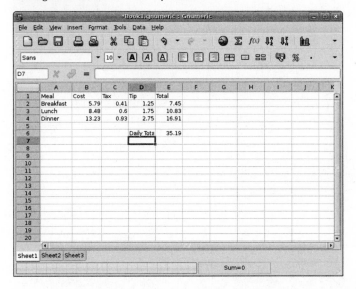

Note that the value "Daily Total" doesn't quite fit in the cell. To fix this, you can adjust the column width. To adjust the width of a column in a spreadsheet, left-click the column heading (D, in this case) to select it. Next, position the cursor over the line at the right edge of that column, hold down the left mouse button to select that edge, and drag it to the right to increase its size. As you drag the column edge, a tool tip appears that displays the current column width, as shown in Figure 11.11.

Once you've resized the column so that all of your text is visible, release the left mouse button to complete the resize operation. The column displays on the screen with its new width, as shown in Figure 11.12.

FIGURE 11.11

Resizing a column in the spreadsheet

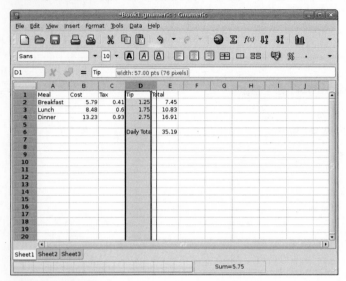

FIGURE 11.12

The resized column

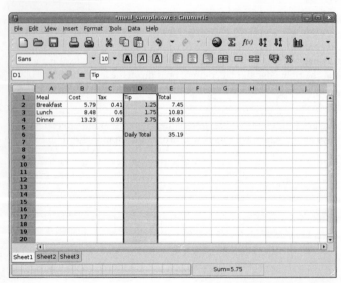

Next, clean up the formatting a bit. It's normal to want to visually differentiate labels from data values, so you can make all of the headings and labels bold. You can do this easily by multi-selecting all of them and applying bold formatting. To do this, hold down the Control key to indicate that you want to select multiple items, click on the row heading for row 1, the column heading for column A, and the cell containing the "Daily Total" label. Your screen should look like Figure 11.13.

FIGURE 11.13

Multi-selecting all labels in the spreadsheet

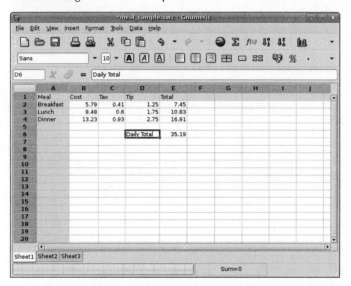

Next, click the bold button in the formatting toolbar. All selected items are formatted in bold, and your screen should look like the spreadsheet shown in Figure 11.14.

The last thing to do after you've done any work is to save your file, which you can do by selecting the File ➪ Save command. Because your spreadsheet only has a temporary name at this point, whatever spreadsheet you're using will display a dialog that enables you to specify a name for your spreadsheet (and optionally navigate to a specific directory location to save the spreadsheet).

Of course, there's much more to today's spreadsheets than the simple actions described in this tutorial, but this should be enough to get you started. All of the spreadsheets discussed in this chapter provide excellent online help, and plenty of books are available that explain how to use spreadsheets. Though few books are available on Linux-specific spreadsheets (yet), both Gnumeric and OpenOffice.org Calc are designed to be compatible with and similar to more common spreadsheets such as Microsoft Excel, so you should be able to get a lot of information out of almost any book on common spreadsheets such as Excel.

FIGURE 11.14

Updated formatting in the spreadsheet

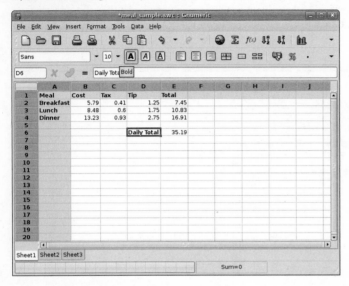

Using Gnumeric

As mentioned in the introduction to this chapter, spreadsheets are often as important to home computer users as they are to business users. This is especially true once a year for those of us in the United States, when tax time for anyone who itemizes deductions means trotting out all of your receipts for the past year, entering them into a spreadsheet, and totaling up anything that is legally deductible.

A recent poll by one of the Linux publications queried readers about what software they'd most like to see ported to Linux, and my vote went to TurboTax, because otherwise I'll have to have at least one Mac OS X machine around the house for the next twenty years or so. Until the TurboTax folks heed my plea (or, more likely, recognize Linux as a growing market opportunity), spreadsheets will have to do for tracking my personal business expenses. Luckily, Linux provides some excellent spreadsheet packages, one of which (Gnumeric) is installed by default on your Ubuntu Linux systems.

Gnumeric, a component of the GNOME Office Suite (which was introduced in Chapter 10), was one of the first spreadsheets available for Linux and, like a fine wine, has only continued to improve with age.

NOTE Previous Ubuntu Linux Desktop installs included Gnumeric, but Gnumeric is no longer installed by default. You can install Gnumeric on your system by using any of the software update utilities (apt-get, aptitude, or Synaptic) discussed in Chapter 20, "Adding, Removing, and Updating Software." However, if you want to use a spreadsheet that is preinstalled on your system, skip ahead to the discussion of OpenOffice.org Calc, which is discussed later in this chapter.

Starting Gnumeric

After you install Gnumeric on your system, a menu item for it is present on the Applications ➪ Office menu. To start Gnumeric, select this menu item. The application starts, displaying an empty document, as shown in Figure 11.15.

FIGURE 11.15

Starting Gnumeric

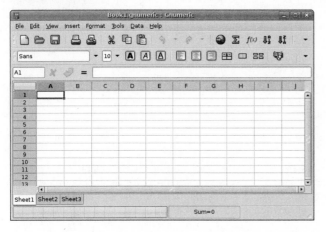

Taking a Quick Tour of Gnumeric

Gnumeric provides excellent online help, so I won't bore you by walking you through each menu and entry that it contains. However, as a quick overview of the Gnumeric interface, the callouts in Figure 11.15 highlight the following areas:

- **Menus:** The drop-down menus in Gnumeric are organized much like the menus in Microsoft Excel to provide a familiar user experience. Menu items with an arrow at their right edge lead to other, related submenus.

- **Toolbars:** By default, Gnumeric displays the Standard and Format toolbars, which provide one-click access to specific commands when you click on the appropriate icon. Depending on the size of the window in which Gnumeric is being displayed, you can access other commands that didn't fit on the current view of the toolbar by clicking on the down-arrow located at the far right. You can also display other toolbars or deactivate the default toolbars by selecting toolbars from the View ➪ Toolbars submenu.

- **Row and column headings:** These headings identify the current row and column for the cells that you're viewing. They can be useful when manually entering cells or ranges in a formula.

- **Context-sensitive menu:** Right-clicking on a call in any spreadsheet that you are working on in Gnumeric displays the context-sensitive menu shown in Figure 11.16. This menu provides quick access to several cell manipulation commands.

FIGURE 11.16

Gnumeric's context-sensitive menu

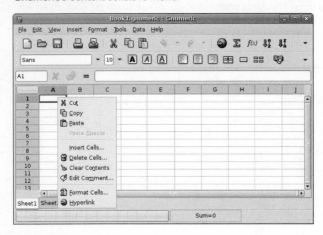

Gnumeric provides extensive online help, available by selecting Contents from the Help menu, or by pressing the F1 key on your keyboard at any time. Figure 11.17 shows the main page for Gnumeric's online help, which provides both a searchable index and a list of popular, general topics from its initial display window (at right).

FIGURE 11.17

Gnumeric's online help

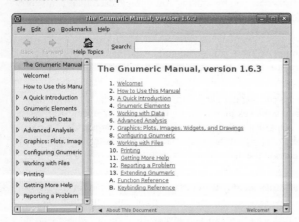

You can also select the Help menu's Gnumeric on the Web menu item to display Gnumeric's home page on the Internet, as shown in Figure 11.18, from which you can always access a variety of online documentation and other resources for working with Gnumeric.

Gnumeric's home page on the Web

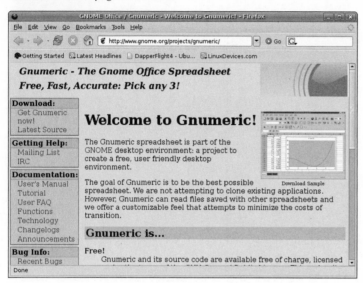

Invoking Functions in Gnumeric

The tutorial given earlier in this chapter explained how to manually enter a function, which is fine if you are using a simple function that you happen to know the name of. Gnumeric supports an extensive collection of functions that you can easily select from the Insert ➪ Function dialog using the mouse. Figure 11.19 shows this dialog with the sum function selected from the complete list of available formulas.

As you can see, selecting any function from the Function dialog displays abbreviated help for that function in the pane at the bottom of the dialog.

FIGURE 11.19

Available functions in Gnumeric

Specifying the Type of Data in a Cell

The spreadsheet tutorial in this section used fairly straightforward types of data that Gnumeric could easily recognize — sequences of characters from the alphabet and spaces are probably words, while numbers and decimal points are probably numeric values. Knowing the type of data that is contained in a cell (generally referred to as its *data type* or *data format*) is fairly important, especially when you subsequently want to invoke functions that calculate values from the contents of various cells.

When you enter values in a spreadsheet without specifying their type, spreadsheets such as Gnumeric assign them a general data format, which performs a best-guess of their data format based on the type of characters that they contain. However, you can also manually specify the format of any cell (or cells) by selecting those cells and using the commands on the Format ➪ Cells dialog, shown in Figure 11.20.

As an example, note that cell C3 in our example spreadsheet (most recently shown in Figure 11.14) doesn't display the traditional number of decimal points that you'd expect to see in a monetary value. This is because Gnumeric's general data format recognized it as a decimal number, but didn't have any way of knowing that this was a monetary value. To correct this, select that cell, select the Format ➪ Cells command, and click Currency in the pane at the left. This displays a list of possible representations for that data format, as shown in Figure 11.21.

FIGURE 11.20

Specifying cell data formats in Gnumeric

FIGURE 11.21

Specifying that a cell contains a currency value

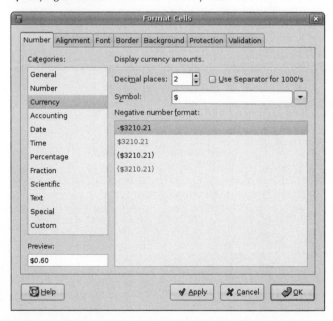

Note that two decimal places is the default for this data type, which is what you are trying to correct. Because this would do the trick, click OK to set cell C3 as a currency value and close the Format Cells dialog. This updates the spreadsheet, which now shows the correct number of decimal places for cell C3, as shown in Figure 11.22.

FIGURE 11.22

The updated spreadsheet showing C3 as a currency value

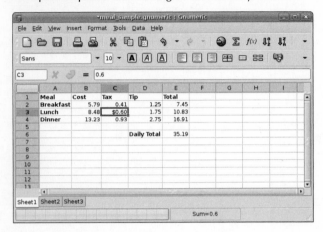

This is fine, except that Gnumeric now recognizes that cell as a currency value but all other numeric cells are still general numeric values, which makes the spreadsheet look a bit odd. You can correct this by multi-selecting all of the numeric values in the spreadsheet (hold down the Control key, click and hold the left mouse button on cell B2, drag the selection box to encompass all cells from B2 through E4, and then also click cell E6 before releasing the Control key), displaying the Format Cells dialog again, selecting Currency, and clicking OK. Voila! The spreadsheet is now consistent, as shown in Figure 11.23.

FIGURE 11.23

The updated spreadsheet showing currency values

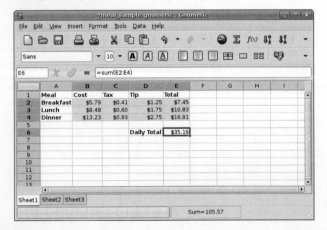

Importing Existing Spreadsheets

Linux folks like me tend to be Linux-centric, but that doesn't mean that we can completely ignore reality. When you're working with existing spreadsheets (and any other office-related documents, to be honest), the chances are pretty good that you created them using more common software packages, such as Microsoft Excel, that run on other operating systems, such as Mac OS X and Microsoft Windows. The folks who wrote and support Gnumeric couldn't ignore this reality either, so Gnumeric provides built-in support for opening Microsoft Excel spreadsheets and workbooks.

> **NOTE** If you have a lot of existing spreadsheets and are wondering how to transfer them to your new Ubuntu system, see Chapter 16, "File Transfer and Sharing on Ubuntu," for detailed information on doing just that. Don't worry—it's really quite easy to do using a network connection or even a traditional mechanism such as a floppy or burning a CD.

For example, to open an existing Excel spreadsheet, simply select the File ➪ Open command. By default, the file selection dialog that opens enables you to select files with any extension, including the `.xls` extension used by Microsoft Excel spreadsheets.

The same mechanism is used to open files in any other format supported by Gnumeric. Gnumeric can open spreadsheets or other data files that have been saved in any of the following formats:

- **Applix** (.as): The spreadsheet files produced by the Applix Office suite, which was discussed in Chapter 10.

- **Comma-Separated Value** (.csv): A standard text-based interchange format, where each row appears on a single line and each field value is separated from the next by a comma. This exchange format does not preserve the calculations required to produce cell values, only the values of the cells themselves.

- **Data Interchange Format** (.dif): Another standard text-based interchange format that does not preserve the calculations required to produce cell values, only the values of the cells themselves.

- **Gnumeric** (.gnumeric): Gnumeric's own format. (No surprise there)

- **Linear and Integer Program Format** (.mps): A text-based interchange format originally developed by IBM in the 16th century. This exchange format does not preserve the calculations required to produce cell values, only the values of the cells themselves, leaving the calculations to the monks who were illuminating the punch cards.

- **Lotus 1-2-3** (.123, .wk1, .wks): The spreadsheet formats used by various versions of Lotus 1-2-3 spreadsheet.

- **Multiplan** (.sylk): The spreadsheet format used by the old Multiplan spreadsheet.

- **OpenOffice.org Calc** (.ods): The open document spreadsheet format used by OpenOffice.org Calc and other forward-thinking spreadsheets.

- **Quattro Pro** (.wb1, wb2, .wb3): The spreadsheet formats used by various versions of Borland's Quattro Pro spreadsheet.

- **Xbase** (.dbf): The database file format used by a variety of Dbase III-compatible applications such as Microsoft FoxPro, Dbase III and later, and so on.

As you can see, the open source developers who are responsible for Gnumeric have made a very significant effort to ensure that you can import any of your existing spreadsheet data files into Gnumeric, so that you're not losing anything other than your dependence on your previous operating system.

Using OpenOffice.org Calc

The previous section explored using Gnumeric, a powerful and well-established spreadsheet application that is a part of the GNOME Office Suite, and is therefore found on most GNOME-based Linux systems, including Ubuntu Linux systems. While very powerful and able to import existing files from many other spreadsheet applications, Gnumeric is still essentially a stand-alone application. The GNOME Office suite is a collection of office applications that depend on the GIMP Toolkit (GTK) graphics library for many of their graphical controls. These have been semantically collected into the GNOME Office suite through their allegiance to GTK and the need for the GNOME folks to have an office suite just like the KDE folks, not necessarily because of any internal similarities or common functionality beyond GTK itself.

This brings us to OpenOffice.org Calc. As the name suggests, OpenOffice.org Calc is a part of the OpenOffice.org Office suite, which is a set of applications that were designed together, share extensive amounts of code, share a similar look and feel, and invoke each other to satisfy certain requirements. For example, as I'll discuss later in this chapter, bulk importing existing spreadsheets into Calc using its Document Converter wizard produces a report of the results of the import process. This file is created in the OpenOffice.org document format used by OpenOffice.org Writer, and can be displayed once the conversion process completes so that you can check for any errors or problems. You can't even select the Document Converter's Show log file button if OpenOffice.org Writer is not installed on your system.

As companies such as Microsoft have discovered, there's a lot to be said for a set of consistent, related applications that know how to leverage each other's capabilities to perform many of the data management tasks required in a modern, computer-oriented office. Unlike Microsoft Office, the OpenOffice.org suite is a high-quality, no-cost solution to your office software requirements. Though I've been a Gnumeric user for years, I tend to use all of the OpenOffice.org applications on my desktop systems nowadays. Because Gnumeric is much smaller and lighter-weight than OpenOffice.org, I still use Gnumeric on my laptops, which has come in very handy both times that I've needed a spreadsheet in a hotel room in recent years.

Installing Files for OpenOffice.org Calc

The OpenOffice.org software, including Calc, is installed by default if you install Ubuntu from the Live CD, from the Alternate Install CD using the Text Mode installer, and from the Alternate installer using the OEM Mode installer. If you want to add Calc or the entire OpenOffice .org suite to a server system that has a graphical user interface, you can install them using `apt-get`, `aptitude`, or `Synaptic`, as explained in Chapter 20, "Adding, Removing, and Updating Software."

One of the things that differentiates Ubuntu Linux from other Linux distributions is its extreme dedication to the user, especially in terms of internationalization. If you are installing Calc for use when creating spreadsheets in languages other than English, you may also want to search for and install the appropriate hyphenation, localization, and thesaurus packages for whatever other locales you are creating spreadsheets for. This is especially important for working with spreadsheets that use non-U.S. currencies.

> **TIP** If you've already installed the localization and internationalization packages for any component of the OpenOffice.org suite, there is no need to install them again. Installing them once installs them as a shared resource that can be used by every component of the suite.

You can easily find these localization and internationalization packages by looking for a string that represents the country code that you are looking for. For example, Figure 11.24 shows the Synaptic Package Manager, displaying specific German language support packages for OpenOffice.org that have been identified by searching for the string "-de."

FIGURE 11.24

Related language packages for OpenOffice.org

You can install complete language support for all applications (without translating the GNOME user interface itself) by installing the appropriate language support meta-package for your target locale(s). These packages have names of the form language-support-country-code (for example, language-support-de), and include the dictionaries for the specified locale. To fully translate the GNOME interface and all internationalized applications, select the appropriate language pack. The names of the language packs are of the form language-pack-country-code. Once you've installed multiple dictionaries, and so on, you can set the default language for your document using the Tools ⇨ Options ⇨ Language Settings ⇨ Language drop-down list.

See Chapter 20, "Adding, Removing, and Updating Software," for more detailed information on installing applications using the Synaptic Package Manager.

Starting Calc

You can start Calc from any command line by executing the command `oocalc`, but it is usually easier to start it from your GNOME menus. A menu item for Calc is provided in the Applications ⇨ Office menu. To start Calc, select the OpenOffice.org Spreadsheet menu item. The application starts, displaying an empty document, as shown in Figure 11.25.

FIGURE 11.25

Starting Calc

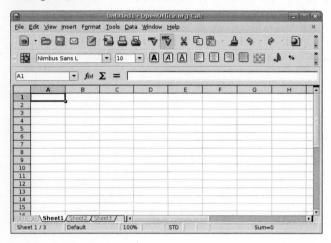

Taking a Quick Tour of Calc

OpenOffice.org Calc provides excellent online help, as do all of the tools in the OpenOffice.org suite, so I won't bore you by walking you through each menu and entry that it contains. However, as a quick overview of the Calc interface, the callouts in Figures 11.25 and 11.26 highlight the following areas:

- **Menus:** The drop-down menus in Calc are organized much like the menus in Microsoft Excel to provide a familiar user experience. Menu items with an arrow at their right edge lead to other, related submenus.

- **Toolbars:** By default, Calc displays the Standard and Formatting toolbars, which provide one-click access to specific commands when you click on the appropriate icon, and a Formula Bar, in which you can view and edit any functions or formulas for selected cells. You can modify the list of icons displayed on a toolbar by clicking on the control for that toolbar, located at the far right. You can display other toolbars or deactivate the default toolbars by selecting the names of those toolbars from the View ➪ Toolbars submenu.

- **Row and column headings:** These headings identify the current row and column for the cells that you're viewing. They can be useful when manually entering cells or ranges in a formula.

- **Context-sensitive menu:** Right-clicking on any cell in a spreadsheet that you are working on in Calc displays the context-sensitive menu shown in Figure 11.26. This menu provides quick access to several cell manipulation commands.

Calc provides extensive online help, available by selecting OpenOffice.org Help from the Help menu, or by pressing the F1 key on your keyboard at any time. Figure 11.27 shows the main page for Calc's help, which provides both a searchable index and a list of popular, general topics from its initial display window (at right).

FIGURE 11.26

Calc's context-sensitive menu

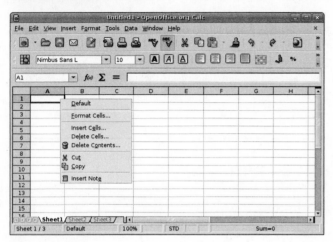

FIGURE 11.27

Calc's online help

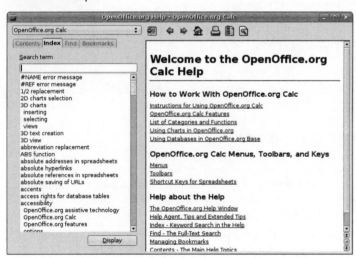

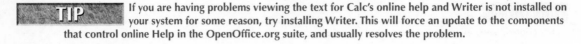

TIP If you are having problems viewing the text for Calc's online help and Writer is not installed on your system for some reason, try installing Writer. This will force an update to the components that control online Help in the OpenOffice.org suite, and usually resolves the problem.

Invoking Functions in Calc

The tutorial given earlier in this chapter explained how to manually enter a function, which is fine if you are using a simple function that you happen to know the name of. Calc supports an extensive collection of functions that you can easily select from the Insert ➪ Function dialog using the mouse. Figure 11.28 shows this dialog with the SUM function selected from the complete list of available formulas.

FIGURE 11.28

Available functions in Calc

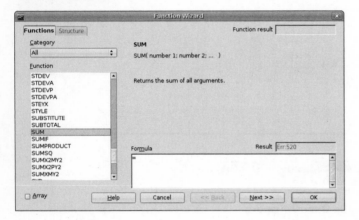

As you can see, selecting any function from the Function dialog displays abbreviated help for that function in the pane at the right of the dialog.

Specifying the Type of Data in a Cell

The spreadsheet tutorial in this section used fairly straightforward types of data that Calc could easily recognize — sequences of characters from the alphabet and spaces are probably words, while numbers and decimal points are probably numeric values. Knowing the type of data that is contained in a cell (generally referred to as its *data type* or *data format*) is fairly important, especially when you subsequently want to invoke functions that calculate values from the contents of various cells.

When you enter values in a spreadsheet without specifying their type, spreadsheets such as Calc assign them a general data format, which performs a best-guess of their data format based on the type of characters that they contain. However, you can also manually specify the format of any cell (or cells) by selecting those cells and using the commands on the Format ➪ Cells dialog, shown in Figure 11.29.

FIGURE 11.29

Specifying cell data formats in Calc

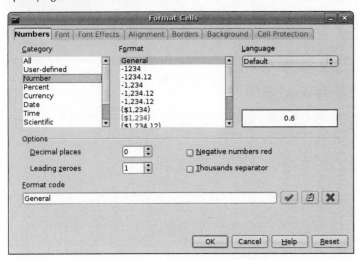

As an example, note that cell C3 in your example spreadsheet (most recently shown in Figure 11.14) doesn't display the traditional number of decimal points that you'd expect to see in a monetary value. This is because Calc's general data format recognized it as a decimal number, but didn't have any way of knowing that this was a monetary value. To correct this, select that cell, select the Format ➪ Cells command, and click Currency in the pane at left. This displays a list of possible representations for that data format, as shown in Figure 11.30.

FIGURE 11.30

Specifying that a cell contains a currency value

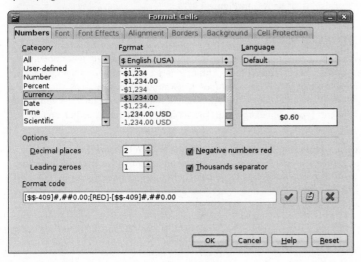

Note that two decimal places is the default for this data type, which is what you are trying to correct. Because this would do the trick, click OK to set cell C3 as a currency value and close the Format Cells dialog. This updates the spreadsheet, which now shows the correct number of decimal places for cell C3, as shown in Figure 11.31.

FIGURE 11.31

The updated spreadsheet showing C3 as a currency value

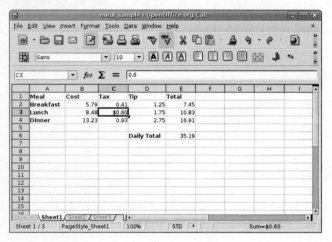

This is fine, except that Calc now recognizes that cell as a currency value but all other numeric cells are still general numeric values, which makes the spreadsheet look a bit odd. You can correct this by multi-selecting all of the numeric values in the spreadsheet (hold down the Control key, click and hold the left mouse button on cell B2, drag the selection box to encompass all cells from B2 through E4, and then also click cell E6 before releasing the Control key), displaying the Format Cells dialog again, selecting Currency, and clicking OK. Voila! The spreadsheet is now consistent, as shown in Figure 11.32.

Importing Existing Spreadsheets

Linux folks like me tend to be Linux-centric, but that doesn't mean that we can completely ignore reality. When you're working with existing spreadsheets (and any other office-related documents, to be honest), the chances are pretty good that you created them using more common software packages, such as Microsoft Excel, that run on other operating systems, such as Mac OS X and Microsoft Windows. The folks who wrote and support the OpenOffice.org suite and OpenOffice.org Calc couldn't ignore this reality either, so Calc provides built-in support for opening Microsoft Excel spreadsheets and workbooks.

NOTE If you have a lot of existing spreadsheets and are wondering how to transfer them to your new Ubuntu system, see Chapter 16, "File Transfer and Sharing on Ubuntu," for detailed information on doing just that. Don't worry—it's really quite easy to do using a network connection or even a traditional mechanism such as a floppy or burning a CD.

FIGURE 11.32

The updated spreadsheet showing currency values

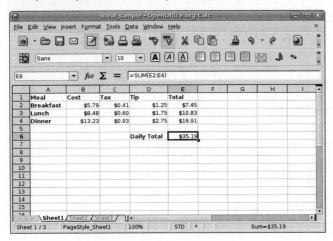

For example, to open an existing Excel spreadsheet, simply select the File ⇨ Open command. By default, the file selection dialog that opens enables you to select files with any extension, including the `.xls` extension used by Microsoft Excel spreadsheets.

Supported Import Formats

The same mechanism as described earlier in this chapter can be used to open files in any other format supported by Calc. Calc can also open spreadsheets or other data files that have been saved in any of the following formats:

- **Comma-Separated Value** (.csv): A standard text-based interchange format, where each row appears on a single line and each field value is separated from the next by a comma. This exchange format does not preserve the calculations required to produce cell values, only the values of the cells themselves.

- **Data Interchange Format** (.dif): Another standard text-based interchange format that does not preserve the calculations required to produce cell values, only the values of the cells themselves.

- **Lotus 1-2-3** (.123, .wk1, .wks): The spreadsheet formats used by various versions of Lotus 1-2-3 spreadsheet.

- **Microsoft Excel** (.xls, .xlt, .xlw, .xml): All of the common spreadsheet formats used by versions of Excel.

- **Multiplan** (.sylk): The spreadsheet format used by the old Multiplan spreadsheet.

- **Open/StarOffice Calc** (.ods, .sdc): The open document spreadsheet format used by Calc and other forward-thinking spreadsheets.

- **Quattro Pro** (.wb1, wb2, .wb3): The spreadsheet formats used by various versions of Borland's Quattro Pro spreadsheet.

- **Pocket Excel** (.pxl): The spreadsheet format used by versions of Microsoft Excel for PDAs.

- **Xbase** (.dbf): The database file format used by a variety of Dbase III-compatible applications such as Microsoft FoxPro, Dbase III and later, and so on.

As you can see, the open source developers who are responsible for Calc have made a very significant effort to ensure that you can import any of your existing spreadsheet data files into Calc, so that you're not losing anything other than your dependence on your previous operating system.

Importing Spreadsheets Using the Document Converter

As you can see from the previous section, Calc can open spreadsheets produced by many other spreadsheet applications. It can also open spreadsheet files with Microsoft Excel extensions directly. After working on them, you can then save them directly in the new, open OpenDocument spreadsheet format (`http://en.wikipedia.org/wiki/OpenDocument`) that is used by Calc.

Repeating this process is fine if you have only one or two spreadsheets that you want to update, but if you are moving all of your work to Ubuntu, you may find that you have hundreds of spreadsheets that you want to update to Calc format. Luckily, Calc provides a wizard for this that will not only import all of your Microsoft Excel spreadsheets, but also will import and convert any existing or attached templates that it detects.

To bulk import your existing Microsoft Excel (or older OpenOffice.org) documents, do the following:

1. Select File ⇨ Wizards ⇨ Document Converter. The dialog shown in Figure 11.33 displays.

FIGURE 11.33

Specifying the input format when converting documents

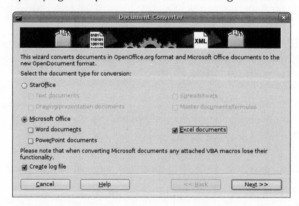

---

2. To bulk import Microsoft Excel files and templates, select the Microsoft Office radio button and the Excel Documents checkbox. To import existing SDC spreadsheets from StarOffice or a version of OpenOffice.org prior to 2.0, leave the StarOffice radio button selected and click the Spreadsheets and Master Documents checkboxes. Click Next to proceed. The dialog shown in Figure 11.34 displays.

FIGURE 11.34

Specifying document and template locations when importing

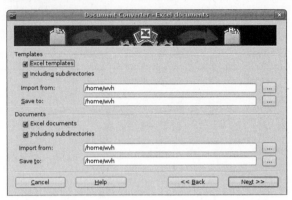

3. Specify the directories in which you want the wizard to search for the specified document types, and the locations to which converted documents should be saved. You may want to update the location to which converted templates should be saved — I typically use my home directory, and subsequently move the files around manually. Once you've checked the directory locations, click Next to proceed. A status dialog displays, summarizing the conversions that are about to take place. Click Convert to begin the conversion process. The dialog shown in Figure 11.35 displays as the conversion process progresses. When the conversion process completes, the Close and Show log file buttons are activated on the dialog.

FIGURE 11.35

Monitoring the document conversion process

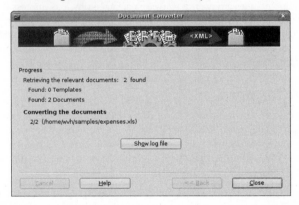

Congratulations — the conversion process is complete! Your converted spreadsheets and templates are ready for use in Calc. Before clicking Close, it's a good idea to click the Show log file button, which opens the log file in OpenOffice.org Writer. (This button will not be selectable if OpenOffice.org Writer is not installed on your system for some reason.) As shown in Figure 11.36, the log file for the conversion process lists successful conversions, and also identifies spreadsheets that should be fine-tuned or corrected before they can be used with Calc. This is often the case with spreadsheet template files or spreadsheets containing complex macros, which may contain statements that are not completely compatible with anything other than Microsoft's own Visual Basic.

FIGURE 11.36

A log file of the spreadsheet conversion process

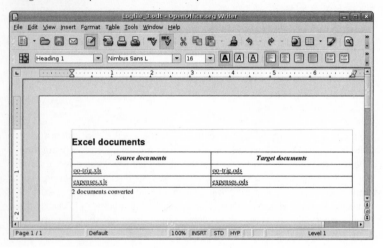

Using OpenOffice.org Impress

The OpenOffice.org office suite includes a powerful software package known as Impress for creating and editing presentations. While you may not need to create presentations on your home computer, presentations are a fact of everyday life in business today, and no suite of office applications would be complete without this type of package. As mentioned earlier, I'll simply refer to OpenOffice.org Impress as Impress throughout the remainder of this section.

Installing Files for Impress

The OpenOffice.org software, including Impress, is installed by default if you install Ubuntu from the Live CD, from the Alternate Install CD using the Text Mode installer, and from the Alternate installer using the OEM Mode installer. If you want to add Impress or the entire OpenOffice.org suite to a server system that has a graphical user interface, you can install it using `apt-get`, `aptitude`, or `Synaptic`, as explained in Chapter 20, "Adding, Removing, and Updating Software."

One of the things that differentiates Ubuntu Linux from other Linux distributions is its extreme dedication to the user, especially in terms of internationalization. If you are installing Impress for use when creating presentations in languages other than English, you may also want to search for and install the appropriate hyphenation, localization, and thesaurus packages for whatever other locales you are creating spreadsheets for.

If you've already installed the localization and internationalization packages for any component of the OpenOffice.org suite, there is no need to reinstall them. Installing them once installs them as a shared resource that can be used by every component of the suite.

You can easily find these localization and internationalization packages by looking for a string that represents the country code that you are looking for. For example, Figure 11.37 shows the specific German language support packages for OpenOffice.org that have been identified by searching for the string "-de."

FIGURE 11.37

Related language Packages for OpenOffice.org

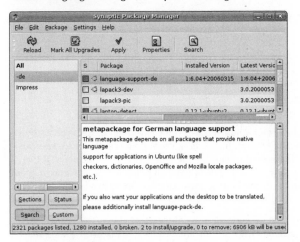

> **TIP**   You can install complete language support for all applications (without translating the GNOME user interface itself) by installing the appropriate language support meta-package for your target locale(s). These packages have names of the form language-support-country-code (for example, language-support-de), and include the dictionaries for the specified locale. To fully translate the GNOME interface and all internationalized applications, select the appropriate language pack. The names of the language packs are of the form language-pack-country-code. Once you've installed multiple dictionaries, and so on, you can set the default language for your document using the Tools ➪ Options ➪ Language Settings ➪ Language drop-down list.

See Chapter 20, "Adding, Removing, and Updating Software," for more detailed information on installing applications using the Synaptic Package Manager.

Starting Impress

You can start Impress from any command-line by executing the command ooimpress, but it is usually easier to start it from your GNOME menus. A menu item for Impress is provided in the Applications ➪ Office menu. To start Impress from the menus, select the OpenOffice.org Presentation menu item.

Using the Presentation Wizard

Unlike other OpenOffic.org applications that you may have looked at previously, when Impress starts, it runs a Wizard that walks you through creating a presentation. Let's follow along.

Figure 11.38 shows the initial screen of the Impress Presentation Wizard.

FIGURE 11.38

The first screen of the Impress Presentation Wizard

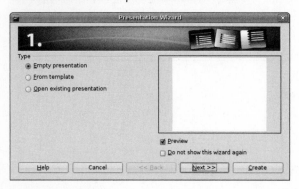

TIP When you start Impress and see the Presentation Wizard, you can opt out of the Presentation Wizard by selecting the Open existing presentation radio button. If you select Open, you can select an existing Impress or Microsoft PowerPoint presentation using the Open dialog that displays. If the presentation that you want to open is located in your home directory, you can double-click its name to open it. If it is located in another directory, click Open to display a dialog that enables you to browse for the presentation that you want to open.

You can permanently opt out of starting Impress with the wizard in the future by clicking Do not show this wizard again before you proceed. Impress will remember this setting and display a blank presentation the next time that you start Impress.

If you do not have any existing presentations that you want to open and simply want to open a new, blank presentation without using the wizard, click the Create button while the Empty presentation radio button is selected.

Assuming that you haven't opted out of the Presentation Wizard, click Next to begin creating your new presentation. The second Presentation Wizard screen displays, as shown in Figure 11.39.

Select one of the available backgrounds for your presentation from the list (or keep the <original> setting to continue without a background) and identify the output medium that you are targeting for this presentation: an on-screen presentation, overhead slides, paper, photographic slides, and so on. Specifying the output medium modifies some internal settings to maximize the appearance and usable area in your presentation. Once you've made any desired changes to these settings (I selected the Dark Blue with Orange presentation background for this example), click Next to continue. The third Presentation Wizard dialog displays, as shown in Figure 11.40.

This screen enables you select an effect that Impress should use when changing from one slide to the next. These include many different sweeping movements, rotations, and so on. Rather than trying to describe them all here, I'll just suggest that you experiment with them. Selecting any effect from the list while the Preview checkbox is selected (which it is by default) shows a preview of the selected effect in the preview window on this screen of the wizard.

FIGURE 11.39

Specifying a background in the Presentation Wizard

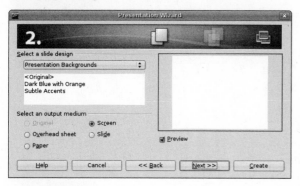

FIGURE 11.40

Providing presentation details in the Presentation Wizard

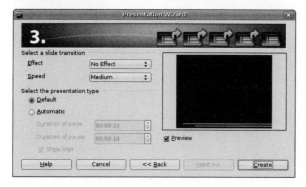

The other values on this wizard screen enable you to specify the speed of any selected effect, and the type of presentation that you are creating. Default presentations change slides only when you press a key or otherwise indicate that they should change — Automatic presentations change slides after a specified period of time, and are intended for use in kiosks or at trade shows where you want a regular, possibly repeating series of slides to serve as an attractor.

Once you've changed any of the settings on this screen that you want to take advantage of, click Create to create your new presentation and complete the Presentation Wizard. The standard Impress screen displays, as shown in Figure 11.41.

FIGURE 11.41

The standard Impress screen displaying a new presentation

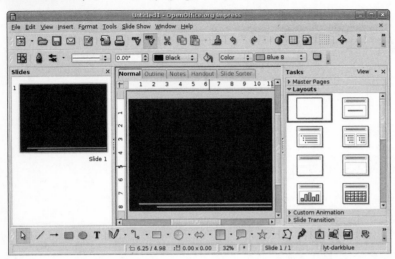

Taking a Quick Tour of Impress

Impress provides excellent online help, as do all of the tools in the OpenOffice.org suite, so I won't bore you by walking you through each menu and entry that it contains. However, as a quick overview of the Impress interface, the callouts in Figures 11.41 and 11.42 highlight the following areas:

■ **Menus:** The drop-down menus in Impress are organized much like the menus in Microsoft PowerPoint to provide a familiar user experience. Menu items with an arrow at their right edge lead to other, related submenus.

■ **Toolbars:** By default, Impress displays the Standard, Presentation, Drawing, and Lines and Filling toolbars, which provide one-click access to specific commands when you click on the appropriate icon. You can modify the list of icons displayed on a toolbar by clicking on the control for that toolbar, located at the far right. You can display other toolbars or deactivate the default toolbars by selecting the names of those toolbars from the View ➪ Toolbars submenu.

■ **Preview pane:** By default, the pane at the left displays a preview of all of the slides in the current presentation.

■ **Edit pane:** By default, the central pane displays your working copy of the current slide. You can change the way in which this slide is displayed by selecting the other tabs at the top of this window.

■ **Layouts pane:** By default, the pane at the right displays the predefined layouts that can be applied to the current slide. You can change the contents of this window by selecting other presentation-related tabs, such as Templates, Master Pages, Custom Animations, and Slide Transitions.

- **Context-sensitive menu:** Right-clicking on the slide that you are working on in Impress displays the context-sensitive menu shown in Figure 11.42. This menu provides quick access to several cell manipulation commands.

FIGURE 11.42

The context-sensitive menu for Impress

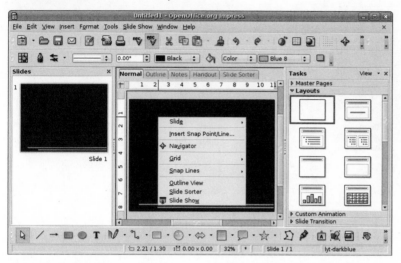

> **TIP** Though not displayed by default, you can display a Styles and Formatting window at any time by pressing the F11 key on your keyboard. (You can press F11 again to close this window.) The Styles and Formatting window provides easy access to the styles that are available in the current presentation, and is especially convenient if you choose not to display the formatting toolbar. Figure 11.43 shows Impress with the Styles and Formatting window displayed. Like any floating window in OpenOffice.org applications, you can dock this window by double-clicking on the grey portion of the window heading, making it a part of the default OpenOffice.org interface rather than a floating window. You can undock the window by double-clicking on the heading of the docked area.

Impress provides extensive online help, available by selecting OpenOffice.org Help from the Help menu, or by pressing the F1 key on your keyboard at any time. Figure 11.44 shows the main page for Impress help, which provides both a searchable index and a list of popular, general topics from its initial display window (at right).

> **TIP** If you are having problems viewing the text for the online help in Impress and OpenOffice.org Writer is not installed on your system, try installing OpenOffice.org Writer. This will force an update to the components that control online Help in the OpenOffice.org suite, and usually resolves the problem.

FIGURE 11.43

Impress showing the Styles and Formatting window

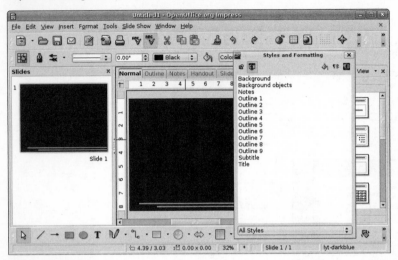

FIGURE 11.44

Online help for Impress

Creating a Presentation

Creating presentations in Impress is easy, though fine-tuning them can be as challenging as it is in any software for creating presentations.

To apply any of the available formats to the current slide, select that format in the Layouts window. The selected layout is applied to the current slide. You can then click in any of the text boxes and enter the appropriate text for that region. Figure 11.45 shows a slide that uses the Title Slide layout at the upper right in the Layouts window.

FIGURE 11.45

Creating a title slide in Impress

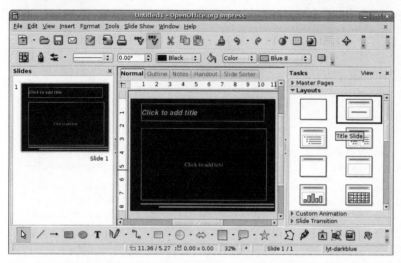

Impress provides many sample layouts, including title slides, slides that provide headings and text areas, slides that provide headings and areas for graphics, and so on. You can identify the intent behind any of the available layouts by positioning the cursor over that layout and viewing the tool tip that displays. As an example, the Title Slide tool tip is shown in Figure 11.45.

Once you've entered your text or other content in the current slide, you can add a new slide by selecting the Insert ➪ Slide command. A new slide displays in the editing window, and the preview window is updated to display the new slide and any previous slides. Figure 11.46 shows a new slide with the Title, Text format applied, and a preview of the previous and current slides. This figure also shows the tool tip for the currently selected format.

FIGURE 11.46

Adding a new slide in Impress

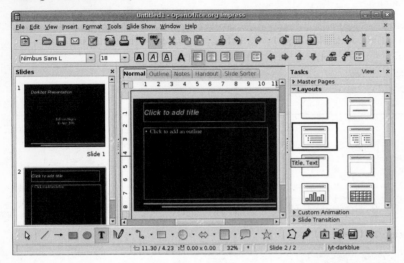

Once you've added some number of slides to your presentation, you should save it using the File ⇨ Save command. If this is a new presentation, you will be prompted to supply a name for the presentation.

After saving your presentation, you will probably want to see what it looks like so far. To preview your actual presentation, select View ⇨ Slide Show or press the F5 key on your keyboard. Your presentation displays on your screen, using any transition effects and timing that you specified when you created the presentation.

 **When previewing your presentation, the preview starts at the first slide selected in the preview pane. To see your entire presentation, select the first slide in the presentation before requesting a preview.**

Importing Existing Presentations

Impress can open existing presentations produced by Microsoft PowerPoint (and those produced by itself or StarOffice, of course). After working on these, you can then save them directly in the new, open OpenDocument presentation format that is used by Impress.

Repeating this process is fine if you have only one or two presentations that you want to update, but if you are moving all of your work to Ubuntu, you may find that you have many presentations that you want to update to Impress format. Luckily, Impress provides a wizard for this that will not only import all of your Microsoft PowerPoint presentations, but also will import and convert any existing or attached layout files and master documents that it detects. This wizard is known as the Document Converter.

The Document Converter used to convert presentations works identically to the Document Converter used to bulk import spreadsheets, as explained earlier in this chapter, so I won't waste space by repeating those instructions here. For information on using the Document Converter Wizard to bulk-import documents of any supported type, see "Importing Spreadsheets Using the Document Converter" earlier in this chapter.

The only real difference when importing presentations rather spreadsheets (or word processing documents, as explained in Chapter 10) is that you must select Microsoft Office and PowerPoint documents on the initial screen of the wizard, as shown in Figure 11.47

FIGURE 11.47

Specifying the input format when converting presentations

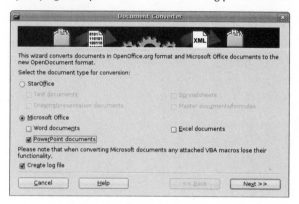

Summary

This chapter discussed common types of office software that you may need to use to complete your move to Ubuntu Linux. Linux often gets a bad rap in the press for not having a rich set of application software — as this books shows, this is entirely false. Not only is a good selection of powerful office software available for Linux, the open source nature of Linux gives you many alternatives in terms of the package that you want to use — and all at the same low, low price, which is $0 thanks to the hard work and time spent by the open source community and the folks who bring you Ubuntu Linux.

This chapter discussed two of the most popular spreadsheets for Ubuntu Linux, Gnumeric and OpenOffice.org Calc. As you can see from the sections that discuss them, they are quite similar in both appearance and capabilities. The chapter concluded by discussing OpenOffice.org Impress, which is a powerful software package for creating, working with, and managing presentations that is a part of the OpenOffice.org suite of office applications.

Now that we've explored creating documents, spreadsheets, and presentations, the next chapter discusses the software that enables you to create and convert various types of graphics files on Ubuntu Linux Desktop systems.

Chapter 12

Working with Graphics

A s a writer, I've always somewhat resented the old saying, "a picture is worth a thousand words." Can't I just do the thousand words and we can all move on?

I'm kidding of course — there are many times when a picture is worth far more than any number of words, such as the screen shots in this book, photographs and artwork in advertising, or various publications that specialize in glorifying the human form. No one has ever described a text-heavy document as eye-catching, even despite the best efforts of typographers and the layout artists at *Wired*. Even if you're not a graphics artist, there are times when everyone needs software for editing graphics and creating drawings, whether you just want to remove the terminal case of red-eye from all of your vacation photographs or produce simple illustrations for a card, letter, or presentation.

If you've worked with graphics packages such as Adobe Photoshop, Adobe Illustrator, or CorelDRAW, or Corel's Paint Shop Pro (formerly from JASC), you'll be happy to know that open source packages with most of the capabilities that you'll need to do the same sort of work are freely available for Ubuntu Linux. Some are pre-installed, and some are located in Ubuntu repositories and are therefore just a download away.

This chapter helps you make some sense out of the maze of acronyms, general terminology, and specialized jargon that aficionados use to describe digital graphics, and explains how to use the software available for Ubuntu Linux to create and edit drawings, images, and other types of computer graphics.

Overview of Digital Graphics Terminology

Even if you're not a graphics artist (and I certainly am not), everyone with a Web site or a digital camera has some familiarity with digital graphics. Terminology-wise, digital graphics is basically nothing more than storing images in files on your computer, regardless of whether these files contain pictures from your summer vacation, fancy buttons or other images that you're using on your Web site, artwork and drawings that you've created using graphics software, pictures that you've used a scanner to capture, images captured directly from your computer screen, or just about anything else that you can store in a file and display in a graphics application.

The following provides a quick dictionary of graphics terms that you may encounter as you start to work with online, digital graphics:

- **anti-aliasing:** A technique used to reduce the jagged appearance of the edges of objects and text in graphical images. Anti-aliasing softens those edges by blending them with the colors or areas that appear beside them in an image.

- **bitmap:** A graphical image that is composed of multiple picture elements, each representing one bit of that image. Each bit in a bitmap has its own color value, generally expressed as a combination of red, green, and blue (RGB) color values. Bitmaps are one of the two main formats for digital images — the other is vector graphics. Bitmaps are also referred to as raster images.

- **BMP:** A graphics format originally developed by Microsoft that supports a variety of resolutions and color depths. A file in BMP format contains a single bitmap/raster image.

- **color depth:** The maximum number of colors contained in an image or that can be displayed by a given device or graphics card. Common color depths are 256 colors, 16-bit (65,535 colors), 32-bit (4,294,967,296 colors, generally simply referred to as "millions of colors"), and so on. The greater the color depth of an image, the greater its size, because the color of each pixel requires the associated number of bits to represent each of the red, green, and blue portions of its color. Color depth is often defined in "bits per pixel" (BPP). For example, high color uses 15 or 16 bpp: 5 bits for blue, 5 bits for red, and 5 or 6 bits for green.

- **dithering:** The process of displaying pixels of different colors in a portion of an image to give the visual impression of a single color. Dithering is often used to give lower-resolution images the smoother appearance of a higher-resolution image.

- **GIF:** A popular lossless graphics format, Graphics Interchange Format files were formerly quite popular on the Web because they produced relatively high-quality, small file size images through the use of a compression technique known as Lempel-Ziv-Welch (LZW) compression, which is patented by Unisys. Because of licensing issues, most Web sites now use JPEG or PNG graphics. The primary advantage of the GIF format is that a single GIF file can contain multiple images that can be configured to display in sequence. These multi-image GIF files are known as "animated GIFs." To avoid patent and licensing issues, most animated Web graphics today are done using file formats such as Flash, QuickTime or Shockwave, or are done using Java-based animation techniques.

- **grayscale:** An image that is composed of various shades of gray. The number of bits used to hold the color value for each pixel determines the number of shades of gray that the image can use. If the number of bits is one, then the image is simply black and white, which is also known as *monochrome*. Grayscale is typically used in newspapers or books that are printed in black and white, where a halftone is used to print the different shades of gray.

- **halftone:** The simulation of a continuous-tone image (shaded drawing, photograph) by using different-sized dots to make up different portions of the image. Smaller dots per print area are used for lighter areas, and larger dots are used for darker areas. Halftones are typically used for relatively high-resolution reproduction of black and white images in print, such as in a newspaper or magazine.

- **jaggies:** The term for the staircase effect seen on the edges of bitmapped objects, also sometimes referred to as "aliasing." This unpleasant visual effect is usually eliminated by the use of techniques such as anti-aliasing.

- **JPEG:** A popular bitmapped image format consisting of 24-bit color and developed by the Joint Photographic Experts Group. JPEG is a lossy format, which is often used for graphics on Web pages to provide a good balance of good image resolution and small file size.

- **layers:** Most complex graphics files are internally composed of multiple image layers that are superimposed to create the final image. Working with different portions of an image (background, each component of an image, and so on) not only make it easy to interact with each graphics element without disturbing others, but also make it easy to quickly build up complex graphics by separating them into different logical elements that can be reused across similar graphics.

- **lossless formats:** File formats that are not lossy, i.e., file formats that provide all of the information that was present in the audio, graphics, or video information as it was originally recorded, drawn, or captured.

- **lossy formats:** File formats that sacrifice image quality to reduce file size. The term *lossy* refers to the data compression algorithm used to reduce file size, where some of the information that was present in the original file is actually eliminated to produce the smaller, compressed file, and therefore the original file can never be completely reconstructed from the compressed version. In the case of graphics, lossy images typically reduce both the available palette of colors and the number of pixels in the image. Lossy formats are quite common in graphics, audio, and video files because they can often reduce file size by eliminating information that is beyond the range of the human eye, the human ear, or both.

- **metadata:** Data about other data. In graphics files, metadata typically provides information about file data elements, file attributes (name, size, location, color depth, data type, and so on), or free-form comments. Metadata simplifies the use and analysis of graphics files by providing a higher-level interface to the file than just the raw data itself.

- **monochrome:** Images and text that are displayed using only black and white pixels. The term comes from the fact that there is only one chromatic (i.e., color) value used in the image: black is a pixel that is set to that color value, while white is a pixel that is not set to black.

- **PCL:** A Printer Control Language originally developed by Hewlett-Packard (HP) and now used in thousands of different printers. Files in PCL format can be printed directly on HP and compatible printers with no preprocessing.

- **pixels:** the smallest graphical element in a digital image that can be displayed on your computer screen. Each pixel has its own color, generally expressed as a combination of red, green, and blue (RGB) color values. The term *pixel* stands for "picture element." Most graphical images, such as digital photographs, contain millions of pixels — hence the term megapixels. The more pixels an image contains, the more detail it provides and the higher its resolution.

- **PNG:** Portable Network Graphics, a graphics file format originally designed as an alternative to the GIF format and its attendant licensing problems. PNG files are lossless, supporting up to 48-bit color or 16-bit grayscale images without losing any detail during compression.

- **PostScript:** a printer control language developed by Adobe and used in thousands of high-quality laser printers. PostScript files support both bitmaps and drawing primitives, and therefore typically produce high-quality images. PostScript was inspired by an earlier printer control language called InterPress, which was developed at Xerox PARC, as were other handy things such as Ethernet, laser printers, bitmapped displays, and so on.

- **prepress:** the process of preparing documents for printing. Nowadays, this generally refers to the use of computers to prepare documents and illustrations for printing as opposed to previous analog techniques such as producing photographic negatives, manual page layout, manual typesetting, and the manual production of printing plates.

- **raster graphics:** another name for bitmap graphics. The term *raster* refers to a position in the grid of coordinates that make up a computer display.

- **resolution:** the output quality of an image, defined in terms of dots, lines, pixels, or samples per inch, depending on your output device. PPI (pixels per inch) refers to screen resolution, DPI (dots per inch) refers to printer resolution, SPI (samples per inch) refers to the resolution at which images are obtained from a scanner, and LPI (lines per inch) refers to halftone resolution. High-resolution images contain 300 or more units per inch, and are intended for printed output. Low-resolution images generally contain 100 or fewer units per inch and are generally intended for on-screen or Web-based display.

- **stair-stepping:** another term for jaggies.

- **TIFF:** Tagged Image File Format, a popular lossless graphics file format. Files in TIFF format often have the extensions .TIF or .TIFF.

- **vector graphics:** a digital graphics representation and associated file format that defines an image by identifying each object in that image and describing that object in terms of characteristics such as its outline, shape, color palette, associated text, gradients, patterns, and element grouping. Vector graphics are resolution independent because they can be redrawn at the highest quality supported by a graphics application or display device.

For more complete information, the best site I've found on the Web as a general source of information about digital graphics is About.com's Graphics Software section at `http://graphicssoft.about.com`. This site contains everything from a great dictionary of graphics terms to hundreds of useful tutorials, articles, and discussions. It's truly amazing! The only problem with this site is that it is titled, "About Graphics Software for PC or Mac." Hey, what about the rest of us? Luckily, as you'll see throughout this chapter, the graphics tools available for free on your Ubuntu system are more than sufficient for almost every graphics task.

Using GIMP

GIMP stands for GNU Image Manipulation program and is the premiere open source graphics package for Linux systems. GIMP originally stood for General Image Manipulation Program and was originally created by Spencer Kimball and Peter Mattis. From the beginning, GIMP was designed to be easily extendible by the addition of plug-ins that could be written, compiled and maintained separately, but which would work seamlessly within the GIMP framework. Like any other open source package, GIMP has subsequently bene-fited from the contributions of others, especially in terms of plug-in development. GIMP is a shining exam-ple of a powerful and successful open source package, having also been ported to Microsoft Windows and Apple's Mac OS X and used extensively on those platforms. For all of the gory details of GIMP history, see `www.gimp.org/about/ancient_history.html`.

GIMP is also legendary among GNU software packages, especially as far as the GNOME desktop environ-ment goes, because the toolkit on which much of the GNOME user interface is based is GTK, the GIMP Tool Kit. Without restating everything on the GIMP ancient history page, let's just say that GIMP started out using another X Window system toolkit, but its authors decided to create their own, which was full-featured enough to be adopted by many other projects. Biblically, GIMP begat GTK, which begat GTK+, which begat GNOME, which now supports GIMP. I hope that's clear — there will be a quiz later.

NOTE   People often refer to GIMP simply as gimp or the gimp (not to be confused with the character from Quentin Tarantino's *Pulp Fiction*), because that's the name of the command that you type at the command-line to start the program. Throughout this chapter, I'll use GIMP as a way of generally referring to the program, using `gimp` (lowercase) only when I'm specifically referring to the command-line command.

Starting GIMP

GIMP is automatically installed as part of a basic Ubuntu system install, so no special installation process is required. You can start GIMP manually in a variety of different ways, the most basic of which are:

- by selecting GIMP Image Editor from the Applications ⇨ Graphics menu.

- by typing the `gimp` command in a GNOME Terminal or xterm window and pressing return.

When starting GIMP for the first time, a usage tip displays, and various GIMP panels are also displayed, as shown in Figure 12.1.

NOTE If you've used other versions of GIMP, you may remember that GIMP formerly displayed a sequence of startup dialogs that enabled you to customize some aspects of GIMP's initial configuration. Because most people simply accepted all of the defaults, these introductory panels have been done away with. If this is your first time starting GIMP, things are better now.

The first thing that most people do when using GIMP is to customize the various panels and dialogs that display each time you start GIMP. The next section explores each of the panels available in the default GIMP interface.

FIGURE 12.1

Starting GIMP for the first time

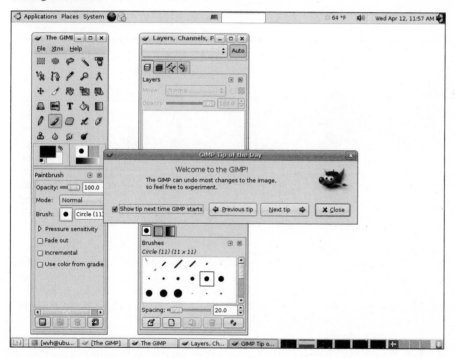

A Quick Tour of GIMP

Figure 12.1 showed what GIMP looks like the first time you execute the program. I typically disable the startup tips (you can access them from a GIMP menu command, anyway), which leaves the GIMP's startup screen as shown in Figure 12.2.

As you can see, GIMP initially displays two windows. A single window can actually contain multiple dialogs that are combined into one dialog window — this is known as a *dockable* dialog. To make things even more flexible, dialogs can be either docked together or combined as multiple tabs within a single dialog. The default screen shown in Figure 12.2 displays the following windows. Each window description includes a list of the dialogs contained in that window:

- **Main Toolbox window:** The window at the left contains two dialogs: at the top, the Main Toolbox dialog and below it, the Tool Options dialog. The Main Toolbox dialog provides access to all GIMP commands and dialogs. The Tool Options Dialog provides access to the configurable aspects of the GIMP tool that is currently selected in the Main Toolbox dialog.

- **Layers and Brushes window:** The window at the right contains two dialogs: at the top, the Layers, Channels, and Paths dialog and below it, the Brushes, Patterns, and Gradients dialog. The interesting thing about this window is that each of the dialogs that it contains actually consists of multiple dialogs that have been docked together as tabs. The top dialog consists of the Layers, Channels, Paths, and Undo dialogs docked together, while the bottom dialog consists of the Brushes, Palettes, and Gradients dialogs docked together.

FIGURE 12.2

Basic GIMP windows

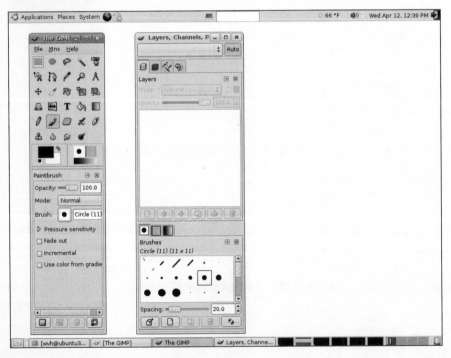

TIP GIMP's Main Toolbox dialog must always be visible — closing this dialog causes GIMP to exit. Similarly, most GIMP users find it extremely useful to always have the Layers dialog available so that they have easy access to the portions of an image that are contained on different layers.

Docking and undocking dialogs is a fairly simple process. To undock dialogs, select the header for that dialog and drag it out of the window in which it is currently displayed. An icon identifying that dialog follows the cursor, as shown in Figure 12.3, in which the Tool Options dialog header has been dragged out of the window shown at the left in Figure 12.2.

FIGURE 12.3

Undocking a GIMP dialog

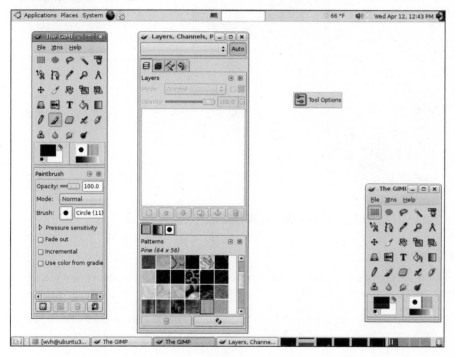

Releasing this icon on the screen at the point where you want the undocked dialog to appear results in a screen like that shown in Figure 12.4. The Tool Options dialog displays as a separate window, and the portion of the Main GIMP Toolbox window that it formerly occupied is now empty. You can resize the window that formerly contained this dialog to remove the empty space by selecting and dragging a corner.

FIGURE 12.4

The GIMP Tool Options dialog, undocked

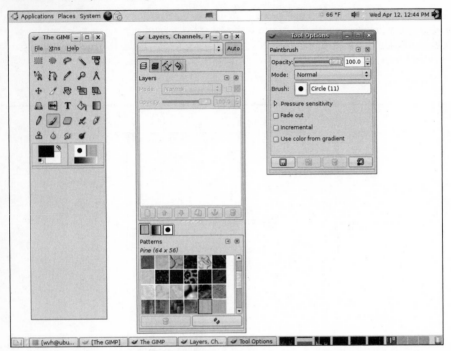

Sample GIMP Tasks

As I confessed earlier, I am not a graphics artist. Many people who are serious artists have created extensive sets of tutorials on using GIMP, and I'd be insulting them (and you) by either parroting those or by trying to pretend that I have major graphics skills. That said, I do use GIMP regularly for a variety of common tasks that you may find useful, so I'll discuss those in the next two sections. For tutorials on using GIMP to do serious graphics work, see some of the URLs in "More Information About GIMP," later in this section.

Taking Screen Shots Using GIMP

As you may have noticed so far, this book contains several screen captures that show the entire screen, specific windows, or certain portions of the screen. My graphics friends have finally convinced me that a picture is indeed worth a thousand words, or should at least accompany them. All of the screen shots in this book were done with GIMP, which is an excellent tool for screen and window captures. You may think that you'll never need to do a screen capture yourself, but that's not necessarily the case — screen captures are very useful when you're submitting problem reports and trying to share what you're seeing on your screen with a friend, and so on.

Capturing a screen shot in GIMP is quite easy:

1. Select File ➪ Acquire ➪ Screen Shot from the main GIMP Toolbox window. The dialog shown in Figure 12.5 displays.

The Screen Shot dialog

2. Select the radio button that identifies whether you want to capture a specific window or the entire screen.

3. Select any delay that you want to take place before you capture a specific dialog or the entire screen. Specifying a delay enables you to pull down menus, set specific values, hide other dialogs, and so on — anything that you want to do to capture a screen or window shot that displays exactly what you want it to.

4. Click Grab to initiate the capture process. After any interval that you have specified elapses, the screen capture takes place. (If no delay was specified, it happens as soon as you click Grab.) If you specified that you wanted to capture a single window, the cursor turns into a set of crosshairs, and you must click on the window that you want to capture. Once the capture takes place, the result displays on the screen in its own GIMP window, as shown in Figure 12.6, which shows the full screen capture from which Figure 12.5 was taken.

5. Once you have a full screen or window capture, the next step is to save it in a lossless format that you or someone else can use. To save the screen capture, right-click in the capture window and select File ➪ Save As. (You can also do this by selecting the File ➪ Save As menu command.) A dialog like the one shown in Figure 12.7 displays.

FIGURE 12.6

A full screen capture in GIMP

FIGURE 12.7

GIMP's first Save As dialog

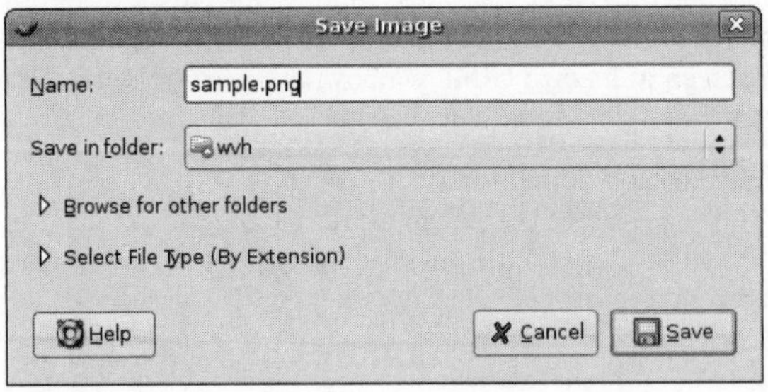

6. Dialogs like the one shown in Figure 12.7 enable you to save your screen shot in a specific graphics format, which is determined by the file extension. After entering your file name and the file extension that you want to use, click Save to display an additional, format-specific dialog, as shown in Figure 12.8.

GIMP's format-specific Save dialog

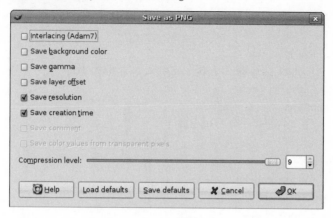

7. The options associated with each graphics format differ, so the available options on dialogs like the one shown in Figure 12.8 are specific to your target file format. Once you have made any changes to the default values that GIMP associates with your target output format, click OK to save your screen capture.

GIMP not only supports a wide variety of output graphics formats, but it also makes it quite easy to capture high-quality screen images and fine-tune the characteristics of the files that you create.

Converting and Reducing Images Using GIMP

Most of us nowadays have a Web page where we share information and pictures with our friends. Most digital cameras save images in JPEG format, which can provide a great combination between small file size (so that Web pages containing images will load in our lifetimes) and good quality (so that you appear to know what you're doing with your digital camera). Regardless, there are going to be times when you have images in larger file sizes that you want to reduce in size and convert to other formats. For example, the TIFF files produced by most scanning software today can't be displayed on a Web page, and are huge. Similarly, most digital cameras today capture photos in megapixels, which are great for printing but are overkill on a Web page.

Because GIMP supports so many different graphics file formats, it is an excellent tool for converting images to formats that you can use elsewhere (most notably on the Web), and for reducing file size without sacrificing too much quality. The sidebar entitled "Graphics Formats Supported by GIMP" shows all of the graphics file formats and associated file extensions that are supported by GIMP.

The following are some tips about using GIMP to reduce the file size of your images so that you can easily put them on a Web page or even mail them to loved ones:

■ Save your files in a lossy format that supports compression. PNG files are an attractive choice because they support up to 48-bit color, but I've found JPEG files easiest to exchange with users of other types of computer systems (and supported in all Web browsers). Make sure to save the modified files with a different name so that you still have your originals in case you want to print them or edit them in some other tool.

Graphics Formats Supported by GIMP

Gimp enables you to save graphics files in the following formats, each identified by one or more associated file extensions:

- Adobe Photoshop image — `.psd`
- Alias/Wavefront PIX image — `.pix, .mask, .matte, .alpha, .als`
- ASCII Art — `.txt, .ansi, .text`
- Autodesk FLIC animation — `.fli, .flc`
- Bzip archive — `.xcf, .bz2, .bz2, .xcfbz2`
- C source code — `.c`
- C source code header — `.h`
- Digital image and Communications in Medicine image — `.dcm, .dicom`
- Encapsulated PostScript image — `.eps`
- Flexible Image Transport System — `.fit, .fits`
- GIF image — `.gif`
- GIMP Brush — `.gbr`
- GIMP Brush (animated) — `.gih`
- GIMP Compressed XJT image — `.xjt, .xjtgz, .xjtbz2`
- GIMP pattern — `.pat`
- GIMP XCF image — `.xcf`
- Gzip archive — `.xcf, .gz, .gz, .xcfgz`
- HTML table — `.html, .htm`
- JPEG image — `.jpg, .jpeg, .jpe`
- KISS CEL — `.cel`
- Microsoft Windows icon — `.ico`
- MNG animation — `.mng`
- PGM image — `.pgm`
- PNG image — `.png`
- PostScript document — `.ps`
- PPM image — `.ppm`
- Silicon Graphics IRIS image — `.sgi, .rgb, .bw, .icon`
- TarGA image — `.tga`
- TIFF image — `.tif, .tiff`
- Windows BMP image — `.bmp`
- X Bitmap image — `.xbm, .icon, .bitmap`
- X Pixmap image — `.xpm`
- X Window dump — `.xwd`
- Zsoft PCX image — `.pcx, .pcc`

■ When editing or converting JPEG images, experiment with reducing the quality level of your image. In most cases, you won't be able to tell the difference, and neither will your viewers. To reduce the quality level of a JPEG image, click File ➪ Save As, enter the new, unique name and click Save. The Save As JPEG dialog displays, as shown in Figure 12.9. By default, this dialog selects an image quality level of 85, and shows you the size of your resulting output file. Click the Show Preview in image window checkbox and experiment with dragging the slider to see how your image changes and how the file size changes with lower quality images. Once you're happy with the new image, click OK to save the updated image.

FIGURE 12.9

Reducing JPEG quality when saving files

■ For Web graphics, reduce the size of your images by scaling them down from the physical size captured by your camera or scanner to a size that is better suited to viewing on a Web page. To scale images in GIMP, select Image ➪ Scale. The dialog shown in Figure 12.10 displays. Enter a new value in the Width field and press return — the Height value will change automatically to preserve the current aspect ratio of your image. Click scale to rescale the image and update the preview of your image.

FIGURE 12.10

Scaling images for better Web-page display

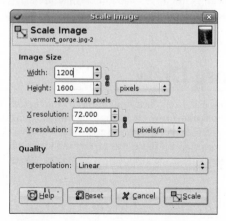

Using these simple techniques, I've been able to reduce images from the ~500KB size that my digital camera captures down to less than 50KB, with no obvious loss of quality. Well, maybe someone with better eyesight than mine could notice a significant difference, but I certainly can't.

> **TIP** Ubuntu Linux also provides several command-line tools that can quickly and easily manipulate images. One of my favorites is the `convert` utility, which reduces the color depth in an image. The `convert` utility is one of the graphics tools provided in the ImageMagick set of graphics tools that are installed by default on your Ubuntu system. For more information about the convert utility or ImageMagick in general, use the `man` command to see the online reference information for these commands.

GIMP has many, many more great features and capabilities — this section has only scratched the surface to encourage you to experiment. See the next section for links to some great online sites that provide detailed information and tutorials about GIMP. Tutorials provide a great way to accomplish a specific task quickly and feel good about your growing proficiency.

More Information About GIMP

Hundreds of sites on the Web provide information about using GIMP. The following are some of my favorites:

- `www.gimp.org`: The GIMP home page. Because this is the GIMP mother ship, this is a great starting point for checking the latest documentation, making sure that you have the latest version of GIMP, finding GIMP tutorials, and getting pointers to other online resources.

- `http://empyrean.lib.ndsu.nodak.edu/~nem/gimp/tuts/`: Nem W. Schlecht has put together a great site that provides pointers to a huge collection of GIMP tutorials on various subjects.

- `http://gimp-savvy.com/BOOK/index.html`: An excellent, though slightly older, book about GIMP that is available online. Though it doesn't have the latest and greatest GIMP information, it is still an excellent resource (and a book well worth having if you're going to be doing lots of work with GIMP).

- `http://gimps.de/en/tutorials/gimp/picture-photo-image/index.htm`: A great set of GIMP tutorials for photo retouching.

> **TIP** If you're a digital photography fan, an excellent package that's well worth checking out is Bibble (`www.bibblelabs.com`). Bibble comes in two versions, Lite and Professional. Bibble is not included in your Ubuntu Linux installation because it is a commercial program, though still relatively inexpensive, costing $70 for the Lite version and $130 for the more full-featured Pro version. Bibble is an example of the growing amount of commercial software for Linux that makes it the equal of any personal computer operating system.

Using OpenOffice.org Draw

OpenOffice.org (`www.openoffice.org`) is a suite of office applications including a word processor (Writer), a spreadsheet (Calc), this drawing program, software for creating presentations (Impress), and a database program called BASE. This section focuses on the drawing application — other chapters in this book discuss the OpenOffice.org word processor, spreadsheet, and presentation software. For some background about the OpenOffice.org suite in general, see the introductory section of " Word Processing with OpenOffice.org Writer" in Chapter 10.

Draw is primarily focused on creating drawings in OpenDocument Drawing (.odg) format. Like Inkscape (discussed later in this chapter), OpenOffice.org Draw enables you to create drawings in SVG format, though its ability to import existing SVG graphics is very limited at this point. Stay tuned!

To save repeating the phrase "OpenOffice.org Draw" more times than necessary, I'll refer to it simply as Draw or as oodraw (the name of the application that you must type to execute OpenOffice.org Draw from a command-line interface) throughout the rest of this section.

Installing OpenOffice.org Draw

Draw is installed by default if you install Ubuntu from the Live CD, from the Alternate Install CD using the Text Mode installer, and from the Alternate installer using the OEM Mode installer. Draw is also installed automatically if you manually install the OpenOffice.org presentation software, Impress.

To install Draw on a system where it is not already present, start the Synaptic Package Manager from the System ➪ Administration menu, select Search, enter **Draw** in the Search box that displays, and click Search. Once the search completes, scroll down in the list of packages in the new Draw category until you see OpenOffice.org Draw, and right-click to select that item for installation from the pop-up menu, as shown in Figure 12.11.

FIGURE 12.11

Installing OpenOffice.org Draw in the Synaptic Package Manager

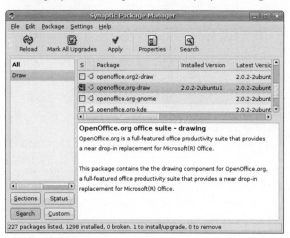

Depending on what software you have previously installed on your Ubuntu system, a dialog may display that lists other packages that must also be installed and it may ask for confirmation. Click Mark to accept these related (and required) packages.

After you are finished making your selections, click Apply in the Synaptic toolbar to install Draw on your system. Once the installation completes, you're ready to begin working with Draw!

See Chapter 20, "Adding, Removing, and Updating Software," for more detailed information on installing applications using the Synaptic Package Manager or the command-line apt-get or aptitude software management utilities.

Starting Draw

In Ubuntu 6.06 LTS, no menu item is provided on the Office menu for OpenOffice.org Draw, so you must start the program by typing the `oodraw` command in a GNOME Terminal or xterm window and pressing return. You can add a menu item for Draw using the Alacarte Menu Editor, as explained in Chapter 5.

When Draw starts, it displays an empty document, as shown in Figure 12.12.

FIGURE 12.12

Starting OpenOffice.org Draw

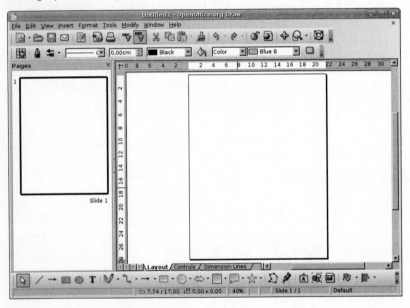

A Quick Tour of Draw

OpenOffice.org Draw provides excellent online help, as do all of the tools in the OpenOffice suite, so I won't bore you by walking through each menu and entry that it contains. However, as a quick overview of the Draw interface, the callouts in Figure 12.12 highlight the following areas:

- **Menus:** The drop-down menus in Draw are organized much like those in other drawing packages to provide a familiar user experience. Menu items with an arrow at their right edge lead to other, related submenus.

- **Toolbars:** By default, Draw displays the Standard, Line and Filling, and Drawing toolbars, which provide one-click access to specific commands when you click on the appropriate icon. You can modify the list of icons displayed on a toolbar by clicking on the control for that toolbar, located at the far right. You can display other toolbars or deactivate the default toolbar by selecting toolbars from the View ➪ Toolbars submenu. Draw provides a great selection of drawing-oriented toolbars, such as a 3D objects toolbar, so that you can quickly and easily create and modify the geometry of 3D images.

- **Rulers:** These rulers display the horizontal and vertical location of the cursor in the current drawing. The grayed-out portions of each ruler reflect the page margins used in the current document. You can disable these rulers by deselecting the View ⇨ Ruler menu command.

- **Styles and Formatting window:** Though not displayed by default, you can display this window at any time by pressing the F11 key on your keyboard. (You can press F11 again to close this window.) The Styles and Formatting window provides easy access to the styles that are available in the current drawing, and is especially convenient if you choose not to display the formatting toolbar. Like any floating window in OpenOffice, you can dock this window by double-clicking on the gray portion of the window heading, making it a part of the default OpenOffice interface rather than a floating window. You can undock a window by repeating this process in the docked area.

- **Context-sensitive menu:** Right-clicking on the background of any drawing that you are working on in OpenOffice.org Draw displays the context-sensitive menu shown in Figure 12.13. This menu provides quick access to several commonly-used commands and submenus, including those for modifying the current page format, displaying a grid, and controlling snapping to grid points.

FIGURE 12.13

OpenOffice.org Draw's context-sensitive menu

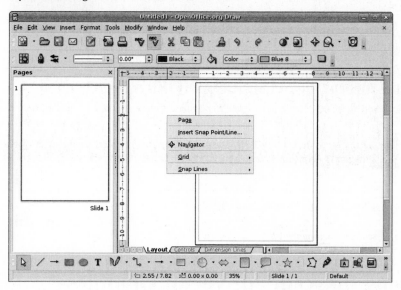

Draw provides extensive online help, available by selecting OpenOffice.org Help from the help menu, or by pressing the F1 key on your keyboard at any time. Figure 12.14 shows the main page for Draw's help, which provides both a searchable index and a list of popular, general topics from its initial display window (at the right).

FIGURE 12.14

OpenOffice.org Draw's online help

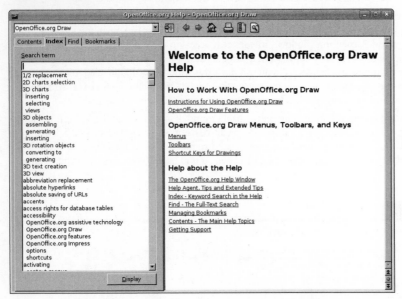

More Information About OpenOffice.org Draw

As the OpenOffice Suite continues to grow in popularity, more and more free resources are available for helping you with each of its components. Some of my favorite Draw-related sites on the Web are the following:

- `http://oooauthors.org/en/members/tutorials/draw/`: Drawing tutorials and Frequently Asked Question (FAQ) files in a variety of languages.

- `www.openoffice-support.net/#draw`: A few tutorials and a CLUE sheet that I've found very handy. Some of the information on the site is from Sun (and thus says StarOffice), but it is still appropriate for standard OpenOffice users.

- `www.openoffice.org`: The OpenOffice mother ship, this site provides access to mailing lists, sample documents, FAQs, and much more.

Using Inkscape for Vector Graphics

Standard document and graphics formats were less important before personal computers became the latest household appliance and the Internet provided a common platform for exchanging and presenting text and illustrations. The sections of previous chapters that discussed Web browsing using Firefox and document creation using OpenOffice.org stressed the importance and value of open standards for the written word such as HTML and the Open Document format. Similar standards are emerging in the area of graphics and illustration, where older formats such as GIF and JPEG are being expanded by the emergence of open raster graphics standards such as Portable Network Graphics (PNG) and an equally powerful, open standard for vector graphics such as the W3C standard Scalable Vector graphics (SVG) format. (For more information about the SVG standard, see `www.w3.org/Graphics/SVG/`.)

Inkscape is an open source application for creating and editing vector graphics, and is similar to traditional applications such as Adobe Illustrator, Aldus (Adobe) Freehand, and CorelDraw. Inkscape can also import graphics in a variety of raster graphics formats that it can use as components of its SVG output. Inkscape can even export PNG graphics for compatibility with raster-only applications and older Web browsers. In addition to the standard elements of scalable vector graphics files, Inkscape also supports Web-oriented Creative Commons metadata and direct XML creation and editing.

TIP Although OpenOffice.org Draw, discussed earlier in this chapter, can export images in SVG format and has some import capabilities, Inkscape was designed for SVG graphics. The OpenDocument Drawing format used by Draw is an excellent format to use if your focus is on producing drawing for use with the other components of the OpenOffice.org suite. If your focus is on creating stand-alone artwork for Web pages, I'd suggest that you use Inkscape.

Installing Inkscape

Because not everyone needs to create vector graphics images (and many people may have already decided to do this using OpenOffice), Inkscape isn't installed by default on a Ubuntu Linux system. Luckily, that's easy enough to fix!

To install Inkscape, start the Synaptic Package Manager from the System ➪ Administration menu, select Search, enter **Inkscape** in the Search box that displays, and click Search. Once the search completes, select Inkscape from the new Inkscape category (it will be the only entry), and right-click to select that item for installation from the pop-up menu, as shown in Figure 12.15.

FIGURE 12.15

Installing Inkscape in the Synaptic Package Manager

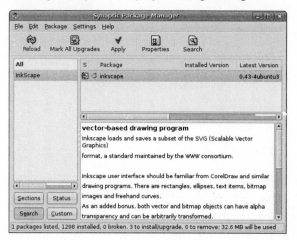

A dialog displays that lists other packages that must also be installed for Inkscape to work correctly and asks for confirmation. Click Mark to accept these related (and required) packages.

After you are finished making your selections, click Apply in the Synaptic toolbar to install Inkscape on your system. Once the installation completes, you're ready to begin working with Inkscape! See Chapter 20, "Adding, Removing, and Updating Software," for more detailed information on installing applications using the Synaptic Package Manager.

Starting Inkscape

After installing Inkscape, you can start the program in a variety of different ways, the most basic of which are:

- by selecting Inkscape Vector Illustrator from the Applications ➪ Graphics menu.
- by typing the `inkscape` command in a GNOME Terminal or xterm window and pressing return.

The application starts, displaying an empty document, as shown in Figure 12.16.

FIGURE 12.16

Starting Inkscape

A Quick Tour of Inkscape

Inkscape provides great online help, and even includes some tutorials that are available from its help menu. The callouts in Figure 12.16 highlight the basic components of the Inkscape interface, which are the following:

- **Menus:** The drop-down menus in Inkscape are organized to provide easy access to commands related to the basic elements of SVG drawings, such as Layers, Objects, Paths, and Text. The Inkscape designers have done at great job at minimizing the number of submenus used in the program — almost every command is directly available from a top-level menu.

- **Toolbars:** Inkscape provides two toolbars. The top toolbar provides access to some standard file and clipboard manipulation commands, and also provides access to a variety of commands for zooming, copying, and grouping selected objects. The bottom toolbar provides easy access to rotation, layer manipulation, and scaling commands.

- **Rulers:** These rulers display the horizontal and vertical location of the cursor in the current document.

- **Context-sensitive menu:** Right-clicking on any component of a drawing that you are working on in OpenOffice.org Draw displays the context-sensitive menu shown in Figure 12.17. This menu provides quick access to several commonly used commands and submenus, including those for duplicated a selected object, grouping and ungrouping, undo operations, and a general object properties panel for the selected object.

FIGURE 12.17

Inkscape's context-sensitive menu

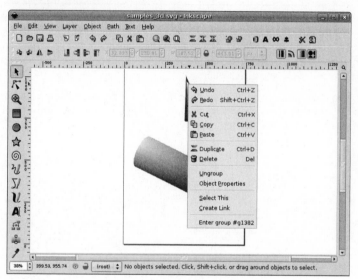

More Information About Inkscape

I'm not the best graphics artist, so I'll let people speak who are. Some of my favorite Inkscape-related sites on the Web are the following:

- `www.inkscape.org/`: The home page of the Inkscape project, this page provides access to many Inkscape resources, such as mailing lists, articles, collections of images, and so on.

- `www.inkscape.org/mailing_lists.php`: Inkscape-specific mailing lists. The Inkscape-user list is a great place for asking questions and searching for solutions to whatever problem you're experiencing (with Inkscape, that is). The Inkscape-announce list is a low-traffic list, but is worth subscribing to so that you are notified of new major and patch releases of Inkscape.

- `http://tavmjong.free.fr/INKSCAPE/MANUAL/html/index.php`: Tavmjong Bah is writing a book about Inkscape that is freely available on the Web. This is a great book with a fantastic selection of information.

- `www.angelfire.com/mi/kevincharles/inkscape/index.html`: An unofficial (but extremely useful!) user manual for Inkscape written by Kevin Wixson.

- `www.openclipart.org/`: Open Clip Art Library Web site, which provides a huge collection of clip art that can be freely used. The majority of these graphics are stored in SVG format, though some are found in formats such as PDF or WMF.

As with every popular open source package, more resources and sources of related information for Inkscape are probably appearing on the Web as I type this. If you find a great Inkscape resource that I've missed in this quick summary, please let me know. Inkscape is a great program!

Summary

This chapter explored tools for creating and manipulating various types of graphics files on Linux systems. Linux has a great selection of powerful graphics tools that you can use to do real work that is only constrained by your artistic skills. (I personally will still require a "mental image to graphics file" application, but that's my problem.) GIMP is one of the shining examples of just how excellent and powerful open source software can be.

The Chapter 13 explores how to work with audio and video on Ubuntu, ranging from how to configure sound on your Ubuntu system to how to work with CDs, DVDs, and the alphabet soup of digital audio and video file formats that one finds on the net today.

Working with Multimedia

MP3, WMA, OGG, FLAC, SHN, APE: this may look like a blast from a shotgun loaded with three letter acronyms (TLAs), but it's really a list of the most popular formats for digital audio nowadays. The same is true of digital video, where acronyms such as MPG, MPEG, and VOB are king. There are also some really ugly acronyms such as DRM, MPAA, and RIAA, which stand for groups of self-interested thugs trying to deny the rights of the consumer, but we won't go into that here.

The great thing about digital audio and video is that you no longer need specialized devices to play your music or watch a movie. You can listen to a music CD or play a video CD or DVD on your computer. Once you buy a CD or DVD, it is completely legal for you to transfer its contents to your computer and watch it there. This eliminates the need to carry around the original media, and you can safely leave them behind at home as backups in case your computer crashes.

This chapter helps you make some sense out of the maze of acronyms, general terminology, and specialized jargon that aficionados use to describe digital audio and video, and explains how to use the software available for Ubuntu Linux to listen to music, watch movies, and even create your own CDs and DVDs. I love being able to check into a hotel room and relax while listening to my favorite tunes because I've brought them along on my favorite modern multimedia device—a computer running Ubuntu Linux.

IN THIS CHAPTER

Understanding multimedia terminology

Configuring sound on Ubuntu

Installing the GNOME sound framework

Playing, ripping, and burning CDs

Working with audio files and Internet radio

Playing, ripping, and burning DVDs

Overview of Digital Audio and Video Terminology

As mentioned in the introduction to this chapter, digital audio and video is an area in which the computer industry's tendency towards using jargon and three-letter acronyms makes many conversations and reference information almost incomprehensible to the novice. Though I've been a record collector, CD collector, and musician for years, I still encounter terms that I either have to look up or decrypt, and there is no single source of this sort of terminology outside of all-encompassing sites like Wikipedia.

This section therefore provides a basic glossary for the most common audio, video, and digital multimedia terminology and acronyms that I am familiar with and see often. It isn't necessarily easy reading, but it should be a great reference for the rest of the chapter, where these terms will be used.

- **AAC (Advanced Audio Coding):** A lossy codec originally developed by Dolby Laboratories that is similar to MP3 files in file size but provides slightly higher quality. AAC is now often, and incorrectly, referred to as the Apple Audio Codec because of Apple's use of a protected version of the AAC format to impose DRM on its iTunes customers.

- **ABR (Average Bit Rate):** A type of encoding in which the user specifies the target bit rate for sampling and playback, and the encoder calculates the appropriate VBR (Variable Bit Rate) values necessary to achieve the average.

- **AIFF (Audio Interchange File Format):** A lossless audio codec originally developed by Apple Computer, and therefore commonly used on Macintosh systems.

- **ALAC (Apple Lossless Audio Codec):** A proprietary lossless audio code developed by Apple Computer. This format is frequently confused with the M4A format, which is essentially a container file that can deliver files in ALAC and other formats.

- **APE:** The file extension for audio files encoded using the proprietary lossless Monkey's Audio codec. This codec provides slightly better compression (i.e., slightly smaller file sizes) than the FLAC or SHN codecs, but at the cost of slower encoding/decoding. APE files are primarily used for lossless compression and archival on Microsoft Windows platforms because no official Linux port of the Monkey's Audio codec exists. For more information about the Monkey's Audio codec, see www.monkeysaudio.com/.

- **bit rate:** The number of bits per time interval that make up an audio signal. The most common time interval used in bit rate calculations is one second (BPS). High-speed data communications is often measured in Kbps (kilobits — thousands of bits per second). This is overkill for digital audio.

- **burn:** The term for writing files to recordable or rewritable CD or DVD media. The term *burn* comes from the fact that data is written to CDs and DVDs using a laser that inscribes miniscule pits on their surface to represent digital information.

- **CBR (Constant Bit Rate):** A codec that uses a fixed number of bits per second as opposed to ABR or VBR codecs.

- **CD (Compact Disc):** A storage device capable of holding approximately 650MB of prerecorded/prewritten digital information.

- **CD-R (Compact Disc/Recordable):** A storage device capable of holding approximately 650MB of digital information, but where each portion of the disc can be written to once by home computers with compatible drives. Writing a CD-R disc can be done in multiple sessions, where each session writes a different portion of the disc. Mike Richter's *Primer on CD-R* at www.mrichter.com/cdr/primer/primer.htm is a tremendous resource for everything you ever wanted to know about CD-R (and more). Similarly, Andy McFadden's CD-Recordable FAQ at www.cdrfaq.org/ is another tremendous resource with tons of detailed information about CD software. Web documents like these are true testimonials to the power of the Internet and the expertise and dedication of its users. My hat goes off to these guys!

- **CD-RW (Compact Disc/Rewritable):** A storage device capable of holding approximately 650MB of digital information, which can be written to multiple times by home computers with compatible drives. Only CD-RW drives can read CD-RW discs.

- **CDDA (Compact Disc Digital Audio):** The format used on most non-copy-protected audio CDs. Sometimes also referred to as CDA because of Microsoft Windows' inability to use four-character file extensions.

- **CDDB (CD Database):** A commercial, online database that provides identification information and track listings for commercial CDs.

- **codec (compressor/decompressor):** An algorithm by which digital signals are compressed so as to lose a minimum amount of quality, and decompressed for playback.

- **DAT (Digital Audio Tape):** A digital recording tape medium used in recording studios and by audio professionals.

- **DAE (Digital Audio Extraction):** The process of cloning prerecorded digital media by directly copying it to files rather than by playing it, converting the resulting analog audio output, and saving that information to a digital storage device.

- **disc-at-once:** A CD/DVD burning mechanism that writes the entire surface of the CD or DVD disk rather than simply the amount of storage required to hold the information that you are recording.

- **DMCA (Digital Millenium Copyright Act):** Legislation passed in the United States in which the supposed goal was to preserve copyrights for digital media, but which has been used to squash reverse engineering, eliminate free-speech discussions of encryption technology, and rob users of the free reuse of legitimately purchased audio and video files; a good idea gone bad.

- **DRM (Digital Rights Management):** A technique for denying legitimate users of audio and video files the ability to freely copy and use them.

- **DSP (Digital Signal Processing):** Using various algorithms to convert or modify digital audio and video signals. DSP can be done in hardware, software, or a combination of both.

- **DVD (Digital Video Disc):** A storage device capable of holding approximately 4.7GB of digital information.

- **EQ (Equalize):** A recording effect that increases or decreases the volume of different frequency ranges in an audio signal. Equalizing frequency ranges smoothes the audio signal by preventing extreme differences in volume across different frequency rangers.

- **FFP (FLAC Footprint):** Checksum files that are typically distributed with FLAC-encoded files to enable you to verify their integrity. See the entry for MD5 in this glossary for more information about checksums.

- **FLAC (Free Lossless Audio Codec):** A lossless audio codec that typically achieves compression rates of 30% to 50% without any reduction in quality from the original recordings.

- **Freedb (Free DB):** An open source alternative to CDDB that enables users to contribute information about CDs.

- **ID3 tags:** 128-byte header information in MP3 files that is used to provide information about the audio file. ID3v1 tags provide album, artist, general comments, genre, and title information. ID3v2 tags provide this information and more in a more free-form fashion, permitting larger, user-defined tags that support all ID3v1 tags but can also include information such as lyrics and images.

- **ISO (International Standards Organization):** In the context of CDs and DVDs, ISO refers to the three-letter file extension added to CD and DVD images to show that the contents of the file conform to the ISO9660 specification, which defines CD and DVD formats. People often refer to conformant image files that contain complete CD or DVD images as ISOs.

- **lossless formats:** File formats that are not lossy, i.e., file formats that provide all of the information that was present in the audio, graphics, or video information as it was originally recorded, drawn, or captured.

- **lossy formats:** File formats that sacrifice quality to reduce file size. The term lossy refers to the data compression algorithm used to reduce file size, where some of the information that was present in the original file is actually eliminated to produce the smaller, compressed file, and therefore the original file can never be completely reconstructed from the compressed version. In the case of audio files, lossy images typically reduce both the bit rate and the frequency ranges at which audio is recorded, the theory being that the majority of this information is inaudible to most people.

- **M4A:** An audio file container format that can contain AAC or (more commonly) ALAC files. Protected versions of M4A files that have been subjected to Digital Rights Management are delivered as M4P files.

- **MD5:** A popular mechanism, known as a *checksum*, used to verify the integrity of digital data files, especially lossless audio files. Files with this extension are plain text files that typically contain unique 32-character ID numbers for one or more companion data files. An MD5 checksum value is unique to the data file that accompanies it, and therefore is often used to fingerprint (i.e., uniquely identify) that file and thus verify its integrity. If you generate an MD5 checksum (using a Linux application such as md5sum) and that checksum value matches the checksum value delivered with the file, the file has not been modified.

- **MP3 (MPEG-1 Audio Layer 3):** The most popular audio format used today, MP3 is a proprietary lossy codec that produces relatively high quality sound from relatively small audio files.

- **MP3 CD:** A compact disc that contains MP3 files rather than traditional CDDA audio. Because MP3 files are smaller than CDDA files, MP3 CDs can hold much more music than other CD formats, and are quite popular nowadays even though they usually cannot be played in standard CD players.

- **MPAA (Motion Picture Association of America):** The motion picture industry's equivalent of the RIAA, a group of industry thugs bent on maximizing industry income at the expense of the end user and often the artist.

- **MPEG (Motion Picture Experts Group):** An Industry consortium responsible for defining standards for audio and video formats.

- **MPEG-4:** The latest generation of MPEG standard at the time that this book was written, MPEG-4 is a standard file format for delivering audio, video, and other multimedia objects.

- **noise reduction:** Audio processing techniques used to clean up audio files by removing, filtering, or equalizing specific frequency bands.

- **normalize:** An audio processing technique that identifies the loudest range of an audio file, and then uses that as a baseline for the volume used when playing back the rest of the file. Normalizing audio data does not change relative volumes within a song, just the baseline volume.

- **OGG (Ogg Vorbis):** A popular, open source lossy codec and associated container format that provides a powerful, royalty-free alternative to lower quality codecs such as MP3. Ogg Vorbis was developed by the Xiph.org foundation, a foundation dedicated to developing and promotion free, open source multimedia formats. (Ogg is the file format, while Vorbis is the actual codec, though files encoded using this codec typically have the .ogg file extension.) For more information about Ogg Vorbis, see `www.xiph.org` or `www.vorbis.com`. If your software or audio player does not support Ogg Vorbis, contact the manufacturer.

- **P2P (Peer-to-Peer):** A popular data exchange and delivery mechanism where each client (peer) identifies other peers and exchanges data with them without the use of a central server. Popular P2P applications are BitTorrent, GNUtella, LimeWire, and so on.

- **PCM (Pulse Code Modulation):** An audio and video data format that provides a true representation of the recorded signal by sampling it at regular intervals. PCM is the standard form for digital audio in computers, compact discs, and in digital video.

- **RealAudio:** A popular streaming audio format developed by Real.com and often used on the Web. For more information, see `www.real.com`.

- **RIAA** (Recording Industry Association of America): A group of industry thugs bent on maximizing industry income at the expense of the end user and often the artist.

- **rip:** The generic term used to describe the process of converting CD and DVD discs to files that can be used on a computer system.

- **SHN** (Shorten codec): A popular lossless audio codec frequently used for distributing authorized live recordings on the Internet. Shorten delivers slightly larger file sizes than FLAC, its primary "competitor." Interestingly, the Shorten codec also offers a lossy mode, though I don't see why anyone would use that. For more information about the Shorten codec and Linux software for working with SHN files, a great resource is the SHN Resources page at `http://research.umbc.edu/~hamilton/shnlinks.html`. The Shorten codec is a commercial product of SoftSound Ltd, but has a user-friendly personal use license. For more information, see `www.softsound.com/Shorten.html`.

- **skin:** An alternate user interface for graphical applications. New skins can be applied to an existing application without recompilation or any actual changes to the application other than its configuration information. Many audio players (such as XMMS and the venerable WinAmp for Microsoft Windows systems, which pioneered skinnable applications) are skinnable, which enables fans to easily customize their appearance.

- **streaming:** A method of delivering digital content over a network such that an application (such as an audio player) receives information as it is needed without the need to store that data on the machine. The most common examples of streaming media players are the RealPlayer and RealOne applications from RealAudio. For more information, see `www.real.com`.

- **SVCD** (Super Video CD): The successor to Video CDs (VCDs), an SVCD contains MPEG-2 video and MPEG-1 or MPEG-2 audio recorded on a normal VCD. Most DVD players can also play SVCD discs because DVD players support the MPEG-2 codec required to decode the MPEG-2 video data.

- **track-at-once:** A CD/DVD burning mechanism that writes on track of a CD or DVD disk but leaves the remainder of the CD or DVD available for further recording at a later stage.

- **transcode:** The process of converting from one encoding format to another, typically used when referring to converting a media file or object from one format to another, as is done when creating DVDs from MPEG files in other formats (or vice versa).

- **TTA** (True Audio codec): A free lossless audio codec offering an average of 30% to 40% file size reduction without any loss of quality. I haven't encountered this codec much on the Net, but some people swear by it. For more information about the True Audio codec, see `www.true-audio.com/`.

- **VBR** (Variable Bit Rate): A type of encoding that attempts to reduce file size without sacrificing significant quality by varying the bit rate at which audio information is recorded. More complex audio is recorded at a higher bit rate, while simpler audio passages are recorded at a lower bit rate.

- **VCD** (Video CD): A storage device capable of holding approximately 650MB of prerecorded/prewritten digital video and audio information that are encoded in MPEG-1 format. Most DVD and CD players can play VCDs because they support the MPEG-1 codec used to decode the video and audio data.

- **WAV:** A digital audio file format originally developed by Microsoft and IBM that has become the standard format for distributing lossless audio (waveform) files. WAV files consist of chunks of data that can actually be encoded using any codec, but most commonly contain raw pulse-code modulation (PCM) audio data, which is lossless and therefore huge. WAV files are often used by audio professionals to ensure maximum quality and complete fidelity to the original recordings.

- **Wavpack:** A free lossless audio codec used primarily on Windows systems but also available for many different Linux distributions, architectures, and applications such as XMMS. I haven't encountered Wavpack much outside of the Windows community, but your mileage may vary. Wavpack is extremely quick at compressing and decompressing files with no loss of quality. For more information about Wavpack, see `www.wavpack.com/`.

- **WMA** (Windows Media Audio): A popular codec for Microsoft Windows users that is the default audio codec used by the Windows Media Player. Lossy, lossless, and DRM versions of the WMA codec are available. The most important thing that Linux users need to know about WMA is how to convert audio files encoded with this codec into more reasonable formats.

- **WMV** (Windows Media Video): A popular lossy codec for Microsoft Windows users that is the default video codec used by the Windows Media Player. The most important thing that Linux users need to know about WMV is how to convert video files encoded with this codec into more reasonable formats.

Unless you have plenty of free brain cells and nothing else to do with them, there's no need to memorize these terms — that's what books like this one are for. However, now that you have expanded your digital multimedia terminology, let's move on to something more important — actually playing sound and video on an Ubuntu Linux system.

Configuring Sound Devices, Levels, and System Sounds

Most of the setup for your Ubuntu system's audio components is done automatically when you install your Ubuntu Linux system. Ubuntu's installer has excellent hardware detection capabilities and automatically installs and configures the ALSA (Advanced Linux Sound Architecture) utilities, drivers, and libraries that Ubuntu uses to provide excellent, high-quality audio playback. The following sections enable you to test your system's sound capabilities, customize the sounds your system plays in response to various system events, and tell you how to set sound levels on your system.

Testing and Customizing System Sounds

By default, your system is configured to play a "welcome" sound when you log in. To verify that sound is working on your Ubuntu Linux system, first check the obvious things, such as whether your speakers are plugged into your sound card's audio out port (usually a light green socket — the central one — of the three sound ports on the back of your system or on your sound card), the speakers are turned on, and so on. Next, select the System ➪ Preferences ➪ Sound command. The Sound preferences utility displays, as shown in Figure 13.1.

FIGURE 13.1

Default system sound settings in the Sound Preferences utility

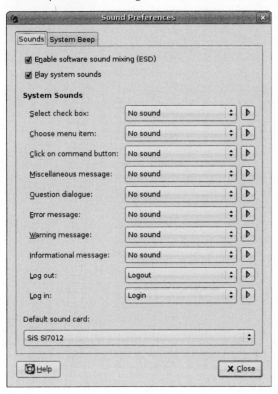

The Sound Preferences utility enables you to verify the system activities for which your system will play an associated sound. By default, only the Log in and Log out sounds should be enabled, as shown in Figure 13.1. To play the sound that is currently associated with any system event, click on the right-arrow button to the right of any system action that currently has a sound associated with it (i.e., does not display the No sound label). If you hear a sound, congratulations! Sound is working correctly on your Ubuntu system.

TIP If your system has multiple sound cards (or a built-in sound card and a stand-alone sound card that you installed yourself), make sure that the sound card listed at the bottom of the dialog shown in Figure 13.1 lists the sound card to which you have connected your speakers. If it does not, click the drop-down list of available sound cards, select the correct sound card, and try playing a system sound again.

If you want to associate a sound with any other system event, click the No sound label beside that event and select the sound you want to play from the pop-up list that displays, as shown in Figure 13.2.

FIGURE 13.2

The pop-up list of available system sounds

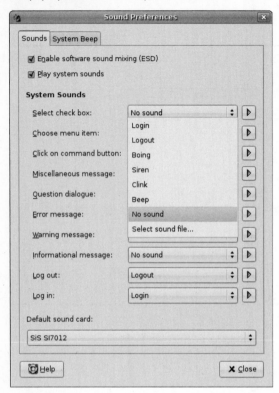

If you have a sound file that you want to play when that system event occurs, click the Select sound file entry and navigate to the sound file in the dialog that displays, as shown in Figure 13.3.

Setting System Sound Levels

The section of Chapter 5 entitled "Customizing Panel Contents" discussed how to add various applets to your GNOME desktop's panels. One of the more useful applets that is preinstalled for you on your Ubuntu Desktop is the Volume Control applet, whose icon looks like a small speaker and is usually displayed at right in the top panel, just to the left of the date.

To customize your system's volume settings for the current session, right-click on this icon. The slider shown in Figure 13.4 displays.

FIGURE 13.3

Associating a personal sound file with a system event

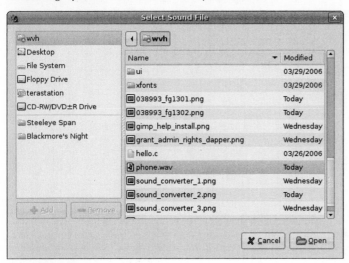

FIGURE 13.4

Quickly changing current volume settings

To change your current volume settings, drag the slider up or down to the value that you prefer.

To get access to more detailed volume settings, left-click the volume control icon and select the Open volume control command to display the dialog shown in Figure 13.5.

FIGURE 13.5

Detailed playback volume control settings

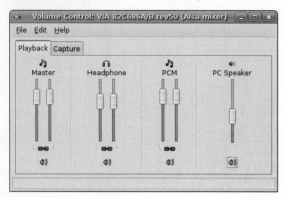

NOTE   The volume settings displayed in the dialog shown in Figure 13.5 are based on the capabilities of your sound card. Based on the sound card that your system is using, you may see additional settings. The settings shown in Figure 13.5 are for an integrated VIA sound card that is built into the motherboard on one of my test systems.

If your system has multiple sound cards (or a built-in sound card and a stand-alone sound card that you installed yourself), make sure that the sound card you are changing settings for is the card to which your speakers are attached and which is listed in the header of the Volume Settings dialog shown in Figure 13.5. To change the sound device that you are configuring, select File ⇨ Change Device and select the radio button beside the correct sound interface, as shown in Figure 13.6.

FIGURE 13.6

Changing your default sound device

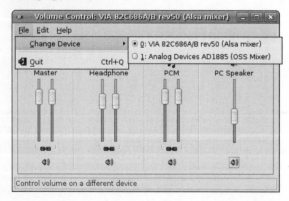

The basic playback volume settings that you can adjust for any sound card are the following:

- **Master:** the volume setting for all audio playback from any sound-enabled application
- **Headphone:** the volume settings for audio playback from the headphone jack on a sound card, if present
- **PCM:** the volume setting for WAVE files, which are typically in PCM format
- **PC Speaker:** the volume setting for you PC's internal speaker, which is generally pretty useless

These are settings for audio playback. Two icons display below each slider:

- The chain icon determines whether the two sliders for each output (the left and right channels) must move together or can be set separately. A linked chain means that the channel sliders will move together. A broken chain indicates that they can be set separately. Click the icon to toggle whether the sliders are linked together or not.
- The speaker icon determines whether the output is muted or not. If a red X is displayed over the speaker icon, that output is currently muted. Click the icon to toggle whether an output is muted or not.

To adjust the input volumes settings used for recording sounds, click the Capture tab. A dialog like the one shown in Figure 13.7 displays.

FIGURE 13.7

Detailed sound capture volume settings

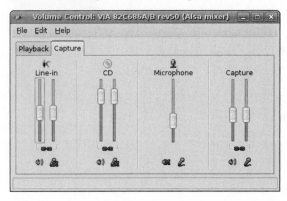

The basic capture volume settings that you can adjust for any sound card are the following:

- **Line-in:** the volume setting for any external device connected to your sound hardware's line-in port
- **CD:** the volume setting for any CD-ROM drive that is directly connected to your sound hardware
- **Microphone:** the volume setting for any microphone that is connected to your sound hardware's microphone-in port
- **Capture:** the volume setting for any audio that is currently playing on your system

In addition to the icons displayed below the sliders on the Playback tab, the Capture tab also displays a Microphone icon that indicates that a specific input source is being used for sound capture. If a red X is displayed over this icon, that input source is currently disabled. Click the icon to toggle whether an input/capture source is active.

Once you have modified any volume settings that you want to change, select File ➪ Quit to close the Volume control applet.

Getting Detailed Information About Your Sound Hardware

If you've gotten to this point and sound still isn't working on your Ubuntu system, it may be time to explore your system's sound hardware to see if it is set up correctly and to give you the information that you need to ask for help. Information about your system's hardware, including your sound hardware, is available in Ubuntu's Device Manager application, shown in Figure 13.8, which you can display by selecting the System ➪ Administration ➪ Device Manager menu command.

FIGURE 13.8

Sound hardware entries in the Device Manager

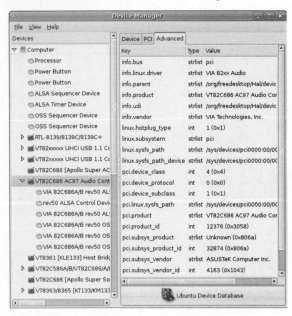

The entries in the Device Manager for your sound hardware will tell you whether Ubuntu has been able to identify the device, what it has identified it as, and whether valid entries for that device exist in the /sys filesystem, which is a virtual filesystem that provides direct access to various aspects of your system hardware.

> **TIP** If your system sounds play correctly, but you can't play CDs, make sure that your CD player is correctly connected to your sound hardware. This connection typically consists of a two or three pin cables that run from the back of your CD drive to your sound card or the sound hardware that it built into your motherboard. Some sound cards and motherboards support several input sound devices, and it's quite possible that your CD drive is connected to the wrong port or that the connector has become dislodged.

If the entries in the Device Manager appear to match your hardware, it's time to search the Web, starting with various Ubuntu resources listed in the section of Chapter 1 entitled "Support for Ubuntu Linux." Paid support is always an option, but your best (and certainly cheapest) bet is to begin by searching the various forums for information about your sound hardware or the specific problem that you are seeing. If you don't find any relevant or helpful information, try posting to the Ubuntu Users mailing list. As emphasized throughout this book, one of the best aspects of Ubuntu Linux is its huge, helpful user community. You're also welcome to ask me, but my response time is certainly going to be slower than that of the thousands of continuous participants in the Ubuntu forums and mailing lists.

Setting CD and DVD Preferences

Now that few people bother with floppy disks anymore, CDs and DVDs are the most common examples of removable media that you'll use with your computer system. Removable media is the generic term for any media that contains digital data and which is not a mandatory part of your computer system. Removable disks, flash drives, and other devices that show up as disk drives (like an iPod) are not exactly the same things as far as Ubuntu is concerned, and are discussed in Chapter 17, "Consumer Electronics and Ubuntu," as well as in Chapter 23, "Adding Hardware and Attaching Peripherals." This section focuses on how you can configure what your system does when you insert a prerecorded or blank CD or DVD.

When you insert a blank CD or DVD in your Ubuntu system, the system does two things:

- displays an appropriate icon for the type of blank media that you have inserted
- displays a dialog asking what you would like to do with that media

Figure 13.9 shows the icon and dialog displayed when you insert a blank CD-R or CD-RW disc in a compatible drive on your system. Figure 13.10 shows the icon and dialog displayed when you insert a blank DVD-R disc into a compatible drive on your system.

FIGURE 13.9

Dialog and icon for blank CD-R/RW insertion

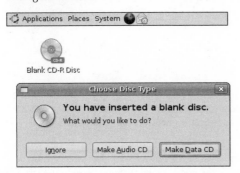

FIGURE 13.10

Dialog and icon for blank DVD-R insertion

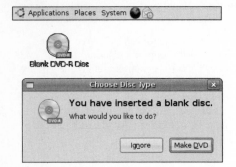

In either case, clicking Ignore closes the dialog without starting an application. However, specifying that you want to burn any media starts the applications that are currently associated with those actions and media types, which are defined on the dialog shown in Figure 13.11.

FIGURE 13.11

Setting preferences for blank CD or DVD insertion

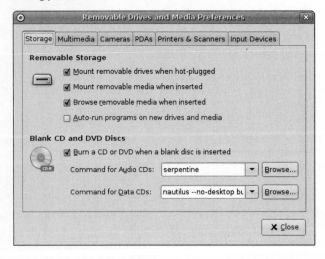

You can start the application shown in Figure 13.11 by selecting the System ➪ Preferences ➪ Removable Drives and Media menu command. The default panel of this application controls the settings associated with blank but writable CD and DVD media.

To prevent your system from displaying the dialogs shown in Figures 13-9 and 13-10, deselect the Burn a CD or DVD when a blank disc is inserted checkbox. To modify the applications that your system uses to create audio or data CDs, leave this checkbox selected and click browse beside the correct entry to select another application. By default, Ubuntu uses the same application — the Nautilus file manager — to create DVDs as it does to create data CDs.

How your Ubuntu system reacts when you insert a prerecorded CD or DVD depends on the preferences settings on the Multimedia panel of the application shown in Figure 13.11. To display this panel, click the Multimedia tab. This displays the panel shown in Figure 13.12.

FIGURE 13.12

Preferences for prerecorded CD or DVD insertion

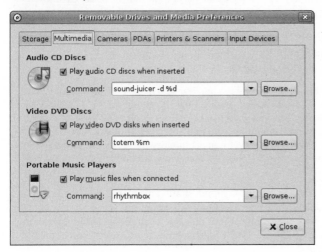

To disable automatically starting a specified application, deselect the checkbox beside the appropriate type of media. To change the application that starts automatically when prerecorded media is inserted, click Browse beside the correct entry to select another application. By default, Ubuntu uses the same application — Totem — to display both prerecorded Video CDs and DVDs. (More about that later!)

Installing the gstreamer Framework and Plug-ins

Most GNOME audio and video applications use an underlying open source multimedia framework called gstreamer (http://gstreamer.freedesktop.org/). Gstreamer makes it easy to integrate codecs by writing simple plugins that integrate with its framework. As good, forward-looking GNOME party members, most of the applications discussed in this chapter leverage the gstreamer framework for codec support via plug-ins. For this reason, you should use the Synaptic Package Manager to install the latest versions of gstreamer and associated sets of plug-ins before starting Rhythmbox, attempting to convert sound files, or attempting to play a DVD with Totem. If you do not, you will be extremely disappointed in Ubuntu's audio and video capabilities.

As explained in Chapter 1, the Ubuntu folks are very strict about the legal and licensing requirements of the packages that they include in the default Ubuntu distribution. Because of copyright and licensing issues, many of the codecs that are commonly used by audio applications on other platforms are not installed by default on your Ubuntu Linux system. The best example of this is anything having to do with the MP3 audio format. Not everyone needs to play the most common audio files format found in the known universe, right? I can't blame them for this perspective, but in this case, it doesn't meet my needs.

> **NOTE**   Chapter 20, "Adding, Removing, and Updating Software," explains the processes of adding repositories and using the Synaptic Package Manager in much more detail. The following instructions are intended as an "I just need to do it, not understand it" quick-reference.

To make your Ubuntu Linux system able to play and convert audio files in MP3 format and DVDs, you must install gstreamer and the relevant sets of plug-ins, but before doing that, you will need to change the type of software that your Ubuntu system's Synaptic Package Manager looks for. To do this, edit the /etc/apt/sources.list file using your favorite text editor, using a command like the following:

```
$ sudo vi /etc/apt/sources.list
```

Remove the hash marks at the beginning of the lines that enable the universe repositories, add the word **multiverse** to the end of these lines, and save the updated file.

> **NOTE**   Just to be perfectly clear, by telling you to add the universe and multiverse repositories to the places where your system looks for software, I am enabling you to add software that may have licensing requirements that you or the company that you work for find odious (such as MP3-related software), for which support is not guaranteed by the Ubuntu folks (even if you purchase support, there are no commitments to support it), and which may be difficult to get support for anywhere. I use all of the software discussed in this book, and am therefore my very own test case for everything this book discusses, but your mileage may vary.

Next, start the Synaptic Package Manager from the System ➪ Administration menu and click the Reload button to refresh Synaptic's idea of what packages are available. Once this completes, select Search, enter **gstreamer** in the Search box that displays, and click Search. Once the search completes, scroll down in the list of packages in the new gstreamer category until you see the following items, and select each of them:

- gstreamer0.10-alsa (should already be selected)
- gstreamer0.10-esd (should already be selected)
- gstreamer0.10-ffmpeg
- gstreamer0.10-gl
- gstreamer0.10-gnomevfs (should already be selected)
- gstreamer0.10-pitfdll
- gstreamer0.10-plugins-bad
- gstreamer0.10-plugins-bad-multiverse
- gstreamer0.10-plugins-base (should already be selected)
- gstreamer0.10-plugins-base-apps (should already be selected)
- gstreamer0.10-plugins-good (should already be selected)
- gstreamer0.10-plugins-ugly
- gstreamer0.10-plugins-ugly-multiverse
- gstreamer0.10-tools (should already be selected)
- gstreamer0.10-x (should already be selected)
- gstreamer0.8-dv
- gstreamer0.8-dvd

- `gstreamer0.8-faac`
- `gstreamer0.8-faad`
- `gstreamer0.8-flac`
- `gstreamer0.8-lame`
- `gstreamer0.8-mad`
- `gstreamer0.8-misc`
- `gstreamer0.8-mpeg2dec`
- `gstreamer0.8-musepack`
- `gstreamer0.8-speex`
- `gstreamer0.8-swfdec`
- `gstreamer0.8-vorbis`
- `gstreamer0.8-xvid`
- `totem-gstreamer` (should already be selected)

To select these, right-click on each of them and select Mark for Installation from the pop-up menu to schedule that item for installation.

> **TIP** You may not need all of these unless you are doing sound conversion. I'm assuming that you would rather err on the side of caution — i.e., installing a version of the gstreamer framework that is as full-featured as possible, at the expense of a bit of disk space.

Depending on the versions of the packages that you are installing and the other software that you have already installed on your system, marking any of these packages for installation may display an additional dialog that lists any other packages that must also be installed, and asks for confirmation. Click Mark to accept these related (and required) packages.

Once you have selected all of these packages and their requirements, click Apply to install all of the specified packages. Once these packages have installed successfully, you can close the Synaptic Package Manager.

Installing Microsoft Windows Codecs on Your System

Many proprietary audio and video formats are used on Microsoft Windows systems. To be able to play many of these on your Linux system, you can install freely available Windows codecs on your system and use them via the `gstreamer0.10-pitfdll` package, which you installed in the previous section. There are two ways to install these:

- by downloading a Debian package containing them and installing it on your system using the `dpkg` utility
- by downloading an archive file containing them and installing it as `/usr/lib/win32` on your Ubuntu system

To get and install a Debian package containing these codecs, do the following:

1. Enter the following command (all on one line, no spaces anywhere after http):

```
wget -c
http://packages.freecontrib.org/ubuntu/plf/pool/dapper/i386/non-
free/w32codecs/w32codecs_20060611-1plf1_i386.deb
```

2. Install the package using the following command:

```
sudo dpkg -i w32codecs_20060611-1plf1_i386.deb
```

To get the codecs through a Web interface and install them manually, do the following:

1. Visit the page at www.mplayerhq.hu/design7/dload.html, search for the **Codecs** section, and download the file essential-20060611.tar.bz2 (or any newer version) from the mirror site nearest you.

2. Extract the contents of the archive using a command like the following

```
tar jxvf essential-20060611.tar.bz2
```

3. Rename the directory created by the previous command, essential-20060611, to be /usr/lib/win32, using a command like the following:

```
mv -v essential-20060611 /usr/lib/win32
```

Regardless of which of these two approaches you take, you will find that you will now be able to play many more audio files in applications such as Rhythymbox, which use the gstreamer framework.

Installing Software to Play Encrypted DVDs on Your System

Though it technically has nothing to do with gstreamer, installing the library necessary to read encrypted DVDs is related to being able to take advantage of the complete capabilities of gstreamer, so let's install it now.

 **In my personal opinion, installing the CSS** (http://en.wikipedia.org/wiki/ Content_Scramble_System) **software that enables you to play commercial DVDs on your Ubuntu Linux system is a right, not a privilege or a crime. However, I am not a lawyer. Installing this software on your system may someday cause jackbooted enforcers from the MPAA to kick down your door and drag you off to be forcibly reeducated. You should make sure that you are comfortable with installing this software, and should probably never install it on a business system.**

To install this library, execute the following command from a GNOME terminal or xterm command line:

```
$ sudo /usr/share/doc/libdvdread3/examples/install-css.sh
```

As always, you'll be prompted for your password by the sudo command, which will then execute the specified shell script. The install-css.sh script will both retrieve the decss library and install it on your system for you.

Congratulations! You can now watch your favorite DVDs in the privacy of your Ubuntu Linux system.

TIP **For up-to-date information on using gstreamer-based applications to play proprietary audio and video formats, see** https://help.ubuntu.com/community/RestrictedFormats.

Working with CDs

I still have a few friends who use Windows voluntarily, and one of their favorite rationales is the statement, "It just works!" Thanks to the efforts of all the contributors and testers who are associated with the Ubuntu project, playing music on Ubuntu Linux has this same mantra — I have never had a problem with an internal CD drive on any desktop or laptop system where I have installed Ubuntu Linux.

By default, inserting a prerecorded CD into your Ubuntu system's CD drive does two things in response to the default settings for removable media on your system (as discussed in the previous section):

- displays an audio disk icon on your Ubuntu desktop
- starts an application called Sound Juicer which enables you to play or rip your audio CDs

If Sound Juicer doesn't start for you automatically when you insert a CD, you can start it manually by selecting the Applications ➪ Sound and Video ➪ Sound Juicer CD Extractor menu command.

Playing CDs Using Sound Juicer

Once Sound Juicer starts, it initially tries to look up any CD that you insert in the MusicBrainz online CD information database. If it finds a matching entry, it displays information about the CD and the tracks that it contains, as shown in Figure 13.13.

FIGURE 13.13

Information about a CD from MusicBrainz

If the CD is not listed in MusicBrainz, Sound Juicer displays a similar screen, using generic entries like *Unknown Artist* and *Unknown Title*, and assigning each track a generic name such as *Track 1*, *Track 2*, and so on.

If the CD you are playing (or ripping, as discussed in the next section) is a commercial CD for which information is not yet available in MusicBrainz and you want to be a good Internet citizen, you can select the Disc ➪ Submit Track Names menu command, which will connect you to a Web site called musicbrainz.org, where you can create an account and enter information about that CD, as shown in Figure 13.14. This is definitely the right thing to do if you have the time, because the next person who tries to look up this CD in MusicBrainz will benefit from the information that you have entered.

FIGURE 13.14

Contributing CD information to Free DB

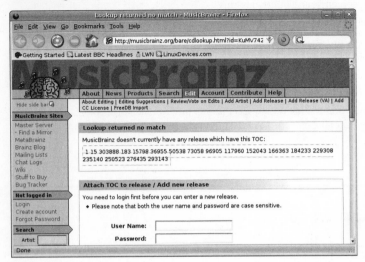

If you simply want to play the CD (or are finished entering information about it), click Play to play the CD. It just works!

TIP You can play selected tracks from the CD by deselecting the checkmarks to the left of the tracks that you do not want to hear before clicking Play.

Once you're done playing your CD, you can select the Disc ➪ Eject commands to eject this CD and insert another or simply quit Sound Juicer.

Ripping CDs Using Sound Juicer

Ripping CDs is almost exactly like playing them, with the exception of the fact that you click the Extract button rather than the Play button. While Sound Juicer is extracting the contents of an audio CD and converting each track to a file, it displays a progress dialog as shown in Figure 13.15.

Before ripping a CD, however, you may want to specify the format of the audio files that Sound Juicer creates, the location in which it creates them, and so on. This is done through Sound Juicer's Preferences dialog, which is shown in Figure 13.16. To display this dialog, select the Edit ➪ Preferences menu command.

FIGURE 13.15

Ripping an audio CD in Sound Juicer

FIGURE 13.16

Sound Juicer preferences for ripping CDs

This dialog enables you to change the following Sound Juicer settings:

- **Device:** If your system contains multiple CD or DVD drives, this drop-down menu displays all available drives so that you can be sure to rip the contents of the right drive.

- **Music Folder:** Enables you to select the folder in which you want extracted audio to be stored. I tend to create a specific folder called music in my home directory, so that everything ends up in one place and doesn't clutter up my home directory. This also simplifies backups!

- **Track Names:** Enables you to specify the folder hierarchy in which Sound Juicer creates the audio files that it extracts. By default, the tracks of each CD are written in a folder with the name of the CD, which is itself a subdirectory of a folder with the artist's name. The name of the file for each track is preceded by the track number, which simplifies playing extracted audio in the same order as the tracks on the original CD. I find the default organization to be very useful in organizing my music collection, but you may want to adopt some different conventions.

- **Format:** Enables you to specify the file format in which extracted audio files are written. Your choices are CD Quality, Lossless (using the FLAC codec), CD Quality, Lossy (using the Ogg container format and Vorbis codec), Voice, Lossless (using the standard WAV file format), and Voice, Lossy (using the Ogg container format and Vorbis codec, but at a lower quality level). You may want to specify the CD Quality, Lossless setting if you are extracting the contents of a tradable live recording that you want to share with others.

I rarely change any of these settings with the exception of the default Music Folder, but it's always nice to know that the flexibility to change them is present if you so desire.

Burning CDs Using Serpentine

GNOME's Serpentine application makes it easy to create audio CDs from selected audio files on your system. Ubuntu automatically starts Serpentine for you when you insert a blank CD and specify that you want to create an audio CD (in the dialog shown in Figure 13.9). Serpentine's initial screen is shown in Figure 13.17.

Once this screen displays, click Add to display a navigation dialog that enables you to select the audio tracks that you want to put on the CD. This navigation dialog is shown in Figure 13.18.

FIGURE 13.17

The first step in burning an audio CD

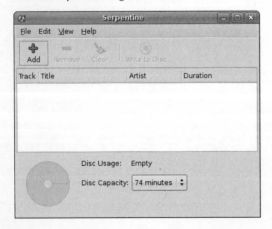

FIGURE 13.18

Track selection when burning an audio CD

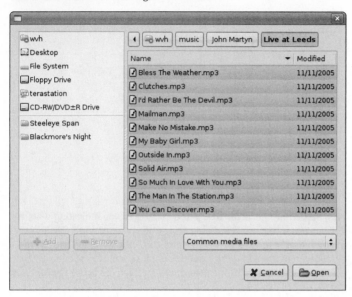

As with most other graphical applications, you can select multiple tracks at one time using Control+left+click or Control+Shift to select a range of songs. After selecting tracks in this dialog, click Open to add those tracks to the proposed contents of your CD. The dialog shown in Figure 13.17 redisplays, showing the tracks that you've added so far and displaying information about the remaining amount of time available on the CD.

>  **If your system contains more than one writable CD or DVD drive, make sure that Serpentine is configured to use the right one before attempting to burn a CD. You can do this by selecting the Edit ➪ Preferences menu command and making sure that the correct CD/DVD device is specified at the top of the Preferences dialog.**

When you're ready to burn your CD, click Write to Disc. The dialog shown in Figure 13.19 displays, requesting confirmation.

FIGURE 13.19

Confirmation request before burning an audio CD

Do you want to record your music?
You are about to record a media disc. Canceling a
writing operation will make your disc unusable.

✗ Cancel   Write to Disc

Click Write to Disc to proceed, and the CD burning operation proceeds. As the process proceeds, Serpentine displays a status dialog, as shown in Figure 13.20.

FIGURE 13.20

The progress dialog when burning an audio CD

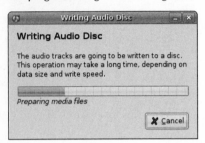

When writing your audio CD completes, Serpentine ejects the disc and displays a dialog indicating whether writing the disc was successful or not. Click Close to close this dialog and return to Serpentine. If you want to burn another CD with the same contents, simply insert a new blank disc and click Write to Disc again. If you want to burn another audio CD with different contents, you can click Clear to remove the current track listing and start another one. If you're finished creating CDs for the moment, you can select the File ⇨ Quit menu command to close Serpentine.

Working with Other Audio Sources

Thanks to the Internet, portable music players, podcasting, and greater amounts of local disk space to devote to online audio files, playing audio on your computer isn't just about playing CDs anymore. A huge variety of alternate audio sources are available today, including streaming broadcasts over the Internet, downloaded podcasts (which are nothing more than MP3 files), and ripped audio files (so that you can store your original CDs safely away somewhere as backups). This section explains how to use GNOME's Rhythmbox application to play audio in sources that it understands, and how to use the excellent Sound Converter application to convert audio files from their original formats into formats that you can more easily use on your computer system.

Playing Audio Files and Internet Radio Using Rhythmbox

Rhythmbox is a GNOME application that is oriented toward audio delivered in a variety of file formats, whether as a stream that you can read over the Internet or a physical file that you downloaded or ripped, stored on your computer system, and subsequently want to play.

To start Rhythmbox, select the Applications ⇨ Sound and Video ⇨ Rhythmbox Music Player menu command.

NOTE   The first time that you start Rhythmbox, it walks you through three configuration dialogs that enable you to specify the location of any online collection of audio files that you may already have. Because it only shows you these once and you can also set this value using its Preferences dialog, I suggest that you simply click Forward in the first configuration dialog, select Skip this Step and click Forward in the second one, and click Apply in the third one. I'll explain how to specify the location of your music library later in this section.

Figure 13.21 shows the default Rhythmbox interface with no audio libraries, podcasts, or other audio sources specified.

FIGURE 13.21

Rhythmbox with no imported audio sources

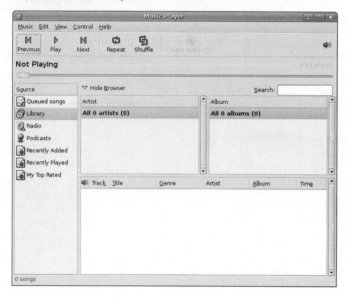

Next, add information about the location of your audio files. To do this, select the Edit ➪ Preferences menu command. Click the Library tab of the dialog, which is shown in Figure 13.22.

FIGURE 13.22

Identifying the location of music files in Rhythmbox

Click and hold on the Library location button to see a list of potential directories where Rhythmbox will look for music files. To specify a directory that is not listed, select Other and navigate to that folder in the resulting dialog.

Once you've specified the directory where your music files are located, select the Watch my library for new files checkbox to ensure that Rhythmbox notices any new audio files that you create or put in that directory, and click Close to exit the Preferences dialog. Rhythmbox begins the import process, updating its display as new files are added to its list of available music files. Any problems that Rhythmbox encounters during this process are displayed in a separate window so that you can examine them. In most cases, these are file corruption problems, but at least you can delete the offending files in your library and reextract them from your original CDs. Figure 13.23 shows Rhythmbox after importing the contents of my music library.

FIGURE 13.23

Rhythmbox after loading music files from a library

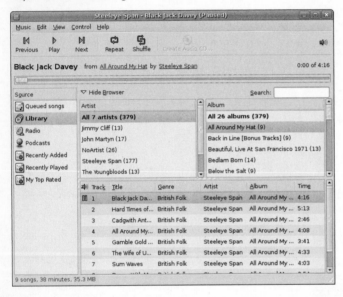

Once you've told Rhythmbox about your library, you can see that it creates summary entries for each artist across all of the directories in your library, and also creates per-directory listings that correspond to a playlist for each Album/CD in your library. To play a particular Album, select its name from the Album list and click Play. To see all of the Albums available from a specific artist, click the name of that artist in the Artist window. You can then select the Album that you want to listen to and click Play. Once you're playing a specific Album, you can also skip from track to track by clicking the name of the track that you want to play in the track listing

Creating Playlists

If you're like me, you may own a lot of music, but only truly love a few tracks on each album. Rhythmbox makes it easy for you to create your own "Greatest Hits" collections by making it easy to create playlists that contain specific songs from any of the Albums in your library.

To create a new playlist and add songs to it, select the Music ⇨ Playlist ⇨ New Playlist menu command (or type Control+N). A new playlist displays at the bottom of the Source pane at the left of the Rhythmbox window. To assign it a specific name, left-click its blank name and enter the name that you want the new playlist to have. To change the name later, right-click on its name and select Rename from the pop-up menu. You can then type its name and press Return to give it the new name.

To add songs to a playlist, simply browse your library and drag and drop the tracks that you want to add to the name of the playlist that you want to add them to in the sources window. Figure 13.24 shows the contents of a playlist containing my favorite tracks by the band Steeleye Span. My favorite tracks today that is — one of the great things about creating your own playlists is that you can easily add and remove tracks from them to match your current mood or favorite tracks.

FIGURE 13.24

A custom playlist in Rhythmbox

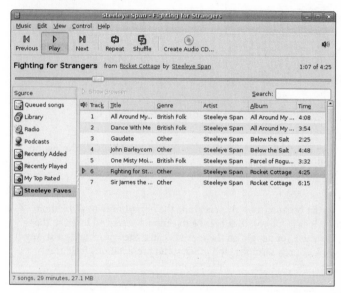

To remove a song from a playlist, right-click on its name and select remove from the pop-up menu. This only removes the song from the playlist, not from your library — you can always add it to the playlist again if you want to hear it again.

Adding Internet Radio Stations

Internet radio is a revolutionary step for broadcast media because it enables people anywhere to listen to their favorite radio stations regardless of whether you can physically receive their signal (or even have a radio, for that matter).

To subscribe to an Internet Radio station, right-click the Radio entry in the Rhythmbox Source pane, and select New Internet Radio Station from the pop-up menu. A dialog displays, in which you can enter the URL of the Internet radio station that you're interested in. Click Add to add that station to your list of current radio stations, as shown in Figure 13.25.

FIGURE 13.25

Playing Internet radio in Rhythmbox

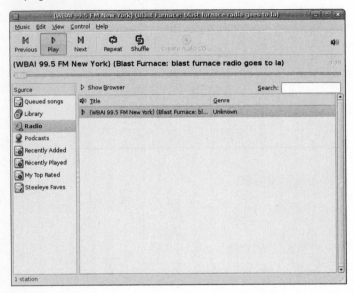

You can then click on the Radio entry to show all of your Internet radio stations, and listen to the station you're interested in by simply double-clicking on its name.

Adding Podcasts

Podcasts are revolutionizing broadcast media because they give everyone the opportunity to share their opinions with anyone else. Podcasts make it easy for you to subscribe to certain shows and listen to them at your leisure. Podcasts are especially attractive for people on the move because they provide a great way for people anywhere to keep up with news, church sermons, and other audio presentations from their hometown.

To subscribe to a Podcast, right-click the Podcast entry in the Rhythmbox Source pane, and select New Podcast feed from the pop-up menu. A dialog displays, in which you can enter the URL of the feed for a podcast you're interested in. Click Add to add that feed to your list of current Podcast feeds, as shown in Figure 13.26.

You can then click on the Podcast entry to show all of your Podcast feeds, and download any available podcast by right-clicking on an available podcast and clicking Download episode from the popup-menu. Once a podcast has downloaded, you can listen to it by simply double-clicking on its name.

You can customize where your downloaded podcasts are stored and the frequency with which Rhythmbox looks for new podcasts by selecting the Edit ⇨ Preferences menu command and clicking the Podcast tab. This displays the dialog shown in Figure 13.27, which enables you to update those settings.

FIGURE 13.26

Downloading and playing podcasts in Rhythmbox

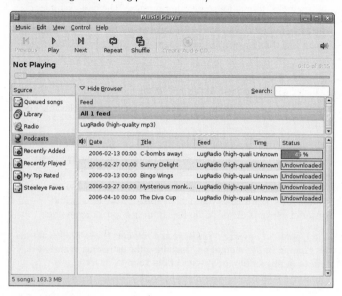

FIGURE 13.27

Customizing podcast settings in Rhythmbox

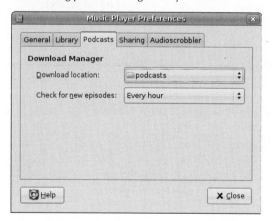

Converting Audio File Formats

It's inevitable that you'll eventually get some great music from free downloads, off the Internet, or after ripping it from your CDs, only to find that it isn't in "the right" format for some other purpose. The best examples of this are things like:

- ripping CDs into Ogg Vorbis format and then wanting to play them on an iPod, which can't play OGG files

- downloading live concert recordings in FLAC format, only to find that this format is not usable with today's iPod (and probably never will be because of the size of the FLAC files)

- wanting to create a greatest hits CD for your car, only to find that you can't create a playable audio CD from MP3, OGG, or FLAC files

Regardless of which corner you find yourself in, it's irritating to have music that you can play on your desktop system but which you can't use in portable music players, to burn CDs, and so on. The problem that these examples expose is the fact that specific devices and types of media require specific audio formats. Apple's iPods can only play files in MP3 or Apple's own formats; audio CDs must contain WAV files, and so on. Luckily, Ubuntu Linux provides a great solution to these sorts of problems through an application called Sound Converter. As the name implies, Sound Converter converts digital audio files from one format to another.

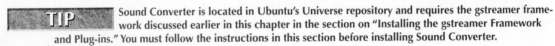

TIP Sound Converter is located in Ubuntu's Universe repository and requires the gstreamer framework discussed earlier in this chapter in the section on "Installing the gstreamer Framework and Plug-ins." You must follow the instructions in this section before installing Sound Converter.

Installing Sound Converter

Because not everyone will be using their Ubuntu system for serious audio work, Sound Converter isn't installed by default. To install Sound Converter, start the Synaptic Package Manager from the System ⇨ Administration menu, select Multimedia (universe) from the package lists at the left (or just search for it), and scroll through the window at the right until you see Sound Converter. Once you find the package, right-click on its name to select that item for installation from the pop-up menu, as shown in Figure 13.28.

FIGURE 13.28

Installing Sound Converter in the Synaptic Package Manager

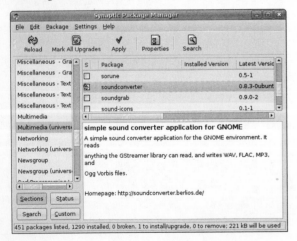

Depending on the versions of the packages that you are installing and the other software that you have already installed on your system, marking any of these packages for installation may display an additional dialog that lists any other packages that must also be installed, and asks for confirmation. Click Mark to accept these related (and required) packages.

Next, click Apply in the Synaptic toolbar to install Sound Converter on your system. Once the installation completes, you're ready to convert your existing audio files to whatever formats you require!

See Chapter 20, "Adding, Removing, and Updating Software," for more detailed information on installing applications using the Synaptic Package Manager.

Using Sound Converter

Once you've installed Sound Converter, you can execute it by selecting Applications ⇨ Sound and Video ⇨ Sound Converter. Its primary dialog displays, as shown in Figure 13.29.

FIGURE 13.29

Starting Sound Converter

To add the files that you want to convert, click Add File to display the dialog shown in Figure 13.30. (You can also click Add Directory to select and add an entire directory of files.)

This dialog enables you to navigate to and select the files that you want to convert to another format. Once you've selected those files, click Open to close the navigation dialog. The files that you selected display in the main Sound Converter dialog, as shown in Figure 13.31.

FIGURE 13.30

FIGURE 13.30

Selecting files for format conversion

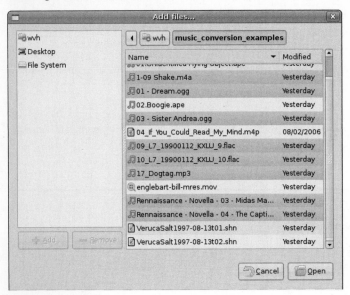

FIGURE 13.31

Files slated for conversion

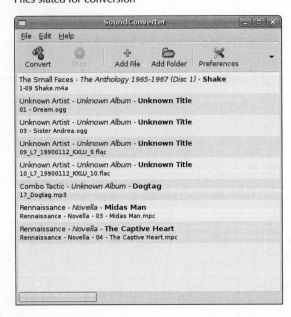

Next, specify your format conversion preferences. The files that I've selected in Figure 13.31 are all MP3 files, but my goal is to write a CD, which requires WAV files. Not a problem — I just need to specify WAV as the target output format. To do this, click Preferences to display the dialog shown in Figure 13.32.

FIGURE 13.32

Specifying format conversion preferences

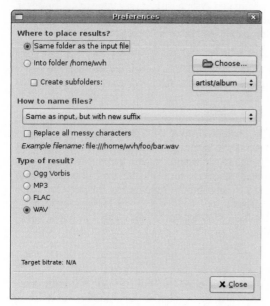

The Where to place results? section of Figure 13.32 determines where the converted output files are located. (I tend to leave them in the same directory so that I know what they are.) The Type of Result? section of this dialog shows that I am converting the files I selected in Figure 13.31 to WAV format, as desired. Click Close to exit the Preferences dialog. Once this dialog closes, you can click Convert to begin the conversion process.

Once the format conversion is complete, the converted files are ready to be burned to your target media, copied to your target device, or whatever else you want to do with them.

TIP One of the few audio formats that isn't somehow supported on Ubuntu Linux systems is Shorten (SHN), a free lossless audio codec that is quite popular in live recording circles. To work with files of this type, you can download a plug-in for XMMS (and install the XMMS audio player) so that you can play them directly, or you can use Synaptic to install the `shntool` package, a command-line utility that can convert them to WAV files so that Sound Converter can convert to your favorite output format.

Working with DVDs on Ubuntu

The only thing that could possibly make anyone nostalgic for videotapes is how badly the entertainment media is trying to screw DVD users. Region-specific DVDs. Video encryption. Licensed codecs. Suing young adults and prohibiting free speech for academicians just because both are smarter than their research staff. Need I say more?

For all of these reasons (and more), playing DVDs on a computer system isn't an easy thing to do. However, Ubuntu provides a great DVD player called Totem that leverages the gstreamer framework that I discussed earlier in this chapter to provide high-quality playback capabilities. The next section describes how to set up and use Totem, which is impressively easy to do.

The rest of this section explains how to rip and create DVDs. Ripping DVDs is even simpler than playing them, because I tend to use a popular command-line utility called dd, which is available on any Linux system. Creating an ISO image from an existing DVD using dd (for backup purposes, of course) is only slightly slower and certainly more cost effective than buying a second copy.

This section concludes by discussing how to copy DVDs, burn DVDs from DVD images, and how to assemble files onto data or video DVDs. To do any of these tasks, I strongly suggest that you use the k3b software package. I can almost hear the screams from GNOME fanatics everywhere, because k3b is a KDE-based package. In a nutshell, my perspective on that is — so what? Though I am a GNOME fan and prefer its simple interface and ease of use over KDE, I am much more a fan of using the right tool for the job. The simple fact is that k3b is exponentially better than any GNOME-based tool that I've ever seen for working with DVDs. It also does a great job with CDs, but I think that the GNOME tools are essentially equivalent there. At any rate, more about k3b later — time to play a DVD!

Playing DVDs

The GNOME Totem application (`http://hadess.net/totem.php3`) is a full-featured DVD and video file player that relies on underlying technologies such a gstreamer (the default) or Xine (another video display and codec engine) for many of its low-level capabilities. Totem is preinstalled on Ubuntu Linux systems, as it is on all GNOME-based Linux distributions.

Using Totem to play a DVD is easy. Because most prerecorded DVDs feature some sort of encryption, you should install the gstreamer framework and associated libraries before trying to play a DVD. For details on how to do this, see "Installing the gstreamer Framework and Plug-ins," earlier in this chapter.

As explained earlier in this chapter, Ubuntu's GNOME desktop comes preconfigured to start Totem for you when it detects that you have inserted a prerecorded DVD. Therefore, if you haven't changed any of those settings, the only remaining step in playing a prerecorded DVD is the following: Insert it into your DVD drive. GNOME starts Totem automatically for you, and you'll see a screen like that shown in Figure 13.33. (The DVD that displays will probably be different, of course.)

TIP You can also start Totem manually at any time by selecting the Applications ➪ Sound and Video ➪ Movie Player menu command, or by typing *totem* in a GNOME Terminal or xterm terminal session.

FIGURE 13.33

A prerecorded DVD playing in Totem

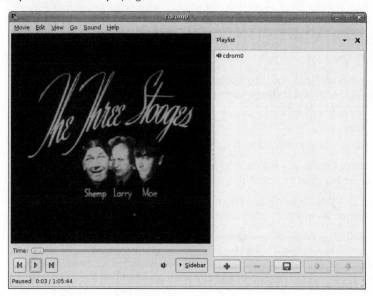

Like most GNOME applications, Totem supports a variety of keyboard commands that make it easy for anyone to use. Some of the more common keyboard commands in Totem are the following:

- **B:** Skip back to the previous chapter or movie on the DVD.
- **F:** Switch to full-screen mode. In full-screen mode, Totem displays an icon in the upper-right corner of the screen that you can click on to return to the original display mode shown in Figure 13.33.
- **H:** Hide Totem's controls. Pressing H again redisplays them.
- **N:** Skip to the next chapter or movie on the DVD.
- **F9:** Hide Totem's contents sidebar. Pressing F9 again redisplays the sidebar.
- **Page-Up:** Increase the volume.
- **Page-Down:** Decrease the volume.

Once you have watched a movie in Totem, you can select the Movie ➪ Eject menu command (or press Control+E) to eject the current disk. If you choose to watch another, you can select the Movie ➪ DVD command to open and begin playing that DVD. If you do not want to watch another, you can exit from Totem by selecting the Movie ➪ Quit menu command.

TIP Totem is still actively under development, and some versions have problems opening certain prerecorded DVDs using the menu commands. If Totem complains about not being able to locate the codecs required to play a DVD in response to the Movie ➪ DVD command, exit Totem, eject the DVD, and let GNOME start Totem correctly for you when you reinsert the DVD.

Ripping DVDs

Though a variety of different applications are available in the Ubuntu repositories and on the Internet to rip DVDs under GNOME, most of them involve chains of other applications. As a long-time Unix/Linux geek, my primary desire in ripping DVDs is to back them up so that I still have a copy after our Rottweiler finishes using the original and its case as a chew toy. Therefore, my favorite command to rip DVDs is the following:

```
$ dd if=/dev/dvd of=name_of_output_file.iso
```

This command is simple, works on every Linux and Unix system in the known universe, and produces an output file that is an exact image of the original DVD. You can mount the output file just like an actual DVD if you're interested, using commands like the following:

```
$ sudo mkdir /mnt/dvd
$ sudo mount -o loop -t iso9660 name_of_output_file.iso /mnt/dvd
```

The first of these commands creates a directory on which to mount the ISO image; the second actually mounts it and makes it available like any other mounted filesystem.

Once you create an ISO image of a DVD with the `dd` command, you can also immediately burn the image to a blank DVD-R using an application such as k3b, as explained in the next section.

> **TIP** If you absolutely need to rip DVDs in some fashion other than by simply cloning them to an ISO file, the `dvd::rip` application is a popular package that gets my vote. It's also written in Perl, which ought to count for something. The `dvd::rip` package is available in the Ubuntu repositories (under the name dvdrip). Installing this package also installs 10 to 20 other packages that it requires, and even this doesn't complete the `dvd::rip` food chain — you'll also have to manually install helper packages that it invokes, such as `xcdroast`, `mplayer`, and so on. For more information about `dvd::rip` and its requirements without actually installing and trying it, see its home page at `www.exit1.org/dvdrip/`.

Copying DVDs and Burning DVD Images Using k3b

As stated in the introduction to this section, I think that the best and easiest Linux tool for copying DVDs, burning DVDs from DVD images, and assembling random files onto data or video DVDs is k3b, a KDE-based software package. Installing and using k3b requires that you install many KDE-related libraries and much of its infrastructure, but I think that the value you get from high-quality applications like k3b is well worth the time and disk space. Besides, with today's relatively huge disk drives, what's a hundred megabytes between friends?

The rest of this chapter explains how to install k3b and how to perform some simple tasks with it, such as copying DVDs and burning DVD images to DVDs. k3b is capable of much more, but it's easy enough to use that creating data and video DVDs manually isn't all that difficult. k3b also has good documentation and a great selection of fan sites, which I'll list at the end of this section as sources for more detailed information about k3b.

Installing k3b

To install k3b, start the Synaptic Package Manager from the System ⇨ Administration menu, select Search, enter k3b in the Search box that displays, and click Search. Once the search completes, select k3b from the new k3b category, as shown in Figure 13.34.

FIGURE 13.34

Selecting the k3b package for installation

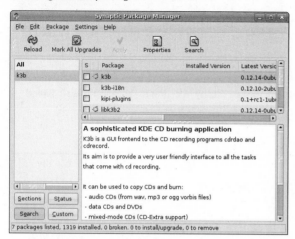

Marking the k3b package for installation displays an additional dialog that lists many other packages that must also be installed, and asks for confirmation. Don't be surprised at the number of these packages — after all, k3b is a KDE application, and you'll need to install lots of KDE libraries and a few fundamental applications to make k3b happy. Click Mark to accept these related (and required) packages.

FIGURE 13.35

Satisfying package requirements for k3b

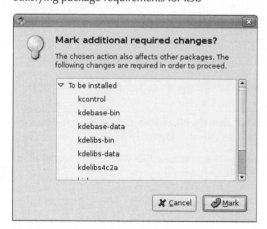

Once you have marked k3b and all of its requirements for installation, click Apply to install all of the selected packages. A summary dialog displays, asking for confirmation. Click OK to proceed. Once all of the selected packages have been downloaded and have installed successfully, you can close the Synaptic Package Manager.

See Chapter 20, "Adding, Removing, and Updating Software," for more detailed information on installing applications using the Synaptic Package Manager.

Burning an ISO Image to DVD with k3b

Once you've installed k3b and friends, the easiest way to start it is by selecting the Applications ⇨ Sound and Video ⇨ k3b menu command. This displays the initial k3b window, as shown in Figure 13.36.

FIGURE 13.36

The initial k3b window

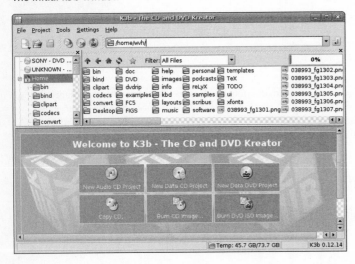

To burn an ISO image to a DVD, select the Tools ⇨ Burn DVD ISO Image menu command. The dialog shown in Figure 13.37 displays.

To navigate to the directory where your ISO image is located, click the folder icon at the right of the Image to Burn text box. A standard KDE navigation dialog displays, as shown in Figure 13.38.

Once you've selected your ISO image, click OK to close the navigation dialog. k3b checks the integrity of the ISO image file and calculates an MD5 checksum to use when verifying the copy.

FIGURE 13.37

The k3b dialog for burning an ISO image

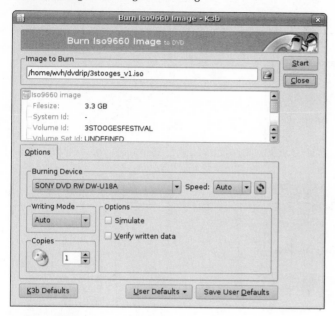

FIGURE 13.38

Selecting a DVD ISO image in k3b

Next, if you have more than one writable CD or DVD drive on your system, make sure that the Burning Device specified in this dialog is the device to which you actually want to write the image. By default, k3b autodetects all writable CD and DVD drives on your system and presents them as options on the Burning Device pop-up menu.

To begin writing the image to a DVD, insert one into the specified drive and click Start. A dialog like the one shown in Figure 13.39 displays as k3b fills its internal buffers and begins the write process.

FIGURE 13.39

Status information while burning an ISO image to DVD in k3b

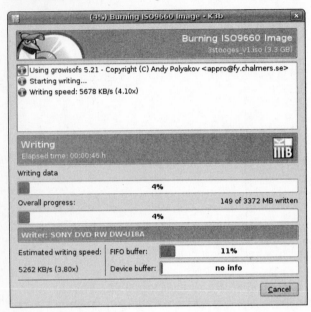

Once writing completes, k3b displays a status dialog that enables you to double-check any messages emitted by k3b during the write process, which can be useful for debugging. I typically just click Close to terminate this dialog. This redisplays the dialog shown in Figure 13.37. To return to the main k3b dialog, click Close.

Copying a DVD with k3b

The k3b DVD copy process consists of several steps: k3b first creates an ISO image of the DVD, ejects the original DVD, requests the new DVD, and then writes the ISO image to the new CD.

> **TIP** You may want to disable auto-mounting DVDs and automatically starting Totem on DVD inser-tion when copying DVDs. This is done using the System ➪ Preferences ➪ Removable Drives and Media Preferences dialog, as explained earlier in this chapter. This eliminates potential conflicts for con-trol of your DVD device(s) between k3b and Totem. You can always undo this when you're done using k3b.

To copy an existing DVD using k3b, start k3b and select the Tools ➪ Copy DVD menu command. The dia-log shown in Figure 13.40 displays.

After verifying that the source and destination devices for reading and writing the DVD (respectively) are correct, click Start to begin the copy process. The dialog shown in Figure 13.41 displays.

FIGURE 13.40

The DVD Copy dialog in k3b

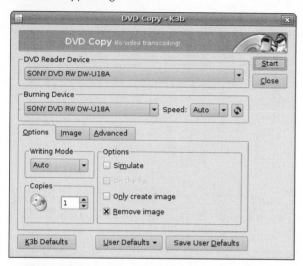

FIGURE 13.41

Status information while copying a DVD in k3b

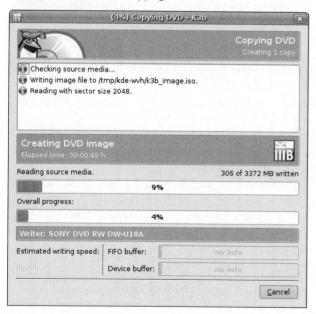

After k3b reads the disc and creates its ISO file, it will display a request for DVD insertion if the source and destination drives are the same, as shown in Figure 13.42.

A request for a blank disc when copying a DVD in k3b

Insert the new disc and click Load to continue. The media request dialog closes, and k3b writes its ISO file to the blank CD. Voila, an exact copy!

Once writing completes, k3b displays a status dialog that enables you to double-check any messages emitted by k3b during the write process, which can be useful for debugging. I typically just click Close to terminate this dialog. This redisplays the dialog shown in Figure 13.40. To return to the main k3b dialog, click Close.

More Information about k3b

I'm not the only fan of k3b—it's a very popular application with many people (not all of whom are KDE fanatics). Some of the better sites I've found for k3b information, tutorials, and tips and tricks are the following:

- www.k3b.org: The k3b application's home page, this site provides a FAQ and access to the latest and greatest releases, as well as the k3b subversion repository if you just can't wait for the next official release.

- www.novell.com/coolsolutions/feature/2746.html: A nice article from Novell entitled "CD Burning in Linux Made Easy with k3b," written by Jason Jones.

- http://sourceforge.net/projects/k3b/: The k3b project's home page at SourceForge.

- www.newsforge.com/software/03/10/20/1340254.shtml?tid=82: A nice article and review of k3b from the NewsForge folks, written by Joe Barr.

- www.pclinuxonline.com/wiki/K3b: A detailed but informal article from the "PCLinuxOS New User Guide" on using k3b.

- http://en.wikipedia.org/wiki/K3b: The k3b entry in the Wikipedia. Cool!

Summary

This chapter covered a lot of general audio and digital media ground to help you get the most out of your Ubuntu system. It began with a Rosetta Stone for the most common terms and acronyms associated with digital audio and video, whether it is stored on a CD, DVD, or in files on your computer. Subsequent sections explored how to configure the bleep, boops, and boings your Ubuntu system can emit when various events occur, and explored the gstreamer framework that provides the underpinnings of all GNOME-based audio and video applications, explaining the somewhat torturous set of packages that you'll want to install to deal with the zillions of audio file formats used on personal computer systems today. Other sections discussed how to play, rip, and burn CDs and DVDs, how to play streaming audio from Internet radio stations, and how to play and convert online audio files. When I buy a CD or DVD nowadays, I rip it and toss the original in a box in the attic. Who wants to juggle CDs and DVDs all day anyway? Finding my online audio and video archives is always exponentially easier for me than finding the CD that I accidentally used as a coaster in my office or the DVD that was accidentally buried under a stack of magazines. This sucks up a lot of disk space, but as far as I'm concerned, disk space is cheap compared to my time — both in terms of finding things and trying to keep them organized.

Chapter 14 explores one of everyone's favorite pastimes, playing computer games. Sad to say, most game manufacturers don't release their wares for Linux platforms. Luckily, this doesn't mean that you can't play games on Linux systems, just that you may not be able to play the latest and hottest 3D shooters, version of Grand Theft Auto, or other games that fans of the Spanish Inquisition like Jack Thompson are trying to ban. A huge variety of classic card and board games are preinstalled on Ubuntu Linux Desktop systems, as well as several clever (and fun) video games. Hundreds more are available on the Internet or are just a Synaptic Package Manager session away.

Chapter 14

Would You Like to
Play a Game?

Games on Unix-like systems such as Linux have come a long way from
"*Hunt the Wumpus*," a text-oriented adventure and exploration game that
I spent many an hour playing in 1982 on a PDP-11 running primordial
Unix. Today, as you'd hope, Linux games are sophisticated graphical applications
with plenty of performance and eye candy. One thing that you'll see in many
of the games discussed in this chapter is that Linux games also have a sense of
humor, which I always find refreshing. Losing and laughing is almost as good
as winning (at least, that's what I tell myself).

As emphasized throughout this book, Ubuntu is a Linux distribution for people,
and people are supposed to relax and have fun at times. Computer games are the
aspect of desktop computer systems that give us all the opportunity to escape
and relax without leaving our desks — hmmm, I'm not sure that this is exactly
where I wanted to go when discussing relaxation, but c'est le way it is.

Ubuntu comes with a good complement of games preinstalled as part of your basic
distribution. A huge number of other Linux games are available in the Ubuntu
repositories and in source and package form on sites across the Internet. This chapter discusses the games that come with Ubuntu, highlighting the fact that you can
get work done and have fun with the exact same machine. The first section of the
chapter explores the games that come with a default Ubuntu system; the latter part
of the chapter discusses popular games and types of games, and how to locate and
play these on your Ubuntu Linux system.

Default GNOME Games

As shown in Figure 14.1, a default Ubuntu Linux desktop installation comes
with a variety of different games across the gaming spectrum, which I classify as
board games, card games, and video games.

FIGURE 14.1

The Games menu in a default Ubuntu installation

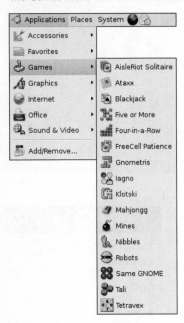

The rest of this section highlights the different games that come with a default Ubuntu desktop installation, providing a screen shot of each and an overview of the game. Because these all come with a default desktop installation at absolutely no cost and everyone enjoys different types of games, you'll quickly be able to figure out which games appeal to you and try them out yourself.

Card Games

Who hasn't walked past the desk of a Windows user sometime during the past twenty years and seen the quick flash as a Solitaire window was being minimized? Nowadays, this same surreptitious time sink is completely cross-platform, as Ubuntu Linux comes with some great card games. Once you master these, many more are available in the Ubuntu repositories. The following sections provide an overview of the card games that come with a default Ubuntu Linux desktop installation.

AisleRiot Solitaire

I've played solitaire since I was a kid, and somehow thought that there was only one solitaire game — that being, of course, the one that I'd learned to play, which turned out to be Klondike. I became more enlightened recently when my wife asked me what other versions of solitaire were available. Googling told me that there were indeed a few zillion solitaire games, so I bought her an analog data storage device that came pre-loaded with information about solitaire — i.e., a book on the subject.

I was similarly enlightened when I suggested that she play AisleRiot Solitaire, which sports a mean game of Klondike (shown in Figure 14.2) and is installed on her Ubuntu-based laptop. Unlike me, she read the online help, which immediately told her that AisleRiot Solitaire actually provides 81 different solitaire games. (Ironically this was a higher number than the ones discussed in the book I bought her.)

FIGURE 14.2

AisleRiot solitaire showing a standard Klondike game

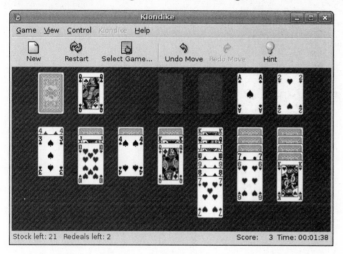

If you're a solitaire aficionado who knows more than one game, you'll be happy to know that AisleRiot Solitaire provides the following games: Agnes, Athena, Auld Lang Syne, Aunt Mary, Backbone, Bakers Dozen, Bakers Game, Beleaguered Castle, Block Ten, Bristol, Camelot, Canfield, Carpet, Chessboard, Clock, Cover, Cruel, Diamond Mine, Doublets, Eagle Wing, Easthaven, Eight Off, Elevator, Escalator, First Law, Fortress, Fortunes, Fourteen, Freecell, Gaps, Gay Gordons, Glenwood, Golf, Gypsy, Helsinki, Hopscotch, Isabel, Jamestown, Jumbo, Kansas, King Albert, King's Audience, Klondike, Labyrinth, Lady Jane, Maze, Monte Carlo, Neighbor, Odessa, Osmosis, Peek, Pileon, Plait, Poker, Quatorze, Royal East, Saratoga, Scorpion, Scuffle, Seahaven, Sir Tommy, Spider, One Suit Spider, Two Suit Spider, Spiderette, Straight Up, Streets and Alleys, Ten Across, Thieves, Thirteen, Thumb and Pouch, Treize, Triple Peaks, Union Square, Valentine, Westhaven, Whitehead, Will o' the Wisp, Yield, Yukon, and Zebra.

If you're like me and just love Klondike, it's in there, and it's a great implementation of the classic game.

Blackjack

Whether you're a blackjack lover and want to play a few thousand games without actually winning or losing money, or just want to practice your card-counting skills prior to a vacation in Vegas, Ubuntu's default desktop install comes with a nice online version of Blackjack, as shown in Figure 14.3.

FIGURE 14.3

Online, Vegas-strip-style blackjack

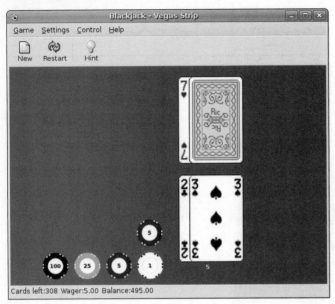

This version of Blackjack is a pretty standard multideck, casino-style blackjack game that also supports more advanced blackjack moves such as doubling down or splitting your hand. It uses Vegas Strip rules by default but can also be configured to use Atlantic City, Ameristar, or Vegas Downtown rules so that you can prepare for almost any gambling vacation.

Freecell Patience

Freecell Patience is a fairly popular card game thanks to its appearance in various versions of Microsoft Windows over the years. Figure 14.4 shows the GNOME games version of Freecell, highlighting the fact that the toolbar for many GNOME games provides a Hint button that is always handy as a last resort.

Implementation-wise, presenting this game as being stand-alone is a bit misleading, because this menu item just starts the AisleRiot Solitaire application but pre-loads a different card game.

FIGURE 14.4

Freecell

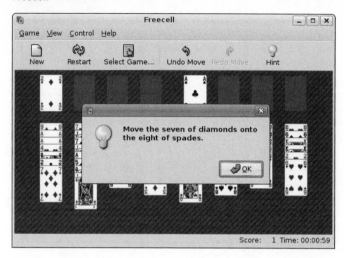

Tali

Tali is an online version of a dice game that essentially emulates a card game (poker). Figure 14.5 shows the beginning of a GNOME Tali game.

FIGURE 14.5

Tali

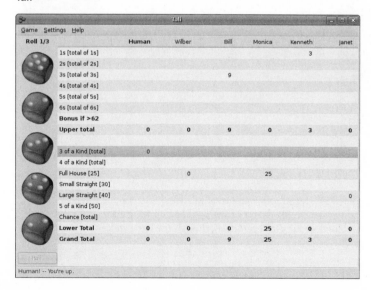

If you're familiar with a popular analog game called Yahtzee from Hasbro, Inc., Tali may not be a complete shock to you, and may instead appear to be a familiar friend. By default, Tali is configured to enable one human player (you) to take on four computer-generated opponents, but you can easily configure your preferences to support multiple human players and reduce or eliminate the computer-generated opponents. I especially like the default prompt at the bottom of the screen when it's my turn: "Human! — You're up." Yes, Mr. Borg, sir!

Board Games

Board games have always been quite popular and don't have the sinful connotation that some people attach to card games. Though some of the games in this section are Linux implementations of existing computer games, I've defined board games as any game that uses a grid or could conceivably be played on a board.

Ataxx

Ataxx is a disc-flipping game that is similar to the Iagno computer game, which is also included in the GNOME games package and is therefore provided as part of a default Ubuntu desktop installation. Figure 14.6 shows the starting screen for a game of Ataxx.

FIGURE 14.6

Ataxx

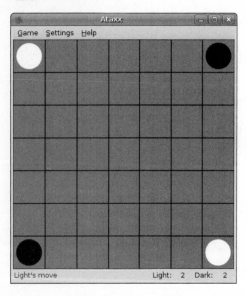

As you can see from Figure 14.6, Ataxx (like Iagno) is a conceptual relative of the popular category of existing board games such as Othello and Reversi. Unlike Iagno or analog disc-flipping games, Ataxx discs start in the corners and require slightly different strategy and gameplay, though the basic concept of capturing adjacent discs of opposing colors is still the same.

Five or More

Five or More is a GNOME version of a well-known Windows game called Color Lines. Figure 14.7 shows a Five or More game that has just started.

Five or More

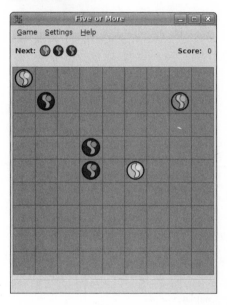

Like many good games, gameplay in Five or More is elegant in its simplicity. Each turn, three additional shapes appear on the screen in random locations. Your goal is to move existing shapes to try to arrange sequences of five matching discs, which removes them from the ever-crowding game field, something like a slow-motion, nonlinear version of Tetris.

Unfortunately, Five or More is missing the Boss Alert key that was present in the Windows versions of this game, which was one of my favorite features. Pressing this key displayed a system utility screen that would make it look like you were doing real work while your boss was within range of your monitor. Fortunately, the game is just as addictive as Color Lines — you'll just have to hide the screen yourself when the boss approaches.

Iagno

Iagno is a disc-flipping game that is similar to the Ataxx computer game, which is also included in the GNOME games package and is therefore provided as part of a default Ubuntu desktop installation. Figure 14.8 shows the starting screen for game of Iagno.

FIGURE 14.8

Iagno

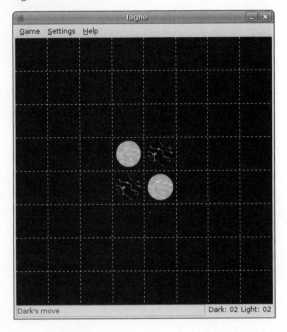

As you can see in Figure 14.8, Iagno is a conceptual relative of the popular category of existing board games such as Othello and Reversi, and offers much the same sort of gameplay.

Klotski

Klotski, the game with one of the least pleasant names I've ever heard, is another game that many Windows escapees will be familiar with, though it has its roots in analog games from France, Thailand, and most directly from Poland, where "Klocki" is the word for blocks. Figure 14.9 shows the GNOME version of Klotski.

Klotski is a strategy game in which the object is to maneuver a large square out of the enclosed area by moving the smaller squares that surround it. It's quite fun to play and comes with a number of pattern variants, each of which tells you in advance how many moves should be required.

FIGURE 14.9

Klotski

Mahjongg

GNOME Mahjongg is a single-player version of the classic Chinese Mahjongg game, which was apparently developed as a combination of earlier Chinese games. Figure 14.10 shows the GNOME version of Mahjongg.

FIGURE 14.10

Mahjongg

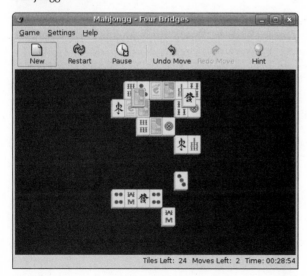

Mahjongg was extremely popular in the United States and Great Britain in the early 20th century, and is still popular today. The object of the game is to remove tiles by matching pairs that display the same pattern. Mahjongg tile patterns are extremely intricate and can be quite beautiful, as they are in the graphics for this version of the game. The GNOME Mahjongg game is quite fun and addictive, and also features a nice Hint button for use when your eyes blur after staring at too many intricately patterned, but very similar tiles.

Mines

Mines is the GNOME version of the popular Microsoft Windows Minesweeper game. Figure 14.11 shows a sample Mines game in progress.

FIGURE 14.11

Mines

Clicking on a square reveals the number of mines in area around that square. Once you identify a square as containing a mine, you mark it by planting a flag on that square. If you clear or mark all squares on the board without clicking on a mine, you win. You are then judged on the time that it took for you to reach the end.

I've never particularly understood why so many people find this game interesting, but I feel exactly the same way about the GNOME and Windows versions, so I suppose that this means that the GNOME version is quite faithful to the original.

Tetravex

Tetravex is an interesting game where you place squares with numeric values beside existing squares where the values on each edge match. Figure 14.12 shows a Tetravex game in progress.

Tetravex

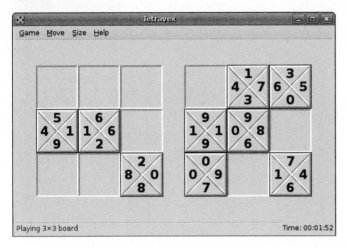

I find Tetravex to be quite fun — and like the kindest GNOME games, its File menu provides a Hint key that hastens the learning process and lets you win early on, while you're still evolving your strategy.

Video Games

Video games have probably gotten more kids interested in computers than any other motivator. After all, it's not surprising to see a video game in a bar or grow up staring at your PlayStation and find yourself thinking, "I wish I could create something like that." This is a far more likely scenario than staring at a huge report in your father or mother's briefcase and thinking, "I wish I could write a program that would produce neat reports like that!"

The GNOME games pack installed on Ubuntu Linux desktop systems has some great implementations and different takes on some classic video games, and many well-known games such as Quake are directly supported under Linux. For information about actually playing some arcade classics on Linux, see the "MAME, MESS, and Friends" sidebar later in this section.

Four-in-a-Row

Four-in-a-Row is an interesting and addictive cross between tic-tac-toe and Tetris, which should help keep you from doing real work for many hours. Figure 14.13 shows the initial Four-in-a-Row screen.

FIGURE 14.13

Four-in-a-Row

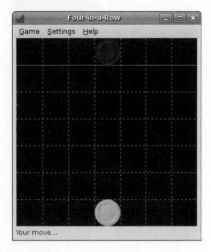

Your goal in Four-in-a-Row is to be the first to arrange a row of four pieces of your color while preventing your opponent (or computer opponent) from doing so. You click in a row to drop and stack a piece in that row, adding to your sequence or blocking your opponent's.

Gnometris

Gnometris is a GNOME implementation of Tetris, probably the most famous computer game of all time. Invented in Russia, it has all of the elements of a great game — it's simple to grasp, easy to play, and when you lose you always find yourself thinking, "I was so close — I can beat this next time!" Figure 14.14 shows a game of Gnometris in progress.

FIGURE 14.14

Gnometris in action

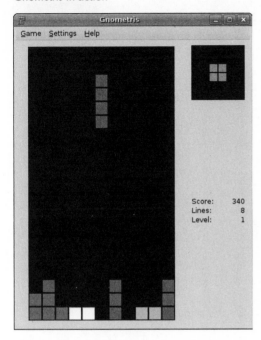

In case you grew up in a cave or under a rock, the object of all Tetris-like games is to orient falling shapes so that they complete rows, which you then score points for as they disappear. The pace of the game accelerates as time passes, and once a shape reaches the top row of the screen without completing a row, the game is over. Simple, fun, fast, and addictive.

Nibbles

Nibbles is a simple but classic game in which the user controls the movements of a snake that travels around the screen, eating diamonds of various colors and growing in length as the game progresses. Figure 14.15 shows a game of Nibbles in progress.

FIGURE 14.15

Nibbles in progress

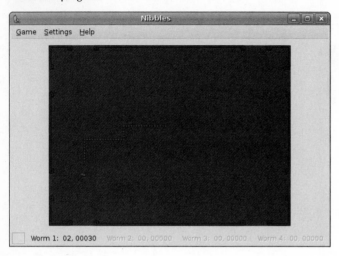

Each player has three lives, one of which is used up each time the snake hits a wall or itself. If you're playing by yourself, the game ends when you run out of lives.

Nibbles is interesting because it is also network-aware, which is configured as shown in Figure 14.16.

FIGURE 14.16

Networked Nibbles configuration

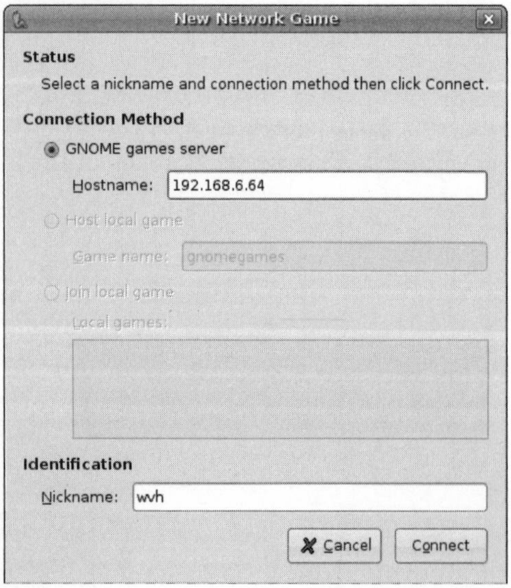

Using this panel, you can define a system that is a games server, and can therefore play Nibbles against other users who also have access to that server. As we'll see later in this chapter, many of the classic board games such as Chess and Go also feature networked modes, but Nibbles is a simple and fun example of a game that you and your friends can play together over a network, each from the comfort of your own console.

Robots

GNOME Robots is a graphical version of the many text-based hunt-and-kill games available on older Unix systems. Figure 14.17 shows a simple Robots game in progress.

FIGURE 14.17

Robots hunting your character

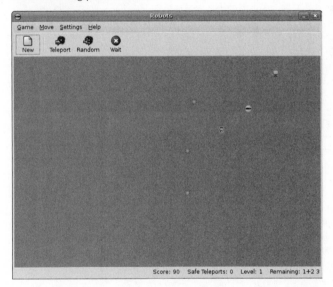

All of the robots in the game want to kill you, and your motivation is simple. First of all, you must survive, and second, you must trick the robots into destroying themselves, either by colliding with each other or by colliding with the wreckage left behind by a previous collision. This game can be surprisingly addictive.

Same Gnome

Same Gnome is a puzzle game that combines aspects of Tetris, Five or More, and similar games, in which you remove areas of similarly-colored pieces on a grid by clicking on them, which causes the pieces around them to drop down or over, hopefully increasing the size of other similarly-colored areas which you can then remove, and so on. Figure 14.18 shows a game of Same Gnome in progress.

This is really a fun little game, and can be surprisingly addictive. It's so simple that you'll continue to think, "I can beat this!" long after every other living creature in your house or apartment has fallen asleep.

FIGURE 14.18

Same Gnome in progress

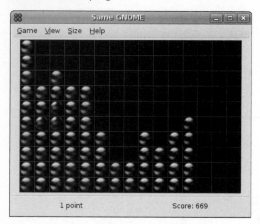

Other Popular Games in the Ubuntu Repositories

The GNOME games pack installed as part of a default Ubuntu Linux desktop installation is really just the tip of the iceberg as far as games on Ubuntu Linux is concerned. The main, universe, and multiverse repositories each offer many other games that are just a few clicks of the Synaptic Package Manager away. Trying to describe each of these games would bloat this book far beyond its purpose of helping you to get up and running with all aspects of Ubuntu Linux, so this section focuses on how to find equivalents or clones of some well-known games that many people would enjoy playing on their Ubuntu systems if they only knew what they were called and how to use them. For information on the Synaptic Package Manager, see Chapter 20, "Adding, Removing, and Updating Software." The remainder of this chapter focuses on explaining what to look for if you're interested in a specific game or type of game.

Billions and Billions of Versions of Chess

In the world of open source computing, chess has two things going for it: it's incredibly popular, and nobody owns it. The fact that chess and its ancestors have been popular for a few thousand years as a thought-provoking strategy game makes it no surprise that versions of computer chess have existed since computers had enough memory to manage any sort of sophisticated gameplay. The fact that nobody owns the rights to the name "chess" means that there are no royalty or licensing entanglements, so any computer chess game can actually be called chess without having to resort to camouflage names or slight changes to the rules to escape corporate greed.

A simple search for chess against package names and descriptions in the Synaptic Package Manager shows 26 packages. These include local and network-enabled chess games, chess-playing engines that you can compete against, a chess game that you can play inside emacs, special fonts for typesetting chess moves and even boards that you can format using TeX and LaTeX (discussed in Chapter 10), and much, much more.

MAME, MESS, and Friends

MAME is an acronym that stands for Multiple Arcade Machine Emulator, and is also the name of a software package that enables you to play old video arcade games by providing the MAME software with the location of zipped images of the ROMs from those machines. It is a truly amazing piece of software and is the only way that you can hope to play many of the old arcade machines nowadays without access to a time machine or a very friendly computer museum. MAME isn't installed by default as part of an Ubuntu Linux desktop installation because it is not true open source software by the GPL definition. Its source code and binaries are freely available, but commercial use and redistribution are prohibited. That said, the X Window system package for the emulator, called xmame, is available in the Ubuntu repositories. MAME supports playing the ROM sets from over 5000 old video games, and does an amazing job of running these games, down to faithfully playing the sounds that the machines originally made, as well as the attractors that they would play to try to entice passersby to play. "Coin detected in pocket!" Versions of MAME are available for most modern platforms, including Linux (xmame), Mac OS X (MacMame), and Microsoft Windows.

As you might suspect, the only hiccup in using MAME lies in getting copies of the ROMs for these old games. In theory and in most cases, you have to actually own the original game (or its board set) to legally play the game in MAME, regardless of where you got the compressed ROM images. I actually own the boards for Centipede (my all-time favorite arcade game) and Millipede as part of my computer collection, and many of my friends have actual arcade machines, but I suspect that this is not all that common. It's a shame that, because of corporate greed, the companies who developed these games originally and already made millions from them won't release the ROM images into the public domain, but that usually seems to be the case. Perhaps there is still a drop or two of blood in those turnips, but it's a shame that this kind of legal crapola is keeping people from legally enjoying the beauty, artwork, and clever gameplay of many classic machines.

For more information about MAME, see the following:

- `http://en.wikipedia.org/wiki/MAME`: general information about MAME as well as a detailed explanation of its legal status and that of MAME ROM images
- `www.mameromlinks.com`: a convenient site where people who own old arcade machines or their board sets can freely download a huge selection of ROM images in MAME format rather than having to have their own PROM reader
- `www.mamedev.org`: the primary MAME development site, with the latest version of the MAME software and related tools in case you want to roll-your-own, bleeding edge version of MAME
- Google search for "MAME ROMs": search results return a few million hits

If you ever squandered any time at all playing video games, or wonder just what your parents used to do with all of their quarters, you owe it to yourself to check out MAME. MESS is a similar emulation effort, but focuses on old home computer and game console emulation. Equally fun, equally impressive, and equally conducive to statements like "how the heck did it get to be four in the morning?"

> **TIP** If you're a true chess fan, your competition is no longer limited to friends, family, and neighbors thanks to the Internet. You can find several chess servers on the Internet, through which you can play remote opponents from the convenience of your own workstation. For more information, see Web sites like the Free Internet Chess Server site at `www.freechess.org` and Tim Mann's great summary of worldwide chess servers at `www.tim-mann.org/ics.html`. There are also a variety of chess servers that require some sort of payment or subscription to use their services and play against their subscribers.

Figure 14.19 shows gnome-chess, a GNOME-based graphical interface for playing chess.

FIGURE 14.19

The gnome-chess interface

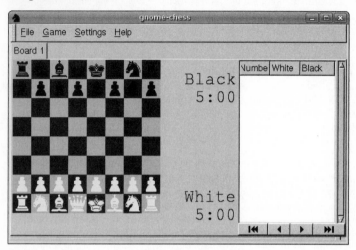

Gnome-chess is just an interface for displaying chessboards and recording and tracking moves. To do any-thing interesting with gnome-chess, you have to identify the chess-playing engine that you want to play against or identify an Internet chess server through which you want to locate and play an opponent. In gnome-chess, both of these are set using the Settings ➪ Preferences dialog, which enables you to define both of these. Figure 14.20 shows a definition for the gnuchess chess-playing program, which is also available in the Ubuntu repositories and is probably the best-known local chess engine for Linux (and most) systems, because it is GNU software and therefore free as in beer. Other chess-playing engines available in the Ubuntu repositories are fruit and phalanx.

FIGURE 14.20

Identifying a chess-playing program in gnome-chess

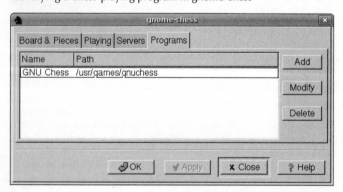

Once gnome-chess knows how to find a chess-playing program or chess server, you simply select which one you want to play against from either the File ➪ Programs or File ➪ Servers menus, a new game board displays, and you're off.

> **TIP** For some reason, the version of the `gnome-chess` package that was available at the time that this book was written doesn't add an entry for `gnome-chess` to the Applications ➪ Games menu. You'll have to either start gnome-chess manually from a GNOME terminal or `xterm` command-line (as explained in Chapter 6), or add a menu entry for `/usr/bin/gnome-chess` to the Games menu, as explained in the section of Chapter 5 entitled "Customizing Menus."

As mentioned previously, the Ubuntu repositories offer many different applications for playing chess. Figure 14.21 shows `xboard`, which is another graphical interface that can play against the `gnuchess` engine or an Internet chess server. Installing the `xboard` package adds an entry for this game to the standard Applications ➪ Games menu.

FIGURE 14.21

An xboard game in progress against the gnuchess engine

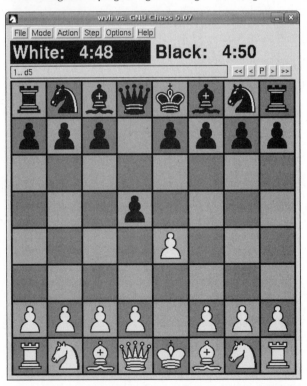

Another popular chess display application is `eboard`, which is probably the most customizable of the three, and can be easily installed from the Ubuntu repositories. If you're a KDE fan, you should look at `knights`, which is certainly my favorite among the KDE-oriented chess display engines.

Of course, you may have already beaten Bobby Fisher or Big Blue or simply may be bored with standard chess. For you, Ubuntu offers the `3D chess` package (shown in Figure 14.22), which displays three chessboards and can automatically play against you if you start the game with the `--play white|black` argument, which specifies the color that you want the computer to play.

FIGURE 14.22

A 3D chess game in progress

Installing the `3D chess` package doesn't add an entry for the game to the Applications ➪ Games menu so you'll need to start the `/usr/games/3Dc` binary from the command-line, optionally specifying the color that you want the computer to play if you can't find a human opponent that can grasp 3D chess. Unless you're already familiar with 3D chess, you'll want to read the documentation in `/usr/shared/doc/3dchess/3dc-rules.html` so that you understand how this particular implementation of the game is played.

TIP   Fans of other versions of chess such as Japanese Shogi, will be glad to know that you can install both the `xshogi` display program and the `gnushogi` shogi-playing engine from the Ubuntu repositories.

Go

Besides chess, one of the most historically popular strategy games in the known universe is Go, a game with a demonstrable history of several thousand years. Just like chess, Go has the advantage of being wildly popular and free, so it matches chess in the open source space in terms of the number of free front-ends for displaying games, a clever GNU go-playing engine (gnugo), and a number of free Go servers on the Internet that you can access to play Go any time of the night or day against opponents throughout the Internet universe. A simple search for "go" against package names and descriptions in the Synaptic Package Manager shows many packages — the ones that I'll discuss in this section are cgoban (a playing interface) and gnugo (a Go-playing engine).

Figure 14.23 shows the startup screen shown by the cgoban graphical interface for Go.

FIGURE 14.23

Initial game selection and configuration in cgoban

This screen enables you to determine if you want to play against IGS (Internet Go Server), NNGS (No Name Go Server), or if you want to use the Go Modem protocol to play against the gnugo program or even another human if your ISP is down. Figure 14.24 shows how to use the Go Modem dialog to specify that one of the two players is human and the other is the /usr/games/gnugo program.

FIGURE 14.24

Player specification in cgoban

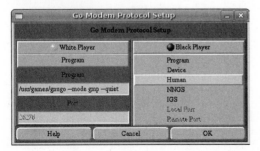

Figure 14.25 shows an actual game of Go in progress after filling out additional details about a local Go game in a per-game configuration dialog that enables you to specify rule sets, board size, per-player handicaps, and komi.

A Go game in progress against the gnugo engine

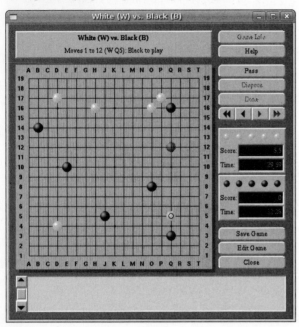

If you're interested in Go, the best site I've found for general information about Go is the British Go Association's (BGA) page at www.britgo.org/index.html, which provides information about applications, the history of the game, competitive Go, and a list of Internet Go servers. A great general site is the International Go federation's page at www.nihonkiin.or.jp/igf/, which I have never found as friendly as the BGA page, but has a great set of pointers to Go sites all over the world. Sensei's Library of Go Servers at http://senseis.xmp.net/?GoServers also provides a fairly large list of online servers that speak various protocols.

Monopoly Clones

Like chess and Go, Monopoly is a board game that is incredibly popular. Unfortunately for us, Monopoly is indeed owned by Hasbro (who bought Parker Brothers, Inc. who originally developed the game — see www.hasbro.com/monopoly), who has not seen fit to provide a Linux port of an online version of Monopoly. However, fear not, open source fans! An excellent Monopoly-like game called Atlantik is available in the Ubuntu repository, as is a game-playing engine that enables you to play Atlantik against other players over the network. To find Monopoly-related packages in the Ubuntu repositories, use the Synaptic

Package Manager to search for "Monopoly" in package names and descriptions. GNOME users will want to install the gtkatlantik package from the resulting list, while KDE fans will want to install the original Atlantik package because Atlantik was originally developed for KDE. Regardless of the desktop you are using you will also want to install the monopd package if you ever want to actually host a game using your machine as a server (which you probably will).

> **NOTE** Atlantik is a network-aware game that can use a server, but it does not offer automated game-play against a computer opponent. This means that you will either have to contact a remote opponent from a default Atlantik server, or you will have to install the monopd package and enable users to connect to your server to play the game.

After you install the appropriate packages on your Ubuntu system, you can start Atlantik by selecting it from the Applications ⇨ Games menu. Figure 14.26 shows Atlantik being played using the gtkatlantik interface.

FIGURE 14.26

A game of Atlantik in progress

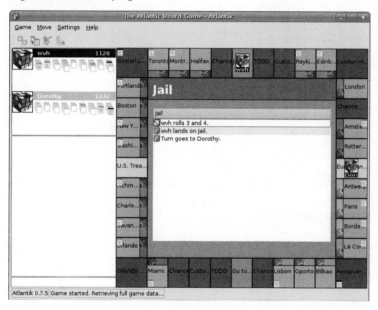

By way of comparison, Figure 14.27 shows a game of Monopoly in progress using the gtkatlantik inter-face. There are few play-related differences between this and the Atlantik game shown in Figure 14.26. The primary difference is the game board used — the rules are identical by default though you can customize them in Atlantik's Game Configuration screen, which is discussed later.

FIGURE 14.27

A game of Monopoly in progress using Atlantik

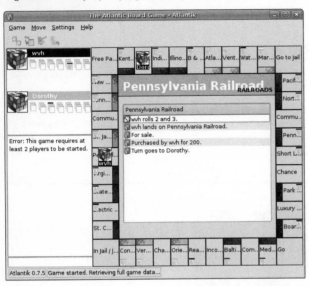

Getting to the point where you actually see a game screen can be slightly confusing. When you first start `gtlatlantik`, click Enter to get past the splash screen, and a game selection dialog such as the one shown in Figure 14.28 displays.

FIGURE 14.28

Creating or joining a networked game of Atlantik

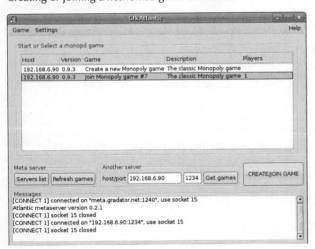

Enter the hostname or IP address of the `monopd` server that you want to contact in the Another server text box. Click Get games, and a list of the games available at that server displays. If one is available, select that game from the list and click CREATE/JOIN GAME, at which point the screen shown in Figure 14.27 or Figure 14.28 displays. The actual game that you see depends on the type of game(s) that the server is hosting, and the one that you connected to.

If no game is available and you are running the `monopd` server, you will need to start one and wait for someone to connect to it. This is almost the same process as joining an existing game, except that you would select one of the Create a new Monopoly game or Create a new Atlantik game entries in the game list. Your system will display a Game Configuration dialog until someone remotely connects to your game, at which point you will see the game board as the game begins.

> **TIP** Installing the `monopd` **server package starts the** `monopd` **server on your system. If you cannot contact a remote** `monopd` **server or simply want to run your own, you can check its status using a command like** `ps alxww | grep monopd`**. If this doesn't show any** `monopd` **processes running, you can start one with a command like** `sudo -u nobody /usr/sbin/monopd`**.**

A game board editor for Atlantik, called Atlantik Designer, is also available as a separately installable package. Figure 14.29 shows the initial Atlantik Designer screen with a blank board that you can customize, save, and use.

FIGURE 14.29

Using the Atlantik Designer to create your own game board

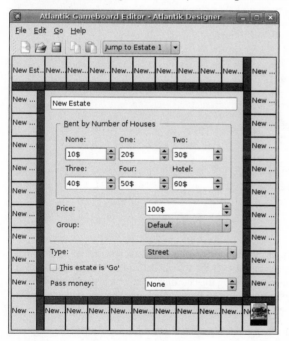

Using the Atlantik Designer in conjunction with Atlantik can be a lot of fun, because you can create your own game boards to reflect the streets and corporate landmarks in your own area. Who doesn't want to rule (or at least own) their neighborhood?

Atlantik is the easiest way to become a capitalist without actually crushing anyone under your boot heels, and is great fun, just like the original Monopoly board game. Frankly, I wish that Hasbro would release an official Linux version because I believe in rewarding companies for fun games, but until then Atlantik is just all right with me.

Scrabble Clones

Scrabble is another classic board game that is extremely popular but suffers from the same commercial ownership and corporate malaise as Monopoly. Scrabble is owned by Milton Bradley, which is also a wholly owned subsidiary of Hasbro. Microsoft Windows and Macintosh versions of Scrabble are available, but until Hasbro sees fit to release a Linux version, we'll just have to content ourselves with the unofficial Linux version provided by Ubuntu Linux. To locate this, simply use the Synaptic Package Manager to search for Scrabble in package names and descriptions, which has exactly one match. After installing this package, you can run Scrabble from the command-line in a GNOME terminal or xterm. Figure 14.30 shows the Ubuntu Linux version of Scrabble.

FIGURE 14.30

The standard version of Scrabble for Ubuntu Linux

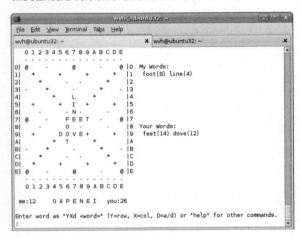

Holy ASCII Art, Batman! It turns out that the standard version of Scrabble for Linux systems uses a terminal-oriented interface. This isn't actually a problem once you get over the initial GUI shock, because the game is eminently playable in this form once you get used to identifying the coordinates at which you want to position each of your words. The Scrabble game comes with a fairly intelligent game-playing engine which is fun to use and often more clever than some of us (namely me) if you can't interest anyone else in a game.

> **TIP**   Other versions of Scrabble that actually provide a graphical interface are available for Linux systems, though not currently in a pre-packaged form that can be easily installed on an Ubuntu system. You can get the tarballs for `xscrabble`, an X11-based version of Scrabble, at `ftp://ftp.ac-grenoble.fr/ge/educational_games`. You may also want to look at a Java-based Scrabble game called Jduplicate, which is available at `http://jduplicate.sourceforge.net`.

Summary

An Ubuntu desktop system provides a great selection of computer games, ranging from classic card and board games to more modern video games. Beyond the default set installed with an Ubuntu desktop system, the Ubuntu repositories provide many, many more, including some very sophisticated, graphically oriented video games and simulations. Whether you want to play games like Go or Chess, which have been around for thousands of years, or you simply want to shoot aliens, Ubuntu Linux can keep you occupied and happy until you finally have to give in to sleep deprivation or the need to go to work.

Chapter 15 explores how you can connect to other machines on your network. Whether you need a command-line login session or a remote graphical console to execute commands directly on a remote machine, or simply need to transfer files back and forth between multiple machines, most of the tools you'll need are installed by default on Ubuntu desktop systems. Anything else that you may need is only a few clicks and a download away in your favorite Ubuntu repository.

Chapter 15

Connecting to Other Systems

Not too long ago, networking meant either talking with groups of friends or sending e-mail and surfing the Web from your home computer. Today's multicomputer households are much more sophisticated than that, often featuring home or SOHO networks of computers that share files, are often centrally administered, and to which multiple people want or need access. Although networked access to shared resources such as file servers and printers has been common in enterprise and SMB environments for a long time, this is now a common requirement for the modern, enlightened household.

This chapter discusses various command-line and graphical solutions provided by Ubuntu Linux for directly connecting to remote systems, either by logging in on them directly or by obtaining remote, graphical access to a desktop session. This chapter doesn't explore connecting to remote file servers and file sharing—that's discussed in Chapter 16, "File and Transfer Sharing on Ubuntu."

IN THIS CHAPTER

Establishing secure connections

Enabling secure connections to your machine

Accessing remote windows and Mac OS X consoles

Using virtual network computing

Establishing Secure Connections to Other Systems

The traditional Unix application used to establish a terminal connection to a remote machine over the network is known as *telnet*. The `telnet` application connects to a `telnet` daemon running on a remote system and creates a login session once the proper authentication credentials have been exchanged. Unfortunately, authentication information and all other data exchanged between a `telnet` client and server is exchanged in the clear, meaning that it is readily visible to anyone with access to your network, a packet sniffer, and sufficient curiosity or other motivation. There are ways around this, of course: You can use `telnet` through an encrypted virtual private network (VPN) or tunnel, or install a version of `telnet` that uses Kerberos authentication, but why cling to an old application and protocol when there are newer, more secure alternatives available?

The `telnet` client is installed as a part of a default Ubuntu installation because you may need the `telnet` client to connect to older systems or systems that simply do not support more sophisticated remote connections, but a `telnet` server is not officially supported by Ubuntu. If you must, you can still explicitly install the `telnet` server — known as `telnetd` — from a "universe" repository by using the Synaptic Package Manager.

If you're an old-time Unix fan, you may remember the Berkeley r-command suite, which provided commands like `rsh` and `rcp`. These commands had the same security problems as the older `telnet` command, namely that they transmitted passwords and other information in the clear. Although these commands appear to be available on Ubuntu Linux systems, they are mapped to the corresponding SSH commands (`ssh` and `scp`, respectively) using the alternative system that is discussed in Chapter 20, "Adding, Removing, and Updating Software."

Logging in to Remote Systems Using ssh

The newer, more modern, and secure replacement for `telnet` is `ssh`, the secure shell application, which uses SSH, the Secure Shell protocol. The `ssh` application is installed as part of a default Ubuntu Linux installation, along with other applications that use the same protocol and authentication information, and which shares much of the same command-line syntax, such as `sftp` (secure FTP) and `scp` (secure copy). Using `ssh`, you can establish a remote login session on any machine that is running an `ssh` daemon. An `ssh` daemon must be running on the remote system. If you try to connect to the remote system and see a message like the following, the `ssh` daemon is either not running on that system or it is running on some port other than the default port 22:

```
$ ssh ulaptop
ssh: connect to host ulaptop port 22: Connection refused
```

The remainder of this section discusses how to use `ssh` to connect to remote systems that are actually running the daemon. For information on how to enable the SSH daemon on an Ubuntu system, see the next section.

Using `ssh` to connect to a remote system as the current user is as simple as typing the `ssh hostname` command, where hostname is the name or IP address of the host that you want to connect to. The first time that you attempt to connect to a remote system that you have never connected to before, you will see a message like the following:

```
$ ssh ulaptop
The authenticity of host 'ulaptop (192.168.6.90)' can't be established.
RSA key fingerprint is 07:e6:3a:50:4b:6d:e6:d8:f1:80:c6:b2:da:02:a3:da.
Are you sure you want to continue connecting (yes/no)?
```

To continue connecting to this system, type yes and press return. The `ssh` utility adds the RSA key for the remote system to its list of known hosts (to prevent some other machine from impersonating the remote machine in the future), and prompts you for your password, as in the following example:

```
Warning: Permanently added 'ulaptop' (RSA) to the list of known hosts.
wvh@ulaptop's password:
```

If you're curious, RSA stands for Rivest, Shamir, and Adleman, the developers of the type of public key encryption technology that is used by default by the OpenSSH implementation of the SSH protocol. For more information about public key infrastructure (PKI) and related encryption technologies, see a Web site such as Wikipedia's PKI information at `http://en.wikipedia.org/wiki/Pki`.

At this prompt, enter your password on the remote system and press return. Assuming that you typed the correct password, you'll see a successful login message from the remote system, and that system's prompt will display, as in the following example:

```
Linux ubuntu32 2.6.15-21-386 #1 PREEMPT Fri Apr 21 16:43:33 UTC 2006

The programs included with the Ubuntu system are free software;
the exact distribution terms for each program are described in the
individual files in /usr/share/doc/*/copyright.

Ubuntu comes with ABSOLUTELY NO WARRANTY, to the extent permitted by
applicable law.
Last login: Wed May 1 20:15:16 2006
wvh@ubuntu32:~$
```

Once you've established an ssh connection to a remote machine, you can do anything from this login prompt that you could do from a direct connect to that machine, including starting graphical applications that display on your local system if you set the DISPLAY environment variable correctly, as discussed in the section of Chapter 5 entitled "What's a Desktop? Graphical Environments for Linux." When you're done working on the remote system, you can log out by pressing Control+D or by typing the exit command.

All of this is well and good assuming that you have the same login name on all of the systems that you want to connect to, or that you always want to connect as yourself. Luckily, the ssh command provides an easy way to connect to another system as another user by using a command such as ssh user@host, where *user* is the name of the user that you want to log in as, and *host* is the name of the host to which you want to connect as that user. For example, the command ssh joeuser@ulaptop would use ssh to connect to the remote host ulaptop as the user joeuser. Assuming that you know this user's password, you can log in there as the specified user and perform any actions that they are authorized to do.

The ssh command has many other options, few of which you'll probably ever need to use. For complete information on the ssh command, see the online reference information for the command that is available through the man ssh command.

Enabling the SSH Daemon on Your System

As mentioned previously in this chapter, the SSH daemon, sshd, must be running on your system if you want to be able to connect to it remotely using any command that requires the SSH protocol. The version of the SSH server that is available for Ubuntu is the OpenSSH server (www.openssh.org), an open source SSH server that is actively maintained by the people who also support the OpenBSD project (www.openbsd.org), an Open Source Unix-like operating system inspired by the original Berkeley Unix distributions that is well-known for its focus on system security. The OpenSSH server is not installed by default as part of a standard Ubuntu installation but (like everything else in Ubuntu) is easy enough to add using the Synaptic Package Manager.

To install the OpenSSH server, start the Synaptic Package Manager from the System ➪ Administration menu, select Search, enter **OpenSSH Server** in the Search box that displays, and click Search. Once the search completes, select openssh-server from the new OpenSSH Server category, as shown in Figure 15.1.

Once you have marked the openssh-server package for installation, click Apply to install the package. A summary dialog displays, asking for confirmation. Click OK to proceed. Once the package has been downloaded and installed successfully, you can close the Synaptic Package Manager.

FIGURE 15.1

Locating the OpenSSH Server in Synaptic

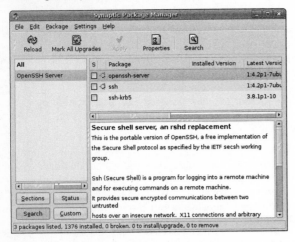

See Chapter 20, "Adding, Removing, and Updating Software," for more detailed information on installing applications using the Synaptic Package Manager.

As part of installing the OpenSSH server, Ubuntu installs a control for it in the administrative Services application, which you can start by selecting Services from the System ⇨ Administration menu. As shown in Figure 15.2, the Remote shell server is automatically enabled when you install it.

FIGURE 15.2

Verifying the state of the SSH server in the Services application

Should you ever want to stop enabling remote users to attempt to log in on your Ubuntu system, you can deselect the checkbox beside the Remote shell server entry in this application and click OK to deactivate the SSH daemon.

Connecting to Other Systems Using VNC

If you have multiple computer systems on a single network, getting up and going to the console of a specific machine to run a program there quickly becomes old. Yes, perhaps it's lazy, but you'd think that there would be a way that a graphical computer system could connect to another graphical computer system over the network and display that machine's console inside a window on the first machine. Actually, there is, and it's included in a standard Ubuntu Linux distribution by default.

Virtual Network Computing (VNC) makes it easy for you to work on multiple graphical computer systems by enabling you to export their graphical displays across a network to another machine. VNC is a cross-platform technology originally developed by Olivetti Research Labs in Cambridge, England, which was later acquired by AT&T. A VNC server runs on one computer system and exports a system desktop that can be accessed by a VNC client running on another system. VNC servers are typically password-protected, which makes VNC an optimal environment for accessing and running graphical administrative and monitoring applications remotely. VNC servers export their virtual displays via network ports starting at 5900 plus the number of the graphical displays that they are exporting. For example, a VNC server running on the X Window system display :1 will use port 5901.

VNC is released under the GPL, and many of the original VNC developers now work for a company called RealVNC (www.realvnc.com), which distributes and supports a commercial VNC implementation but also makes the source code for its version of the VNC server and client freely available, as required by the GPL. Their VNC client is named vncviewer, and is the VNC client provided with a standard Ubuntu installation. Using a vncviewer client to connect to another system's graphical display is explained later, in the section entitled "Using vncviewer." Another extremely popular VNC distribution is TightVNC, an optimized VNC client and server, which is also available for Ubuntu but is not installed by default.

Getting VNC Client and Server Software for Your Other Platforms

Before trying to use the vncviewer to connect to a remote system, you have to have a VNC server to connect to. This section explains how to enable the VNC server provided by Ubuntu, as well as how to get VNC client and server software for popular platforms such as Mac OS X and Microsoft Windows.

> **TIP**   Regardless of the platform on which you are running a VNC server, you must make sure that the network ports that it uses are not being blocked by other network software. For example, if your system does packet filtering or your network uses a firewall, you must make sure that you do not block ports 590x (used to export VNC server displays), 6000 (used to communicate with Linux or Unix X Window system servers), or 580x (used to communicate with a VNC server over the Web).

The vino VNC server for Ubuntu

Connecting to another Ubuntu system on your local network is quite simple — the software that you need to connect to the current graphical console is already installed. This is a GNOME-specific VNC server called vino (the actual executable is called vino-server), which was originally created by Mark McLoughlin.

Little other information about vino is available beyond the initial check-in document at `http://cvs` `.gnome.org/bonsai/cvsblame.cgi?file=vino/docs/remote-desktop.txt` and the minimal information in `/usr/share/doc/vino` on your Ubuntu system. However (luckily), in my experience it "just works," and therefore I guess we don't really need to know much more.

NOTE Vino works differently from most VNC servers, in that once it is enabled, the GNOME session manager automatically starts it for you whenever you log in. It can therefore only export the display of a user that is currently logged in, unlike more standard VNC servers that typically display a system's login screen and therefore support remote access to your system by random users. I'll discuss the high points of more traditional VNC servers later in this section, in the sidebar "How Other VNC Servers Work."

To make sure that the vino VNC server is enabled for you, select the System ➪ Preferences ➪ Remote Desktop menu item, which displays the dialog shown in Figure 15.3. To enable remote access to your desktop, select the Sharing section's Allow other users to view your desktop checkbox. This enables remote users to view the desktop but not to actually do anything there — you must select the Allow other users to control your desktop checkbox to enable a remote VNC viewer to control the mouse and use keyboard shortcuts.

FIGURE 15.3

Configuring the vino VNC server on a Ubuntu system

When configuring the vino server, you should always set a remote desktop password in the Security section of the dialog shown in Figure 15.3. To do this, select the Require the user to enter this password checkbox and enter a password. You can optionally select the Ask you for confirmation checkbox, which displays the dialog shown in Figure 15.4.

In general, I don't recommend enabling this option, because it largely defeats the purpose of supporting remote VNC connections in the first place, and second, because access to your VNC server should always be password-protected.

Once you've enabled remote access using the Remote Desktop Preferences dialog, the GNOME desktop starts the `vino-server` process, and will start it automatically for you whenever you subsequently log in on this Ubuntu system.

How Other VNC Servers Work

Most VNC servers are started by a shell or Perl script called `vncserver` and export their own displays rather than the desktop of the currently logged-in user. The `vncserver` script provides a more flexible mechanism for passing arguments to the server, displays status information once the server has started and detached, and also builds in the ability to use a startup script to identify the window manager and any X applications that the VNC server should start. The VNC server's startup script is usually the file `~/.vnc/xstartup`. If this directory and the startup file do not exist the first time that you start a VNC server, the directory is created and the startup script is cloned from the default X Window system startup file `/etc/X11/xinit/xinitrc`.

Exporting a graphical console that is independent of any physical one and using a startup script to do so enables traditional VNC servers to follow the same somewhat convoluted chain of X Window startup files that are normally used: `~/.xinitrc`, `~/.Xclients` on some systems, `/etc/X11/xinit/xinitrc`, `/etc/X11/Xsession`, and so on. These startup files can start various desktop environments and window managers by using environment variable settings, and also provide a final fall-through to starting the `twm` window manager.

VNC servers that follow this more traditional model and are available for Ubuntu include the `vnc4server` and `tightvncserver` packages, which you can install using the Synaptic Package Manager. If you install one of these, you should de-install the `vino` VNC server at the same time to eliminate possible conflicts.

FIGURE 15.4

A remote connection request on an Ubuntu desktop

VNC Clients and Servers for Mac OS X

A variety of VNC clients and servers are available for Mac OS X. My favorite VNC server for Mac OS X is the OSX VNC server, which is available at `http://sourceforge.net/projects/osxvnc`. You can download this as a Mac disk image file that will mount automatically and start the installer. Once it is installed, you can configure OSX VNC using the dialog shown in Figure 15.5, which displays after you start the OSX VNC Server.

Configuring this utility is much the same as configuring any other VNC server, enabling you to set a password (recommended) and tweak other aspects of the OSX VNC configuration (not recommended).

FIGURE 15.5

Configuring the OSX VNC Server on a Mac OS X system

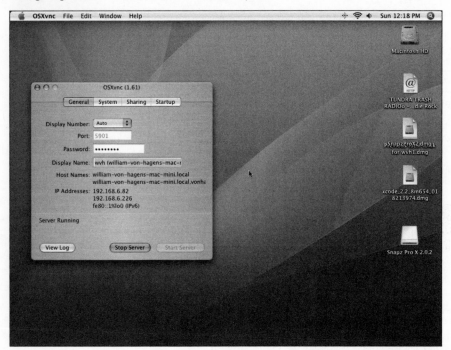

As far as VNC clients go, my favorite for Mac OS X is called "Chicken of the VNC." It's a small, fast VNC client with a funny name — and how can you beat that combination? The latest version of the Chicken of the VNC client is available from the project's SourceForge site at the URL http://sourceforge.net/projects/cotvnc.

VNC Clients and Servers for Windows

TightVNC is a small, highly optimized VNC client and server. TightVNC makes efficient use of network bandwidth through some clever tricks using JPEG compression for the display and differentiating between local cursor movement and cursor movement that needs to be communicated back to the VNC server. TightVNC also provides security features that RealVNC does not, including automatic SSH tunneling for security purposes. Although RealVNC clients and servers are available for Windows, I really like Tight VNC and therefore recommend using it. Both stable and bleeding edge versions of TightVNC are downloadable from www.tightvnc.com/download.html or from their SourceForge site at http://sourceforge.net/projects/vnc-tight.

The downloadable EXE file from either of these sites provides both the VNC client and server. After downloading and installing the executables, you can start the VNC server from the standard menus. The VNC server displays the administrative dialog shown in Figure 15.6, which enables you to set a password that you will need to use to connect to the VNS server (recommended) and to change other server settings (not recommended).

FIGURE 15.6

Configuring the TightVNC Server on a Windows system

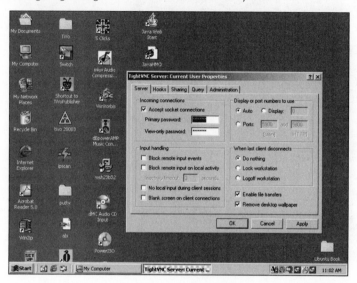

One of the options when configuring a VNC server on Windows is to display a VNC icon in the Windows system tray when the server is running. This is extremely convenient, because it both lets you know when a server is running and also provides instant access to the configuration dialog shown in Figure 15.6 by clicking on the icon in the system tray.

Using vncviewer

Once a VNC server is running on one of your systems, you can connect to it from any remote system by executing the command vncviewer host:display, where host is the host on which the VNC server is running, and display is the number of the system display on which the VNC server is running. If the remote system that you are trying to connect to is a Windows or Macintosh system, you usually do not need to specify the number of the display unless the VNC server running on those systems was configured to use a nonstandard display number. Figure 15.7 shows a VNC connection from one of my desktop Ubuntu systems to an Ubuntu laptop using vncviewer.

FIGURE 15.7

A vncviewer connection to another Ubuntu system

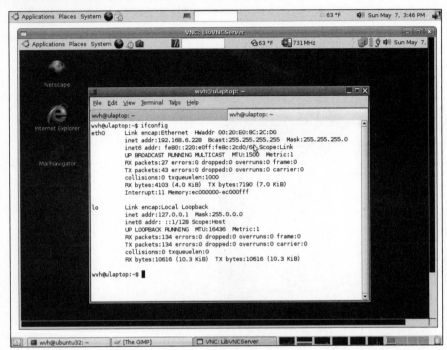

As mentioned previously, once you are running a VNC server on any system, you can connect to it from your Ubuntu system, which simplifies system administration, problem solving, and can generally confuse and amaze your kids if they don't know that you're connecting to their machines. Figure 15.8 shows a VNC connection to a remote Mac OS X system using vncviewer.

FIGURE 15.8

A vncviewer connection to a Mac OS X system

Figure 15.9 shows a VNC connection to a remote Microsoft Windows 2000 system using vncviewer.

FIGURE 15.9

A vncviewer connection to a Windows 2000 system

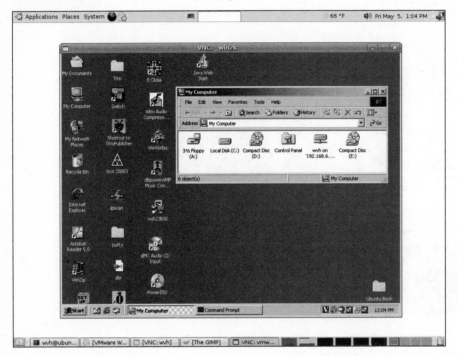

Connecting to Remote Windows Terminal Servers

For most of us, needing to interact with systems running Microsoft Windows is a fact of corporate, and occasionally personal, life. In the home networking environment, most Windows connectivity can be handled quite nicely using the VNC server and client discussed earlier in this chapter, but if you need to connect to a remote Windows system at work or your home computing budget is a bit higher than mine, you may need to access Windows systems that are running a Windows Terminal Server.

If you need to give users occasional, personal access to a Windows system but want to minimize costs and administrative hassles rather than installing one machine per user, a good solution is to install Windows Terminal Services on a reasonably beefy Windows system, and purchase a small pool of Client Access Licenses that are distributed by the server, as needed. Remote clients can then attach to the Terminal Services server and run virtual Windows sessions in a window on their desktops. You then install the software that people need to use on the terminal server or in shares defined in your user profiles, and any remote user connected to the server can access it to run the software that they need. Luckily, remote access to Windows Terminal Services doesn't even require a Windows system any more. Linux users can easily access Windows Terminal Servers using `rdesktop` or `tsclient`, two open source software packages that speak the Remote Desktop Protocol (RDP) used by Windows Terminal Services.

If you centralize Windows services by running Terminal Services on a Microsoft Windows Domain Controller or server, you'll need to make sure that the users who want to connect to it have the "Log in Locally" user right or belong to a group with that right. Otherwise, users will receive the message "The local policy of this system does not permit you to log on interactively" and you may still have to give everyone a Windows box.

Using rdesktop for Terminal Server Connections

The rdesktop package (www.rdesktop.org) is a remote desktop package for Linux and most other Unix and Unix-like systems that run the X Window system. The rdesktop package is installed by default on Ubuntu Linux systems, and provides an excellent, high-power client with a few really cool features as described in this section. The rdesktop package is available from the standard Ubuntu repositories, but you can always get the latest version of its source code and installable packages for other types of systems from its SourceForge site at http://sourceforge.net/projects/rdesktop.

You must start rdesktop from a GNOME or xterm terminal window, though you can certainly add it to your GNOME menus as explained in Chapter 5. The simplest rdesktop command line that you can use to connect to a remote system running Windows Terminal Services is rdesktop host, where host is the name or IP address of the system running Windows Terminal Services. A window displays on your Linux desktop, showing the standard Windows login screen as shown in Figure 15.10.

FIGURE 15.10

A Windows Terminal Services login prompt in rdesktop

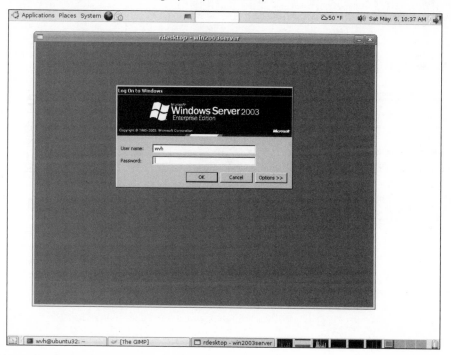

After logging in and specifying the domain that you want to log in to (if necessary), your `rdesktop` window displays the standard Windows desktop as shown in Figure 15.11, which demonstrates an interesting example of recursion, because it shows me editing this chapter of this book in Microsoft Word using a Samba connection to the Ubuntu system where the Word file is actually located. (For more information about Samba, see Chapter 32, "Setting Up a Samba Server.")

The `rdesktop` application provides you with several options that can simplify access to Windows Terminal Services. Some of my favorites are the following:

- `-d`: The domain that you want to authenticate to.
- `-f`: Full-screen mode. This displays `rdesktop` in a decoration-free window that takes over your desktop. You can toggle decorations (and therefore window controls) by pressing Ctrl+Alt+Enter.
- `-p`: Your password in the remote domain.
- `-u`: The name of the user that you want to log in as.

FIGURE 15.11

A Windows 2000 desktop in rdesktop

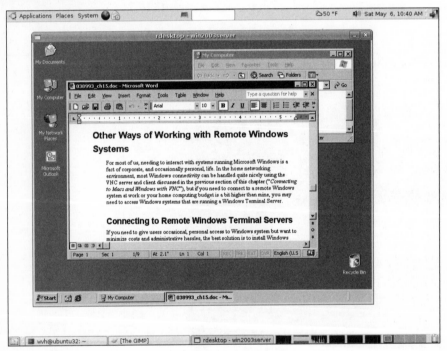

If the system running Windows Terminal Services is running Windows XP or a newer version of Windows, one especially handy option not listed in the previous section is the `-r` option, which lets you directly map resources on your Linux system to your Windows Terminal Services connection. This is especially useful when you want to map a local print queue to a virtual printer in your Windows Terminal session, or when you want to access a local drive to your terminal session. The syntax for these is `-r printer:local-queue-name` and `-r disk:share-name=/device/path`, respectively. For example, to attach PRN1 to a local print queue named SuperScript-660i, you would add `-r printer:SuperScript-660i` to your command-line options when executing the `rdesktop` command. Figure 15.12 shows how your local print queue shows up in a generic Windows print dialog.

Similarly, to map your local CDROM drive to a share called cdrom, you would add `-r disk:cdrom=/dev/cdrom` to the `rdesktop` command-line. If you still use floppies, you could map your local floppy drive to a share called floppy by adding `-r disk:floppy=/dev/fd0` to your `rdesktop` command-line. The name that you specify as the share must be eight characters or less.

FIGURE 15.12

A local printer connected to a remote print queue in rdesktop

Using tsclient for Terminal Server Connections

In case you don't like `rdesktop` for some reason, Ubuntu also provides another Windows Terminal Server client as part of a default Ubuntu installation. This is the `tsclient` (Terminal Services Client) application (`http://gnomepro.com/tsclient`). The `tsclient` application is a GNOME-centric Terminal Server client that provides some optimization and also enables you to save information about a terminal server connection in a file that you can quickly and easily reload instead of manually specifying all of your settings each time that you want to connect. Though the latest version of `tsclient` for Ubuntu is always available from the Ubuntu repositories, you can get the latest source code and packages for other GNOME-based systems at the `tsclient` SourceForge project site at `http://sourceforge.net/projects/ts-client`.

To start the `tsclient` application, select Applications ➪ Internet ➪ Terminal Server Client, which displays the dialog shown in Figure 15.13.

FIGURE 15.13

The tsclient startup screen

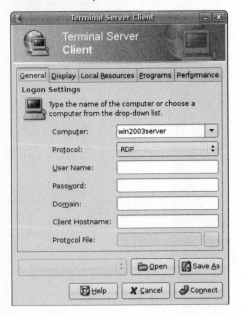

If you only enter the name of the terminal server that you want to connect to and click Connect, the standard Windows Terminal Server login screen displays in a new `tsclient` window, as shown in Figure 15.14. You must then log in normally.

FIGURE 15.14

A terminal server session shown in tsclient

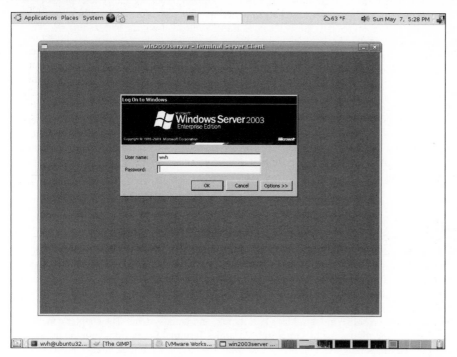

To simplify future connections to terminal servers that you may contact frequently, you can fill out all of the particulars for a connection on the screen shown in Figure 15.13, click Save As, and enter the name that you want to associate with this connection. The `tsclient` application will save all of this information (except for your password) in a file by that name with the `.rdp` extension, and store it in the directory `~/.tsclient` in your home directory. In the future, you can select one of these files after starting `tsclient`, enter your password, and quickly establish a connection to the indicated terminal server.

Using Other Remote Connection Software

Though it is not supplied as part of a default Ubuntu Linux installation, another popular software package for graphically connecting to remote systems is the free version of NoMachine NX, known as FreeNX. This package (named `freenx`) is not provided in the Ubuntu repositories and is not installed by default on a standard Ubuntu system, primarily because its Linux clients are KDE-based, and therefore install many KDE libraries. However, versions of FreeNX are available from some of the additional, user-supported repositories listed in Chapter 20, "Adding, Removing, and Updating Software." See that chapter for additional information.

FreeNX is a free, GPL implementation of NoMachine's NX (NoMachine NX) Server (www.nomachine.com). NoMachine has developed a compression technology that substantially reduces the size of X Window system communications and adds other performance improvements through caching and general protocol optimization. The NX client applications for Linux are included in the `freenx` package — the clients for Microsoft Windows, Mac OS X, and Solaris are available as free downloads from the NoMachine site. The free and commercial versions of the NX server primarily differ in terms of capabilities (and, of course, cost). FreeNX provides all of the core capabilities of the commercial NX server for remote connection, but does not currently include the SMB and printing (CUPS) support provided by the commercial NX server.

If you're already a VNC fan, NX is definitely worth a look for its superb compression technologies and associated performance improvements, and also because it inherently uses SSH for secure communications between client and server. FreeNX is effectively equivalent to VNC, and also supports Linux Terminal Server (www.ltsp.org), Windows Terminal Server, Citrix Metaframe, and standard X Window system XDMCP (X Display Manager Control Protocol) connections. However, it is not part of any official Ubuntu repository from Canonical, so you won't be able to get support from them if you encounter any problems. (You may still get free sympathy, though.)

Summary

Networking is a given in today's academic, business, and even home computing environments. The need to access more and different systems goes hand in hand with that. This chapter discussed secure command-line mechanisms for connecting to remote Linux and Unix systems and explained installing the SSH server on your system so that people can securely connect to your system. I then explored the excellent VNC (Virtual Network Computing) clients and servers that enable you to remotely connect to the consoles of graphical systems such as Microsoft Windows, Mac OS X, Linux, and Unix systems. The chapter concluded by discussing mechanisms for connecting to a Microsoft Windows Terminal Server from your Ubuntu system, and then introduced the popular NX and FreeNX software that enables you to securely connect to just about any remote graphical console service.

Chapter 16 discusses the related topic of connecting to remote file servers to access files that are stored on them, and explains how to share files from your Ubuntu system so that other systems on your network can quickly and easily access them. Music server, anyone?

Chapter 16

File Transfer and Sharing on Ubuntu

IN THIS CHAPTER

Transferring files between systems

Sharing files with window systems

Sharing files with Linux and Unix systems

Peer-to-peer file sharing

Sooner or later, you're going to want to copy a file to or from another computer system. In pre-networking and pre-e-mail days (which you may not even remember), this usually involved writing a copy of the file to removable media of some sort, such as a floppy disk, carrying that floppy from one system to the other, and then copying the file from the floppy disk to the other system. This was known as "sneaker net" — you just can't beat that nerd humor!

Today, thanks to the fact that networking is almost ubiquitous and that most businesses and many homes have their own networks, electronic file transfer is an important capability. As you'd expect, there are many ways to transfer or copy files between systems, ranging from point-to-point file transfers to the peer-to-peer (P2P) file transfers much beloved of the music and film industries. In point-to-point file transfers, you explicitly copy a file from one system to another, and you therefore know the addresses or identities of both hosts. In peer-to-peer file transfer, groups of systems share files with each other without necessarily knowing or caring about the specific systems from which they are getting the files or to which they are sending them. In peer-to-peer file transfers, somebody obviously has to know what hosts are sharing what files, but this is usually built into the software — more about that later in this chapter.

The first section of this chapter discusses popular point-to-point file transfer solutions that are built into your Ubuntu Linux system. The second section of this chapter, "Peer-to-Peer File Sharing on Ubuntu," discusses various P2P solutions that are easily installed and used on your Ubuntu system.

NOTE You may have noticed by now that I am not a lawyer and that I have significant disdain for industry groups that try to suppress technologies just because they can be used to do something that may be illegal. Heck, I could conceivably club someone to death with my laptop, but does that mean that we should outlaw laptops? There is absolutely nothing inherently illegal about Peer-to-Peer file sharing. P2P is a great way to efficiently share and transfer large files between multiple systems, with everyone sharing part of the load. What you do with it is your business. Explaining how you can use it is mine.

Transferring Files to Other Systems

As noted in the introduction to this chapter, this section discusses how to copy files between systems in cases where you know the identities of the machines involved in the transfer. Common examples of this sort of file transfer are "I need to copy this file from my laptop to the machine on my desk," "I want to put this file on our home media server so we can play it from any machine in the house," or "I need to put this spreadsheet on the corporate file server so that my boss can see that I'm actually working from home." In each of these cases, you have authorized access to the machines at both ends of the transfer and you know their names, whether by fully qualified hostname (`ftp.vonhagen.org`), IP address (207.44.142.34), or by their local hostname on your network (laptop, server1, and so on).

In addition to having authorized access to the system that you're transferring files to, the appropriate service already must be running on the remote system, holding up a sort of electronic catcher's mitt that can receive the files that you're transferring there. This chapter focuses on the client-side of file transfers — transferring files to something that's ready to receive them, and doing anything you need to do to enable your local machine to reach them. This chapter doesn't explain how to set up services such as an FTP server or shared directories on Microsoft Windows or Linux systems. For information on sharing Linux directories so that you can reach them directly from a PC running Microsoft Windows, Mac OS X, or Linux, see Chapter 32, "Setting Up a Samba Server." For information on sharing Linux directories so that you can reach them directly from a PC running Mac OS X or Linux, see Chapter 31, "Setting Up an NFS Server." (You can also contact NFS Servers from Microsoft Windows, but only by installing special software that doesn't come with Windows by default.) Information about setting up an FTP server is provided as a sidebar in Chapter 31.

TIP Another common file transfer scenario is "my brother would really like a copy of this file." In that case, I'd suggest just attaching the file to an e-mail message and sending it to him. You don't know the name of his machine, its IP address, and you probably don't have direct access to the machine anyway.

Using FTP

FTP in uppercase letters stands for File Transfer Protocol, and is the oldest existing way of transferring files over a network using the standard TCP/IP protocol that is the basis of the Internet. In lowercase letters, `ftp` is the name of a command-line program that you can run to connect to a remote FTP server so that you can transfer a file in either direction. As I'll explain in this section, Ubuntu makes it easy to transfer files using FTP in a variety of ways: the GNOME desktop provides built-in support for FTP connections; Ubuntu comes with the command-line `ftp` client; and the Ubuntu repositories provide stand-alone, graphical FTP applications if neither of the previous solutions meets your needs.

FTP is an old protocol and the commands that you need to know are simple, even from the command-line. You may never need to use `ftp` from the command-line at all, because many equivalent command-line tools such as `wget` and `curl` exist that use newer protocols such as HTTP to retrieve files by directly specifying their URLs. In general, I prefer to err on the side of caution in this book — if you don't need certain information, that's fine and you can skip over it. However, if you do need to use FTP and information about it wasn't present in the book, both of us would be unhappy.

Connecting to an FTP Server from the GNOME Desktop

Ubuntu's Places menu provides the Connect to Server command, which makes it easy to create an icon on your desktop for an FTP server, and then to connect to that share using the Nautilus file manager. Selecting Places ➪ Connect to Server displays the dialog shown in Figure 16.1.

FIGURE 16.1

Defining a connection to a Public FTP server

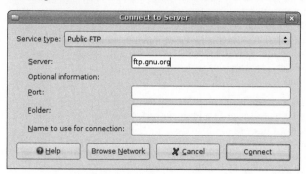

The default selection, Public FTP, is not the one that you want to use if the FTP server that you want to connect to requires authentication (a specific username and password), which is usually the case. (I'll explain how to do that a little bit later in this section.) As you might suspect, Public FTP servers are servers that do not require authentication, and are traditionally known as *anonymous FTP servers*. However, if you are actually connecting to an anonymous FTP server, you must at least enter the name or IP address of the FTP server that you want to connect to. If you want to provide your own name for the desktop icon that this command will create, you can enter that in the Name to use for connection field, but I rarely do this because the default name of the icon is the name of the FTP server. You need to specify a specific port only if the remote FTP server is running on a nonstandard TCP/IP port, and you need to specify the name of a remote directory only if you want to automatically connect to some directory other than the default one that the FTP server associates with the anonymous user. Click Connect to create a desktop icon for that FTP server.

To specify that you want to connect to an FTP server that requires authentication, click the Service type menu at the top of this dialog and select the FTP (with login) entry to display the dialog shown in Figure 16.2.

FIGURE 16.2

Defining a connection to an FTP server that requires authentication

Connect to Server		
Service type:	FTP (with login)	
Server:	192.168.6.64	
Optional information:		
Port:		
Folder:		
User Name:	wvh	
Name to use for connection:		
Help	Browse Network	Cancel	Connect

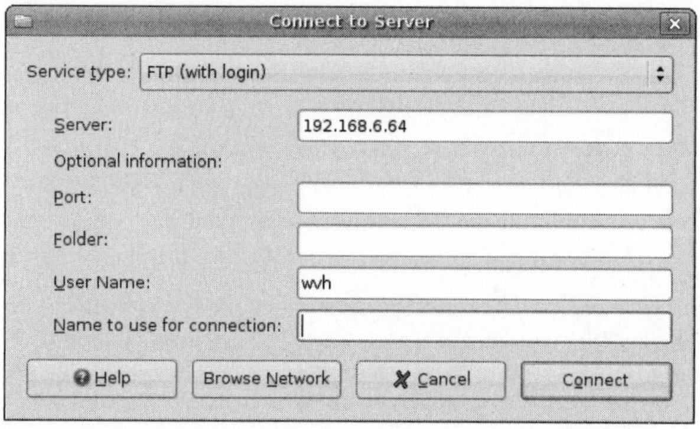

As with an anonymous FTP server, you must at least enter the name or IP address of the FTP server that you want to connect to. Similarly, you can provide your own name for the desktop icon that this command will create, but I rarely do this because the default name of the icon is the name of the FTP server. You can also identify the name of the user that you want to connect as, but this is also optional — if you don't specify one, you'll be prompted for that information when you actually connect. As with the Public FTP server, you need to specify a specific port only if the remote FTP server is running on a nonstandard TCP/IP port, and you need to specify the name of a remote directory only if you want to automatically connect to some directory other than the default one that the FTP server associates with any user that you've specified. Click Connect to create a desktop icon for that FTP server.

TIP If you look really closely, you'll see that the icon created for an anonymous or authenticating FTP server by the Connect to Server dialog displays a little network connection beneath it, and displays a small red flag with the letters FTP inside it to its right. If you end up creating lots of files on your desktop and have really good eyesight, this makes it easy to identify the protocol used to connect to various directories. This can come in handy, especially if you also use the Connect to Server mechanism to connect to shared Microsoft Windows directories, which I'll explain later in this chapter.

Simply creating a desktop icon for an anonymous or authenticating FTP server doesn't actually establish the connection. To do that, double-click on the appropriate desktop icon to open it. If you are connecting to an authenticating FTP server, you will see a dialog that prompts you for any required information that you have not specified yet, as shown in Figure 16.3.

FIGURE 16.3

Completing the login information for an FTP server

If you are connecting to an FTP server that requires authentication and didn't specify the name of a user to connect as, the dialog shown in Figure 16.3 still gives you the opportunity to connect anonymously. However, to actually log in, select the Connect as user radio button and enter the login name and password of the user that you want to connect as.

Once you enter the correct user name and login (or successfully connect to an anonymous FTP server), a Nautilus file manager window appears which displays the contents of the default directory associated with the user that you are logged in as, as shown in Figure 16.4.

FIGURE 16.4

A connection to an FTP server in the Nautilus file manager

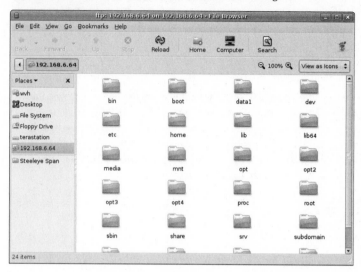

Once the Nautilus file manager displays, copying files in either direction uses the standard Nautilus and GNOME desktop conventions, as discussed in Chapter 5.

Once you are done accessing the FTP server, close the Nautilus file manager window. To discard the desktop icon, right-click on the icon for the FTP server and select Unmount Volume from the pop-up menu to sever the connection and discard the icon. If you want to reuse the FTP server definition in the future, you can simply leave the icon on your desktop when you log out — the next time that you log in, the icon will still be present, but you will have to re-authenticate to access the FTP server again.

Connecting to an FTP Server from the Command-Line

You can also connect to a remote FTP server by typing the ftp command and the name or IP address of the server from any Ubuntu command-line, such as the GNOME Terminal or an xterm. The following example connects to an FTP server running on a system whose IP address is 192.168.6.64:

```
$ ftp 192.168.6.64
Connected to 192.168.6.64.
220-Welcome to Pure-FTPd.
220-You are user number 2 of 10 allowed.
220-This is a private system - No anonymous login
220-IPv6 connections are also welcome on this server.
220 You will be disconnected after 15 minutes of inactivity.
Name (192.168.6.64:wvh):
```

When you connect to an FTP server from the command-line, you see some information about the FTP server and the system that it is running on, and the remote system eventually prompts you for the login that you want to use to connect to it. (How much information an FTP server displays about itself depends on the specific FTP server software that it is running and how the FTP server was configured.)

As you'll see from the last line of the previous example, an FTP server's login prompt usually tries to provide some defaults. In this case, I was logged in as the user "wvh" on the system from which I initiated the FTP connection. If that is the login name that you want to use to connect to the remote FTP server, you can simply press return to accept the default. If you want to connect as another user, type that user's login name and press return, as in the following example where I specify the user name "vonhagen":

```
Name (192.168.6.64:wvh): vonhagen
331 User vonhagen OK. Password required
Password:
```

 You can usually log in on an anonymous FTP server from the command-line by entering the login name "anonymous" and supplying your e-mail address as the password.

After entering your login name, the remote FTP server prompts you for your password on the FTP server. Enter that and press return. If you've entered a valid username and password, you'll see a confirmation message, some optional information about the remote FTP server, and the ftp> prompt from the remote machine, telling you that it's ready to do something, as in the following example:

```
230 Login successful
Remote system type is UNIX.
Using binary mode to transfer files.
ftp>
```

All FTP servers support several commands, which you can see at any time by typing a question mark and pressing return, as in the following example:

```
ftp> ?
Commands may be abbreviated.  Commands are:
!         debug       mdir      qc          send
$         dir         mget      sendport    site
account   disconnect  mkdir     put         size
append    exit        mls       pwd         status
ascii     form        mode      quit        struct
bell      get         modtime   quote       system
binary    glob        mput      recv        sunique
bye       hash        newer     reget       tenex
case      help        nmap      rstatus     tick
cd        idle        nlist     rhelp       trace
cdup      image       ntrans    rename      type
chmod     lcd         open      reset       user
close     ls          prompt    restart     umask
cr        macdef      passive   rmdir       verbose
delete    mdelete     proxy     runique     ?
ftp>
```

Because the chances are good that you'll never use most of these (and you can get a complete explanation of them from the online man page for the ftp command by using the man ftp command from any command-line); I'll just discuss the most basic set of commands required to find and retrieve a file on a remote machine.

All FTP servers export a directory hierarchy, just like any directory on a Linux system. Therefore, you can use familiar commands like pwd to find out the name of the current directory, cd to change to a specified directory, and so on. If you've logged in to an FTP server as a specific user, chances are good that you'll initially find yourself in the system's standard file transfer directory (called /pub) or in that user's home directory.

Once you've navigated to the directory to which you want to transfer a file or from which you want to retrieve one, you issue either the put command (to send a file to the FTP server) or the get command (to retrieve a file from the FTP server). Before actually transferring a file, you should make sure that the file transfer will take place in the appropriate mode. Most FTP servers automatically set the transfer mode so that you can retrieve binary files, such as graphics, archive files (file formats such as zip, tgz, bz2, tar, pax, and so on), music files, and so on. Just in case, I like to always make sure that the file transfer will take place in binary mode by issuing the bin command, as in the following example:

```
ftp> bin
200 TYPE is now 8-bit binary
ftp>
```

If you do not transfer files in binary mode, they will be transferred as ASCII files, which will corrupt any binary file that you transfer and prevent you from opening it correctly. If you transfer a file and then can't view, play, or de-archive it, you may have overlooked this step.

By default, when you send or retrieve a file, the FTP command doesn't display any status information until the transfer completes. Personally, I like a bit of feedback just to know something is actually happening. I therefore always use the FTP server's hash command, which causes the server to display a hash mark ('#') for each kilobyte of data that it transfers. Typing the hash command once activates this feature; typing it a second time deactivates the feature. The following example shows hashing being activated before an FTP file transfer:

```
ftp> hash
Hash mark printing on (1024 bytes/hash mark).
ftp>
```

Now we're finally ready to actually send or retrieve a file. Sending a file to the remote machine is as easy as typing the put command followed by the name of the file that you want to transfer to the FTP server, as in the following example:

```
ftp> put JDSC-0.5.9a.zip
local: JDSC-0.5.9a.zip remote: JDSC-0.5.9a.zip
200 PORT command successful
150 Connecting to port 39972
################################################################
################################################################
################################################################
################################################################
################################################################
################################################################
################################################################
#################
226-File successfully transferred
226 0.202 seconds (measured here), 2.36 Mbytes per second
499668 bytes sent in 0.19 secs (2526.9 kB/s)
ftp>
```

Retrieving a file from the FTP server is equally easy: Type the `get` command followed by the name of the file that you want to retrieve from the FTP server, as in the following example:

```
ftp> get JDSC-0.5.9a.zip
local: JDSC-0.5.9a.zip remote: JDSC-0.5.9a.zip
200 PORT command successful
150-Connecting to port 35431
150 488.0 kbytes to download
##########################################################################
##########################################################################
##########################################################################
##########################################################################
##########################################################################
##########################################################################
##########################################################################
#################
226-File successfully transferred
226 0.105 seconds (measured here), 4.53 Mbytes per second
499668 bytes received in 0.12 secs (4217.0 kB/s)
ftp>
```

> **TIP** When sending or retrieving a file, you can give it a different name on the FTP server or your local machine (respectively), by specifying the new file name after the name of the one that you want to send or retrieve.

Once the file transfer is complete, you can terminate your connection to the FTP server and exit from the `ftp` command by typing the `quit` command, as in the following example:

```
ftp> quit
```

It doesn't get much simpler than that! The nice thing about learning to use the standard command-line `ftp` utility is that it is available on most systems (even from the Microsoft Windows command-line), and the commands are essentially the same everywhere. Learn once, use many, I always say.

Connecting to an FTP Server Using Graphical Clients

If you need to use FTP but would prefer a stand-alone graphical FTP client, a popular one that is available from the Ubuntu repositories is `gtk-gftp`, a GNOME FTP client that uses the GTK graphical interface. This isn't installed on an Ubuntu system by default, but is easy to install using the Synaptic Package Manager. Installing this package will create an entry on the Applications ➪ Internet menu called gFTP. This command makes it easy to graphically transfer files using FTP, and also enables you to bookmark FTP settings (hostname, username, password, and so on) just as you would do in your favorite Web browser. Figure 16.5 shows the `gtk-gftp` application being used to retrieve the same file used in the command-line examples.

FIGURE 16.5

Using the graphical FTP client, gtk-gftp

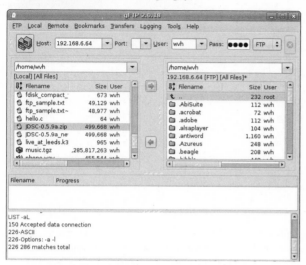

Accessing Shares on Remote Windows Systems

Your Ubuntu Linux system can easily access shared directories on Microsoft Windows systems (commonly known as *shares*) thanks to one of the most popular and useful open source software packages ever created, Samba (www.samba.org). Samba was originally written by Andrew Tridgell who has received numerous awards and accolades for it. Tridgell still works on it today, though thousands of others have contributed to Samba and it is now a team effort. See Chapter 32, "Setting Up a Samba Server," for a bit more background information on Samba.

Samba takes its name from the SMB (Server Message Block) protocol that is the original underlying protocol used for networked file sharing on Microsoft Windows systems. Tridgell created Samba in a massive feat of reverse engineering the protocol and how it worked, because Microsoft's specifications for SMB weren't publicly available (big surprise). Today, thanks largely to Tridgell and Samba, Microsoft has opened up the SMB specification, which is now part of its larger CIFS (Common Internet File System) specification.

As mentioned in the introduction to this part of the chapter, you can also use Samba to share files from a Linux system so that specified directories look like Windows shares and Windows users can access them. This requires that you set up a Samba server, which is explained in Chapter 32. This section focuses on accessing a shared Windows directory from the desktop of your Ubuntu Linux system and copying files to or from that Windows share.

Ubuntu's Places menu provides the Connect to Server command, which makes it easy to create an icon on your desktop for a Windows share and connect to that share using the Nautilus file manager. Selecting Places ➪ Connect to Server displays the dialog shown earlier in Figure 16.1. To specify that you want to connect to an FTP server that requires authentication, click the Service type menu at the top of this dialog and select the Windows share entry to display the dialog shown in Figure 16.6.

FIGURE 16.6

Identifying a Windows share to connect to

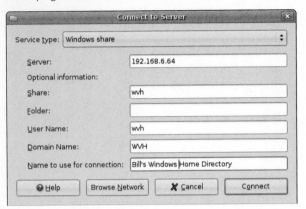

You must at least enter the name or IP address of the Windows server that hosts the share that you want to connect to. If you want to provide your own name for the desktop icon that this command will create, you can enter that in the Name to use for connection field, which can be handy because the default name of the icon is the name of the Windows server, and you may want to connect to multiple shares on the same server. You can also identify the name of the user that you want to connect as, the name of the Windows domain or workgroup that you want to connect as, and the share that you want to connect to, but all of this is optional—you'll be prompted for anything that you don't specify here when you attempt to connect. As you can see in Figure 16.6, I prefer to put as much information as possible here, but that's up to you. Click Connect to create a desktop icon for the Windows share that you have defined.

> **TIP**   If you look really closely, you'll see that the icon created for a Windows share by the Connect to Server dialog displays a little network connection beneath it, and displays a small red flag with the letters SMB inside it to its right. If you end up creating lots of files on your desktop and have really good eyesight, this makes it easy to identify the protocol used to connect to various directories. This can come in handy, especially if you also use the Connect to Server mechanism to connect to FTP servers, as explained earlier in this chapter.

Simply creating a desktop icon for a Windows share doesn't actually establish the connection. To do that, double-click on the appropriate desktop icon to open it. You will see a dialog that prompts you for any required information that you have not specified yet, as shown in Figure 16.7.

Once you enter any remaining information about the share that you want to connect to and the server on which it resides, a Nautilus file manager window appears which displays the contents of the default directory associated with the user that you are logged in as, as shown in Figure 16.8.

FIGURE 16.7

Completing authentication information for a Windows share

FIGURE 16.8

A connection to a Windows share in the Nautilus file manager

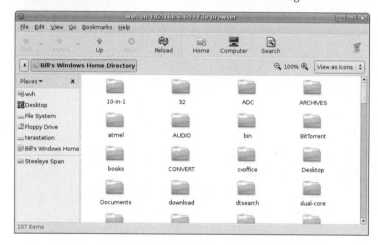

Once the Nautilus file manager displays, copying files in either direction uses the standard Nautilus and GNOME desktop conventions, as discussed in Chapter 5.

Once you are done accessing the Windows share, close the Nautilus file manager window. To discard the desktop icon, right-click on the icon for the Windows share and select Unmount Volume from the pop-up menu to sever the connection and discard the icon. If you want to reuse the share definition, you can simply leave the icon on your desktop when you log out — the next time that you log in, the icon will still be present, but you will have to re-authenticate to access the Windows share again.

Accessing NFS Directories from Linux Systems

Long before Microsoft Windows or the Apple Macintosh existed, Unix systems were sharing files over networks using a Network File System (NFS) that was originally developed by Sun Microsystems, Inc. in the early 1980s. Sun was smart enough to release the specifications for NFS to the known universe, and every other Unix system manufacturer with any common sense since then has also implemented support for NFS on their Unix and Unix-like systems. Today, most of those vendors are gone and even Sun's long-term future is cloudy, but NFS lives on as the default network filesystem and file sharing mechanism that you can find on any Unix or Unix-like system, such as Linux and Mac OS X.

Unfortunately, a whizzy graphical mechanism for mounting NFS filesystems isn't currently supported by the GNOME desktop's Connect to Server tool, so you'll have to mount remote NFS filesystems manually, using the command-line. And you may have thought you could get away with not reading Chapter 6! Luckily, mounting filesystems from the command-line is extremely easy to do. (The mechanism by which you export a filesystem from your local system via NFS is similarly easy, and is explained in Chapter 31, "Setting Up an NFS Server.")

NFS filesystems are identified by the name or IP address of the NFS server on which they live, a colon, and the name of the directory that the server is exporting. For example, 192.168.6.64:/home/wvh identifies the directory /home/wvh that is being exported by the NFS server whose IP address is 192.168.6.64. NFS filesystems are mounted on directories on your local Ubuntu system just like any other filesystem (as explained in Chapter 4).

To mount the remote NFS filesystem that I just mentioned, you therefore need to create a mount point for it. I always create these in the directory /mnt so that they're easily identified as temporarily mounted devices. For example, the following command creates a mount point called /mnt/nfs:

```
$ sudo mkdir /mnt/nfs
Password:
```

After providing your password, the mount point exists, so we can now mount the NFS directory using the standard Linux mount command, as in the following example:

```
$ sudo mount -t nfs 192.168.6.64:/home/wvh /mnt/nfs
```

At this point, you can verify that the directory is successfully mounted by either listing that directory or by simply using the df command, as in the following example:

```
$ df
Filesystem            1K-blocks       Used Available Use% Mounted on
/dev/hda1              77299808   40359464  33013660  56% /
varrun                  257968        136    257832   1% /var/run
varlock                 257968          4    257964   1% /var/lock
udev                    257968         96    257872   1% /dev
devshm                  257968          0    257968   0% /dev/shm
192.168.6.64:/home/wvh
                      160010496  151044928   8965568  95% /mnt/nfs
```

The mounted directory is now available so that you can access the files that it contains and create new files there. Of course, because NFS filesystems are Linux (or Unix) directories, you must have sufficient permissions to read and write files there. In most NFS environments, user identities are synchronized across systems so that you appear to be the same user on both the remote and local system. If this is not the case, you can always use the sudo command (if necessary) to copy files or directories to the NFS filesystem, as in the following example:

```
$ sudo cp resume.xml /mnt/nfs
```

Synchronizing user identities across multiple systems and understanding how Linux systems recognize users in general is discussed in Chapter 21, "Managing Users, Groups, Authentication, and Advanced Permissions."

Once you're done accessing the files in an NFS filesystem, you can unmount it using the standard Linux umount command, as in the following example:

```
$ sudo umount /mnt/nfs
```

Note that this command isn't "unmount," but umount. Why type that extra "n" if you don't have to?

Peer-to-Peer File Sharing on Ubuntu

Let's say that you have a tarball or ISO of the greatest open source software package ever, everyone who hears about it wants a copy, and you want to make it freely available to all users. The classic solution to this problem was for you to put it on your FTP or, more recently, Web server, and then to advertise its existence to the known universe. Regardless of how fast your servers are, how many you have, and how fast your connection to the Internet is, it's easy to spot the problem with this approach: Eventually too many people show up to download the file, consuming all of the resources on your site until new people who've just heard about your whizzy software package can't get to it anymore; the delivery of your files to the people who are already in the process of downloading them slows to a crawl; and your servers fall over from the load. It's the downloading equivalent of being mentioned on SlashDot (www.slashdot.org).

The key to this problem is that there is only one place to get the magic files and everyone who wants them has to get them there. The entire load for grabbing these magic files is dumped on that single site, which turns it from a one-stop-shopping experience into a huge bottleneck. Even if you have an arsenal of replicated servers serving up your files and you have the world's best load-balancing software managing the traffic, your resources are finite, while the load may be effectively infinite.

Peer-to-Peer (P2P) file sharing is an impressively cool solution to this problem. As mentioned in the introduction to this chapter, peer-to-peer (P2P) file sharing differs from traditional point-to-point file transfers in that P2P file transfers are essentially a community effort, a cooperative distribution network in which systems (peers) share files with each other without the user having to know which specific systems are involved in the transfer. Obviously, somebody has to know what hosts are sharing what files, or else no host would know where to get anything from, but there are some cool solutions to this problem. The legal Achilles heel of the pioneering P2P mechanism, Napster, was that it used a central database to track which peers were offering which files. Some legal idiots decided that this meant that Napster was effectively condoning all of the P2P traffic on the network, some of which involved sharing audio files that users might otherwise have had to pay for. They therefore forced Napster to shut down its central server, which effectively decapitated the original Napster network. Alas, poor Napster v1, I knew thee well.

Fortunately, performing a computer science autopsy of this "legal" fiasco has helped the second wave of P2P solutions come up with some great work-arounds. These primarily revolve around peers dynamically monitoring and querying other peers or a network in its entirety to find out who has the files that you're looking for. The key to the success of the next wave of P2P solutions has been, and will continue to be, the effective anonymity of which peer is sharing what with whom. Without directly querying each and every peer, you can never get a complete picture of a modern, anonymous P2P network. Which is a good thing.

Today, there are many popular P2P protocols, file-sharing networks, protocols, and clients. Some of the most popular are the following:

- **BitTorrent:** www.bittorrent.com
- **eDonkey2000:** www.edonkey2000.com
- **FastTrack (essentially Kazaa):** www.kazaa.com
- **Freenet:** http://freenet.sourceforge.net
- **Gnutella:** www.gnutella.com

The next two sections explain how to be part of the free speech revolution by installing and using P2P clients such as gtk-gnutella, a popular Linux client for the Gnutella file-sharing network, and gnome-btdownload, a simple but complete Linux client for BitTorrent downloads. As in the rest of this chapter, these sections focus on using client software to retrieve files, not on how to explicitly publish files from your system — you're sharing them while this is happening, of course, but the focus here is on retrieving them.

Installing and Using gtk-gnutella

The Gnutella network (not to be confused with Nutella, the yummy European hazelnut and chocolate spread) is a widespread, immensely popular P2P network. Many people do not realize that popular P2P applications such as LimeWire and BearShare are actually just Gnutella clients. One of the coolest things about Gnutella clients is their search feature, which I'll explain later and which makes it easy to query the entire network for shared files that match your search terms. As explained in the introduction to this section, the search feature does not consult a single centralized database because that would make it too easy to terminate Gnutella traffic. Instead, it uses a very cool friend-of-a-friend mechanism. Your query initially goes to a single Gnutella node, which passes on your original query to the other nodes it knows about, each of which passes on your original query to the other nodes it knows about, until much of the Gnutella network is buzzing with your search request.

Installing gtk-gnutella

Because not everyone wants or needs to do P2P file sharing, the gtk-gnutella client isn't installed by default on an Ubuntu Linux system. To install gtk-gnutella, start the Synaptic Package Manager from the System ➪ Administration menu, select Search, enter **gnutella** in the Search box that displays, and click Search. Once the search completes, scroll down in the list of packages in the new Gnutella category until you see gtk-gnutella, and right-click to select that item for installation from the pop-up menu, as shown in Figure 16.9.

Depending on what software you have previously installed on your Ubuntu system, a dialog may display that lists other packages that must also be installed, and asks for confirmation. If you see this dialog, click Mark to accept these related (and required) packages.

After you are finished making your selections, click Apply in the Synaptic toolbar to install gtk-gnutella on your system. Once the installation completes, you're ready to join the Gnutella network! See Chapter 20, "Adding, Removing, and Updating Software," for more detailed information on installing applications using the Synaptic Package Manager.

FIGURE 16.9

Installing gtk-gnutella in the Synaptic Package Manager

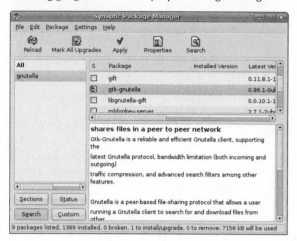

Using gtk-gnutella

Installing `gtk-gnutella` as described in the previous section creates a menu item on the Applications ⇨ Internet menu. To start `gtk-gnutella`, click the Gtk-Gnutella item on this menu, which starts the application and displays a window like the one shown in Figure 16.10.

FIGURE 16.10

The gtk-gnutella startup window

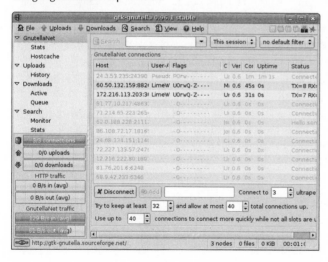

The first time that you start `gtk-gnutella`, it will create the `gtk-gnutella-downloads` directory in your home directory, which is where it will store the files that it downloads. This directory contains three subdirectories: `complete`, which is where successfully downloaded files are stored when a download completes; `incomplete`, which is where in-progress downloads are stored; and `corrupt`, which is where downloaded files that do not match Gnutella's official checksum for the files are stored. Files in the `corrupt` directory are probably bad, but just in case...

Aside from the standard menu bar, the most interesting parts of the `gtk-gnutella` screen shown in Figure 16.10 are the following:

- **graphical summary area (lower left):** An area that displays status information about the number of connected clients, the number of uploads and downloads in progress, the local HTTP (Web) traffic that the application sees, and the amount of Gnutella traffic it sees passing by on the network at the moment.

- **details window (upper left):** A window containing collapsible/expandable entries that enable you to get detailed information about any of the items that it lists: the state of the network, active and completed uploads, active and queued downloads, and the state of any searches that you have initiated.

- **search bar (upper right, just below the menu bar):** Enables you to search for files whose names match a specific sequence of characters.

- **connection status window (middle right):** Shows the status of any active connections, the results of a search when performing a search, and the status of any active downloads when you view active or queued downloads. The type of information displayed in this window depends on the item selected in the control window.

- **control window (bottom right):** Enables you to control the number of connections that are supported to and from your machine.

The interesting parts of `gtk-gnutella` are actually searching for something, seeing what matches you find, and then downloading the result. So let's first start a search. To demonstrate that there is plenty of legal and useful content out there, I'll search for "Linux ISO." To do this, put the cursor in the search field of the search bar, enter **Linux ISO**, and press return. The search begins, with any matches for the search string displaying in the connection status (now a search results) window. Once search results are displayed, you can see summary information about any of them by positioning the cursor over its name, as shown in Figure 16.11.

Once you've spotted a file that you want to download, you can select it for downloading by right-clicking on its name and selecting Download selected files from the pop-up menu, as shown in Figure 16.12.

Once you've started a download, you can view its status at any time by selecting the Downloads ⇨ Active entry in the details window. If the download is not listed there, it is queued, and you can select the Downloads ⇨ Queue entry in the details windows to see what it is waiting for. Figure 16.13 shows an in-progress download that is just beginning.

Search results in gtk-gnutella with detailed information

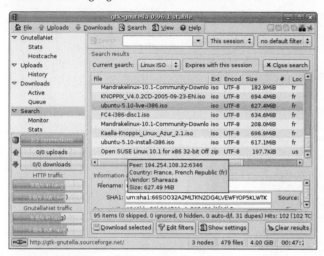

Initiating a download in gtk-gnutella

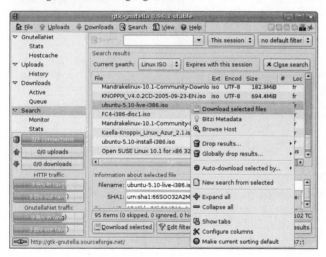

FIGURE 16.13

An in-progress download in gtk-gnutella

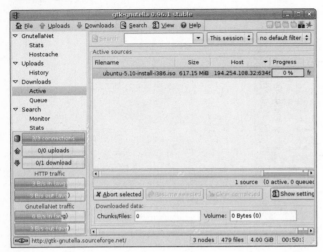

Many systems in the Gnutella network offer many files for downloading and will therefore match search requests, but may already be delivering as many downloads as they have been configured to deliver by their operators. You may have to wait a while for a download to move from queued to active status. Frankly, if I find several matches for a specific file that I'm looking for, I often begin downloading more than one of them to ensure that I can get the file as quickly as possible. Once one of them actually begins to download, you can terminate the others so that you don't waste Gnutella bandwidth.

> **TIP**   If you have problems getting `gtk-gnutella` to successfully download files, make sure that any firewall that you are running does not block TCP ports 5634, 6346, 6347, 6348, 6349, and 6355, which are the ports that are used by the current version of Gnutella. If you are seeing performance problems and are behind a configurable gateway or router, you may want to forward those ports from your external Internet interface directly to the host on which you are running your BitTorrent client. A general discussion of port forwarding on a variety of routers is available at `www.portforward.com/routers.htm`.

Using BitTorrent on Ubuntu

BitTorrent, originally written by Bram Cohen, has been around for a few years and is an incredibly popular protocol and tool for P2P file sharing. Bram's original BitTorrent software is GPL and was written in Python. Frankly, I still primarily use the command-line version of BitTorrent (`btdownloadheadless.py`) because "it just works." Don't worry, I'm not going to make you follow my lead here — though a version of the Python BitTorrent software is installed on every Ubuntu system, a simple graphical interface called `gnome-btdownload` is also installed, which is what I'll focus on in this section.

The special sauce in the BitTorrent P2P mechanism is the use of torrent files, which provide information about the files that are to be distributed as part of a *torrent* (the generic BitTorrent term for each collection of files that are shared as a group), and the use of a computer system that tracks the current activity related to a torrent (known to BitTorrent devotees as a *tracker*). Unlike Napster's old use of a central server, a BitTorrent tracker doesn't know anything about the contents of a torrent, but simply knows what peers are currently involved in downloading, uploading, and sharing a particular torrent. The tracker initially choreographs communications between any peers interested in a specific torrent — once peers are communicating with each other, the tracker is no longer necessary. As you'd expect, when initiating a torrent, at least one peer must provide a complete set of the files in the torrent, which is known as *seeding* in BitTorrent vernacular.

One interesting optimization in BitTorrent is that peers retrieve and share the files in a torrent in a random sequence of chunks. This means that, while many peers may be in the process of downloading the collection of files that make up a torrent, it's normal to expect that no two of them are sharing the same portions of those files. This makes torrents quite durable — even if the tracker and the host that is seeding a torrent goes away, it's quite possible that all of the peers together have a complete set of the files in the torrent — they all just have to trade missing chunks with each. This is known as a *distributed copy* in BitTorrent terms.

BitTorrent is a great piece of software, an excellent software distribution mechanism, and a good example of how P2P file sharing can help guarantee the free sharing of data of any kind over the net. It is also free. However, if you find it useful, you may want to consider donating funds to help guarantee its continued existence and development. I have. You can contribute to the future of free speech and free data on the net via PayPal at `http://bittorrent.com/donate.myt`.

Using gnome-btdownload

Because `gnome-btdownload` and the Python BitTorrent distribution are installed with a basic Ubuntu distribution, you don't have to do anything special to access or configure them. Unfortunately, no menu item is provided for `gnome-btdownload`, so you'll have to start it from an Ubuntu command-line such as the GNOME Terminal or an xterm. After starting `gnome-btdownload`, you'll see the initial dialog shown in Figure 16.14.

FIGURE 16.14

The initial gnome-btdownload dialog

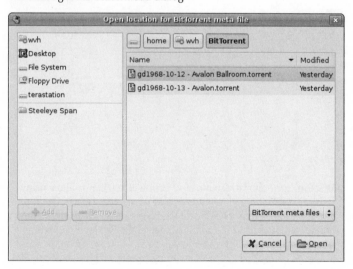

TIP If you find yourself using `gnome-btdownload` frequently, you may want to add a menu item for it, as explained in Chapter 5.

Use the dialog shown in Figure 16.14 to navigate to the directory that contains the torrent files that you have downloaded, select one, and click Open to begin downloading and sharing its contents. The dialog shown in Figure 16.15 displays.

FIGURE 16.15

Selecting a directory in which to save files

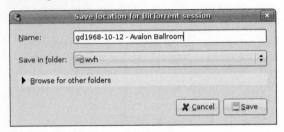

You can either save your files in the current directory (which, by default, is the directory that you were working in when you executed the `gnome-btdownload` command) or use this dialog to navigate to some other folder using the Browse for other folders control button. Click Save to begin saving the files that make up the torrent in the currently selected directory. The dialog shown in Figure 16.16 displays.

FIGURE 16.16

Downloading in progress in gnome-btdownload

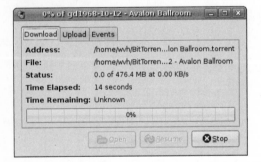

The dialog shown in Figure 16.16 enables you to monitor the status of your download, control how many peers you will share this file with (using the Upload tab), and monitor exactly what your client is doing at any given time (using the Events tab). The most interesting statistics are the Status entry, which shows the amount of the torrent that you've currently downloaded and the complete size of the files in the torrent, and the Time Remaining entry, which is an estimate of how long the download will take based on the current download rate, number of peers, and so on. Because the Time Remaining statistic changes based on the number of peers that are participating in the download, and because different peers can be configured to download/share at different rates, this statistic can drop dramatically as other peers join in.

TIP If you have problems getting BitTorrent to work at all, make sure that any firewall that you are running does not block TCP ports 6881-6999, which are the ports that are used by the current version of BitTorrent. If you are seeing performance problems and are behind a configurable gateway or router, you may want to forward those ports from your external Internet interface directly to the host on which you are running your BitTorrent client. Michael Ingram has a great article on solving slow download problems and configuring specific routers and gateways at www.slyck.com/news.php?story=493. A general discussion of port forwarding on a variety of routers is available at www.portforward.com/routers.htm.

Happy file sharing! If you find the gnome-btdownload interface too minimal for your tastes, a variety of other graphical BitTorrent clients are available in the Ubuntu repositories. Some of the best known of these are azureus, a Java-based client that also includes a tracker and can therefore be used to seed torrents; bittornado-gui, a fast and powerful but relatively lightweight client; and qtorrent, a graphical client that uses the QT graphical interface. KDE fans may be interested in ktorrent, a KDE-based BitTorrent client.

Finding Torrents

At this point, I hope that you're thinking, "Well, BitTorrent sounds like the best thing since sliced bread, but where do I get these torrents from?" Because BitTorrent doesn't provide the same sort of search features as P2P networks such as Gnutella, you have to have a torrent file to actually use it. You may have noticed that the torrent I used as an example in the previous section is a live recording by the Grateful Dead, who are well known for allowing fans to freely share their live concert recordings. A quick search on the net for "Grateful Dead" and "torrent" turns up zillions of hits, but that's hardly the most efficient search mechanism when looking for a live recording by your favorite band or some other freely-available downloads.

Luckily, many sites provide search engines that are specifically designed for finding torrents. Some of my favorites are the following:

- **BtBot:** www.btbot.com
- **isoHunt:** http://isohunt.com
- **Torrent Search:** www.torrentsearch.com
- **Torrent Spy:** www.torrentspy.com

Because BitTorrent is such an efficient P2P mechanism, many Linux distributions (including Ubuntu) provide torrents for their most recent distributions as well as supporting the standard, slow Web-based downloads. You can grab a torrent for your favorite Linux distribution. (I'm hoping that this is Ubuntu, but you may want to experiment with one of the Ubuntu derivatives such as Kubuntu or Xubuntu, or the Ubuntu Server. You can find links to sites that provide torrents for the latest Ubuntu releases at www.ubuntu.com/download.)

Getting More Information About BitTorrent

Because this is a general-purpose book about Ubuntu, not a bible for BitTorrent itself, this section has only scratched the surface of available information about BitTorrent. I'm betting that once you've started to use BitTorrent, you'll have additional questions or simply want to know more. Some great sources of dedicated information about BitTorrent are the following:

- **Official BitTorrent FAQ:** www.bittorrent.com/faq.myt. The FAQ from the BitTorrent mother ship.
- **Guide to Distributing Files via BitTorrent:** www.bittorrent.com/guide.myt. Useful if you want to package and distribute your own torrents.
- **Brian Dessent's FAQ:** www.dessent.net/btfaq. Though somewhat dated, this alternate FAQ still provides a good deal of useful information.

Summary

Business and academic environments typically provide file servers where centralized collections of corporate documents, project directories, and even supported software are stored. Many networked home computing environments do the same thing to provide a central location for family photos, music, and documents. This chapter began by explaining how to access remote file servers running on Microsoft Windows, Mac OS X, and Linux systems using software such as Samba and NFS. The last section of this chapter discussed peer-to-peer (p2p) file sharing on Ubuntu, the most popular and resource-friendly mechanism for sharing files that is in common use today.

Chapter 17 discusses how to retrieve and install files on consumer electronics devices such as iPods and other music players, digital cameras, and PDAs. The types of consumer electronics devices are basic accessories for most people today, but they aren't very useful if you can't update their contents or, in the case of a digital camera, retrieve your current photos to free up space for capturing your next vacation or family get-together.

Chapter 17

Consumer Electronics and Ubuntu

Linux is the embedded operating system of choice for many modern *embedded devices*. Embedded devices is the industry term for things that have computers or control systems running inside them. Twenty years ago, popular embedded devices were things like power plants, factories and assembly lines, and spacecraft. Today, the list still features those same technological chestnuts, but now also includes things like your car, your home gateway or router, your TiVo or other Digital Video Recorder (DVR), your Personal Digital Assistant (PDA), your MP3 or other digital audio player, and so on. Today, many consumer electronics devices contain a full-blown operating system to support their configuration and communication requirements.

Although the fact that Linux is the operating system of choice for most new embedded devices may not matter to you personally, it has a good deal of significance for you as a consumer and as a user of a desktop Linux distribution. There are a few major reasons for the popularity of Linux in the embedded world. The fact that Linux is free and therefore requires no payment of royalties or licensing costs is extremely important to embedded hardware vendors who are planning on making a few million devices. First, if they had to pay some sort of royalties on the operating system they used, that cost would ordinarily be something that they would have to pass on to the consumer (you and me). Second, the flexibility of Linux makes it easy to adapt to a huge number of devices, which means that the support in Linux for the device drivers that control those devices and their peripherals continues to expand. And finally, the openness of Linux makes it easy for Linux to access files stored in almost any modern type of filesystem and communicate with just about any other operating system. This is good news if, for example, a company is building a new digital audio player wants the freedom and power of Linux, but needs their customers to be able save and sync their personal audio collections to it from their Mac OS X or Microsoft Windows systems. Read and write support for popular Windows filesystems? It's in there. Support for USB connections, wireless connections, or serial ports? Free. I think that you see where I'm going here...

The fact that you and I are using Linux on the desktop puts that same power and flexibility in our hands. As you'll see in this chapter, you can talk to just about anything from a Linux system. Users of other operating systems require that the makers of specific consumer electronics devices or third-party software vendors provide the software that enables an operating system to talk to a specific device. Microsoft Windows users would find their iPods to be nicely designed paperweights if Apple didn't provide iTunes for Windows. PDA users who use Macs and Windows boxes would find their digital assistants to be remarkably deaf and dumb if Apple, Palm, and various third parties didn't provide synchronization software for them. Sometimes this software is free, and sometimes it costs money — but never the latter for you and me.

As you'll see in this chapter, your Ubuntu Linux system can talk to, sync, and exchange files and data with almost anything. In the world of Linux, all it really takes is a motivated hacker with the latest widget from Spacely Sprockets, and sooner or later you'll be able to download and install a free sprockinator package that will make it easy for you to keep that widget in sync with your Ubuntu Linux system. It may require a bit of tweaking to do so, but you can never beat the price.

Configuring Your System for Consumer Electronics Devices

The section of Chapter 13 on "Setting CD and DVD Preferences" explained how to configure your system's behavior when a blank, audio, or data CD and DVD is inserted using the System ➪ Preferences ➪ Removable Drives and Media Preferences dialog. CDs and DVDs may be the type of removable media that you'll use most frequently with your computer system, but consumer electronics devices are probably a close second. This same dialog provides tabs that enable you to configure how your system handles digital cameras, PDAs, digital audio players, and so on. How your system interacts with removable media of any sort is discussed in detail in Chapter 23, "Adding Hardware and Attaching Peripherals." The next few sections focus on how you can configure what your system does when you attach various types of consumer electronics devices to your Ubuntu system.

Configuring Digital and Digital Video Camera Recognition

Configuring how your system recognizes digital cameras and video records is done by selecting System ➪ Preferences ➪ Removable Drives and Media Preferences, and then selecting the Cameras tab, as shown in the dialog in Figure 17.1.

This dialog provides two settings that simplify working with digital still and video cameras:

- **Digital cameras:** Selecting the Import digital photographs when connected checkbox tells Ubuntu to automatically start the specified application when the system detects that a digital camera has been attached to the USB or FireWire ports. By default, the gnome-volume-manager-gthumb shell script and associated gthumb application are installed as part of a basic Ubuntu installation, and the shell script is selected as the application used to display and retrieve digital photos. You can specify another application or shell script by clicking Browse and navigating to that application in the Select program to import photos dialog that displays.

■ **Digital video cameras:** Selecting the Edit video when connected checkbox tells Ubuntu to automatically start the specified application when the system detects that a digital video camera has been attached to the USB or Firewire ports. No default application for editing video is installed as part of a basic Ubuntu installation. The most popular applications for retrieving and editing digital video are `dvgrab` and `Kino`, which you can install from an Ubuntu repository using `apt-get` or the Synaptic Package Manager, as described in Chapter 20, "Adding, Removing, and Updating Software."

Using the `gnome-volume-manager-gthumb` script and associated `gthumb` application with digital cameras is discussed later in this chapter, in the section entitled "Digital Cameras and Ubuntu," which also provides suggestions for how to work with cameras that are not recognized by this application.

<hr>

FIGURE 17.1

Settings for digital cameras and video recorders

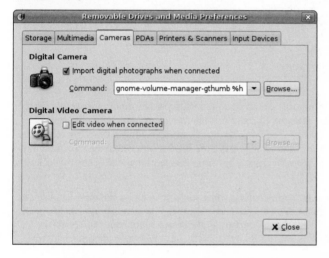

Configuring iPod and Other Digital Audio Player Recognition

Depending on the amount and type of storage that they provide, most digital audio players are recognized as USB (or Firewire) storage or media devices when attached to your Ubuntu Linux system. Configuring how and if your system recognizes removable drives and media is done by selecting System ⇨ Preferences ⇨ Removable Drives and Media Preferences, and then selecting Storage tab, as shown in the dialog in Figure 17.2.

FIGURE 17.2

Settings for removable storage and media

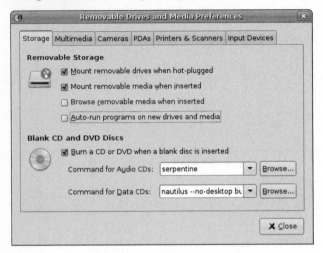

You will want to activate both the Mount removable drives when hot-plugged and Mount removable media when inserted options to provide the widest possible coverage for different types of digital audio players. If you are using a digital audio player other than an iPod (which your Ubuntu system can uniquely recognize, and can therefore handle in a specific way), you should also select the Browse removable media when inserted option — this may not be necessary for your device, but simplifies working with many digital audio players (and can't hurt).

TIP If you want to automatically start an application when you connect a portable media player to your Ubuntu system, select the Multimedia tab and make sure that an application is specified in the Portable Music Players section. By default, the Rhythmbox application is associated with portable media players, but you may want to change this to `gtkpod` or `gtkpod-aac`, which are discussed later in this chapter.

Configuring PDA and Smart Phone Recognition

The GNOME desktop recognizes PDAs running the Palm OS, PDAs running Microsoft Windows CE, PDAs running Microsoft Windows, Pocket PC edition, and most types of smart phones running any of these operating systems, and can be configured to automatically run specific applications when a device running the Palm OS or some teeny, tiny version of Windows is connected and you request synchronization. These are all considered to be PDAs by Ubuntu Linux. Configuring how and if your system recognizes different types of PDAs is done by selecting the System ➪ Preferences ➪ Removable Drives and Media Preferences, and then selecting the PDAs tab, as shown in the dialog in Figure 17.3.

FIGURE 17.3

Settings for PDA synchronization

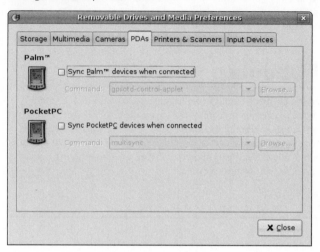

- **PDAs running Palm OS:** Select the Sync Palm devices when connected checkbox to activate a specified application when you request synchronization from your Palm. When this checkbox is selected, Ubuntu is configured to run the `gpilotd-control-applet` panel applet when a Palm Sync event is detected. You can specify another application or shell script to run on sync by clicking Browse and navigating to that application in the Select program to sync Palm device dialog that displays.

- **PDAs running Microsoft Windows:** Select the Sync PocketPC devices when connected checkbox to activate a specified application when you request synchronization from your PocketPC or other Windows CE device. When this checkbox is selected, Ubuntu is configured to run the `multisync` application when a PocketPC Sync event is detected. You can specify another application or shell script to run on sync by clicking Browse and navigating to that application in the Select program to sync PocketPC device dialog that displays.

Depending on the operating system that your PDA uses, you must configure the `gpilotd-control-applet` or `multisync` applications before you can successfully synchronize data in either direction. See "PDAs, Smart Phones, and Ubuntu" later in this chapter for details.

Configuring Flash Card and Other Digital Media Recognition

Some digital cameras and media players do not offer USB or Firewire ports for directly connecting those devices to your computer to extract or update them. However, such devices typically provide removable media in the form of a CompactFlash or SD card that you can attach to your system using a USB CompactFlash or SD card reader. Configuring how and if your system recognizes removable media is done by selecting the System ➪ Preferences ➪ Removable Drives and Media Preferences, and then selecting Storage tab, as shown earlier in this section in Figure 17.2.

You will want to activate the Mount removable media when inserted option to be able to automatically mount these types of storage cards. You may also want to activate the Browse removable media when inserted option when working with these types of media — this will automatically start the Nautilus file browser, displaying the contents of your card to simplify copying files to or from these types of storage media. See "Reading CompactFlash and SD Cards" later in this chapter for more information.

Digital Cameras and Ubuntu

If you've followed the instructions in the section entitled "Configuring Digital and Digital Video Camera Recognition" earlier in this chapter, your Ubuntu system is preconfigured to use the GNOME and a shell script named gnome-volume-manager-gthumb to use the gthumb image viewer to import, organize, and display your photographs. When you attach your digital camera to a USB port on your Ubuntu system and turn on the camera, your Ubuntu system displays the dialog shown in Figure 17.4, identifying the fact that the camera has been detected and asking how you want to proceed.

FIGURE 17.4

Your Ubuntu system detecting a digital camera

Click Import Photos to proceed or click Ignore to ignore the event. If you always want to automatically import photos whenever your camera is detected, you can select the Always perform this action checkbox before clicking Import Photos. If you click Import Photos, your Ubuntu system loads the appropriate drivers for your camera, and then loads the gthumb application preparatory to provide you with a few options before actually importing your photos. The dialog shown in Figure 17.5 displays.

FIGURE 17.5

The gthumb application preparing to import your photographs

The dialog shown in Figure 17.5 provides several options that you may want to consider before importing the photographs from your camera:

- **Destination:** Change where your imported photos are stored. By default, the gthumb image viewer will import your photographs into a subdirectory in your home directory that is named based on the date and time that you imported your photographs (for example, the directory 2006-05-18 - 12.31.43 would contain photographs that you imported on May 18, 2006 at 12:31:43 in the afternoon). You can change the location in which this directory is created by using the Destination drop-down menu to select or navigate to another location. I personally prefer to organize all of my photos in date/time subdirectories in a directory that I've named photos, to better organize my home directory, but you can choose whatever suits you best or simply accept the default value of your home directory.

- **Film:** Provide a name for this group of imported photos — as noted in the previous bullet, the names of the directories that gphoto creates to hold your imported photos are normally based on the date and time that you imported a set of photographs. The Film text area provides a free-form text-area in which you can enter your own name for the directory that will be created to hold the current set of photos that you are importing. This directory will be created in the location identified by your Destination setting.

■ **Categories:** Categorize the imported photos. The gthumb viewer provides several logical categories that you can use to help you locate conceptually related types of photos in the future. Click the Categories selector to display the dialog shown in Figure 17.6. This dialog enables you to select an existing category or define your own.

FIGURE 17.6

Categorizing photos during the import process

■ **Delete imported images from the camera:** Selecting this checkbox will purge the photos from your camera after they have been imported successfully, freeing up the storage on your camera for your next set of photos.

■ **Keep original filenames:** By default, gthumb will number each set of photos sequentially as it imports them, restarting this numbering each time you import photos and relying on the unique directories that it creates to differentiate them. If you want to keep the names of the photos as they were created on your camera (which are unique to each storage card used with your camera), you can select this checkbox to prevent gthumb from renaming the file names for your photos.

After making any changes to these settings that you want to use, click Import to import your photos or click Cancel to close the dialog without importing your digital photographs. If you click Import, a gthumb dialog like the one shown in Figure 17.7 displays once your photos have been successfully imported.

FIGURE 17.7

Categorized photos after the import process

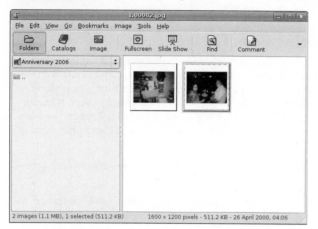

Be very careful when specifying that imported images be deleted after importing. I usually import photos once with the delete option deactivated and then verify that the import worked correctly before actually purging the images from my cameras and storage media. The `gnome-volume-manager-gthumb` script is quite simple, and only detects images that are organized in a specific way. If this script doesn't work for you and you're a bit adventurous, you may want to consider replacing it with another script such as Peter Parkkali's import-photos script, available at `http://pfp.iki.fi/gnome/import-photos`. Similarly, if your camera features removable storage media, you can always import and delete photos manually, as discussed later in this chapter in the section entitled "Reading CompactFlash and SD Cards."

> **TIP**   Many digital cameras automatically power down after a short period of time with no activity. This is great for saving battery life, but may cause import failures if the camera powers down while the `gthumb` application is waiting for input. If you are importing photos and `gthumb` creates files that do not contain your photos, try repeating the import process.

PDAs, Smart Phones, and Ubuntu

Personal Digital Assistants are a great tool for simple tasks such as managing calendars and making quick notes. If yours is network-enabled and your eyesight is good enough, it's also possible to browse the Web, send and receive e-mail, and even work with documents in a variety of popular desktop software formats, all from a device that you can easily tuck into a purse or shirt pocket. All of the software that you need to synchronize a PDA that runs the Palm OS comes preinstalled on your Ubuntu system, and the software to synchronize a Microsoft Windows for PocketPC or Microsoft Windows CE PDA is just a repository away. The next two sections discuss how to install, configure, and use the software that you'll need to synchronize almost any PDA with the data stored on your Ubuntu Linux system.

> **TIP** If you are going to be synchronizing PDAs using a serial port, you must be a member of the dialout group on your Ubuntu system. You can list the groups to which you belong by running the `groups` command at any Ubuntu command prompt. For information about adding users to groups, see Chapter 21, "Managing Users, Groups, Authentication, and Advanced Permissions."

Configuring and Synchronizing Palm OS Devices

As discussed in "Configuring PDA and Smart Phone Recognition" earlier in this section, a standard Ubuntu Linux installation includes a panel applet called `gpilot`. (This application is also sometimes referred to as `gnome-pilot`, its package name, or as `pilot-link`.) The section of Chapter 5 entitled "Customizing Panel Contents" explained how to add an applet to the panel—in a nutshell, click on the panel, select the applet that you want to add from the dialog that displays, and drag it to the panel location where you want it to appear. The panel applet synchronizing with PDA running the Palm OS is called "Pilot Applet," and is located in the utilities section of the Add to Panel dialog.

Once you add the `gpilot` applet to your panel, you'll need to configure how it communicates with your Palm.

> **TIP** The first time that you start the `gpilot` applet, it displays a wizard that walks you through the configuration process. These steps are the same as those discussed in this section and occur in the same sequence. This section discusses them as manual steps because the `gpilot` wizard only runs the first time that you start `gpilot`—if you ever need to reconfigure or modify your synchronization settings, you'll need to do that manually, as described in this section.

To configure your synchronization settings, click the `gpilot` icon in the panel. The dialog shown in Figure 17.8 displays.

FIGURE 17.8

Configuring synchronization with Palm OS PDAs

Before doing anything, you must verify and possibly define the connection to your PDA. Your alternatives are Serial, USB, IrDA (Infrared), and Network connections. If you're using a serial or USB connection to attach PDA to your Ubuntu system, attach the PDA to your Ubuntu system. Then, regardless of the type of connection that you are using, turn on the PDA and wait a few moments for your Ubuntu system to create any device nodes that are necessary. Finally, click the Devices Tab and click Add to define the entry for how the gpilot applet will communicate with your PDA. The dialog shown in Figure 17.9 displays.

FIGURE 17.9

Configuring device settings for communicating with Palm OS PDAs

Select the appropriate communication Type on the screen, and select an appropriate Port for communicating with the PDA. Unless you are using a serial connection, you can simply select /dev/pilot as the Port — if you are using a serial port, you should select the appropriate port, usually /dev/ttyS0.

TIP The default name for the device you are using is Cradle — if you are going to be synchronizing multiple PDAs with your Ubuntu system, you may want to change this name to something that uniquely identifies each PDA.

Click OK to save these settings and return to the dialog shown in Figure 17.8. Next, click the Pilots tab and click Add to provide user information about your connection to the PDA. The dialog shown in Figure 17.10 displays.

FIGURE 17.10

Setting user information for your Palm PDA

Click Get from pilot to retrieve your user name and identification information from the PDA. On your PDA, start the HotSync application and press the Sync button when you see a `gpilot` dialog instructing you to do so. Your PDA will exchange user information with your Ubuntu system, as shown in Figure 17.11.

FIGURE 17.11

User information retrieved from your Palm PDA

The last step in the configuration process is to define the types of information that you want to synchronize between your Ubuntu system and your Palm PDA. Each type of information that you want to synchronize is known as a *conduit*. The `gpilot` applet comes with a variety of predefined conduits that know how to communicate with various Ubuntu Linux applications, but all of these conduits are initially deactivated. To activate selected conduits, click the Conduits tab. The dialog shown in Figure 17.12 displays.

FIGURE 17.12

Defining the information to sync with your Palm PDA

The conduits provided by the `gpilot` applet are the following:

- **Backup:** Backs up all of the databases on your PDA to the backup location selected on the Pilots tab.
- **EAddress:** Synchronizes address book information between your PDA and the Evolution mailer discussed in Chapter 8.
- **ECalendar:** Synchronizes calendar information between your PDA and the Evolution mailer discussed in Chapter 8.
- **EMemos:** Synchronizes the memo list between your PDA and the Evolution mailer discussed in Chapter 8.
- **EToDo:** Synchronizes the TODO list between your PDA and the Evolution mailer discussed in Chapter 8.
- **Expense:** Extracts data in various formats from your PDAs expenses database.
- **File:** Installs specific files on the PDA.
- **MAL:** Synchronizes PDA data with AvantGo (`www.avantgo.com`) information.
- **MemoFile:** Synchronizes your PDA memos to local files on your Ubuntu system.
- **Sendmail:** Sends e-mail queued on the PDA using the sendmail application on your Ubuntu system.
- **Test:** Tests communication between the PDA and your desktop system. Useful for diagnosing synchronization problems.
- **Time:** Synchronizes the time on your PDA with that on your Ubuntu system. This conduit only works on PDAs running Palm OS 3.3 or better.

All of these conduits can be either disabled (as they are by default) or enabled, in which case they can be configured by clicking the Settings button, which displays a dialog like the one for EAddress synchronization shown in Figure 17.13.

FIGURE 17.13

Defining conduit-specific settings

The Settings dialog for any configurable conduit provides the following synchronization options:

- **Action:** The status of the conduit. When a conduit is enabled, you can select Disabled to turn it off; Synchronize, which supports bi-directional data exchange with the PDA; and Copy to pilot which simply enables you to clone the data from your desktop applications to the PDA.

- **One Time Action:** Enables you to specify the action that will occur for a conduit the next time that you synchronize with the PDA. Your options are None to do nothing the next time that you sync your PDA; Synchronize, which supports bi-directional data exchange with the PDA; and Copy to pilot which simply enables you to clone the data from your desktop applications to the PDA.

Other conduits provide other settings that are relevant to the type of data that you are exchanging. For example, the EAddress conduit shown in Figure 17.13 lets you identify the address book that you want to synchronize with, whether or not you want to sync private data as well as public address information, and which PDA address book you want to update or use.

Once you've configured the `gpilot` applet, actually synchronizing with your PDA is easy. Connect the PDA to your Ubuntu system, turn it on, start the HotSync (or other) synchronization application, and press the Sync button. You will see a dialog like that shown in Figure 17.14 while synchronization occurs.

FIGURE 17.14

The synchronization process

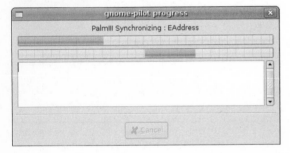

That's all there is to it — congratulations! If you have problems with `gpilot` or simply want to explore alternatives, my first suggestion is to try the `multisync` application described in the next section, installing the Palm Sync plug-ins to enable it to synchronize data with Palm devices. The `multisync` package is an extremely powerful, flexible solution for synchronizing your Ubuntu Linux desktop with almost anything short of your stove and refrigerator.

If you want to experiment with other open source, Palm-centric synchronization applications, the Ubuntu repositories provide two other Palm OS synchronization applications that you may be interested in experimenting with. These are `jpilot`, a graphical, Java-based alternative to the Palm Desktop that comes from your PDA vendor, and `kpilot`, a KDE-based graphical synchronization application. Of these, `jpilot` is nice because it is completely independent of GNOME and KDE and therefore works identically in both environments. However, my favorite of the two is `kpilot` — even though installing it will drag along the entire base KDE libraries, it's an excellent application that is quite user-friendly and therefore easy to use (as you'd expect from the KDE folks). Its primary downsides are that it focuses on the KDE Office suite and therefore does not currently sync with all of the information from GNOME applications such as the Evolution mailer, and the fact that it is in the process of being replaced by KitchenSync from the OpenSync folks (www.opensync.org).

Synchronizing Data with Microsoft Windows Devices

This section discusses how to synchronize PDAs and smart phones running Microsoft Windows, Pocket PC edition, or Microsoft Windows CE with your Ubuntu Linux system. The application required to do this, multisync, is an incredibly powerful and flexible application that uses a plug-in framework, which makes it simple to support multiple shrunk-down flavors of Microsoft Windows for mobile devices, and also enables it to support syncing with devices running Palm OS, PDAs running Linux such as the Sharp Zaurus, and almost every other modern PDA. The home page of the multisync project is http://multisync .sourceforge.net/news.php.

> **TIP** Support for syncing to a Windows-Based PDA using multisync is very fragile, in my experience. Ironically, I have had far better and more consistent results syncing using a traditional 9-pin serial cradle as opposed to a USB cradle — I used a serial cradle in this example because I could not get my USB cradle to work with my iPaq. Different versions of multisync and its synchronization plug-ins each seem to have their own quirks. This section was tested with my favorite Windows-Based PDA, an iPaq 3650 running Windows CE 3.0.11171, which is my favorite PDA because it is easy to install Linux on. Other Windows-Based PDAs probably have different quirks. Always remember that search engines like Google and Clusty are your friends.

The multisync package is not installed by default as part of a standard Ubuntu installation, primarily because of its flexibility and the number of associated plug-in packages. It is difficult to anticipate which set(s) of plug-ins any given user will want to install to suit the requirements of the PDA that they know and love, so it's left to us to install multisync if we want (or need) to use it. Luckily, that's a simple enough task on Ubuntu Linux, so let's get started!

> **NOTE** The successor to multisync is the OpenSync project, which provides a more generalized framework for synchronizing with a wide variety of devices, applications, and protocols using a more easily extended plug-in model. For more information about OpenSync, see www.opensync.org. Debian packages for the OpenSync library, a new version of multisync (required), and new plug-ins are available there, but are still being tested and are not officially ready for prime time. If you want to switch to OpenSync, you may want to build the latest and greatest "version" directly from its source code, which is available at www.opensync.org/wiki/download.

Installing Multisync, Plug-ins, Libraries, and Related Tools

To install multisync, related plug-ins, and associated tools and libraries, start the Synaptic Package Manager from the System ➪ Administration menu, select Search, enter **multisync** in the Search box that displays, and click Search. Once the search completes, scroll down in the list of packages in the new multisync category until you see the multisync package itself, and right-click to select that item for installation from the pop-up menu. Figure 17.15 shows the multisync package being selected for installation.

> **TIP** You must have enabled the universe repository to install the multisync application. See Chapter 20, "Adding, Removing, and Updating Software," for information about adding and enabling other repositories.

FIGURE 17.15

Installing multisync and related packages

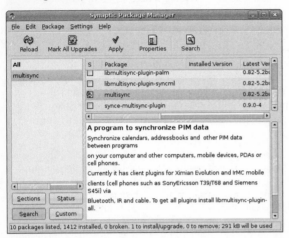

You will also need to select the packages that contain any plug-ins that you will use to synchronize data with your PDA. At a minimum, you should select the `libmultisync-plugin-all` package, which contains all of the standard plug-ins used with multisync (which includes the `libmultisync-plugin-evolution` package so that you can synchronize data to/from the evolution mailer), and the `synce-multisync-plugin` package that is required for synchronizing with devices running Windows CE rather than Windows PocketPC edition. You should also scroll through the list of available multisync-related packages and look for any that are related to the specific type of PDA that you are using, the operating system that it runs, or unique synchronization mechanisms such as SyncML.

Depending on what software you have previously installed on your Ubuntu system and what you select in Synaptic, dialogs may display that list other packages that must also be installed, and asking for confirmation. If you see such dialogs, click Mark to accept these related (and required) packages.

Next, search for "synce" in Description and Name in the Synaptic Package Manager and mark the `librra0-tools`, `synce-dccm`, and `synce-serial` packages for installation.

After you are finished making your selections, click Apply in the Synaptic toolbar to install multisync and friends on your system.

TIP   As packages are installed, Synaptic displays a dialog that enables you to configure the `synce-serial` package. By default, its Serial Interface field displays the device associated with a USB cradle connection. If you are using an old-school 9-pin serial connection (which is the only thing that works for me on my iPaq, you will want to change this field to specify the Serial Interface device `/dev/ttyS0`. You do not need to change any of the other entries. If you subsequently want to change them, you can do so by using `sudo` to execute the `synce-serial-config` command, providing the correct values for your environment.

Once the installation completes, you're ready to sync (after the obligatory configuration step, of course).

See Chapter 20, "Adding, Removing, and Updating Software," for more detailed information on installing applications using the Synaptic Package Manager.

Defining Synchronization Pairs

Known as conduits in the Palm environment, synchronization pairs are sets of input and output plug-ins that define each type of synchronization that you want to perform. Although this provides a very flexible mechanism for configuring the exact types of synchronization that you want to occur, this also means that multisync requires a bit more configuration than applications such as those used to sync with Palm OS devices, as described earlier in this chapter. This section explains how to create a synchronization pair that enables you to synchronize your PocketPC or CE address book with the one used by the Evolution mailer on your Ubuntu Linux system. You will almost certainly want to create additional synchronization pairs, but the set and number of synchronization pairs that you will want to create depends on both the type of PDA that you're using and the application data that you care about synchronizing.

Installing multisync on your Ubuntu system creates the Applications ➪ Accessories ➪ Multisync menu item, which you can use to start multisync. Selecting this menu item starts multisync, which displays the initial multisync dialog shown in Figure 17.16.

FIGURE 17.16

The initial multisync dialog

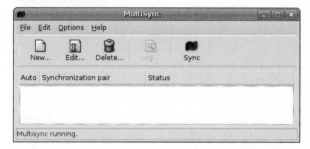

Click new to begin defining a new synchronization pair, which displays the dialog shown in Figure 17.17.

FIGURE 17.17

Defining source and target plug-ins

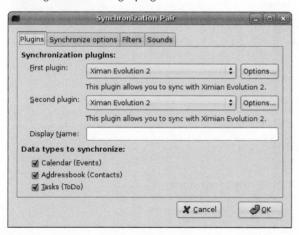

Since you're synchronizing from Evolution to your PDA, select SynCE plug-in from the drop-down Second plug-in list. Now, define the details of the portions of Evolution that you want to synchronize to the PDA. Though the bottom of the dialog shown in Figure 17.17 identifies that you want to sync the Calendar, Addressbook, and Tasks lists, you'll need to define the names of the specific Calendar, Addressbook, and Task (ToDo) lists that multisync should sync with. Click Options beside the First plug-in entry to display the dialog shown in Figure 17.18.

NOTE When syncing with Evolution, the names of alternate Calendars, Addressbooks, and Tasks lists are shown in this dialog only after you have configured the Evolution mailer on your system. For information about configuring Evolution, see Chapter 8.

FIGURE 17.18

Identifying specific synchronization targets

When this dialog first displays, it shows entries for No Calendar, No Addressbook, and No Tasks list. Click the drop-down lists for each of Calendar, Addressbook, and Tasks, and select the specific list that you want to synchronize. This is usually the Personal list, as shown in Figure 17.18. Click OK to save the selected list and return to the dialog shown in Figure 17.17. Click OK to close this dialog and return to the main multi-sync dialog, which should now look something like Figure 17.19.

FIGURE 17.19

The main multisync dialog after defining a synchronization pair

Our new synchronization pair is now configured, so it's time to actually synchronize some data!

Synchronizing Devices Using Multisync

Once you've installed the multisync software and configured one or more synchronization pairs, synchronizing your Ubuntu desktop system with your Windows Pocket PC or CE PDA is quite straightforward.

First, use sudo to run the sync-serial-config tool from an Ubuntu command-line to define the connection to your iPaq's cradle, as in the following example:

```
$ sudo synce-serial-create /dev/ttyS0
You can now run synce-serial-start to start a serial connection
```

This example defines the PDA as being connected to my first serial port — if yours is connected via USB, you would use a device name like /dev/ttyUSB0. (You can use the command tail /var/log/messages to identify the serial port to which your PDA is connected.) If you see any other message than the one shown here, there was a problem establishing the connection. Check that you've identified the device associated with the PDA's cradle correctly, and try reseating the PDA in its cradle.

Next, start the dccm daemon, which handles the connection to your PDA, starting the PPP daemon to communicate with the PDA and ensuring that it stays alive as long as necessary. To do this, simply execute the dccm command from the command line as yourself, not using sudo. The dccm command starts in daemon mode, and immediately appears to exit. You can verify that it is running using a command like ps alxww | grep dccm, as in the following example:

```
$ ps alxww | grep dccm
1  1000 16371    1 16  0  1928  780 -       Ss  ?      0:00 dccm
0  1000 16771 16431 16  0  2876  800 pipe_w S+  pts/2  0:00 grep dccm
```

Next, use sudo to execute the synce-serial-start command. This displays output like the following:

```
$ sudo synce-serial-start
synce-serial-start is waiting for your device to connect.
```

Unless you reconfigured or disabled system sounds on your PDA, you should hear a chime as it connects to the Linux system. If you don't hear this and have not reconfigured system sounds on your PDA, remove and reseat the PDA in its cradle.

TIP Once connected, you can use the synce-pstatus command to get information about your PDA, such as the version of Windows that is installed, and so on. The successful execution of this command will also verify that your PDA and Linux system are connected correctly. The output of this command looks like the following (shortened so as to show just the essentials):

```
$ synce-pstatus
Version
=======
Version:   3.0.11171 (Merlin: Pocket PC 2002)
Platform:  3 (Windows CE)
Details:   ""

System
======
Processor architecture: 5 (ARM)
Processor type:         2577 (StrongARM)
Page size:              0x10000
[additional output trimmed]
```

Next, start the ActiveSync application on your PDA (Start ⇨ ActiveSync), which should display a status message saying that it is connected.

Then start the `multisync` application by selecting Applications ⇨ Accessories ⇨ Multisync, make sure that the synchronization pair that you selected is highlighted, and press the Sync button. The Status field will display various messages as it connects and synchronizes your PDA. After a few moments, congratulations — you're in sync!

> **TIP**   If you have problems using the `multisync` application, try starting it from an Ubuntu command line as `/usr/bin/multisync` instead of using the menu item. The `multisync` application produces a good deal of verbose output that you'll be able to see in your terminal window, which should help you diagnose the problem.

iPods, Other Digital Audio Players, and Ubuntu

Digital audio players of various sorts have largely replaced other portable music players such as cassette decks and CD players. Digital audio players don't skip, are extremely small, require little power, and are hard to damage because they have few moving parts. On the other hand, when those moving parts are a disk drive and the drive goes bad, that damage is usually fatal — which makes it all the more important to have backups of your digital audio collection on your desktop machine, where it is safer (and where you hopefully have more disk space).

This section explains how to work with different types of digital audio players, a huge universe of devices that I have neatly divided into iPods and "not iPods." The next section explains how to use easily-installed software called gtkpod to copy files, music, create playlists, and do just about anything else with your iPod. The section after that explains how to work with other types of digital audio players.

ID3 Tag Editing on Ubuntu

As discussed in Chapter 13, most of the popular audio file formats such as MP3 support ID3 tags to provide information about file contents such as the artist, album title, song title, date recorded, and so on. All digital audio players can extract and display this information from supported audio file formats, and most use it to enable you to sort, search, and organize the files on a digital audio player. Before transferring audio files to your audio player, you should verify that they have valid ID3 tags, or else it may be hard to figure out exactly who performs `Track03.mp3`. You can usually verify the ID3 tag information by simply playing your audio files in a graphical audio application such as Rhythmbox or xmms on your Ubuntu system, because these applications automatically display ID3 information as they play each audio file.

Most CD-ripping applications will automatically fill out ID3 tag information during the ripping process, but you may occasionally encounter a CD that is not in the Internet CD databases, and for which you will therefore have to manually supply ID3 information. The Ubuntu repositories provide several applications for filling out or updating ID3 and ID3v2 tags. Good candidates from the Ubuntu repositories are `id3`, `id3v2`, and `id3tool`, all of which are command-line utilities; `mp3info`, a terminal-oriented interactive application; and kid3, a graphical, KDE-based ID3 tag editor. Installing kid3 requires installation of all of the KDE libraries and so on, but you also get the traditional KDE user-friendliness and ease-of-use.

Working with an iPod from Ubuntu

Apple Computer could conceivably be a footnote today were it not for Mac OS X and, more relevant to this section, the runaway success of its iPod digital audio player and attendant iTunes applications and music store. The iPod is a great example of what happens when people who understand industrial design meet people who understand software and usability. In many households, the iPod has replaced the automobile as the device most likely to be buffed, polished, and accessorized.

That said, there are some downsides to the software side of the iPod. First, it supports odious digital rights management song formats, which are designed to prevent users from freely reusing the music that they have purchased. Secondly, iPods that have disk drives can be formatted using either the Macintosh HFS filesystem or the Microsoft Windows filesystem. Macs (and Ubuntu Linux systems, of course) can read both types of filesystems, but Microsoft Windows systems can only understand the latter. Even though these are conceptual and political problems for some people, the bottom line is that it's hard to argue with success. However, more importantly, the iTunes application, which is the default software from Apple Computer that is used to managing music on an iPod, isn't available for Linux. However, as a famous Linux person once said, "We don't need no steenking iTunes." As you'll see throughout this section, the free, open source `gtkpod` application (GIMP Tool Kit iPod) is an excellent replacement for iTunes as far as I'm concerned, doing everything I've ever wanted to do with my iPods.

> **NOTE** Although `gtkpod` is a replacement for iTunes as far as synchronizing music and creating playlists goes, it does not (of course) enable you to buy music from Apple's online music store. Music purchased from the iTunes store is protected with DRM software, so is conceptually evil in the first place. I have purchased sample tunes there for experimentation purposes, but in general, I get my music by ripping CDs that I have purchased, and then dumbing down my OGG files to MP3 so that my iPod can play them. This section explains how to move music, playlists, and other data to/from your iPod and create playlists using `gtkpod`. For information about how to work with DRM-protected m4p files on a Linux system and via `gtkpod`, see sites such as `http://all-streaming-media.com/streaming-media-faq/faq-playing-DRM-protected-m4p-AAC-Apple-iTunes-files.htm` or search the Web for keywords like "Linux iTunes " or "Linux gtkpod DRM."

You may be wondering why you need to install a separate `gtkpod` application to work with audio files on the iPod, when Rhythmbox already serves as a central digital audio media manager. iPods are indeed being integrated into Rhythmbox, and the version of Rhythmbox delivered with the initial Ubuntu Dapper release can read from an iPod and play iPod playlists. Rhythmbox will soon support iPods in both read and write mode, but for now, `gtkpod` is the best graphical solution available for both reading and writing to iPods in my opinion. It is stable, readily available in the Ubuntu archives, and has been around for a few years, so it is well-tested. The `gtkpod` application will always be an excellent alternative to Rhythmbox, and is well worth learning if you have to use Linux systems other than Ubuntu, which do not provide suitable versions of Rhythmbox.

Installing gtkpod

To install the `gtkpod` application used to work with your iPod, start the Synaptic Package Manager from the System ➪ Administration menu, select Search, enter **iPod** in the Search box that displays, select Description and Name, and click Search. Once the search completes, scroll down in the list of packages in the new iPod category until you see the `gtkpod` package, and right-click to select that item for installation from the pop-up menu. Figure 17.20 shows the `gtkpod` package being selected for installation.

> **TIP** If you have music that you purchased from the iTunes music store that is in Apple's AAC DRM-protected format, you may want to install the `gtkpod-aac` package rather than the `gtkpod` package. The `gtkpod-aac` package claims support for AAC DRM-protected music, which I no longer have any of.

FIGURE 17.20

Installing gtkpod

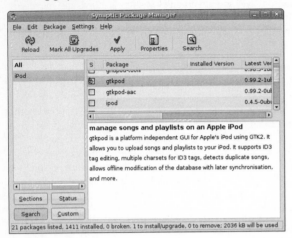

Depending on what software you have previously installed on your Ubuntu system and what you select in Synaptic, dialogs may display that list other packages that must also be installed, and ask for confirmation. If you see such dialogs, click Mark to accept these related (and required) packages.

After you are finished making your selections, click Apply in the Synaptic toolbar to install gtkpod (or gtkpod-aac) on your system. Once the installation completes, you're ready to start managing your iPod from your Ubuntu Linux desktop.

See Chapter 20, "Adding, Removing, and Updating Softwared," for more detailed information on installing applications using the Synaptic Package Manager.

Attaching Your iPod

Before attaching your iPod to your Ubuntu Linux system with a USB or Firewire cable, make sure that you followed the instructions in the section entitled "Configuring iPod and Other Digital Audio Player Recognition" earlier in this chapter. When you attach your iPod to your Ubuntu system, it will show up as a removable storage device, it will automatically be mounted at /media/ipod, and a desktop icon for it will automatically be created.

WARNING   When you attach an iPod to your Linux system, its screen will display an international No symbol and a Do not disconnect! message. Believe it. Follow the instructions in the section called "Safely Disconnecting Your iPod" later in this chapter, to safely remove your iPod without risking damage to its disk and the files that it contains.

If your iPod is successfully detected by your Ubuntu system, attaching it will also start the Rhythmbox application that, as mentioned earlier, provides the ability to play music stored on your iPod and will eventually support writing to your iPod. If you are going to be creating playlists or transferring new music to your iPod using `gtkpod`, you can simply close the Rhythmbox application. If you just want to play music that is stored on your iPod, there's no need to start `gtkpod`—you can just use Rhythmbox.

If you do not see the iPod icon on your desktop and are sure that you followed the instructions in the section entitled "Configuring iPod and Other Digital Audio Player Recognition," see Chapter 22, "Backing Up and Restoring Files," for general debugging and troubleshooting tips. If you see the desktop icon but have problems writing to your iPod after attaching it, you should check the device nodes that are created for it from the command line. First, check where it is mounted by using the `df` and `ls -l` commands, as in the following example:

```
$ df | grep ipod
/dev/sda2              19448804     275924   19172880    2% /media/ipod
$ ls -al /dev/sda*
brw-rw---- 1 root plugdev 8, 0 2006-05-22 16:04 /dev/sda
brw-rw---- 1 root plugdev 8, 1 2006-05-22 16:04 /dev/sda1
brw-rw---- 1 root plugdev 8, 2 2006-05-22 16:04 /dev/sda2
```

Next, verify that you are a member of the `plugdev` group by using the `groups` command from the command line, as in the following example:

```
$ groups
wvh adm dialout cdrom floppy audio dip video plugdev lpadmin scanner
admin
```

If your iPod is mounted as `/media/ipod`, is owned by the `plugdev` group, and you are a member of the `plugdev` group, all is well, and you can skip the rest of this section.

However, if your iPod is being mounted at some other mount point or is owned by some other group (which might be the `disk` group), you may need to add yourself to that group. The `disk` group is the Ubuntu permissions group that is used to grant read/write access to standard disk devices. To add yourself to this group, execute the following command from any Ubuntu command line, where `username` is your login name:

```
$ sudo adduser username disk
```

This step is rarely necessary, and actually is just a workaround for occasional problems that I've encountered in the past. This can solve several possible problems, but is truly a last resort. Note, however, that this gives you read/write access to any device that is owned by the `disk` group, so you should be careful! For more information about Ubuntu groups, see Chapter 21, "Managing Users, Groups, Authentication, and Advanced Permissions."

Using gtkpod

Installing `gtkpod` on your Ubuntu system creates the Applications ➪ Sound and Video ➪ gtkpod menu item to help you remember the somewhat cryptic name of this application. Selecting this menu item starts `gtkpod`, which displays the initial dialog shown in Figure 17.21.

If your iPod was mounted and accessed successfully, it should be listed in the pane at the left of the gtkpod window. To see the actual contents of your iPod and begin working with it, select its name from this pane. The other gtkpod windows will update to show the contents of your iPod, as shown in Figure 17.22.

FIGURE 17.21

The gtkpod startup screen

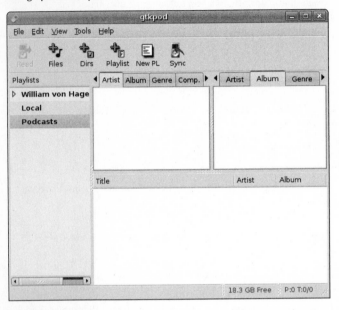

FIGURE 17.22

The contents of an iPod in gtkpod

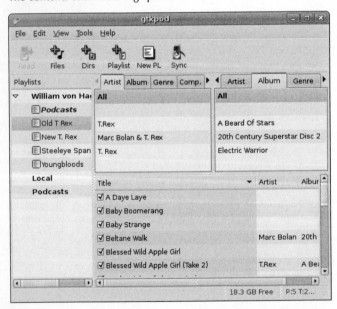

If you do not see your iPod listed in the left gtkpod pane, select the Edit menu's Edit Preferences command, which displays the dialog shown in Figure 17.23. Verify that the entry in the iPod Mount Point field is the directory where your iPod is actually mounted, and change it if necessary. If you change this field, you will have to exit from and restart gtkpod to have it check the new mount point. You may also have to click the Read icon on the gtkpod toolbar to force the gtkpod application to read the database information from an iPod that is mounted in a new location.

FIGURE 17.23

Verifying the mount point for an iPod in gtkpod

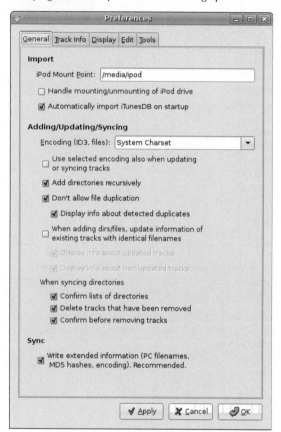

The next few sections discuss how to do some common tasks with gtkpod. You can, of course, do much more — after all, there are entire books on iTunes — but the suggestions in the following sections will get you started and are the most common tasks that I do in gtkpod.

Adding Music to your iPod

You can add MP3 files to your iPod in two different ways, either as single files or by adding complete directories of MP3 files. To add single files to your iPod, click the Files button in the gtkpod menu bar to display the dialog shown in Figure 17.24.

FIGURE 17.24

Adding single MP3 files to your iPod

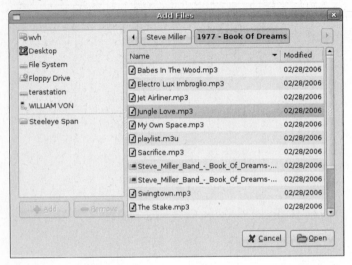

Once this dialog displays, navigate to the directory containing the file that you want to add, select that file, and click Open. That file will be added to your iPod, and the Artist and Album information will be added to the iPod (if it is present in ID3 tags in the audio file), as shown in Figure 17.25.

More commonly, you will want to add all of the audio files associated with a single album to your iPod at one time after you've ripped your latest CD acquisition. To do this, click the Dirs button to display the dialog shown in Figure 17.26.

FIGURE 17.25

Updated Artist and Album information after adding a file

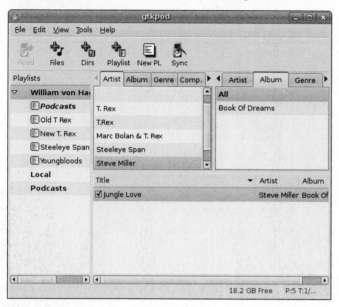

FIGURE 17.26

Adding directories of MP3 files to your iPod

Use the dialog shown in Figure 17.26 to navigate to the directory that you want to add and click Open to add that entire directory to your iPod. The main gtkpod window updates to reflect the addition of the new directory (entire album), as shown in Figure 17.27.

Updated Artist and Album information after adding a directory

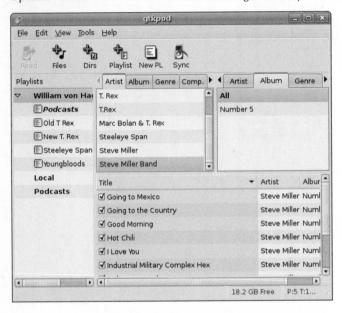

Even though the main gtkpod dialog shows the files and directories that you've added to your iPod, only the files have been copied there. The databases that your iPod uses to track file, song, and artist information aren't actually updated until you resynchronize the gtkpod database with the iPod's database by clicking Sync, as described in "Writing Changes to Your iPod" later in this section.

Creating and Editing Playlists on Your iPod

Creating playlists that contain your favorite music du jour is part of the fun of having and using an iPod. At a minimum, you'll probably want to create a playlist for each album that you add to your iPod, so that you can recreate the experience of hearing the tracks in the order that the artist intended.

The gtkpod application makes it easy to create many different types of playlists. There are also various ways of creating playlists, but you can access all of them from the Edit ➪ Create Playlists menu, shown in Figure 17.28.

FIGURE 17.28

Different types of playlists in gtkpod

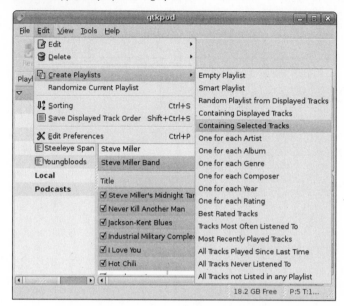

For example, to create a playlist that contains all of the tracks associated with a certain album, navigate to that album in gtkpod and select all of the tracks that it contains (you can use the standard GNOME Control+A shortcut to select all of the files). Once you've done that, select Edit ⇨ Create Playlists ⇨ Containing Selected Tracks. The dialog shown in Figure 17.29 displays, which enables you to specify a meaningful name for the new playlist (the default value is the catchy name "New Playlist," which isn't all that memorable).

FIGURE 17.29

Naming a newly created playlist

As you can see from Figure 17.28, gtkpod supports a wide variety of playlists. Once you've created a new playlist, its name displays in the left-most pane in the main gtkpod dialog. You can then select the playlist to show its current contents and sequence of tracks, as shown in Figure 17.30, which displays my newly created playlist for the ancient Steve Miller Band album, Number 5.

FIGURE 17.30

Examining a specific playlist

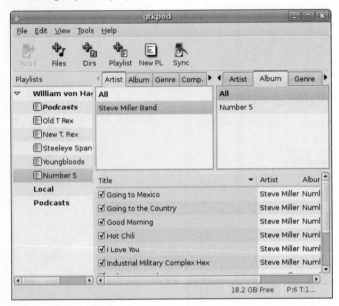

You can rename this playlist at any time by clicking its name in the left pane and entering a new name, or you can delete it and start over by selecting Edit ➪ Delete ➪ Selected playlist. More often, you'll simply want to modify it somehow. To remove tracks from a selected playlist or otherwise manipulate the files that one contains, you can right-click on any entry in the playlist to display the menu shown in Figure 17.31.

To remove a track from the playlist without removing the associated audio file from your iPod, select the Delete From Playlist command, which is highlighted in Figure 17.31. To remove the selected track from both the playlist and the iPod, select the Delete From iPod command.

You can manipulate existing playlists several other ways. For example, you can re-sort the playlist in different ways by clicking on any of the headings shown in the track-listing pane at the bottom of the gtkpod application. You can add other tracks to an existing playlist by navigating to those tracks and dragging them from the track-listing pane to the name of the playlist in the left pane. The gtkpod application provides a tremendous amount of control over playlists, making it easy for you to create playlists that enable you to hear what you want, when you want, in the order that you want.

FIGURE 17.31

The context-sensitive menu in gtkpod

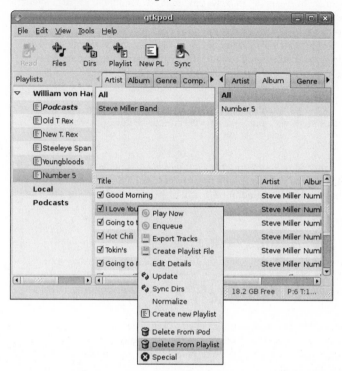

Writing Changes to Your iPod

Once you've finished adding music to your iPod, creating and editing playlists, and so on, you will certainly want to save all of those changes to your iPod. Although files and directories of audio files, new playlists, and other new items are added to your iPod at the time that you create them, the database that your iPod uses to track these new and modified items isn't updated until you explicitly synchronize the information in gtkpod with those databases on your iPod. You should always synchronize gtkpod with your iPod after making any changes to ensure that those changes are not lost or saved in some incomplete, intermediate state. After all, updating playlists or adding new music to your iPod doesn't do you much good if you can't access the new information!

To synchronize this information, click the Sync button in the gtkpod toolbar. A dialog displays as the information is synchronized. Once this dialog closes, it is safe to disconnect your iPod from your Ubuntu system, as described in the next section.

Safely Disconnecting Your iPod

Simply writing your changes to your iPod and exiting from gtkpod doesn't disconnect your iPod from your Ubuntu Linux system. Like any storage device on a Linux system, an iPod is mounted as part of your Linux filesystem so that you can access it as part of the standard directory hierarchy. By default, iPods are mounted on the directory /media/ipod when you attach them to your system. Although it is mounted as a part of your Ubuntu system's filesystem, an iPod's screen will display an international No symbol and a "Do not disconnect!" message. To safely disconnect an iPod from the filesystem, you must first unmount it to guarantee that all disk updates have been saved and that the iPod's filesystem is marked as up-to-date and clean.

Linux provides the eject command to cleanly unmount a disk partition or mounted device. Before disconnecting your iPod from your Ubuntu system, you should always execute the following command:

```
$ sudo eject /media/ipod
```

After you supply your password, this command will unmount the iPod filesystem, remove the desktop icon for the iPod, and will cause your iPod's screen to stop displaying the international No symbol and "Do not disconnect!" Message. When an iPod has been safely unmounted, it will display the standard iPod menus, and you can physically disconnect it from your Ubuntu system.

Working with Other Digital Audio Players

Attaching any sort of digital audio player to your Ubuntu system is just like attaching an iPod to your Ubuntu Linux system. First, make sure that you followed the instructions earlier in this chapter in the section entitled "Configuring iPod and Other Digital Audio Player Recognition" if you are using a digital audio player.

When you attach any sort of digital audio player to your Ubuntu system using a USB or Firewire cable, it will show up as a removable storage device and a desktop icon for it will automatically be created. If the Nautilus file browser doesn't automatically open to enable you to browse its contents, you can open the browser by double-clicking on the desktop icon for your audio player.

The Ubuntu repositories provide various software packages to simplify working with various types of MP3 players. For example, if you are using an MP3 player from Sonic Blue, Diamond MultiMedia, or Digital Networks, you may want to install and use the tools provided in the rio and rioutils packages, which you can easily install from the Synaptic Package Manager, as shown in Figure 17.32.

Most digital audio players enable you to simply drag and drop files in supported audio formats to them. However, searching the Ubuntu repositories and doing a quick Google search for Linux and the name of your audio player is always a good idea. Some digital audio players use an internal database to track files and playlists (as the iPod does), and these databases may not be updated automatically after you simply drag and drop files to the associated device icon on your desktop.

Once you are finished working with your digital audio player, you should eject it by right-clicking on its desktop icon and selecting the Eject command from the context-sensitive menu. This ensures that any pending changes are actually written to your device and that it is cleanly dismounted so that it can be safely disconnected form your Ubuntu system.

Utilities for working with MP3 players in Synaptic

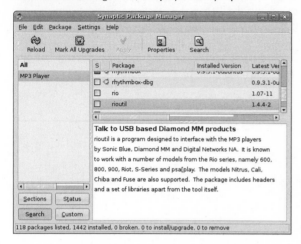

Reading CompactFlash and SD Cards

Though Ubuntu Linux can recognize a tremendous selection of digital cameras, PDAs, and other devices, you may encounter a situation where Ubuntu doesn't recognize a specific device or that device doesn't provide a USB or Firewire port to enable you to connect it to your Ubuntu system. Luckily, most of these devices provide removable storage such as CompactFlash or Secure Digital (SD) memory cards that can be accessed from your Ubuntu Linux system using a generic USB media reader. These devices are quite common nowadays and can be purchased on eBay or at most camera stores. Using these devices with Ubuntu Linux is quite simple, and makes it possible for you to copy your precious photos, files, or other information from just about anything to the safety of your Ubuntu Linux desktop system.

First, make sure that you followed the instructions in "Configuring Flash Card and Other Digital Media Recognition" earlier in this chapter. Next, after ejecting the removable storage media from your camera, PDA, or other device, insert it into the media reader and attach that device to your system. If your Ubuntu system can identify the media as a storage device from a digital camera (in other words, if the flash card contains a directory called DCIM), it will display a dialog like the one shown in Figure 17.33.

Handling removable flash media that contains digital photographs

If you see this dialog and click the "Import Photos" button, Ubuntu will start the gthumb application and follow the import process described earlier in this chapter in the section entitled "Digital Cameras and Ubuntu." See that section for detailed information about the import process. In some cases, the automatic import may fail because no valid camera was detected, just the flash card. In that case, you can simply copy the files off the media using Nautilus, an xterm, or the GNOME Terminal application.

Regardless of the contents of your removable media card, if you followed the instructions in "Configuring Flash Card and Other Digital Media Recognition," a desktop icon for your removable media should appear, as should a Nautilus file manager dialog like the one shown in Figure 17.34.

FIGURE 17.34

Removable flash media in the Nautilus file manager

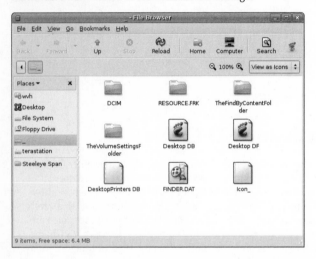

The Nautilus file manager makes it easy for you to copy selected files and directories to your desktop system as described in the section of Chapter 5 entitled "Using the Nautilus File Manager." If the Nautilus file manager doesn't automatically open to enable you to browse its contents, you can open it by double-clicking on the desktop icon for your removable media. If the CompactFlash or SD card that you are exploring is from a digital camera, your photos will be located in subdirectories of the media's DCIM directory.

Once you are finished working with your removable media card, you should eject it by right-clicking on its desktop icon and selecting the Eject command from the context-sensitive menu. This ejects the card from the Linux filesystem—it doesn't physically remove it from your media reader. The Eject command ensures that any pending changes are actually written to your storage card and that it is cleanly dismounted so that it can be safely disconnected form your Ubuntu system.

Summary

Portable consumer electronics devices like PDAs, digital music players, digital cameras, and smart phones are essentially high-tech jewelry today. Almost everyone has at least one. Therefore, this chapter covered a lot of digital media ground, including how to sync various types of PDAs with your Ubuntu system, how to work with an iPod from Ubuntu, and how to work with digital cameras or directly with removable CompactFlash or Secure Digital storage cards. Though I've been using Linux for over a decade now, the quality, power, and even (nowadays) the ease-of-use of its application ecosystem still impresses me. After reading this chapter, I hope that you feel the same way.

Chapter 18 moves into territory that is the traditional bugaboo of Linux systems — how to compile your own software on an Ubuntu system. Ubuntu systems do not include a compilation environment in their default installations because not everyone needs them, but more importantly because the Ubuntu repositories provide such a great selection of software that you rarely have to do this unless you want to (or are a developer). The need to roll your own versions of applications on Linux systems is a traditional part of the FUD (Fear, Uncertainty, Doubt) that Linux detractors use to support their claims that Linux is hard to use and only for nerds. This is not true at all. Not only is building your own applications optional nowadays but, as you'll see in Chapter 18, package management software like `apt-get`, `aptitude`, and `Synaptic` make it easy to install build tools and a powerful IDE if you need them.

Chapter 18

Software Development on Ubuntu

As pointed out on the Web site and throughout this book, Ubuntu is a distribution for everybody. And that includes developers! Just because Ubuntu is easy to use doesn't mean that serious, hard-core developers can't get real work done on an Ubuntu system — quite the contrary, actually. A good, recursive proof of this is the Ubuntu distribution, which is built by Ubuntu developers on Ubuntu systems. In addition, the fact that Ubuntu offers such a great user experience means that the time that you might ordinarily spend tweaking and fine-tuning your Linux desktop and installed software can be devoted to more productive pursuits, such as working on your personal code projects. The whole world may be waiting for your software!

Linux in general has a bad rep among many of the users of other platforms such as Microsoft Windows and Mac OS X, who often see Linux users as cave dwellers using VT100 terminals and living at the command line. Although there's a lot to be said for the command line, modern Linux systems such as Ubuntu strike just the right balance between providing graphical utilities for just about everything, with command-line access when and if you need it. The modern Linux model is strikingly similar to the user model provided by Mac OS X, and new versions of Microsoft Windows include "new" tools that provide support for extensive use of the command line and sophisticated command-script support. Does any of that ring a bell?

This chapter explains how to install the packages that you'll need for most Linux software development projects, starting with the fundamentals of installing the world's best compiler (gcc, the C compiler that is provided as part of the Free Software Foundation's GNU Compiler Collection, GCC), related tools that you'll need to provide a complete software build environment on your Ubuntu system, and then branches out to discuss other software packages that many people use when creating and maintaining software on Linux systems. These other packages include Integrated Development Environments (IDEs) that put an easy-to-use face on modern software development, and source code control and management software so that you can easily track changes to your software.

Installing and Using Development Software on Ubuntu

Ubuntu systems don't provide a software build environment out of the box because many people don't want to do software development. After all, Ubuntu provides a great user solution and a tremendous selection of software packages "out of the box," so many people will never need to build their own software. Providing the software that users need, and providing it in an integrated, easy-to-install, and easy-to-manage way, is what Linux distributions are all about in the first place.

For me, the most important part of the term *software* is the word *soft*. Software is flexible. Different people need different software packages to reflect their interests. When you're writing your own program to do "the right thing" that no one else seems to understand the need for, or simply want to use a special-purpose package that you can't live without from some random Web site, you may need to compile software yourself.

The traditional Linux build environment is composed of several different software packages, providing compilers, a linker, an assembler, an archiver for building and working with libraries, a utility to simplify building complex software packages, and much more. As you'd expect, Ubuntu makes it easy to install all of these core components as one simple über-package. As explained in the next section, installing this single package pulls together all of the basic ingredients of a Linux build environment, which you can subsequently augment with any other favorite tools that you've come to know and love when building software on your Linux system.

Installing GCC Compilers, make, and Friends

Ubuntu makes it especially easy to install the core elements of a Linux build environment by providing a package called build-essential that pulls in the GCC C and C++ compilers, mandatory libraries, the make utility, and the current set of Linux kernel headers. To install this meta-package on an Ubuntu system without a GUI, use the apt-get install build-essential or aptitude -r install build-essential commands. If you use these commands to install the build-essential package, you can skip the rest of this section. For more information about these commands, see Chapter 20, "Adding, Removing, and Updating Software."

To install this meta-package on an Ubuntu Desktop system or other Ubuntu system with a GUI, start the Synaptic Package Manager from the System ➪ Administration menu, select the Development group from the left pane, and scroll the upper right-hand window until you see the build-essential package. Right-click this package and select Mark for Installation to select that package for installation from the pop-up menu. Figure 18.1 shows the build-essential package being selected for installation.

Depending on what software you have previously installed on your Ubuntu system and what you select in Synaptic, a dialog may display that lists other packages that must also be installed, and asks for confirmation. If you see this dialog, click Mark to accept these related (and required) packages.

After you are finished making your selections, click Apply in the Synaptic toolbar to install gcc, g++, make, and friends on your system. Once the installation completes, you're ready to compile an application.

Depending on the build requirements of the software or package that you are compiling, you may find that you will subsequently need to install other packages. For example, configuration-related utilities such as autoconf and automake are not included in the build-essential package. Similarly, the build-essential package only provides the GCC C and C++ compilers—if you want to compile applications written in any of the other languages supported by GCC, you will have to install those compilers and any associated libraries separately. These additional packages can always be installed, as needed, using the Synaptic Package Manager or other Ubuntu package management commands.

FIGURE 18.1

Installing the build-essential package

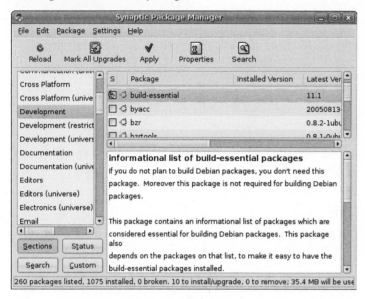

See Chapter 20, "Adding, Removing, and Updating Software," for more detailed information on installing applications using the Synaptic Package Manager and Ubuntu's other software package management tools.

Retrieving Source Packages

Throughout this book, the information on installing software packages has always focused on retrieving and installing binary packages, which are the packages that contain executable programs, related precompiled libraries, and associated configuration data that may be either text or binary. Because this chapter discusses installing build tools, it seems reasonable to at least touch on how to retrieve the source code associated with any Ubuntu binary package. In a nutshell, there are essentially two steps to this, both of which are most easily done using the command-line apt-get utility:

1. Retrieve the source code for the package that you want to build.
2. Satisfy any dependencies on other software, libraries, and so on that are required to build a specific package.

To retrieve the source code for any Ubuntu package, use the apt-get source package command, where package is the name of the package that you want to build from source code. To install any other tools, libraries, header files, and so on that are required to actually build that package from its source, you use the apt-get build-dep package command, where package is the name of the package that you want to build.

See Chapter 20, "Adding, Removing, and Updating Software," for a more detailed discussion of satisfying build dependencies and retrieving package source code using the apt-get utility.

GCC Compiler Overview

In uppercase letters, GCC is an acronym for the GNU Compiler Collection, formerly known as the GNU Compiler Suite. In lowercase letters, gcc is a specific compiler from the GNU Compiler Collection, the GNU C Compiler. GCC is a collection of compiler front-ends to a common back-end compilation engine. The list of compilers provided by GCC includes C (gcc), C++ (g++), Objective C (gcc with a special library), Fortran (gfortran), and Java (gcj). GCC also has front ends for Pascal, Modula-3, and Ada 9x. The C compiler speaks several different dialects of C, including traditional and ANSI C. The C++ compiler is a true native C++ compiler — in other words, it does not first convert C++ code into an intermediate C representation before compiling it, as older C++ compilers did. GCC's C++ compiler, g++, creates native executable code directly from the C++ source code.

GCC is a GNU Project, which is directed by the Free Software Foundation (FSF). The FSF holds the copyright on the compilers and licenses the compilers under the terms of the GPL. Either individuals or the FSF hold the copyrights on other components, such as the runtime libraries and test suites, and these other components are licensed under a variety of free software licenses. The FSF also handles the legal concerns of the GCC project.

Using GCC's C Compiler

The gcc compiler supports a tremendous number of command-line options to control its behavior. It accepts both single-letter options, such as -o, and multiletter options, such as -ansi. Because it accepts both types of options, you cannot group multiple single-letter options together as you may be used to doing with many GNU and Unix/Linux programs such as ps, ls, and so on. For example, the multiletter option -pg is not the same as the two single-letter options -p -g. The -pg option creates extra code in the final binary that outputs profile information for the GNU code profiler, gprof. On the other hand, the -p -g options generate extra code in the resulting binary that produces profiling information for use by the prof code profiler (-p) and causes gcc to generate debugging information using the operating system's normal format (-g).

Despite its sensitivity to the grouping of multiple single-letter options, you can freely mix the order of options and compiler arguments on the gcc command line. The following two commands are identical in terms of what they tell gcc to do:

```
$ gcc -pg -fno-strength-reduce -g hello.c -o hello
$ gcc hello.c -o hello -g -fno-strength-reduce -pg
```

In most cases, the order of options and their arguments does not matter. In some situations, order does matter if you use several options of the same kind. For example, the -I option specifies the directory or directories to search for include files. So if you specify -I several times, gcc searches the listed directories in the order specified.

Compiling a single source file, hello.c, using gcc is easy — just invoke gcc, passing the name of the source file as the argument as shown in the following example:

```
$ gcc hello.c
```

By default, the result is an executable file named a.out in the current directory, which you execute by typing ./a.out. To define the name of the output file that gcc produces, use the -o option, as in the following example:

```
$ gcc hello.c -o runme
```

If you are compiling multiple source files using gcc, you can specify them all on the gcc command line, as in the following example, which leaves the compiled and linked executable in the file named `showdate`:

```
$ gcc showdate.c helper.c -o showdate
```

If you want to compile these files incrementally and eventually link them into a binary, you can use the -c option to halt compilation after producing an object file. You can then use a single gcc command to link them all together and specify the name of the output file, as in the following example:

```
$ gcc -c showdate.c
$ gcc -c helper.c
$ gcc showdate.o helper.o -o showdate
```

It should be easy to see that a project consisting of more than a few source code files would quickly become exceedingly tedious to compile from the command line, especially after you start linking in external libraries, adding optimization commands, and providing other miscellaneous gcc options. The solution to this command-line tedium is the `make` utility, which is discussed in the next section.

Creating Simple Makefiles

Since the dawn of Unix time, most Unix applications have been built using a rule-driven application called `make`, which invokes the compilers and other utilities necessary to produce an executable from all the components of a program's source code. The `make` program also serves as the cornerstone of building C and C++ applications on Linux and all other Unix-like systems. The `make` program does the following:

- enables developers to identify relationships and dependencies between the source modules, include files, and libraries that are required for successful compilation
- specifies the sequence in which things must be compiled to build an application successfully
- avoids recompilation by limiting compilation to the portions of an application that are affected by any change to source code or statically linked libraries

The `make` program was originally written by Stu Feldman at AT&T for an early version of Unix. As a part of AT&T Unix, the source code for the `make` program was not freely available, and has therefore largely been replaced by the GNU `make` program. GNU make provides all of the features of the original `make` program and a host of others. Subsequent references to the `make` program throughout this chapter therefore refer to GNU make.

The rules used by any `make` program are stored in text files named Makefile, which contain dependency rules and the commands necessary to satisfy them. As you might expect, the Makefiles for complex applications can themselves be extremely complex as well as platform-specific, because they need to invoke platform-specific libraries and utilities that may be located in different directories or have different names on different systems. The simplest possible Makefile is the one for a simple application that is compiled from a single source code file, such as the legendary C language "Hello, World!" application. The Makefile for this application looks like the following:

```
hello: hello.c
gcc hello.c -o hello
```

The first line identifies the binary target (hello) that this Makefile builds, and the fact that this binary must be regenerated whenever the source file `hello.c` is modified. The second line (which begins with a tab) specifies the command necessary to produce that binary target. To invoke this Makefile, you simply execute the `make` command in the directory containing the Makefile. The `make` program automatically looks for a file named Makefile and follows any build rules that it contains.

> **TIP** The fact that all lines containing a build rule must begin with a tab is one of the most common problems with handcrafted Makefiles.

Although this example shows the true basics of a Makefile, it is also a trivial example that doesn't show off any of the real benefits that Makefiles can provide in terms of simplifying and automating compilation and recompilation. Let's consider another example. In the previous section, one of the examples I used compiled a single binary from two object modules, using the following command lines:

```
$ gcc -c showdate.c
$ gcc -c helper.c
$ gcc showdate.o helper.o -o showdate
```

A Makefile for this application would look something like the following:

```
showdate: showdate.o helper.o
  gcc showdate.o helper.o -o showdate

showdate.o: showdate.c
  gcc -c showdate.c
helper.o: helper.c
  gcc -c helper.c
```

This example highlights how a Makefile can reduce the amount of recompilation necessary when you have only modified some of the files associated with a project. For example, this Makefile states that the showdate binary depends on the two object modules `showdate.o` and `helper.o`, and provides a rule for generating the binary by using gcc to link the two object files. It then continues to highlight that each of these object modules depends on its associated C language file, and provides a rule for using gcc to regenerate each of the object modules.

This sample Makefile can simplify recompilation if, for example, only one of the C files was modified. The Makefile would regenerate to object module for only the C file that has been modified, and then relink the existing object file with the new object file to regenerate the binary.

As your projects become larger, you will want to take advantage of other Makefile features, such as defining and using variables, using some truly cryptic symbols to simplify make rules, and so on. Some good sources for more advanced information about the make program and Makefiles are the following:

- `www.linuxdevcenter.com/pub/a/linux/2002/01/31/make_intro.html`: A nice article on using make from O'Reilly & Associates Linux Development Center.
- `www.tldp.org/HOWTO/Software-Building-HOWTO-3.html`: The section on using make from the Linux Documentation project's guide to Linux software development.
- `www.gnu.org/software/make`: The home page for GNU make, which also includes links to the official make documentation.
- `www.gnu.org/software/make/manual`: The official online home of the documentation for GNU make, which is available in various formats.

Using an Integrated Development Environment

An *integrated development environment* (*IDE*) is a unified set of tools that typically provides an editing environment, compiler, build environment, and debugger that work together in a single framework. IDEs typically also provide infrastructure for creating and managing software projects composed of multiple source files, include files, and libraries. Most modern IDEs are graphical tools that work in desktop environments such as the X Window system, GNOME, KDE, Microsoft Windows, or Mac OS X. For this reason, many modern IDEs therefore also include tools for creating user interfaces and the other graphical elements of graphical desktop applications.

The key aspect of an IDE is the integration between the different tools that make up the development environment that it provides. Most IDEs give the impression of being a single tool, regardless of how many features and components they provide.

As I'll discuss in the next section, IDEs are traditionally oriented toward the requirements of developers working in a specific language or a set of related languages. Recently, general-purpose IDEs such as Eclipse have become more popular, because they provide a single framework that standardizes the developer experience regardless of the language in which a developer is working, and support a plug-in model that enables them to easily be extended.

Popular IDEs for Linux

As you might expect from an operating system that is used for the development of applications in a huge number of languages, and one in which everyone has their own idea of how development should be done, Linux is knee-deep in IDEs. Ubuntu provides a large selection of IDEs for different languages in its repositories. Some of the more widely known IDEs provided in the Ubuntu repositories are the following:

- **Eclipse:** Eclipse is a multipurpose IDE written in Java. Eclipse was originally developed as an IDE framework for developing Java applications, but has been extended to support development in other languages. The fact that Eclipse is written in Java makes it very portable and usable on a variety of different graphical environments and operating systems. For more information about Eclipse, see the rest of the discussion of IDEs in this chapter or the Eclipse home page at www.eclipse.org.

- **KDevelop3:** A graphical IDE for C and C++ applications that is based on the KDE desktop environment. KDevelop is an extremely popular and easy-to-use IDE that provides wizards, which simplify creating standard command-line Linux applications, as well as graphical applications that use the Qt, GNOME, and KDE graphical environments. For more information about KDevelop, see its home page at www.kdevelop.org. Figure 18.2 shows a version of the traditional C language "Hello, World!" application in KDevelop.

- **Motor:** The motor IDE is a text-based integrated development environment for C, C++, and Java applications that works well within any terminal application, such as an xterm or the GNOME Terminal. The motor IDE provides integrated support for various GCC compilers and the GNU debugger, gdb. For more detailed information about Motor, see its home page at http://konst.org.ua/motor.

FIGURE 18.2

A sample C application in KDevelop

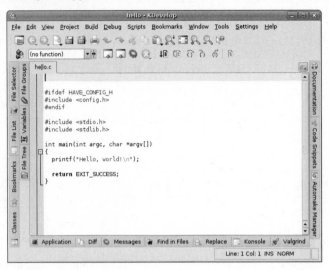

- **Pida:** The pida IDE (Python Integrated Development Application) is a GTK-based IDE for developing text-mode or graphical application written in the Python scripting language. The pida IDE is quite popular and supports easy integration of familiar development tools within its unified development framework. For more information about pida, see its home page at `http://pida.berlios.de`.

- **Sbcl:** The sbcl IDE (Steel Bank Common Lisp) is a graphical development environment for applications written in the Lisp programming language. The `sbcl` IDE was originally based on the Common Lisp development environment provided by Carnegie Mellon University's CMU Common Lisp, but is actively being maintained and enhanced. The sbcl IDE features provide a native Lisp code compiler and a sophisticated debugger. For more information about sbcl, see its home page at `http://sbcl.sourceforge.net`.

- **Free-java-sdk:** The Free Java SDK is an IDE created by combining and integrating best-of-breed open source tools to provide an alternative to the development environment provided by the standard Java Development Kit from Sun Microsystems, Inc. The `free-java-sdk` package was assembled from various open source projects by the developers of the Debian Linux distribution and has therefore been inherited by Ubuntu Linux.

This list is just a subset of the IDEs available in the Ubuntu repositories, but highlights the number of different IDEs available and the fact that many IDEs focus on specific programming languages. My favorite IDE is the Eclipse IDE, which was originally developed by IBM as an easily-extended framework for Java development, but was released by IBM as open source, and has soared in popularity since then. Eclipse is now released and supported by the Eclipse Foundation (`www.eclipse.org`), a not-for-profit organization dedicated to promoting Eclipse and helping guide its development and acceptance throughout the software development industry. Eclipse provides a plug-in based framework that makes it easy to create, integrate, and support tools that provide specific functionality or target certain sets of developers. This plug-in model also gives developers the freedom to select and integrate plug-ins from different projects or commercial vendors and thereby assemble an IDE that does exactly what they need it to do. Eclipse is available for Linux, HP-UX, AIX, Solaris, QNX, Mac OS X, and Microsoft Windows systems.

As you might suspect from the previous paragraph, the rest of this part of the chapter focuses on installing and using the Eclipse IDE.

Installing Eclipse

To install Eclipse and related packages, start the Synaptic Package Manager from the System ➪ Administration menu, select Search, enter **eclipse** in the Search box that displays, make sure that Description and Name is selected for the search type, and click Search. Once the search completes, scroll down in the list of packages in the new eclipse category and select each of the following packages. Not all of these are mandatory, but they're all suggested — my rationale for each follows the name of the package in this list:

- `eclipse`: (Mandatory) This is the core Eclipse package, and provides everything you need to use the standard Eclipse IDE to develop Java applications.

- `eclipse-cdt`: (Optional) Eclipse C Developer's Toolkit. This package is required if you want to build C or C++ applications in the Eclipse IDE. This package provides plug-ins, wizards, and Eclipse features to simplify developing and debugging C and C++ applications using Eclipse.

- `eclipse-ecj-gcj`: (Optional) Eclipse Compiler for Java package that provides support for native compilation using gcj, the GNU Compiler for Java, which is part of the Gnu Compiler Collection (GCC).

- `eclipse-pydev`: (Optional) Python Developer's plug-ins for Eclipse. This package is only necessary if you want to do Python development using Eclipse.

Right-click and select Mark for Installation from the pop-up menu to select each of these packages for installation. Figure 18.3 shows the eclipse and related packages being selected for installation.

FIGURE 18.3

Installing eclipse and related packages

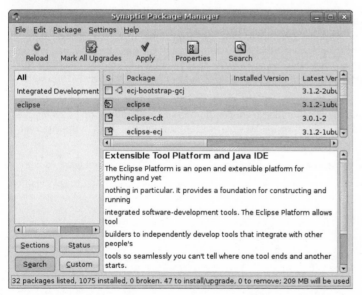

Depending on what software you have previously installed on your Ubuntu system and what you select in Synaptic, dialogs may display that list other packages that must also be installed, and ask for confirmation. If you see such dialogs, click Mark to accept these related (and required) packages.

After you are finished making your selections, click Apply in the Synaptic toolbar to install the Eclipse IDE and friends on your system. Once the installation completes, you're ready to begin developing applications using the most popular cross-platform IDE available today.

See Chapter 20, "Adding, Removing, and Updating Software," for more detailed information on installing applications using the Synaptic Package Manager.

Using Eclipse for C Application Development

This section provides two examples of using Eclipse: one which shows how to create a simple application from scratch, and one that shows how to import the source code for an existing software package into Eclipse to take advantage of its compilation, debugging, and usability features. Entire books are available about using Eclipse, and these introductory sections are hardly equivalent to those, but they should help you get a feeling for the power, capabilities, and ease-of-use of the Eclipse IDE.

NOTE The examples in the next two sections are both C programs, and therefore assume that you took my advice in the "Installing Eclipse" section and installed both the `eclipse` and `eclipse-cdt` packages, because the latter provides the support for C application development that these examples take advantage of. The examples in this section also assume that you followed the instructions in the "Installing GCC Compilers, make, and Friends" section, and installed the `build-essential` package, which provides the versions of gcc and `make` that Eclipse requires to build C applications.

Starting Eclipse for the First Time

Installing Eclipse on your Ubuntu system creates the Applications ➪ Programming ➪ Eclipse menu entry, which you can use to start the Eclipse IDE. The first time that you start Eclipse, it displays a Welcome screen, as shown in Figure 18.4.

The first time that you start Eclipse, it also creates the `workspace` and `.eclipse` directories in your home directory. Eclipse uses the `workspace` directory to store the projects that you create, and uses the `.eclipse` directory to store information about your configuration settings, the organization of the Eclipse UI the last time you used it, and so on. You can start Eclipse using a different workspace directory by using the `-data` command-line argument, followed by full pathname of the workspace directory that you want to use.

The Welcome screen provides some convenient links to sources of information about working with Eclipse, such as tutorials, sample code, and so on. To close the Welcome screen, simply click the X in the Welcome tab. You can reopen it at any time by selecting Help ➪ Welcome.

After closing the Welcome screen, the standard Eclipse user interface displays, as shown in Figure 18.5.

At this point, the Eclipse environment is remarkably empty because you haven't created any projects. The next two sections describe how to fix that.

FIGURE 18.4

The welcome screen in Eclipse

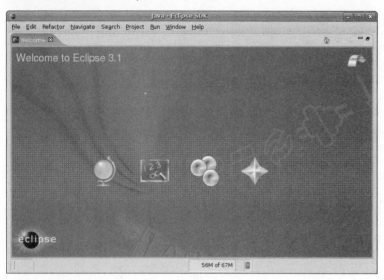

FIGURE 18.5

The standard Eclipse user interface

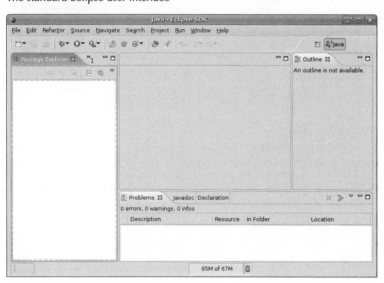

Eclipse Terminology

The Eclipse framework was originally developed by IBM, which seems to have also developed its own language to refer to the elements of the Eclipse user interface and framework. This shouldn't be much of a surprise to anyone who has worked with IBM in the past. The following are a few terms that you'll encounter when using Eclipse — like most languages, they make perfect sense once you have been assimilated, but they can be confusing at first:

- **editor:** A window that enables you to edit a specific type of file or other resources. The Eclipse toolbar and menus provide different options based on the editor that is currently active.

- **feature:** A packaged set of one or more plug-ins that make up a product.

- **perspective:** A set of windows within the Eclipse GUI that are associated with a specific plug-in or task, and which are organized in a specific way.

- **plugin:** Code that performs a specific function or set of functions and can be integrated into the Eclipse framework.

- **view:** A window within the Eclipse GUI that can support an editor or provide access to a certain type of resource. Each view has a titlebar that provides tabs to select different resources that are open in that view, and also often provide their own menus and icons, which are available by right-clicking or selecting an icon in the titlebar.

- **workbench:** One of the two key plug-ins provided with the Eclipse IDE, the workbench plug-in provides the basic user interface, menu structure, event notification mechanism, and mechanisms for creating new windows and views. This plug-in also provides the extension points that developers can use to create menus, menu items, events, editors, and views for their plug-ins. From the user's point of view, the workbench is simply the Eclipse user interface.

- **workspace:** The second of the two key plug-ins provided by the Eclipse IDE, the workspace plug-in enables you to interact with external resources such as project directories, files, and so on. The term workspace may also be used to describe a directory used by Eclipse to hold projects.

These are my interpretations of official "Eclipse-speak." The online help for Eclipse provides the official definitions for these terms in its Workbench User Guide section.

Creating a New Source Project in Eclipse

After starting Eclipse, you create new projects or project components by selecting File ➪ New, and selecting the appropriate item from this menu. To create and work with an application in Eclipse, you must first create a project to hold your source code. Eclipse provides wizards to simplify creating projects of different types. Wizards are sets of graphical screens that walk you through the process of creating a specific type of project, making sure that you don't miss any of the steps in the process.

Selecting File ➪ New ➪ Project displays the wizard selection dialog shown in Figure 18.6.

FIGURE 18.6

Selecting a project creation wizard in Eclipse

Because I'm creating a C source project in this section, I've double-clicked on the C entry to see the wizards available for creating C projects, and have selected the Managed Make C Project wizard. Eclipse supports two different types of C projects — a Managed Make project in which Eclipse will automatically generate and maintain the project's Makefile for you, and a Standard Make project in which you must create and maintain your own Makefile. I'll use a Managed Make project in this example — the example in the next section shows how using a Standard Make project can simplify importing and continuing to work with existing source projects in Eclipse.

After selecting Managed Make C Project, click Next to proceed to the wizard for this particular type of project. The dialog shown in Figure 18.7 displays.

Enter the name that you want to associate with this project ("hello" in this example). You can then click Finish to create a project with default attributes (which is configured to produce a stand-alone Linux executable) or click Next to specify that your project produces some other type of object code, such as a shared or static library for Linux. Because this is a simple example, I'll just click Finish. The wizard creates my new "hello" project and displays a dialog asking if I want to display my new project in the C/C++ Perspective that is associated with C projects. Click Yes to display the default structure and content of the project in Eclipse's C/C++ perspective, as shown in Figure 18.8, in which I've expanded the contents of the project to highlight its default contents.

FIGURE 18.7

Specifying the name of your project in Eclipse

FIGURE 18.8

A newly created project in Eclipse

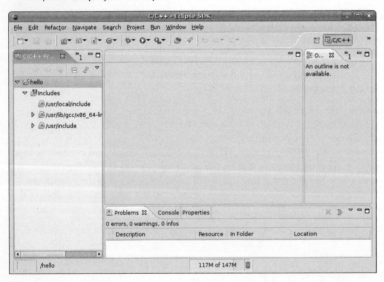

The default views and editors displayed in Eclipse's C/C++ Perspective are the following:

- **Navigator:** The view at the left, which enables you to navigate through and work with your project and the files and other resources that it contains.

- **Editor:** The pane at the top center, which differs based on the open resources in the Navigator view.

- **Console:** The bottom right view, in which messages about interactions with Eclipse are displayed. This view also provides a Problems tab that identifies any errors or warning associated with the current project, and a Properties tab that enables you to examine any properties associated with the current project.

- **Outline:** The view at the right, which shows an outline of the files and functions referenced and defined in the active project.

One thing missing from my sample C project is any C files, so I'll use the File ⇨ New ⇨ Source File menu command to create one, which displays the dialog shown in Figure 18.9. You can also create new resources for a project by right-clicking on the name of the project and selecting the type of item that you want to create from the pop-up menu's New submenu.

FIGURE 18.9

Creating a new C source file in Eclipse

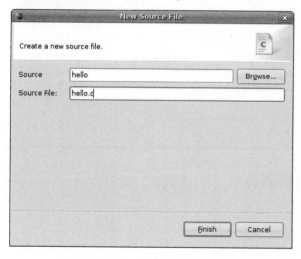

Creating a new source file in a project opens the new file in the type of editor associated with that source file, as shown in Figure 18.10.

When you create your first source file in a Managed Make C Project, you'll notice that the Console view's Problems tab displays (located below the editor pane), which points out the fact that the project (which only contains one empty file) does not yet provide a main routine. Well, I suppose that's helpful — this message displays because Eclipse tries to automatically build your project each time that you change it. You can prevent this level of "helpfulness" by deselecting the Build Automatically item on the Project menu. After deselecting this option, Eclipse will only build the project when I tell it to, which is fine with me.

FIGURE 18.10

A new source file in an editor in Eclipse

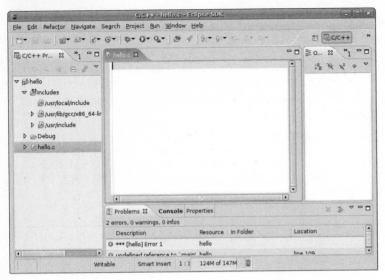

Next, type the source code for this module in the editor pane. Eclipse provides many keyboard shortcuts to simplify moving around in its editors. You can see the list of current key bindings for the workbench by selecting Window ➪ Preferences, and selecting General ➪ Keys in the dialog that displays, as shown in Figure 18.11.

FIGURE 18.11

Viewing current key bindings in Eclipse

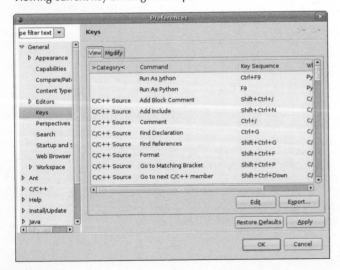

If your fingers have already been trained to use a specific set of editor commands (as mine have been trained by the emacs text editor), you can select different sets of key bindings by clicking the Modify tab in the dialog shown in Figure 18.11, which displays a dialog that enables you to customize your key bindings. From this tab, you can select reasonable (i.e., emacs) key bindings by clicking the Scheme selector and selecting Emacs from the drop-down menu, as shown in Figure 18.12. You may not want to do this if you're not an emacs aficionado, but it works for me. Click OK to close this dialog and return to the C/C++ perspective.

FIGURE 18.12

Customizing key bindings in Eclipse

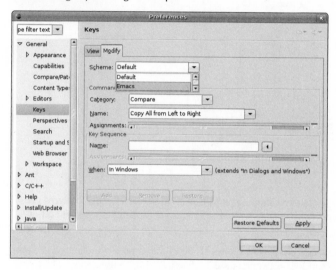

Now that you know what commands to use to move around in the editor, type in the source code for your application (the familiar "Hello, World!" application, in this example). As you enter your source code, you'll notice that Eclipse automatically indents new lines, matches brackets, parentheses, and does the sort of code highlighting that you'd expect in a modern IDE. As you enter your code, you'll also notice that the Outline view to the left of the editor updates to identify any external references in your code, any functions that you have defined (including "main"), and so on. Figure 18.13 shows Eclipse after entering a complete "Hello, World!" program.

FIGURE 18.13

A sample application and its outline in Eclipse

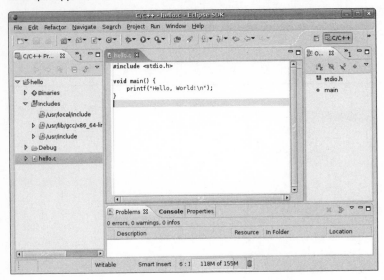

At this point, select File ➪ Save to save your application. As part of the save process, Eclipse analyzes your code and identifies any possible problems that it sees. Common problems are missing newlines at end-of-file, missing return values, and so on.

Now it's time to build the project. If I hadn't deselected the Project ➪ Build Automatically menu item, Eclipse would have built the project for me automatically after operations such as a Save operation. As it is, I have to build the project manually, by selecting Project ➪ Build Project (or right-clicking on the project and selecting Build Project from the pop-up menu). If you're lucky, you will not see any error or warning messages in the Console view's Problems tab, located below the editor.

The final step in this example is to actually run the application and see its output. To do this, select one of the Run commands from the Run menu. Eclipse enables you to define multiple Build and Run configurations, enabling you (for example) to define sets of compilation and execution parameters for debugging your application, executing it normally, and so on. (The default Build configuration is to build for debugging, with symbols present, and so on.) In this case, I'll select the default way of running the application, which is as a stand-alone, local C/C++ application by selecting Run ➪ Run As ➪ Run Local C/C++ Application, as shown in Figure 18.14.

Selecting this command displays the dialog shown in Figure 18.15, which enables you to select how to run this program. Because the default Build configuration used in Eclipse projects is a Debugging configuration, this dialog enables you to select whether you want to run this in the context of a local Gnu debugger (gdb) or a gdb server so that you could connect to it remotely.

FIGURE 18.14

Running a project binary in Eclipse

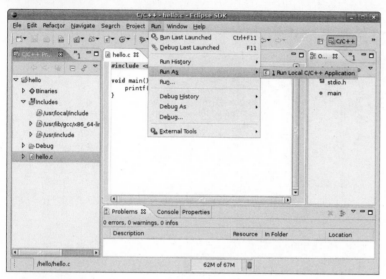

FIGURE 18.15

Selecting a run configuration for debugging in Eclipse

Select GDB Debugger and click OK. Eclipse runs the application and refreshes the Console view, displaying the Console tab in which the output from the sample application displays, as shown in Figure 18.16.

FIGURE 18.16

Running the sample application in Eclipse

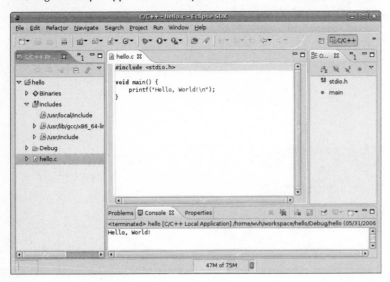

To simplify running your sample application, you could create special Run configurations that would execute the application in Eclipse's other default Build configuration, which is called Release and enables you to build the application without debugging symbols, and so on, which is somewhat outside the scope of this simple tutorial. You've created a project, a source module, watched Eclipse do its magic, and even executed the application. Not bad for 10 minutes or so.

Importing an Existing Source project into Eclipse

Creating new projects in Eclipse is one thing, but you can also take advantage of the capabilities of Eclipse in existing projects by importing them into Eclipse. This example shows how to do just that, using one of my favorite open source applications as an example, which is the pop3check application that enables you to list the headings for any mail that is pending for you on a remote POP mail server. I often use this as a quick, command-line way of seeing if anything interesting has come in without risking being sucked into the black hole of actually reading all of my incoming mail. The pop3check application was written by Steven Radack and Simon Liddington, and is available from http://sourceforge.net/projects/pop3check.

In my opinion, the easiest way to import an existing project into Eclipse is as a tarball that contains the source. This enables you to import a pristine version of the source code, and also provides a convenient way for you to keep track of exactly what was in the project when you moved it into Eclipse, by archiving the tarball. Preparatory to beginning the import process, cd to the top-level of your source project directory, clean the project to remove object code, backup files, and any other items that you don't actually want to import. You'll want to generate a source tarball for your project from the top level of its source code directory so that the files that comprise your project are imported into the top level of your Eclipse project rather than being created in a subdirectory, which would happen if you imported a vanilla tarball that you retrieved from the Web or created as a backup of your project. In my case, I prepare the tarball with commands like the following:

```
$ cd pop3check-0.100.3
$ make clean
$ tar czf ../pop3check.tgz *
```

Tarball in hand, start Eclipse using the Applications ⇨ Programming ⇨ Eclipse command, and create an Eclipse project that corresponds to the source project that you are importing by using File ⇨ New ⇨ Project wizard selector. Because you're importing an existing project that already includes a Makefile, I typically select Standard Make C Project, as shown in Figure 18.17.

FIGURE 18.17

Creating a standard C make project in Eclipse

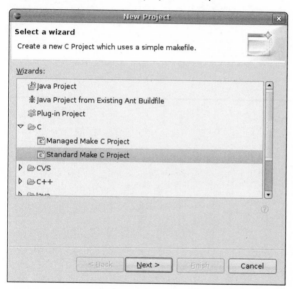

After specifying the name of the project and clicking Finish, the new project displays in Eclipse, as shown in Figure 18.18.

Because the project you've just created is a standard make project rather than one in which Eclipse will generate and manage the make information, you'll notice that the project is initially empty. Next, to import the tarball you prepared earlier, you would right-click on the name of the project and select Import. This displays the dialog shown in Figure 18.19.

FIGURE 18.18

An empty standard make project in Eclipse

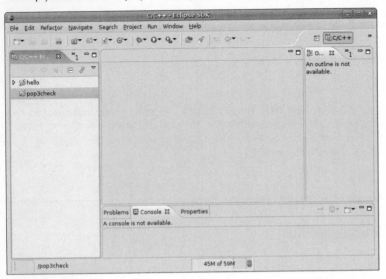

FIGURE 18.19

Specifying how to import an existing project into Eclipse

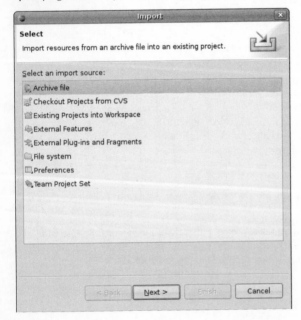

Because you're importing from a tarball, select Archive File and click Next. The dialog shown in Figure 18.20 displays, in which you've browsed for and selected the tarball that you prepared earlier.

FIGURE 18.20

FIGURE 18.20

Selecting the tarball for importing into Eclipse

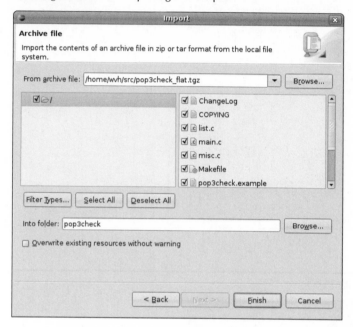

You'll note that this dialog shows an expanded view of the tarball, which enables you to verify that it contains everything you need and that Eclipse can open it successfully. Click Finish to begin the import process. Once the import completes, the contents of the imported tarball are added to the selected project, as shown in Figure 18.21.

After importing a project into Eclipse, it's a good idea to verify that the Makefile uses the build targets that Eclipse expects to find, which are all and check. You can tell Eclipse about other build targets by right-clicking on the Makefile and selecting Create Make target, but I find it easiest to start out with the standard ones. To check the Makefile, double-click its name in the Navigator view, which displays the Makefile in an editor, as shown in Figure 18.22.

FIGURE 18.21

An imported project in Eclipse

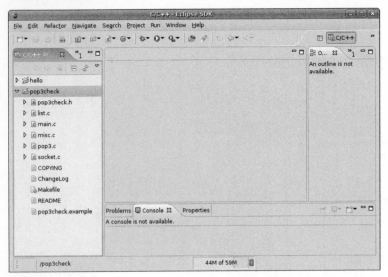

FIGURE 18.22

Editing the Makefile for a standard make project in Eclipse

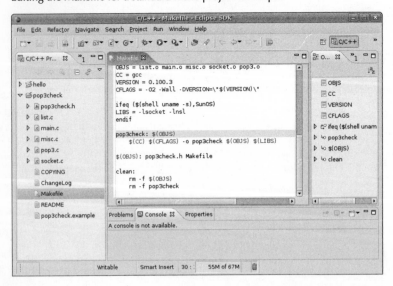

In this case, the default target is pop3check, which you'll change to all in order to simplify things. After selecting File ➪ Save to save your changes, you can build the project in the standard fashion, by selecting Project ➪ Build All. Hooray! In this case, your newly imported project built correctly and successfully, as shown in Figure 18.23.

FIGURE 18.23

Console output from a build of an imported project in Eclipse

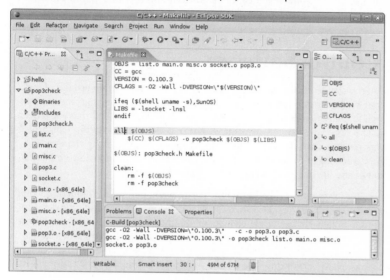

As you might expect, your mileage may vary when importing existing source projects into Eclipse, but the ease with which you can do so makes it easy for you to move your existing application development efforts into Eclipse so that you can take advantage of its many capabilities and take advantage of the ease-of-use that a modern IDE such as Eclipse provides.

Getting More Information About Eclipse

Eclipse is a powerful, full-featured IDE, which means that the examples in the previous two sections can only scratch the surface of its capabilities and bells and whistles. For more detailed information about using Eclipse, see one of the many books on using Eclipse that are available, or visit some of the following resources on the Web:

- www.eclipse.org: home page of the Eclipse mothership
- www.eclipse.org/documentation/main.html: eclipse documentation site
- http://planeteclipse.org/planet/: Planet Eclipse, frequented by Eclipse developers, contributors, hackers, and users
- www.eclipseplugincentral.com: Eclipse Plug-in Central, from which you can download many free Eclipse plug-ins

The next section talks about Source Code Control Software, highlighting the Subversion SCCS. As an example of the wide range of free plug-ins available for Eclipse, the following are two free Subversion plug-ins for Eclipse:

- Subversive Plug-in at `www.polarion.org`
- Subclipse Plug-in at `http://subclipse.tigris.org`

Not only do these plug-ins provide an easy way to work with Subversion repositories in Eclipse, but they also provide a great example of how all of this open source stuff tends to fit together nicely. And you certainly can't beat the price!

Source Code Control Software

If you've ever accidentally deleted a source file that you were working on, lost the software version of the great American novel when your system crashed and lost its disks, or worked on a joint project with someone who was thoughtful enough to overwrite all of your new code, you might have wished that you'd been using a source code control system once you finished swearing. A source code control system, popularly known as an *SCCS*, is a software package that manages a repository of source code, tracking changes to existing code, managing different versions of that code (often known as *branches*), and providing a mechanism for recovering any version of any file in the repository at any point in time.

If I had to count the number of times that an SCCS had saved my bacon when doing development, I would quickly run out of fingers and toes. This doesn't necessarily mean that I'm sloppy. When multiple developers work on the same sets of files, conflicts between their changes are bound to occur. An SCCS provides a mechanism for identifying and resolving conflicting sets of changes (known as *merges*). Similarly, a source code control system facilitates experimentation with code by providing a safety net that you can use to fall back to versions of files that you know to be working, just in case your latest bright idea didn't turn out to be very illuminating after all.

> **WARNING**   One common misconception is that an SCCS is a replacement for backups. Not really true. An SCCS may be a replacement for backing up your own files, because you can check them in and retrieve them later if your machine bursts into flames. However, the SCCS repository itself must be backed up regularly — if anything, a central repository used across a project or enterprise provides a single, critical point of failure.

The next two sections discuss the two most popular source code control systems for Linux, the Concurrent Versioning System (CVS) and the Subversion Project. I have used CVS for years, but am purposely giving it short shrift here — Subversion is often referred to as CVS++, and for good reason. Not only is Subversion a more modern implementation with a richer set of commands than those provided by CVS, Subversion is based on modern protocols and is more easily integrated into Web browsers, integrated development environments, graphical computer interfaces, and is actively under development. Alas, poor CVS, I knew thee well...

The Concurrent Versioning System (CVS)

My humorous comments about CVS in the previous section are meant to be just that, and should not be taken to mean that CVS is not a time-tested, stable SCCS. CVS has been in use and under development for years, and is still often used to provide access to the source code for open software projects over the Internet. That said, most projects that I'm aware of which have traditionally depended on CVS are mobbing to Subversion, and that's a trend that I believe will continue, if not accelerate. Because neither CVS or Subversion is installed as part of a basic Ubuntu installation, I'd strongly suggest that you install and use Subversion rather than CVS.

However, if you're a CVS fanatic or your current projects already work with CVS, you can use the Synaptic Package Manager to install CVS, and then see sites such as the following for information about setting up and Web-enabling CVS repositories:

- `www.faqs.org/docs/ldev/0130091154_198.htm`: The Linux Development FAQ's section on CVS.

- `www.freeos.com/articles/4608`: A nice (and short!) article by Mahantesh. M.Vantmuri on setting up and configuring CVS and synchronized copies of CVS repositories. Though this article is a few years old, not much has changed — we are talking about CVS, after all.

- `www.flexwiki.com/default.aspx/FlexWiki/ConfiguringCVS.html`: A nice Wiki that provides a lot of good information about understanding and using CVS.

CVS is a fine system, and I've used it extensively at many companies. However, I feel that if you're going to set up an SCCS from scratch on your Ubuntu system, you may as well use the more modern and powerful Subversion SCCS.

Installing and Using Subversion

Subversion (`http://subversion.tigris.org/`) is a relatively new, yet extremely popular source code control system (SCCS). Aside from its power and rich command set, much of Subversion's popularity lies in the fact that it is based on WebDAV (Web Distributed Authoring and Versioning), a Web-based protocol that enables you to view and access subversion repositories in any Web browser. This includes the ability to drag and drop files from your Web browser to your desktop to check them out, and vice versa to check them in. As you'll see in the next few sections, setting up a Subversion repository and integrating it into your Web server is quite easy to do, just as subversion is easy to use from the desktop or the command line.

Installing Subversion

To install subversion and related packages, start the Synaptic Package Manager from the System ⇨ Administration menu, select Search, enter **subversion** in the Search box that displays, make sure that Description and Name is selected for the search type ("Look in"), and click Search. Once the search completes, scroll down in the list of packages in the new subversion category and select each of the following packages. Not all of these are mandatory, but they're all suggested — my rationale for each follows the name of the package in this list:

- `libapache2-svn`: (Optional) This package is necessary only if you want to provide a Subversion repository that users can access through your Web server. Selecting this item causes the Apache2 Web server and related files to be installed on your system. I always find it handy to be able to access my repository over the Web, it's easy to configure everything at once, and the extra disk space that Apache2 consumes is always worth it to me. However, you can always add this in later. See Chapter 26, "Setting Up a Web Server," for information about manually installing different versions of the Apache Web server.

- `rapidsvn, esvn, or kdesvn`: (Optional) Graphical clients for Subversion. Only necessary if you want to use a graphical client. The rapidsvn client is quite popular and is a GNOME client. The esvn client uses the Qt graphical interface and therefore doesn't have much baggage in either the GNOME or KDE desktops. The kdesvn client is a KDE client and therefore requires that the KD libraries be installed on your system, but is the only Subversion client that accepts command-line arguments. The kdesvn client can therefore be handy to use if you want to integrate a graphical subversion client into Firefox to handle svn: URLs. See the sidebar entitled "Handling svn: URLs in Firefox" later in this chapter, for more information about doing this.

■ `subversion`: (Mandatory) This is the core Subversion package, and provides everything you need to use Subversion from the command line on your local system.

■ `subversion-helper-scripts`: (Optional) This is a set of scripts that simplify working with Subversion repositories. This is a small but handy package, well worth the disk space that it requires (less than 200KB).

> **TIP** You may also find it handy to install the `subversion-tools` package when installing subversion. This package provides a few tools for sharing subversion repositories between users and doing more sophisticated imports of existing source code directories into subversion. However, if you have not already installed a mail server on your system, selecting this package for installation causes the exim mail server and related files to be scheduled for installation on your system. This is the mail server that I use anyway, so I'm OK with that, but your mileage may vary. See Chapter 27, "Setting Up a Mail Server," for general information about the different mail servers that are available on Ubuntu and why exim is a good choice.

Right-click and select Mark for Installation from the pop-up menu to select each of these packages for installation. Figure 18.24 shows subversion and related packages being selected for installation.

FIGURE 18.24

Installing subversion and related packages

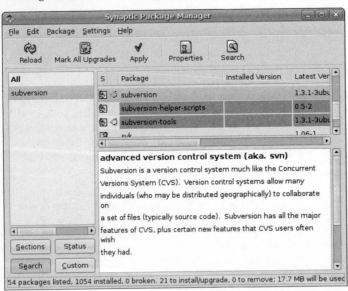

Depending on what software you have previously installed on your Ubuntu system and what you select in Synaptic, dialogs may display that list other packages that must also be installed, and ask for confirmation. If you see such dialogs, click Mark to accept these related (and required) packages.

After you are finished making your selections, click Apply in the Synaptic toolbar to install subversion and friends on your system. Once the installation completes, you're ready to set up your repository and, if you installed the `libapache2-svn` package, configure Apache2 to support subversion.

See Chapter 20, "Adding, Removing, and Updating Software," for more detailed information on installing applications using the Synaptic Package Manager.

Setting Up a Subversion Repository

Creating a subversion repository is done with the `svnadmin create` command, which creates the directory structure that makes up a Subversion repository. This command takes one argument, which is the name of the directory in which you want your subversion repository to be created.

One important thing to remember when creating a Subversion repository is that, because Subversion depends on WebDAV, which depends on the HTTP protocol, your subversion repository must be owned by the user and group that is used for communication via this protocol. On Ubuntu, this is the www-data user and the www-data group.

> **TIP** If you are creating a Subversion repository named `svn` and plan to export it through a Web server by that name, you must not create it in your Web server's `DocRoot` directory. As you'll see later in this section, you specify the full pathname to the Subversion repository in Apache's Subversion configuration file. Trying to use a repository named `svn` that is located in your Web server's `DocRoot` directory will result in the error `301 Moved Permanently (http://server-name)`, which isn't exactly intuitive.

For example, to create a Subversion repository in the directory /var/svn, you would execute the following command:

```
$ sudo -u www-data svnadmin create /var/svn
```

After supplying your password, the `svnadmin create` command creates your repository and populates it with the subdirectories it requires, all owned by the proper user and group. You can verify this by listing the contents of the specified directory, as in the following example:

```
$ ls -l /var/svn
total 28
drwxr-xr-x 2 www-data www-data 4096 2006-05-29 12:31 conf
drwxr-xr-x 2 www-data www-data 4096 2006-05-29 12:31 dav
drwxr-sr-x 5 www-data www-data 4096 2006-05-29 12:31 db
-r--r--r-- 1 www-data www-data    2 2006-05-29 12:31 format
drwxr-xr-x 2 www-data www-data 4096 2006-05-29 12:31 hooks
drwxr-xr-x 2 www-data www-data 4096 2006-05-29 12:31 locks
-rw-r--r-- 1 www-data www-data  229 2006-05-29 12:31 README.txt
```

Of course, an empty Subversion repository isn't all that exciting. The next section explains how to add an existing project to your repository, so that you actually have some source code to control.

Importing Projects into a Subversion Repository

A Subversion repository is simply a catcher's mitt for the files and directories that make up different projects. You can simply check your existing files directly into a Subversion repository, but it's far better to check files in using a separate directory hierarchy for each project.

To check a project directory into Subversion, first remove all nonsource files such as object files, intermediate files, binaries, and so on from that directory. Next, you simply import the project into subversion using Subversion's `svn import` command, as in the following example where you import a project that contains the canonical C program, "Hello, World!":

```
$ svn import hello file:///var/svn/hello -m "Creating hello project"
Authentication realm: <http://192.168.6.90:80> Subversion Repository
Password for 'wvh':
Adding          hello/hello.c
```

The arguments to the svn import command are the project that you want to import, the Subversion URL of the location in the repository where you want the project to be created, and the -m (message) option, followed by a string that contains the initial check-in message for the project, enclosed within quotation marks. The -m option is optional, of course, but it saves time because you would otherwise have to enter this message in a text editor that the svn command would start for you.

Once you've created a project or checked any files into Subversion, you can use the svn list command to display the contents of the repository, as in the following example, which uses the -R option to this command to recursively display the contents of the repository:

```
$ svn list -R file:///var/svn
hello/
hello/hello.c
```

You'll notice that this example uses a URL beginning with file:///, which provides access to a local repository. This is necessary at this point because you haven't started a Subversion server, so all URLs must be specified relative to the current filesystem. Trying to access your Subversion repository using any Web-based URL would display an error message at this point, either svn: PROPFIND of '/svn': could not connect to server (if you do not have a Web server running), or svn: PROPFIND of '/svn': 405 Method Not Allowed (if you have a Web server running but no subversion repository is available). The next section explains the two Subversion servers that are provided for use on Ubuntu systems, and how to configure them to make your repository available from other machines.

Setting Up a Subversion Server

Though Subversion is based on WebDAV and therefore uses the HTTP protocol for basic communications between clients and servers, you can access a local subversion repository (i.e., one that is physically located on the same machine that you are using) without running a subversion server. However, you will need to be running a Subversion server on machines whose repositories you want to access from other systems. There are two common types of Subversion servers:

- **Apache2:** An Apache Web server with integrated support for Subversion. Support for Subversion and WebDAV is easily added to an Apache or Apache2 Web server, which enables you to access your Subversion repository over the Web using URLs like http://host-name/repository or https://host-name/repository (if you configure SSL support into Apache2 and Subversion). The examples in this chapter discuss Apache2 integration and configuration, because Apache2 is the more modern and powerful Apache Web server.

- **Svnserve:** A stand-alone subversion server that enables you to access your Subversion repository over the Web using URLs like svn://host-name/repository. The svnserve binary is installed as part of the subversion package.

These two servers are not mutually exclusive, and can easily run on the same machine at the same time, providing access to the same repository if correctly configured. The next two sections explain how to configure each of these to provide access to the sample repository that you set up and populated in previous sections.

Configuring Apache2 for Subversion Support

Configuring the Apache2 Web server to support Subversion is quite easy, only requiring that you install and integrate the right Apache module, configure that module, and create the authentication file that will control write access to the repository.

Installing the Apache2 Web server's support for Subversion was described earlier in this chapter in the section entitled "Installing Subversion," and is done by installing the `libapache2-svn` package using the Synaptic Package Manager or the `apt-get` utility. The Apache2 Web server's support for Subversion integration with Apache2 is loaded by the file `/etc/apache2/mods-available/dav_svn.load`. The configuration file for this module is the file `/etc/apache2/mods-available/dav_svn.conf`.

After installing the Apache2 Web server's support for Subversion, edit this file using `sudo` and your favorite text editor. Your configuration options are the following:

1. Update the `<Location /svn>` element if you want to make your repository available through any URL other than `http://Web-server/svn`.

2. Uncomment the `DAV svn` entry to enable the repository.

3. Edit the `SVNPath` entry to identify the full pathname of your Subversion repository in the server's directory structure.

4. To use basic HTTP authentication (which I will use in this example), uncomment the following three lines:

    ```
    AuthType Basic
    AuthName "Subversion Repository"
    AuthUserFile /etc/apache2/dav_svn.passwd
    ```

5. Modify the pathname in the `AuthUserFile` entry to identify the HTTP password file that you want to use for HTTP authentication.

6. Purge any existing HTTP password file for Subversion and create the HTTP password file using the following commands, where `user-name` is the name of the first user for whom you want to create a password entry:

    ```
    $ sudo rm -f /etc/apache2/dav_svn.passwd
    $ sudo htpasswd2 -c /etc/apache2/dav_svn.passwd user-name
      New password:
      Re-type new password:
    ```

7. Add any other users to the HTTP password file using the following command:

    ```
    $ sudo htpasswd2 /etc/apache2/dav_svn.passwd user-name
    ```

After editing this file, a sample `dav_svn.conf` file looks like the following example. I've removed the comments to make things easier to read:

```
<Location /svn>
  DAV svn
  SVNPath /var/svn
  AuthType Basic
  AuthName "Subversion Repository"
  AuthUserFile /etc/apache2/dav_svn.passwd
  <LimitExcept GET PROPFIND OPTIONS REPORT>
    Require valid-user
  </LimitExcept>
</Location>
```

At this point, all you have to do is restart the Apache2 Web server, which you can do using the `sudo /etc/init.d/apache2 restart` command, and your repository will be available from other machines through the URL `http://Web-server/svn`. See "Checking Files Out of a Subversion Repository" later in this section, for information about using this URL to check out the files for your projects.

Configuring the svnserve Server

As mentioned earlier, Subversion's svnserve server enables Subversion clients to use URLs that use the svn protocol directly rather than the HTTP protocol. The svnserve server is installed as a part of the basic Subversion package.

You can start the svnserve server manually or through an Internet services daemon such as inetd or xinetd. The svnserve server doesn't require any special configuration because you identify the root of your subversion repository on the command line or in the configuration files for any Internet services daemon that you want to use. To start the svnserve daemon from the command line to provide access to the repository you created earlier in this chapter, you would simply execute the following command:

```
$ sudo -u www-data /usr/bin/svnserve -r /var -d
```

This starts the svnserve server as the user `www-data`, uses the `-r` option to identify the root of the Subversion repository as `/var`, and uses the `-d` option to start the `svnserve` process as a daemon that runs in the background.

As mentioned previously, you can also configure an Internet services daemon to handle incoming requests for svn: URLs on demand, rather than starting the svnserve daemon manually each time that you log in or explicitly add it to your Ubuntu system's startup files. Internet services daemons wait for incoming requests for services on certain ports and start associated daemons on demand, rather than requiring that the daemons are always running. Ubuntu provides two Internet services daemons, inetd and xinetd. The inetd daemon is the original Internet services daemon, while the xinetd daemon is a more modern and flexible Internet services daemon. Neither of these is installed by default on a basic Ubuntu system, so you will have to manually install whichever one you choose (I suggest xinetd) using the Synaptic Package Manager or `apt-get`.

If you install the xinetd Internet services daemon, you will also have to create the file `/etc/xinetd.d/svn`, which is the configuration file that tells the xinetd daemon what to do when an incoming svn request is received on port 3690, as defined in the file `/etc/services`. An `/etc/xinetd.d/svn` file that provides access to the repository that you created earlier in this chapter would look like the following:

```
service svn
{
    disable = no
    socket_type = stream
    protocol = tcp
    wait = no
    user = www-data
    server = /usr/bin/svnserve
    server_args = -i -r /var
}
```

After creating this file, you must restart the xinetd daemon using a command like the following:

```
$ sudo /etc/init.d/xinetd restart
```

Handling svn: URLs in Firefox

Trying to access a URL that begins with svn: in Firefox will display a dialog with the message "Firefox doesn't know how to handle this address because the protocol (svn) isn't associated with any program." If you want to be able to handle these URLs in Firefox, you'll need to create a small wrapper script that invokes your favorite graphical Subversion client with that URL as an argument. For example, I use the following script to automatically start the kdesvn client (the only Subversion client that accepts command-line arguments at the moment) when I click on an svn: URL:

```
!#/bin/bash
/usr/bin/kdesvn "$1"
```

After saving this script in a file and making it executable, I modified Firefox to call it when I click on an svn: URL by doing the following:

1. Type about:config in the Firefox location bar and press Peturn.
2. Right-click in the Preference Name window and select New ⇨ String.
3. Enter network.protocol-handler.app.svn as the name of the string. Click OK.
4. Enter the full pathname of the script as the value of the string.

This isn't especially exciting, but it does prevent occasional frustration when clicking on svn: URLs. It would be nice if esvn or rapidsvn took command-line arguments, because kdesvn is a KDE application and installs a ton of KDE libraries if you haven't already installed other KDE applications on your Ubuntu system. One of these days...

Checking Files Out of a Subversion Repository

Now that you've configured one (or two) Subversion servers, you can access the sample repository from any machine that can reach your server. Sample checkout commands that would retrieve the entire hello project are the following:

- svn co file:///var/svn/hello: This is the standard command to retrieve the hello project. You can use this command only from the machine on which the Subversion repository is located.
- svn co http://192.168.6.90/svn/hello: This command retrieves the hello project using the HTTP protocol, and will work only if you have a Web server running on the host where the Subversion repository is located, as described in the section entitled "Configuring Apache2 for Subversion Support."
- svn co svn://192.168.6.90/svn/hello: This command retrieves the hello project using the SVN protocol, and will work only if you have the Subversion server running on the host where the Subversion repository is located, as described in the section entitled "Configuring the svnserve Server."

Executing any of these commands will create a directory named hello in your current working directory, and will populate that directory with the file hello.c. Congratulations—you're using Subversion!

Committing Changes to a Subversion Repository

Once you have checked files out of your Subversion repository and modified them, you'll want to check them back into the repository from where they came — providing one true location for the latest and greatest version of your source code and being able to track changes to it is the whole point of source code control in the first place.

Subversion makes it very easy to check modified files back in because it automatically keeps track of version information and the repository from which checked-out files came in the first place. If you do a long listing (`ls -al`) of any directory that you've checked out of subversion, you will see a directory named `.svn` that holds this information.

Because Subversion maintains this information for you, all you have to do to check a file back into subversion is to use the `svn ci` (check in) command, as in the following example, which checks in a new, improved version of the file `hello.c` and shows the output from the `svn` command's check-in operation:

```
$ svn ci hello.c -m "Added comment"
Sending        hello.c
Transmitting file data .
Committed revision 7.
```

The `-m` option enables you to specify your check-in message on the command line. If you do not use this option, the `svn` command will automatically start a text editor in which you can enter a check-in message, and will proceed with the check-in once you exit the editor.

Getting More Information About Subversion

Subversion is a powerful source code control system, with many more commands and options than I've needed to discuss in the previous few sections. Some great Web sites for additional information about Subversion are the following:

- **Subversion Book** (`http://svnbook.red-bean.com`): An online version of the O'Reilly book *Version Control with Subversion*. Though this is available online for your convenience, it's always nice to buy a copy (`http://svnbook.red-bean.com/buy/p`), because we all understand that authors like to be compensated for their work other than through "good vibes" and "thank you" messages.

- **Subversion FAQ** (`http://subversion.tigris.org/faq.html`): The Subversion FAQ, which is a great source of answers to common questions and general information about Subversion.

- **Subversion Home Page** (`http://subversion.tigris.org`): This is the home page for Subversion, with as much information as you'd expect from the Subversion mothership.

- **Subversion IRC:** If you need answers *now* and are a fan of Internet Relay Chat, a dedicated channel for subversion users is available at irc.freenode.net, channel #svn.

- **Subversion Mailing Lists:** The tigris.org folks provide a variety of mailing lists for Subversion information. The announce@subversion.tigris.org mailing list is a low-traffic, read-only list to which release and update announcements are posted. The dev@subversion.tigris.org list is a mailing list for Subversion developers. The users@subversion.tigris.org list is a high-traffic list for Subversion users where you can ask questions and help out other Subversion users. To subscribe to any of these lists, send mail to listname-subscribe@subversion.tigris.org and follow the instructions that you receive in the response mail that you receive. These mailing lists are moderated, so there may be a delay before any posts that you make actually appear on the lists.

Many other Subversion-related pages and sites are available on the Web; a simple Google or Clusty search for Subversion will keep you knee-deep in reading material for weeks. The Indian *Linux For You* magazine (www.linuxforu.com) published a nice article on Subversion, which I couldn't find in the archives on their site, but is available from the authors' site at http://mia.ece.uic.edu/~papers/publications/subversion_final.pdf.

Summary

You don't have to build your own Linux applications anymore unless you want to—providing a precompiled, integrated set of Linux applications, libraries, and a kernel is the whole point of a Linux distribution. However, you may sometimes want to build your own, bleeding edge versions of existing software to get the latest and greatest features, or you may be a developer and want to write some of your own tools (hopefully open source) because that's what you do. This chapter explained how to install the tools that you'll need to compile most C and C++ applications on an Ubuntu system, including related software such as the make build tool and various libraries. The chapter also explored many of the most popular IDEs available for Linux systems, primarily focusing on the popular, powerful, and open source Eclipse IDE. The chapter concluded by discussing source code control systems and how to set up your own Subversion repository and server, and how to quickly and easily make your Subversion repository available through a local Apache Web server.

Chapter 19 discusses the sequence of events that occur when you boot or shut down your Linux system. Understanding the system startup process is important to successfully integrate new services and capabilities into an existing system. Knowing where and how various services are started is also important when optimizing your system, because this enables you to easily disable specific services that you don't really need and which are therefore wasting CPU time on your system. Understanding the system shutdown process is important in terms of understanding how to cleanly shut down various services, in the right order, so that you avoid various system cleanup and housekeeping tasks the next time you boot your system.

Part III

Ubuntu for System Administrators

Chapter 19

Understanding the Ubuntu Startup and Shutdown Processes

IN THIS CHAPTER

Understanding the Linux boot process

Monitoring the Linux boot process

Optimizing the Linux boot process

Understanding the Linux shutdown process

Nowadays, booting an Ubuntu Linux system involves watching a friendly splash screen display a variety of system status messages and progress bars as it proceeds through the various commands that are part of the boot, initialization, and startup processes. This is all well and good, but sometimes it's nice to know what's actually going on under the hood. It's similarly interesting to know how your Ubuntu system performs an orderly shutdown, which is what happens when you select System ➪ Quit, and select the Shutdown icon. (Describing what happens when you do a disorderly shutdown by pulling the plug is much easier — poof! The system's off, but the boot process next time will be a tad slower as the system checks for filesystem problems and repairs everything that it can.)

This chapter describes the general phases of the Linux boot process and any things that are specific to Ubuntu Linux. It then discusses how you can get detailed information about all of the processes executed when your system starts, so that you can look for ways to speed up your system's boot process, and discusses upcoming improvements that will further speed up the boot process in general. The chapter concludes with an explanation of what happens when you shut down your system, which is relatively short, because this is really just the reverse of the last stage of the boot process.

Overview of the Ubuntu Linux Startup Process

This section describes the process of booting an Ubuntu Linux system, from the time that you turn it on to the point at which your operating system of choice (hopefully, Ubuntu Linux) is running. I've tried to provide a detailed description of the boot process for most of the hardware that is capable of running Linux, which means that some of the following subsections will not apply to all hardware. If you are running Ubuntu Linux on a desktop or server system that has an x86-compatible processor, all of the following sections are relevant.

The Boot Monitor or BIOS

When you first turn on a computer system, it loads a boot monitor or Basic Input/Output system (BIOS) from storage on the motherboard. This storage is usually a programmable, read-only memory chip (PROM) or a section of flash memory that is present on the board. The BIOS or boot monitor is a very low-level, hardware oriented application that does some basic hardware initialization, performs some amount of hardware testing and verification (often optional), waits for keyboard or console input for some predetermined period of time, and then usually begins to execute a set of predetermined instructions to load another program into memory. These instructions load another program into memory from a predetermined location such as a portion of flash memory or the Master Boot Record (MBR) of a storage device such as a hard drive or CD-ROM, and then specify the memory address at which to begin executing the program once it has been loaded successfully.

On systems with limited hardware resources, such as many embedded systems, the program loaded into memory by a boot monitor is the Linux kernel, which is described in a subsequent section. However, the boot process is slightly more involved on most desktop and server computer systems. On these types of systems, an intermediate program is loaded into memory from the MBR that provides additional configuration and customization options for the boot process. On modern x86, PPC, and SPARC systems, the program that is loaded into memory at this point is known as a *boot loader*, which is a configurable application that provides higher-level options for loading an operating system on the computer. The boot loader that is most commonly used on modern x86 systems (including 64-bit systems) is the Grand Unified Boot Loaders (GRUB) though some Linux distributions still use an older, simpler boot loader known as the Linux Loader (LiLo). Desktop PPC and SPARC systems that run Linux do not use these boot loaders, but instead load system-specific boot loaders that work with their boot monitors.

The Boot Loader

Boot loaders typically consist of two stages: a minimal first-stage boot loader and a more elegant, second-stage boot loader. The size of a first-stage boot loader is constrained by the size of the MBR on a storage device, which is a single sector (512 bytes). The first-stage boot loader therefore primarily contains enough information to locate and load the second-stage boot loader, which is where all the action is.

As mentioned earlier, Linux offers two boot loaders, LiLo and GRUB. The LiLo boot loader was developed long before GRUB, and does not understand Linux filesystem formats — it identifies its second-stage boot loader (/boot/boot.b) and other boot-related information through direct offsets into the device where these files are stored. The GRUB boot loader, which is the boot loader used by Ubuntu, follows a similar process, but uses an intermediate step in the boot process, first loading what GRUB calls a *stage 1.5* boot loader that understands a specific type of Linux filesystem, and can therefore load GRUB's text-format configuration file directly from your machine's root filesystem. GRUB provides many different stage 1.5 boot loaders as follows:

- **e2fs_stage1_5**, for booting from a partition containing an ext2 or ext3 filesystem
- **fat_stage1_5**, for booting from a partition containing a DOS or Microsoft Windows VFAT filesystem
- **ffs_stage1_5**, for booting from a partition containing a Berkeley Fast filesystem
- **iso9660_stage1_5**, for booting from a partition containing an ISO9660 filesystem, such as a CD-ROM
- **jfs_stage1_5**, for booting from a partition containing a JFS filesystem
- **minix_stage1**, for booting from a partition containing a Minix filesystem
- **reiserfs_stage1_5**, for booting from a partition containing a ReiserFS filesystem

- **ufs2_stage1_5**, for booting from a partition containing a traditional Unix filesystem
- **vstafs_stage1_5**, for booting from a partition containing a Plan 9 VSTa filesystem
- **xfs_stage1_5**, for booting from a partition containing an XFS filesystem

By default, Ubuntu systems include stage 1.5 boot loaders for booting from ext2/ext3, JFS, Minim, ReiserFS, VFAT, and XFS filesystems.

The stage 1.5 boot loader then loads GRUB's second-stage boot loader and associated configuration files directly from the type of filesystem on which they are located.

> **NOTE** The fundamental difference between LiLo and GRUB is whether they load boot loader configuration and menu data from a filesystem, or whether the location of this information needs to be built into the boot loader. Though both boot loaders use a configuration file, you must rerun the LiLo command (/sbin/lilo) each time you modify LiLo's configuration file (/etc/lilo.conf), so that LiLo can repackage information about available menu options and kernels into the boot.b file that it locates by a direct filesystem offset, and so that it can update the location of this file in the MBR. GRUB's stage 1.5 boot loaders work around this problem by enabling GRUB to locate its configuration information and associated files in a filesystem. There is no need to rerun GRUB after modifying its configuration data.

A second-stage boot loader typically provides access to a menu that enables you to choose between different ways of loading an operating system on your computer. Both GRUB and LiLo can be configured to display this menu for a short period of time, to display it only in response to specific keyboard input (such as pressing the Escape key), or to not display it at all. Once your system boots Linux, you can modify the configuration of the boot loader to automatically display a menu by modifying the boot loader's configuration file, which is either /etc/lilo.conf for LiLo or /boot/grub/menu.1st for GRUB.

> **NOTE** Ubuntu Linux systems use the GRUB boot loader, so that's the primary focus of this section. For more information about LiLo (which is still used by some other Linux distributions, such as Xandros Linux), see www.freshmeat.net/projects/lilo, which is the FreshMeat project page for LILO.

By default, the GRUB boot loader on Ubuntu systems is configured to boot a default configuration without displaying a menu, but you can press the Escape key when GRUB first starts (do it quickly—you have five seconds) to display a menu that shows all of the available GRUB boot options. Figure 19.1 shows a sample menu from the GRUB boot loader on one of my Ubuntu systems. If you do not press Escape during the boot process, GRUB will automatically boot the default configuration that its file directs it to use.

FIGURE 19.1

A sample GRUB boot menu

Some Linux distributions, such as Fedora Core, provide prettier GRUB menu screens than the one shown in Figure 19.1. My perspective on that is simple: "Who cares? I don't really want to deal with those screens anyway." You will have to interact with the GRUB menu if you set up a dual-boot machine and want to boot your other operating system for some odd reason, but other than that, GRUB boot menus should be something that you never need to see.

TIP   Each time that you install a newer version of the Linux kernel on your system, such as through the Update Manager, the package installation process automatically updates your GRUB configuration to boot the new kernel and associated files. The GRUB menu entry for the previous kernel is still available on the GRUB boot menu. If you experience problems with a new kernel on a system, you can reboot a previous kernel by pressing Escape during the GRUB boot process, using the arrow keys to select the kernel that you want to boot, and pressing Return.

GRUB configuration files typically contain multiple definitions for ways to boot your system. Each set of related entries is referred to as a stanza, and looks like the following:

```
title           Ubuntu, kernel 2.6.15-23-386
root            (hd0,0)
kernel          /boot/vmlinuz-2.6.15-23-386 root=/dev/hda1 ro quiet
splash
initrd          /boot/initrd.img-2.6.15-23-386
savedefault
boot
```

Each line in a stanza begins with a keyword that identifies the aspect of the boot process that it described. In the preceding example, these entries have the following meanings:

- `title`: provides the name for this entry displayed on the grub menu
- `root`: identifies the absolute location of the runtime root filesystem using GRUB's own nomenclature
- `kernel`: identifies the kernel to boot and provides command-line boot parameters for that kernel
- `initrd`: identifies an initial RAM disk or initial RAM filesystem image that should be loaded by the kernel during the boot process
- `savedefault`: identifies this entry as the default GRUB boot entry
- `boot`: tells GRUB to boot using the configuration described in the current stanza

These keywords are only a subset of the keywords supported by GRUB. For complete information about GRUB configuration files, see the online documentation for GRUB, which is provided in the `grub-doc` package, which you must install manually using the Synaptic Package Manager or the `apt-get` application. Once you have installed this package, the complete GRUB documentation is available by typing **info grub** from any Ubuntu command line. For even more information about GRUB, see the GRUB home page at www.gnu.org/software/grub. This page also discusses the new, improved family-size version of GRUB, GRUB2, which is currently under development.

Loading the Kernel

A kernel specified in a GRUB stanza is typically a compressed kernel image that is loaded directly into memory. This compressed kernel is prefixed by some instructions that perform initial hardware and execution environment setup (stack definition, page table initialization, starting the swapper, and so on), uncompress the kernel image into high memory, store any initial RAM disk or initial RAM filesystem in memory for subsequent access, and then begin execution of the uncompressed kernel.

The kernel sets up interrupts, performs additional hardware initialization, and then uncompresses and mounts any initial RAM disk or filesystem that is found in the kernel image or is specified using GRUB's `initrd` keyword. If an initial RAM disk or filesystem is found or specified, the system follows the sequence of events described in the next section, "Loading and Using an Initial RAM Disk or RAM Filesystem." If no initial RAM disk or initial RAM filesystem is found in the kernel or identified using the `initrd` parameter, the kernel mounts the root filesystem identified on the command line using the disk identifiers specified in GRUB's root entry, and then starts the standard system initialization process, as described later in this chapter in the section entitled "The Init Process."

Loading and Using an Initial RAM Disk or RAM Filesystem

Many Linux systems use a special type of filesystem as part of the boot process, before actually mounting the nontransient storage devices that are attached to your system. These initial filesystems are optional, and come in two different flavors: an *initrd* (initial RAM disk) or *initramfs* (initial RAM filesystem). On most desktop and server computer systems, these initial filesystems are typically used to load kernel modules, such as specialized device drivers that the kernel needs but which are not built into the kernel, and to perform specialized hardware and software initialization functions. On desktop and server systems such as Ubuntu Linux systems, an initial RAM disk or initial RAM filesystem is almost always a transient part of the boot process. On embedded Linux systems with sufficient memory, the `initramfs` or `initrd` might be the actual root filesystem used when Linux is running.

Initial RAM disks are the traditional mechanism used by many 2.6 and all earlier Linux kernels to enable the kernel to load drivers and execute processes that must be available to boot successfully. Initial RAM disks are compressed files that provide an initial filesystem for use by the Linux kernel at boot time. Initial RAM disks are compressed files that contain an actual filesystem in a format such as ext2, romfs, and so on. Initial RAM disks are uncompressed into a pre-allocated portion of memory and are then mounted for use by the kernel. The primary problem with initial RAM disks is that they consume a substantial amount of system memory and, because they are actual block devices, require the kernel to contain drivers for whatever type of filesystem they use.

The Linux 2.6 kernel introduced the idea of initial RAM filesystems that exist directly in the kernel's file and directory cache. Initial RAM filesystems are identified or built into the kernel in the same way that initial RAM disks are, but consist of compressed archive files in the format produced by the Unix/Linux `cpio` command. These archive files contain all of the files and directory entries for the initial RAM filesystem, and are directly unpacked into the kernel's file and directory entry cache, which is then mounted as a filesystem. Using the file and directory cache as a filesystem substantially reduces the amount of memory required for the initial RAM filesystem because files and directories live in the kernel's page and directory entry (dentry) cache, where they would be copied anyway if they were used from a filesystem located on a block device. An initial RAM filesystem is an instance of the Linux `tmpfs` filesystem.

Linux systems that boot with an initial RAM disk execute the file `/linuxrc` from that filesystem after uncompressing and mounting the filesystem. This file is typically a command file, but can also be a version of the `/sbin/init` program that follows the standard initialization process described later in this chapter in the section entitled "The Init Process." (This is typically done when the initial RAM disk will be your runtime filesystem, as in embedded systems.) Linux systems that boot with an initial RAM filesystem execute the file `/init` from that filesystem after loading it into the file and directory entry cache. Like the `/linuxrc` file used with initial RAM disks, `/init` is typically a command file, but can also be a version of the init program that follows the standard initialization process described in the next section.

Comparing Initial RAM Disks and RAM-based Filesystems

Some of the more significant ways in which initial RAM disks and initial RAM filesystems differ are the following:

- You do not need any special privileges to build an initial RAM filesystem file or a kernel that contains one. Building an initial RAM disk typically requires root privileges unless you do so using an external application such as the genext2fs application.

- Initial RAM disks (initrd) are compressed files containing a filesystem in a specific format such as ext2, romfs, cramfs, squashfs, and so on. Initial RAM filesystems (initramfs) are compressed archive files in the format used by the Linux/Unix cpio application.

- Initial RAM disks must be prepared outside the kernel and identified during the kernel build process if you want to link them directly into the kernel. Initial RAM filesystems can be prepared outside the kernel and identified during the kernel build process, but can also be automatically created during the kernel build process. Versions 2.6 and later kernels enable you to identify a directory that contains the files that you want to have in your initial RAM filesystem or a configuration file that describes their contents.

- Initial RAM disks allocate and require a fixed amount of memory that is specified when building the kernel, regardless of the actual size of the files and directories that they contain. Any space not used by files and directories in the initial RAM disk is completely wasted. Initial RAM filesystems are directly allocated in the kernel's page and dentry cache, and therefore only require allocating the amount of memory that is required by the files and directories that they contain.

- You can easily add a new script or file to an initial RAM filesystem that is specified as an external file in GRUB by using the gunzip application to uncompress the cpio archive, using the cpio -- append command to add the new file to the archive, and using the gzip command to recompress the archive. You should only do this for testing purposes, because your modification will go away the next time you build a kernel or receive an update. You can permanently add the file or script to future initial RAM filesystems that you build by adding that file or script to the directory or script pointed to by the CONFIG_INITRAMFS_SOURCE kernel configuration variable for your kernel.

- Initial RAM disks automatically execute the file /linuxrc from the RAM disk. Initial RAM filesystems automatically execute the file /init from the RAM filesystem. The /init file in an initramfs filesystem runs with process ID 1, just like the init process in a standard Linux system.

The contents of an initial RAM disk or initial RAM filesystem differ based on the hardware, system capabilities, and type of Linux system that you are using. Desktop Linux systems typically use these filesystems to provide loadable device drivers or mandatory system setup procedures that are required to proceed with the boot process. Embedded Linux systems often use initial RAM disks or RAM filesystems as their actual runtime filesystems in the absence of usable disk, flash, or compact Flash storage. Both initial RAM disks and initial RAM filesystems provide only transient storage that does not enable you to save files across system restarts, but initial RAM filesystems are much more efficient and place fewer requirements on the kernel.

On desktop and server systems that use physical root filesystems, the last step in the /linuxrc or /init instructions is to mount the real root filesystem (identified in the kernel or using the root= kernel boot parameter), begin using that root filesystem as the new root filesystem (by using a pivot_root or chroot command), and start the init process, as described in the next section.

The Init Process

After loading the kernel and mounting their runtime root filesystem, traditional Unix and Linux systems execute a system application known as the *init* (initialization) process, which is typically found in /sbin/init on Linux systems. Typically, the init process is process number 1 on the system, as shown in a process status listing produced using the ps command, and is therefore the ancestor of all other processes on your system. The init process reads the file /etc/inittab to identify the way in which the system should boot and defines all of the other processes and programs that it should start.

> **NOTE** The init binary is part of a package of applications known as the SysVInit package. The SysVInit package uses a package of related command scripts known as the *initscripts* package, to identify the processes that are started when a system boots into different run levels and the order in which they are started.

Most desktop and server Linux systems use the concept of *run levels* to identify the applications that the system executes and the order in which they are executed. Different run levels are simply a way of defining a set of applications that the system administrator believes should be run when the system is being used in a certain way. For example, run level 1 is usually known as single-user mode, and is used for system maintenance. Only the core set of applications required for a system administrator to contact the system and perform maintenance tasks are running when the system is in run level 1. The run levels used by Ubuntu are the following:

- **0**: halt
- **1**: single-user
- **2**: default multiuser run level on Ubuntu/Debian systems
- **3-5**: other multiuser run levels, used for customized run levels
- **6**: reboot

> **NOTE** Most Linux distributions other than Ubuntu and other Debian-inspired distributions use run level 3 as the default, nongraphical multiuser run level. These distributions use run level 5 as the default graphical multiuser run level.

Systems that use both the SysVInit and initscripts packages boot in the following sequence: Once the kernel is loaded and begins executing from its runtime root filesystem, it invokes a process known as the /sbin/init (initialization) process, which reads the file /etc/inittab to identify the basic processes and programs that it should start.

In the /etc/inittab file, the default run level for your system is identified with a line containing the string initdefault, as in the following example:

    id:2:initdefault:

In this case, the default run level is 2. An additional entry in the /etc/inittab file identifies a command script that is run to initialize the system itself, as in the following example:

    si::sysinit:/etc/init.d/rcS

> **NOTE** On Ubuntu systems, the /etc/init.d/rcS command actually runs the /etc/init.d/rc command with an argument of S, which executes all of the scripts in the directory /etc/rcS.d that begin with an uppercase S, as described in the rest of this section. On some other Linux distributions, the system initialization script is a single script to which you manually add any initialization commands that you want to run.

After the system initialization script is run, Linux distributions that use the SysVInit and initscripts packages then define what occurs when the system enters a specific run level. For example, a few lines later in the /etc/inittab file, you might see additional information about run boot level 2 in an entry like the following:

```
12:2:wait:/etc/init.d/rc 2
```

This line specifies that when the system enters run level 2, the /etc/init.d/rc command will be executed with an argument of 2. This causes the rc (run command) command to execute all of the appropriate files located in the directory /etc/rc2.d. The files in this directory have names of the form SNNname or KNNname, and are usually executable shell scripts (or are links to a common set of scripts) that contain lists of other system commands to execute. Files beginning with the letter S are executed when the system starts a specified run level. Entries beginning with the letter K are executed when the system leaves a specified run level. Commands are executed in the numerical order specified by the number NN. The "name" portion of an entry is user-defined, but is generally evocative of the program or subsystem that the file starts.

Two standard assumptions that you can make about the startup scripts on your Ubuntu system are the following:

- All device drivers have been initialized, local filesystems have been mounted, and networking is available after all of the S40* scripts have completed.
- The system clock has been set, NFS filesystems have been mounted (if any are listed in /etc/fstab or you use the automounter, which is started later), and all filesystems have been checked for consistency after all of the S60* scripts have been executed.

You should keep these rules in mind when adding your own startup scripts to the startup sequence for any of your system run levels.

Because Linux systems start many of the same commands at different run levels, the entries in the run level directory for all run levels are usually just symbolic links to the master collection of system startup and shutdown scripts located in the directory /etc/init.d. The names of the symbolic links in the different run level directories use the SNNname and KNNname naming convention to impose a sequence on their execution. The names of the scripts in /etc/init.d that the run level directories link to have generic names. Using symbolic links rather than explicit startup and shutdown scripts for each run level makes it easy to add or remove services from a given run level without duplicating the master scripts, and leaves /etc/init.d as a single, central location where you can modify any of these scripts to propagate your changes to the startup/shutdown process for all of the associated run levels.

As the last step of the startup process for any multiuse run level, the init process runs the script /etc/rc.local, which is provided so that you can customize the startup process for a specific machine without making general changes to the startup scripts and symbolic links for that machine.

See "Optimizing the Ubuntu Boot Process," later in this chapter, for a discussion of some applications that can help you manage the startup/shutdown scripts and links associated with different Ubuntu run levels.

Examining the Boot Process with Boot Chart

Boot chart (www.bootchart.org), by Ziga Mahkovec, is an impressive and useful utility that monitors the boot process, creating data files that it uses to generate a graphical representation of your system's boot process, a portion of which is shown in Figure 19.2.

FIGURE 19.2

A section of Boot chart output

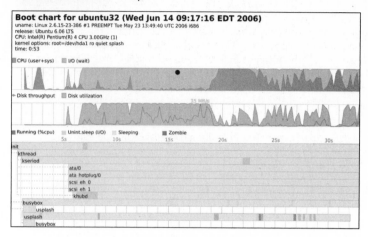

Boot chart isn't installed by default on Ubuntu systems, but you can install it manually using either the Synaptic Package Manager or the apt-get utility. When installed on Ubuntu systems, Boot chart adds itself to the initial RAM filesystem used by your kernel to capture data about the boot process, and then adds a script to your runtime root filesystem's startup process (/etc/init.d/stop-bootchart, sym-linked to /etc/rc2.d/S99stop-bootchart) that processes the collected data and generates the graphical record of the boot/startup process.

> **TIP** On Linux distributions that do not yet use an initial RAM filesystem (but still use an initial RAM disk), you can still use Boot chart by installing it on your system and modifying the GRUB boot entry for your kernel to include an init=/sbin/bootchartd entry so that the system runs the Bootchart data collection script before starting the /sbin/init program and executing the normal sequence of startup scripts.

Boot chart uses a Java application to generate a Portable Network Graphics (PNG) graphics file in /var/log/bootchart. This file is named based on the day that it was created and a version number, so that multiple files created on the same day don't overwrite each other. You can configure Boot chart to produce graphics in SVG or EPS formats (or to preserve the data files that it creates) by modifying the /etc/init.d/stop-bootchart script.

Not only is it really cool to have a graphical record of the boot process, but that graphical record can be very valuable in terms of helping you identify startup scripts that are running that you don't want or need to run, extra invocations of system or X Window system processes, and so on. Boot chart adds very little over-head to your system's startup process, but the view of the system startup process that it provides can be invaluable.

Optimizing the Ubuntu Boot Process

The section earlier in this chapter entitled "The Init Process" described how the /sbin/init process uses an entry in /etc/inittab for your system's default run level to run scripts that start various services at boot time. You can manually customize the run levels at which various services start, but this is tedious at best. As you might expect, the Ubuntu repositories provide a number of applications that simplify editing the startup and shutdown scripts associated with different run levels. Ubuntu comes with an application (System ⇨ Administration ⇨ Services) that promises to provide coarse control over which services are started at boot time, but does not provide granular control over the run levels with which these services are associated or the sequence in which they are started. (This is odd because it used to do this. I guess that progress is not always forward.)

My two favorite tools for modifying the scripts started at various Ubuntu run levels are the following:

- **sysv-rc-conf**: An application that runs in any Ubuntu terminal application, such as an xterm or the GNOME Terminal, as shown in Figure 19.3. The SysV Runlevel Config application provides a simple interface for enabling or disabling services at various run levels, and includes on-screen help for its user interface.

FIGURE 19.3

The sysv-rc-conf application running in a GNOME terminal

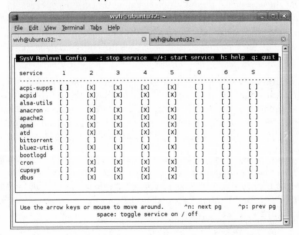

- **Boot-Up Manager**: A graphical application that provides an excellent user interface for enabling and disabling startup/shutdown scripts at various run levels. Figure 19.4 shows the Boot-Up Manager.

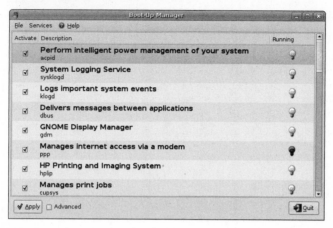

FIGURE 19.4

The Boot-Up Manager application

Neither the `syv-rc-conf` or Boot-Up Manager applications are installed automatically as part of a default Ubuntu installation, but can easily be installed using the Synaptic Package Manager or the command-line `apt-get` application. See Chapter 20, "Adding, Removing, and Updating Software," for detailed information about using these applications.

The Boot-Up Manager is by far the more interesting of these two applications (as long as you're running an X Window system desktop or window manager). Installing this application adds the System ⇨ Administration ⇨ Boot-Up Manager menu item, which you can use to start the application. Like most administrative applications, you'll need to supply your password to run this application. The Boot-Up manager requires a fair amount of time to start, as it must read and process every startup script in the `/etc/init.d` directory and must read every symbolic link in any of your `/etc/rc` directories. This additional startup time is worth it in terms of usability.

Once the Boot-Up Manager is running, Figure 19.4 shows that it provides some basic information about each of the startup scripts that your system is running, which helps you make intelligent decisions about the services that you want to enable or disable. However, clicking the Advanced checkbox on its main dialog displays two additional tabs that provide access to the real power of the Boot-Up Manager. You can click either of these tabs to display more detailed information about the topic with which it is associated, or click the Summary tab to display the standard Boot-Up Manager screen shown in Figure 19.4.

Figure 19.5 shows the Boot-Up Manager's Services tab, which provides a detailed description of the services that are stopped and started by available run level scripts, and the different run levels with which each is associated.

You can start or stop any existing service, remove it from the startup and shutdown sequence, or modify the sequence in which that script is executed during the startup or shutdown processes by right-clicking any entry in the Services tab to display the pop-up menu shown in Figure 19.6.

FIGURE 19.5

The Boot-Up Manager's Services tab

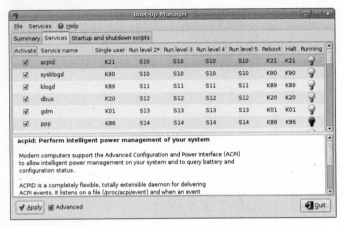

FIGURE 19.6

The pop-up menu for modifying services in Boot-Up Manager

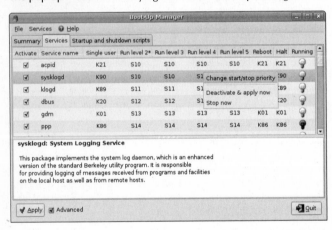

To change the sequence in which a script is executed during the startup and shutdown processes, select Change start/stop priority from the pop-up menu. (Identifying a script's sequence number as its priority is somewhat misleading, but c'est le vie.) The dialog shown in Figure 19.7 displays, in which you can enter the new numeric identifier for the sequence in which you want this script to run during the startup or shutdown process.

Modifying a service's sequence in the Boot-Up Manager

After modifying these values, click OK to save your changes and return to the Services tab or click Cancel to return to the Services tab without making any changes. Any changes that you specify are made to your system immediately. (The current Boot-Up manager doesn't update its internal display to use the new sequence number until the next time that you start the Boot-Up Manager, which is certainly a bug.)

In addition to enabling you to modify the startup and shutdown scripts associated with various system services, clicking the Boot-Up Manager's Advanced checkbox also displays a tab on which you can examine the startup and shutdown scripts that are run during the boot process through the system initialization script identified by the `sysinit` entry in your `/etc/inittab` file. Click the Startup and shutdown scripts tab to see a list of these other scripts and the part of the system startup or shutdown sequence that they are associated with, as shown in Figure 19.8.

The Boot-Up Manager's Startup and shutdown scripts tab

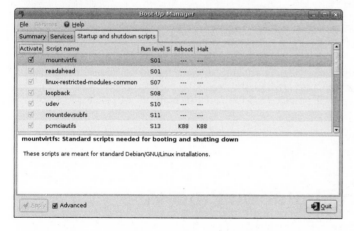

Init, the Next Generation

The SysVInit process is well-known and well-established, but has been used for years without any substantial modifications. Its biggest problem is that all of the scripts that it executes are executed sequentially, which means that your system's startup process can take much longer than it needs to, assuming that there are no major dependencies between startup scripts. Jimmy Wennlund's initng (Init, Next generation) replacement for the standard `/sbin/init` process is a great step in the right direction, supporting parallel execution of startup scripts whenever possible. The InitNG program also enables you to collect additional statistics that may be useful to you when analyzing your system's startup performance. See the InitNG home page, `http://initng.thinktux.net`, for more information about this project (and the source code).

InitNG is actively under development and is still maturing, but you can experiment with it by building and installing it on your system, and then modify your GRUB kernel command line to include the statement `init=/sbin/initng`. This enables you to experiment with InitNG without risking any problems with your current, traditional initialization sequence.

Because these scripts are associated with the core system initialization process, this dialog only enables you to see the scripts associated with the system initialization process. Attempting to deactivate any of these scripts displays the slightly irritating warning dialog shown in Figure 19.9. (You'll notice that the Apply button is also deactivated on this tab.)

FIGURE 19.9

Boot-Up Manager's warning regarding system initialization scripts

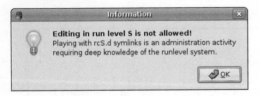

I am being kind by calling this warning dialog "slightly irritating," because modifying your system's startup and shutdown scripts in any way is an administrative task that requires some knowledge of what you're doing. I'm sure that editing these scripts will be added in a future release of the Boot-Up Manager. This is open source, after all!

To accept and permanently apply any changes that you have made to various services, click the Boot-Up Manager's Apply button before exiting, and then click OK.

The Ubuntu Linux Shutdown Process

To shut down your Ubuntu Linux system, you can select the System ⇨ Administration ⇨ Quit menu item, which displays the dialog shown in Figure 19.10.

FIGURE 19.10

Ubuntu's system shutdown dialog

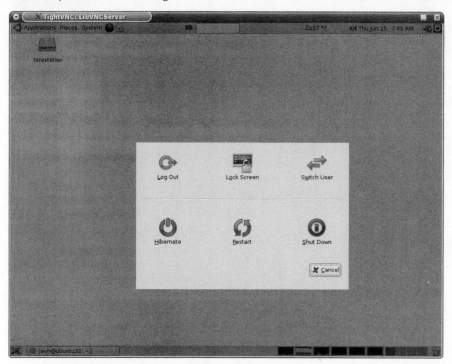

Clicking Shut Down in this dialog begins the system shutdown process, which is essentially the opposite of the startup process. After selecting this item, the system logs you out, and the /sbin/init process begins to run the shutdown scripts associated with your current run level, which are the scripts beginning with the letter K in the /etc/rcNN.d directory, where NN is your current run level. The system then runs any shutdown scripts in the system initialization directory, and turns off your system.

As a nod to x86-based PC tradition (and as a relatively quick silver bullet), the init process intercepts the traditional Control+Alt+Delete key combination and can perform a specific action when this key combination is pressed. This key combination is known as the "three-finger salute" to many PC lovers.

The line in the /etc/inittab file that identifies what happens when the Control+Alt+Delete key combination is pressed is identified with the crtlaltdel keyword, and looks like the following on Ubuntu systems:

```
ca:12345:ctrlaltdel:/sbin/shutdown -t1 -a -r now
```

This command tells the system to run the /sbin/shutdown command with options that tell it to wait one second between sending a shutdown warning and actually terminating processes (-t1), use the /etc/shutdown.allow text file to determine the users that can shut down the system using this key combination (-a), to reboot after shutting down (-r), and to do everything now (now). For more detailed information about the /sbin/shutdown command, see the online reference information available for this command by typing the man shutdown command from any xterm or GNOME Terminal window. You should probably do this at least once before actually shutting down your system — one second isn't a lot of time to read a man page during the actual shutdown process.

Summary

This chapter dove down into the details of how Linux systems boot, and the specific steps that your Ubuntu system follows when it boots. The Linux boot process is a very cool combination of hardwired and flexible steps that make it easy to customize the services that are started on your system and the order in which they are started.

Chapter 20 explores how to add, remove, and update software on your Ubuntu system. All Ubuntu installations come with a great initial selection of software but, as you've seen throughout this book, a huge amount of additional, useful software is readily available in the Ubuntu repositories. The next chapter explains how to retrieve that software, how to browse it, and how to figure out which software packages you need to install to find specific files or fulfill other requirements.

Chapter 20

Adding, Removing, and Updating Software

I f you looked around the universe before settling on Ubuntu Linux, one of the things that you were sure to notice is that "billions and billions" of Linux distributions are available, each with its own installer, favorite desktop environment and/or X Window system window manager, set of core applications, and some way of updating, expanding, and maintaining the software that comes with the distribution. When you come right down to it, the last item is the most significant aspect of a Linux distribution aside from the size and involvement of its user and development communities. There's actually an interesting loop between ease-of-use/ease-of-maintenance and the size of the user community. A Linux distribution that makes it easy to keep existing software up to date, install new software, and figure out what's on your system in the first place is a Linux distribution that more people are apt to use. (This assumes that someone is actually keeping the distribution up to date.)

As discussed in Chapter 1, I find the Ubuntu Linux community the most exciting, dynamic, and energetic Linux community that I've ever encountered. The Ubuntu community is a committed community of both users and developers. Updates and bug fixes to existing software are frequent, which is a good thing. A vast pool of software is available for easy download and installation.

Access to new and updated software is similarly easy. Ubuntu's Update Manager automatically lets you know when updates are available to software that's installed on your system, and keeping your system up-to-date requires three or four mouse clicks. Not too shabby! The dpkg, apt-get, aptitude, and synaptic tools make it almost easy to install new software, and Synaptic Package Manager makes it easy to search for software that's relevant to your interests. Who could ask for anything more?

The key to all of this simplicity and ease-of-use is the excellent DEB (for Debian) package format, developed for the Debian Linux distribution and therefore used by Ubuntu. The DEB package format put other software package formats, such as RPM, to shame — I personally would appreciate some electroshock therapy to

IN THIS CHAPTER

Package management overview

Using Ubuntu repositories

Finding things on your system

Using apt-get, aptitude, and Synaptic

Using the Ubuntu Update manager

Cleaning up your system

forget the needless hours I've wasted trying to untangle twisty mazes of dependencies and requirements between various RPM packages. If you don't know what RPM is, you're lucky. Let's keep it that way.

NOTE If you're familiar with RPM-based Linux distributions such as Fedora Core, Mandriva, Red Hat, or Yellow Dog, you're probably thinking, "Silly Human, yum solves most RPM problems!" Although this is probably true in a court of law, I don't feel that providing additional layers of syntactic sugar on top of a frustrating package management system such as RPM is the "right thing" or an actual solution. I prefer using smarter package formats such as DEB and smarter utilities such as the ones discussed in this chapter that were designed to do the right thing in the first place rather than continually shaving JoJo the dog-faced boy to make him look more human.

TIP If you must deal with packages that were created for other Linux distributions and are therefore in other package formats, see the section entitled "Converting Packages from Other Package Formats" later in this chapter for information about converting package.

Tools such as dpkg, apt-get, and aptitude are knee-deep in online manual pages and Web sites that explain every conceivable combination of command-line options, so I'm not going to bore you by repeating those in this chapter. This chapter explains how to do common tasks using these tools, focusing on helping you get your work done rather than on duplicating existing reference material. The first section of this chapter provides an overview of the package management utilities used on Ubuntu systems (and thus discussed in this chapter) so that you have a clear idea of "what does what" as you read through this chapter. The next section explains how the Ubuntu software that you can download from the repositories is organized, and provides some tips about other, unofficial repositories that you might find useful. After this, the hands-on sections of this chapter begin by explaining how to find out what's on your system, figure out what package provided specific files that are already on your system, and how to figure out what package you might want to install if you're looking for a specific file. This is most easily done from the command line, so that's our focus in this section.

Subsequent sections of this chapter focus on using the apt-get (command-line), aptitude (terminal-oriented), and synaptic (fancy graphics) tools to locate and install new packages on your system. The last two sections discuss how to use the Ubuntu Update Manager to keep your system up-to-date and how to identify and remove packages on your system that are no longer required because they were installed to satisfy dependency requirements for packages that are no longer installed.

Overview of Ubuntu Package Management Software

A standard Ubuntu Linux installation provides several different utilities for managing and querying Ubuntu software packages, ranging from low-level command-line tools to tools with sophisticated graphical interfaces. The basic user-level tools provided as part of a standard Ubuntu installation are the following:

- apt-get: A command-line utility that provides subcommands which enable you to install, remove, and manage packages on your system, both as individual packages and as components of a distribution.

- aptitude: A terminal-oriented utility that serves as a front end to lower-level utilities such as apt-get and dpkg. The aptitude utility provides both a quasi-graphical, menu and screen-oriented user interface and the ability to install, remove, query, and manage packages from the command-line.

- dpkg: The basic Ubuntu and Debian command-line tool for installing, removing, querying, and generally managing packages. This utility uses even lower-level utilities, such as dpkg-deb, to perform package installation, removal, and manipulation, and dpkg-query, to search for packages, but these lower-level packages are not discussed in this chapter. Although handy to use directly .0001% of the time, the rest of the time, I find it more convenient to think of the capabilities provided by these low-level utilities as functionality that is provided by the dpkg utility itself.

- dselect: A terminal-oriented front-end to the dpkg utility that provides quasi-graphical menus and an interactive display within the context of an xterm, GNOME Terminal, or other Ubuntu command-line environment. The dselect utility also accepts command-line options and arguments that you can use to initiate selected operations without selecting them from menus. This application isn't discussed in this chapter, because its functionality is available in other tools.

- synaptic: A graphical, X Window system tool for installing, removing, querying, and managing software packages on Ubuntu. This is my preferred package management utility for all day-to-day package installation operations.

- update-manager: A graphical, X Window system tool for identifying and installing updated versions of packages that are already installed on your Ubuntu Linux system.

NOTE The dpkg, apt-get, and aptitude utilities all use different databases to store information about installed packages, and therefore all use different mechanisms for identifying and resolving conflicts and dependencies between software packages. The dpkg utility stores its information about installed and available packages in files and directories under /var/lib/dpkg. The apt-get utility stores the information that it uses in files and directories under the directory /var/lib/apt. The aptitude utility stores the information that it uses in files and directories under the directory /var/lib/aptitude. When using either apt-get or aptitude, it is important that you run either the apt-get update or aptitude update commands in order to ensure that the package state and availability information used by these applications is up-to-date. Similarly, if you want to experiment with dselect after having installed packages using apt-get, aptitude, or synaptic, you must use the dselect update command before using dselect, to ensure that dselect (and therefore dpkg) is aware of the state of all installed and available software.

The apt-get, aptitude, and Synaptic Package Manager utilities also depend on the information about available repositories and associated packages maintained in a storage area which is generically known as the "apt cache". The apt cache actually consists of several files that, by default, are located in the directory /var/cache/apt on your Ubuntu Linux system.

This chapter focuses on discussing the apt-get, aptitude, dpkg, synaptic, and update-manager tools in the context of performing common tasks that each is best suited for, based on my experiences with them. As a fan of graphical tools that "do the right thing," most of the examples of installing packages throughout this book use the Synaptic Package Manager tool, which I find both powerful and easy to use. In general, however, the mantra for this chapter is "use the right tool for the job."

NOTE Another popular graphical interface for package management on Ubuntu systems is adept, which is a graphical interface found on the Kubuntu Ubuntu derivative. The adept application is an excellent, easy to use application that is not discussed in this chapter because this book focuses on the standard Ubuntu Linux distribution, not variants such as Edubuntu, Kubuntu, or Xubuntu.

All of the automated aspects of the package management utilities available on Ubuntu systems rely on obtaining packages from Ubuntu software repositories. The next section explains software repositories, how they are organized, the system configuration file that identifies them, and how to work with this file to ensure that your system has access to all of the latest and greatest software that is available for it.

Ubuntu Repositories and Components

A repository is exactly what the name suggests, a storage site for objects of some sort. In the case of the Ubuntu repositories, the objects stored therein are all of the source and binary packages that make up a variety of Ubuntu Linux distributions. When you download an ISO image (an image of a CD or DVD that conforms to the International Standards Organization 9660 standard for CD-ROM filesystem), the CD that you burn from this image and then use to install Ubuntu Linux provides the CD boot environment (known as *Isolinux*), an installer and the applications required to support it, a basic set of packages, and some documentation. As part of the install process, your system retrieves the majority of the Ubuntu Linux distribution from the Ubuntu repository over the Internet.

Making ISO images of Linux distributions available over the Internet is nothing new — it's the standard way of distributing most Linux distributions nowadays. Putting the Ubuntu repositories directly on the net has two primary advantages for Ubuntu fans:

- keeping the Ubuntu installation media down to a single CD and ISO image
- making every part of Ubuntu Linux instantly available to any computer that is connected to the Internet, anywhere, including the latest updates and additions

To organize its repositories along lines that are important to the Ubuntu folks, to many individuals, and to many corporations, the Ubuntu repositories are organized into four components, which are basically ways of classifying Linux software along support and licensing guidelines. The Ubuntu repositories contain four basic components:

- **main:** The main component contains binary packages (and source packages, in most cases) for Linux software that is officially supported by Canonical, Ltd., and can be freely redistributed. This does not mean that everything in the main repository component is GPL — the main repository component can include software that is distributed in binary format, such as firmware and binary fonts. The main portion of the repository is designed to provide everything that most people will need for a fully functional Linux desktop or server system that is fully supportable by Canonical, Ltd.

- **restricted:** The restricted component contains source and binary packages for commonly-used software that is not available under a completely free license. Packages in the restricted repository component are not guaranteed to be completely supportable by Canonical, Ltd., but are provided because they are necessary to use Linux on certain hardware. For this reason, some items from the "restricted" repository are included on Ubuntu installer CDs in subdirectories of `CD/dists/dist-name/restricted` and `CD/pool/restricted`. With the 6.06 (Dapper) release, restricted items include drivers for specific network interface cards (NICs) and video cards.

- **universe:** The universe repository component contains binary and source packages for the rest of the free and open source software that is commonly associated with Linux systems, but which is available under a variety of different licenses and is not guaranteed to be supported by Canonical, Ltd. There's simply too much software in the universe (pardon the expression) for Canonical to guarantee support for all of the software that it contains

- **multiverse:** The multiverse repository component contains binary and source packages for software that is not released under a license that meets the Ubuntu guidelines for free and open source software (`www.ubuntu.com/ubuntu/licensing`). This software is not supported by Canonical, Ltd., and it is your responsibility to verify that you satisfy the requirements imposed by software from the multiverse component.

NOTE The official descriptions of the Ubuntu repositories are located at `www.ubuntu.com/ubuntu/components` — I've tried to distill them down to their essentials, but if you're a licensing fan, there's plenty of good reading there.

One additional repository component also exists, known as the *backports* repository. The backports repository component contains updated or bleeding-edge versions of Linux software, including software that may already have an "official" version in one of the other repository components. Software in this repository component is not supported by Canonical but is provided because newer versions of existing software packages often provide some critical feature that users may require.

> **TIP** If you are curious about the packages that are installed or available in the Ubuntu repositories for different Ubuntu releases, see the Web page at `http://packages.ubuntu.com`. **This page enables you to select the distribution that you are interested in, and then view a list of all of the packages, organized into various logical categories. It also provides a search capability so that you can search for specific packages.**

Enabling Additional Repository Components

The most common example of a situation in which you will want to access repository components other than the main and restricted components is when working with audio and video applications. The wide variety of CODECs (compressors/decompressors) used to encode digital audio and video, the platform-specific roots of many of these CODECs, and the hoops that many media companies make you jump through in order to actually play many digital audio and video formats on an Ubuntu Linux system make it necessary to push the boundaries of free software licensing.

By default, only the main and restricted components of the Ubuntu repositories are enabled when you install an Ubuntu Linux distribution. "Enabled" means that the online sources of these repository components are included in the default `/etc/apt/sources.list` file, which is the file that all of the package installation and management utilities discussed in this chapter consult when looking for new and updated software. This file is a text file that contains entries, which describe the location and name of different online repositories and the repository components that are available there. The general format of an entry in the `/etc/apt/sources.list` file is the following:

```
deb  URI distribution component-or-package(s)
```

The `deb` field identifies the package format, the URI is a universal resource identifier for the location where the repository can be found, and is typically an FTP or HTTP URL. The distribution field is typically the name of a standard Ubuntu distribution, but can be anything that is used to identify a subdirectory at the URI where associated packages can be found, and the component-or-package is one (or more) names of repository components or packages that are also used to navigate the directory tree at the URI and locate available packages. If multiple component-or-package names are provided, each identifies a different directory at the URI.

As examples, the entries in the `/etc/apt/sources.list` file for the main and restricted repository components of the 6.06 (Dapper) release of Ubuntu Linux are the following:

```
deb http://archive.ubuntu.com/ubuntu/ dapper main restricted
deb-src http://archive.ubuntu.com/ubuntu/ dapper main restricted
```

The first of these identifies the source of binary packages, while the second identifies the source of source packages. A similar pair of entries provides access to updated versions of the packages in these repository components:

```
deb http://archive.ubuntu.com/ubuntu/ dapper-updates main restricted
deb-src http://archive.ubuntu.com/ubuntu/ dapper-updates main
restricted
```

The examples in this section reflect the `/etc/apt/sources.list` settings for the Ubuntu 6.06 (Dapper) release. If you are working with another Ubuntu distribution, you should replace the word "dapper" in these examples with the name of the Ubuntu release that you are using, such as breezy (the 5.10 release that preceded "dapper") or "edgy" (the release that follows "dapper"), and so on. You should not mix repository entries for different Ubuntu releases in an `/etc/apt/sources.list` file, because the repositories for a newer release will typically provide the same software as the repositories for older releases, and will be compiled against a set of system libraries that are found on the newer release. See the section entitled "Mixing Ubuntu and Debian Repositories" later in this chapter, for information about some cases in which you may want to have entries in your `sources.list` file that are not consistent with the Ubuntu release that you are using.

Finally, a similar pair of entries provides access to security fixes for the packages in these repository components:

```
deb http://security.ubuntu.com/ubuntu dapper-security main restricted
deb-src http://security.ubuntu.com/ubuntu dapper-security main
restricted
```

Lines beginning with a hash mark (#) in the `/etc/apt/sources.list` file are comments. If you look through the entries in the default `/etc/apt/sources.list` file on your Ubuntu system, you will note that entries for access to the universe repository are already present in this file, but commented out. You can enable access to this repository by using `sudo` to edit this file in your favorite text editor. To do this, edit the `/etc/apt/sources.list` file using your favorite text editor, using a command like the following:

```
$ sudo emacs /etc/apt/sources.list
```

Remove the hash marks at the beginning of the lines that enable the universe repositories, add the word "multiverse" to the end of these lines, and save the updated file. The updated entries in a sample `sources.list` file would look like the following:

```
deb http://archive.ubuntu.com/ubuntu/ dapper universe multiverse
deb-src http://archive.ubuntu.com/ubuntu/ dapper universe multiverse
```

You could, of course, simply add these entries to the end of the lines that already provide access to the main and restricted components of the Ubuntu repositories, but I prefer to keep them separate just for clarity regarding licensing differences — and because that stays closest to the original format of the default `sources.list` file.

Just to be perfectly clear, by suggesting that you may want to add the universe and multiverse repositories to the places where your system looks for software, I am enabling you to add software that may have licensing requirements that you or the company that you work for find odious (such as MP3-related, or video-related software), for which support is not guaranteed by the Ubuntu folks (even if you purchase support, there are no commitments to support it), and which may be difficult to get support for anywhere. If you are configuring systems for enterprise use, you should make sure that your firm is comfortable with the licenses provided with non-free software in the universe and multiverse repositories. I use all of the software discussed in this book, and am therefore my very own test case for everything this book discusses, but your mileage (and your responsibilities) may vary.

Enabling Additional Repository Sources Using a Text Editor

As you can see from the examples in the previous section, the standard Ubuntu repositories are all hosted on systems that are in the ubuntu.com domain. This makes perfect sense, because this is the only way that the Canonical folks can guarantee the integrity of their repository and the adherence of various components and their contents to the associated licensing guidelines. However, additional repositories of Ubuntu software

are also available on the Internet (I know that's a surprise), maintained by various groups and individuals. These alternate repository sites may simply mirror the contents of the official Ubuntu repositories to "share the load," or may provide software that is not found in the official Ubuntu repositories. In the latter case, this software may provide even newer versions of popular software than is found in the backports repository component, or may provide up-to-date versions of locally maintained software. As mentioned earlier, if you are interested in working with audio and video on your Ubuntu system, you may find that these alternate repository sites provide versions of related software with bleeding-edge features that you need.

Some well-known alternate repositories for Ubuntu and the software that they provided at the time that this book was written are the following:

- FreeNX: A repository of the latest version of the FreeNX client and server software. FreeNX is an alternative to the vnc-server, vino, and vnc-viewer software. The `/etc/apt/sources.list` entries for this repository are the following:

```
deb http://mirror3.ubuntulinux.nl/ dapper-seveas freenx
deb-src http://mirror3.ubuntulinux.nl/ dapper-seveas freenx
```

- Multimedia Support: A repository providing Windows CODECs and other software necessary for playing various digital audio and video files on your Ubuntu system. The `/etc/apt/sources.list` entries for this repository are the following:

```
deb ftp://cipherfunk.org/pub/packages/ubuntu/ dapper main
deb-src ftp://cipherfunk.org/pub/packages/ubuntu/ dapper main
```

> **NOTE** You will have to import the GPG key for this site to access and install the packages that it provides. You can retrieve this key from `http://subkeys.pgp.net`; the fingerprint of the appropriate GPG key is 33BAC1B3.

- Penguin Liberation Front: This repository builds and provides packages that may be subject to patents, or other mechanisms for preventing free access to software. The `/etc/apt/sources.list` entries for this repository are the following:

```
deb http://packages.freecontrib.org/ubuntu/plf dapper free non-free
deb-src http://packages.freecontrib.org/ubuntu/plf dapper free non-free
```

- Wine: A repository providing the latest versions of WINE, the Windows API support environment for Linux that enables you to install and run much Windows software directly on your Linux system. The `/etc/apt/sources.list` entries for this repository are the following:

```
deb http://wine.budgetdedicated.com/apt dapper main
deb-src http://wine.budgetdedicated.com/apt dapper main
```

If you're interested in exploring other repositories and want to use a truly cool application, see `www.ubuntulinux.nl/source-o-matic`. This site provides a Web-based sources application that generates a sources.list file for you based on your selections of available repositories.

Enabling Additional Repository Sources Using the Software Properties Tool

Editing a text-format configuration file is pretty old school Linux, and is the sort of thing that you may not want to mention to your Windows or Mac OS X friends. (You'll still want to be able to do it, because it's fast and easy, but we'll keep that sort of thing our little Linux secret, OK?) For fans of graphical interfaces, Ubuntu provides a Software Preferences tool that gives you a graphical view of the entries in your `/etc/apt/sources.list` file and makes it easy for your to enable, disable, or add entries with a few mouse clicks.

To start the Software preferences utility, select the System ➪ Administration ➪ Software Properties menu item. After supplying your password to enable access to this administrative tool, the Software Preferences tool's main dialog displays, as shown in Figure 20.1.

FIGURE 20.1

The main Software Preferences dialog

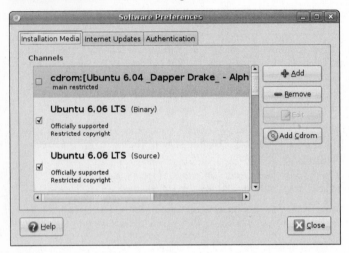

As you can see in Figure 20.1, the main software preferences dialog displays all of the entries in your current /etc/apt/sources.list file, regardless of whether they are commented out or not. Each of these is identified as a channel. Entries that are commented out, such as the cdrom entry shown in Figure 20.1, are displayed as inactive — in other words, the checkbox beside their name is not selected. This gives you an convenient overview of all of the valid repository entries in your /etc/apt/sources.list file.

To add a new repository or repository component to the list of repositories that your system will search for software packages, click Add. This displays the dialog shown in Figure 20.2.

FIGURE 20.2

Adding a repository in the Software Preferences tool

574

The drop-down Channel menu shown in Figure 20.2 enables you to select any of the standard Ubuntu repositories and associated components — by default, only the main and restricted entries for any repository are enabled, but you can add the universe and multiverse components to any standard repository in which they are available by selecting the Community Maintained (Universe) or Non-free (Multiverse) checkboxes.

The dialog shown in Figure 20.2 also enables you to add entries for custom repositories by clicking the Custom button, which displays the dialog shown in Figure 20.3.

FIGURE 20.3

Adding a custom repository in the Software Preferences tool

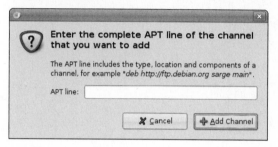

Though not particularly elegant, this dialog makes it easy for you to cut and paste a repository identification entry from a mail message or browser session where you found it, and automatically add it to your /etc/apt/sources.list file. To return to the dialog shown in Figure 20.2 without adding a custom repository entry, click Cancel. To save a new entry after typing it in or cutting and pasting, click Add Channel, which adds the new entry and returns you to the dialog shown in Figure 20.1, which now contains an entry for the channel that you just added.

The Software Preferences tool provides three tabs that let you manage different aspects of your repositories and the update process. The first, the Installation Media tab, is the initial tab shown when you start the Software Preferences tool. The others, the Internet Updates and Authentication tabs, enable you to manage different aspects of system updates and how your system identifies valid repositories.

Figure 20.4 shows the Software Preferences tool's Internet Updates tab, which enables you to specify when your system checks for updates and how it responds to any available updates that it detects.

By default, your system automatically checks for updates on a daily basis, displaying an "Available Updates" icon in the GNOME panel at the top of your screen when updates are available (see Figure 20.28). If you are using a laptop or other system that only connects to the Internet infrequently, you may want to decrease the frequency with which your system checks for updates by selecting another value from the Check for updates automatically entry's drop-down menu, or disable this item entirely. If you disable this item, you can always check for updates manually using Ubuntu's Update manager, which is discussed later in this chapter in the section entitled "Using the Ubuntu Update Manager." If you are performing regular checks for updates and are using a system that is often (or always) connected to the Internet, you may want to select the Download updates in the background, but do not install them to make sure that packages are already available on your local system when you actually execute the update process. Similarly, you may want to select the Install security updates without confirmation option if you want to automatically retrieve security updates and install them so that your system is always secure against any known attacks or software exploits.

FIGURE 20.4

The Internet Updates tab in the Software Preferences tool

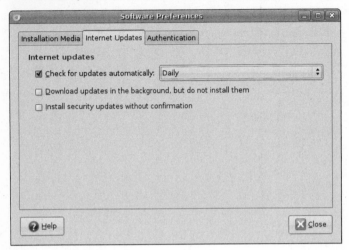

Figure 20.5 shows the Software Preferences tool's Authentication tab, which simplifies the process of importing identification keys for new repositories into the keyring used by Ubuntu's package management utilities.

FIGURE 20.5

The Authentication tab in the Software Preferences tool

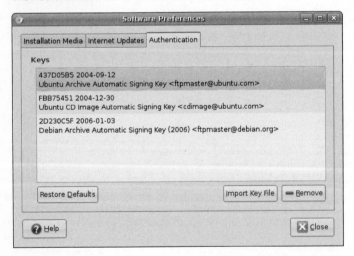

Each package in any repository is signed with the key for that repository to verify its authenticity and validity. The Ubuntu package management tools will not retrieve packages from unauthorized or unidentifiable repositories. Adding the authentication key that identifies a nonstandard repository as a valid package source requires several steps from the command line, using hard-to-remember options to the gpg command in conjunction with the apt-key utility. Clicking the Import Key File button enables you to navigate to and select any file that contains an ASCII representation of a PGP authentication key and import it for use by Ubuntu's package management tools.

After making any changes that you desire to the list of repositories available to your system, the way in which system updates are performed, or the Authentication keys available to the Ubuntu package management utilities, click Close to exit the Software Properties application. If you have made any changes, the Software Preferences tool will display a dialog informing you that your channel (repository) information is out of date, as shown in Figure 20.6.

FIGURE 20.6

Change notification when exiting the Software Preferences tool

To automatically update the cache information used by Ubuntu's package management utilities, click Reload. To exit without updating the cache, click Close. If you exit without reloading the cache information, you will need to run apt-get update or use the Check option in Ubuntu's Update manager or the Synaptic Package Manager before you are guaranteed that your system is aware of all available packages in all valid repositories.

Problems Adding or Accessing Nonstandard Repositories

After modifying your system's /etc/apt/sources.list file, you may find that packages from new repositories that you've added aren't actually showing up in the list of available packages. First, make sure that you've run apt-get update or used Synaptic's Check button to refresh the list of available repositories and packages. This should identify any inaccessible repositories and outright syntax errors in the sources.list file.

Next, when running apt-get update to update your system's idea of repository contents, seeing messages like the following means that your system does not have the right authentication keys to add packages from a specified repository to its cache:

```
Ign http://ftp.us.debian.org sarge Release
Ign http://ftp.us.debian.org unstable Release
```

Similarly, you may see messages at the end of the output from apt-get update. These are related to the previous messages, but are somewhat less subtle, because they explicitly identify missing keys and associated repositories

```
W: GPG error: http://ftp.us.debian.org testing Release: \
     The following signatures couldn't be verified because the public
     key is not available: \
     NO_PUBKEY 010908312D230C5F
W: GPG error: http://ftp.us.debian.org unstable Release: \
     The following signatures couldn't be verified because the public
     key is not available: \
     NO_PUBKEY 010908312D230C5F
```

In these cases, the associated entries in /etc/apt/sources.list point to repositories whose keys are not present in the keyring used by the Ubuntu package management utilities. See the man page for the apt-key application for information on retrieving and installing keys into this keyring. For an example of the process of retrieving remote repository keys and integrating them into the keyring used by Ubuntu's package management system, see the next section.

Mixing Ubuntu and Debian Repositories

Because the Ubuntu Linux distribution has its conceptual and packaging roots in the Debian project, the Ubuntu and Debian projects both use the /etc/apt/sources.list file to identify sites where packages for those distributions are located, and both use the DEB package format for distributing, installing, and maintaining packages. This makes it tempting to add Debian repositories to the /etc/apt/sources.list file on your Ubuntu system in order to get access to even more software. The best general rule for mixing and matching Ubuntu and Debian repositories can be summed up in a very simple rule: DON'T!

That said, the rest of this section explains how to mix Ubuntu and Debian repositories for the people who are going to ignore my warnings and know what they're doing (or think that they do). Just in case, here are a few more warnings: Mixing Ubuntu and Debian repositories may break your Ubuntu system, irritate both your Debian and Ubuntu friends, create a confused system on which the source of various software packages is remarkably unclear, and cause cancer in rats. I am not responsible if your once-pretty Ubuntu system turns into a smoking crater of unbootable software. You've been warned (again).

As noted in the previous section, you can add new repositories to your /etc/apt/sources.list file using Synaptic or by directly modifying the underlying configuration files used by Synaptic, aptitude, and apt-get. This section explains how to manually modify these files and make other changes necessary to use selected Debian repositories.

To add Debian repositories to the list of repositories where your system looks for software packages, do the following:

1. Add the appropriate entries for the repositories that you want to use to your /etc/apt/sources .list file, Debian repositories use Debian release or branch names and contain different components than Ubuntu repositories, named "main," "non-free," and "contrib." When adding Debian repositories to the repositories used on your Ubuntu system, you will probably want to add the testing and unstable Debian branches. Entries for these repositories in the form required by the /etc/apt/sources.list file are the following:

   ```
   deb http://ftp.us.debian.org/debian testing main contrib non-free
   deb-src http://ftp.us.debian.org/debian testing main contrib non-free
   deb http://ftp.us.debian.org/debian unstable main contrib non-free
   deb-src http://ftp.us.debian.org/debian unstable main contrib non-
   free
   ```

2. When adding nonstandard repositories, you will want to explicitly set the priorities that the apt and Synaptic utilities use when checking repositories for new and update packages. This information is stored in the file /etc/apt/preferences, which usually does not exist on a standard Ubuntu system. Create this file using sudo and your favorite text file, and enter the relative priorities of the repositories that are present in your /etc/apt/sources.list file. The values in mine are the following:

```
Package: *
Pin: release a=dapper
Pin-Priority: 900
 Package: *
Pin: release o=debian a=testing
Pin-Priority: 500
 Package: *
Pin: release o=debian a=unstable
Pin-Priority: 400
```

Priority values below 1000 have special meanings to Ubuntu's package management utilities. The sample values shown above assign anything in a Dapper repository the highest priority, assign packages in Debian's testing branch a lower priority, and assign the lowest priority to packages found in Debian's unstable branch. Different priority ranges have special meanings in the preferences file. Because my goal is not to rewrite the man page for the preferences file (see man apt_ preferences), the values for the Debian testing and unstable branches in the previous example prevent packages from these repository components from being installed if there is a version of the same package in Dapper or the currently installed version is newer.

3. Modify the file /etc/apt/apt.conf to increase the size of the memory-mapped file used for storing the data structures that hold package information. Adding entire Debian repositories to the standard Ubuntu repositories requires lots of storage. The default size of this file is 4MB (4194304 bytes). I'd suggest changing this to 16MB, just to be safe, by adding the following entry to /etc/apt/apt.conf:

```
APT::Cache-Limit "16777216";
```

4. You'll have to retrieve and import the PGP key for the Debian repositories into the keyring used by the Ubuntu package management utilities. Ubuntu will not retrieve packages from unauthorized repositories. Adding the keys that identify nonstandard repositories as valid repositories requires several steps. First, list the keys available on the Debian public key server using the gpg command's --list-keys option. The appropriate command and its output look like the following:

```
$ gpg -v --keyserver keyring.debian.org --list-keys
gpg: using classic trust model
----------------------------
[existing key output deleted]
 pub   1024D/2D230C5F 2006-01-03 [expires: 2007-02-07]
uid       Debian Archive Automatic Signing Key (2006)
<ftpmaster@debian.org>
```

NOTE You can also retrieve the current Debian key in ASCII format using a command like wget http://ftp-master.debian.org/ziyi_key_year.asc (where year is the current year, such as 2006), and then import it into your keyring manually, but this isn't quite as secure as getting the key directly from a key server.

5. Retrieve the specified key by its fingerprint (2D230C5F in the previous example) into your local keyring using the gpg command's --recv-keys option. The appropriate command and its output look like the following:

```
$ gpg -v --keyserver keyring.debian.org --recv-keys 2D230C5F
gpg: requesting key 2D230C5F from hkp server keyring.debian.org
gpg: armor header: Version: GnuPG v1.4.1 (GNU/Linux)
gpg: armor header: Comment: Key ID: 0x2D230C5F
gpg: pub  1024D/2D230C5F 2006-01-03  Debian Archive Automatic Signing
Key (2006) <ftpmaster@debian.org>
gpg: using classic trust model
gpg: key 2D230C5F: public key "Debian Archive Automatic Signing Key
(2006) <ftpmaster@debian.org>" imported
gpg: 2 keys cached (7 signatures)
gpg: 1 keys processed (1 validity counts cleared)
gpg: 3 marginal(s) needed, 1 complete(s) needed, classic trust model
gpg: depth: 0  valid:   1  signed:   0  trust: 0-, 0q, 0n, 0m, 0f, 1u
gpg: Total number processed: 1
gpg:                 imported: 1
```

6. Once you've retrieved the key successfully, you can then export it into the keyring used by the Ubuntu package management utilities using the gpg, sudo, and apt-key commands together, as in the following example:

```
$ gpg --armor --export 2D230C5F | sudo apt-key add -
OK
```

The --armor option wraps the key that you are exporting in the standard ASCII descriptors for a key file, while the --export option uses the argument that follows this option to identify the key that you want to export.

> **TIP** You can use the gpg --armor --export command to export any key in your keyring to an ASCII file, by simply redirecting its output into a text file. You can then use these files with tools that require ASCII key files, such as Ubuntu's Software Properties tool, described earlier in this chapter in the section entitled "Enabling Additional Repository Sources Using the Software Properties Tool."

At this point, you can now execute the command apt-get update to update the Ubuntu package management utilities cache of repositories and packages. You can then install any packages that any of these repositories provide. Good luck!

> **TIP** If you have problems after changing the Preferences file, you can use the apt-cache policy package-name command to see information about the priority associated with the specified package from various sources. See the online reference information for the apt-cache command (using the command man apt-cache) for more information.

Exploring Your System Using dpkg and Friends

Package management software not only simplifies software installation, removal, and updates, but also provides great opportunities for asking questions about the software that is installed, or could be installed, on your system. Some of the command-line package management utilities that are installed on your system make it easy to find out exactly what software is installed on your system, what a specific package contains, what packages provided certain files, and so on. The next few sections describe how to answer some basic questions about existing files and available packages on your Ubuntu system.

Listing the Packages that are Installed on Your System

The dpkg command's -1 option provides the easiest way of listing the packages that are installed on your system. (This option can also be specified in verbose option format as --long.) You can execute this command with no other argument to produce a (long) listing of every package that is installed on your system, which looks something like the following:

```
$ dpkg -1
Desired=Unknown/Install/Remove/Purge/Hold
| Status=Not/Installed/Config-files/Unpacked/Failed-config/Half-
installed
|/ Err?=(none)/Hold/Reinst-required/X=both-problems (Status,Err:
uppercase=bad)
||/ Name               Version            Description
+++-================-==================-
===================================
ii  3dchess           0.8.1-11.1         3D chess for X11
ii  acpi              0.09-1             displays information on ACPI
devices
ii  acpi-support      0.84               a collection of useful events
for acpi
ii  acpid             1.0.4-1ubuntu11    Utilities for using ACPI power
mgmnt
ii  adduser           3.80ubuntu2        Add and remove users and groups
[much more output deleted]
```

The first few lines above the actual package listing identify the meaning of the various fields on each line and the symbols that they contain. This information is provided in a fairly cryptic fashion that is mandated by the terminal-oriented output produced by the dpkg utility. The entries for package name, package version, and package description are pretty straightforward, but the first field requires some serious explanation. The characters in the first field have the following meaning and possible values:

- The first character in the first field indicates the desired status of the package, which is the state that the packaging system thinks the package should be in. Available indicators in this position are h (the package is marked as being on hold, and cannot be updated or removed), i (the package should be installed), p (the package and all associated configuration information is supposed to be purged), r (the package is supposed to be removed, but associated configuration files will be preserved), and u (the package has never been installed on this system, so its state is unknown).

- The second character in the first field indicates the actual status of the package on your system. Available indicators in this position are c (the configuration files for the package are installed, but the package is not), f (the script used to complete the configuration of this package, known as a post-installation script, failed for some reason, and the package is therefore not guaranteed to be correctly installed), h (the package is partially installed because the installation process was interrupted), i (the package is correctly installed), n (the package is not installed), and u (the package was retrieved, unpacked, and is partially installed, but its post-installation script was not executed).

- The third character highlights any errors that are associated with the package. Available indicators in this position are a space (no errors, which looks remarkably like there is nothing in this position), H (the package has been marked as being on hold by a the package management system itself, which usually means that other packages that this package requires are not installed), R (reinstallation is required), and X (the package both requires re-installation and has been automatically put on hold by the package management system itself).

Now that I've explained what each character position in the first field of a package entry means, it's easy to see what the ASCII art in the dpkg output heading means. This is not exactly the same thing as being "intuitive," but that's hard to do in the limited number of characters that you can display and easily use from the command line.

Listing the Packages that are Available for Your System

The previous section explained how to figure out what packages are installed on your system. While that's interesting, a more interesting question perhaps is, "What packages are available for my system that I have not yet installed?" As mentioned in the previous section, the dpkg command's -l option with no other arguments shows the list of installed packages. You can supply an argument to this command to list available packages that match that argument, whether installed or un-installed. For example, the dpkg -l emacs command should list all of the packages that have the string emacs in their package name. Let's try that:

```
$ dpkg -l emacs
No packages found matching emacs.
```

Well, that seems odd, because I'm actually typing this in emacs on my Ubuntu system. The problem is that any argument that you supply to dpkg is used as a pattern match, and there are apparently no packages installed on my system whose exact name is "emacs." Let's try that again, using a standard Linux wildcard to say that you want to list any packages with a name that begins with emacs, as in the following example:

```
$ dpkg -l 'emacs*'
Desired=Unknown/Install/Remove/Purge/Hold
| Status=Not/Installed/Config-files/Unpacked/Failed-config/Half-
installed
|/ Err?=(none)/Hold/Reinst-required/X=both-problems (Status,Err:
uppercase=bad)
||/ Name                    Version          Description
+++-=================================-================-
=================================
ii  emacs-chess             2.0b5-1          a client/library for playing
Chess
ii  emacs-chess-pieces      2.0b5-1          XPM images of chess pieces
ii  emacs-goodies-el        26.4-1           Miscellaneous add-ons for
Emacs
un  emacs-goodies-extra-el  <none>           (no description available)
ii  emacs21                 21.4a-3ubuntu2 The GNU Emacs editor
ii  emacs21-bin-common      21.4a-3ubuntu2 The GNU Emacs editor's
shared...
ii  emacs21-common          21.4a-3ubuntu2 The GNU Emacs editor's
shared...
un  emacs21-el              <none>           (no description available)
un  emacs21-nox             <none>           (no description available)
un  emacsen                 <none>           (no description available)
ii  emacsen-common          1.4.17           Common facilities for all
emacsen
```

That's more like it! Note that when using wildcards in a dpkg specification, you have to protect them from expansion on the command line by enclosing your dpkg wildcard specification within quotation marks of some sort.

The previous output showed some emacs packages, but I could swear that there were others on my Ubuntu system. Let's try a more general wildcard that searches for packages that contain the string "emacs" anywhere in their names:

```
$ dpkg -l '*emacs*'
Desired=Unknown/Install/Remove/Purge/Hold
| Status=Not/Installed/Config-files/Unpacked/Failed-config/Half-
installed
|/ Err?=(none)/Hold/Reinst-required/X=both-problems (Status,Err:
uppercase=bad)
||/ Name                        Version            Description
+++-=========================-===============-===========================
ii  emacs-chess                 2.0b5-1            a client/library for
Chess ii  emacs-chess-pieces             2.0b5-1            XPM images of
chess pieces
ii  emacs-goodies-el            26.4-1             Miscellaneous add-ons
un  emacs-goodies-extra-el      <none>             (no description
available)
ii  emacs21                     21.4a-3ubuntu2     The GNU Emacs editor
ii  emacs21-bin-common          21.4a-3ubuntu2     The GNU Emacs shared...
ii  emacs21-common              21.4a-3ubuntu2     The GNU Emacs shared...
un  emacs21-el                  <none>             (no description
available)
un  emacs21-nox                 <none>             (no description
available)
un  emacsen                     <none>             (no description
available)
ii  emacsen-common              1.4.17             Common facilities for
emacsen
un  xemacs                      <none>             (no description
available)
un  xemacs-support              <none>             (no description
available)
un  xemacs-widget               <none>             (no description
available)
ii  xemacs21                    21.4.18-1ubuntu1 highly customizable text
editor
[additional output deleted]
```

Even better! Thanks to the explanation of the characters in the first field of your dpkg output (provided in the previous section of this chapter), it's clear that I need to install xemacs on this system.

Because this is a Linux system, you can pipe your dpkg output through other commands to answer questions like, "What packages are not yet installed on my system whose names contain the string emacs anywhere in their names," which I can do using grep to look for lines that begin with the string "un," as in the following example:

```
$ dpkg -l '*emacs*' | grep '^un'
un  emacs-goodies-extra-el      <none>             (no description
available)
```

```
un  emacs21-el             <none>      (no description
available)
un  emacs21-nox            <none>      (no description
available)
un  emacsen                <none>      (no description
available)
un  xemacs                 <none>      (no description
available)
un  xemacs-support         <none>      (no description
available)
un  xemacs-widget          <none>      (no description
available)
un  xemacs21-gnome-mule    <none>      (no description
available)
un  xemacs21-gnome-mule... <none>      (no description
available)
un  xemacs21-gnome-nomule  <none>      (no description
available)
un  xemacs21-mule-canna-wnn <none>     (no description
available)
un  xemacs21-nomule        <none>      (no description
available)
un  xemacs21-supportel     <none>      (no description
available)
```

Other Ubuntu package management utilities provide similar search features, particularly the aptitude utility. Though most commonly associated with it's terminal-oriented, quasi-graphical interface (discussed later in this chapter in the section entitled "Using aptitude to Add and Remove Software," aptitude also provide a command-line mode with many powerful commands. To locate packages, aptitude provides a search keyword that enables you to specify a substring to search for (no wildcards necessary), and displays information about any installed or available package that is present in any repository listed in your /etc/apt/ sources.list file. Some sample output from a search for emacs using aptitude is the following:

```
$ aptitude search emacs
p   acl2-emacs           - A Computational Logic for Applicative Comm
p   aleph-emacs          - The Aleph programming language - emacs mod
p   cxref-emacs          - Generates latex and HTML documentation for
p   emacs                - The GNU Emacs editor
i   emacs-chess          - a client and library for playing Chess fro
i   emacs-chess-pieces   - XPM images of chess pieces for emacs-chess
p   emacs-color-themes   - Color themes for Emacs
p   emacs-extra          - emacs configuration
i   emacs-goodies-el     - Miscellaneous add-ons for Emacs
i   emacs21              - The GNU Emacs editor
i   emacs21-bin-common   - The GNU Emacs editor's shared, architectur
i   emacs21-common       - The GNU Emacs editor's shared, architectur
[additional output deleted]
```

You'll notice that the aptitude utility finds more packages than the dpkg -l search command that was described earlier.

Another very convenient application for searching for packages is the apt-cache utility, which is a command-line utility that provides subcommands that enable you to search and manipulate the cache of packages that are installed or available for installation on your system and the metadata that is associated with those packages. You must enable the universe repository in order to install the apt-cache utility. The apt-cache utility can also be used to search the packages in any repository that is active in your /etc/apt/sources.list file, and find even more matching packages because it searches within the package name and both the short and long descriptions of all available packages, whether installed or not. Some sample output from an apt-cache search for our favorite string, emacs, is the following:

```
$ apt-cache search emacs
acl2-emacs - A Computational Logic for Applicative Common Lisp: emacs
interface
ada-mode - Ada mode for GNU Emacs and XEmacs
af - An Emacs-like mail reader and composer
aleph-emacs - The Aleph programming language - emacs mode
anjsp - A major mode to edit JSP and PSP code with Emacs
anthy-el - A Japanese input method (elisp fronted)
apel - portable library for emacsen
aplus-fsf-el - XEmacs lisp for A+ development
artist - Emacs Lisp drawing package
asn1-mode - Emacs mode for editing ASN.1 specification files
bhl - Emacs mode for converting brut text to HTML and LaTeX
bigloo-ude - Bigloo Unified Development Environment for Emacs
biomode - [Biology] An Emacs mode to edit genetic data
[additional output deleted]
```

As you can see, the apt-cache and aptitude utilities are easiest to use when searching for packages, and return the most verbose results.

Listing Information About a Package

Once you've found a package that you're interested in, there are an equivalent number of ways to get more detailed information about the package and its contents. However, because the apt-cache and aptitude utilities return the best search results, it makes sense to use them to display information about any packages that they've identified. For example, to find out detailed information about the xemacs21 package that was listed in the previous section, you could use either the apt-cache show xemacs21 or aptitude show xemacs21 commands, both of which return almost identical information. The following example shows the output from the aptitude show xemacs21 command, which is slightly more verbose:

```
$ aptitude show xemacs21
Package: xemacs21
New: yes
State: installed
Automatically installed: no
Version: 21.4.18-1ubuntu1
Priority: optional
Section: universe/editors
Maintainer: OHURA Makoto <ohura@debian.org>
Uncompressed Size: 49.2k
Depends: xemacs21-mule (= 21.4.18-1ubuntu1) | xemacs21-mule-canna-wnn
        (= 21.4.18-1ubuntu1) | xemacs21-nomule (= 21.4.18-1ubuntu1) |
```

```
                    xemacs21-gnome-mule (= 21.4.18-1ubuntu1) |
                    xemacs21-gnome-mule-canna-wnn (= 21.4.18-1ubuntu1) |
                    xemacs21-gnome-nomule (= 21.4.18-1ubuntu1)
Conflicts: xemacs, xemacs-widget
Replaces: xemacs, xemacs-widget
Provided by: xemacs21-nomule, xemacs21-mule-canna-wnn, xemacs21-mule,
                    xemacs21-gnome-nomule, xemacs21-gnome-mule-canna-wnn,
                    xemacs21-gnome-mule
Description: highly customizable text editor
 XEmacs is a full fledged programming language with a mail reader, news
 reader, info browser, Web browser, calendar, specialized editor for
more
 programming languages and other formats than most people encounter in
a
 lifetime, and much much more.
   This package exists to cause the installation of the real XEmacs
packages.
```

This output probably provides more than you want to know about the specified package, but it's always better to err on the side of caution.

Listing the Contents of a Package

In some cases, you may want to list all of the files associated with a package that is installed on your system. To do this, you can use the dpkg command's -L option, followed by the name of the package whose contents you want to list. Sample output that lists the contents of the emacs21 package on my Ubuntu system is the following:

```
$ dpkg -L emacs21
/.
/usr
/usr/bin
/usr/bin/emacs21-x
/usr/share
/usr/share/emacs
/usr/share/emacs/21.4
/usr/share/emacs/21.4/etc
/usr/share/emacs/21.4/etc/DOC-21.4.1
/usr/share/applications
/usr/share/applications/emacs21.desktop
/usr/share/doc
/usr/share/doc/emacs21
/usr/share/doc/emacs21/README.Debian.gz
/usr/share/doc/emacs21/copyright
/usr/share/doc/emacs21/changelog.Debian.gz
/usr/lib
/usr/lib/emacs
/usr/lib/emacs/21.4
/usr/lib/emacs/21.4/i486-linux-gnu
/usr/lib/emacs/21.4/i486-linux-gnu/fns-21.4.1-x.el
/usr/lib/menu
```

Being able to identify the packages provided by a package that is installed on your system can be handy if you are considering removing a package but want to make sure that doing so does not delete a file that you want to preserve. The next section describes how to find out what package does provide a specific file.

> **TIP** You can list the files that are provided by packages that are not yet installed by using the `apt-file` utility with a command such as `apt-file list` package, where package is the name of the package that you are interested in. The `apt-file` utility is described more detail in "Determining What Package Provides a Missing File" later in this chapter.

Determining What Package Provides an Existing File

After working with Ubuntu for a while and installing, updating, and removing some number of packages, you may be curious about which package provides a certain file on your system. This is easy enough to determine using the `dpkg` command's `--search` option, as in the following example, where I'm curious about which package provides the `/usr/bin/ar` archiving utility:

```
$ dpkg --search /usr/bin/ar
binutils: /usr/bin/ar
```

If you know that a utility that you're looking for is in your path but you don't want to have to determine the directory in which it is physically located, you can use the cool shell trick of using the output of an existing command as the input to another one, in this case combining the `which` command, to determine the full pathname of an application and the `dpkg --search` command, which produces exactly the same output:

```
$ dpkg --search `which ar`
binutils: /usr/bin/ar
```

When searching for files, the `dpkg --search` command can't find symbolic links that are created by package post-installation scripts. If you are trying to find a file that you know exists but cannot locate it, make sure that the file is not a symbolic link and, if it is, search for the file that it actually points to. This can sometimes require a few tries, as in the following example:

```
$ dpkg --search /usr/bin/emacs
dpkg: /usr/bin/emacs not found.

 $ ls -l /usr/bin/emacs
/usr/bin/emacs -> /etc/alternatives/emacs

 $ dpkg --search /etc/alternatives/emacs
dpkg: /etc/alternatives/emacs not found.

 $  ls -l /etc/alternatives/emacs
/etc/alternatives/emacs -> /usr/bin/emacs21-x

 $ dpkg --search /usr/bin/emacs21-x
emacs21: /usr/bin/emacs21-x
```

Though sometimes tedious, symbolic links are usually not an actual part of a package and you must therefore ferret out a file that actually is part of a package.

> **TIP** Another handy package management utility that you may want to use when determining what package provides a specific file is the `dlocate` utility. This utility is not installed on Ubuntu systems by default, but can easily be installed using `apt-get`, `aptitude`, or Synaptic Package Manager.

After installing this command, you can search for the package that provides a file using the `dlocate -S` command, as in the following example:

```
$ dlocate -S /usr/bin/emacs
emacs21-bin-common: /usr/bin/emacsclient.emacs21
emacs21: /usr/bin/emacs21-x
emacs21: /usr/bin/emacs21
```

The `dlocate` utility's `-S` option uses the string that you specify as a substring to search for, and can therefore be a bit more helpful when looking for files on your system.

Determining What Package Provides a Missing File

Identifying the package that provides a file that is not installed on your system is somewhat tricky, but is a common question when you are trying to build software whose source code requires an include file that is not present on your system, or you are trying to link software that requires a missing library. Unfortunately, the utility that performs this type of search, the `apt-file` utility, is not installed on Ubuntu systems by default, but can easily be installed using `apt-get`, `aptitude`, or Synaptic Package Manager. After installing this command, you must first update its idea of the available packages in the repositories that you are using by running the command `sudo apt-file update`.

Once this command completes, you can search for the package that provides a file, even if that file is not installed on your system, using the `apt-file search` command, as in the following example, which looks for the package associated with the *libpowersave* library:

```
$ ls -l /usr/lib/*power*
ls: /usr/lib/*power*: No such file or directory
 $ apt-file search libpowersave.so
libpowersave-dev: usr/lib/libpowersave.so
libpowersave10: usr/lib/libpowersave.so.10
libpowersave10: usr/lib/libpowersave.so.10.0.3
```

Installing the `apt-file` utility can save you a tremendous amount of hair-pulling and general frustration when you are trying to build software and have no idea what package provides the missing include file or "the missing link." (Sorry, but I couldn't resist.)

TIP   You can also use the `apt-file` utility to list the contents of packages that are not yet installed by using the apt-file list package command, where package is the name of the package that you are interested in.

Using apt-get to Add and Remove Software

The `apt-get` command is the fundamental user-level command provided as part of the Ubuntu package management suite. The `apt-get` command is a command-line tool that is fast and easy to use.

NOTE   As with any system administrative utility on your Ubuntu system, running the `apt-get` command requires the use of the `sudo` command or an equivalent, such as running `apt-get` under a shell that itself has been executed using the `sudo` command. To simplify examples and the readability of the text, the examples and discussion of using the `apt-get` command throughout this section do not include the `sudo` command.

Much of the basic functionality provided by the apt-get command is quite straightforward. For example, you can install a package and any other packages that it requires using the apt-get install package command. Similarly, you can remove a package by using the apt-get remove package command, specifying the --purge option if you also want to remove any configuration files or other data associated with the package that you're removing. Before using apt-get to install new software or new versions of existing software, you should always first execute the apt-get update command to ensure that apt-get is aware of the latest software packages and versions of that software from all of the repositories listed in your /etc/apt/sources.list file.

When using the apt-get utility to install software, you may occasionally have to provide additional information during the installation process. In these cases, the apt-get utility displays a quasi-graphical screen in the terminal application from which you were running the apt-get utility, an example of which is shown in Figure 20.7.

FIGURE 20.7

Supplying configuration information during package installation

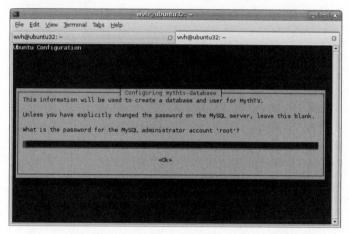

Whenever you see this sort of screen, you must answer any questions that it asks and supply any required information before the installation of your package can complete.

TIP If you are using apt-get to install new software and the apt-get utility informs you that other packages are recommended or suggested for installation, you may want to consider using aptitude's command-line interface to install these packages rather than apt-get. As explained later in this chapter in the section entitled "Using aptitude to Install Recommended Software" aptitude provides options that can automate installing recommended software when installing a new software package.

As mentioned throughout this book, I prefer to use the graphical Synaptic tool to search for, install, and remove packages whenever possible. The apt-get tool provides these same capabilities, but also provides some powerful capabilities that are not duplicated in the Synaptic tool, or are at least much more easily done using apt-get from the command line. Even if you're a Synaptic fan, the next few sections explain how and when you still may want to use apt-get to perform these advanced functions.

Upgrading Your System Using apt-get

The `apt-get` upgrade command searches all of the repositories in your `/etc/apt/sources.list` file for new versions of packages that are currently installed on your system, and downloads and installs those new versions. Before using this command, you should always first execute the `apt-get update` command to ensure that `apt-get` is aware of the latest software packages and versions of that software from all of the repositories listed in your `/etc/apt/sources.list` file.

During the upgrade process, the `apt-get upgrade` command will not change the installation status of any other packages on your system. This is the installation status of a package, not the version of a package. If a new version of a package requires a newer version of another package that is already installed on your system, the `apt-get` upgrade command will also install the updated version of that other package. However, if a newer version of an existing package requires that new packages be installed or that existing packages be removed, the `apt-get upgrade` command will not install the newer version of the existing package. To do this, you will need to use the `apt-get dist-upgrade` command, as described in the next section.

Smart System Upgrades Using apt-get

The `apt-get dist-upgrade` command searches all of the repositories in your `/etc/apt/sources .list` file for new versions of packages that are currently installed on your system, and downloads and installs those new versions. Before running this command, you should always first execute the `apt-get` update command to ensure that `apt-get` is aware of the latest software packages and versions of that software from all of the repositories listed in your `/etc/apt/sources.list` file.

The difference between the `apt-get upgrade` and `apt-get dist-upgrade` commands is that the `apt-get dist-upgrade` command will do what is known as a "smart upgrade." This means that it will do its best to handle any new package requirements or the removal of any existing packages that mandated in order to install the latest versions of all of the software on your system. For example, if a new version of a package requires that a new package be installed on your system, the `apt-get dist-upgrade` command will install both of these, while the `apt-get upgrade` command would not have updated the original software package. Similarly, if installing a new version of an existing package requires the removal of any other package(s) that are currently installed on your system, the `apt-get dist-upgrade` command will remove those packages in order to install the new version of the existing package.

Even if you are a Synaptic fan, you will occasionally need to execute the `apt-get dist-upgrade` command in order to completely upgrade all of the packages on your system. Synaptic provides a "smart upgrade" preference that tries to do this sort of thing for you whenever possible, but the `apt-get dist-upgrade` command is still occasionally required. When using Synaptic, symptoms of the need to use the `apt-get dist-upgrade` command are packages that are mysteriously identified as being held back and not updated — and, of course, the occasional pop-up message that explicitly tells you to run the `apt-get dist-upgrade` command.

Retrieving Package Source Code Using apt-get

Even in the wonderful world of constantly updated repositories with a rich collection of software, you may occasionally want to build your own versions of software packages for your system. The most common situation in which you'll want to do this is when you find patches to an existing software package that fix problems you're experiencing or add enhancements, and you just can't wait for them to appear in the official or backports repositories. You may also have your own ideas about changes that should be made to a package and want to test and work through your ideas. Linux and its ecosystem of utilities and other applications are open source, after all!

The `apt-get` command makes it remarkably easy to retrieve the source code for an installed package. The only requirement for this capability is that your `/etc/apt/sources.list` file includes a `deb-src` entry for the repository from which you retrieved the binary version of that software. For example, if you want to retrieve the source for a package in which the binary version is located in the multiverse repository component, you must have entries like the following (or equivalent entries) in your `/etc/apt/sources.list` file:

```
deb http://archive.ubuntu.com/ubuntu/ dapper multiverse
deb-src http://archive.ubuntu.com/ubuntu/ dapper multiverse
```

Assuming that the right entries are present in your `/etc/apt/sources.list file`, retrieving the source code for a specified package is easy using the `apt-get source` command. The following example shows the retrieval of the source code for one of my favorite packages, the MythTV personal video recorder package:

```
$ apt-get source mythtv
Reading package lists... Done
Building dependency tree... Done
Need to get 9836kB of source archives.
Get: 1 http://.../multiverse mythtv 0.18.1-5ubuntu3 (dsc) [1084B]
Get: 2 http://... dapper/multiverse mythtv 0.18.1-5ubuntu3 (tar)
[9817kB]
Get: 3 http://... dapper/multiverse mythtv 0.18.1-5ubuntu3 (diff)
[17.3kB]
Fetched 9836kB in 1m31s (107kB/s)
dpkg-source: extracting mythtv in mythtv-0.18.1
dpkg-source: unpacking mythtv_0.18.1.orig.tar.gz
dpkg-source: applying ./mythtv_0.18.1-5ubuntu3.diff.gz
```

When retrieving the source code for a package, the `apt-get` source utility actually retrieves multiple files. The extensions of these files are the following:

- `diff.gz`: a compressed file containing any available patches to the standard source archive for the package

- DSC: a description file for the Ubuntu package that identifies the contents of the package, associated binary packages, any package dependencies for that package, and so on

- `tar.gz`: a compressed archive file containing the source code for the official version of this package

After retrieving these files, the `apt-get source` command unpacks the compressed source archive, creating a working directory for your development efforts, and automatically applies any patches that are available in the (optional) compressed patch file.

Chapter 18 discussed how to install the basic packages required for software development on an Ubuntu system. If you are writing your own code or simply compiling existing applications on an Ubuntu system, that may be sufficient — except when you are building complex graphical software or when you are building your own DEB packages from the downloaded source for an Ubuntu package. In these cases, you will quickly encounter frustration such as the fact that today's graphical software has dependencies on libraries, include files, and utilities that you may not be familiar with or even have heard of before. Similarly, building DEB packages requires the use of billions and billions of utilities that may be new to you. Not to worry — you're not the first person to have encountered these issues, and the `apt-get` command provides a handy solution, as explained in the next section.

Satisfying Build Dependencies Using apt-get

Many of the software packages available for Linux have dependencies on other packages, which makes perfect sense — why reinvent the wheel when you can just link your code with it? However, if you decide to work on an existing Linux package, build-time dependencies can be frustrating. They're rarely well-documented, so you tend to encounter them as an iterative set of errors when you try to compile and link the application you're trying to build. This is also true when you begin to work with software packages in the formats used by different package management systems. The DEB packages used on Ubuntu and Debian systems (and derivatives) eliminate the dependency mumbo-jumbo that you often encounter with other package formats (such as RPM), but require the presence of an entire ecosystem of related utilities in order to build and package them successfully. Getting started with these can be tricky — you don't know what you're missing until your build process goes up in flames.

The `apt-get` tool provides a great, automated solution for these sorts of problems through its `build-dep` command-line option. Using this command-line option, followed by the name of the package that you want to build automatically identifies, retrieves, and installs all of the include files, libraries, and tools required to build the specified package. An example of the output from this command when retrieving build dependencies for the MythTV package used as an example in the previous section is the following:

```
$ sudo apt-get build-dep mythtv
Reading package lists... Done
Building dependency tree... Done
The following NEW packages will be installed
   build-essential g++ g++-3.4 g++-4.0 libartsc0-dev libasound2-dev
   libaudio-dev libdvb-dev libgl1-mesa-dev libglu1-mesa-dev
   libjpeg62-dev liblame-dev liblcms1-dev liblircclient-dev
   libmng-dev libmysqlclient14-dev libogg-dev libqt3-headers
   libqt3-mt-dev libstdc++6-4.0-dev libstdc++6-dev libvorbis-dev
   libxmu-dev libxmu-headers libxt-dev libxv-dev libxvmc-dev
   libxxf86vm-dev mesa-common-dev qt3-dev-tools x11proto-video-dev
   x11proto-xf86vidmode-dev
0 upgraded, 32 newly installed, 0 to remove and 0 not upgraded.
Need to get 14.2MB/17.9MB of archives.
After unpacking 63.4MB of additional disk space will be used.
Do you want to continue [Y/n]? Y
[much output deleted]
```

As you can see from this example, it would have taken me many, many iterative compilation attempts to retrieve all of the packages required to build MythTV. Identifying the packages that provide missing include files and libraries can also be time-consuming, even with the help of the `apt-file` application discussed earlier in this chapter in the section entitled "Determining What Package Provides a Missing File." The `apt-get build-dep` command eliminates these sorts of hassles, letting you focus on the software, not the infrastructure required for building it.

Using aptitude to Add and Remove Software

As mentioned earlier in this chapter, the `dpkg` utility provides the conceptual underpinnings of much of the package management software provided on Ubuntu (and Debian) systems. However powerful it may be, it is a command-line utility, and therefore doesn't provide any sort of graphical interface, so the `dselect` utility was developed in order to at least provide a quasi-graphical interface using terminal-oriented cursor-movement libraries such as curses (now ncurses, for new curses). However, dselect couldn't quite let go of its command-line roots, and therefore also provides a command-line interface.

The apt-get application discussed earlier in this chapter provides a simpler, higher-level interface than that provided by the dpkg utility. However, apt-get is YACLU (Yet Another Command-Line utility), and therefore doesn't provide any sort of graphical interface either. The aptitude application was developed to solve this problem, but couldn't quite let go of the command line either. Thus aptitude (like deselect before it) provides both a powerful command-line interface and a terminal-oriented, quasi-graphical interface.

Personally, I find terminal-oriented graphical interfaces quaint, at best. I prefer not to use them unless absolutely necessary, especially when they've been replaced by actual graphical user interfaces such as that provided by the Synaptic Package Manager.

NOTE When using the aptitude utility to install software, you may occasionally have to provide additional, configuration-related information during the installation process. In these cases, the aptitude utility displays the same sort of information requests as those displayed by the apt-get utility and shown earlier in Figure 20.7. Whenever you see this sort of screen, you must answer any questions that it asks and supply any requested information before the installation of your package can complete.

Software can easily be installed by aptitude using the command-line aptitude install command, and removed using the aptitude remove command. As discussed later in the section entitled "Using aptitude to Install Recommended Software," aptitude provides some convenient options that make it attractive to use aptitude from the command line in certain cases. Many people are also fans of the aptitude interface, primarily those who understand it. The next section discusses the absolute basics of the aptitude user interface, focusing on how to make it readable by mere mortals.

Tips and Tricks for Using the aptitude User Interface

Figure 20.8 shows the default aptitude interface that you see the first time that you start aptitude with no arguments in a GNOME Terminal.

FIGURE 20.8

The default aptitude interface in the GNOME Terminal

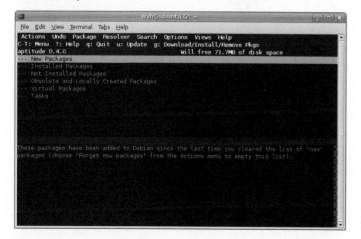

This interface looks essentially the same in an X Window system xterm or any other terminal application that supports color. (It's slightly more psychedelic in an xterm, but I won't bore you with a screen shot.)

If you insist on using this interface but are having problems seeing the text or dealing with the color scheme, you're somewhat out of luck, because the `aptitude` application doesn't offer command-line options for changing the color scheme. However, all is not lost — you can make the interface easier to read by changing your terminal application's underlying notion of the type of terminal in which you are running `aptitude`. A good choice for this is the value `vt100`, which is a classic terminal from the late Digital Equipment Corporation that only supported black and white. To make this change, exit `aptitude` by pressing Q and using the tab key to emphasize that you do actually want to exit from `aptitude`. Next, type the following command in your terminal application:

```
$ export TERM=vt100
```

After executing this command, you can then restart `aptitude`, which will look like the screen shown in Figure 20.9.

FIGURE 20.9

The aptitude interface in black and white

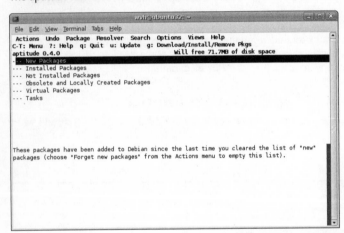

Changing the color scheme doesn't make the `aptitude` interface any more attractive, but (for me) it does at least make it more usable.

Once running `aptitude`, my favorite commands are the following:

- Q: Enables you to exit `aptitude`.
- ?: Displays a panel containing summary information about using the `aptitude` interface.
- `Control-t`: Holding down the control key and pressing T displays `aptitude`'s menus, which you can navigate through using the arrow keys or by pressing the highlighted key shortcut to execute a specific command.

Figure 20.10 displays a menu in aptitude using `aptitude`'s default color scheme. Need I say more? This is the sort of thing that gives Linux applications a bad name.

FIGURE 20.10

A menu in the default aptitude interface

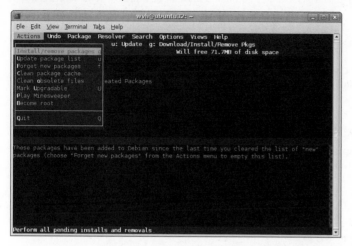

For more detailed (and less opinionated) information about using the `aptitude` user interface, see the online reference information for `aptitude` (`man aptitude`) or search the Web for relevant information.

Using aptitude to Install Recommended Software

If you have been using `apt-get` to install new software and the `apt-get` utility informs you that other packages are recommended or suggested for installation, you may want to consider using `aptitude`'s command-line interface rather than `apt-get`. The DEB packages used by Ubuntu identify various dependences, divided into five different classes:

- **Conflicts:** packages (or package versions) with which a package conflicts, and which cannot therefore be installed on a system when a specified package is being installed

- **Depends:** packages that are mandatory for the correct operation of a package, and which therefore must also be installed when a given package is installed

- **Enhances:** packages whose operation is improved or simplified as a result of installing a package, but between which there is no direct relationship

- **Pre-Depends:** packages that must be completely installed on your system before you can install a given package

- **Recommends:** packages that you should probably have, but which are not absolutely required for the correct operation of a given package

- **Suggests:** packages that may be useful, and which are normally installed on systems where a given package is installed

Requirements marked as Pre-Depends (which are rarely used or necessary) must be satisfied before you can install a given package. Requirements marked as Depends are automatically installed along with a given package. The `aptitude` utility enables you to automatically install packages that are recommended for installation by including the `--with-recommends` command-line option on your `aptitude` install command line.

The `aptitude` utility is the only command-line package installation utility that enables you to automatically install recommended packages along with required packages. Specifying the `--with-recommends` command-line option when installing packages from the command line can be quite convenient and can save you search time in the future if you discover that you want to use a recommended packages. A similar option to aptitude's `--with-recommends` option for `apt-get`, `--recommends`, and a related on for installing suggested packages, `--suggests`, have been "suggested" for `apt-get` for a long time, but are not available in any version of `apt-get` that I've ever seen. As I'll discuss in the section of this chapter on Synaptic, the Synaptic tool provides configuration options for considering recommended packages to be dependencies and automatically installing them; similarly, its interface provides a run-time option for manually selecting suggested packages and including them as part of the package installation process.

Advantages of Using aptitude to Install and Remove Software

Though I am not such a fan of the `aptitude` user interface, `aptitude` itself does provide some significantly useful capabilities. Its search capabilities, discussed earlier in this chapter in the section entitled "Listing the Packages that are Available for Your System," are easy to use and quite powerful — exactly what you want in a utility. Similarly, the current version of `aptitude` has some other advantages when installing and, specifically, when removing packages. The most significant of these are the fact that `aptitude` remembers dependency information when installing packages. Every Ubuntu package management utility understand requirements when installing packages, but `aptitude` remember this information and can therefore use that information should you decide to remove packages.

As an example, the following sample output shows an attempt to remove the PostgreSQL database system from one of my Ubuntu systems using `apt-get`:

```
$ sudo apt-get remove postgresql
Password:
Reading package lists... Done
Building dependency tree... Done
The following packages will be REMOVED
  postgresql
0 upgraded, 0 newly installed, 1 to remove and 0 not upgraded.
Need to get 0B of archives.
After unpacking 45.1kB disk space will be freed.
Do you want to continue [Y/n]? n
Abort.
```

Using `aptitude` to remove the same package is much more useful, because it also offers to remove packages that were installed along with the `postgresql` package, but which are not longer needed on that system if the `postgresql` package itself is removed, as in the following example:

```
$ sudo aptitude remove postgresql
Reading package lists... Done
Building dependency tree... Done
Reading extended state information
Initializing package states... Done
Building tag database... Done
The following packages are unused and will be REMOVED:
  postgresql-plperl-7.4 postgresql-plpython-7.4 postgresql-pltcl-7.4
```

```
The following packages will be REMOVED:
  postgresql
0 packages upgraded, 0 newly installed, 4 to remove and 0 not upgraded.
Need to get 0B of archives. After unpacking 651kB will be freed.
Do you want to continue? [Y/n/?] Y
[much output deleted]
```

For me, this makes aptitude a much more attractive command-line package installation solution than apt-get. Note that aptitude only remembers dependency information for packages that it has installed, so I tend to use aptitude from the command-line for both package installation and removal. Otherwise, if you actively install and remove large numbers of packages, your system tends to accumulate packages that you no longer need, but which you're not aware of. For information about ways of checking for unneeded packages and removing them, see the last section of this chapter, "Keeping your System Lean, Mean, and Pristine."

Using Synaptic to Add and Remove Software

The Synaptic Package Manager is a graphical, GNOME application for installing, removing, and generally managing Ubuntu software packages. In the unlikely event that this is only the second sentence you have read in this book, you may not know that I recommend using the Synaptic package management utility for almost all package management tasks on Ubuntu systems. It's true. Synaptic is the type of administrative application that users of other Linux distributions and other personal computer operating systems wish they had.

Synaptic was originally developed by the folks at Connectiva Linux, a Latin American Linux distribution that was eventually acquired by Mandrake Linux, which then changed its name to Mandriva to highlight that it wasn't your father's Mandrake Linux distribution anymore. Synaptic was originally written using the WINGS toolkit used by the Window Maker X Window system window manager (www.windowmaker .info), which attempted to provide a look and feel familiar to users of NeXT computer systems. Today, Synaptic is now built with the standard GTK+ toolkit used by GNOME. Interestingly, Connectiva was an RPM-based distribution, but Synaptic is now more commonly associated with the DEB packages used by distributions such as Ubuntu and Debian.

The Synaptic package management utility is installed by default as part of any Ubuntu installation. Select the System ➪ Administration ➪ Synaptic Package Manager menu item to start the Synaptic tool. As when trying to run any graphical administrative application on Ubuntu, you will be prompted for your administrative password before Synaptic actually starts. Figure 20.11 shows the dialog displayed when you first start Synaptic.

The left pane of the Synaptic dialog shown in Figure 20.11 shows the conceptual categories into which software is organized based on the default repositories enabled when you first install Ubuntu. Figure 20.12 shows an initial Synaptic dialog when additional repositories have been enabled.

FIGURE 20.11

The startup dialog for the Synaptic utility

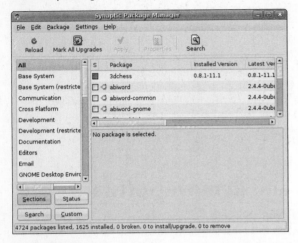

FIGURE 20.12

The startup dialog for the Synaptic utility

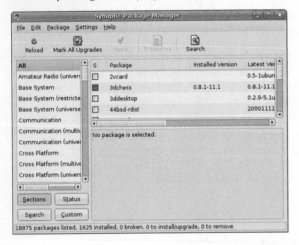

Note that the software listed in the left pane of the main Synaptic dialog is still organized into the same basic categories, but that entries for those categories from each available repository component are also listed. This enables you to identify the software packages that are associated with the various licensing requirements explained in "Ubuntu Repositories and Components" earlier in this chapter.

The basic package-related areas of Synaptic's main dialog are the following:

- **left pane:** Lists available software organized into various conceptual categories based on the repositories listed in /etc/apt/sources.list.

- **upper-right pane:** Lists the software packages that are available in the category that is currently selected in the left pane. By default, the All category is selected in Synaptic's left-pane, so that all available software packages are listed, As I'll discuss later in this chapter, performing a search in Synaptic creates a new category with the name of your search term(s) and hides all other default categories with the exception of the All category.

- **bottom-right pane:** Displays the description of any package that is currently selected in the upper-right pane.

Synaptic provides an excellent online manual, shown in Figure 20.13, that you can access by selecting the Help menu's Contents item.

FIGURE 20.13

The online manual for Synaptic

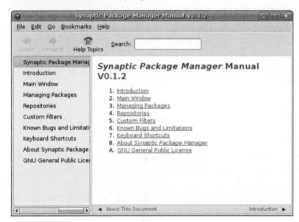

Because Synaptic includes thorough and up-to-date online help, I'm not going to bore you by repeating all of that. The next few sections focus on how to do common tasks in Synaptic, explaining how to configure Synaptic and how to perform basic package management tasks such as searching for and installing packages using Synaptic.

Configuring Synaptic Preferences

The entries on Synaptic's Settings menu enable you to set default values for using Synaptic, identify the repositories available to Synaptic, configure how searches work in Synaptic, configure how the icons are displayed in the Synaptic toolbar, and set internal variables used by Synaptic. Most of the settings that you will want to change are located on the Preferences dialog, which you can display by selecting the Settings menu's Preferences option. Figure 20.14 shows Synaptic's Preferences dialog.

FIGURE 20.14

The Synaptic Preferences dialog

The Synaptic preferences that you will most commonly want to change are all located on the general tab of Synaptic's Preferences dialog. These are the following:

- **Consider recommended packages as dependencies:** Selecting this check box causes Synaptic to always install any packages that are associated with a package that you are installing, but which are identified as recommended, but not required, for package installation. As discussed in more detail in this chapter in the section entitled "Using aptitude to Install Recommended Software," such recommended packages are ones that you will probably want to use with the package that you are installing.

- **System upgrade:** This item should always be set to "Smart Upgrade," which tries to identify other packages that must be installed, updated, or removed when installing or upgrading any package. Synaptic is much more conservative about this than other utilities such as apt-get (where the apt-get dist-upgrade command is a more powerful equivalent for this Synaptic option. Even if you are a Synaptic fan, you will occasionally need to execute the apt-get dist-upgrade command in order to completely upgrade all of the packages on your system. When using Synaptic, symptoms of the need to use the apt-get dist-upgrade command are packages that are mysteriously identified as being held back and not updated — and, of course, the occasional pop-up message that explicitly tells you to run the apt-get dist-upgrade command.

- **Apply changes in a terminal window:** Selecting this option causes Synaptic to always display package installation/update status messages and results in a separate terminal window. As mentioned when discussing installing software using the apt-get and aptitude utilities, you may occasionally have to provide additional, configuration-related information during the installation process. In these cases, the Synaptic utility displays the same sort of information requests as those displayed by the `apt-get` and `aptitude` utilities, as shown earlier in Figure 20.7. Whenever you see this sort of screen, you must answer any questions that it asks and supply any requested information before the installation of your package can complete. The Synaptic utility displays this information in the dialog that you see only when you expand the software installation status window, so it's a good idea to always monitor this window. If you choose not to and notice that Synaptic seems to have stopped installing things, expand this window to see if Synaptic is waiting for additional information.

Once you have change any setting on any of the tabs in Synaptic's Preferences dialog, click Apply to make sure that your changes are saved, and then click OK to close the Preferences dialog and return to the main Synaptic dialog.

Searching for Software in Synaptic

One of Synaptic's most powerful capabilities is providing a powerful and usable package search capability that doesn't involve a command line. To locate packages that are relevant to one or more keywords, click the Search button in the Synaptic toolbar. The search dialog displays, as shown in Figure 20.15.

FIGURE 20.15

Synaptic's Find dialog

Most examples of installing software throughout this book have relied on Synaptic's search capabilities. To locate matching, available packages, you have to make sure that you're searching the right portion of the information that Synaptic has about packages. In almost all cases, you will want to make sure that the Look in value in Synaptic's search dialog is set to Description and Name so that the search looks for matches for your keyword(s) in both package descriptions and package names. However, you may occasionally want to search other portions of the package information that is available via Synaptic. Other search possibilities are the following:

- **Name:** searches only package names for your keyword
- **Maintainer:** looks for a package maintained by one your favorite Ubuntu rock star
- **Version:** finds specific versions, which can be useful when looking for all packages that take their version number from higher-level packages, such as GNOME versions
- **Dependencies:** identifies packages that depend on a given package
- **Provided Packages:** identifies packages based on other packages that they also install.

To search for packages in Synaptic, enter one or more keywords in Synaptic's search dialog and click Search (or press Return). Synaptic will create new category in the left pane with the name of your search term(s) and hides all other default categories with the exception of the All category. Once the search completes, the new category is selected and any matching packages display in the upper-right pane. Figure 20.16 shows the results of a search for "window manager."

FIGURE 20.16

Search results in Synaptic

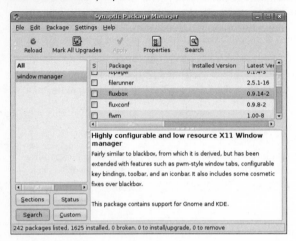

To select a package for installation, scroll down in the upper-right pane until you see the name of the package that you want to install. You can select the name of any package in the upper-right pane to see the description of that package, and can also click the Properties button in Synaptic's toolbar (or select the properties item from the pop-up menu after right-clicking its name) to display a Properties dialog that shows detailed information about the selected item. Figure 20.17 shows the Properties dialog for the package that provides the fluxbox window manager, a lightweight window manager that I like to use on laptops.

FIGURE 20.17

A package Properties dialog in Synaptic

The Common tab, shown by default when you display a package properties dialog, provides general information about the package. The Dependencies tab provides useful information about required, recommended, suggested, and conflicting packages. The Installed Files tab is also very useful, but only contains information on packages that are already installed. (To see information about the files that are included in a package that is not installed, you can use the apt-file application, which is discussed earlier in this chapter in the section entitled "Determining What Package Provides a Missing File.")

After examining any properties of a selected package, click Close to close the properties dialog and return to the main Synaptic dialog.

Installing Packages in Synaptic

After locating a package that you want to install, right-click on its name in the upper-right pane and select Mark for installation from the pop-up menu, as shown in Figure 20.18.

FIGURE 20.18

Marking a package for installation in Synaptic

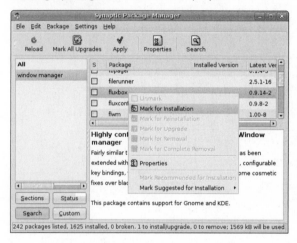

If installing the selected package requires that other packages be installed, Synaptic displays a dialog like that shown in Figure 20.19.

This dialog lists all packages whose installation is required by the package that you have selected. If you checked the Consider recommended packages as dependencies item in Synaptic's Preferences dialog, this list will also include any packages that are recommended, but not required, for installation. Click mark to accept the installation of these other packages and close this dialog.

Next, right-click the package name again and check whether any packages are listed on a sub-menu of the Mark Suggested for Installation command at the bottom of Synaptic's pop-up menu, as shown in Figure 20.20.

FIGURE 20.19

Identifying other packages required for installation

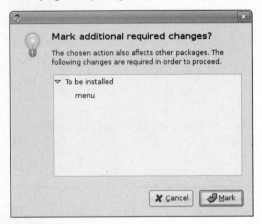

FIGURE 20.20

Marking suggested packages for installation in Synaptic

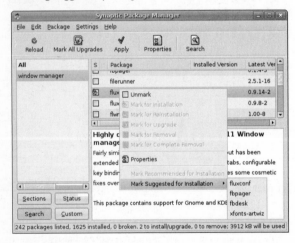

This sub-menu identifies packages that are normally installed with the primary package that you have selected for installation, but which are not required or expected. You can select any of the additional packages listed on this menu (one by one) to also schedule them for installation.

Once you have selected any suggested packages that you want to install with the primary package that you have selected for installation, click Apply in the Synaptic toolbar to begin the actual installation process. This displays the dialog shown in Figure 20.21, which summarizes all of the activities associated with installing the selected package(s).

FIGURE 20.21

A package installation summary in Synaptic

To proceed, click Apply. At this point, Synaptic begins retrieving the selected packages from the repository where they are located, displaying the progress dialog shown in Figure 20.22.

FIGURE 20.22

The download status dialog during Synaptic package installation

Once the download process completes, Synaptic begins installing and configuring the downloaded packages. If you did not select the Apply changes in a terminal window item in Synaptic's Preferences dialog, Synaptic displays a simple status dialog, as shown in Figure 20.23.

You can display a small terminal window that lists the status of Synaptic's installation and configuration processes by clicking the arrow to the right of the Terminal option on this dialog. When the installation and configuration of your packages completes, the dialog shown in Figure 20.24 displays.

FIGURE 20.23

A simple installation and configuration status dialog in Synaptic

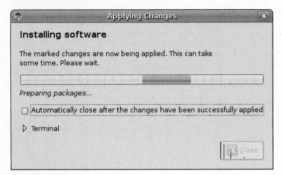

FIGURE 20.24

A simple completion dialog in Synaptic

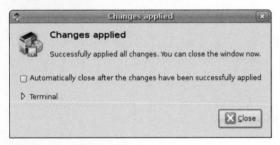

> **TIP** When using the Synaptic utility to install software, without having configured Synaptic to always display configuration status in a Terminal window, it is useful to display a Terminal to see information about the status of software installation on your system. You may occasionally have to provide additional, configuration-related information during the installation process. In this case, the Synaptic utility displays the same sort of information requests as those displayed by the apt-get and aptitude utilities, as shown earlier in Figure 20.7. Whenever you see this sort of screen, you must answer any questions that it asks and supply any requested information before the installation of your package can complete. The Synaptic utility displays this information in the dialog that you see only when you expand the software installation Terminal window, so it's a good idea to always monitor this window. If you choose not to and notice that Synaptic seems to have stopped installing things, expand this window to see if Synaptic is waiting for additional information.

If you selected the Apply changes in a terminal window item in Synaptic's Preferences dialog, Synaptic displays a single large terminal window during its installation and configuration phases, shown in Figure 20.25, instead of the dialogs shown in Figures 20.23 and 20.24.

FIGURE 20.25

A terminal window showing installation and configuration status

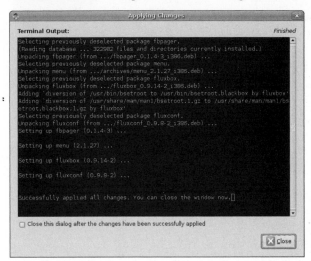

Regardless of which of the dialogs you see when package installation and configuration completes, click Close to close that dialog and return to Synaptic's main dialog.

Once you have finished installing any packages that you are interested in, you can exit from Synaptic by selecting the File menu's Quit command (or pressing the Control-q key sequence).

Removing Packages in Synaptic

Removing software in Synaptic is very similar to the installation process. You must first locate the package(s) that you want to remove by selecting the appropriate category from Synaptic's left pane and scrolling through the package lists in the upper-right pane, or by searching for that package and then selecting it from the upper-right pane. Either way, once you have located the package that you want to remove, right-click on its name to display the pop-up menu shown in Figure 20.26.

Marking a package for complete removal removes the package and any configuration files for the application that you may have modified, while Mark for Removal removes the package but leaves the configuration files on your system.

> **TIP**   Unfortunately, Synaptic does not automatically remove other packages that were required by a package that you are selecting for removal, or which you installed as a result of their being suggested for installation. You must select all of these packages manually in order to remove them. You can also not worry about them and use the process described in the last section of this chapter, "Keeping your System Lean, Mean, and Pristine" to remove them at some point in the future.

FIGURE 20.26

Marking a package for complete removal in Synaptic

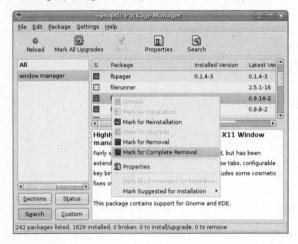

Once you have selected any packages that you want to remove and marked them for removal, click Apply to proceed with the installation process. This displays the confirmation dialog shown in Figure 20.27.

FIGURE 20.27

The confirmation dialog for package removal in Synaptic

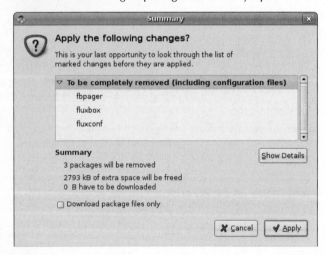

Click Apply to proceed. As the removal process proceeds, Synaptic dialog displays status dialogs similar to those shown during the package installation process, as described in the previous section. Once package removal completes, click Close to close the final status dialog and return to Synaptic's primary dialog.

Once you have finished removing packages from your system, you can exit from Synaptic by selecting the File menu's Quit command (or pressing the Control+q key sequence).

Using the Ubuntu Update Manager

Ubuntu's Update Manager checks the active repositories listed in your /etc/apt/sources.list file and notifies you if updated to any installed packages are available. The Update Manager uses an associated panel applet to let you know when updates are available by displaying a small orange icon and a pop-up dialog when updates are found. Figure 20.28 shows this pop-up and the icon that is associated with the availability of system updates.

FIGURE 20.28

The icon and dialog that notify you of available updates

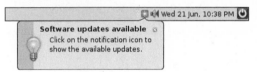

Clicking on this icon starts the Update Manager itself, which is shown in Figure 20.29.

Using the Update manager is simple — just click Install Updates. The Update manager then automatically retrieves, installs and configures all available updated packages, displaying progress and status dialogs that are very similar to those used by the Synaptic Package Manager. When the update process completes, click Close to terminate the Update Manager and begin doing real work.

TIP As when using the Synaptic utility, you should watch for configuration questions or requests for additional information that are required during the package update process. If the update process seems to have halted or is taking a long time, click the **Terminal** button in the Update manager's status dialogs to see if any configuration questions are pending.

FIGURE 20.29

The Ubuntu Update Manager

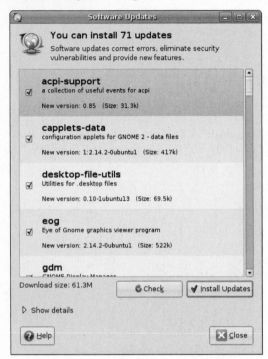

Converting Packages from Other Package Formats

Though the Ubuntu repositories contain most of the add-on software packages that anyone could ever want, there are cases when you must deal with pre-packed software that is provided in the package formats used by distributions other than Ubuntu. This is often the case with commercial software whose Linux releases are distributed in formats such as RPM and LSB. Luckily, an easy solution to this sort of problem is provided by the alien application (www.kitenet.net/~joey/code/alien.html), which is a Perl script that can covert between different package formats. Most importantly, alien can convert most package formats to the DEB package format that is used by the Ubuntu and Debian installation and update tools that are discussed in this chapter. Depending on the format of the package that you are converting from, alien may need some additional software to be installed on your Ubuntu system — more about that in a second.

 You must run alien as root (preferably using the sudo program) so that it can correctly set ownership and file permissions on the files in the converted package.

The alien application can convert packages to and from the following formats:

- **DEB:** When converting packages to DEB format, the `debhelper`, `dpkg`, `dpkg-dev`, `gcc`, and `make` packages must be installed on your system. (The `gcc`, `make`, and `dpkg-dev` packages are installed as requirements for the build-essential package, as discussed in Chapter 18. Installing `alien` installs the `debhelper` package.) If you're stuck with using some distribution other than Ubuntu on one or more of your systems, you can use `alien` to convert DEB packages to the appropriate format for your other distribution(s) until you can replace them.

- **LSB:** The package format used to distribute applications and entire distributions that are compliant with the Linux Standard Base specification (`www.freestandards.org/en/LSB`). Because the LSB specification mandates RPM packages, LSB packages are a superset of RPM packages, the RPM Package Manager software must be installed on your Ubuntu system in order to convert LSB packages. (The rpm software is automatically installed for you when you install `alien`, because it is listed as a requirement for the `alien` package.) If you are converting an LSB package that depends on other packages, the conversion process will correctly translate those dependencies, but will also introduce a new dependency on the `lsb` package, which is available in the Ubuntu repositories. You should also install the `lsb-rpm` package, which is suggested but not required by the `alien` package, if you are converting from LSB packages.

- **PKG:** The package format used by Solaris. Converting PKG files into other package formats requires Solaris-only tools such as `pkginfo` and `pkgtrans`. If you also install the rpm software from one of the Sun Free Software CDs, you can then use `alien` on your Solaris system to convert PKG packages into RPMs. This is probably only useful for packages composed of scripts, source code, or command files, since you can't execute Solaris binaries on a Linux system.

- **RPM:** The package format used by distributions such as Red Hat, Fedora Core, Mandrake, Yellow Dog, and so on. To convert packages from the RPM format, the RPM Package Manager, formerly known as the Red Hat Package Manager, software must be installed on your Ubuntu system. (The rpm software is automatically installed for you when you install `alien`, because it is listed as a requirement for the `alien` package.)

- **SLP:** The package format used by the extinct Stampede Linux distribution, which ceased development in 2002. I can't believe that this option is still actively supported, but since Stampede Linux is dead, I don't suppose much is changing in its package format.

- **TGZ:** The software distribution format used by most open source software projects and the Slackware Linux distribution, a TGZ file is a `tar` archive that has been compressed using the `gzip` compression tool, whether from the command line or by `tar` itself when creating the archive. Compressed tar archives are often simply referred to as *compressed tarballs*. Package files that are generated from TGZ files simply contain the same files as the compressed tarball, plus the package database information for the target package format.

> **TIP** For more information about Linux package formats and a general comparison of their capabilities, see `http://kitenet.net/~joey/pkg-comp`.

Using `alien` to convert from one package format to another is easy. The `alien` application provides options such as `--to-deb`, `--to-lsb`, `--to-rpm`, and `--to-tgz` to specify the target output format. The following is an example of converting the RPM package for Adobe Acrobat Reader, which some of you may have heard of, to DEB format:

```
$ sudo alien --scripts --to-deb AdobeReader_enu-7.0.0-2.i386.rpm
Password:
adobereader-enu_7.0.0-3_i386.deb generated
```

Not much to see there, actually. The `--scripts` option tells `alien` to convert any pre- or post-installation scripts found in the package, though the validity of the converted scripts can't be guaranteed — you should watch carefully to make sure that nothing goes amiss when you install the converted package. The `--to-deb` option tells `alien` to generate a Debian package from the input package. If you want to see detailed output, you can add the `-v` option to the `alien` command line, but you're likely to see way more output than you actually care about.

Before installing a converted package, you can verify its integrity using `dpkg`, as in the following example:

```
$ dpkg --info adobereader-enu_7.0.0-3_i386.deb
 new debian package, version 2.0.
 size 37932742 bytes: control archive= 7436 bytes.
     484 bytes,     11 lines         control
   20061 bytes,    207 lines         md5sums
    1340 bytes,     60 lines     *   postinst            #!/bin/sh
     980 bytes,     45 lines     *   postrm              #!/bin/sh
     211 bytes,      7 lines         shlibs
 Package: adobereader-enu
 Version: 7.0.0-3
 Section: alien
 Priority: extra
 Architecture: i386
 Installed-Size: 92316
 Maintainer: root <root@vmdesktop>
 Description: Adobe Reader for Linux. An application that reads a PDF
 document.
   Adobe Reader 7.0.0 can read documents in PDF format. Adobe Reader
 also allows you to search within PDF files, search for PDF files on the
 internet and participate in collaborative document reviews.

   .
   (Converted from a rpm package by alien version 8.64.)
```

This matches quite nicely with information about the original RPM package that was produced on one of my other systems:

```
$ rpm -q --info -v -p AdobeReader_enu-7.0.0-2.i386.rpm
Name         : AdobeReader_enu            Relocations:
/usr/local/Adobe/Acrobat7.0
Version      : 7.0.0                      Vendor: Adobe Systems,
Incorporated
Release      : 2                          Build Date: Mon 28 Mar 2005 06:34:42
AM EST
Install date: (not installed)            Build Host:
acrolinux2.corp.adobe.com
Group        : Applications/Publishing    Source RPM: AdobeReader_enu-
7.0.0-2.src.rpm
Size         : 97613446                   License: Commercial
Signature    : (none)
Packager     : Adobe Systems, Incorporated
URL          : www.adobe.com
```

```
Summary     : Adobe Reader for Linux. An application that reads a PDF document.
Description :

Adobe Reader 7.0.0 can read documents in PDF format. Adobe Reader also
allows you to search within PDF files, search for PDF files on the
internet and participate in collaborative document reviews.
Distribution: (none)
```

For more information about the `alien` package, see its online reference information, which is available by typing the man `alien` command (after installing the package, of course).

> **WARNING** You should never use `alien` in order to install packages containing low-level system utilities or system libraries. Though they may convert and install successfully, these packages will probably not work correctly on your Ubuntu system and you risk reducing your Ubuntu system to a dysfunctional heap of slag that will not boot correctly.

Keeping your System Lean, Mean, and Pristine

If you like to play with different software packages as much as I do, you'll find yourself installing lots of random packages on your system, playing with them for a while, and then forgetting about them unless they solve some major problem for you. You may occasionally even be thoughtful enough to remove packages that you aren't planning on using anymore. Unfortunately, this doesn't remove packages that were required, recommended, or suggested by the packages that you've removed (unless you use `aptitude` to both install and remove those package).

Every now and then, it is therefore useful to run a utility that scans all of the packages that are installed on your system and looks for packages that are not used or required by any other package on your system, and which are also not a part of some system installation process. Good examples of programs that you can use to check your system in this way are the `deborphan` and `debfoster` packages. Neither of these packages is installed by default on an Ubuntu system, but you can easily install either of them using your favorite package installation utility.

The core difference between these two packages is that the `deborphan` utility simply produces a list of packages that are not used or referred to by any system package on your system, while the `debfoster` package builds its own database of which packages are required, tries to be smart about things that you may not need, and also asks lots of questions the first time you run it. For all of these reasons, I prefer the `deborphan` package, but I suggest that you investigate both and see which utility best suits your needs and modus operandi.

As mentioned previously, the `deborphan` utility simply lists packages that are no longer required by or associated with any other package. To do something useful with this list, you can either redirect it into a file and use that file as the basis for a shell script that will remove the packages that you actually want to remove. Another solution, much more wizardly, is to feed this list to the `apt-get remove` command using the Linux `xargs` command, as in the following example:

```
$ sudo deborphan | xargs apt-get remove --purge -y
```

Before running this sort of command, you should examine the `deborphan` output to make sure that it isn't removing anything that you still want.

Running either the `deborphan` or `debfoster` commands periodically will help you reduce the amount of software package detritus that tends to accumulate on any running system. Keeping your system as free of unneeded packages as possible can help guarantee that the maximum amount of free disk space is available on your system, which you can then devote to "real work" such as your online music archives or collection of artistic digital photographs.

Summary

Package management is a wonderful thing, enabling your system to identify installed packages and, with the help of excellent package formats such as DEB, identify and satisfy any requirements for successfully installing a completely functional software package. This chapter discussed Ubuntu's four primary package management utilities (dpkg, apt-get, aptitude, and synaptic), and discussed how you can use these and related utilities to install and query packages, figure out other packages that you need, and many more interesting package management tricks.

Chapter 21 continues with system-related topics, discussing how to create and manage users and groups on your Ubuntu system, and why this is important. It also discusses advanced topics related to file and directory protection, such as Access Control Lists, that are above and beyond the traditional user/group protection model but give you even finer control over who can access your data (and don't require system administration privileges to do so).

Chapter 21

Managing Users, Groups, Authentication, and Advanced Permissions

Though many people install and use Ubuntu as the operating system on a truly personal computer, Linux is designed and implemented as a multi-user computer system from the group up. Even if you're the only user of an Ubuntu system, that system still has multiple user and group accounts and runs many processes using the rights granted to those accounts. Similarly, the login process seems simple, but actually invokes several user and group checks under the hood, as do other commands that require specific permissions.

This chapter explains how to manage users and groups on Ubuntu systems. Chapter 4 provided a basic introduction to the classical Ubuntu and general Linux concepts of users, groups, file permissions, and performing privileged operations. Following is a quick review:

- The section of Chapter 4 entitled "Basic Concepts: Users and Groups" provided an overview of how users and groups work on Ubuntu and other Unix-like systems, explaining the content and organization of the system files that hold user and group information.

- The section of Chapter 4 entitled "File and Directory Permissions Under Linux" introduced file and directory permissions and explained what the cryptic protection entries in a long file listing actually mean.

- The section of Chapter 4, "Performing Privileged Operations in Ubuntu" explained how Ubuntu handles the execution of privileged commands, which is a slight departure from how other Linux and Unix-like systems work.

This chapter delves into related topics in more detail. The information in this chapter ranges from a hands-on discussion of how to create and modify user and group accounts using graphical tools to more detailed discussions of how users and groups actually interact with your Ubuntu system and the files and directories that it contains. The first section discusses the graphical and command-line tools used to create and manage user and group accounts. The following section explains how authentication works when a user logs in, which should be of

IN THIS CHAPTER

Creating users and groups

Understanding standard Linux authentication

Configuring the sudo command

Using ACLs from the command line

Editing ACLs graphically

interest to Ubuntu system administrators in enterprise or academic environments that may require changes to the standard authentication process to support custom authentication mechanisms. This chapter also discusses the details of how Ubuntu handles the execution of privileged commands, which is a slight departure from how other Linux and Unix-like systems work. The final section in this chapter discusses ACLs, which provide fine-grained control over who can access selected files, and includes an ACL-to-earth dictionary to understand the cryptic ACL commands, their obscure output, and their motto, which seems to be, "Is that gibberish on the screen, or are you just glad to see me?"

Creating and Managing Users and Groups

Users and groups are primarily ways of granting different permissions to different individuals or sets of individuals, respectively. These permissions include the ability to read, write, and access specific files and directories, the ability to access specific devices in different ways, and the ability to read or write special-purpose resources such as filesystems, portions of memory, and kernel resources.

Ubuntu provides a convenient graphical tool for creating users, creating groups, and adding users to groups. Select the System ➪ Administration ➪ Users and Groups menu entry to execute this tool. After you supply your password, the dialog shown in Figure 21.1 displays.

FIGURE 21.1

Ubuntu's Users and Groups tool

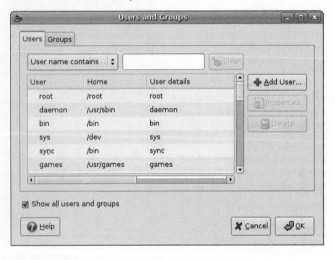

In this figure, I've checked the Show all users and groups to list all system users and groups, not just the accounts for individual users.

> **TIP** Ubuntu also provides command-line tools for quick user and group creation, modification, and removal. For more information about these tools, see the online reference information for the `adduser`, `useradd`, `userdel`, `usermod`, `groupadd`, `groupdel`, and `groupmod` commands. I prefer to use the graphical Users and Groups tool when creating single users to take advantage of capabilities such as its default privilege settings and associated group memberships. The command-line tools are quite useful in scripts, but they are also well documented, and I don't see much point in simply recreating that documentation here. One tip, though — when you're using these commands to add users to existing groups, either use the `adduser` command (`adduser user-name group-name`) or make sure that you specify the `-a` option when using the `usermod` command (`usermod -a -G group-name user-name`). Forgetting to use the `-a` option with `usermod` will make the specified `user-name` a member of `group-name` and only that group — it will remove `user-name` from all other groups. I can personally attest to the fact that it is painful to remember and add back all of the other group memberships that most desktop users require.

The text box and drop-down menu above the list of users enables you to search for users based on criteria such as substrings of the username (User Name Contains), substrings of a user's default group (Group Name Contains), the user's user ID (UID is), and the user's default group ID (Group ID is).

For information about using the Users and Groups tool beyond what is discussed in the next few sections, see its online manual, shown in Figure 21.2, which you can access at any time by clicking Help on any panel of the main Users and Groups dialog.

FIGURE 21.2

The online manual for Ubuntu's Users and Groups tool

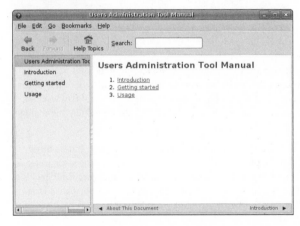

Creating New Users

To add a new user using the Users and Groups tool, click Add User to display the User Account Editor dialog shown in Figure 21.3.

FIGURE 21.3

The User Account Editor dialog

Only the Username and Password fields are mandatory on this dialog, but you should generally provide as much information as possible when creating a user account — you may not be the only administrator of the system that you're working on, so you should be kind to your fellow sysadmins who may one day wonder, "Who is this person?" After populating the fields of this dialog, click the Advanced tab to display the dialog shown in Figure 21.4.

This dialog enables you to define some basic settings for the new account that you're creating, but its most interesting capability is the ability to associate a specific profile with that user. A profile (not the same thing as the .profile file discussed in the section of Chapter 6 entitled "Exploring the Bash Configuration File") is a complete group of environment and privilege settings that are used when a new user is created. The standard profiles provided by the Users and Groups tool are named Default, Desktop, and Administrator. Each of these profiles specifies things such as the devices that a user has access to, basic user capabilities, and the default groups that the user belongs to. You can determine the capabilities associated with any of the default user profiles by clicking Edit User Profiles, which displays the dialog shown in Figure 21.5.

FIGURE 21.4

The Advanced tab of the User Account Editor dialog

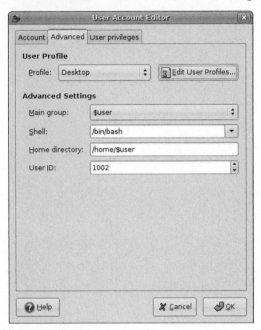

FIGURE 21.5

The User Profiles dialog

To examine the settings associated with any existing user profile, select the name of that profile and click Properties, which displays a dialog like the one shown in Figure 21.6.

FIGURE 21.6

Exploring the privileges associated with a user profile

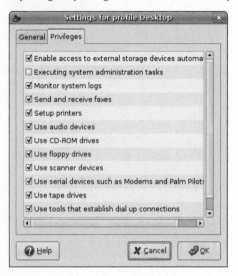

Figure 21.6 displays the default privileges associated with a standard Ubuntu Desktop user. As you can see from this dialog, all privileges and capabilities are enabled for a desktop user with the exception of the ability to execute system administration tasks. This dialog also provides access to more general settings associated with this user profile, which you can view by selecting the General tab that is shown in Figure 21.7.

As you can see from Figure 21.7, this dialog provides many of the settings that are displayed by the User Account Editor's Advanced tab (shown earlier in Figure 21.4), such as the way in which a user's home directory is constructed (/home/ plus the username), the user's default login group (the same as the username), and how the user's UID is derived (the first available UID in the range that is specified in Figure 21.7).

The ability to associate several settings with a specific type of user is convenient for home users, where the basic profiles provided with Ubuntu installation are probably sufficient. However, the ability to create your own profiles can be very handy in enterprise or academic environments where you may want to create large numbers of users with similar capabilities.

To close the profile settings dialog and return to the User Profiles dialog without saving any changes that you may accidentally have made, click Cancel. You can then click Close to close the User Profiles dialog and return to the standard User Account Editor dialog.

The Users and Group tool also enables you to customize privileges on a per-user basis, using the command available by clicking the User Account Editor's User Privileges tab, shown in Figure 21.8.

FIGURE 21.7

General settings for a user profile

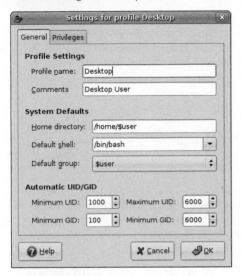

FIGURE 21.8

Setting User Privileges during account creation

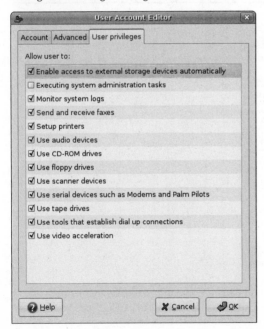

You'll note that the initial settings in this dialog are the same as those on the user profiles associated with the current user (shown in Figure 21.6). These dialogs show how the privilege settings in a selected profile set defaults for user account privileges, just as the General tab in the profile provide general settings that are used on the Advanced tab.

Once you have customized the account settings for the user account that you are creating, click OK on the main User Account Editor dialog to create the new account. The User Account Editor dialog closes, all system files (such as /etc/passwd, /etc/group, and /etc/shadow) are updated, and the new account is added to the list in the main Users and Groups dialog.

Managing Existing Users

In addition to simplifying the creation of new accounts, the Users and Groups tool also simplifies updating (or deleting) an existing account. To update or delete an existing account, start the Users and Groups tool by selecting the System ➪ Administration ➪ Users and Groups menu entry to execute this tool. After supplying your password, the dialog shown in Figure 21.1 displays.

> **NOTE** The most common administrative task done after an account has been created is to add that account to other groups or remove it from groups of which it is currently a member. This is not done by modifying the settings for the account using the dialogs described in this section, but is done using the procedures described later in this chapter in the section entitled "Managing Existing Groups."

To modify or delete an existing account, scroll through the list of available accounts and select the account that you want to update or delete. Selecting the name of an existing account activates the Properties and Delete buttons, as shown in Figure 21.9.

FIGURE 21.9

Selecting an account for modification or deletion

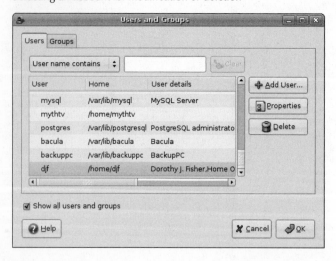

To delete the selected account, click Delete. The Users and Groups tool displays a dialog that requests confirmation that you actually want to delete the account, and which also explains that deleting an account just removes the entries for that user from the password, group, and shadow files—it does not remove any files and directories that are associated with the user, such as the user's home directory. To delete the selected user, click Delete in the dialog. To return to the Users and Groups tool without deleting the account, click Cancel. This also deselects the account that you had selected in the Users and Groups tool.

To modify an existing account, click Properties. This displays essentially the same dialogs as those used by the User Account Editor in the previous section, with a few differences:

- All dialogs are now titled "Setting for User *username*" rather than "User Account Editor."
- Fields that cannot be edited, such as the username and user ID, are disabled.
- You cannot change the profile associated with this account, because the profile is only used to provide default settings during account creation.

Figure 21.10 shows the Advanced tab displayed when modifying the properties of an existing account, which is equivalent to the User Account Editor's Advanced tab (shown in Figure 21.4).

FIGURE 21.10

Modifying Advanced settings for an existing account

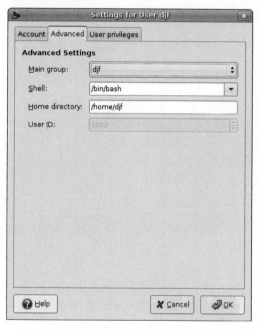

To change the privileges associated with the selected account, click the User Privileges tab, which displays the same dialog as shown in Figure 21.8.

Once you have made any changes that you wish to make to the account, click OK to close the Settings dialog and return to the main Users and Groups dialog.

Creating New Groups

Creating a new system group is usually done as a part of the installation process for any software that requires a group that does not yet exist on your Ubuntu system. System groups is the term used to refer to groups that are created to support a specific software subsystem or application, such as groups that control access to printers, databases, and various types of hardware. On Ubuntu Linux, the group IDs of system groups are less than 1000.

You may want to create your own groups to do things like identify project members, to limit access to selected directories to a group, or to use a group to limit the people who can execute selected binaries. Ubuntu's Users and Groups tool provides a graphical interface to simplify both group creation and group management (the latter is discussed in the section after this one). To start this tool, select the System ⇨ Administration ⇨ Users and Groups menu entry to execute this tool. After supplying your password, the dialog shown in Figure 21.1 displays. To access the group-oriented portions of this tool, click the Groups tab, which displays a dialog like the one shown in Figure 21.11.

FIGURE 21.11

The Groups tab in the Users and Groups tool

To create a new group, click Add Group. The dialog shown in Figure 21.12 displays.

Enter the name of the new group that you want to create in the Group name box. Next, you can optionally modify the group number associated with this group, which you may want to do in NFS file-sharing environments that do not use NIS. (See the section of Chapter 16 entitled "Accessing NFS Directories from Linux Systems" and Chapter 31, "Setting Up an NFS Server," for more information about NFS and NIS.)

At this point, you can also add selected users to the group that you are creating by clicking their names in the All users list and clicking Add to add them to the list of Group members for the new group. If you change your mind about adding a specific user to your new group, simply select their name in the Group members list and click Remove to remove them from the list.

FIGURE 21.12

The Create New Group dialog

Once you are finished changing settings and adding members to your new group, click OK to create that group and return to the Groups tab of the Users and Groups application. If you are finished creating or modifying groups, you can click OK to exit the application.

Managing Existing Groups

In addition to simplifying the creation of new groups, the Users and Groups tool also simplifies adding and removing users from those groups. To update groups memberships, start the Users and Groups tool by selecting the System ➪ Administration ➪ Users and Groups menu entry to execute this tool. After supplying your password, the dialog shown in Figure 21.1 displays. Click the Groups tab to display the dialog shown in Figure 21.11.

In this dialog, click the name of the group that you want to add or remove users from and click Properties. This displays the dialog shown in Figure 21.13.

As you can see, this dialog is essentially identical to the settings dialog that is provided when you create a new group, down to the fact that you can change its name and group ID. However, its primary purpose is to enable you to add and remove group members.

> **TIP** You should rarely, if ever, use the group settings dialog to change group IDs. Changing the group ID in this dialog changes the entry for this group in the file `/etc/group`, but does not change the group ID of any files that may happen to already be owned by that group. This could prevent any per-group protections that are already in use from working correctly, preventing users that should be authorized from accessing files or directories associated with their group.

FIGURE 21.13

The group settings dialog

To add a user to an existing group, select that user's username in the scrollable list at the left of the dialog shown in Figure 21.13. Selecting a user in this list activates the Add button, which you can click to add that user to the current group.

Similarly, to remove a user from an existing group, select that user's username in the scrollable list of group member at the right of the dialog shown in Figure 21.13. Selecting a user in this list activates the Remove button, which you can click to remove that user from the current group.

Any membership, name or group ID changes that you make in the dialog shown in Figure 21.13 are not written to the /etc/group file (and updated in the /etc/passwd file, if necessary) until you click OK. You can click Cancel at any time to discard your changes. Clicking either of these buttons closes the group settings dialog and returns you to Groups portion of the main Users and Groups dialog, as shown in Figure 21.11. Once you have finished making any changes to group memberships or other properties, click OK to close the Users and Groups tool.

PAMs and the Linux Authentication Process

Many different Linux and Unix applications require authentication or special privileges of one type or another to access special devices, files, or to start processes as a specific user and group. In the early days of Linux/Unix, each authentication-aware application was compiled with hardwired information about the authentication mechanism that it required. Changing or enhancing a system's authentication mechanism therefore required that all such applications be updated and recompiled, which is tedious at best even if you have the source code for all of the relevant applications on your system.

To resolve this problem, the folks at Sun Microsystems developed the idea of Pluggable Authentication Modules (PAMs), which provide a flexible and dynamic mechanism for authenticating any application or service that uses them. This model has since been adopted by most Linux and Unix-like operating systems, including Ubuntu Linux. Applications or services compiled with the Linux-PAM library use text-format configuration files to identify and describe their authentication requirements and the specific shared library modules used to implement them. The PAM model lets you modify the authentication requirements of existing applications by simply adding entries to the PAM configuration file that is used by a specific application or service. Applications that use PAMs are typically referred to as PAM-aware applications, and PAMs are usually simply referred to as PAM modules.

PAMs satisfy different parts of the authentication requirements for PAM-aware applications, much like reusable code and libraries do for applications in general. For example, a PAM-aware version of the login program can invoke several PAMs that check things such as whether the user logging in as root is on a terminal listed as a secure terminal, whether users are allowed to log in on the system at the moment, and other similar, authentication requirements. Because PAMs are shared library modules, a PAM-aware version of the `ssh` command can reuse the same "are users allowed to log in on the system now" PAM as the PAM-aware version of login, but then apply other rules that are more relevant to ssh than to login.

The files that describe the sequence of PAMs associated with specific applications or services are located in the directory `/etc/pam.d`. The shared-library PAM modules themselves are stored in the directory `/lib/security`. In older PAM implementations, the PAM modules used by all applications on a system were defined in a central configuration file, `/etc/pam.conf`. This file is still used, but only as a fall-back if no PAM configuration file for a specific application is found in `/etc/pam.d`.

Many different PAM libraries are available in the Ubuntu repositories, some of which are installed by default and many that are associated with specific authentication mechanisms such as LDAP or Kerberos. Searching the repository for packages that match the string "`libpam`" and extracting the names of unique package names shows that there are (currently) 31 PAM-related packages, as the following example shows:

```
$ apt-file search libpam | sed -e 's;:.*;;' | grep libpam | \
  grep -v dev | sort | uniq
libpam0g
libpam-ccreds
libpam-chroot
libpam-cracklib
libpam-doc
libpam-dotfile
libpam-encfs
libpam-foreground
libpam-heimdal
libpam-krb5
libpam-ldap
libpam-modules
libpam-mount
libpam-musclecard
libpam-mysql
libpam-ncp
libpam-openafs-kaserver
libpam-openafs-session
libpam-opie
libpam-p11
libpam-passwdqc
```

```
libpam-pgsql
libpam-pwdfile
libpam-pwgen
libpam-radius-auth
libpam-runtime
libpam-smbpass
libpam-ssh
libpam-tmpdir
libpam-umask
libpam-unix2

$ apt-file search libpam | sed -e 's;:.*;;' | grep libpam | \
  grep -v dev | sort | uniq |  wc -l
31
```

The PAM modules used by specific, nonstandard authentication mechanisms are identified as requirements for the packages that provide the applications and daemons associated with those authentication mechanisms, and are therefore only installed when those authentication mechanisms are installed.

PAM Configuration Files for Applications and Services

The PAM configuration files in /etc/pam.d have the same name as the PAM-aware application or service that they are associated with, and define the sequence of PAM modules invoked, in order, during the authentication and validation process for that application or service. In addition to PAM rules and related statements, the files in /etc/pam.d can contain blank lines (which are ignored) and comments — any characters on a line that follow the traditional hash mark (#) are interpreted as a comment.

Each noncomment line in one of the files in /etc/pam.d is either an @include statement that includes (inserts) the contents of another PAM definition file at this point, or is an actual PAM rule for how a specific PAM module is used as part of the authentication process for the associated application or service. Included files are used to simplify PAM configuration files, enabling a common set of PAM rules to be included by other PAM configuration files. Each PAM rule can consist of four fields separated by white space, the first three of which are mandatory. These fields have the following meaning and content:

- module-type: The type of PAM module defined on that line. A module's type defines how a specific PAM module is used during the authentication process. Valid values are the following:

  - auth: Identifies modules that verify user identity or that system requirements have been met. Common system requirements are that a service can be started at the current time (for example, that /etc/nologin does not exist when a user is trying to log in), that an acceptable device is being used (the device is listed in the file /etc/securetty), that the user is already the root user, and so on.

  - account: Identifies modules that verify if the user can authenticate based on system requirements such as having a valid account that is able to log in at the current time (based on per-account policies, not general system constraints), has access to the requested application or service, and so on.

  - password: Identifies modules that verify that a user can authenticate to the system.

  - session: Identifies modules associated with tasks that must be done before the associated service or application is activated, or just before the termination of that service or application. Modules of this type typically perform system functions such as mounting directories, logging audit trail information, or guaranteeing that system resources are available.

- control-flag: The control-flag specifies the implications of different return values from the specified PAM module. Valid values are the following:

  - optional: Indicates that success of the PAM module is not critical to the application or service unless this PAM is the only PAM for a specified module type. If it is, its success or failure determines the success or failure of the specified module type.

  - required: Indicates that success of the PAM module is mandatory for the specified module type. The failure of any PAM marked as required for a specific module type (such as all modules labeled as auth) is reported only after all required PAMs for that module type have been executed.

  - requisite: Indicates that failure of the PAM module immediately returns failure to the associated application or service.

  - sufficient: Indicates that success of the PAM module satisfies the authentication requirements of this module type. If no previous required PAM has failed, no other PAMs for the associated module type are executed after a module labeled as sufficient has succeeded. Failure of a PAM identified as sufficient is ignored as long as any subsequent modules that are identified as required for that module type return success. If a previous required PAM has failed, the success of a PAM marked as sufficient is ignored.

- module-name: The name of the PAM module associated with this entry. By default, PAM modules are located in /lib/security, but this field can also identify modules located in other directories by specifying the absolute path and filename of a PAM module.

- arguments: Optional, module-specific arguments.

The next section provides an example of the structure and organization of a PAM configuration file by examining the PAM configuration file used by the login process on Ubuntu systems.

Example: PAMs Used by the Login Process

To see how a PAM file actually works, let's look at an actual example. The configuration file for the PAMs used by the login program is the file /etc/pam.d/login. After removing blank lines and comments, the meaningful parts of this file on an Ubuntu system are the following:

```
 1:  auth       requisite   pam_securetty.so
 2:  auth       requisite   pam_nologin.so
 3:  session    required    pam_env.so readenv=1
 4:  @include   common-auth
 5:  auth       optional    pam_group.so
 6:  @include   common-account
 7:  @include   common-session
 8:  session    required    pam_limits.so
 9:  session    optional    pam_lastlog.so
10:  session    optional    pam_motd.so
11:  session    optional    pam_mail.so standard
12:  @include   common-password
```

NOTE   The actual /etc/pam.d/login file does not include line numbers (and cannot). I've added the line numbers to make it easier to match up the PAM entries with the explanations that follow.

Each line of this sequence of PAMs does the following:

1. Invokes the PAM module `pam_securetty.so` to check whether the user is logged in on a secure terminal as defined in the file `/etc/securetty`. This check must succeed, but is not sufficient to enable a user to log in.

2. Invokes the `pam_nologin.so` PAM module to check whether logins are allowed on the system at the current time, which is usually done by checking for the file `/etc/nologin`. If this file is present, the system is in a maintenance state or in the process of being shut down, and logins are disabled. This check must succeed (i.e., the file must not exist), but is not sufficient to enable a user to log in.

3. Invokes the `pam_env.so` module, which reads a list of environment variables to set or unset from the file `/etc/security/pam.conf` (which does not contain any noncommented entries on an Ubuntu system, and is therefore somewhat meaningless). This PAM must succeed (i.e., be able to read its configuration file), but is not sufficient to enable a user to log in.

4. Includes the contents of the file `/etc/pam.d/common-auth`, which provides a common set of PAM rules for system authentication. On Ubuntu 6.06 systems that use standard `/etc/passwd` and `/etc/shadow` password authentication, this file contains the following PAM rule:

   ```
   auth       required   pam_unix.so nullok_secure
   ```

   This rule invokes the `pam_unix.so` to verify that the user has a valid entry in the `/etc/shadow` file. The `nullok_secure` argument indicates that null (empty) passwords are acceptable on this system when coming from the terminals listed in `/etc/securetty`. This PAM must succeed, but is not sufficient to enable a user to log in.

   On Ubuntu systems where other authentication mechanisms, such as LDAP or Kerberos, have been installed, this file would invoke the PAMs specific to checking authentication as required by those services.

5. Invokes the `pam_group.so` module, which verifies that the user is a member of one or more groups and that a group with the numeric identifier for the user's login group actually exist in the `/etc/group` file. This PAM module is executed but is optional — its success or failure does not matter unless it was the only auth module for the login service (which it is not), and is therefore not sufficient to enable a user to log in.

6. Includes the contents of the file `/etc/pam.d/common-account`, which provides a common set of PAM rules for verifying that the user has a valid account on the system. On Ubuntu 6.06 systems that use standard `/etc/passwd` and `/etc/shadow` password authentication, this file contains the following PAM rule:

   ```
   account    required   pam_unix.so
   ```

   This rule invokes the `pam_unix.so` module to perform the traditional Linux authentication mechanism check that the user's account is not marked as expired in the file `/etc/shadow`. This PAM must succeed, but is not sufficient to enable a user to log in.

   On Ubuntu systems where other authentication mechanisms, such as LDAP or Kerberos, have been installed, this file would invoke the PAMs specific to verifying accounts as required by those services.

7. Includes the contents of the file `/etc/pam.d/common-session`, which provides a common set of PAM rules for interactive and noninteractive login sessions. On Ubuntu 6.06 systems that use standard `/etc/passwd` and `/etc/shadow` password authentication, this file contains the following PAM rules:

   ```
   session    required   pam_unix.so
   session    optional   pam_foreground.so
   ```

The first rule invokes the `pam_unix.so` module to create a log entry to the syslog service identifying the beginning of a user's login session on the current system. This PAM must succeed, but is not sufficient to enable a user to log in. The second rule invokes the `pam_foreground.so` module to create a lock file named `/var/run/console/user:tty-number` for the user that is logging in. This file identifies the user as the owner of the specified console and enables software such as the GNOME Volume manager to determine if the user is logged in on the current foreground console. This PAM module is executed but is optional — its success or failure does not matter unless it was the only session module for the login service (which it is not), and is therefore not sufficient to enable a user to log in.

8. Invokes the `pam_limits.so` module to set user limits specified in the configuration file `/etc/security/limits.conf` (which does not contain any noncommented entries on an Ubuntu system, and is therefore somewhat meaningless). This PAM must succeed (i.e., be able to read its configuration file), but is not sufficient to enable a user to log in.

9. Invokes the `pam_lastlog.so` module to add an entry for the user to the file `/var/log/lastlog`, adding an entry when opening a session and terminating that entry when a session is closed. This PAM module is executed but is optional — its success or failure does not matter unless it was the only session module for the login service (which it is not), and is therefore not sufficient to enable a user to log in.

10. Invokes the `pam_motd.so` module to display the contents of the `/etc/motd` file on the login console. This PAM module is executed but is optional — its success or failure does not matter unless it was the only session module for the login service (which it is not), and is therefore not sufficient to enable a user to log in.

11. Invokes the `pam_mail.so` module to examine the user's mail directory and display a message if there is any pending mail. This PAM module is executed but is optional — its success or failure does not matter unless it was the only session module for the login service (which it is not), and is therefore not sufficient to enable a user to log in.

12. Includes the contents of the file `/etc/pam.d/common-password`, which provides a common set of PAM rules for actually checking a password. On Ubuntu 6.06 systems that use standard `/etc/passwd` and `/etc/shadow` password authentication, this file contains the following PAM rules:

```
password    required    pam_unix.so nullok obscure min=4 max=8 md5
```

This rule invokes the `pam_unix.so` module to check `/etc/passwd` for a valid user and test the password for that user against the encrypted password entry found in the file `/etc/shadow`. The `nullok` argument indicates that null (empty) passwords are acceptable on this system. The `obscure` argument specifies that, when changing a password, certain checks will be performed, such as verifying that the new password is not a palindrome or rotated version of the old password, that the new password does not differ from the old one simply in terms of case, that the new password is of the length specified by the `min` and `max` arguments, and that the new password is not "too similar" to the old one. I personally have never looked at the code to see how similarity is determined, but its rules seem to be fairly obscure themselves.) This PAM must succeed, but is not sufficient by itself to enable a user to log in.

NOTE Some other password checking and password-strength checking PAMs are listed in the file `/etc/pam.d/common-password`, but are commented out. You may want to uncomment these and comment out the original `pam_unix.so` entry if, for example, you want to take advantage of the dictionary checks performed by the `pam_cracklib.so` module, which are irritating but ensure that a password is not a word that is commonly found in a dictionary.

Once all of the PAMs specified in the /etc/pam.d/login file (and files that it included) have completed successfully, the login process continues, the user's login shell is created, and any other startup actions specified in the user's login configuration files are executed.

The PAM authentication process can be complex and conducive to migraine headaches. Even though it is a pain, security is one of any sysadmin's most important responsibilities. You will rarely, if ever, want to muck with the PAM configuration files on a home Linux system, but you may want to modify them (and should certainly understand them) when using Ubuntu in an enterprise or academic environment. If it's any consolation, think how complex the code to implement all of this would have been without the flexibility that PAMs provide.

Configuration Files for Various PAMs

The text-format files in /etc/pam.d control the PAMs associated with each authentication-aware application or service. As mentioned when exploring the /etc/pam.d/login file in the previous section, some of these PAMs use optional configuration files to further refine their behavior. The configuration files for individual PAMs are located in the directory /etc/security. Though these files must exist, they do not need to contain any useful information — they are there in case you want to take advantage of the advanced configuration options that they provide. Here is a list of the files in this directory which are found on a default Ubuntu 6.06 system:

- access.conf: Provides fine-grained access control for logins, and is used by the pam_access.so module.
- group.conf: Provides per-session group membership control, and is used by the pam_group.so module.
- limits.conf: Provides a per-user mechanism for setting system resource limits, used by the pam_limits.so module.
- pam_env.conf: Provides a mechanism for setting environment variables to specific values, used by the pam_env.so module.
- time.conf: Provides a mechanism for imposing general or user-specific time restrictions for system services and applications, used by the pam_time.so module.

If you install other authentication systems and their associated PAMs, other configuration files associated with those PAMs may also be installed in /etc/security. This section only lists the default configuration files provided by a standard Ubuntu installation.

What If PAM Configuration Files Are Missing?

PAMs provide a very powerful mechanism for authenticating various applications and making sure that only the right users are running them from the right devices. It is therefore easy to see that the correct configuration of application-specific PAMs is very important. But what if an application uses PAMs and you forget to create its PAM configuration file or that file is somehow accidentally deleted? To cover these cases, the Linux-PAM library provides a default configuration file for any applications and services that do not have their own configuration files. This is the file /etc/pam.d/other, which has the following valid entries on a standard Ubuntu 6.06 system:

```
@include common-auth
@include common-account
@include common-password
@include common-session
```

The contents of each of these included files was discussed earlier in this chapter, in the section entitled "Example: PAMs Used by the Login Process." On Ubuntu systems, by default, the `/etc/pam.d/other` PAM configuration file provides a reasonable set of defaults for verifying that random applications are at least being executed by someone who can successfully log in and authenticate to the system, and guarantees that various log entries for that user are created.

> **TIP** Because a missing PAM configuration file generally indicates a misconfigured system or that someone has imported a PAM-aware binary without thinking things through, you can use the `/etc/pam.d/other` file to disallow access and impose extremely paranoid security, by changing it to contain the following entries:

```
auth        required    pam_deny.so
auth        required    pam_warn.so
account     required    pam_deny.so
account     required    pam_warn.so
password    required    pam_deny.so
password    required    pam_warn.so
session     required    pam_deny.so
session     required    pam_warn.so
```

Because subsequent required entries for a given module type are still executed, each module-type entry first executes the `pam_deny.so` PAM, which denies access to the requested service, and then also executes the `pam_warn.so` PAM, which enters a warning message to the system log. These log entries will help you identify the problem if a cranky user hasn't already surfaced and asked why they can no longer run some obscure binary that they've imported.

Customizing the sudo Command on Ubuntu Systems

As introduced in the section of Chapter 4 entitled "Performing Privileged Operations in Ubuntu," Ubuntu does not use the traditional root account to perform privileged operations, but instead enables users who are members of the admin group to perform all privileged operations by specifying their own passwords. The rationale for why the root account (and it's traditional friend, the `su root` command) are disabled on Ubuntu systems is discussed in the official online Ubuntu documentation at `https://help.ubuntu.com/community/RootSudo`. To save you a Web lookup, this is basically viewed as a security improvement, which it certainly can be. Regardless of whether you like this approach, hate it, or are simply puzzled by it, that's the way that Ubuntu Linux works. Even if you passionately believe that this is an odd approach, you are probably not going to be able to persuade the entire Ubuntu community that it is wrong. Save your breath.

> **TIP** The page at `https://help.ubuntu.com/community/RootSudo` explains how to change an Ubuntu system to re-enable the traditional root account. Although this is possible, I strongly suggest that you do not do this unless you have an excellent, site-specific reason to do so and are willing to have your Ubuntu system(s) be fundamentally different than all other Ubuntu systems in the known universe.

This section explains the internals of the `sudo` command, its configuration file, and discusses how to grant administrative privileges to other users in various forms.

The following list highlights some of the ways in which the `sudo` command works and should be used on Ubuntu systems:

- `sudo` is a command that enables you to execute privileged command-line utilities, such as `apt-get`, `aptitude`, `dpkg`, and so on. If you want to execute graphical commands with administrative privileges on a standard Ubuntu system, you should use the `gksudo` command instead.

  The problem with running graphical applications using `sudo` rather than `gksudo` is that they may change the ownership of the `.ICEauthority` file in your home directory, which many KDE, GNOME, and Standard X Window system applications use to track the applications that are authorized to access a specific X Window system display. If you accidentally use `sudo` to start a graphical application and cannot execute subsequent graphical apps, you can remove the `.ICEauthority` file in your home directory using the command `sudo rm .ICEauthority`, and then use `gksudo` to start your graphical applications.

- Once you have executed the `sudo` or `gksudo` commands to run any privileged commands, your authorization is stored for 15 minutes, so that you don't have to provide your password over and over for each privileged command that you want to execute. During this time, you must still supply the `sudo` or `gksudo` commands, but you will not be prompted for a password. After 15 minutes, using `sudo` or `gksudo` again will prompt you for a password again, and the cycle repeats.

> **TIP** If you are really lazy (as I have been known to be), a quick hack for using `sudo` is to use the `sudo` command to execute the bash shell, as in the command `sudo bash`. After supplying your password, this will give you a root shell in which you no longer have to specify the `sudo` or `gksudo` command to execute privileged operations. This is convenient, but is bad form and will generate verbal abuse from any other Ubuntu fans that see you doing this. Please be clandestine if you should ever want to do this.

The operation of the `sudo` command is controlled by the file `/etc/sudoers`, which is a text file that cannot be viewed by mere mortals for security reasons. To view this file, you should therefore use the `visudo` command to display it using a command like the following:

```
$ sudo visudo
```

The `visudo` command is a special version of the `vi` command that ensures that only one person is modifying the `/etc/sudoers` file at a time. You therefore do not need to identify the file `/etc/sudoers` as an argument — the command knows what file it is designed to edit. You can, of course, open this file in any text editor, but you won't get the protection against simultaneous edits that the `visudo` command provides.

As you will see, the `/etc/sudoers` file can contain blank lines (which are ignored) and comments-—any characters on a line that follow the traditional hash mark (#) are interpreted as a comment. The meaningful entries in the `/etc/sudoers` file on a standard Ubuntu 6.06 system are the following:

```
Defaults    !lecture,tty_tickets,!fqdn
root        ALL=(ALL) ALL
%admin      ALL=(ALL) ALL
```

The first of these lines specifies settings that identify default values for how the `sudo` command behaves. The entries in Ubuntu's `/etc/sudoers` file for the following;

- `!lecture`: Turns off the display of a short lecture explaining the use and implications for the `sudo` command. This would truly be a pain on an Ubuntu system, so this default behavior is disabled.

Fixing a Broken sudo Command

Installing some versions of Ubuntu in expert mode uses the standard root mechanism, which can leave your system in a state where normal users cannot use the sudo command to execute privileged commands. Similarly, even on a normal Ubuntu system, somehow losing the contents of your /etc/group or /etc/sudoers files can leave anyone unable to perform any privileged operation. In the latter case, you can reboot your system, press the Escape key to see the GRUB boot menus, and select the Recovery Mode entry from the GRUB menu. This will reboot your system and bring up a root shell.

Once you are logged in as root on your Ubuntu system, check to see that your /etc/group file contains the admin group and that any users who you want to be able to perform administrative operations are indeed members of that group. If you do not have an admin group, you can add it using the Users and Groups tool explained earlier in this chapter or by a command-line command (as the root user) such as the following:

```
# addgroup --system admin
```

Next, make sure that the /etc/sudoers file contains the entry that grants administrative privileges to the admin group, which is:

```
%admin ALL=(ALL) ALL
```

If this entry is not present in your /etc/sudoers command, you can use the visudo command to edit that file and add the entry.

After making sure that the admin group exists and is referenced in the /etc/sudoers file, all you have to do is add any user that you want to be able to run protected applications to the admin group. You can do this using the Users and Groups tool discussed earlier in this chapter or from the command-line using a command such as the following:

```
# adduser djf admin
```

This command would add the user djf to the admin group, enabling them to run privileged operations using sudo and gksudo in the future.

- tty_tickets: Specifies that users must authenticate on a per-tty or per-pty basis. For example, if you are logged in and running the Terminal application, this flag requires that you must separate sudo from each shell that you are running as a separate tab. In other words, the authentication information that is cached by the sudo command is only valid within the context of a specific shell.

- fqdn: Disables support for fully-qualified domain names in the /etc/sudoers file, which would otherwise enable this file to contain references to specific hosts from which users could execute privileged commands. Using fully-qualified domain names in the /etc/sudoers file would make the sudo command rely on successful DNS name lookups, which could be a bad thing for a system, such as Ubuntu, that uses sudo as its primary administrative interface if your DNS server goes down.

The next two lines are the really interesting ones. The following entry states that root can do anything and execute any command on the system:

```
root    ALL=(ALL) ALL
```

The following line states that all members of the admin group (as defined in the `/etc/group` file) can also do anything (i.e., run any command as root):

```
%admin    ALL=(ALL) ALL
```

To enable other users to perform privileged operations, all you have to do is add them to the admin group in the `/etc/group` file using the Users and Groups utility (as explained earlier in this chapter) or by using the `sudo` command to execute a command-line utility such as `adduser`, as in the following example:

```
$ sudo adduser djf admin
```

This command would add the user `djf` to the admin group and enable that user to execute any commands using `sudo` or `gksudo`.

Using ACLs for Sophisticated File Sharing

Standard Linux/Unix file permissions are fine if you have a relatively small number of users with limited requirements for sharing and working on the same files. The section of Chapter 4 entitled "Basic Concepts: Users and Groups" introduced the idea of groups, while the section of Chapter 4 entitled "File and Directory Permissions Under Linux" introduced file and directory permissions and explained the portions permissions that are relevant to the group that owns a file or directory.

Linux groups are the traditional way of enabling access to selected files and directories by multiple users. Unfortunately, using groups to control shared access requires the intervention of a system administrator every time you want to add a new user to the group or remove an existing user, as well as set up the initial shared directories. Access Control Lists (ACLs), which are supported in most modern versions of Linux including Ubuntu Linux, eliminate this hassle by providing a fine-grained set of permissions that users can impose on their own directories, and which go far beyond the permissions and protections provided by standard Linux groups. ACLs have been around for a long time on Linux and other Unix-like systems, but have never become as popular as they might be because of the arcane syntax of the command-line tools that are traditionally used to view and manage them. As you'll see later in this chapter, graphical tools for working with ACLs are now available, and Ubuntu users can now set and modify ACLs with ease.

Simply put, an ACL is a list of Linux users and/or groups and the access rights that they have to a specific file or directory. ACLs enable you to define totally granular permissions such as "only the users wvh and djf can write this file, but the user juser can at least read it" without requiring that you create any special-purpose Linux groups. The key item of interest about ACLs is that you can set and manage the ACLs on any files that you own, giving random users and groups access to those files without requiring the intervention of anyone with administrative privileges. ACLs truly put you in the driver's seat as far as file and directory access goes.

If you're playing a round of acronym bingo, Access Control Lists (ACLs) as implemented on Linux systems today are defined by the draft Portable Operating System Interface (POSIX) standard 1003.1e, draft 17, from the Institute of Electrical and Electronics Engineers (IEEE). This is not an official standard, but it is publicly available and has become the foundation for ACL implementations for modern operating systems such as Linux.

The rest of this chapter explains how to install the commands necessary to use ACLs, other system requirements that may be associated with using ACLs on your systems, and how to use various command-line and graphical tools to examine, set, update, and remove ACLs from your files and directories.

 This section does not discuss extended file attributes, which are often presented as a companion topic to ACLs, though they do something completely different.

Overview of Linux ACLs

Linux supports two basic types of ACLs:

- ACLs used to control access to specific files and directories
- Per-directory ACLs known as *mask* ACLs that define the default ACLs that are assigned to any files created within that directory

ACLs are represented in a standard format consisting of three colon-separated fields:

- The first field of an ACL entry is the entry type, which can be one of user (u), group (g), other (o), or mask (m).
- The second field of an ACL entry is a username, numeric UID, group name, or numeric GID, depending on the value of the first field. If this field is empty, the ACL refers to the user or group that owns the file or directory. This field is empty for ACLs of the mask and other types.
- The third field is the access permissions for this ACL. These are represented in two forms:
  - A standard Unix-like permissions string rwx (Read, Write, and eXecute permissions, where eXecute permissions on directories indicate the ability to search that directory). Each letter may be replaced by a – (dash), indicating that no access of that type is permitted). These three permissions must appear in this order.
  - A relative symbolic form that is preceded by a + (plus) sign or a ^ (caret) symbol, much like the symbolic permissions that are designed for use with the chmod command by people who are octally challenged. In this ACL representation, the + or ^ symbols are followed by single r, w, or x permission characters, indicating that these permissions should be added to the current set for a file or directory (the plus symbol) or that these permissions should be removed from the current set (the caret) for a given file or directory.

When listed or stored in files, different ACL entries are separated by white space or new lines. Everything after a # character to the end of a line is a comment and is ignored.

Installing ACL Commands on Ubuntu

Special-purpose commands such as those used to create and manage ACLs aren't installed as part of a default Ubuntu installation because, let's face it, not everybody needs (or wants) to use ACLs. However, as with all software packages on Ubuntu, they can easily be installed using apt-get or aptitude on systems without a graphical user interface or using Synaptic on a standard Ubuntu Desktop system. The user-level commands for ACL support are located in the acl package.

To install this package using apt-get or aptitude, use the commands sudo apt-get install acl or sudo aptitude -r install acl.

To install this package using Synatpic, start the Synaptic Package Manager from the System ⇨ Administration menu and supply your password to start Synaptic. Once the Synaptic application starts, click Search to display the search dialog. Make sure that Description and Name are the selected items to search through, enter **Access Control Lists** as the string to search for, and click Search. After the search completes, scroll down in the search results until you see the acl package, right-click its name, and select Mark for Installation to select that package for installation from the pop-up menu. Figure 21.14 shows the acl package being selected for installation.

FIGURE 21.14

Installing the ACL utilities in Synaptic

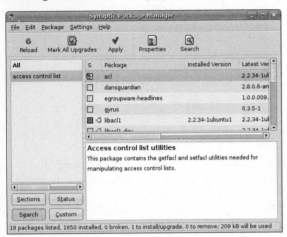

After you have selected the `acl` package, begin another search, this time for the term ACLs. After the search completes, scroll down in the search results until you see the `eiciel` package, which is a graphical utility for setting and managing ACLs. Right-click its name, and select Mark for Installation to select that package for installation from the pop-up menu. More about the `eiciel` application is discussed later in this chapter.

After selecting `eiciel` for installation, click Apply in the Synaptic toolbar to install the user-level commands necessary to set and manage Access Control Lists on your files and directories. When the installation completes, you can exit from Synaptic. Almost there!

Activating Filesystem Support for ACLs

To use ACLs to enhance the granularity of permissions on your system, any filesystems that contain files and directories with which you want to use ACLs must be mounted with ACL support. This is not done by default on Ubuntu systems, but is easy enough to change. Filesystems mounted with support for ACLs will have the `acl` keyword in the mount options portion of your `/etc/fstab` file. Because this is not enabled by default on Ubuntu systems, the entry in `/etc/fstab` for your filesystems will probably look something like the following:

```
/dev/hda1    /      ext3    defaults,errors=remount-ro       0 0
```

You can edit this file to enable ACL support when that filesystem is mounted by adding the `acl` keyword to the mount options for that filesystem. You can do this using your favorite text editor and a command like the following:

```
$ sudo emacs /etc/fstab
```

Changing this entry to add support for ACLs would look like the following:

```
/dev/hda1    /      ext3    defaults,acl,errors=remount-ro   0 0
```

Updating this file only means that support for ACLs will be enabled the next time your system automatically mounts that filesystem, which is typically the next time that you reboot your system. If you want to get started using ACLs right away, you can enable ACL support in the currently mounted version of the filesystem on /dev/hda1 without rebooting your system, by executing a command such as the following, which would remount the example ext3 filesystem /dev/hda1, activating ACL support:

```
$ sudo mount -o remount,acl /dev/hda1
```

Now, as they say in the Worldwide Wrestling Federation, "Get ready to ACL!"

Working with ACLs from the Command Line

As you'll see in this section, ACLs are ugly on the command line, often being indistinguishable from typing on a broken keyboard or displaying the contents of a binary file in a terminal window. Regardless of this, it is useful to understand their command-line representation and the command-line commands used to manipulate them. If you ever need to write a shell script to perform ACL manipulation, you'll be proud to say, "Of course I know how to use ACLs from a shell prompt."

Overview of Command-Line Utilities for ACLs

The Linux acl package provides the following three utilities for ACL creation, modification, and examination:

- chacl: lets you change, examine, or remove user, group, mask, or other ACLs on files or directories
- getfacl: lets you examine file access control lists for files and directories
- setfacl: lets you set file and directory access control lists

The next few sections explain how (and when) to use these commands.

Displaying Current ACLs from the Command Line

As an example of using ACLs, let's use a directory with the following contents and permissions:

```
$ ls -al
total 49
drwxr-xr-x    2 wvh wvh      80 2006-06-26 04:59 .
drwxr-xr-x  106 wvh wvh    5288 2006-06-26 23:11 ..
-rw-r-----    1 wvh wvh   44032 2006-06-26 04:58 resume.xml
```

The default ACL for this directory is the following:

```
$ getfacl .
# file: .
# owner: wvh
# group: wvh
user::rwx
group::r-x
other::r-x
```

The default ACL for the file resume.xml is the following:

```
$ getfacl resume.xml
# file: resume.xml
```

```
# owner: wvh
# group: wvh
user::rw-
group::r--
other::---
```

The default ACL for a file in a directory for which no default ACL has explicitly been set is derived from the default file protections associated with the user that created the file. A user's default file protections are derived from the user's umask, which is discussed in more detail in the section of Chapter 4 entitled "Default Permissions When Creating Files and Directories."

Setting ACLs from the Command Line

There are three common ways to change the ACL of a file or directory:

- By explicitly setting it to a specific value using the setfacl command, which overwrites any existing ACL settings
- By using the setfacl command with the –m (modify) option to modify an existing ACL
- By using the chacl command to modify an existing ACL

In the next few examples, I'll use the chacl command to change ACLs, because it is safer and easier to use because it doesn't overwrite any existing ACL. It also provides a bit more information about how ACLs really work than the setfacl command does.

For example, to add the user djf as someone who could read the file resume.xml, I would use a chacl (change ACL) command like the following:

```
$ chacl u::rw-,g::r--,o::---,u:djf:r--,m::rw- resume.xml
```

No, that isn't a typo or misprint — that's the way that ACLs look in real life. You wanted power, didn't you? It comes at a price. As mentioned previously, ACLs consist of three colon-separated fields that represent the permission of the user (owner of the file), group (the group ownership to the file), and others. When changing an ACL with the chacl command, you need to specify the ACL of the file, and then append the changes that you want to make to that ACL. The u::rw-,g::r--,o::--- portion of the ACL in this example is the existing ACL of the file; and the u:djf:r--,m::rw- portion specifies the new user that I wanted to add to the ACL for that file and the effective rights mask to be used when adding that user's ACL. The effective rights mask is the union of all of the existing user, group, and other permissions for a file or directory. You must specify a mask when adding a new user to the ACL for a file.

Note that the name of the user that I am adding to this ACL appears between the two colons in the u portion of the ACL entry. Using the getfacl command to retrieve the ACL for my resume.xml file shows that the user djf has indeed been added to the list of people who have access to the file:

```
$ getfacl resume.xml
# file: resume.xml
# owner: wvh
# group: wvh
user::rw-
user:djf:r--
group::r--
other::---
mask::rw-
```

Using the `ls -al` command shows that the visible, standard Unix file and directory permissions haven't changed:

```
$ ls -al
total 49
drwxr-xr-x     2 wvh wvh        80 2006-06-26 04:59 .
drwxr-xr-x   106 wvh wvh      5288 2006-06-26 23:11 ..
-rw-r-----     1 wvh wvh     44032 2006-06-26 04:58 resume.xml
```

Even more interesting and useful than just giving specific individuals read access to files is the ability to give specific users the ability to write specific files. For example, to add the user djf as someone who could both read and write the file `resume.xml`, I would use a `chacl` command like the following:

```
$ chacl u::rw-,g::r--,o::---,u:djf:rw-,m::rw- resume.xml
```

Note, again, that the name of the user that I am adding to this ACL appears between the two colons in the u portion of the ACL entry. Using the `getfacl` command shows that the user djf now has both read and write access to the file:

```
$ getfacl resume.xml
# file: resume.xml
# owner: wvh
# group: wvh
user::rw-
user:djf:rw-
group::rw-
other::---
mask::rw-
```

It's unfortunate that ACLs are so ugly, but that's because there is a fair amount of information packed into them. You may not find it odd that typos are common when typing ACLs. Now if there were only a friendly, graphical tool for ACL control…

Working with ACLs Using Graphical Tools

Yes, Virginia, there is a Santa Claus, and in this case his name is Roger Ferrer Ibanez. Roger is the primary author of the `eiciel` GNOME File ACL editor. What does eiciel mean? Try pronouncing it slowly with a fake French accent, and you'll hear that it sounds like Maurice Chevalier discussing his favorite computer science topic, the ACL.

The `eiciel` ACL editor provides a graphical interface for setting, updating, and removing ACLs in ext2, ext3, XFS, JFS, and ReiserFS filesystems, and should work equally well with any other filesystems that support POSIX ACLs.

You installed `eiciel` as part of the installation of your ACL software earlier in this chapter, in the section entitled "Installing ACL Commands on Ubuntu." Unfortunately, installing `eiciel` doesn't also create a menu item for it, so you must initially start `eiciel` from any GNOME command line, such as the GNOME Terminal or an xterm window, or by creating a desktop launcher for it. You can always create your own menu item for `eiciel` by following the instructions the section of Chapter 5 entitled "Customizing Menus." Figure 21.15 shows the `eiciel`'s initial dialog.

FIGURE 21.15

The initial dialog for the eiciel ACL Editor

If you are starting `eiciel` from the command line, you can supply the name of the file or directory for the ACLs you want to set or modify as a command-line argument. To open a file or directory manually, click Open in `eiciel`'s upper-right-hand corner, navigate to the file or directory of the ACLs you want to set or modify, and click Open to open the ACLs for that file or directory. Figure 21.16 shows the ACL for the file `resume.xml` (which was used as an example in the command-line discussion of ACLs earlier in this chapter).

FIGURE 21.16

The ACLs for a sample file in eiciel

The top portion of the Eiciel dialog displays the current ACLs for the file or directory that you opened in eiciel. By default, the bottom half of the Eiciel dialog provides a list of all of the nonsystem users on your system. If you want to add a group to an ACL rather than a single user, select the Group radio button. To add system users and groups (i.e., those with UIDs and GIDs less than 1000), select the Also show system participants checkbox near the bottom of the Eiciel dialog.

To add a specific user or group to the ACLs for the file or directory that is currently displayed in eiciel, select the name of that user or group from the list in the bottom half of the Eiciel dialog. This activates the Add button, as shown in Figure 21.17.

FIGURE 21.17

Selecting a user to add to an ACL

To add the user to the ACL, click Add. The name of that user is added to the list in the top of the Eiciel dialog, and is immediately added to the ACL for the file or directory that you are editing.

If you look closely at the ACL that I just added, you'll note that the Execute bit is labeled as being an ineffective permission. This is because the file itself isn't executable.

At this point, you can select the various settings for any user on the ACL displayed in the window at the top half of the Eiciel dialog. Any changes that you make to the ACL take place immediately — there is no need to explicitly save them. When you are finished using `eiciel`, click Quit to exit.

The `eiciel` editor is an excellent piece of software, and a great example of how the latest generation of Linux tools can remove much of the wizardry, typos, and barriers-to-use that are often the companions of complex command-line tools and twisted syntax. For more information about using `eiciel`, click Help in the Eiciel dialog to see its online manual. For information about the latest and greatest `eiciel` developments, see its home page at `http://rofi.pinchito.com/eiciel`. Thanks for a great piece of software, Roger!

FIGURE 21.18

The ACL entry for a newly added user

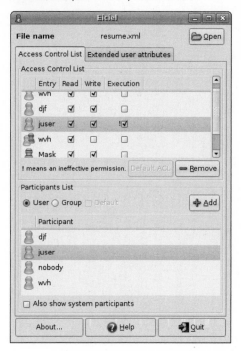

Summary

This chapter started off by explaining the concepts of login users and protection groups on Ubuntu systems. It explained how Linux systems use Pluggable Authentication Modules to verify a user's identity, that a user is authorized to log in at a specific time, and perform other authentication-related tasks when logging in on an Ubuntu system. It explained the basics of file and directory protection using users and groups on Ubuntu systems, and then discussed how users perform tasks that require system privileges on Ubuntu systems using the sudo command. The last section of the chapter explained Access Control Lists, a more powerful and modern mechanism for enabling or denying access to specific files and directories.

Chapter 22 discusses various mechanisms for backing up and restoring files, starting with commands that enable you to create archives of specific files and directories, and then discussing mechanisms for backing up and synchronizing files and directories to other systems using the network. It also provides a detailed discussion of BackupPC, a powerful network-oriented application that makes it easy to automatically back up systems over the network to a central backup server.

Chapter 22

Backing Up and Restoring Files

Backups are spare copies of the files and directories that are found on a computer system, written to and stored on removable media that is preferably stored somewhere other than beside your computer. Doing backups is a time-consuming, but absolutely mandatory task if you place any value at all on the files, e-mail, and other data that you have stored on your computer.

Backups are exactly like auto insurance policies — well, almost exactly, because they're not a legal requirement to own a computer system (in most states). You rarely need them, and you hope that you never do. They are usually just time-consuming and expensive (your time has some value, right?). However, one rainy night when you discover that you've just accidentally deleted your home directory or when a user comes to you and says that they've accidentally deleted your company's personnel records, payroll data, or the source code for your company's products, you'd better have a good answer. The right answer, of course, is, "I'll restore that from backups immediately."

It's hard to think of anything that so thoroughly combines the mundane and mandatory as backing up your data. It's boring. It's time-consuming. And, of course, it's critical. This chapter is oriented toward you as a systems administrator, regardless of how many systems you're responsible for. As system administrators, our responsibility is to provide secure, well-maintained, and rigorously backed up systems for the benefit of the users of the computer systems we're responsible for. You should feel even more responsible if you're only supporting a user community of one (yourself), because you won't even have anyone else to blame if a catastrophe occurs. Even if you're a community of one, I'm sure that you feel that whatever you do on your computer system is important. Backups keep it safe.

This chapter explains a variety of solutions for creating backups on Ubuntu Linux systems, ranging from command-line solutions to some impressive graphical tools. It also covers the flip side of making backups, restoring files from them, which is what makes backups worthwhile in the first place.

Backups 101

Before discussing the different tools used to actually create backups, it's useful to review some of the basic issues and approaches in backing up any kind of computer system. Though you may already be totally familiar with these concepts and occasionally mumble backup and restore commands in your sleep, providing a clear picture of what you're trying to accomplish in doing backups and how backup systems are usually designed provides a firm foundation for discussing the various tools discussed later in this chapter. Because I have no way of knowing whether you're reading this book because you're using Ubuntu on your home computer or because you're deploying Ubuntu Linux throughout your business, I'm going to err on the side of caution and discuss many topics that are overkill for a home computing environment but are mandatory in multisystem business or academic environments.

Why Do Backups?

In an ideal world, backups would not be necessary. Computer hardware and software would always work correctly, users would never make mistakes, and I'd be a rock star. Unfortunately, in the real world, things are different. Computer system administrators and other members of an MIS/IT department do backups for many reasons, helping protect you against the following types of problems:

- Natural disasters such as fires, floods, and earthquakes that destroy computer systems
- Hardware failures in disk drives or other storage media that make it impossible to access the data that they contain
- System software problems such as filesystem corruption that might cause files and directories to be deleted during filesystem consistency checks
- Software failures such as programs that crash and corrupt or delete the files that you're working on
- Pilot error, AKA the accidental deletion of important files and directories

> **NOTE**   Many people tend to confuse RAID (Redundant Array of Independent Disks) arrays with backups. They are not the same thing at all. RAID arrays can be a valuable asset in keeping your existing data online and available in the face of disk failures, but they do not protect against any of the problems identified in the previous list. All of the drives in a RAID array will burn evenly in case of a fire or other natural disaster.

In addition to protecting you against these sorts of problems accessing the data they, you, and any other users of your systems require, there are a variety of procedural and business reasons to back up the data on your computer systems. Complete and accurate backups provide:

- A complete historical record of your personal, corporate, or organizational business and financial data. Sadly enough, this includes serving as a source of information that you, your company, or your organization may someday need to defend itself or to prove its case in a lawsuit or other legal proceedings.
- A source of historical information about research projects and software development.
- A way of preserving data that you do not need to make continuously available online, but which you may need to refer to someday. This includes things like projects that you've completed, the home directories of users who are no longer using your systems, and so on.

A final issue where backups are concerned is the need for off-site storage of all or specific sets of your backups. The history of personal, business, and academic computing is littered with horror stories about people

A Few Words About Backup Media

Backups take a significant amount of time and require a significant investment in both media and backup devices. Nowadays, even home computer systems store tens or hundreds of gigabytes of information, which means that you either need to have fast, high-capacity backup devices, or you must prepare yourself for a laborious day or two or loading CDs, DVDs, or tapes. Other, more historical solutions such as Zip disks, Jazz disks, LS-120 disks, and so on, provide such a small amount of storage that they're really only useful for backing up individual files, directories, or sets of system configuration files, and are therefore not discussed in this chapter.

If the mention of backup tapes causes flashbacks to mainframe computer days or old sci-fi movies, you may want to rethink that. Even for home use, today's backup tape drives are fast, store large amounts of data, are relatively cheap, and use tapes that fit in the palm of your hand. Though disk-to-disk backups are becoming more and more common, especially in networked environments, backup tapes are still quite popular and cost-efficient.

CD-Rs and DVD-Rs are eminently suitable for backups of home computer systems because they are inexpensive and typically provide enough storage for backing up the selected files and directories that comprise most home backups. For home use, I prefer CD-R and DVD-R media over their rewritable brethren because of the cost difference and the fact that rewritable CDs and DVDs are only good for a limited number of writes. On the other hand, CD-Rs and DVD-R's are rarely appropriate for enterprise backups because even DVD-Rs are not large enough to back up complete systems, it's tricky to split backups across DVD-R media, and DVD-R's are relatively slow to write to. They can be useful when restoring a system because of their portability, because you can take them directly to the system you're restoring without having to move a tape drive, do a network restore, and so on. However, I personally prefer removable hard drives or tapes in enterprise or academic environments.

who did backups religiously, but stored them in a box beside the computer. After a file or natural disaster, all that the administrators of those systems were left with were poor excuses and unemployment benefits. Off-site storage is critical to your ability to recover from a true physical catastrophe, but it also raises another issue — the need for appropriate security in the storage location you select.

For the same reasons that you wouldn't leave the door to your house propped open and then go on vacation and wouldn't put a system that didn't use passwords on the Internet, you shouldn't store your backups in an insecure location. This is especially important if you are in charge of computer systems that are being used for business. Wherever you store your company's current and historical backup media should have a level of security comparable to wherever your computers are in the first place. Though your local cat burglar might not actively target a stack of CDs, removable disks, or storage locker full of backup tapes, any competitors you have would probably be ecstatic to be able to read and analyze the complete contents of your company's computer systems. Why not just save everybody time and mail them your source code and customer lists?

Different Types of Backups

Now that I've discussed why to do backups and some of the basic issues related to storing them, let's review the strategy behind actually doing backups. As mentioned previously, backups take time and have associated costs such as backup media, but there are a variety of ways to manage and minimize those costs.

There are three basic types of backups:

- archive backups, which provide a complete snapshot of the contents of a filesystem at a given time
- incremental backups, which reflect the changes to the contents of a filesystem since a previous backup
- spot backups, which provide a snapshot of specific files or the contents of one or more important directories at a given time

NOTE   **Spot backups are the most common type of backups done by home computer users, because writing a copy of your current projects, mail folders, or even your entire home directory to a few CD-Rs or DVD-Rs is relatively fast and cheap. There isn't all that much to say about this approach, because it can easily be done using drag and drop, so the rest of this section focuses on the classic backup models of archives and incremental backups. I'll discuss some techniques for doing spot backups later in this chapter.**

Archive backups, often referred to as archives or full backups, are the ultimate source for restoring data, because they usually contain a copy of every file and directory on a specific filesystem or under a certain directory on your computer at the time that the backup was done. In an ideal world, it would be great to be able to do daily archive backups simply because this would guarantee that no one could ever lose more than a day's work, regardless of the type of calamity that occurred to your computer system. Unfortunately, archive backups have some drawbacks:

- They take the maximum amount of time that backups could require because they make a copy of every file and directory on every filesystem on all of your computer systems.
- The volume of data that is preserved by an archive backup means that they use the maximum amount of space on your backup media.
- Producing the largest possible volume of backup media maximizes the amount of storage space required to store it, and makes your record keeping as complex (and as critical) as it possibly could be.
- Archives are best done when no one is working on a computer system. This reduces the amount of time that it takes to do the backups (because they're not competing with anyone for computer time), and also guarantees the consistency of the files and directories that are being copied to your backup media, because nothing can be changing. This may not be a big point in a home computing environment, but in a business environment, making sure that no one is using a computer system so that you can do an archive backup is often impractical (as on systems that run 24×7 services such as Web servers, database systems, and so on) or, best case, reduces the availability of a computer system to the company and your customers.

Although the advantages of archive backups as a complete record of everything are significant, these kinds of issues keep archives from being a reasonable approach to daily backups for any home computer, business, or organization. You could always do them less often than daily, but reducing the frequency of your backups increases your exposure to losing a significant amount of data if your disks fail or your computer bursts into flames.

Enter incremental backups. As mentioned before, incremental backups are backups that contain a copy of all of the files and directories that have changed on a computer system since some previous backup was done. If a problem occurs and you need to restore files and directories from backups, you can restore an accurate picture of those files and directories by first restoring from an archive backup, followed by restoring from some number of incremental backups up through your most recent ones, which should restore whatever you've backed up to the date of your most recent incremental backups. When combined with archives, incremental backups provide the following advantages:

- They help minimize the amount of disk space or other backup media required to do backups. Archives usually require large quantities of most types of backup media, while incrementals inherently require less because they aren't preserving as much data.

- They can be done more quickly, because they are copying less data than an archive backup would.

- The backup media to which incremental backups are written requires less storage space than archive backups, because there's less of it.

- Even in business and academic environments, incremental backups can be done while the computer systems and filesystems you're backing up are available for use.

Another nice feature of incremental backups is that they record changes to the files and directories on your computer systems since some previous backups, which are not necessarily archives. In corporate environments, most systems administrators organize their backup media and associated procedures in a way similar to the following:

- Archives are done infrequently, perhaps every six months or so, or just before any point at which major changes to your filesystems or computer systems are being made.

- Monthly incremental backups are made of all changes since the previous archive. If your budget and backup storage capabilities are sufficient, you usually keep the monthly incremental backups around until you do another archive backup, at which point you can reuse them.

- Weekly incremental backups are made of all changes since the previous monthly backup. You can reuse these each month, after you do the new monthly backups.

- Daily backups are made of all changes since the previous weekly backup. You can reuse these each week, after you do the new weekly backups. Some installations even just do dailies since a previous daily or the daily done on some previous day of the week.

No backup system can make it possible to restore any version of any file on a computer system. Even if you were lucky or compulsive enough to be doing daily archives of all of your computer systems, files that exist for less than a day can't be restored, and it isn't possible to restore a version of a file that is less than a day old. Sorry. When designing a backup schedule and the relationships between archive and various incremental backups, you have to decide the granularity with which you might need to restore lost files. For example, the general schedule of archives, monthlies, weeklies, and dailies doesn't guarantee that you can restore a version of a file that is newer than the previous archive. For example:

- If the file was deleted one day before the first set of monthly backups were done based on the archive, it would be present on the archive and on the weekly backups for a maximum of one month. At that point, the weekly tape containing that file would be overwritten and the newest version of the file that could be restored was the version from the archive.

- If the file was deleted one day after the first set of monthly backups were done based on the archive, it would be present on the archive and on the first monthly backup for a maximum of seven months — a new archive would be done at that point, and the monthly tape wouldn't be overwritten until one month after the new archive. At that point, the monthly tape containing that file would be overwritten and the newest version of the file that could be restored was the version from the most recent archive.

Selecting a backup strategy is essentially a calculation of how long it will take someone to notice the absence of one or more files and request a restore, taking into account the level of service that you need to provide and the cost of various levels of service in terms of media, backup time, and storage/management overhead. Sometimes you will notice missing files immediately, such as when you accidentally delete the great American novel that you're actively working on. Other problems, such as lost files because of gradual disk failures or filesystem corruption, may not surface for a while.

Almost all backup systems generally provide automatic support for doing incremental backups since a previous incremental or archive backup. The Linux dump program, which I'll discuss in the next section, assigns different numbers to different backup "levels," and keeps track of which levels of backups have been done based on the name of the device on which the filesystem is located.

A final issue to consider when doing backups and restoring files is when to do them, and what privileges are required. It's generally fastest to do backups during off-peak hours when system usage is generally at a minimum, so that the backups can complete as quickly as possible, and when people are less likely to be modifying the files that you're backing up. In an enterprise environment, this may mean that you'll want to have a graveyard shift of operators. In this case, you'll need to think about how to make sure that operators have the right set of privileges. Being able to back up user files that may be heavily protected, or using a backup system that accesses the filesystem at the filesystem level generally requires root privileges. Many people use programs such as sudo (which is already our friend on Ubuntu systems) or set s-bits on privileged binaries such as backup and restore programs so that they don't have to give the administrative password to the operators or part-time staff that generally do backups at off-peak hours. See the section of Chapter 21 entitled "Customizing the sudo Command on Ubuntu Systems" for some suggestions on how to assign different privileges to different groups of individuals on your Ubuntu system.

Verifying and Testing Backups

Just doing backups isn't a guarantee that you're safe from problems, unless you're also sure that the backups you're making are readable and that files can easily be restored from them. Though it's less common today, there's always the chance that the heads in a tape drive may be out of alignment. This either means that you can only read the tapes back in on the same tape drive that you wrote them on, or that they can't be read at all. You should always verify that you can read and restore files from backups using another device than the one on which they were made. You don't have to check every tape every day, but random spot checks are important for peace of mind and for job security. Similarly, tapes can just stretch or wear out from use — be prepared to replace the media used to do various types of incremental backups after some set amount of time. Nobody appreciates WORN backup media — write once, read never — even though its storage capacity is apparently infinite.

One of the problems inherent to backups is that every type of computer media has a shelf life of some period of time, depending on the type of media, the environment in which it is stored, and how lucky you are. No backup media has infinite shelf life. For example, backup tapes can last for years, but they can also be unreadable after a much shorter period of time. Long-lived media such as write-once CD-Rs and DVD-Rs are attractive because of their supposed longevity, but they have other problems, as mentioned earlier in the sidebar entitled "A Few Words About Backup Media." Media such as these may only be suited for certain types of backups, depending on whether your backup software writes to the backup device as a filesystem or as a raw storage device. Also, no one yet knows exactly how long those types of media will last, but they certainly take up less room than almost any kind of tape or stack of hard drives. In addition to spot-checking the backup media that you are currently using, you should always make a point to spot-check old archives every few years to make sure that they're still useful.

TIP   Aside from the fact that backups can be subject to the vagaries of the device on which they're written, having those devices available when you need to restore backups is an important point to consider. It's a well-known nerd fact that many government and military sites have huge collections of backup data written on devices that don't exist anymore, such as super low-speed tape drives and 1" or 7-track tapes. Even if the devices exist, the data is often not recoverable, because it's written in some ancient, twisted backup format, word size, and so on. When you retire a computer system, deciding if you'll ever need to restore any of its archive data is an easily overlooked issue. If you're lucky, you'll be able to read in the old archives on your new system and write them back out to some newer backup media, using some newer backup format. If you're not, you've just acquired a huge number of large, awkward paperweights that will remind you of this issue forever.

Deciding What to Back Up

Aside from cost-saving issues like using higher-density media such as CD-ROMs for archive purposes, another way to reduce the number of old backups that you have to keep around, as well as minimizing the time it takes to do them, is to treat different filesystems differently when you're backing them up. For example, system software changes very infrequently, so you may only want to back up the partitions holding your operating system when you do an archive. Similarly, even locally developed application software changes relatively infrequently, so you may only want to back that up weekly. I can count on one hand, with one finger, the number of times that I've needed to restore an old version of an application. On the other hand, you may not be so lucky.

Keeping backups of your operating system and its default applications is important, and is certainly critical to restoring or rebuilding an entire system should you ever need to do so (which is known in backup circles as a *bare-metal restore*). In terms of backups (and thanks to the excellence of the Ubuntu Update Manager), you can usually just preserve your original installation media (or even re-retrieve it over the net) if it is ever necessary to completely restore the system software for your Ubuntu system. However, if your systems run a custom kernel or use special loadable kernel modules, you should always make sure that you have a backup of your current configuration and all of the configuration files in directories such as /etc that describe the state of your system. You'll be glad you did if the disk on which your finely tuned and heavily tweaked version of an operating system bursts into flames late one night.

The issues in the first few sections of this chapter often give system administrators and system managers migraines. Losing critical data is just as painful if you're only supporting yourself. Thinking about, designing, and implementing reasonable backup policies, schedules, and disaster recovery plans is an important task no matter how many people will be affected by a problem. Backups are like insurance policies — you hope that you never need to use them, but if you do, they had better be available.

Backup Software for Linux

Many backup utilities are available for Ubuntu systems. Most of these are traditional command-line utilities that can either create archive files or write to your backup media of choice in various formats, but some interesting open source graphical solutions are also beginning to appear.

The next few sections discuss the most common open source utilities that are used to do backups on Linux systems, grouping them into sections based on whether they create local backup files or are inherently network-aware. As discussed in the previous section, off-site storage of backups is an important requirement of a good backup strategy. In today's networked environments, off-site storage can be achieved in two basic ways: either by writing to local backup media and then physically transporting that media to another location, or by using a network-aware backup mechanism to store backups on systems that are physically located elsewhere.

Commercial Backup Solutions for Linux

Commercial application vendors have also been moving into the Linux backup space, because of the popularity of Linux in server environments. In my opinion, commercial backup solutions for Linux are unnecessary in the home computing environment, but are well worth considering if you are using Ubuntu in a multisystem enterprise or academic computing environment. Before you scoff at using commercial software for backups on a free, open source operating system, consider just how critical backups are to the computers that you maintain. This book doesn't cover commercial backup solutions, but you may want to investigate the following vendors if you need or want a commercial, supported backup solution:

- **Arkeia Software:** Arkeia's Network Backup and Smart Backup applications are well-known cross-platform packages that also support backing up Microsoft Windows systems, and have been bundled with a variety of commercial Linux distributions such as Red Hat, SUSE, and Mandrake. For more information, see www.knox-software.com.

- **Lone Star Software:** Lone Star's LONE-TAR software has been providing backup solutions for Unix and Linux systems for over a decade. They also offer an X Window system interface, LTX, for LONE-TAR. For more information, see www.cactus.com.

- **MicroLITE:** MicroLITE's BackupEDGE and RecoverEDGE software is a nice high-performance package that supports local and remote backups and provides some interesting bare-metal restore capabilities. For more information, see www.microlite.com.

- **Storix:** Storix's System Backup Administrator is a graphical tool for Linux (and AIX) backups that also supports Microsoft Windows backups via SMB network access and features some interesting bare-metal restore capabilities for Linux systems. For more information, see www.storix.com.

- **Symantec/Veritas:** Veritas's Backup Exec software, now owned by Symantec, is a well-known backup solution for Microsoft Windows systems that is also supposedly available for Linux. For more information, see www.symantec.com/enterprise/veritas.

None of these vendors explicitly state that they support Ubuntu, but they all advertise Linux support and I'm sure that they'd at least be happy to discuss Ubuntu support with you.

Local Backup and Restore Software for Linux

The roots of the core set of Linux utilities lie in Unix, so it's not surprising that versions of all of the classic Unix backup utilities are available with all Linux distributions. Some of them are starting to show their age, but these utilities have been used for years and guarantee the portability of your backups from any Linux system to another.

The classic Linux/Unix backup utilities available in the Ubuntu distribution are the following, in alphabetical order:

- cpio: The cpio utility (copy input to output) was designed for doing backups, taking a list of the files to be archived from standard input and writing the archive to standard output or to a backup device using shell redirection. The cpio utility can be used with filesystems of any type, because it works at the filesystem level and therefore has no built-in understanding of filesystem data structures.

- dd: The original Unix backup utility is called dd, which stands for *dump device*, and it does exactly that, reading data from one device and writing it to another. The dd utility doesn't know anything about filesystems, dump levels, or previous runs of the program — it's simply reading data from one source and writing to another, though you can manipulate the data in between the two to do popular party tricks like converting ASCII to EBCDIC. The dd utility copies the complete contents of a device, such as a disk partition to a tape drive, for backup purposes. It wasn't really designed to do backups, though there are situations in which dd is the perfect tool: For example, dd is the tool for you if you want to copy one partition to another when a disk is failing, make on-disk copies of the partitions on a standard boot disk for easy cloning, or use an application that reads and writes directly to raw disk partitions which you can only backup and restore as all or nothing. Because dd reads directly from devices and therefore doesn't recognize the concept of a filesystem, individual file restores are impossible from a partition archive created with dd without restoring the entire partition and selecting the files that you want.

■ dump/restore: The dump and restore utilities were designed as a pair of utilities for backup purposes, and have existed for Unix since Version 6. Although cpio and tar combine the ability to write archives with the ability to extract files and directories from them and dd can't extract anything except an entire backup, the dump program only creates backups and the restore program only extracts files and directories from them. Both dump and restore work at the filesystem data structure level, and therefore can only be used to backup and restore ext2 and ext3 filesystems (at the moment, at least). However, the dump/restore programs can accurately back up and restore any type of file that is found in ext2 and ext3 filesystems, including device-special files and sparse files (without exploding their contents and removing their "sparseness"). The dump/restore utilities can only be used to back up entire filesystems, though they have built-in support for doing incremental backups, keeping a record of which filesystems have been backed up and which level of backups has been performed for those filesystems. All of this information is tracked in an easily understood text file named /etc/dumpdates. Archives created with the dump utility can automatically span multiple tapes or other media if the devices support end-of-media detection, but can also span cartridge or magnetic tape media by using command-line options that tell dump the length or capacity of the tape. The most entertaining feature of the restore program is its ability to execute it in interactive mode, in which case it reads the information from the tape necessary to create a virtual directory hierarchy for the archived filesystem that it contains. You can then use standard commands such as cd to explore the list of the files on the tape and mark specific files and directories to be restored.

NOTE The dump/restore **programs are not installed as part of a default Ubuntu distribution, but can easily be installed using** apt-get **(both are located in the** dump **package)**

■ tar: Probably the most widely used and well-known Unix backup utility, the tar command (tape archiver) takes a list of files and/or directories to be backed up and archives those files to an output device or to standard output. The GNU version of tar, once known as gtar to differentiate it from the version of tar that came with the Unix operating system (back when anyone cared), is yet another amazing piece of work from the Free Software Foundation. GNU tar provides capabilities far and above the abilities of classic Unix tar, including the built-in ability to read from compressed tar archives created with gzip, support for incremental backups, support for multivolume archives, and much more. The tar program is filesystem-independent and accesses files and directories without needing to know their low-level data structures. The tar program is far and away the most popular free archiving utility available for Linux, and is used to archive almost every free software package. The DEB and RPM archive formats actually contain tar files that are compressed using the gzip utility, and files with the .tgz or .tar.gz (also gzipped tar files) are commonly used to distribute most Linux source code.

The utilities discussed in this section all create local archive files or write their archives to local storage devices. Of course, when you're using a network-aware operating system such as Ubuntu Linux, the term *local storage devices* actually includes anything that appears to be local to your system, which therefore includes network storage that is mounted on a directory of the system that you are using. Common examples of this are NFS-mounted directories or directories that are mounted on your Linux system via Samba. Directories that are mounted over the network enable you to integrate remote storage with local backup commands in ways such as the following:

- Back up remote directories to local archives by mounting the remote directories on your local system and including them in the backups that you do.

- Write your backup files to remote storage by creating your backup archives in remote directories that are mounted on your system as local directories.

Both of these scenarios provide ways of satisfying the basic off-site requirement of backups through the use of network-mounted directories.

Network-Oriented Backup Software for Linux

The utilities discussed in the previous section all create local archive files or write their archives to local storage devices (or storage that appears to be local). The backup utilities discussed in this section are slightly different — they are inherently network-aware, and therefore enable you to create and manage local backups of the contents of remote systems.

The following are some of the more commonly used, network-aware backup systems that are available for Ubuntu. There are many more, which you can find by starting the Synaptic Package Manager and doing a Description and Name search for the term **backup**. The following are my personal favorites:

- **Amanda:** The Advanced Maryland Automated Network Disk Archiver is an open source distributed backup system that was originally developed for Unix systems at the University of Maryland in the early 1990s. Amanda makes it quite easy to back up any number of client workstations to a central backup server, supports Windows Microsoft backups via Samba, and provides a complete backup management system for your Ubuntu system. Amanda supports multiple sets of backups with distinct configurations, supports disc and tape backups, tracks backup levels and dates on its client systems, produces detailed reports that are automatically delivered via e-mail, and keeps extensive logs that make it easy to diagnose and correct the reason(s) behind most problems. Communication between Amanda clients and servers is encrypted to heighten security. Amanda is not installed by default on Ubuntu systems, but is available in the Ubuntu repositories and can easily be installed using `Synaptic`, `apt-get`, or `aptitude`. Amanda consists of two packages, `amanda-server` and `amanda-client`. Amanda's home Web site is at `www.amanda.org`.

- **BackupPC:** BackupPC is a nice backup system that provides a Web-based interface that enables you to back up remote systems using smb, tar, or rsync. Figure 22.1 shows the Web page of a sample BackupPC server. BackupPC creates backups of your remote systems that are stored and managed on your BackupPC server, and also enables authorized users to restore their own files from these archives, removing the number one source of migraines for system administrators. Configuration data for each client system is stored on the BackupPC server, which enables you to back up different types of systems using different commands or protocols, and to easily identify which remote directories or filesystems you want to back up. One especially nice feature of BackupPC is that it uses standard Linux commands on the server to create backups, and therefore doesn't require the installation of any software on client systems, though some client-side configuration may be necessary for certain backup commands.

FIGURE 22.1

A BackupPC server's home page in Firefox

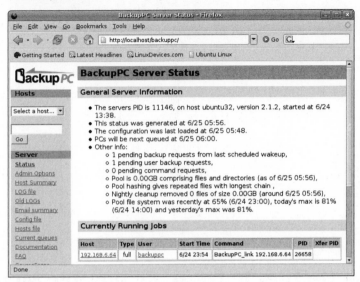

BackupPC's home page is at `http://backuppc.sourceforge.net`. See "Installing and Using the backuppc Utility," later in this chapter for more information about installing, setting up, and using BackupPC.

■ **Bacula:** Bacula is an extremely powerful set of programs that provide a scalable network backup and restore system that supports Linux, Unix, and Microsoft Windows systems. Its power and flexibility easily match that of Amanda, but it is more flexible in terms of how and where backups are stored. Bacula is not installed by default on Ubuntu systems, but is available in the Ubuntu repositories and can easily be installed using `Synaptic`, `apt-get`, or `aptitude`. Bacula is quite powerful, but can be complex—if you're interested in exploring Bacula, you may want to start by installing the `bacula-doc` package and reading its documentation to determine if it is right for your environment. Bacula is primarily command-line oriented, but provides a graphical console, shown in Figure 22.2, as a wrapper around its command-line interface. Bacula's home page is `www.bacula.org`.

■ `Rsync`: Rsync (remote sync) is a command-line file and directory synchronization program that makes it easy to copy files and directories from one host to another. When both a local and remote copy of a file or directory hierarchy exist, `rsync` is able to leverage built-in features that help reduce the amount of data that needs to be transmitted to ensure that the local and remote copies of those files and directories are identical. The remote-update protocol used by the `rsync` utility enables `rsync` to transfer only the differences between two sets of files and directories. The `rsync` program is automatically installed as part of a default Ubuntu installation, but requires some configuration on the remote systems that you want to copy to your local host.

FIGURE 22.2

The GNOME console for Bacula

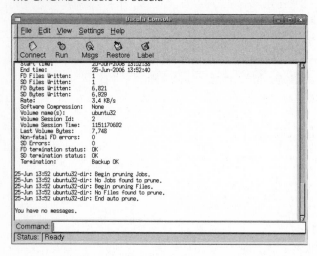

Backing Up Files to Local, Removable Media

The section of this chapter entitled "Backups 101" introduced the basic concepts of backups, many of which may seem impractical for home use. Whether or not they are really impractical depends on the problems that you want to be able to solve using your backups. If you're mostly interested in protecting yourself against disk failures or the accidental deletion of critical files that you're working on, you may not need to worry about doing archive and incremental backups — doing spot backups of important files and directories to a CD-R or DVD-R may suffice. Similarly, if you don't need to be able to restore any file from any point in time, but just need to have recent copies of your files, then spot backups of the directories that you want to back up may be sufficient, done with whatever frequency you're comfortable with. If you're not concerned about losing all of your data if your house or apartment is destroyed, then you don't have to worry about things like storing backups off-site.

The bottom line is that I can't tell you what you're comfortable with — that's up to you, and defines your backup strategy. The next few sections highlight how you can use some of the utilities mentioned earlier in this chapter (and even the standard Linux cp command) to create backup copies of important files.

TIP For home use, the most popular backup method is simply dragging and dropping directories to CD-R or DVD-R media to create spot backups of those directories. The second most popular way of backing up your system is to use hard drives that you can attach to your systems via USB or FireWire ports. On the plus side, unless you're using a really small removable hard drive, this gives you a larger pool of available storage for backups than a CD or DVD, and enables you to either store more backups of important files and directories or create a single copy of each important directory on removable storage which you can then just update each time you do backups. On the minus side, a removable hard drive is much more expensive than CD-R or DVD-R disks and is more of a pain to store off-site and retrieve each time you do backups.

Archiving and Restoring Files Using tar

The `tar` program is one of the oldest and most classic Linux/Unix utilities. Though it can write to a backup device, such as a tape drive, the `tar` command is most commonly used to create archive files, such as source code, that can easily be shared with others. Archive files created using the `tar` command typically have the `.tar` file extension. The GNU `tar` command, which is the version of `tar` found on Ubuntu and all other Linux systems, provides built-in compression capabilities, being able to automatically compress `tar` archives on the fly. Compressed `tar` archives typically have either the file extension `.tgz`, indicating that they are compressed (and can be uncompressed) using the `gzip` application, or the file extension `.tar.bz2`, indicating that they are compressed (and can be uncompressed) using the `bzip2` application. Archive files produced using the `tar` utility are typically referred to as *tarballs*.

> **NOTE** Because of its age, you have to be kind when passing arguments to the `tar` command, because in some cases they must be specified in a particular order.

Creating an archive file using `tar` is easy. For example, to create a tarball called `home_dir_backup.tgz` that contains all of the directories in `/home`, you could use commands like the following:

```
$ cd /home
$ sudo tar czvf /tmp/home_dir_backup.tgz *
```

> **NOTE** Note that you want to write the backup file somewhere other than the directory that you are backing up. Creating a backup file in the directory that you're working in would cause the `tar` command to back up the file that it was creating, which would both not work correctly and waste tremendous amounts of space.

The `tar` options in this command have the following meanings:

- c: Create a new archive file. If a file by the specified name already exists, it will be overwritten and its original contents will be lost.

- z: Compress the archive file using the same techniques used by the `gzip` application.

- v: Be verbose, displaying the name of every file added to the archive file as it is added.

- f: Write the output of the `tar` command to the file whose name appears as the next argument on the command-line. In this example, the output of the `tar` command would be written to the file `/tmp/home_dir_backup.tgz`.

After a significant amount of output, the file `/tmp/home_dir_backup.tgz` will be created, containing a complete recursive copy of all files and directories under `/home`. You can then copy this file to backup media such as a CD or DVD, or to a removable hard drive.

After you've created a tarball of a given set of directories, you can easily create another tarball that only contains files and directories that have changed since a specific date (such as the date on which the first tarball was created) using commands like the following:

```
$ cd /home
$ sudo tar czvf /tmp/home_dir_backup.tgz * --newer "2006-06-23"
```

This command produces extremely verbose output, even if you drop the v option, which is puzzling at first. This is an artifact of the format used in `tar` files. Even when used with the `--newer` option, the tar file header must contain the complete directory structure in which it is looking for files newer than the specified date. This is necessary so that the `tar` command can create extracted files in the right directory location. In other words, if you use the `tar` command to extract the entire contents of a tarball created using the `--newer` option, it will create an empty directory hierarchy that only contains files that are newer than the date that was specified when the tarball was created.

Creating tarballs isn't much fun without being able to retrieve files from them. You can extract various things from a tarball:

- Its entire contents. For example, the following command would extract the entire contents of the tarball `home_dir_backup.tgz`, creating the necessary directory structure under the directory in which you executed the command:

      $ sudo tar zxvf home_dir_backup.tgz

- One or more directories, which recursively extracts the complete contents of those directories. For example, the following command would extract the directory `Ubuntu_Bible` and all the subdirectories and files that it contains from the tarball `home_dir_backup.tgz`, creating the necessary directory structure under the directory in which you executed the command:

      $ sudo tar zxvf home_dir_backup.tgz Ubuntu_Bible

- One or more specific files, which extracts only those files but creates all of the directories necessary to extract those files in their original location. For example, the following command would create the directory `Ubuntu_Bible` and extract the file `chap22.txt` from the tarball `home_dir_backup.tgz`, creating the `Ubuntu_Bible` directory under the directory in which you executed the command:

      $ sudo tar zxvf home_dir_backup.tgz Ubuntu_Bible/chap22.txt

For more detailed information on the `tar` command, see its online reference information (man `tar`). As one of the oldest Linux/Unix commands, it has accumulated a huge number of command-line options over the years, many of which you will probably never use. However, command-line options are like bullets — you can never have too many.

Making an Up-to-Date Copy of a Local Directory Using cp

If you're only backing up a few directories and are primarily concerned with keeping copies of the files that you are actively working on, it's often simplest to just keep copies of those directories on removable media. The traditional Linux/Unix cp command provides options that make it easy to create a copy of a specified directory, and then to subsequently update only files that have been updated or that do not already exist in the copy. For example, to back up all of the directories in /home to a removable drive mounted at /media/LACIE (LACIE is a popular manufacturer of prepackaged USB hard drives), you could use a command like the following:

    $ sudo cp –dpRuvx /home /media/LACIE/home

The cp options in this command have the following meanings:

- d: Don't de-reference symbolic links, i.e., copy them as symbolic links instead of copying what they point to.
- p: Preserve modes and ownership of the original files in the copies.
- R: Copy the specified directory recursively.
- u: Copy files only if the original file is newer than an existing copy, or if no copy exists.
- v: Display information about each file that is copied. (You may not want to use this option, but it's interesting, at least the first few times you do this.)
- x: Don't follow mount points to other filesystems.

After running this command, you will have a copy of every directory under /home on your system in the directory /media/LACIE/home. You can then detach your removable drive and store it somewhere safe (preferably off-site). Any time that you want to update your backup, retrieve the drive and update this copy at any time by simply rerunning this command.

Making an Up-to-Date Copy of a Remote Directory Using rsync

As mentioned earlier, rsync is a commonly used command-line utility that enables you to push or pull files to or from remote systems. The rsync program must be configured on the remote systems before you can push or pull file or directories to or from those systems.

To use rsync on an Ubuntu system, you must first enable it so that the system starts rsync as a background process, and then also modify the rsync configuration file to add entries for specific directories that you want to be able to read from and write to remotely. To enable rsync, edit the file /etc/defaults/rsync using your favorite text editor and a command like the following:

```
$ sudo emacs /etrc/default/rsync
```

In the line that begins with RSYNC_ENABLE, change false to true, and then save the updated file. Next, create the rsync configuration file before actually starting the rsync daemon.

NOTE Most Linux systems use an Internet service manager such as inetd or xinetd to manage incoming requests for on-demand services such as ftp, tftp, rsync, and vnc. These Internet service managers automatically start the appropriate daemon when an incoming request is received. Though these Internet service managers are available in the Ubuntu repositories, they are not installed by default. On Ubuntu systems, a specific system startup file that starts rsync in daemon mode is provided as /etc/init.d/rsync. If you subsequently install xinetd and want to use it to manage rsync requests, you will want to disable this file and create the file /etc/xinetd.d/rsync to make sure that the rsync service is enabled on your system.

The /etc/defaults/rsync file just determines whether rsync is enabled or not. The actual configuration information for rsync itself is stored in the file /etc/rsyncd.conf, which does not exist by default on an Ubuntu system. To create this file, use your favorite text editor and a command like the following:

```
$ sudo emacs /etc/rsyncd.conf
```

A minimal rsync configuration file that contains a definition remotely synchronizing the directories under /home on your system would look something like the following:

```
uid = root
transfer logging = true
log format = %h %o %f %l %b
log file = /var/log/rsyncd.log
hosts allow = 192.168.6.255/3

[homes]
    path = /home
    comment = Home Directories
    auth users = wvh
    secrets file = /etc/rsyncd.secrets
```

The first section of this file sets parameters for how the `rsync` dameon runs. In order, the `rsync` daemon runs as root (`uid`), logs all transfers (`transfer logging`), uses a specific log file format (`log format`) and log file (`log file`), and allows access from any host whose IP address is on the 192.168.6.*x* subnet (`hosts allow`). The second section of this file identifies a synchronizable entity known as home that maps to the directory /home on that system. Synchronization to or from this directory is done as the user wvh, whose password must be supplied in the file `/etc/rsyncd.secrets`.

After saving this file, use the `sudo` command and your favorite text editor to create the file `/etc/rsync.secrets`, with a command like the following:

```
$ sudo emacs /etc/rsyncd.secrets
```

This file should contain an entry for each `auth users` entry in the `/etc/rsync.conf` file, in this case wvh. Each entry in this file contains the name of a user, a colon, and the plain-text password for that user, as in the following example:

```
wvh:hellothere
```

Next, save this file and make sure that it is readable only by the root user on your system using a command like the following:

```
$ sudo chmod 600 /etc/rsyncd.secrets
```

You can now start the `rsync` daemon using the following command:

```
$ sudo /etc/init.d/rsync restart
```

You can now create a local copy of the /home directory on your Ubuntu system using a command like the following, where `ubuntu-system` is the name or IP address of the system on which you just configured the `rsyn` daemon:

```
$ rsync -Havz ubuntu-system-addr::home /media/LACIE/home
```

The arguments to the `rsync` command in this example have the following meaning:

- H: Preserve hard links if these exist in any directories that are being copied.
- a: Use archive mode, which preserves ownership, symbolic links, device files, and so on, and is essentially a shortcut that saves you specifying several other options.
- v: Be verbose, identifying each file that is copied or considered for copying. (You may not want to use this option, but it's interesting, at least the first few times you run `rsync`.)
- z: Use compression when transferring files, which improves throughput.

If you have problems using `rsync`, you should check the `/var/log/rsyncd.log` file (on the system that you are trying to retrieve files from) for error messages and hints for resolving them. If you are not using the verbose option on the host where you are retrieving these files, you may want to use it to see if you can identify (and resolve) any other errors that the host that is trying to retrieve files is reporting.

NOTE   The `rsync` configuration file created in this section is just a minimal example, and is not particularly secure. For details about all of the options available in an `rsync` configuration file and information about making `rsync` more secure, see the man page for the `rsyncd.conf` file (`man rsyncd.conf`).

Installing and Using the backuppc Utility

This section explains how to install, configure, and use the backuppc utility to back up a variety of hosts on your local network to a central Ubuntu server. Introduced earlier in this chapter, backuppc is a great application that is both easy to use for a system administrator and empowering for any authorized user. Any authorized user can initiate backups of the machines that they have admin rights to and can also restore files from existing backups of those machines, all using a convenient Web interface,

If you have more than one machine on your home network, or if you're working in a multimachine enterprise or academic environment, the BackupPC software is well worth a look. Its Web-based interface is easy to set up and use; various types of supported backups are easy to configure, initiate, and monitor; it can back up your Linux, Unix, Windows, and Mac OS X systems; and the fact that it doesn't require that you install any special software on the systems that you want to back up makes backuppc a great package.

The backuppc utility supports four different backup mechanisms (known in the BackupPC documentation as *backup transports*) to enable you to back up different types of systems. These are the following:

- rsync: Back up and restore via rsync via rsh or ssh. This is a good choice for backing up Linux, Unix, or Mac OS X systems, and you can also use it to back up Microsoft Windows systems that support rsync, such as those running the Cygwin Linux emulation environment.

- rsyncd: Back up and restore via rsync daemon on the client system. This is the best choice for Linux, Unix, and Mac OS X systems that are running an rsync daemon. You can also use this mechanism to back up Microsoft Windows systems that support rsyncd, such as those running the Cygwin Linux emulation environment.

- smb: Back up and restore using the smbclient and the SMB protocol on the backuppc server. This is the best (and easiest) choice to use when backing up Microsoft Windows systems using backuppc, and you can also use it to back up Mac OS X systems or Linux and Unix systems that are running a Samba server.

- tar: Back up and restore via tar, tar over ssh, rsh, or nfs. This is an option for Linux, Unix, and Mac OS X systems. You can also use this mechanism to back up Microsoft Windows systems that support tar, ssh, rsh, and/or nfs, such as those running the Cygwin Linux emulation environment.

A default backup transport value for all backups is set in the primary backuppc configuration file, /etc/backuppc/config.pl. The specific mechanism used to back up any particular host can be identified in that host's configuration file, as discussed later in the sections entitled "Defining a Backup Using rsyncd" and "Defining a Backup Using SMB."

NOTE Although backuppc does a great job of backing up systems running Microsoft Windows and Mac OS X, you should be aware of a few issues. First, backuppc is not suitable for backing up Windows systems so that you can do a bare-metal restore. Backuppc uses the smbclient application on your Ubuntu system to back up Windows disks, so it doesn't back up Windows ACLs and can't open files that are locked by a Windows client that is currently running (such as, most commonly, things like Outlook mailboxes). Similarly, backuppc doesn't preserve Mac OS file attributes. See http://backuppc.sourceforge.net/faq/limitations.html for a list of current limitations in using backuppc. It's a surprisingly short document!

Installing backuppc

Special-purpose backup solutions such as `backuppc` aren't installed as part of a default Ubuntu installation because they're probably overkill for most people. However, as with all software packages on Ubuntu, the Synaptic Package Manager makes it easy to install `backuppc` and the other software packages that it requires. To install `backuppc`, start the Synaptic Package Manager from the System ⇨ Administration menu and supply your password to start Synaptic. Once the Synaptic application starts, click Search to display the search dialog. Make sure that Description and Name are the selected items to search through, enter **backup** as the string to search for, and click Search. After the search completes, scroll down in the search results until you see the `backuppc` package, right-click its name, and select Mark for Installation to select that package for installation from the pop-up menu. Figure 22.3 shows the `backuppc` package being selected for installation.

Depending on what software you have previously installed on your Ubuntu system and what you select in Synaptic, a dialog may display that lists other packages that must also be installed, and asks for confirmation. If you see this dialog, click Mark to accept these related (and required) packages.

After you are finished making your selections, click Apply in the Synaptic toolbar to install `backuppc` and friends on your system. Once the installation completes, the configuration phase starts. During this phase, Synaptic automatically runs a script that sets up the initial account that you will use to access `backuppc` via your Web server. This process displays a dialog like the one shown in Figure 22.4, which tells you the initial password for the Web-based `backuppc` interface.

FIGURE 22.3

Installing the backuppc package

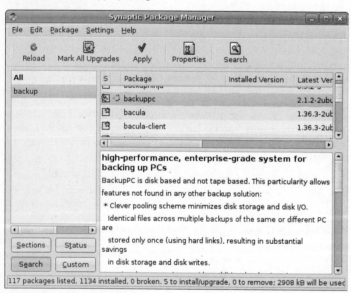

FIGURE 22.4

FIGURE 22.4

The initial password for the backuppc interface

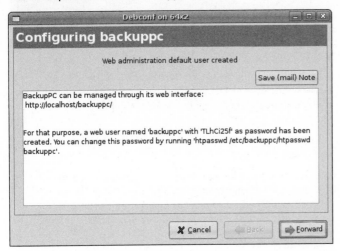

Once you see this dialog, write down the password for the `backuppc` interface and click Forward. Once the remainder of the installation and configuration process completes, you're ready to back up the system you're using and the other systems on your network.

See Chapter 20 for more detailed information on installing applications using the Synaptic Package Manager.

Configuring backuppc

On Ubuntu systems, `backuppc` stores its configuration information in two locations. General `backuppc` configuration information and passwords are stored in files in the directory `/etc/backuppc`. Backup files themselves and host-specific backup configuration information is stored in subdirectories of `/var/lib/backuppc`.

> **TIP** Backups of a single system take a significant amount of space, which is only compounded when you begin to back up other hosts to a central backup server. If you didn't specify using logical volumes when you installed your Ubuntu system, you may want to add a new disk to your system before starting to use `backuppc` and format that disk as a logical volume. You can then copy the default contents of `/var/lib/backuppc` to the new disk (preserving file permissions and ownership), and mount that disk on the directory `/var/lib/backuppc` on the system that you are using for backups. When you need more space to store backups in the future, this will enable you to add other disks to your system and add their space to the logical volume used to store backups. The `backuppc` utility also provides an archive capability that enables you to migrate old backups to other hosts for archival purposes, freeing up disk space on your primary backup server. Though not discussed in this book, setting up archives hosts is discussed in the BackupPC document — which is great, by the way!

The first thing that you should do is to change the `backuppc` password to something easier to remember than the random string generated during the `backuppc` installation process. You can do this by issuing the following command:

```
$ sudo htpasswd /etc/backuppc/htpasswd backuppc
```

This sequence uses `sudo` to run the `htpasswd` command to change the password for the user `backuppc` in the file `/etc/backuppc/htpasswd`. When you are prompted for a new password, enter something easier to remember than "TLhCi25f," which was the default password generated for my `backuppc` installation, as shown in Figure 22.4. You will be prompted to reenter the new password to make sure that you typed it correctly.

Identifying Hosts to Back Up

Each host that you want to back up must be identified in the file `/etc/backuppc/hosts`. Like all `backuppc` configuration files, this file is easy to update. Any characters in any lines in this file that follow a hash mark are comments, which help explain the meaning of the various fields used in the file. A minimal `backuppc` configuration file looks like the following:

```
host            dhcp    user            moreUsers
localhost       0       backuppc
```

The first noncomment line in `/etc/backuppc/hosts` defines the names of the various fields in each line, and should therefore not be modified. (This is the line beginning with the word "host" in the example.) All other lines represent entries for hosts that will be backed up. The first actual host entry, for `localhost`, is a special entry used for backing up system configuration information on the `backuppc` server, and should not be changed.

The fields in each entry that define a host have the following meanings:

- The first field identifies a particular machine, either by hostname, IP address, or NetBios name.
- The second field should be set to 0 for any host whose name can be determined by DNS, the local hosts file, or an nmblookup broadcast. This field can be set to 1 to identify systems whose names must be discovered by probing a range of DHCP addresses, as is the case in some environments where DHCP and WINS are not fully integrated. Setting this field to 1 requires changes in the host-specific configuration file's `$Conf{DHCPAddressRanges}` variable to define the base IP address and range of IP addresses that should be probed.
- The third field identifies the name of the person who is primarily responsible for backing up that host. This primary user will receive e-mail about the status of any backup that is attempted. I tend to leave this as the `backuppc` user, so that this user maintains an e-mail record of all backup attempts, but you can set this to a specific user if you wish.
- The fourth field (which is optional) consists of one or more users who also have administrative rights to initiate backups or restore files for this machine. The names of multiple users must be separated by a comma.

As an example, the hosts file on one of my `backuppc` servers looks like the following:

```
host            dhcp    user            moreUsers
localhost       0       backuppc
192.168.6.64    0       backuppc        wvh
64bit           0       backuppc        wvh,djf
64x2                    0               backuppc        juser

win2k                   0               backuppc        wvh,djf
```

TIP | The `backuppc` program checks the timestamp on the `/etc/backuppc/hosts` files each time the `backuppc` process wakes up, and reloads this file automatically if the file has been updated. For this reason, you should not save changes to the hosts file until you have created the host-specific configuration files, as described in the examples in the next two sections. If the `backuppc` process reloads the hosts file before you have created the host-specific configuration data and another authorized user initiates a backup of this system, you will either back up the wrong thing or a backup failure will occur. You can always make changes to the hosts file and leave them commented out (by putting a # as the first character on the line) until you have completed the host-specific configuration.

Defining a Backup Using rsyncd

The section earlier in this chapter entitled "Making an Up-to-Date Copy of a Remote Directory Using rsync" explained how to set up `rsync` in daemon mode on an Ubuntu system and how to define synchronization entries that can be remotely accessed via `rsync`. The sample `rsync` configuration file created in that section defined a synchronization entry called `homes` that would enable an authorized user to synchronize the contents of all directories under `/home` on a sample Ubuntu system. We'll use that same configuration file in the example in this section.

The previous section showed how to define entries in the `/etc/backuppc/hosts` file for the various hosts that you want to back up via `backuppc`. The first step in host-specific configuration is to use the `sudo` command to create a directory to hold host-specific configuration data, logs, and so on. Throughout this section, I'll use the sample host entry `64bit`, which I defined in the section entitled "Identifying Hosts to Back Up" as an example.

The first step in host-specific configuration is to use the `sudo` command to create the directory `/var/lib/backuppc/64bit`, as in the following command:

```
$ sudo mkdir /var/lib/backuppc/64bit
```

Next, use the `sudo` command and your favorite text editor to create a host-specific configuration file named `config.pl` in that directory, using a command like the following:

```
$ sudo emacs /var/lib/backuppc/64bit/config.pl
```

The contents of this file should be something like the following;

```
$Conf{XferMethod} = 'rsyncd';
$Conf{CompressLevel} = 3';
$Conf{RsyncShareName} = 'homes';
$Conf{RsyncdUserName} = 'wvh';
$Conf{RsyncdPasswd} = 'hellothere;
```

The first line identifies the backup mechanism used for this host as `rsyncd`, which overrides the default backup mechanism specified in the generic `/etc/backuppc/config.pl` file. The second line sets the compression level for this host's backups to level 3, which provides a good tradeoff between the CPU load and time required to do compression and the amount of compression that you actually get. The last three entries in this file correspond to the synchronization entry in the sample `rsyncd.conf` and associated `rsyncd.secrets` file created in "Making an Up-to-Date Copy of a Remote Directory Using rsync" earlier in this chapter.

> **TIP** When using `backuppc` to do automated backups, I like to create a separate authorized user to use `rsync` for backup purposes, so that the system logs show who actually requested a remote sync operation. To do this, you would add this user (I usually use `backuppc`) to the `auth users` entry in the remote host's `/etc/rsyncd.conf` file and create an appropriate username/password pair in the remote host's `/etc/rsyncd.secrets` file. You would then modify the host-specific `backuppc` configuration file to use this username and password. I didn't do this here for simplicity's sake, but doing this would provide more accurate log data on the client system.

If the remote system uses an `rsync` binary other than the default `/usr/bin/rsync` or the `rsync` program is listening on a port other than the standard port (873), you should add correct definitions for these to the host-specific configuration file. The default settings for the associated configuration parameters are the following;

```
$Conf{RsyncdClientPort} = 873;
$Conf{RsyncClientPath} = '/usr/bin/rsync';
```

Next, change the ownership and group of the `/var/lib/backuppc/64bit` directory to `backuppc` and change the protection of the configuration file `/var/lib/backuppc/64bit/config.pl` so that it is not publicly readable (because it contains password information) using the following commands:

```
$ sudo chmod -Rv backuppc:backuppc /var/lib/backuppc/64bit
$ sudo chmod 600 /var/lib/backuppc/64bit/config.pl
```

The last step in creating a host-specific backup definition for `backuppc` is to cause the `backuppc` process to reread its configuration data, which you can do by explicitly reloading the configuration file, explicitly restarting the `backuppc` process, or by sending the associated process a hang-up (HUP) signal. You can force `backuppc` to reload the configuration file using the following command:

```
$ sudo /etc/init.d/backuppc reload
```

The definition for your backup host can now be selected via the `backuppc` Web interface. At this point, you can follow the instructions in the section entitled "Starting Backups in backuppc" to back up this host.

The example in this section only backs up the home directories of users on the remote machine. To recursively back up other directories, you would simply create other synchronization entities for those directories in the remote host's `/etc/rsyncd.conf` file, and then add entries for those synchronization entities to the host-specific configuration file. For example, to back up synchronization entries named `homes`, `/`, and `/boot`, you would change the host-specific `RsyncShareName` entry to look like the following:

```
$Conf{RsyncShareName} = ['/', 'homes', '/boot'];
```

If you back up multiple filesystems or synchronization points, you may create a custom set of arguments to the `rsync` command in the host-specific configuration file. This enables you to add options such as `--one-file-system`, which causes `backuppc` to back up each filesystem separately, simplifying restores. You can also add options to exclude certain directories from the backups, which you will certainly want to do if you are backing up a remote system's root directory ('/'), as in following examples:

```
$Conf{RsyncArgs} = [
        # original arguments here
        '--one-file-system',
        '--exclude', '/dev,
        '--exclude', '/proc',
        '--exclude', '/media',
        '--exclude', '/mnt',
        '--exclude', '/lost+found',
];
```

These settings would prevent backups of /dev, which contains device nodes and is dynamically populated at boot time on modern Linux systems, /proc, which is the mount point for an in-memory filesystem that contains transient data, directories such as /media and /mnt on which removable media is often temporarily mounted, and /lost+found, which is a directory used during filesystem consistency checking. You can also exclude directories from rsync backups using the BackupoFilesExclude directive, as in the following example:

```
$Conf{BackupFilesExclude} = ['/dev', /proc', '/media', '/mnt', '/lost+found'];
```

The backuppc program reads the configuration settings in /etc/backuppc/config.pl first, and then loads host-specific configuration settings, which enables the /etc/backuppc/config.pl file to provide default settings for all backups. After you have used backuppc for a while and are comfortable with various settings, you may want to consider modifying the default settings in the /etc/backuppc/config.pl file for configuration variables such as $Conf{RsyncArgs}, $Conf{BackupFilesExclude}, and $Conf{CompressLevel}, to minimize the number of entries that you have to create in each of your host-specific configuration files.

Defining a Backup Using SMB

The section of this chapter entitled "Identifying Hosts to Back Up" showed how to define entries in the /etc/backuppc/hosts file for the various hosts that you want to back up via backuppc. The first step in host-specific configuration is to use the sudo command to create a directory to hold host-specific configuration data, logs, and so on. Throughout this section, I'll use the sample host entry win2k from the sample hosts file as an example. As you might gather from its name, this is indeed a system running Microsoft Windows 2000. There's no escaping from the Borg.

The first step in host-specific configuration is to use the sudo command to create the directory /var/lib/backuppc/win2k, as in the following command:

```
$ sudo mkdir /var/lib/backuppc/win2k
```

Next, use the sudo command and your favorite text editor to create a host-specific configuration file named config.pl in that directory, using a command like the following:

```
$ sudo emacs /var/lib/backuppc/win2k/config.pl
```

The contents of this file should be something like the following;

```
$Conf{XferMethod} = 'smb';
$Conf{CompressLevel} = 3';
$Conf{SmbShareName} = ['wvh', "djf'];
$Conf{SmbShareUserName} = 'backuppc;
$Conf{SmbSharePasswd} = hellothere';
```

The first line identifies the backup mechanism used for this host as smb, which overrides the default backup mechanism specified in the generic /etc/backuppc/config.pl file. The second line sets the compression level for this host's backups to level 3, which provides a good tradeoff between the CPU load and time required to do compression and the amount of compression that you actually get. The last three entries in this file define the Windows shares that you want to back up, the name of an authorized user who has access to these shares, and the password for that user.

TIP When using `backuppc` to back up Microsoft Windows systems, you should create a Windows user that you will only use to do backups, and then add this user to the standard Windows Backup Operators group. This prevents you from having to put your Windows administrator password in the `backuppc` configuration files. Even though you'll protect those files so that randoms can't read them, the fewer places where you write down a password, the better, especially one with the keys to your entire Windows kingdom.

Next, change the ownership and group of the `/var/lib/backuppc/win2k` directory to `backuppc` and change the protection of the configuration file `/var/lib/backuppc/win2k/config.pl` so that it is not publicly readable (because it contains password information) using the following commands:

```
$ sudo chmod -Rv backuppc:backuppc /var/lib/backuppc/win2k
$ sudo chmod 600 /var/lib/backuppc/win2k/config.pl
```

The last step in creating a host-specific backup definition for `backuppc` is to cause the `backuppc` process to reread its configuration data, which you can do by explicitly reloading the configuration file, explicitly restarting the `backuppc` process, or by sending the associated process a hang-up (HUP) signal. You can force `backuppc` to reload the configuration file using the following command:

```
$ sudo /etc/init.d/backuppc reload
```

The definition for your backup host can now be selected via the backuppc Web interface. At this point, you can follow the instructions in the section entitled "Starting Backups in backuppc" to back up this host.

The example in this section only backs up shares that correspond to the home directories of selected users on the remote machine. As mentioned earlier in this chapter, `backuppc` backups do not support bare-metal restores of Windows systems, and I therefore typically don't back up shares such as `C$`, which is a default Windows share that represents your system's boot drive. You may find it useful to do so to make sure that you have backup copies of drivers, the registry, and so on, but I find it simpler to start from scratch when reinstalling Windows. Windows systems accumulate so much crap in their filesystems over time that doing a fresh installation from your distribution media often frees up a surprising amount of space. If you have several identical systems, restoring partition images created with Norton Ghost or the Linux `partimage` or `g4u` utilities is always the fastest way to rebuild a Windows system without having to locate the drivers for every device that you will ever want to use with your rebuilt system and reinstalling all of your favorite applications.

TIP The `backuppc` program reads the configuration settings in `/etc/backuppc/config.pl` first, and then loads host-specific configuration settings, which enables the `/etc/backuppc/config.pl` file to provide default settings for all backups. After you have used `backuppc` for a while and are comfortable with various settings, you may want to consider modifying the default settings in the `/etc/backuppc/config.pl` file for configuration variables, such as `$Conf{CompressLevel}`, to minimize the number of entries that you have to create in each of your host-specific configuration files.

Starting Backups in backuppc

Thanks to `backuppc`'s Web orientation, starting backups, viewing the status of those backups, and checking the backup history for any host is impressively easy. To start a backup in `backuppc`, connect to the backuppc Web interface using the URL `http://hostname/backuppc`, where `hostname` is the name of the host on which the `backuppc` server is running. A dialog displays in which you are prompted for the login and password of an authorized user. Once you enter the `user/password` combination for a user listed in the file `/etc/backuppc/htpasswd`, the `backuppc` server's home page displays, as shown in Figure 22.5.

FIGURE 22.5

FIGURE 22.5

The backuppc Web interface

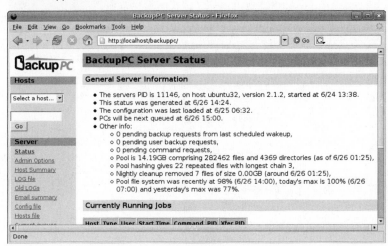

Once this screen displays, click the Select a host... drop-down box and select one of the hosts from the list that displays, as shown in Figure 22.6.

Selecting the name of any host takes you to a summary page for that host, which provides status information, lists authorized users who can back up and restore files to this host using `backuppc`, and displays the last e-mail that was sent about this host, as shown in Figure 22.7.

FIGURE 22.6

Selecting a host to back up

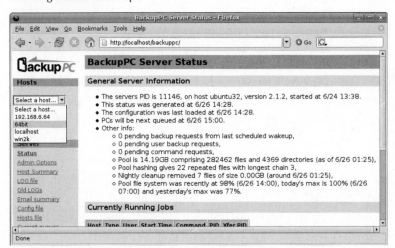

FIGURE 22.7

A per-host page in the backuppc Web interface

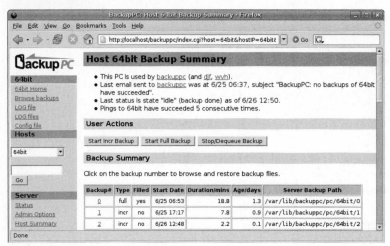

> **NOTE**   Each system's home page displays the subject of the last e-mail sent to the owner of this host. E-mail is only sent occasionally, so seeing a historical problem report does not mean that this problem is still occurring.

Once this page displays, you can scroll down on the page to see additional status information about available backups, any transfer errors that occurred during backups, and other tables that show the status of the pool where backup files are archived and the extent to which existing backups have been compressed to save disk space.

To start a backup, click either Start Full Backup to start a full (archive) backup of the system, or Start Incr Backup to start an incremental backup containing files that have changed since the last full backup. The confirmation page shown in Figure 22.8 displays.

Clicking Start Full Backup (or Start Incr Backup for an incremental backup) queues the backup and displays a link that you can click to return to the main page for that host to monitor the state of the backup.

Restoring from Backups in backuppc

Thanks to backuppc's Web orientation and the fact that backuppc backups are stored online on the backup server, restoring files from backuppc can be done online, by any authorized user whose name is associated with that host in the /etc/backuppc/hosts file. Backuppc enables you to browse through online backups, interactively select the files and directories that you want to restore, and restore them in various ways.

To begin restoring files or directories, click the name of the full or incremental backup in which they are located. A screen like the one shown in Figure 22.9 displays.

FIGURE 22.8

Confirming the start of a full backup

FIGURE 22.9

Restoring files and directories in the backuppc Web interface

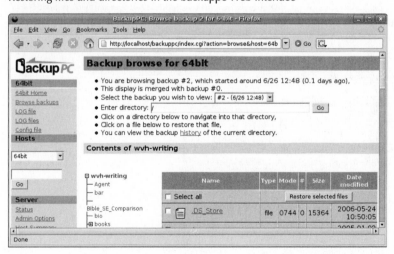

The bottom of the screen shown in Figure 22.9 displays a hierarchical listing of the files and directories that are contained in the full or incremental backup that you selected. If you selected an incremental backup, the contents of that incremental backup are overlaid on the contents of the previous full backup to give you an accurate snapshot of the contents of your system when the backup was done. You can drill down into the backup by selecting directories from the tree view at the left, or you can drill down into individual directories by selecting from the view of the current directory shown at the right of the main window.

To mark files and directories for restoration, select the checkbox beside their names, as shown in Figure 22.10.

FIGURE 22.10

Selecting files and directories for restoration

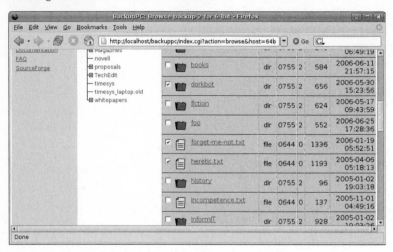

Once you have selected all of the files and directories that you want to restore, scroll to the bottom of the restore page and click restore selected files. A page that enables you to specify how you want to restore those files displays, as shown in Figure 22.11.

FIGURE 22.11

Specifying the restore method in backuppc's Web interface

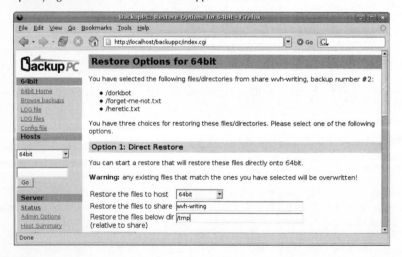

You have three options when restoring files using the `backuppc` Web interface:

- **Direct restore:** Selecting this option restores files directly to the host from which they were backed up. When doing a direct restore, you have the option of restoring files in the locations from which they were originally backed up, or into a subdirectory that `backuppc` will create for you if it does not already exist. (The latter is almost always a good idea so that you don't accidentally overwrite any files that you don't actually mean to.) To select this option, enter the name of any subdirectory that you want to use (I usually specify one called `tmp`) and click Start restore.

- **Download Zip archive:** Selecting this option restores the selected files and directories into a zip-format archive that you can download to your desktop and manually extract the contents of. When selecting this option, you can optionally specify the compression level used in the zip file, which can be important if you are restoring large numbers of files. To select this option, click Download Zip file.

- **Download Tar archive:** Selecting this option restores the selected files and directories into a tar-format archive that you can download to your desktop and manually extract the contents of. To select this option, click Download Tar file.

If you selected the Direct restore option, `backuppc` displays a confirmation screen like the one shown in Figure 22.12.

FIGURE 22.12

Confirming a restore directly to a remote system

This lists the files and directories that you selected for restoration and confirms the location to which they will be restored, including the name of any subdirectory that you specified. To proceed, click Restore,

If you selected the Zip or Tar archive options, the `backuppc` application displays your Web browser's standard file download dialog after the archive file has been created. Figure 22.13 shows this dialog for a `tar` format restore.

FIGURE 22.13

Downloading a tarball of files restored by backuppc

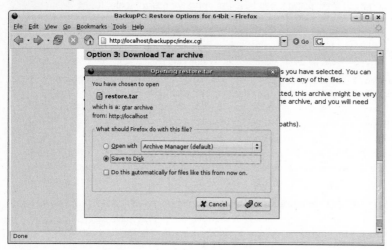

As you can see from this section (and the preceding sections), `backuppc` provides a powerful, flexible interface for backing up and restoring files on many different systems to a single `backuppc` server. All you need are a few configuration files and sufficient disk space, and lost files (and the lost time that is usually associated with them) can be a thing of the past.

Summary

This chapter discusses backups, which are the most time-consuming, boring, and valuable things that you need to do with your personal computer system. Ubuntu is knee-deep in excellent software that you can use to do various types of backups, ranging from backing up to files that you can store on removable media or simply move to other systems. It then discusses doing simple backups over the network, and concludes by discussing BackupPC, an excellent open source backup application for doing regular, networked backups of multiple systems to a central backup server.

Chapter 23 discusses how to add various types of hardware to your Ubuntu system. Like most modern personal computer systems, Ubuntu does a great job of automatically recognizing and providing access to new printers, scanners, and removable storage such as USB sticks, USB hard drives, FireWire devices, and so on. Adding new internal drives requires a bit more work, but is a key element of permanent system upgrades and is easy enough to master given the general commands explained in Chapter 23.

Chapter 23

Adding Hardware and Attaching Peripherals

Support for a tremendous variety of hardware is a key issue for any desktop computer system. As computer hardware becomes more and more of an end-user commodity, where desktop computer users feel more and more comfortable adding cards and external peripherals to their computer systems, the extent to which an operating system supports all of this new hardware has increasingly higher visibility. An increasing number of devices that are designed as external plug-and-play devices using interfaces like USB and FireWire are available at the local Best Buy, CompUSA, or Stop-n-Go. People expect to buy these things, take them home, plug them in, and find that "they just work." And rightly so.

All hardware requires pieces of kernel software called device drivers in order to be accessed and correctly used by the operating system. This is true for the Microsoft Windows kernel (yes, it has one), the Mac OS X kernel, and the Linux kernel. The fact that CDs labeled "Windows Drivers" fall out of the boxes containing almost every piece of modern hardware might make you think that you'll have a problem using this hardware with Linux. After all, there is no companion coaster labeled "Linux Drivers." What gives?

Luckily, the answer is that the device drivers for most hardware are already available as part of the Linux kernel as installed on your Ubuntu system. Device drivers are usually either compiled into the kernel or are available as kernel modules that are loaded when specific hardware is detected. (Hence, the generic term for such on-demand drivers: *loadable kernel modules*.) This is true for a vast amount of hardware — after all, in the open source world, all it takes is one motivated Linux user with driver development skills and a piece of hardware that "doesn't quite work right," and a working driver usually surfaces shortly thereafter.

Though I am an Ubuntu and general Linux advocate, I can't deny that the lack of device-specific drivers can sometimes be a problem. To get the absolute best performance out of some pieces of new hardware — most specifically things like graphics and audio cards — you may need special drivers. Unfortunately, most hardware manufacturers are motivated by projected sales numbers based on market analysis, and the Windows market is currently at least fifty to a hundred times larger than the Linux market. This is why you get a "Windows Driver" mini-Frisbee free with almost all new hardware. Open source support for these high-performance drivers may lag behind Windows support, though more and more hardware manufacturers are providing Linux drivers in one form or another, often only available for download from their Web sites.

The good news is that, for the most part, drivers that are required for most new hardware come with your Ubuntu Linux distribution. Some specialized drivers that are not open source or which have licensing or other encumbrances are available as updates from portions of the Ubuntu repository such as the restricted, universe, or multiverse components, as discussed in Chapter 20. You may have to retrieve other drivers directly from a corporate Web site. The bottom line is that, usually, things will indeed "just work" with Linux.

This chapter explores using different types of hardware devices with your Ubuntu Linux system, focusing on the types of hardware that most desktop and laptop computer users will be interested in. Hardware detection and support under Ubuntu Linux is constantly improving. Regardless, when researching or buying new hardware, it's always a good idea to spend a bit of time in your favorite search engine, looking for information about Linux support for your hardware. More information is always a good thing, regardless of what the U.S. government says nowadays.

Adding a Printer

Most modern printers connect to your system via its USB interface, though some still connect to the classic parallel port. Regardless of the type of printer you are connecting to your system, the first things to do are to connect it to your system and turn it on. If it is a USB printer, you can verify that the printer is visible to your system by executing the lsusb (list USB) command, which provides the information like the following:

```
$ lsusb
Bus 004 Device 001: ID 0000:0000
Bus 001 Device 001: ID 0000:0000
Bus 003 Device 001: ID 0000:0000
Bus 002 Device 004: ID 04b8:0005 Seiko Epson Corp. Stylus Printer
Bus 002 Device 001: ID 0000:0000
```

From this output, you can see that an Epson Stylus printer is attached to this system via USB.

> **TIP** If you have not purchased a printer yet and want to get information about Linux support for a specific printer, check out the LinuxPrinting.org site at www.linuxprinting.org. This site provides an easy interface that enables you to get information about how well specific printers (or all of the printers from a specific manufacturer) work with the Linux printing system. For more information about printing on Linux, see Chapter 30, "Setting Up a Print Server."

The System ➪ Preferences ➪ Removable Drives and Media menu item enables you to define how you want your system to react when a new Printer is attached or detected. After selecting this menu item, select the Printers and Scanners tab from the preferences dialog. The Printers and Scanners tab is shown in Figure 23.1.

FIGURE 23.1

Setting printer detection preferences

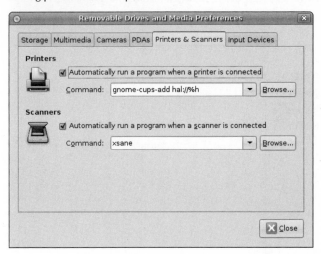

Selecting the Automatically run a program when a printer is connected checkbox with its default value of `gnome-cups-add hal://%h` (which calls the `gnome-cups-add` application with an ID retrieved from Ubuntu's hardware availability layer) displays the dialog shown in Figure 23.3. (For information about using these dialogs, skip ahead to the text that follows that figure.)

If you disable automatically running `gnome-cups-add` when a new printer is detected or auto-detection fails for some reason, you can still add a new printer to your Ubuntu system manually. To do this, select the System ➪ Administration ➪ Printing menu item. This displays a dialog like the one shown in Figure 23.2, which lists all of the printers that are currently defined on your system and also provides a New Printer icon that we'll use to define and configure the new printer.

FIGURE 23.2

The Ubuntu Printers utility

Double-click the New Printer icon or select the Printer ⇨ Add Printer menu command to start the wizard that helps configure a new printer. After the Printers utility processes and parses its database of available printers, the first dialog for New Printer configuration displays as shown in Figure 23.3.

FIGURE 23.3

Specifying the printer and connection type

If your Ubuntu system was able to automatically detect information about your new printer, it will automatically populate this dialog with the appropriate information about the printer and the way in which it is connected to your system. For example, the dialog shown in Figure 23.3 displays preconfiguration information for an Epson Stylus Photo R200 printer attached to one of my test systems via USB. If this information is correct, click Forward to proceed to the second printer configuration dialog, shown in Figure 23.4.

TIP If your printer is not automatically detected, you can manually specify a printer by selecting the Use another printer by specifying a port radio button and selecting the port to which your printer is attached from the Printer Port drop-down list.

If you printer was automatically (and correctly) detected, the appropriate driver for that printer is displayed in the dialog shown in Figure 23.4. Click Forward to proceed to the dialog shown in Figure 23.5.

TIP If the driver for your printer was not automatically detected, you can manually select a driver by clicking on the Manufacturer drop-down list, selecting the manufacturer of your printer, and selecting the model of your printer in the Model dialog.

FIGURE 23.4

Selecting a printer driver

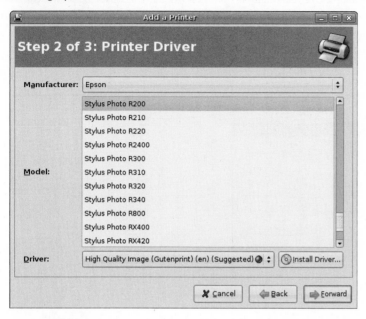

FIGURE 23.5

Providing printer information

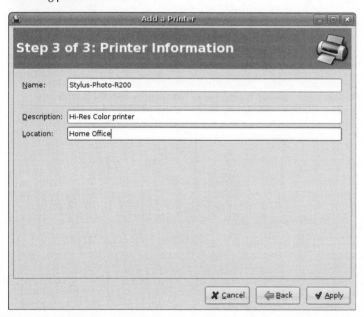

The dialog shown in Figure 23.5 enables you to provide some meaningful (but optional) information about your printer and to optionally change the name assigned to that printer. Once you are happy with the values on this screen, click Apply to complete the definition for your new printer. This closes the printer configuration dialog and displays an icon for your new printer in the dialog shown in Figure 23.2.

To test your new printer, right-click on its name and select Properties from the pop-up menu. This displays a Properties dialog like the one shown in Figure 23.6.

FIGURE 23.6

A printer's Properties dialog

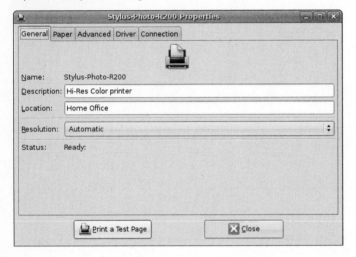

To verify that your printer is working correctly, click Print a Test Page. This queues and prints a test page for your printer. If the test page does not print, use the other tabs in the Properties dialog to verify that the correct connection settings are being used, and that the right printer manufacturer and the driver for your printer are specified. You should then be able to successfully print a test page.

TIP   **If your printer is not automatically detected or cannot be made to print to with any manual setting specified in the Add printer dialog, try rebooting your system with the printer connected and turned on. In some rare cases, Ubuntu's printer and device subsystems may not correctly detect a device unless it is present and active when you boot your system.**

Using a Scanner

Most modern scanners are USB devices and are well supported on Linux systems, as are older scanners that use a real SCSI interface. Scanners are supported on Linux systems through the SANE (Scanner Access Now Easy) interface and associated front-end and back-end applications. The home of the SANE project is www.sane-project.org. If you are still shopping for a scanner or are interested whether support for a specific scanner is available under Linux, see the page at www.sane-project.org/sane-supported-devices.html, which also provides access to an easy-to-use search engine application that provides data about specific scanners.

Ubuntu systems preinstall the XSane Image Scanner software that uses the SANE drivers but provides a graphical display of the scanning process, supports a variety of scanner configuration options, and provides both quick preview scans for alignment purposes and final scans at a variety of scan resolutions. Through the rest of this chapter, I'll simply refer to the XSane Image Scanner as XSane to save a few words.

> **NOTE**   This section is not a complete guide to every nuance of scanning software for Linux. The focus in this section is to introduce the software and common controls necessary to get a scanner working reasonably on your Ubuntu system.

The System ➪ Preferences ➪ Removable Drives and Media menu item enables you to define how you want your system to react when a Scanner is attached or detected. After selecting this menu item, select the Printers and Scanners tab from the preferences dialog. The Printers and Scanners tab is shown in Figure 23.7.

FIGURE 23.7

Setting scanner detection preferences

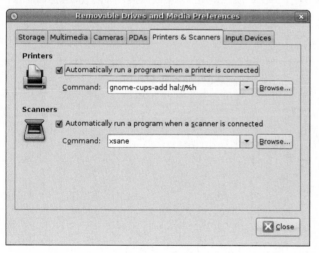

Selecting the Automatically run a program when a scanner is connected checkbox with its default value of xsane starts the XSane application for you automatically.

If you disable automatically running XSane when a new scanner is connected or auto-detection fails for some reason, you can still start XSane manually. To start the XSane application, select Applications ➪ Graphics ➪ XSane Image Scanner. This displays several dialogs, all of which you can initially close except for the one shown in Figure 23.8, which is the primary XSane dialog.

FIGURE 23.8

The primarily XSane dialog

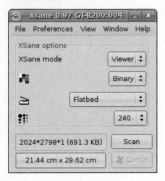

To determine how your scanner was recognized by your Ubuntu system, select File ➪ Info to display the dialog shown in Figure 23.9.

FIGURE 23.9

Information about your scanner in XSane

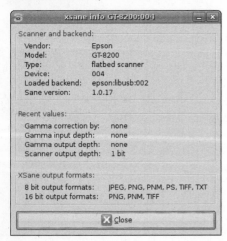

This Info dialog identifies the vendor and model of the scanner that was detected on your system, as well as some general information about the SANE driver that is being used and the output formats that are supported by XSane. Click Close to close this dialog and return to the main XSane dialog.

To get a preview scan (which is a low-resolution scan that is typically used to verify that your scanner is working, the document that you are scanning is correctly aligned, and so on), select Window ⇨ Show Preview, which initially displays the dialog shown in Figure 23.10.

FIGURE 23.10

The initial XSane Preview window

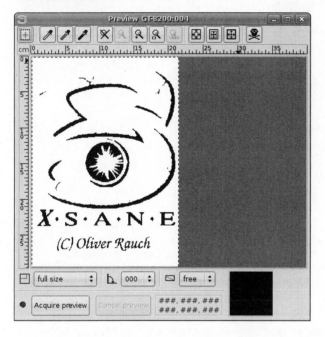

To get a quick preview of the document that you are scanning, click Acquire Preview in the dialog shown in Figure 23.10. Your scanner should wake up, scan your document, and display a preview of that scan, as shown in Figure 23.11.

FIGURE 23.11

A low-res, black and white preview in XSane

Don't panic at this point — so far, I've just used XSane's default resolution and scan settings, which are quite minimal. However, if the preview is acceptable, you can proceed to do a full scan of your document. In most cases, the preview will not be of sufficient quality, so you should return to the main XSane dialog shown in Figure 23.8 to set some common scanning configuration options. The most common settings that you will want to change are:

- **Scan Mode:** Enables you to select different scanning modes. Available options are binary (black and white, which is the default setting), grayscale (many shades of gray, plus black and white), and color (a full-color scan). Selecting either grayscale or color scan modes refreshes the main XSane dialog and shows additional configuration items that you can use to control brightness, contrast, colors, and so on. Figure 23.12 shows the main XSane dialog for color scans.

- **Scan Resolution:** Enables you to control the resolution at which the image is scanned. Possible values range from 50 DPI (dots per inch) to 3200 DPI. The range of possible values depends on the scanner you are using.

The combination of the scan mode and the scan resolution determines the size of the image file that will be produced by XSane when you do a final scan. For example, a black and white scan of a U.S. Letter-sized (8½×11 inches) document at 72 DPI produces an image file that is 63KB. A color scan at that same resolution using default color settings produces an image file that is 1.5MB. Scanning that same document at a resolution of 240 DPI increases the file size to 16MB. Apparently, quality does indeed come at a price.

Once you have changed your settings, you should preview your image again by clicking Acquire Preview again in the Preview window, which should show a substantial improvement over your initial preview, as shown in Figure 23.13.

FIGURE 23.12

Additional controls for color scans in XSane

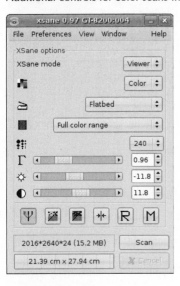

FIGURE 23.13

A substantially improved preview in XSane

Look, there are actually people in the test document that I am scanning! Assuming that the new preview looks as though it will be sufficient for your purposes, close the Preview window and click Scan in the main XSane dialog. The document will be scanned using the current settings. Once the scan completes, XSane will display the scan in its standard View window, as shown in Figure 23.14.

FIGURE 23.14

A final scan in the XSane viewer

You may want to iterate through several scans, adjusting things like contrast and brightness using the controls on the main XSane dialog. Whenever you get a scan that you are happy with, you can save the scanned image by clicking File ➪ View, which displays a dialog that enables you to specify a filename and also the image format in which the scan will be saved.

For general information about SANE and scanners on Linux, see:

- Linux Scanner HOWTO: `http://tldp.org/HOWTO/Scanner-HOWTO/index.html`
- SANE FAQ: `www.xs4all.nl/~ljm/SANE-faq.html`
- SANE Project Site: `www.sane-project.org`

TIP   If your Ubuntu system is having a problem locating your scanner or you need to know the name of the device node associated with your scanner, use Synaptic Package Manager to install the `sane-utils` package, which provides a convenient utility called `sane-find-scanner` which does an excellent job of finding SCSI and USB scanners. Installing the package will also install man pages for `sane-scsi` and `sane-usb`, which provide a great selection of useful suggestions for resolving problems locating SCSI or USB scanners.

Using External Disks and CD/DVD Drives

Portable USB and FireWire hard drives are common today, as are USB flash drives (which look like small hard drives to your system). These portable, removable storage devices simplify backups, transporting large amounts of data, and transferring large amounts of data from one system to another. For the most part, these removable devices are correctly identified by Ubuntu Linux systems, which respond to their detection as specified by the storage preferences described in the next section. The section after that, "Troubleshooting Automatic Device Detection" discusses ways of manually identifying the devices associated with newly attached storage devices and mounting or formatting them manually so that they can subsequently be mounted.

Configuring Automatic Device Detection

Chapter 13 provided an overview of how to use the System ➪ Preferences ➪ Removable Drives and Media menu item to define how you want your system to react when a new removable storage device is attached or detected. When first started, this application displays the Storage tab where you can configure your system's responses to detecting new removable storage devices. The Storage tab is shown in Figure 23.15.

FIGURE 23.15

Setting removable storage detection preferences

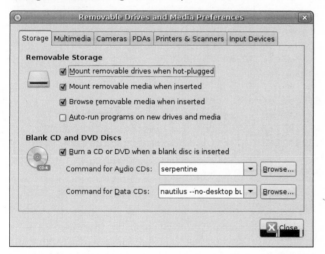

The Removable Storage section of this tab determines what your system does when USB or FireWire disk hard drives are detected, or when nonblank CD or DVD media is inserted into an existing (or newly attached) CD or DVD drive. This provides the following settings for these cases:

- **Mount removable drives when hot-plugged:** automatically mounts the partitions on a removable storage device when one is attached to your system

- **Mount removable media when inserted:** automatically mounts any filesystems available on removable media when such media is inserted into a storage device on your system

- **Browse removable media when inserted:** automatically starts the Nautilus file browser with a view of the filesystem contained on the removable media that has been inserted

- **Auto-run programs on new drives and media:** automatically executes any `autorun.sh` or `autorun.inf` script found on the removable media when it is inserted

The Blank CD and DVD Disks section of this dialog enables you to specify what happens when blank media is inserted into any CD or DVD drive on your system. The Audio CD Disks setting on the Preferences application's Multimedia tab controls auto-playing audio CDs when they are inserted. Similarly, the Video DVD Disks setting on the Preferences application's Multimedia tab controls auto-playing video DVDs when they are inserted.

Troubleshooting Automatic Device Detection

When you attach a removable storage device, whether it is a hard drive, CD or DVD drive, or flash device (which look like IDE storage devices to a Linux system), the kernel automatically logs messages related to the detection of that device, any kernel modules loaded in response to the device, and any device nodes that are associated with the new storage device. If a newly attached device does not mount on your system automatically, you will at least need to know the Linux device nodes associated with that device so that you can attempt to mount it manually.

As an example, the kernel messages associated with attaching a USB hard drive to one of my systems are the following:

```
kernel: usb 4-1: new high speed USB device using ehci_hcd and address 5
kernel: scsi3 : SCSI emulation for USB Mass Storage devices
kernel:    Vendor: WDC        Model: WD2500JB-00GVC0   Rev: 08.0
kernel:    Type:   Direct-Access                      ANSI SCSI
revision: 02
kernel:  3:0:0:0: Attached scsi generic sg1 type 0
kernel: Driver 'sd' needs updating - please use bus_type methods
kernel: SCSI device sda: 488397168 512-byte hdwr sectors (250059 MB)
kernel: SCSI device sda: 488397168 512-byte hdwr sectors (250059 MB)
kernel:   sda: sda1
kernel: sd 3:0:0:0: Attached scsi disk sda
```

NOTE   I've eliminated some superfluous information from the beginning of each of these lines to make them fit on the printed page.

The first six lines of this output have to do with the USB driver and the SCSI emulation driver used to access USB storage. The last four lines are the interesting ones in terms of the device(s) associated with that USB storage. They state that the device is being attached as the first SCSI device, `sda`, and that one partition, `sda1`, was detected on the that device. You can verify this information by using the `fdisk` utility to query the device, as in the following example:

```
$ fdisk -l /dev/sda
Disk /dev/sda: 250.0 GB, 250059350016 bytes
255 heads, 63 sectors/track, 30401 cylinders
Units = cylinders of 16065 * 512 = 8225280 bytes
   Device Boot      Start         End      Blocks   Id  System
/dev/sda1   *           1       30401   244196001    c  W95 FAT32 (LBA)
```

This output confirms that the device /dev/sda has one partition, /dev/sda1, and also tells you that this partition is a FAT32 partition, which means that you'll have to mount it as type vfat if you need to mount it manually. You could do this using a command like the following:

```
$ sudo mount -t vfat /dev/sda1 /mnt
```

Similarly, the kernel messages associated with attaching a USB DVD+RW drive to that same system are the following:

```
kernel: usb 4-2: new high speed USB device using ehci_hcd and address 4
kernel: Initializing USB Mass Storage driver...
kernel: scsi2 : SCSI emulation for USB Mass Storage devices
kernel: usbcore: registered new driver usb-storage
kernel: USB Mass Storage support registered.
kernel:   Vendor: _NEC      Model: DVD+RW ND-1100A   Rev: 1.A3
kernel:   Type:    CD-ROM                             ANSI SCSI
revision: 00
kernel: sr0: scsi3-mmc drive: 40x/40x writer cd/rw xa/form2 cdda tray
kernel: sr 2:0:0:0: Attached scsi generic sg0 type 5
```

In this sample output, the first seven lines have to do with the USB and SCSI drivers loaded to access the USB DVD+RW drive. Again, the last two are the interesting ones. These state that the drive is associated with both /dev/sr0 and /dev/sg0. Looking at these device nodes using ls -l, we can see that one is a block device (/dev/sr0), while the other is a character device (/dev/sg0) that can be used to read any media in the drive directly.

As you can see from this section, the kernel messages can be very useful in identifying both devices that have been newly attached and the devices associated with them. For information about a more user-friendly tool that can help you get the same information, see the last section in this chapter entitled "Examining and Troubleshooting Devices Graphically."

Adding Internal Disks and CD/DVD Drives

This section explains how to add new internal drives to your systems. The most common types of hard drives found in desktop and laptop PC systems today are EIDE/ATA (Enhanced Integrated Drive Electronics/Advanced Technology Attachment) and SATA (Serial Advanced Technology Attachment) drives. Because of the popularity of SATA drives, EIDE/ATA drives are also often known as PATA (Parallel Advanced Technology Attachment) drives, which highlights the basic difference between these two types of drives (parallel vs. serial) and also delivers a nicely parallel acronym at the same time. SCSI (Small Computer System Interface) hard drives are another possibility, but are much less common in desktop systems, though they are still often used in server systems. Most CD and DVD drives are EIDE/ATA drives, using a standard referred to as ATAPI, though SCSI CD and DVD drives are also available.

To add any of these drives internally to your system, you will have to shut down the system and remove its side cover to give you access to the motherboard and to the portions of the case where hard drives can be mounted, which are usually referred to as *drive bays*.

The next few sections explain how to add extra drives of these various types to your system, how to identify the device nodes associated with those drives when you reboot your system, and provide an overview of partitioning and creating filesystems on these devices.

Adding EIDE/ATA Drives

Once your system is turned off and open, locate the IDE cables that are attached to the EIDE interfaces on your motherboard (or, in rare cases, to an IDE or EIDE controller card). IDE cables are flat, 40-pin ribbon cables with two flat, notched connectors near one end and a similar connector at the other end. Most PCs have two IDE interfaces, known as primary (IDE-1) and secondary (IDE-2). The cable from each IDE interface can be attached to a maximum of two hard or CD/DVD drives. If two drives are attached to a single cable, they must be configured as master and slave drives by connecting pins known as *jumpers* that are located on the back or bottom of the hard drive or CD-ROM drive. *Master* is the term used for the first drive on an IDE interface; *slave* is the term used for the second drive on the IDE interface.

To add a new drive to your system, you must set the jumper (or jumpers) on the new drive so that it does not conflict with any existing drive on a given IDE interface in your system. To do so, you must know how the current drives are connected. You can determine how the existing hard drive(s) and CD/DVD drive(s) are connected in one of two ways: automatically (by checking the BIOS settings on your system) or manually (by simply checking the connections and jumpers on the existing drives). Because you've (hopefully) already turned the PC off and the ways of collecting information from a PC BIOS and Macintosh or SPARC boot monitor differ, we'll focus on just looking at the cables and jumpers.

By tracing cables and examining jumpers, you can manually identify how the drives are connected. To do so, follow each of the IDE cables from your motherboard back to any hard drives or CD/DVD drives connected to them. The hard drive that your PC boots from is known as the *boot drive*, and is usually connected as the master on the first IDE interface on your system. If your CD/DVD drive is connected to the same IDE cables as your hard drive, it is probably jumpered as the slave on the primary IDE interface (IDE-1). If your CD-ROM drive is connected to your other IDE cable (IDE-2), it is probably jumpered as the master on that interface.

> **TIP** If there are already two devices attached to an IDE interface and your PC was working correctly before, skip that IDE interface — it's already fully populated and correctly configured.

Once you know how your current drives are connected, you can proceed to jumper your new drive so that it does not conflict with existing drives in your system. A guide to the jumpers on your hard drive that will cause the drive to be recognized as a master or slave drive is usually printed on the top of the hard drive.

> **TIP** Be careful when reading the jumper information; though they are usually written from left to right, just as the jumpers are physically located on the hard drive, some jumper settings are listed relative to a jumper key, which is a single pin on the left or right side of the hard drive jumpers.

After you jumper your new drive, mount it in a drive bay, attach it to the selected IDE cable in your system, and provide power to the drive by connecting it to one of your system's power feeds. At this point, you can power up the system, boot into Linux, and then follow the instructions in the section later in this chapter entitled "Locating, Partitioning, and Formatting New Drives." If you have problems booting your system after adding a new drive, see the section entitled "Troubleshooting Boot Problems After Adding New Drives" later in this chapter.

> **TIP** The most common source of problems when adding a new EIDE/ATA drive to an existing system is jumpering it incorrectly. If a new drive is jumpered to be the same (master or slave) as an existing drive, your system will usually not be able to see either drive. If you are using a PC rather than a Macintosh, you can verify that the new drive is jumpered, attached, and detected correctly by entering the BIOS immediately after rebooting the PC and examining the primary and secondary IDE interfaces.

Adding SATA Drives

SATA drives are much easier to attach and use than EIDE/ATA or SCSI drives, primarily because no jumpering is required. SATA drives are automatically identified by your system based on the number of the SATA port that they are attached to. Most motherboards with SATA support have either two or four SATA ports that feature the small L-shaped SATA connector in their center. Stand-alone SATA controllers are also available that typically provide four SATA ports, but can provide many more.

SATA has many advantages over traditional EIDE/ATA drives (which I'll call PATA drives in the rest of this section). First and foremost, each SATA drive has a separate cable connecting it to the controller, reducing the shared cable, master/slave model used by PATA drives. Though performance is approximately the same between SATA II and PATA drives, the dedicated connection and controller for each SATA drive can provide higher overall throughput in disk-intensive environments. SATA cables can be up to 39 inches long, while PATA cables are supposed to be limited to 19 inches. The fact that SATA cables are much smaller than PATA ribbon cables makes them easier to route aesthetically within the tight confines of many computer cases. And finally, the biggest advantage of SATA over PATA drives is that SATA drives can be hot-swapped, which makes them eminently suitable for use in RAID or other environments with 24x7 availability requirements.

To add another SATA drive to your system, simply mount it in an available drive bay, connect it to an available SATA port and provide power to the drive by connecting either a traditional power connector or a special SATA power connector, depending on the drive that you're using. At this point, you can power up the system, boot into Linux, and then follow the instructions in the section later in this chapter entitled "Locating, Partitioning, and Formatting New Drives." If you have problems booting your system after adding a new drive, see the section entitled "Troubleshooting Boot Problems After Adding New Drives" later in this chapter.

TIP Some motherboards provide two different sets of SATA ports, one set for hardware RAID support and another set of normal SATA ports. Do not use the hardware RAID SATA ports unless you're sure that the hardware RAID controller is well-supported under Linux and you're sure that you want to use hardware RAID. I usually prefer Linux software RAID to Linux hardware RAID because hardware RAID disk layouts are controller-specific. This means that if your motherboard fails, you will have to replace it with an identical motherboard or another with the same hardware RAID controller. In most cases, you will not be able to use that RAID set with a different hardware RAID controller.

Adding SCSI Drives

Alas, poor SCSI, I knew thee well. SCSI drives have long been the traditional drive of choice for RAID boxes or in systems with 24x7 availability requirements. The primary reasons for this are high performance (SCSI drives are still faster than current SATA II drives), SCSI's traditional support for hot-swapping, and higher quality control (some manufacturers even offer longer warranties for SCSI drives for this reason). The downside is that SCSI drives are substantially more expensive than today's SATA II drives, which offer the same hot-swap capabilities. Some people would rather fight than switch — your call. Traditionally, only very high-end motherboards feature integrated SCSI controllers — SCSI controllers in most systems are stand-alone SCSI controller cards.

SCSI connectors and controllers depend on the version of the SCSI standard that they conform to and the number of drives that they can support. Various types of SCSI connectors have evolved over the years, which are roughly associated with different versions of the SCSI standard and are specifically associated with different performance characteristics. The most common of connectors are Centronics-style parallel and IDC-50 connectors (typically associated with 8-bit SCSI-1 drives), DB-50 connectors (typically associated with 8-bit Fast SCSI-2 drives), and DB-68 connectors or SCA-80 (typically associated with 16-bit,

Fast/Wide SCSI-3). SCSI-1 and SCSI-2 controllers support up to seven drives per controller, while SCSI-3 and later SCSI controllers support up to 15 drives per controller.

Each SCSI drive in a system must be uniquely identified by setting it to a unique ID number. In most cases, you must set one or more jumpers on the drive to indicate its ID, but if you have more money than I do and are using a multiport SCSI controller, that controller may identify each drive based on the port that it is connected to. The last SCSI drive in a chain (i.e., drives that are installed sequentially, with each cabled to the next) must also be terminated, though this is done automatically by some drives and SCSI controllers.

To add another SCSI drive to your system, set it to a unique ID if necessary, mount it in an available drive bay, connect it to your SCSI controller or to the next SCSI drive in a chain, and provide power to the drive by connecting a traditional power connector. At this point, you can power up the system, at which point you should see the BIOS on your SCSI controller identify the IDs on all connected SCSI drives. Once you boot into Linux, you can follow the instructions in the section later in this chapter entitled "Locating, Partitioning, and Formatting New Drives." If you have problems booting your system after adding a new drive, see the following section.

Troubleshooting Boot Problems After Adding New Drives

It is common that adding a new hard drive to your system will prevent it from booting immediately. Much of this has to do with settings in your computer's BIOS or other boot environment that enumerate the hard drives that are available and tell it which order to try various disks and interfaces in order to boot. The next few sections discuss a few common problems and how to resolve them.

Changes to BIOS Hard Disk and Boot Device Priority Settings

Most BIOS menus feature a "Boot" or "Boot Settings" menu or screen that contains entries that lead to configuration screens for Hard Disk Drives and Boot Device Priority. The Hard Disk Drives screen usually enumerates all of the hard drives in your system. Frequently, the first hard drive listed is the first that can be identified on the Boot Device Priority screen. Make sure that the first hard drive in this list is the drive that actually contains your operating system. Next, make sure that the hard drive that contains your operating system is actually listed in the Boot Device Priority screen, and that the entries on this screen appear in the right order. Many Boot Device Priority screens only provide three or four slots for possible boot devices, and I usually squander the first two of these for "Floppy Disk" and "CD-ROM" boot devices. Whatever boot device order you prefer, make sure that the hard drive that contains your operating system is present in this list, and appears in the right sequence.

Problems After Adding IDE Drives to a SATA System

Most systems are configured to try to boot from IDE drives before SATA disks. If you have added IDE disks to a system that formerly only contained SATA drives, make sure that the sequence in which your system tries to boot from different disks is correct. I had a humorous experience a while ago when adding some old IDE disks to one of my SATA systems, because I hadn't wiped the IDE disks. I'd forgotten that one of them contained an older Linux installation, and was quite surprised when my Ubuntu system suddenly booted SUSE.

Problems Related to SATA Drive Name Changes

Adding SATA drives to an existing system can temporarily cause boot problems for various reasons, the most amusing of which is because of how SATA drives are detected and named. SATA disks not only use SCSI emulation (and thus have names beginning with /dev/sd), but the letter that follows /dev/sd in their names is assigned based on the sequence number of the specific SATA port that they are attached to. If whoever built your system was careful, your primary SATA disk will be attached to SATA port 1, and thus will always be assigned the name `/dev/sda`. If whoever built your system wasn't so careful and attached your boot drive to SATA port 4, your system will boot fine with a single drive, but adding another SATA drive will cause that drive to be assigned the name `/dev/sda`, and your existing SATA drive will be called `/dev/sdb`. Adding more than one new SATA drive will continue to demote the name of your original SATA disk. This generally confuses both the BIOS, as described in the previous paragraph, and certainly confuses the boot loader used by Ubuntu systems, GRUB.

If you encounter this problem, there are two possible solutions:

- Open up your system again and connect your original drive to the first SATA port on your motherboard. This will guarantee that it will always be named `/dev/sda`. You may still have to change the BIOS settings, but you won't have to modify anything in your drive's boot configuration files.

- Change the boot settings used by the Linux GRUB boot loader to reflect the new name of your drive.

The first option is almost always preferable unless you have a very good reason for simply modifying the GRUB boot settings. If you insist on doing the second, and modifying GRUB, see the following section.

Changing GRUB Boot Loader Information

If you need to change the GRUB boot loader's idea of the root partition on your system, first correct the boot order of the disks in your BIOS as described in the section earlier in the chapter entitled "Changes to BIOS Hard Disk and Boot Device Priority Settings." This will enable your system to begin to boot from your existing hard drive, which will almost certainly fail once GRUB tries to mount its root filesystem, which is probably identified with a name such as `/dev/sda1`, which is still the right partition but is now located on a disk with a different name. To temporarily modify GRUB's boot settings to work around this problem, you must do the following:

1. Press Escape during the boot process to display the GRUB menu.
2. Press "E" to display the boot commands associated with your default boot entry.
3. Use the arrow keys to highlight the line beginning with the word "kernel."
4. Press "E" to edit that entry, and use the arrow keys and the backspace or delete keys to change the name of the partition identified as the root partition (through the `root=` keyword). For example, if your disk was originally `/dev/sda` but is now `/dev/sdd`, the root partition is probably still identified as `/dev/sda1`. Change this to `/dev/sdd1` and press Return to return to the boot options screen.

> **TIP** If your system already had multiple disks and you were normally mounting partitions from all of them, your system may not come up into multiuser mode correctly because any partition names in your `/etc/fstab` file will be wrong. You may also want to temporarily add the word `single` to the end of the GRUB kernel entry to bring up the system in single-user mode so that you can correct the names of the partitions in `/etc/fstab`.

5. Press "B" to boot using your modified GRUB boot options.

Once your system comes up correctly, you can then use a text editor to permanently modify the file `/boot/grub/emnu.lst`, which is GRUB's configuration file. You should not only modify the boot settings for your default GRUB boot selection, but you should also modify the template values in this file that are used to prepare a new entry each time a new kernel is installed on your system.

You should also check the contents of the `/etc/fstab` file on your system and make sure that it reflects the current disk names in use on your system. It is not uncommon for a system to come up without swap space and identify its root partition incorrectly (in commands such as `df`) because entries in the `/etc/fstab` file are incorrect. During the boot process, the root partition is already mounted by the time the `/etc/fstab` file is used to mount other disks.

Problems After Adding SATA Drives to a SCSI System

The last common problem that you may encounter is when adding SATA drives to a system that boots from SCSI disks. Because SATA drives use SCSI emulation, they are assigned names in the same family as the names of actual SCSI devices. SATA disks are also named before SCSI disks during the kernel boot process. The combination of these two facts means that adding one or more SATA disks will cause your SCSI disk to be renamed. For example, if your system was configured to boot from the real SCSI disk `/dev/sda` and you add two SATA drives, the name of your SCSI disk is now `/dev/sdc`. This will lead to the same sort of BIOS and GRUB boot loader problems discussed in the section entitled "Problems Related to SATA Drive Name Changes," but you will have to solve them using the solution described in the section entitled "Changing GRUB Boot Loader Information." See that section for an explanation of how to modify your GRUB settings and resolve this sort of problem.

Locating, Partitioning, and Formatting New Drives

After rebooting your system to locate new internal drives, you'll probably want to use the storage that those new disks provide. This requires that you identify the Linux device nodes associated with them.

The next three sections explain how to use graphical and command-line utilities to figure out what drives are attached to your system and the partitions they contain, how to partition those drives, and how to format those partitions.

NOTE   At the time that this book was written, the graphical Disks utility did not support disk partitioning, and no other graphical partition management utility was provided as part of a default Ubuntu installation. Future releases of the Disks utility should support partitioning, and there is already an ongoing discussion of providing the partition management utility (`partman`) used during the Ubuntu installation process as a package that can also be installed and used in a running system (i.e., not just during installation). Unfortunately, neither of these options is available now, so you will need to partition disks using the command-line `fdisk` utility discussed in the section entitled "Using Command-Line Utilities to Partition and Format Drives."

Using the Graphical Disks Utility to Examine and Format Drives

Ubuntu's Disks utility, installed as a part of a default Ubuntu Linux installation, provides a graphical view of all of the storage devices that are currently installed on your system. This makes it easy for you to determine basic information about their capacity, any partitions that they contain, and the Linux device nodes associated with the device and each partition. It also enables you to format floppy disks and existing hard disk partitions.

Select the System ⇨ Administration ⇨ Disks menu item to start the Disks utility. After you are prompted for your administrative password, the dialog shown in Figure 23.16 displays.

FIGURE 23.16

Device property information in the Disks tool

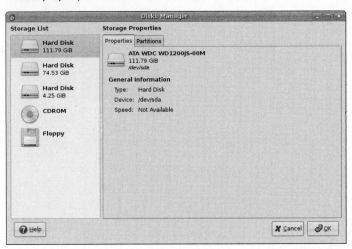

The pane at the left displays all of the available storage devices that are currently detected on your system. Selecting any of these devices in the left pane displays device property information in the pane at the right. This information includes the storage capacity of the device and the Linux device node through which that device can be accessed. Once any device is selected, clicking the Partitions tab displays a summary of how that storage device is currently partitioned, as shown in Figure 23.17.

FIGURE 23.17

Device partitioning information in the Disks tool

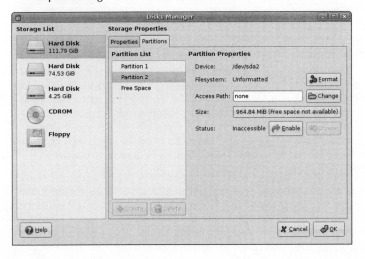

To see information about a specific partition, select its name from the list in the right pane. For example, Figure 23.17 shows information about the partition /dev/sda2, identifying it as currently being unformatted. To format a selected partition, click Format. A dialog like the one shown in Figure 23.18 displays.

FIGURE 23.18

Formatting a selected partition in the Disks tool

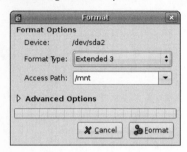

The dialog shown in Figure 23.18 enables you to specify several different types of information about the partition:

- **Format Type:** The type of filesystem that you want to create on the selected partition. Choices are Extended 2, Extended 3, JFS, Memory Swap, ReiserFS, Windows Virtual FAT, and XFS.

- **Access Path:** The point at which the formatted partition can be mounted on the system. This information is stored when you format the partition, but is not actually applied unless you click Enable in the dialog shown in Figure 23.17.

To proceed with the formatting, click Format in the dialog shown in Figure 23.18. This displays a warning dialog, asking if you are sure that you want to format the partition. Click Yes to proceed or click No to return to the dialog shown in Figure 23.17.

Once you are finished examining or formatting the storage devices in your system, click OK in the dialogs shown in Figure 23.16 or 23.17 to exit the Disks utility.

Using Command-Line Tools to Identify Drives and Partitions

The df command provides an easy way to examine all of the disk partitions and associated filesystems that are currently mounted and in use on your system. Unfortunately, commands such as df don't provide information about devices that are newly attached to your system (and that therefore may not contain partitions yet) or devices that are attached to your system but whose filesystems are not mounted. Luckily, Linux provides some easy ways of finding all of the storage devices on your system, regardless of whether they're formatted, partitioned, mounted, or not. You'll have to put up with a small bit of cryptic command-line magic, but you're already at least an apprentice Linux wizard, right? You just put a new drive in your system!

The easiest way to determine the device nodes associated with the storage devices in your system is to look through the kernel boot messages for patterns that match the strings discussed earlier in this chapter in the section entitled "Troubleshooting Automatic Device Detection." That section suggested looking through the system's log files for messages associated with hotplug events, which are the device detection and removal events that are processed by the kernel when a system is running. Luckily, you can also look through the in-memory portion of this message log using a command called dmesg. Because you know that IDE devices have names that begin with hd and are followed by some other letter, and that SATA and SCSI devices have names that begin with sd and are followed by some letter, you can use a pattern such as '[hs]d[a-z]: ' to see what messages match these device names. If you don't speak Linux regular expressions fluently, the string '[hs]d[a-z]: ' means, "match any sequence of characters that begins with an 'h' or an 's', followed by the letter 'd', followed by any character between 'a' and 'z' (inclusive), followed by a colon, followed by a space." That was easy, wasn't it?

The result of searching for this string in the output of the dmesg command on a sample Ubuntu system is pretty much exactly what you'd hope for, as the following example shows:

```
$ dmesg | grep '[hs]d[a-z]: '
[  846.564436] SCSI device sda: 234441648 512-byte hdwr sectors (120034
MB)
[  846.564453] SCSI device sda: drive cache: write back
[  846.564514] SCSI device sda: 234441648 512-byte hdwr sectors (120034
MB)
[  846.564526] SCSI device sda: drive cache: write back
[  846.564531]  sda: sda1 sda2
[  846.575071] SCSI device sdb: 156299375 512-byte hdwr sectors (80025
MB)
[  846.575086] SCSI device sdb: drive cache: write back
[  846.578550] SCSI device sdb: 156299375 512-byte hdwr sectors (80025
MB)
[  846.578826] SCSI device sdb: drive cache: write back
[  846.578830]  sdb: sdb1 sdb2 < sdb5 >
[  848.272430] hdc: DVDRW 16X16X, ATAPI CD/DVD-ROM drive
[  848.952828] hdc: ATAPI 48X DVD-ROM DVD-R CD-R/RW drive, 2048kB Cache
[  852.169148] SCSI device sdc: 8910423 512-byte hdwr sectors (4562 MB)
[  852.170635] SCSI device sdc: drive cache: write back
[  852.171452] SCSI device sdc: 8910423 512-byte hdwr sectors (4562 MB)
[  852.172941] SCSI device sdc: drive cache: write back
[  852.172943]  sdc: sdc1 sdc2
```

On this system, these messages tell you that three storage devices using SCSI device naming have been found, plus an IDE/ATA CD/DVD-ROM drive that is available as /dev/hdc. The first SCSI storage device, /dev/sda, doesn't appear to contain any partitions. The second storage device, /dev/sdb, contains two physical partitions: /dev/sdb1 and /dev/sdb2, and a third virtual partition, /dev/sdb5. (This probably means that the partition /dev/sdb2 is an extended partition that contains the partition /dev/sdb5 — more about that in a moment.) The third storage device, /dev/sdc, contains two physical partitions: /dev/sdc1 and /dev/sdc2.

You can use the fdisk command and its -1 (list) option to get more detailed information about any of these storage devices. For example, fdisk provides the following information about the partitions on it:

```
$ sudo fdisk -1 /dev/sdb
Disk /dev/sdb: 80.0 GB, 80025280000 bytes
255 heads, 63 sectors/track, 9729 cylinders
Units = cylinders of 16065 * 512 = 8225280 bytes

   Device Boot    Start     End      Blocks   Id  System
/dev/sdb1    *        1    9566    76838863+  83  Linux
/dev/sdb2          9567    9729     1309297+   5  Extended
/dev/sdb5          9567    9729     1309266   82  Linux swap / Solaris
```

This shows that, as suspected, the partition /dev/sdb2 is an extended partition, which is a physical partition that can contain other, virtual partitions, and the partition /dev/sdb5 is a partition that was created inside that extended partition.

Executing the same dmesg command as shown previously on a Ubuntu laptop with only IDE storage devices shows you the following:

```
$ dmesg | grep 'hd[a-z]: '
[17179574.600000] hda: HITACHI_DK23DA-30B, ATA DISK drive
[17179576.012000] hdc: UJDA720 DVD/CDRW, ATAPI CD/DVD-ROM drive
[17179576.696000] hda: max request size: 128KiB
[17179576.708000] hda: 58605120 sectors (30005 MB) w/2048KiB Cache...
[17179576.708000] hda: cache flushes supported
[17179576.708000]  hda: hda1 hda2 < hda5 >
[17179576.768000] hdc: ATAPI 24X DVD-ROM CD-R/RW drive, 2048kB Cache,
UDMA(33)
[17179944.340000] hde: LEXAR ATA FLASH, CFA DISK drive
[17179944.676000] hde: max request size: 128KiB
[17179944.676000] hde: 1001952 sectors (512 MB) w/1KiB Cache,
CHS=994/16/63
[17179944.676000] hde: cache flushes not supported
[17179944.676000]  hde: hde1
[17179944.680000] ide-cs: hde: Vcc = 3.3, Vpp = 0.0
```

This listing shows three IDE storage devices, /dev/hda, /dev/hdc, and /dev/hde. The IDE device /dev/hda is an ATA disk drive that contains two physical partitions: /dev/hda1 and /dev/hda2, and a third virtual partition, /dev/hda5. As in the previous example, this probably means that /dev/hda2 is an extended partition that contains the partition /dev/hda5. Next, the device /dev/hdc is an ATAPI DVD-ROM CD-R/RW drive that therefore does not contain any partitions. The third device, /dev/hde, is a Flash card that contains one partition, /dev/hde1. In much the same way that SATA and USB drives look like SCSI disks to a Linux system, Flash storage devices look like IDE storage devices.

Your mind may be a bit numb after the preceding combination of arcane command-line syntax and kernel log messages, but this section has given you some extremely powerful insights into your system and the storage devices that it contains. Because one of these storage devices, the SATA drive /dev/sda in the first example in this section, didn't contain any partitions, it is still quite useless to your system. The next section explains how to partition and format a newly-added disk.

Using Command-Line Utilities to Partition and Format Drives

Chapter 4 introduced basic computer system terms such as disks, partitions, and filesystems. As discussed in this chapter, you cannot use the storage on a disk until it has been partitioned and each of those partitions has been formatted for use, typically as a filesystem. This section explains how to actually do that using the command-line commands fdisk, mkfs, and (occasionally) mkswap. These commands do the following:

- fdisk: Creates and manipulates partitions on a specified disk. We all have our own ideas about what the *f* standards for, but it's probably *format*.

- mkfs: Creates a filesystem of a specified type on a specified partition.

- mkswap: Formats a specified partition for use as a Linux swap partition, which is a special partition that your Ubuntu system can use as virtual memory.

Once you've added a new disk to your system, the first thing that you'll want to do is partition it. The previous section used the fdisk command to simply list the available partitions on a specific storage device —

now let's actually make it do some work. The following example creates two partitions on the disk /dev/sda (actually, the layout of the partitions that you'll create is the same as that shown in Figure 23.17, earlier in this chapter).

To partition a disk using fdisk, do the following:

1. Use the sudo command to start the fdisk command, supplying the name of the disk that you want to partition as an argument, as in the following example:

```
$ sudo fdisk /dev/sda
The number of cylinders for this disk is set to 14593.
There is nothing wrong with that, but this is larger than 1024,
and could in certain setups cause problems with:
1) software that runs at boot time (e.g., old versions of LILO)
2) booting and partitioning software from other OSs
   (e.g., DOS FDISK, OS/2 FDISK)
Command (m for help):
```

The last line of the sample output is fdisk's command prompt, which shows that it is waiting for a command.

2. Use the p (print) command to display a list of any existing partitions that may already be on the disk. After all, you don't want to accidentally try to create partitions on the wrong disk or destroy any existing data. This command and its output looks like the following:

```
Command (m for help): p
Disk /dev/sda: 120.0 GB, 120034123776 bytes
255 heads, 63 sectors/track, 14593 cylinders
Units = cylinders of 16065 * 512 = 8225280 bytes
   Device Boot      Start           End      Blocks   Id  System
Command (m for help):
```

Good. As the total lack of partitions shows, this disk does not currently contain any partitions.

3. Use the n (new) command to define a new partition:

```
Command (m for help): n
Command action
   e   extended
   p   primary partition (1-4)
```

4. Entering this command prompts you for the type of partition that you want to create, either e (extended) or p (physical). Use the p command to create a physical partition:

```
p
Partition number (1-4):
```

5. Specifying that you want to create a physical partition prompts you for the number of the partitions that you want to create. Linux disks can contain only four physical partitions, one of which can be an extended partition. Create partition number 1 by entering 1:

```
1
First cylinder (1-14593, default 1):
```

6. Identifying the number of the physical partitions that you want to create prompts you for the physical disk block at which the partition begins, and displays the range of possible values (1-14593, in this case). Press Return to accept the default value of 1:

```
Using default value 1
Last cylinder or +size or +sizeM or +sizeK (1-14593, default 14593):
```

7. When creating partitions, you can define them in terms of the disk blocks at which they begin or end, or you can define them in terms of the blocks at which they begin and the size of the partition. Enter +30G to indicate that you want to create a 30GB partition:

```
Last cylinder or +size or +sizeM or +sizeK (1-14593, default 14593):
+30G
Command (m for help):
```

8. This completes the information required to create the partition, but doesn't tell you much about whether this actually succeeded. Use the p command again to list any partitions that are currently defined:

```
Command (m for help): p
Disk /dev/sda: 120.0 GB, 120034123776 bytes
255 heads, 63 sectors/track, 14593 cylinders

Units = cylinders of 16065 * 512 = 8225280 bytes
   Device Boot      Start         End      Blocks   Id  System
/dev/sda1               1        3648    29302528+  83  Linux
```

Sure enough, a 30GB partition has been defined as the partition /dev/sda1, the first partition on your disk.

> **TIP** At this point, no physical changes to the partitioning of your disk have been made. Any proposed changes are only in memory at this point, and will be discarded unless you write your changes to disk before exiting the fdisk command.

9. Repeat this process to create a second, smaller partition: No play-by-play this time — the complete sequence of prompts and commands used to do this is the following:

```
Command (m for help): n
Command action
   e   extended
   p   primary partition (1-4)
p
Partition number (1-4): 2
First cylinder (3649-14593, default 3649):
Using default value 3649
Last cylinder or +size or +sizeM or +sizeK (3649-14593, default
14593): +1G
```

10. This completes the information required to create the second partition, but again, doesn't tell us much about whether this actually succeeded. Use the p command again to list any partitions that are currently defined:

```
Command (m for help): p

Disk /dev/sda: 120.0 GB, 120034123776 bytes
255 heads, 63 sectors/track, 14593 cylinders
Units = cylinders of 16065 * 512 = 8225280 bytes

   Device Boot      Start         End      Blocks   Id  System
/dev/sda1               1        3648    29302528+  83  Linux
/dev/sda2            3649        3771      987997+  83  Linux
 Command (m for help):
```

Sure enough, you now have both a 30GB partition and a second 1GB partition.

11. Now, write these changes to disk and exit the `fdisk` command, because these examples are sufficient for my purposes in this section. You use the `w` (write) command to write partition changes to the disk and exit the `fdisk` command:

```
Command (m for help): w
The partition table has been altered!

Calling ioctl() to re-read partition table.
Syncing disks.
```

Congratulations, you've partitioned a disk. Normally, I wouldn't have left unused space on this disk, but I'm only doing this as an example, and I can always rerun `fdisk` to create additional partitions in the remaining space.

The next step is to format each defined partition, either as a filesystem or as additional swap space. To be honest, you'll very rarely create additional swap partitions after you've initially installed your system, but I want to make sure that you know how to do it just in case. 99.9% of the time, you'll be creating filesystems on the partitions of the disks that you add to your system, so that you can mount them to increase the amount of available storage on your system.

Creating a filesystem is done using the `mkfs` utility, which is actually just a wrapper for other commands that create different types of filesystems. On most Linux systems, you will be creating filesystems in any of the following formats: ext2, ext3, JFS, Reiser4, ReiserFS, Windows Virtual FAT (vfat), or XFS. These types of filesystems were explained in the section of Chapter 4 entitled "Local Filesystems: Standard and Journaling." To create any of these types of filesystem using the default options for that type of filesystem, you simply specify the type of filesystem that you want to create using the `mkfs` command's `-t` (type) option. The following example shows the command and output used to create an ext3 filesystem on the partition `/dev/sda1`:

```
$ sudo mkfs -t ext3 /dev/sda1
mke2fs 1.38 (30-Jun-2005)
Filesystem label=
OS type: Linux
Block size=4096 (log=2)
Fragment size=4096 (log=2)
3662848 inodes, 7325632 blocks
366281 blocks (5.00%) reserved for the super user
First data block=0
224 block groups
32768 blocks per group, 32768 fragments per group
16352 inodes per group
Superblock backups stored on blocks:
    32768, 98304, 163840, 229376, 294912, 819200, 884736, 1605632,
        2654208, 4096000

Writing inode tables:   224/224
Creating journal (32768 blocks): done
Writing superblocks and filesystem accounting information: done

This filesystem will be automatically checked every 25 mounts or
180 days, whichever comes first. Use tune2fs -c or -i to override.
```

That's all there is to it! You can now mount this partition temporarily by using the `mount` command, or permanently add it to the list of filesystems that will be mounted each time you boot your system. Both of these concepts were explained in Chapter 4.

The `mkswap` command enables you to format a specified partition in a special way so that it can be used as swap space for use by your system's virtual memory manager. As an example, the command used to create a swap partition on `/dev/sda2` and the output from that command are the following:

```
# mkswap /dev/sda2
Setting up swapspace version 1, size = 1011703 kB
no label, UUID=731c0f53-bf25-4f91-9ac5-73a2b5bef1eb
```

You can begin using this swap space immediately by executing the command `swapon /dev/sda2`. To add this swap space to your system permanently, add it to your system's `/etc/fstab` file, as described in Chapter 4.

Using PCMCIA Cards

PCMCIA (Personal Computer Memory Card International Association) cards are the original mechanism designed to support removable and insertable interfaces in portable computer systems. PCMCIA cards are now often just called PC Cards because no one can ever remember what the acronym means (as suggested by the optional PCMCIA expansion, "People Can't Memorize Computer Industry Acronyms").

PCMCIA cards are available that provide wired and wireless network interfaces, modems, SCSI, USB, and FireWire interfaces for computer systems that don't have them, and so on. With the 2.6 kernel used on Ubuntu systems, the traditional Linux PCMCIA support package has been integrated into the hotplug system to support the creation of appropriate device nodes when PCMCIA cards are inserted.

The primary application that can identify any PCMCIA cards inserted in your system is the `cardctl` application. To see what cards are present in your system and display summary information about them, execute the `cardctl ident` command. This will return something like the following:

```
$ cardctl ident
Socket 0:
  product info: "3Com", "Megahertz 589E", "TP/BNC LAN PC Card", "005"
  manfid: 0x0101, 0x0589
  function: 6 (network)
Socket 1:
  product info: " LEXAR ATA FLASH CARD    ", " STORM ", "TTE01"
  manfid: 0x4e01, 0x0200
  function: 4 (fixed disk)
```

This shows that I have two PCMCIA cards inserted. As in previous section, the output from the `dmesg` command, which shows the most recent kernel status and debugging messages, can help you determine if these two cards can be accessed correctly, and the devices associated with them. For example, searching the `dmesg` output for 3com shows me the following section:

```
[17179870.988000] PCMCIA: registering new device PCMCIA0.0
[17179871.248000] eth2: 3Com 3c589, bio 0x300, irq 5, hw_addr
00:00:86:58:D3:E1
[17179871.248000]   8K FIFO split 5:3 Rx:Tx, auto xcvr
[17179881.916000] eth2: no IPv6 routers present
[17179886.384000] eth2: flipped to 10baseT
```

This shows that my PCMCIA Ethernet card is now associated with the Ethernet interface eth2. I can use the standard ifconfig command with eth2 as an argument to find out the status of that interface, as in the following example:

```
$ ifconfig eth2
eth2      Link encap:Ethernet  HWaddr 00:00:86:58:D3:E1
          inet addr:192.168.6.186  Bcast:192.168.6.255
Mask:255.255.255.0
          inet6 addr: fe80::200:86ff:fe58:d3e1/64 Scope:Link
          UP BROADCAST RUNNING MULTICAST  MTU:1500  Metric:1
          RX packets:22 errors:0 dropped:0 overruns:0 frame:0
          TX packets:11 errors:0 dropped:0 overruns:0 carrier:7
          collisions:0 txqueuelen:1000
          RX bytes:3424 (3.3 KiB)  TX bytes:1878 (1.8 KiB)
          Interrupt:5 Base address:0x300
```

Similarly, the card in my other PCMCIA slot is a LEXAR ATA Flash card that I've inserted into a PCMCIA adapter. Searching the output of the dmesg command shows the following messages:

```
[17179603.088000] hde: LEXAR ATA FLASH, CFA DISK drive
[17179603.424000] ide2 at 0x3100-0x3107,0x310e on irq 3
[17179603.424000] hde: max request size: 128KiB
[17179603.424000] hde: 1001952 sectors (512 MB) w/1KiB Cache,
CHS=994/16/63
[17179603.424000] hde: cache flushes not supported
[17179603.424000]  hde: hde1
[17179603.428000] ide-cs: hde: Vcc = 3.3, Vpp = 0.0
```

This shows that the card is available as the IDE device /dev/hde, and contains one partition, /dev/hde1, which I could mount and use via the mount command.

For more information than you'll probably ever want to know about PCMCIA cards on Linux systems, see http://pcmcia-cs.sourceforge.net/ftp/doc/PCMCIA-HOWTO.html.

Adding PCI Cards

PCI cards are a slightly different animal than most of the devices I've discussed elsewhere in this chapter, because they typically provide support for other devices, such as speakers (PCI sound cards), storage devices (PCI USB, FireWire, or SCSI cards), or support for basic devices such as modems, additional serial or parallel ports, and so on. Your system must be down in order to add a PCI card, and discovering one during the boot process isn't a notable event. The information that may appear in the kernel log related to new PCI cards is the discovery of devices that are attached to them, such as a modem, serial ports, disk drives, and so on.

Nevertheless, it is useful to be able to list the PCI devices found in your system, to verify that cards have been correctly inserted and identified by the system. The command used to do this is the `lspci` command, which displays output like the following:

```
$ lspci
0000:00:00.0 RAM memory: nVidia Corporation C51 Host Bridge (rev a2)
0000:00:00.1 RAM memory: nVidia Corporation C51 Memory Controller 0
(rev a2)
0000:00:00.2 RAM memory: nVidia Corporation C51 Memory Controller 1
(rev a2)
0000:00:00.3 RAM memory: nVidia Corporation C51 Memory Controller 5
(rev a2)
0000:00:00.4 RAM memory: nVidia Corporation C51 Memory Controller 4
(rev a2)
0000:00:00.5 RAM memory: nVidia Corporation C51 Host Bridge (rev a2)
0000:00:00.6 RAM memory: nVidia Corporation C51 Memory Controller 3
(rev a2)
0000:00:00.7 RAM memory: nVidia Corporation C51 Memory Controller 2
(rev a2)
0000:00:02.0 PCI bridge: nVidia Corporation C51 PCI Express Bridge (rev
a1)
0000:00:03.0 PCI bridge: nVidia Corporation C51 PCI Express Bridge (rev
a1)
0000:00:04.0 PCI bridge: nVidia Corporation C51 PCI Express Bridge (rev
a1)
0000:00:05.0 VGA controller: nVidia Corporation C51 PCI Express Bridge
0000:00:09.0 RAM memory: nVidia Corporation MCP51 Host Bridge (rev a2)
0000:00:0a.0 ISA bridge: nVidia Corporation MCP51 LPC Bridge (rev a2)
0000:00:0a.1 SMBus: nVidia Corporation MCP51 SMBus (rev a2)
0000:00:0b.0 USB Controller: nVidia Corporation MCP51 USB Controller
(rev a2)
0000:00:0b.1 USB Controller: nVidia Corporation MCP51 USB Controller
(rev a2)
0000:00:0d.0 IDE interface: nVidia Corporation MCP51 IDE (rev a1)
0000:00:0e.0 IDE interface: nVidia Corporation MCP51 Serial ATA
Controller
0000:00:0f.0 IDE interface: nVidia Corporation MCP51 Serial ATA
Controller
0000:00:10.0 PCI bridge: nVidia Corporation MCP51 PCI Bridge (rev a2)
0000:00:10.1 0403: nVidia Corporation MCP51 High Definition Audio (rev
a2)
0000:00:14.0 Bridge: nVidia Corporation MCP51 Ethernet Controller (rev
a1)
0000:00:18.0 Host bridge: HyperTransport Technology Configuration
0000:00:18.1 Host bridge: [Athlon64/Opteron] Address Map
0000:00:18.2 Host bridge: [Athlon64/Opteron] DRAM Controller
0000:00:18.3 Host bridge: K8 [Athlon64/Opteron] Miscellaneous Control
0000:04:05.0 FireWire (IEEE 1394): VIA, Inc. IEEE 1394 Host Controller
0000:04:08.0 SCSI storage controller: LSI Logic / Symbios Logic 53c895
0000:04:09.0 Ethernet controller: 3Com Corporation 3c595 100BaseTX
[Vortex]
```

Although this output is somewhat ugly, it is easy enough to scan to determine if your new card has been detected. If it has, you should proceed to the configuration utility associated with the capability or type of device that the PCI card provides.

Examining and Troubleshooting Devices Graphically

Ubuntu provides a great graphical utility called Device Manager that enables you to browse, navigate through, and explore the hardware on your system from your Ubuntu system's point of view. Select the System ➪ Administration Device Manager menu entry to start this tool, which displays the initial dialog shown in Figure 23.19.

FIGURE 23.19

Ubuntu's Device Manager

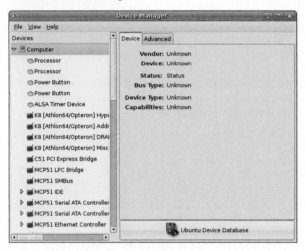

Once the Device Manager displays, you can use the pane at the left to scroll or drill down through your system, enabling you to examine any of the basic devices provided by your system or attached to any of its interfaces. As you select different devices, appropriate tabs display in the Device Manager's right pane. The right pane typically provides a general Device information tab, as shown in Figure 23.19, and an Advanced tab, as shown in Figure 23.20, which provides additional details about a selected device or interface.

FIGURE 23.20

Advanced information in the Device Manager

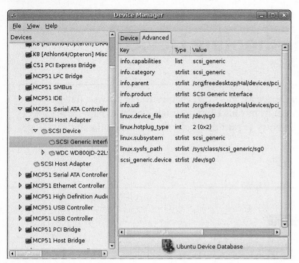

For example, Figure 23.20 shows the details of the SCSI connection established for a SATA interface to which a Western Digital hard drive is attached. This tab also lists the Linux device node associated with the interface, which can simplify locating and accessing newly attached devices.

The Device Manager also enables you to add information about your system and hardware to Ubuntu's central database of supported (and unsupported) hardware. To do this, click the Ubuntu Device Database button at the bottom of the right panel to display the dialog shown in Figure 23.21.

FIGURE 23.21

Submitting information about your system

Once this dialog displays, click Forward to begin walking through a series of dialogs that test various aspects of your system and enable you to supply comments. Submitting information about your system is not only useful to the Ubuntu project and other Ubuntu users, but it also can be personally valuable to you if you are having trouble getting a specific device working correctly. Submitting information about your system is one small way in which every Ubuntu user can contribute to the Ubuntu ecosystem of which we are all now a part.

Summary

This chapter explained how to add various types of hardware to your system, ranging from removable storage that you want to use only temporarily, to more permanently attached devices like printers, new internal hard drives, and scanners.

Chapter 24 explores how to secure your Ubuntu system. Though Linux is generally immune to most of the types of viruses, Trojans, and spyware that infest the Internet (and most Microsoft Windows systems), network security is as critical on a Linux system as it is on any other type of computer system that may be directly connected to the Internet. Hundreds of books are available that are dedicated to network and computer security, but Chapter 24 provides a basic explanation of the key concepts and concerns, explaining basic ways in which you may want to secure your system and highlighting areas that you may want to pursue further.

Chapter 24

Network Configuration and Security

Almost from the very beginning of home computing in the 1970s, personal computers have reached out to touch other types of computer systems. Long before ISPs, and before the Internet even existed, home computer fans used modems to access bulletin board systems, remote mainframe or mini-computers, and ancient content providers like Compuserve and AOL, using various terminal emulation programs to communicate with each other, transfer files, and so on. Early store-and-forward mechanisms such as the Unix-to-Unix Calling Program (UUCP) and fidonet provided great ways of disseminating files and other information across slow networks of computer systems that were networks only in the sense that they knew each other's phone numbers.

The conversion of the ARPANET to the Internet and its resultant commercialization gave birth to the notion of ISPs, commercial Internet Service Providers, who provided a mechanism for home computers to directly access the Internet, albeit through kludgey point-to-point solutions that still depended on a modem and thus provided Net surfing speeds that were only guaranteed (supposedly) to be greater than zero. Regardless, the advent of the ISP ended the concept of the PC as an asynchronous island, making it a real participant in the Internet, even if slowly.

As ISPs surfaced and became a fundamental utility for many home computer users, networking and PC hardware costs continued to drop, approaching the commodity hardware pricing normally associated with toasters and refrigerators. The reality of more and more home computer users, even in the same homes, introduced the notion of home computer networks, often stand-alone or with modems still connecting specific systems to the Internet by functioning as a 9600 or 56KB gateway to the Internet via an ISP. We all owe much to those pioneering users of home computer who were willing to access the Net and download porn though such tragically slow connections.

Broadband Ethernet, even cheaper wired network hardware, and the explosive growth of wireless networking has made networking a true reality for many home computer users. Home computer systems may now have real IP addresses and functional connection speeds to the Internet, and are also commonly members of home computer networks that share those connections to the net using mechanisms such as Native Address Translation (NAT). If you're new to networking, the first section of this chapter provides an overview of basic networking concepts and terminology.

Better networking and network access comes at a price. Ubiquitous networking gives thousands of "randoms" access to your computer system through a real IP address or Web server and other network processes. Most of them could care less, some are simply curious, and others are downright malicious. The last set gives everyone else a bad name by actively trying to break into computer systems to exploit them in some fashion. I have no problem with hackers who are simply curious about what's out there — exploration has always been a fundamental part of the human condition. Real *hackers* are the electronic equivalent of the National Geographic Society or "Star Trek," boldly going where no person has gone before. People who break into systems to damage or exploit them are *crackers* (my apologies to readers in the southern parts of the United States) who give everyone else a bad name.

Unfortunately, there are plenty of unscrupulous crackers who would love to break into your machine and damage it or turn it into some sort of zombie system, either to supposedly demonstrate their cleverness or to somehow make a buck. Sigh. Ubiquitous networking begets the easy availability of tools that enable this sort of thing. The people that use them are often so-called "script kiddies" who use existing tools to demonstrate cleverness in the same way that giving a child an Uzi demonstrates marksmanship.

The bottom line of ubiquitous networking is that security becomes everyone's job. If you live in a small town that considers taking two newspapers from the box on the corner a serious crime, locking your door at night may seem silly. Unfortunately, when you use a personal computer with network access, you are part of the big city known as the Internet. The administrators of enterprise and academic systems that require continuous access to the Internet have known this for a long time. Sadly enough, nowadays your grandmother, parents, and you have to worry about it too. Security is more of a concern today than it has ever been before, and tomorrow will just be worse.

This chapter provides a basic introduction to networking, explains the tools that Ubuntu Linux provides to graphically configure and test your network, and (most importantly) provides some general guidelines on how to secure your system to protect it as best as anyone can. There's an old saying in the IT biz that the only truly secure system is one that isn't connected to anything. Although this is true, it's also impractical. There are easy rules to follow to minimize the chances that your system will be broken into. You're already running Ubuntu Linux, which puts you miles ahead of the millions of vulnerable Windows 98, ME, and 2000 users out there.

Networking 101

Most modern computer systems can communicate with other systems and devices over a type of network called Ethernet, using the Transmission Control Protocol/Internet Protocol (TCP/IP) and Universal Data Packet (UDP) protocols. Ethernet was invented by Xerox Corporation at Xerox PARC (Palo Alto Research Center) in the early 1970s. Like most things they've invented — except for the photocopier — Xerox failed to make money from Ethernet, which was actually commercialized by many companies (like 3COM, which was founded by the inventor of Ethernet networking, Bob Metcalf, who knew a good thing when he invented it).

Until a few decades ago, "the Internet" was a fairly techie term, used only by people whose employers or academic experience offered connectivity to the Internet or its predecessor, the ARPANET. The creation and popular explosion of the World Wide Web and the advent of e-mail as a replacement for phone calls changed all that — suddenly, there was a reason for people to want (or perhaps even need) access to the Internet.

Early home Internet connectivity was primarily done through dial-up connections that emulated TCP/IP connections over dial-up lines using protocols such as Serial Line Internet Protocol (SLIP), Compressed SLIP (CSLIP), or Point-To-Point Protocol (PPP). Unless you were a serious computer geek, developer, or researcher, a home network was somewhat rare, but the advent of broadband access to the Internet through cable and telephone providers changed all that. As mentioned in the introduction to this chapter, home networks are becoming more common but most people have never needed to set one up before now. If you use a single PC, Mac, or workstation as your sole home machine, a straight connection to a cable or DSL modem works just fine. However, the instant you want to enable multiple machines to communicate over a home network, you may encounter unfamiliar terms like hubs, switches, 10-BaseT, RJ45, crossover-cables, uplink ports, packets, gateways, routers, Cat5, and a variety of others that pass for popular nouns among nerdier users. This section provides a quick overview of these terms. It tells you how to set up a simple home network and makes you comfortable with the network-related terms that are used throughout this book. For more detailed information, consult any of the hundreds of books available on home networking.

The basic element of a modern network connection is a standard Ethernet cable, which is just a length of multistrand cable with connectors on either end that enable you to connect a network card in your personal computer (or whatever type) to another network device. The most common connectors used today are plastic connectors known as RJ-45 connectors, which is a transparent plastic jack that looks like a fatter version of a standard telephone cable connector. Ethernet cables that use these connectors are often known as 10-BaseT, 100-BaseT, or even 1000-BaseT, where the numeric portion of the name indicates the speed of your network — the cables are the same. 1000-BaseT is more commonly known as gigabit Ethernet, and is the up-and-coming standard, because things tend to get faster. 10/100 Ethernet (10 megabit or 100 megabit) is the standard nowadays.

> **NOTE** You may also encounter the term 10-Base2 when researching network cards. This is an older type of 10-megabit Ethernet cabling that uses shielded Bayonet Neill-Concelman, or Baby N Connector (BNC) cables, and is not supported by most networking hardware today.

The best way to visualize the Internet or any Ethernet network is as an extremely long piece of cable to which several computers and network devices are attached. In the simplest case, you must use a device called a hub, switch, or router to attach multiple machines to an Ethernet. A *hub* is a device with multiple incoming connectors for attaching the Ethernet cables from different machines, with a single output connector that attaches it to another Ethernet device such as a cable modem, another hub, or a switch, router, or gateway. Network communications on any incoming port of the hub are broadcast to all other devices on the hub and are also forwarded through the outgoing connection. Switches are much like hubs on steroids because they keep track of how network connections between different machines are made and reserve dedicated internal circuitry for established connections. Switches are therefore both typically faster and more expensive than hubs because they do more.

Gateways and routers are similar to hubs and switches, but are designed to provide connectivity between different networks. If a machine that you are trying to connect to isn't immediately found on your local network, the request is forwarded through your gateway, which then sends it on. Network communication is done using discrete units of information that are known as *packets*. Packets contain the Internet Protocol (IP) address of the host that they are trying to contact. IP addresses are in the form of *NNN.NNN.NNN.NNN*, and are the network equivalent of a post office box, uniquely identifying a specific machine. Packets for an unknown local host are sent through your gateway. Routers are expensive, sophisticated pieces of hardware that direct network communication between multiple networks, translate packets between different network communication protocols, and limit network traffic to relevant networks so that your request to retrieve a file from a machine in your son's bedroom isn't broadcast to every machine on the Internet.

The most common way to connect machines on a home network is to use a hub or a home gateway that is connected to your cable or DSL modem. The difference between these is that a hub simply forwards packets through its outgoing connector (known as an *uplink port* because it simply links the network connections on that device with those on another, forwarding network packets to the other device and is, therefore, wired differently). A home gateway may convert internal network addresses to addresses that are compatible with the outside world before sending the information on through its outgoing or uplink connector. If you're using a hub to connect your home network to your cable or DSL modem, each machine on your home network would require an IP address that is unique on the Internet. This can be expensive, because most ISPs charge money for each unique host that can be connected to the Internet from your home at any given time. Home gateways provide a way around this because they enable your home network to use a special type of IP address, known as a nonroutable IP address, to assign unique internal network addresses. The gateway then internally translates these to appropriate external addresses if you're trying to connect to a machine on the Internet. The most common nonroutable IP addresses are in the form of 192.168.*X.Y*, where *X* and *Y* are specific to how you've set up your network.

> **TIP**   If you're really interested, you can get more information about nonroutable IP addresses and address translation in the Internet RFCs (Request for Comment) that defined them, 1597 and 1918. Use your favorite Internet search engine to find relevant information, or check out links such as `www.safety.net/sum1597.html` and `www.howstuffworks.com/nat2.htm`.

IP addresses are assigned to computer systems in two basic ways, either statically or dynamically. Static addresses are unique to your home network that are always assigned to a particular machine. Dynamic addresses are addresses that are automatically assigned to a computer system or network device when you turn it on. Most ISPs use dynamic addresses because only a limited number of IP addresses are available on the Internet. Using dynamic IP addresses enables your ISP to recycle and reassign IP addresses as people turn their machines off and on. Most dynamic IP addresses nowadays are assigned using a protocol called *Dynamic Host Configuration Protocol (DHCP)*, which fills out the network information for your system when it activates its network interface, including things like the IP address of a gateway system and the IP addresses of Distributed Name Service (DNS) servers that translate between hostnames and the IP addresses that they correspond to.

To use static addresses on your home network, you simply assign each machine a unique, nonroutable IP address from a given family of nonroutable IP addresses. For example, most of my home machines have static addresses in the form of 192.168.6.*Y*. Because I use a home gateway, I've configured it to do address translation (more specifically known as *NAT*, or *Network Address Translation*) to correctly translate between these addresses and the external IP address of my home gateway box.

If you want to use Dynamic IP addresses on a home network, one of the machines on your home network must be running a DHCP server. Most home gateways, such as those from DLink or Linksys, have built-in DHCP servers that you simply configure to hand out IP addresses from a specific range of addresses (192.168.6.240 through 192.168.6.250, in my case). Once you activate address translation on your home gateway, your gateway will route packets appropriately. Remember that your home gateway is probably getting its IP address by contacting your ISP's DHCP server, whereas hosts on your internal network will get their IP addresses from your DHCP server. Don't set up hosts on an internal network to contact your ISP's DHCP server unless you have only a single machine on your home network or want every one of your machines to be visible on the Internet. If you are using a home gateway that doesn't provide a DHCP server, want to have more control over what your DHCP server does, or are using Ubuntu Linux in an enterprise or commercial setting, you may want to set up your own DHCP server on an Ubuntu system, which is explained in Chapter 28, "Setting Up a DHCP Server."

A final aspect of networking is how your system identifies and locates specific computer systems on the Internet. This is typically done through the Domain Name Service (DNS), which is explained in the introduction to Chapter 29 and the section of that chapter entitled "Overview of DNS and BIND."

The overview in this section should have familiarized you with basic general and home networking terms and concepts. As you might expect, the Internet is knee-deep in Web sites that provide more general information about home networking. For truly detailed information about setting up and configuring a home network on a specific type of machine and operating system, see any of the hundreds of books on those topics at your local bookstore.

Manually Configuring Your Network Hardware

Configuring the network hardware on your computer system is part of the Ubuntu installation process, which requires network access in order to download the bulk of a vanilla installation of Ubuntu Linux. However, things change. You may install new network hardware, change existing hardware from relying on DHCP to using static IP addresses on your network, prioritize one interface over another in multiport machines such as laptops, or simply want to have a better understanding of how networking works or is configured on your system(s).

Ubuntu provides a convenient tool for reconfiguring existing networking interfaces and configuring new ones. Select the System ➪ Administration ➪ Networking menu item to start this tool (called `network-admin` if you want to execute it from the command line). After supplying your password, a dialog like the one shown in Figure 24.1 displays.

FIGURE 24.1

Ubuntu's networking configuration application

The contents of this dialog depend on the number and type of possible Ethernet interfaces that are available on your system. For example, Figure 24.1 shows this dialog on a system with a single Ethernet interface. By default, the networking application dialog always displays a Point-to-Point Protocol (PPP) item regardless of whether a modem is present in your system, because PPP Ethernet network connections are also possible over standard serial ports. Figure 24.2 shows the initial Networking dialog on a system where both wireless and wired Ethernet adapters are available.

FIGURE 24.2

Networking configuration on a wired/wireless system

> **TIP**   **Systems on which multiple Ethernet connections are available are quite common today. If you are using multiple Ethernet connections simultaneously, it usually only makes sense to have them connected to different network, because network routing is somewhat confusing otherwise. Systems with multiple Ethernet connections where each of these connections are attached to different networks are known as *multi-homed* systems.**

For the rest of this section, I'll use the sample system that provides both wired and wireless Ethernet interfaces, as shown in Figure 24.2, because that is a common configuration that many laptop users will recognize. Desktop computer systems typically provide a single Ethernet interface — providing multiple wired Ethernet interfaces is fairly uncommon, and is normally seen only in systems that route between multiple networks or need a separate network for applications or system development and testing.

Regardless of what the initial Networking dialog looks like on your system, you can select any of the network interfaces displayed in this dialog and click Properties to examine or modify its current configuration. Figure 24.3 shows the Properties dialog for the wireless Ethernet interface shown in Figure 24.2.

FIGURE 24.3

Configuration properties for a wireless network interface

As you can see from Figure 24.3, this dialog provides access to the primary configuration settings for a network interface. For details about using this dialog to configure a wireless interface, see the section of Chapter 25 entitled "Configuring Wireless Ethernet Interfaces."

You'll notice that this Ethernet interface is configured to use DHCP to dynamically obtain an Ethernet address, so many of the network configuration options are not active. Figure 24.4 shows this same network configuration dialog for a wired Ethernet interface that uses a static IP address.

FIGURE 24.4

Configuration properties for a network interface with a static address

Once you've defined the properties for the network interface that you want to configure, click OK to close the properties dialog. If you are not using DHCP, click the DNS tab in the Network settings dialog to display the dialog shown in Figure 24.5.

FIGURE 24.5

Identifying DNS servers

As mentioned in the "Networking 101" section of this chapter and as discussed in more detail in Chapter 29, "Setting Up a DNS Server," most systems today use Domain Name Service (DNS) servers to find out the IP addresses associated with different systems on a network. Though you and I simply want to go to www.google.com, your computer needs to know the numeric network address of that system. The dialog shown in Figure 24.5 enables you to enter the IP addresses of any DNS servers on your home network or which ones are available from your ISP. This dialog is common to all of the Ethernet interfaces on your system, so if you are configuring a second Ethernet interface, you may not need to provide this information. Also, as mentioned previously, this is usually necessary only on systems that do not get their IP addresses via DHCP, because most DHCP servers also provide the IP addresses of DNS servers as part of the general network configuration information that they provide.

NOTE Because DNS servers are the usual source of information that map IP addresses to hostnames, you can enter only IP addresses in this dialog. If you somehow specified a hostname, your system would need to use a DNS server to figure out the IP address associated with that name, which would cause a nasty chicken-and-egg loop.

Once you have entered or verified the DNS information for your network interface, click the Connections tab to return to the main Network settings dialog. You'll note that the network interface that you've just configured is identified as not being active. To activate that interface and make it available for use, click Activate. After a few seconds, the Network settings dialog should resemble the one shown in Figure 24.6, showing that your network interface is configured.

On most systems, your Network settings dialog contains only a single network interface. At this point, you'll probably want to test your new network configuration to ensure that everything is working correctly. Ubuntu provides a nice graphical tool for testing your system's networking capabilities. For information about using that tool, see the section later in this chapter entitled "Network Testing with GNOME's Network Tools."

FIGURE 24.6

FIGURE 24.6

Activating a newly configured network interface

If you are using a system with multiple network interfaces, see the next section for information about making the most of them by using different interfaces in different locations.

Manually Configuring Modem Connections

As mentioned in the previous section, all Ubuntu Linux installations include an option for establishing network connections via PPP , which is a modern way of creating a network interface that runs over a serial or modem connection. Though broadband Internet access is becoming more and more common, dial-up connections using protocols such as PPP are still the way in which most people connect to the Internet. I suspect that this will change, both because people will get tired of waiting for complex Web pages to load, and because telephone and cable companies can make a lot more money from you once you get used to the wire Internet that broadband Internet access provides. Many people, including myself, have both — I use my dial-up account primarily as a fallback whenever the cable in my suburban neighborhood goes out, but it's also generally useful for testing purposes. However, PPP accounts are also useful for portability. Until recently, many of my vacation planning sessions have included getting a free AOL CD and setting up an account so that I can read my mail and submit chapters of books like this one with minimal toll charges from whatever retro paradise my wife and I have chosen to vacation in.

NOTE My personal thanks to Jerry and Nancy Tibbett at the Aurora Inn in Bar Harbor, Maine, for being both gracious hosts and for putting in wireless broadband, thus freeing me from the chains of the 60-foot telephone cable I have had to carry to many other vacation spots. To quote Arnold, "I'll be back!"

At any rate, PPP connections to the Internet via a modem are still very useful in many cases. My first Linux systems required me to write a little script, connect to my ISP, sacrifice a chicken, and hope for the best. Both protocols and ISP support have improved since then. Ubuntu's Network settings utility makes it just as easy to configure a PPP connection as it is to set up a physical network interface.

To configure a dial-up PPP connection to a network, select the Modem Connection item shown in Figures 24.1 and 24.2 and click Properties. The dialog shown in Figure 24.7 displays.

FIGURE 24.7

The initial dialog for configuring a dial-up connection

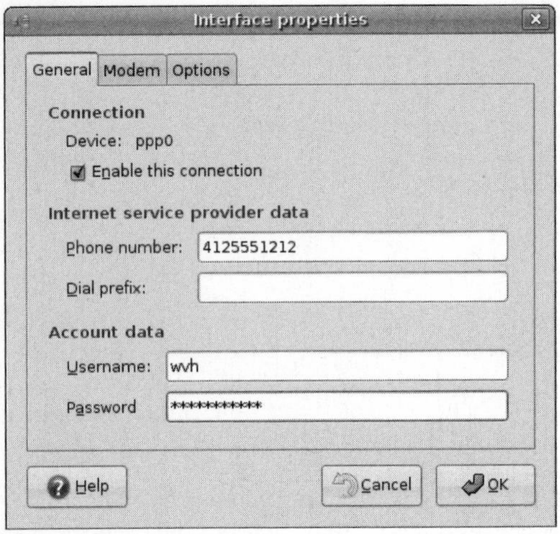

Select the Enable this connection checkbox and fill in the other fields. The content of these fields depends on your ISP. Next, select the Modem tab to display the dialog shown in Figure 24.8.

FIGURE 24.8

Configuring your modem

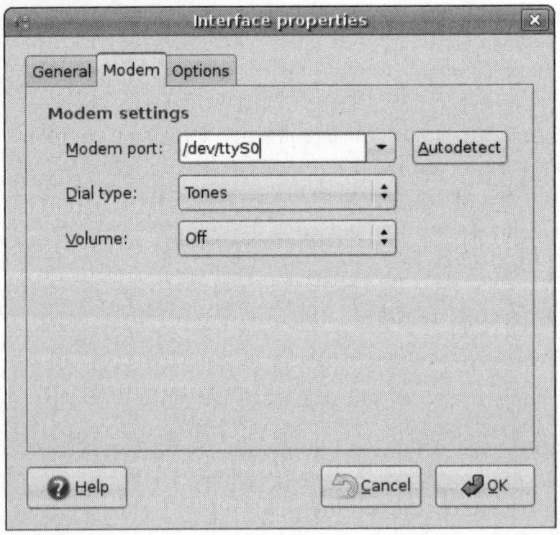

Most modem connections use the first serial port on a Linux system, /dev/ttyS0, as their modem connection, but this varies across machines and modems. To automatically detect your system's modem, connect your computer's modem port to a telephone connector and click Autodetect. This probes a standard set of modem interfaces and selects the one on which a telephone carrier is detected. Most people usually want to leave the Dial type and Volume settings as is, but you can click on either of them to display a drop-down menu that shows other options. Next, click the Options tab to display the dialog shown in Figure 24.9.

FIGURE 24.9

Setting PPP options

The first two options in this dialog are preselected to ensure that your system uses the PPP connection as its default route to the Internet and that DNS information is retrieved from your ISP. I typically also select the third one, which tells the system to try to reestablish the connection if the local phone company drops the connection or can't connect in the first place. Many ISPs use large pools of modems, but have even larger pools of customers. Depending on your ISP, it may be necessary to try to connect a few times before a modem to which you can successfully establish a connection is available.

One you've finished configuring your PPP connection, click OK to close the configuration dialog and redisplay dialogs like the ones shown in Figures 24.1 and 24.2. To activate your PPP connection, simply click Activate and, if all goes well and your ISP has a free modem, you're on the Net!

Defining and Using Multiple Network Configurations

As mentioned earlier, if you're lucky enough to be using a machine with multiple network interfaces, you really don't want to have multiple Ethernet adaptors available on the same network at the same time. This can easily confuse your system when it tries to figure out which interface to use when sending information to that network. The dialogs shown in Figures 24.3 and 24.4 configure interfaces that are on separate networks, so this isn't a problem in my default configuration.

However, having simultaneous access to multiple networks from a single computer system is fairly rare. More commonly, you will either want your system to be on different networks when it is in different locations (home and office, for example), or to use different network interfaces when you are using your system in different locations. Wired Ethernet interfaces are much faster than wireless Ethernet interfaces, so if you are using a laptop with both types of Ethernet interfaces, you'll want to switch to your wired interface whenever possible.

As discussed in the last section of Chapter 25, "Smart Interface Management with Network Manager," a tool called the Network Manager that will do this for you is available from the Synaptic repositories. However, at the time that this book was written, I've had limited success using this application. A similar tool, called whereami, can also be used to do this for you. (See www.ubuntuforums.org/showthread.php?t=24994 for more information about whereami.)

Automatic network reconfiguration is convenient, but can be tricky to set up and, frankly, can be a pain unless you're a networking guru and know every networking buzzword around. Ubuntu's networking dialog makes it easy for you to do this for yourself by defining multiple networking configurations, known as *locations*, which you can easily switch whenever necessary. As described in this section, switching locations is a manual process, but it is also an empirical one that requires no configuration beyond setting up the networking interfaces correctly and creating locations that correctly enable the one that you want to use.

Ubuntu's Network settings tool simplifies defining combinations of network configuration settings on your available network interfaces and then saving them with a unique name, known as a location.

The first step in creating a location is to configure all of your available network interfaces as they would be when your system is in a specific physical location, being used in a certain way. Next, click the Location drop-down menu at the top of the Network settings dialog to display the menu shown in Figure 24.10.

FIGURE 24.10

Creating a new location from the Location menu

Select the Create location menu item, as shown in Figure 24.10. A dialog displays, prompting you for a name for this specific combination of configured/unconfigured network interfaces, as shown in Figure 24.11.

FIGURE 24.11

Entering the name of your new location

Enter a Location name that reflects how and where you anticipate using this network configuration combination, and click OK to save this configuration combination.

In the future, whenever you want to activate this particular combination of network configuration settings, all you have to do is to select the System ➪ Administration ➪ Networking menu item, enter your password, and then select this location from the Location drop-down menu.

TIP Creating new locations doesn't change your existing default networking configuration; it merely adds named combinations to the Locations menu. Once you select a new location, there is no easy way to return to your system's default settings. Therefore, if you're going to use multiple locations, it's a good idea to define a location named Default, which is just a clone of your system's default configuration. You can then return to your system's default settings at any time by selecting that location.

Network Testing with GNOME's Network Tools

To maintain its tradition of easy graphical network tools, Ubuntu Linux also provides a convenient graphical tool that simplifies examining the current configuration of any of your network interfaces. Ubuntu provides GNOME's Network Tools application to give you a graphical display of network configuration information, as well as easy graphical access to a variety of network tools. Select the System ➪ Administration ➪ Network Tools menu item to start the Network Tools application. After supplying your password, you will see a dialog like the one shown in Figure 24.12.

By default, the Network Tools application shows information about your system's loopback interface. To see information about a specific interface, click the Network device drop-down menu and select the Ethernet interface that you're interested in. Figure 24.12 actually shows information about the primary physical Ethernet interface, eth0, on one of my test systems.

The easiest and fastest way to identify the current configuration of one of your Ethernet interfaces will probably always be to run the `ifconfig interface-name` command in an `xterm` or GNOME Terminal window. Figure 24.13 shows the output of the `ifconfig` command examining the Ethernet interface eth0 on a different system, as shown in a GNOME Terminal window.

Information about eth0 in the Network Tools application

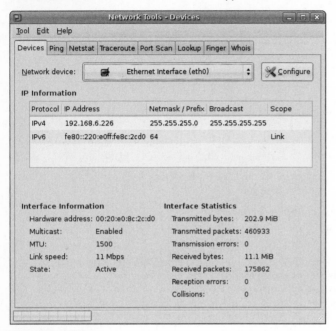

Command-line information about an Ethernet interface

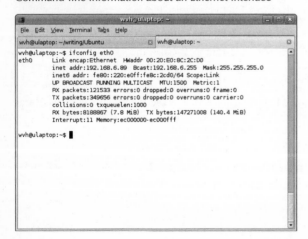

As you can see, the text display of Ethernet interface information provided by the `ifconfig` command still requires a certain amount of interpretation when compared to the friendlier display of information shown in Figure 24.12.

In addition to a more readable display of basic network configuration information, the Network Tools application supports the graphical display of information produced by several standard network utilities, which traditionally operate only in text mode. The tabs provided in the Network Tools application, along with the purpose of each tab, are the following from left to right:

- **Devices:** Displays configuration and traffic summary information for each available network interface on the system. This corresponds to the information provided by the traditional Linux/Unix command-line `ifconfig` application.

- **Ping:** Displays connectivity and availability information by sending packets to a specified host or IP address, and displays elapsed time and success/failure information. This corresponds to the information provided by the traditional Linux/Unix command-line `ping` application.

- **Netstat:** Displays status information about all active and available TCP and UDP network ports on the system. This corresponds to the information provided by the traditional Linux/Unix command-line `netstat` application.

- **Traceroute:** Displays the systems through which communication to a specified host pass and the time required for each intersystem communication, known as a *hop*. This corresponds to the information provided by the traditional Linux/Unix command-line `traceroute` application.

- **Port Scan:** Displays information about available ports and services on a specified remote machine. This roughly corresponds to the information provided by the traditional Linux/Unix command-line `nmap` application.

- **Lookup:** Displays IP address information and available DNS aliases for a specified system. This roughly corresponds to the information provided by the traditional Linux/Unix command-line `nslookup` or `host` applications.

- **Finger:** Displays any available personal information about a specific user or a specified host. This corresponds to the information provided by the traditional Linux/Unix command-line `finger` application. Few hosts provide this information any longer.

- **Whois:** Displays information about the registrant and technical contact for a specified Internet domain. This corresponds to the information provided by the traditional Linux/Unix command-line `whois` or `bwhois` applications.

As an example of the type of information and display provided by the Network Tools application, Figure 24.14 shows DNS hostname lookup information as shown on its Lookup tab for the host `www.google.com`.

FIGURE 24.14

Graphical display of DNS name lookup

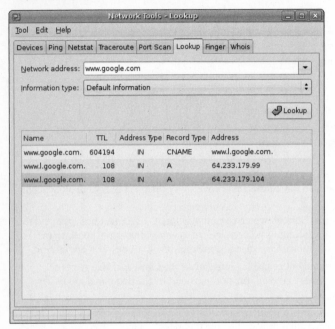

Tips for Securing Your System

System security is an open-ended topic because it has so many different aspects. These include physical security, login authentication, file and filesystem protections, and so on. Entire books have been written about security topics, and more are doubtless on the way. As mentioned in the introduction to this chapter, security in all forms will become an ever-increasing concern because of the increasing ubiquity of networking and the increasing availability of easy-to-use tools for probing, exploring, and breaking into remote machines.

The following are some specific suggestions for increasing the security of your system on a network. As you'd expect, these include some aspects of other security topics but also have their own unique concerns:

- If you are using an off-the-shelf home gateway, change the password before you put it into service. You should also change the name of the authenticated user if possible. If I had a nickel for how many systems have been broken into because people didn't change default passwords, I wouldn't even know how many nickels I had because most of these break-ins go unnoticed.

- Disable any unnecessary services on your system. You can use the Network Tools Port Scan tab to identify ports on your system that are listening from requests for services. Disable any services that you are not using through a tool such as the Boot Up Manager, which was discussed in the section of Chapter 19 entitled "Optimizing the Ubuntu Boot Process."

- Remove accounts for any users that are no longer using your system. This includes system accounts that were created for use by or with services that you are no longer running on your system.

- Always keep your system up to date using the Ubuntu Update Manager. Patches to system and application software are released for a (good) reason.

- Monitor important system log files regularly. The /var/log/messages and /var/log/syslog files can be an important source of information about who is trying to break into your system, and how.

- Change your password regularly. Ubuntu's dependence on the sudo command rather than the traditional root account for system administration tasks is a useful obfuscation, but your dedicated cracker in Beijing often doesn't have anything better to do than try and try again.

As mentioned previously, security is your responsibility. Some interesting applications are available to test and probe your own system, which can be both educational and useful. My long-term favorites are:

- chrootkit: Checks for "root kits," which is the term for precompiled sets of hacked applications that are often installed on systems that have been broken into. These root kits both make it easier for a cracker to get into your system again and also collect additional login/password information from a cracked system.

- nmap: Probes network connectivity on your machine and identifies potential problem points.

As you might expect, both of these applications are available in the Ubuntu repositories and can easily be installed on your system using apt-get, aptitude, or the Synaptic Package Manager.

Installing a Firewall

Firewall is the term used to describe a system that sits between one or more computer systems and monitors and manages network traffic. Just as with the firewall in your automobile, which prevents a fire in the engine compartment from proceeding into the passenger compartment and incinerating its occupants, a network firewall is intended to prevent malicious, spurious, or unnecessary network traffic from moving through it. Many firewalls serve multiple functions, also performing services such as Network Address Translation (NAT), but their primary purpose is to protect against network attacks and other unwelcome intrusions.

On modern Linux systems, firewalling is typically done using kernel modules that support a packet filtering framework known as netfilter, and an associated interface and user-space command known as iptables. *Packet filtering* refers to the ability to analyze network packets and perform various actions based on their source, destination, type, or other information that they contain. Because support for packet filtering is built into the Linux kernel, a Linux system that is directly connected to the Internet can serve as its own firewall, monitoring and managing network traffic before that traffic actually gets to any daemons or network-aware processes that it is running. Of course, a dedicated device or Linux system can also serve as a firewall, and many vendors sell prepackaged solutions that do just that. The fact that many of these off-the-shelf systems run Linux and use the netfilter/iptables mechanism to implement their firewalling solutions is just proof of the power of the Linux kernel's built-in support for packet filtering.

Whether or not an Ubuntu system actually requires a firewall is a hot debate topic among Ubuntu fans. Standard Ubuntu Desktop installations do not expose any open ports to an outside network, so there are no network ports that need to be protected. This is not true, of course, for Ubuntu server systems that expose ports for services such as DNS, e-mail, SSH, a Web server, and so on, so a firewall is always a good idea for any server system.

> **TIP** If you are using your Ubuntu system in an environment that is already protected by a firewall, you probably do not need to set up a firewall on your system. You should, however, make sure that the firewall that your system is located behind is actually doing the right thing by checking with the manufacturer, your IT group in a business or academic environment, or your Internet Service Provider. Just because a box has "Firewall" printed on it doesn't mean that it is actually doing anything.

As far as Ubuntu desktop systems go, you will probably find yourself opening up some ports on a desktop installation as you use your Ubuntu system over time, and a `netfilter/iptables` firewall introduces very little overhead on a desktop system, so I suggest that you always install at least a simple firewall. This way, if you subsequently increase the exposure of your system by opening ports, the firewall will already be in place. You may want to revisit your initial firewall implementation in the future, but you will at least have some protection even if you neglect firewalling in your excitement to make some new service available from your Ubuntu system. Installing a simple firewall by default is also a good idea if you are setting up systems for friends, relatives, or small businesses where you may not always have complete control over what they add to or activate on their systems.

Overview of Linux Firewalling and Packet Filtering

The packet filtering mechanism used by the current Linux kernel (2.6.xx) is a combination of a loadable kernel module framework and API called `netfilter`, and an interface and associated and user-space administrative command called `iptables`. The `iptables` interface is one of several kernel modules based on the `netfilter` framework; others include a module that handles Network Address Translation (which enables multiple machines to share one public IP address), and the module that implements and supports connection tracking. Throughout the rest of this chapter, I will collectively refer to this as `iptables`, because that is the interface that is most commonly associated with modern Linux firewalls and packet filtering.

The `iptables` interface and the `netfilter` framework are actually the fourth generation of Linux packet filtering solutions. The original Linux packet filtering implementation, `ipfw`, was liberated from BSD-based systems and was introduced in Linux by Alan Cox in the Linux 1.1 kernel, and was designed to support the creation of simple IP firewalls and routers through packet inspection and filtering. The `iwfwadmin` tool and associated `ipfw` changes, which simplified creating ipfw-based firewalls, was added to the Linux 2.0 kernel and makes up the second generation. The third generation of Linux packet filtering, consisting of a major rewrite of the entire Linux networking layer and introducing the user-space `ipchains` tool, was introduced in the 2.1 kernel series. The current `netfilter` framework and `iptables` interface were introduced in the 2.4 kernel, and have been the standard mechanism for packet filtering, network address and port translation, and general packet manipulation (often referred to as packet mangling) in the 2.6 series of Linux kernels.

Linux packet filtering works by inspecting incoming and outgoing packets and acting upon them based on filtering rules that have been loaded into the `netfilter` framework's filter table by the `iptables` command.

By default, the `iptables` command supports three default sets of rules, known as *chains*, for filtering network packets using the information stored in the `iptables` filter table. These default chains are the INPUT, OUTPUT, and FORWARD chains. The rules in the INPUT chain are used to examine and process incoming packets intended for ports on the local machine. The rules in the OUTPUT chain are for examining and processing outgoing packets that are being sent from the local machine. The rules in the FORWARD chain are used to examine and process packets that are being routed through the local machine.

Each of the default filtering rule chains can have its own set of filtering rules. You can also define other sets of rules and use them for your own purposes. Many modern Linux and other Unix-like systems come with predefined INPUT, OUTPUT, and FORWARD rule chains and automatically load them at boot time. As discussed later in this chapter, a variety of graphical and command-line software is available for all Linux distributions to make it easy to define your own packet filtering rules.

Other netfilter-based modules use packet-matching tables other than the filter table. The NAT module uses the NAT table, which contains three built-in rule chains: OUTPUT, POSTROUTING, and PREROUTING. Specialized packet manipulation operations use the mangle table, which contains pre-built FORWARD, INPUT, OUTPUT, PREROUTING, and POSTROUTING chains. The connection tracking module uses the raw table, which contains preconfigured OUTPUT and PREROUTING chains.

You must have superuser privileges to examine, create, or modify any netfilter-based rule chains. You can do this by putting `iptables` commands in a script that is executed as part of the system's boot process or by using a command such as `sudo` as a normal user to run the `iptables` commands with root privileges.

Installing and Configuring a Firewall Using Lokkit

As mentioned in the previous section, many different software packages are available to help you configure and activate a firewall on your Ubuntu system. These packages include Lokkit (the package described in this section), Firestarter, Fwbuilder, Guarddog, and many more. I think that Lokkit does a great job of setting up a basic firewall, asks the right questions, and is very easy to use, so that's the package I've chosen to discuss in this section.

Installing Lokkit

Because whether or not you need a firewall is a hot topic among Ubuntu users, a firewall isn't installed as part of any default Ubuntu installation. However, as with all software packages on Ubuntu, both the command-line software maintenance tools such as `apt-get` and `aptitude` and the Synaptic Package Manager make it easy to install a firewall creation and configuration tool. The one that I suggest installing is Lokkit, which is found in the `lokkit` package. I also suggest that you install the `gnome-lokkit` package, which provides an easy-to-use graphical interface that simplifies configuring and customizing a firewall.

To install this package using `apt-get` or `aptitude` (without the graphical configuration tool), use the commands `sudo apt-get install lokkit` or `sudo aptitude -r install lokkit`. There's no point in installing the `gnome-lokkit` package if you don't have a graphical user interface on your Ubuntu system.

To install these packages graphically, start the Synaptic Package Manager from the System ⇨ Administration menu and supply your password to start Synaptic. Once the Synaptic application starts, click Search to display the search dialog. Make sure that "Description and Name" are the selected items to search through, enter **Lokkit** as the string to search for, and click Search. After the search completes, scroll down in the search results until you see the lokkit package, right-click its name, and select Mark for Installation to select that package for installation from the pop-up menu.

After you have selected the lokkit package, you should also select the gnome-lokkit package, which is a graphical GNOME utility for configuring and customizing your firewall. Figure 24.15 shows the gnome-lokkit package being selected for installation.

FIGURE 24.15

Installing Lokkit and friends in Synaptic Package Manager

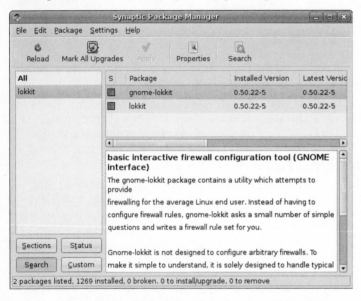

Right-click its name, and select Mark for Installation to select that package for installation from the pop-up menu. Selecting this package will display a dialog that suggests other packages for installation that are required for this package. Click Mark to also accept these packages for installation.

After selecting these packages for installation, click Apply in the Synaptic toolbar to install lokkit and its graphical configuration utility. When the installation completes, you can exit from Synaptic.

Using Lokkit to Set Up a Basic Firewall

Installing lokkit and the gnome-lokkit graphical configuration utility doesn't add a menu item for these commands, because you generally run them only once to set up a basic firewall. To start the graphical gnome-lokkit tool, execute the command gksudo gnome-lokkit from any Ubuntu command line and supply your password in the dialog that displays. An initial gnome-lokkit dialog displays that provides some basic information about Lokkit, as shown in Figure 24.16.

FIGURE 24.16

The initial gnome-lokkit dialog

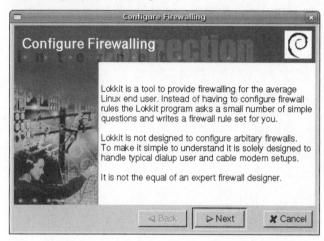

Click Next to proceed. The dialog shown in Figure 24.17 displays.

FIGURE 24.17

Selecting the type of firewall that you want to install

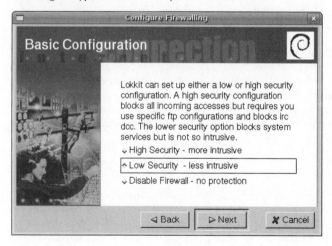

In most cases, the Low Security firewall is your best choice. As discussed earlier, a default Ubuntu Desktop installation doesn't expose any ports to the outside world, so a firewall is simply extra protection in case you subsequently open system ports to the outside world (or install services that do). If you are configuring a firewall on an Ubuntu Server system, you may want to select the High Security option, but you should be prepared to modify the rules created by Lokkit (or specially configure the services that you have installed) to ensure that the services that you want your server to provide are not being blocked by the firewall. Click Next to proceed. The dialog shown in Figure 24.18 displays.

FIGURE 24.18

Trusting hosts on your internal network

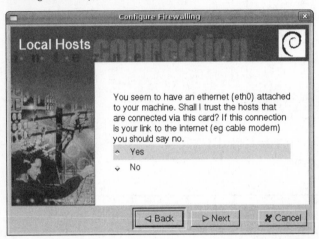

The dialog shown in Figure 24.18 asks if you want to trust hosts on your internal network, i.e., hosts with the same address settings for the first three quads of your system's IP address. For example, if your system's IP address is 192.168.6.6.121, selecting Yes here would enable any hosts with IP addresses of the form 192.168.6.XXX to connect to any services that your system provides. You should select Yes if you have more than one host on your internal network and the system that you are configuring is not directly connected to the Internet. Click Next to proceed. The dialog shown in Figure 24.19 displays.

The dialog shown in Figure 24.19 asks if you want to enable the DHCP port. You should select Yes if you are running (or plan to run) a DHCP server on this system, or if this system gets its IP address from another system using DHCP. Click Next to proceed. The dialog shown in Figure 24.20 displays.

The dialog shown in Figure 24.20 enables you to select services that you are running on your system, and to which you want other systems to be able to connect. If you are not currently running (and do not plan to run) services such as a DNS, FTP, mail, or Web server, select No. If you are running these services or plan to, select Yes. Click Next to proceed. If you selected Yes, subsequent dialogs display that ask, respectively, if you want to enable incoming Web, mail, secure shell, and Telnet services. I suggest that you answer Yes to all of these except for Telnet, which is an older, insecure mechanism for connecting to systems over the network that has largely been replaced by SSH.

FIGURE 24.19

Lokkit's DHCP dialog

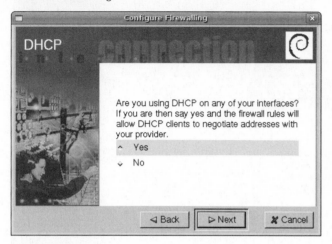

FIGURE 24.20

Enabling inbound services on your system

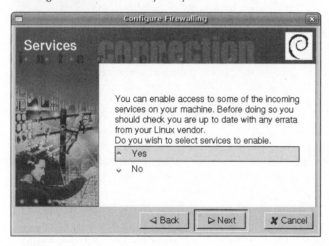

After answering these dialogs, or if you selected No to the dialog shown in Figure 24.20, the dialog shown in Figure 24.21 displays.

FIGURE 24.21

Activating your Firewall

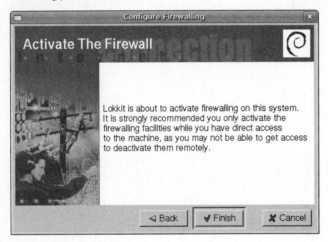

Click Finish to activate your firewall and exit the gnome-lokkit configuration utility. If you've changed your mind, click Cancel—you can always rerun this utility later if you decide that you want to install a firewall. If you select Yes, lokkit will perform some basic tests of your firewall, and will then activate the firewall and add starting the firewall to the series of startup scripts that your system runs when you boot your system, by adding the /etc/init.d/lokkit startup script to the startup sequence for all system run levels.

Summary

This chapter explained the basics of setting up wired, wireless, and modem-based network connections on your Ubuntu system. Ubuntu's GNOME desktop provides easy-to-use graphical tools that simplify configuring these types of interfaces, eliminating the traditional command-line magic required when you are using the ifconfig command. This chapter also provided a basic discussion of securing your Ubuntu system and related networking hardware, and also discussed setting up a simple firewall on your Ubuntu system.

Chapter 25 discusses using wireless technologies on your Ubuntu system in more detail, providing a detailed explanation of setting up and using the wireless network adapters touched upon in this chapter. Chapter 25 also includes a detailed explanation of how to use Windows drivers on your Ubuntu system to make problematic Ethernet and other devices work with Ubuntu Linux.

Chapter 25

Going Wireless

Today's mandatory connectivity requirements would be a farce without the ubiquity of wireless connections, whether these are cell phones leveraging a distant tower, your PDAs syncing to your PC via Bluetooth or Infrared, or your laptops using wireless network connections via an access point hidden in the linen closet in your hotel. It is incredibly liberating to be able to travel without carrying every cable and adapter that could possibly connect device A to device B, especially when airport security seems to frown on suitcases full of cables, power supplies, and connectivity hardware last seen in the laboratory of Victor von Frankenstein (no relation to the author).

Chapter 17 discussed how to connect and synchronize PDAs and smart phones with your Ubuntu system, so this chapter focuses on wireless networking. Like many other hi-tech domains, wireless networking has its own vocabulary and a bewildering set of alphabetically similar but conceptually unique acronyms, protocols, and so on. The first section of this chapter provides a basic overview of wireless networking and associated terminology today. Subsequent sections of this chapter explain how to configure wireless devices that are directly supported by Linux, explain how to work with wireless devices that are not supported by Linux (an impressive trick), and provide tips and tricks for using Microsoft Windows drivers with your Ubuntu Linux system.

Overview of Wireless Technologies

Wireless networking is amazingly useful, both on the job (so that you never have to play rock/paper/scissors over a limited number of Ethernet cables in a conference room), and even more so when traveling, enabling you to connect laptops and PDAs to the Internet in libraries, coffee shops, hotels, and many other public places. Wireless networking also provides an excellent mechanism for connecting networks of computers that are located in inaccessible locations or in existing structures where running new or additional cabling is a problem. Modulo security concerns, wireless networks can prevent the need to drill additional holes through Mount Vernon, the Vatican, or the Louvre.

As used in this chapter, wireless networking refers to technology that enables a computer to communicate using standard network protocols, but without network cabling. Most commonly, wireless networks are local area networks (LANs) whose members use industry standards such as the Institute of Electrical and Electronics Engineers (IEEE) 802.11 to communicate. The original 802.11 standard was released in 1997, and defines the frequencies, data rates, and media access methods used to communicate between the participants in a wireless network. Subsequent standards have defined a potentially bewildering variety of 802.11X standards, which I'll discuss a bit later in this section.

Regardless of the frequency and speed at which participants communicate, there are two basic types of wireless networks: ad hoc wireless networks and managed wireless networks. The characteristics of each (and their differences) are the following:

- **Ad hoc networks**: Also referred to as peer-to-peer wireless networks, consist of some number of computers that each have a wireless networking interface card and that communicate directly with all of the other wireless computers on that network. This enables them to share files and printers, but will not provide access to wired or Internet network resources unless one (or more) of the computers is also connected to those other network resources and is configured to serve as a gateway, bridge, or router to the other network(s). Acronym fans may see Ad hoc networks referred to as IBSS (Independent Basic Service Sets) during the computer bowl.

- **Managed networks**: Also referred to as infrastructure wireless networks, use an access point (sometimes also referred to as a base station) to manage communication between multiple wireless computers, acting much like a hub or switch for the wireless network. An access point is also typically connected to a wired network such as the Internet, and serves as the bridge or gateway between the wireless and wired networks. Access points are traditionally dedicated hardware devices (sometimes referred to as a HAP, a Hardware Access Point), such as Apple's Airports or devices from companies such as LinkSys, NetGear, Cisco, and others, but can also be software solutions (referred to as SAPs, Software Access Points) that run on a computer that is equipped with both wired and wireless network connections. Acronym fans may see managed networks referred to as a BSS (Basic Service Set; N computers and one access point) or ESS (Extended Service Set; N access points and N computers forming one subnet) during the computer bowl.

Large areas that require wireless coverage can accomplish this by providing multiple access points and supporting roaming, which is the ability of a user's connection to transfer from one access point to another. This is usually invisible to the user, though some access points require passwords or other authentication when moving between access points. Many networking hardware vendors also provide specialized hardware known as *extension points* that amplify the signal and therefore extend the range of an existing access point. Whether or not hardware access points support roaming or extension points is dependent on the hardware manufacturer. As with most networking hardware, a good rule of thumb is that buying all of your network hardware from the same vendor increases your chances for compatibility.

Agreement between the low-level wireless networking standards that the computers in your wireless network use is the most important aspect of setting up a successful wireless network. If the computers and access points can't communicate in the first place, you aren't going to be setting up much of anything. Though IEEE 802.11 is a published standard for wireless communication, several different 802.11 protocols and associated standards exist, not all of which are compatible with each other. The following is a current list of popular 802.11 standards, communication speeds, and compatibility promises:

- **802.11a:** A standard for 802.11 communications using the regulated 5.0 GHz frequency, offering maximum communication speeds of 25 to 54 Megabits per second. It is not compatible with any other 802.11 standard.

- **802.11b:** A standard for 802.11 communications using the unregulated 2.4 GHz frequency, offering maximum communication speeds of 5 to 11 Megabits per second. The 802.11b standard is forward compatible with the 802.11g and proposed 802.11n standards.

TIP Some vendors offer wireless cards known as *Dual Band* cards that support both 802.11a and 802.11b, operating in the frequency range and with communications speeds dictated by the type of connection that they establish.

- **802.11g:** A standard for 802.11 communications using the unregulated 2.4 GHz frequency, offering maximum communication speeds of 25 to 54 Megabits per second. The 802.11g standard is backward compatible with the 802.11b standard and forward compatible with the proposed 802.11n standard.

- **802.11n:** A standard for 802.11 communications using the unregulated 2.4 GHz frequency, offering maximum communications speeds of 100 to over 200 Megabits per second. The 802.11n standard is designed to be backward compatible with the 802.11b and 802.11g standards.

WARNING At the time that this book was written, the *n* in 802.11n should stand for "not yet a standard." The 802.11n standard is still under discussion and is not slated for official publication until late 2006 or mid-2007, depending on whom you ask. However, the lack of an official, frozen standard hasn't stopped vendors from releasing supposed 802.11n hardware. Until the official 802.11n standard is published, a good rule of thumb for compatibility between supposed 802.11n devices is "buy everything from the same vendor." Most vendors' hardware will, after all, work with their other hardware. Worst case, you only have one vendor to complain to.

Wireless networks also support a variety of security solutions, ranging from network names to encryption mechanisms. The most common of these are the following:

- **MAC (Media Access Control) filtering:** A security mechanism that requires that access points be programmed with lists of the systems that can connect to them, identified by hardware Ethernet address. MAC security only prevents against unauthorized connections to an access point — it does not secure those communications, once established.

- **SSID (Service Set IDentifier):** An SSID acts as a simple password by providing a unique identifier for a specific wireless network. Access points with a specific SSID can be configured to disallow access to anyone who does not provide that SSID when negotiating the initial connection. SSID security only prevents against unauthorized connections to an access point — it does not secure those communications, once established. An Extended Service Set IDentifier (ESSID) is just an SSID that is (or can be) used on multiple access points to identify the same network.

- **WEP (Wired Equivalent Privacy):** A security mechanism that requires supplying a 48-, 64-, or 128-bit security key when negotiating a connection to an access point. This key is used for encrypting and decrypting wireless communications. If this key is the same as that used by the access point, the two can communicate successfully. WEP security protects against unauthorized access and also provides secure wireless communication, because all communication packets are encrypted.

- **WPA (WiFi Protected Access):** A security mechanism that uses a Temporary Key Integrity Protocol to replace WEP and provides enhanced security on existing hardware. WPA uses a key server or pre-generated key set to encrypt communications on a per-packet basis. Two different WPA standards exist: WPA1, which was developed using a draft of the IEEE 802.11i security standard, and WPA2, which was developed using an approved version of the 802.11i security standard. WPA is not currently supported by all Ubuntu wireless applications, but is the next big thing for wireless network security.

All of these security measures can be used together, in any combination, or separately. Only WEP and WPA provide security for the packets that are being transmitted, but typing in a 128-bit key each time you configure a new wireless interface is both error-prone and incredibly tedious. Many sites therefore use MAC and SSID/ESSID security to establish connections, and then protect transmitted packets by using standard SSH tunneling or VPN technologies on top of the wireless communication layer.

The Linux kernel includes drivers for many popular PCI wireless cards, PCMCIA wireless adapters, and USB wireless adapters. On Ubuntu systems, wireless Ethernet interfaces are configured in the same way as wired Ethernet interfaces, which I'll explain in the next section.

If no Linux driver is available for your wireless card, all is not lost. Thanks to the cleverness of the folks in the open source community, a Linux kernel module and related utilities called `ndiswrapper` enables you to use the Microsoft Windows drivers for much of the networking hardware that is not yet natively supported by Linux. Installing these utilities, installing Windows drivers under Linux, and configuring your system to automatically start loading the kernel module is discussed later in this section.

Using systems that have both wired and wireless interfaces is quite common nowadays. Even though wireless specifications such as 802.11g and the upcoming 802.11n provide high communication speeds, they can't match the speed of wired 100 Megabit or Gigabit Ethernet connections. It's therefore a shame not to use your system's wired connection whenever possible. Ubuntu's administrative Networking application makes this easy enough to do manually, but an automated solution is also available in the Networking Manager application that is discussed in the sidebar later in this chapter.

Configuring Wireless Ethernet Interfaces

As mentioned previously, wireless network adapters are configured in basically the same way as standard networking adapters, except that they require some additional, wireless-specific information. To configure a wireless networking adapter on your Ubuntu system, connect it to your system and select System ➪ Administration ➪ Networking to start Ubuntu's networking administration application (which you can also execute as the `network-admin` command from any Ubuntu command line, using the `sudo` command), as shown in Figure 25.1.

FIGURE 25.1

Configuring a network interface in Ubuntu

When you first start this application, your wireless adapter should be listed in the dialog shown in Figure 25.1, but should be identified as being unconfigured. If no wireless adapter is listed, your wireless adapter may not be directly supported by the Linux kernel. In this case, see the section, "Installing and Using Windows Networking Drivers" later in this chapter for information about installing the Windows drivers that may be necessary for your Ubuntu system to work with your wireless adapter.

Once your wireless adapter is displayed in the dialog shown in Figure 25.1, select the entry for your adapter and click Properties to display the configuration dialog for wireless adapters. Select the Enable this interface checkbox to enable you to enter specific configuration information for your wireless interface, as shown in Figure 25.2.

Configuring wireless Ethernet adapter properties

If you want to join a specific wireless network, enter the ESSID of that network — leaving this space blank will enable your wireless interface to connect to any open, publicly visible access point that does not require authentication, regardless of its name. Similarly, if the wireless network that you are joining uses WEP keys, select the appropriate type of key from the Key type drop-down list, and enter the key in the WEP key field — if the wireless network that you want to join does not use WEP, leave the Plain (ASCII) key type selected, and leave the WEP key field blank. The final configuration step is to enter the appropriate networking information if you want your system to use a static IP address for its wireless connection. If the wireless network that you want to join uses DHCP, click the Configuration entry and select DHCP from the drop-down list.

After completing these settings, click OK to proceed. The Properties dialog closes, and a status dialog displays as your Ubuntu system activates your new wireless adapter. Once the interface is configured, the dialog shown in Figure 25.1 updates to reflect the fact that the interface has been successfully configured, as shown in Figure 25.3.

FIGURE 25.3

Updated Ethernet adapter information

If your system has both wired and wireless adapters and you want to be able to use both together, you should change the Default gateway device setting at the bottom of the dialog shown in Figure 25.3 to identify the Ethernet device over which you want to send packets to random hosts. In most cases, this will be your wired network interface. Depending on your configuration, you may also want to disable the other Ethernet interfaces on your system by selecting each interface, clicking Properties, and deselecting the Enable this connection checkbox. See Chapter 24, "Network Configuration and Security," for information about default gateway devices, routing, and so on.

To complete the wireless configuration process, you can then click OK to save your configuration settings, or click Cancel to close this dialog without saving any of your new configuration settings.

You can verify that the interface is correctly configured by using the `ifconfig` command to query the status of that interface from any Ubuntu command line, which displays output like the following:

```
$ ifconfig wlan0
wlan0     Link encap:Ethernet  HWaddr 00:06:25:07:F7:0E
          inet addr:192.168.6.81  Bcast:192.168.6.255
Mask:255.255.255.0
          inet6 addr: fe80::206:25ff:fe07:f70e/64 Scope:Link
          UP BROADCAST RUNNING  MTU:1500  Metric:1
          RX packets:44 errors:0 dropped:0 overruns:0 frame:0
          TX packets:14 errors:0 dropped:0 overruns:0 carrier:0
          collisions:0 txqueuelen:1000
          RX bytes:7697 (7.5 KiB)  TX bytes:1284 (1.2 KiB)
```

The dialog shown in Figure 25.3 identified the name of the new wireless interface. As you can see from this example, some removable wireless Ethernet interfaces are assigned names beginning with wlan (wireless LAN) and use numeric identifiers to differentiate between multiple wireless interfaces, just like Ethernet interfaces whose names typically begin with eth. The prefix used (wlan or eth) is set inside the device driver.

For additional information about using the networking administration utility and network configuration on Ubuntu in general, see Chapter 24, "Network Configuration and Security."

Command-Line Tools for Wireless Networking

The `wireless-tools` package, which is installed on Ubuntu systems by default, provides several commands for probing and configuring wireless interfaces and networks. You can execute the `man wireless` command to get information about the `wireless-tools` package, learn how and where it is installed by various Linux distributions, and view a list of the commands that this package provides.

The `wireless-tools` commands that I find most valuable are the `iwconfig` and `iwlist` commands. The `iwconfig` command displays information much like the `ifconfig` command, providing information about the wireless status of all or specific Ethernet interfaces on a system. The following example shows the output of the `iwconfig` command, querying the wireless Ethernet interface that was installed in the previous section:

```
$ iwconfig wlan0
wlan0     IEEE 802.11-DS  ESSID:"wvh"  Nickname:"okuwlan"
          Mode:Managed  Frequency:2.427 GHz  Access Point:
00:03:93:E9:89:22
          Bit Rate:11 Mb/s    Tx-Power=15 dBm
          Retry limit:8   RTS thr=1536 B   Fragment thr=1536 B
          Power Management:off
          Link Quality=0/0  Signal level=95/255  Noise level=0/0
          Rx invalid nwid:0  Rx invalid crypt:0  Rx invalid frag:0
          Tx excessive retries:0  Invalid misc:0   Missed beacon:0
```

As you can see, this provides much of the same information as that provided by the `ifconfig` command, but it also includes wireless-specific information. The `iwconfig` command can also be used to set various wireless configuration options from the command line—see the online man page for `iwconfig` (using the command `man iwconfig`) for more information.

The `iwlist` command enables you to scan for wireless networks and examine various characteristics of a wireless interface. For example, scanning for wireless networks around my home using the `iwlist wlan0 scan` command displays the following information:

```
$ sudo iwlist wlan0 scan

wlan0     Scan completed :
          Cell 01 - Address: 00:03:93:E9:89:22
                    ESSID:"wvh"
                    Mode:Master
                    Channel:4
                    Encryption key:off
                    Quality:0/0  Signal level:38/255  Noise level:0/0
                    Bit Rates:1 Mb/s; 2 Mb/s; 5.5 Mb/s; 11 Mb/s
```

This command is useful for verifying that a wireless interface is actually working, and that it can communicate with an access point. The information produced by the `iwlist` command is much more interesting in public areas, where you will usually detect multiple wireless networks, as in the following example from one of my laptops while I was on vacation:

```
$ sudo iwlist eth0 scan
Password:
eth0      Scan completed :
          Cell 01 - Address: 00:09:5B:36:22:38
                    ESSID:"Wireless"
                    Mode:Master
                    Frequency:2.412 GHz (Channel 1)
                    Signal level:20/153   Noise level:12/153
                    Encryption key:off
                    Bit Rates:1 Mb/s; 2 Mb/s; 5.5 Mb/s; 11 Mb/s
          Cell 02 - Address: 00:12:17:A6:E8:CC
                    ESSID:"linksys"
                    Mode:Master
                    Frequency:2.437 GHz (Channel 6)
                    Signal level:83/153   Noise level:13/153
                    Encryption key:off
                    Bit Rates:1 Mb/s; 2 Mb/s; 5.5 Mb/s; 11 Mb/s
          Cell 03 - Address: 00:12:17:A6:E8:CC
                    ESSID:"linksys"
                    Mode:Master
                    Frequency:2.437 GHz (Channel 6)
                    Signal level:81/153   Noise level:13/153
                    Encryption key:off
                    Bit Rates:1 Mb/s; 2 Mb/s; 5.5 Mb/s; 11 Mb/s
          Cell 04 - Address: 00:12:17:79:CF:D3
                    ESSID:"linksysR79cfd3"
                    Mode:Master
                    Frequency:2.437 GHz (Channel 6)
                    Signal level:49/153   Noise level:13/153
                    Encryption key:off
                    Bit Rates:1 Mb/s; 2 Mb/s; 5.5 Mb/s; 11 Mb/s; 18
  Mb/s
                              24 Mb/s; 36 Mb/s; 54 Mb/s
```

In this case, the information provided by the iwlist command was very useful in identifying available wireless access points, their names, and whether they were configured for authentication/encryption. The iwlist command can also query specific wireless configuration details — see the online man page for iwlist (using the command man iwlist) for more information.

Installing and Using Windows Networking Drivers

Device driver support is one of the few areas in which Linux lags behind Microsoft Windows. I hope that my making this statement doesn't induce Linus Torvalds to give me a call and demand the return of my official Linux Bigot decoder ring, but it's a fact. The reason that there are not Linux drivers for every piece of random hardware is not because of any problem or limitation in Linux, but is rather because device manufacturers target their largest potential markets when writing device drivers for their hardware, and at the moment, the main market for random PC hardware is Microsoft Windows systems.

Clever folks in the open source community are writing new device drivers every day, and each new Linux kernel supports more hardware than ever before. However great that is, it doesn't help much when you'd like to use a specific Windows device today. Luckily, a Linux kernel module and related utilities called `ndiswrapper` enables you to use the Microsoft Windows drivers for much of the networking hardware that is not yet natively supported by Linux. How cool is that? Thanks to the `ndiswrapper` package, you can use Windows' own drivers on your superior Ubuntu Linux systems until a native Linux driver becomes available.

One obvious question is, "Why not just buy hardware that works with Linux in the first place?" To be honest, that's my general approach, but there are some very good reasons for wanting (or needing) to use hardware that is supposedly Windows-only. The most significant of these are the following:

- You already have a wireless network adapter that is not yet supported by Linux. Why buy another adapter if you don't have to?

- Dual-boot laptops may include built-in wireless hardware that is not supported by Linux. Similarly, if you are given a laptop as part of your job along with PCMCIA or USB network adapters that are not supported by Linux, using the Windows drivers with Ubuntu enables you to use a real operating system for work without requiring that you spend any money.

- Some wireless protocols, most specifically 802.11a, are poorly supported under Linux but are still used by many businesses. Because 802.11a is also largely extinct, I doubt that this will change. Using the Windows drivers for your 802.11a hardware enables you to run Linux at work, using existing hardware.

The next few sections explain how to install this package and a handy graphical configuration utility, how to install a Windows driver on your Ubuntu system, and provides some tips and tricks for debugging problems and resolving problems using Windows drivers on your Ubuntu system.

> **TIP** Though primarily designed for use with Microsoft Windows drivers for network cards, the `ndiswrapper` package has been used with Windows drivers for many other devices, such as USB serial port devices, wired Ethernet cards, and so on. (For a complete list of devices that people have gotten to work with Windows drivers and the `ndiswrapper` package, see `http://ndiswrapper .sourceforge.net/mediawiki/index.php/List`). If you have a device that came with Windows drivers that you can't get to work natively under Linux, the `ndiswrapper` package is certainly worth a try and is only a Synaptic install away.

Installing NDIS Wrapper and Friends

The `ndiswrapper` Linux kernel module is provided with every Ubuntu Linux kernel, but you'll still want to install some related utilities to simplify installing and configuring Microsoft Windows drivers. The `ndisgtk` package provides a graphical utility that simplifies installing and configuring Windows drivers; the `ndiswrapper-utils` package provides the underlying utilities that it uses, as well as a command-line utility that you can use to install Windows drivers if you're not a GUI fan. These aren't installed by default on an Ubuntu system because not everyone needs them, and why waste disk space if you don't have to?

To install these packages, start the Synaptic Package Manager from the System ⇨ Administration menu, select Search, enter `ndiswrapper` in the Search box that displays, make sure that Description and Name is selected for the search type ("Look in"), and click Search. Once the search completes, select both the `ndisgtk` and `ndiswrapper-utils` packages: Right-click and select Mark for Installation from the pop-up menu to select each of these packages for installation. Figure 25.4 shows these packages being selected for installation.

FIGURE 25.4

Installing the ndisgtk and ndiswrapper packages

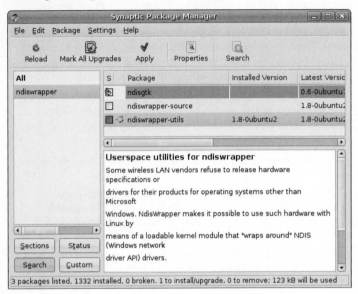

After you are finished making your selections, click Apply in the Synaptic toolbar to install these packages on your system. Once the installation completes, you're ready to install, configure, and use the Windows drivers for your mysterious piece of hardware.

See Chapter 20, "Adding, Removing, and Updating Software," for more detailed information on installing applications using the Synaptic Package Manager.

Installing Microsoft Windows Drivers

This section explains how to install Microsoft Windows drivers using the graphical ndisgtk utility, which (if you'll pardon the expression) puts a friendly wrapper around the ndiswrapper utilities, kernel module, and Ubuntu network configuration. You can also install Windows drivers for use with the ndiswrapper kernel module by using the command sudo ndiswrapper -i name-of-INF-file from any Ubuntu command –line, and then manually modifying some configuration files, but I prefer the graphical one-stop-shopping approach provided by the ndisgtk utility.

NOTE Before installing Windows drivers, you must make sure that they are available on your Ubuntu system. This usually involves either putting the driver CD in your Ubuntu system so that it is available as /media/cdrom (or something similar, depending on the drives in your Ubuntu system), or copying a zip archive containing the drivers to your Ubuntu system and using the unzip command to extract the contents of that archive file into an Ubuntu directory.

Installing the `ndisgtk` package creates the System ➪ Administration ➪ Windows Wireless Drivers menu item, which you can select to start the `ndisgtk` application. Figure 25.5 shows the initial driver installation dialog that is displayed when you first start this application.

FIGURE 25.5

The ndisgtk startup dialog

To install a driver, click Install New Driver. This displays the dialog that enables you to select the INF file associated with a specific Window driver, as shown in Figure 25.6. An INF file is a file with a `.INF` or `.inf` file extension that contains a description of a Windows driver, its installation options, associated files, and so on.

FIGURE 25.6

The INF file selection dialog for a Microsoft Windows driver

Click the Location button to display a standard file dialog that enables you to navigate to the directory containing the Windows driver and select the appropriate INF file, as shown in Figure 25.7. In this particular example, I'm installing the Windows drivers for a NetGear WG121 USB wireless adapter.

After navigating to and selecting the appropriate file, click Open to select that file and close the navigation dialog. The dialog shown in Figure 25.6 redisplays, now listing the name of the selected INF file. Click Install to install the driver and associated files for use by the `ndiswrapper` kernel module. The dialog shown in Figure 25.5 redisplays, now listing the driver that you've just installed and identifying if the hardware associated with that driver was located, as shown in Figure 25.8.

FIGURE 25.7

Navigating to the INF file for a Microsoft Windows driver

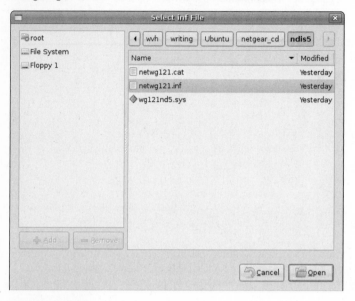

FIGURE 25.8

Loading the driver and detecting associated hardware

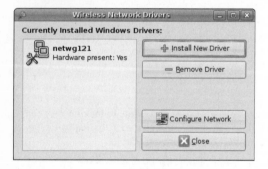

To complete the configuration of your new driver, click Configure Network to display the network configuration dialog discussed in the section of this chapter entitled "Configuring Wireless Ethernet Interfaces." Follow the instructions in that section to configure the new driver for your wireless network.

After configuring your network interface, click OK to close the Network Settings dialog, and click Close to terminate the Windows driver installation process.

To ensure that the `ndiswrapper` kernel module loads each time you restart your Ubuntu system, you must add the `ndiswrapper` to the file that identifies modules that should be loaded at boot time, `/etc/modules`. You can do this using your favorite text editor (which you should start using `sudo` so that you can edit this file), or via a command such as the following:

```
$ sudo echo "ndiswrapper" >> /etc/modules
```

Make sure that you use two angle brackets, not just one! If you accidentally use only one angle bracket, you will overwrite the contents of your existing `/etc/modules` file with a single line containing the name of the `ndiswrapper` module, which will probably certainly cause things like your mouse and printers to misbehave.

NDIS Wrapper Tips and Tricks

As you can see from the previous section, many Microsoft Windows drivers "just work" with the `ndiswrapper` kernel module when installed correctly. Unfortunately, some don't. I won't pretend to have tested every possible piece of wireless hardware and its associated Windows drivers (though I'd be happy to try if you would just send me a sample of the hardware that I can keep), but I have used many different ones with a wide selection of wireless hardware when configuring laptops for a variety of customers, coworkers, and friends.

For me, one of the most frustrating sets of experiences has been with a variety of LinkSys WPC54G wireless PCMCIA cards, all of which I've gotten working, but only after significant driver gymnastics, head-scratching, Google searches, and commiseration with fellow Linux devotees. (I was originally planning to title this section "The LinkSys WPC54G, or How I Spent My Summer Vacation," but I am trying to generalize what I've learned rather than simply provide a single set of instructions.) By the way, these are great cards that support 802.11g (and therefore 802.11b), and because I typically find LinkSys hardware to be inexpensive and reliable, I often recommend them to friends. Unfortunately, a HUGE problem with these cards is that LinkSys has used a variety of wireless chips in them over the years, so they often use different drivers, each of which seems to require its own tweaks to get it to work with the `ndiswrapper` module.

One key item is to make sure that you have the right Windows drivers in the first place. For example, some of the 54G cards use a Realtek 8180 chipset, and therefore only work with these drivers. Others use a Texas Instruments ACX 1xx chipset, while others use the Broadcom BCM43xx, and some newer ones are rumored to use a Marvell chipset. If you can't identify the chipset by reading the product literature, you can usually identify it by using the `lspci` utility to list all of the PCI devices on your system and by scanning the `lspci` output for anything identified as a wireless controller.

As an example of driver and chipset weirdness, the Texas Instruments ACX 1xx chipset is directly supported under Linux using the `acx` and `acx_pci` kernel modules (no `ndiswrapper` module required, though I prefer the `ndiswrapper` approach), but often requires that you play around with different versions of the microcode in `/lib/firware/`*kernel-version*`/acx` until you find the right version and name (see the Ubuntu Forums for some suggestions). If you want to use this version of the 54G with `ndiswrapper`, you have to blacklist the standard Linux kernel modules by adding their names to `/etc/modprobe.d/blacklist` so that they are not loaded during the hardware detection phase of the boot process.

If you're sure that you have the right driver, but still can't get it to work, use the Linux `dmesg` command to display recent kernel messages for error messages related to the `ndiswrapper`, the card that you're using, or any of the chipsets mentioned in the previous paragraph. This can help identify specific problems.

Smart Interface Management with Network Manager

Many systems feature both wireless and wired network adapters, both of which you want to use at different times. You can configure them to talk to different networks without any potential conflicts, but real performance problems will arise if you configure both of them as gateways to the same external networks or as a default gateway to the Internet. You can always deactivate, activate, and reconfigure your network as required, but having to do so quickly becomes irritating.

The GNOME Network Manager (`nm-applet`) that is designed to do automatic network reconfiguration based on the types of connections that your system detects, automatically activates your wired interface when a wired connection is detected, and automatically uses your wireless connection when no wired connection can be found. You can install the Network Manager via the Synaptic Package Manager, by installing the `network-manager` and `network-manager-gnome` package, and verifying that the `wpa_supplicant` package is installed on your Ubuntu system. The Network Manager application supports WPA authentication using the `wpa_supplicant` daemon, which is definitely the next generation of wireless security.

In theory, the Network Manager does the right thing, removing the need for most of the network configuration entries in `/etc/network/interfaces`. However, setting up and using Network Manager is poorly documented (and I'm being kind). I suggest that you search the Ubuntu Forums (`www.ubuntuforums.org`) for updated information about Network Manager — it sounds like it will be a great tool for people who need to roam from network to network and connection to connection, once it works well and is smoothly integrated into Ubuntu.

Personally, I've had little success getting the Network Manager to configure and manage multiple interfaces, and therefore I don't use it. Many people swear by it. I swear at it. Your mileage may vary.

The WPC54G cards that use the Broadcom BCM43xx have a particularly interesting wrinkle — they require a specific microcode firmware driver that is bundled inside the Windows driver (`bcmwl5.sys`), but which must be provided as a stand-alone file in the `/lib/firmware` directory that the Linux kernel checks for firmware microcode. You must therefore use a utility called `bcm43xx-fwcutter` to extract the different firmware files from the driver, and copy them into `/lib/firmware` before you can use this version of the card. If you have this version of the card, you can download the latest version of this utility from the page at `http://developer.berlios.de/project/showfiles.php?group_id=4547`.

As mentioned previously, these are examples of the types of problems that you may encounter when working with a random Windows driver, random wireless hardware, and the `ndiswrapper` package. Many people seem worried about the quality of open source code, but I think that the quality of Windows drivers is just as suspect. However, as my grandfather used to say, "A dysfunctional driver in the hand is worth several driver projects that are under development in the bush." (Or something like that.)

TIP The `ndiswrapper` developers provide as much online help as they can via the resources listed at `http://ndiswrapper.sourceforge.net/support.html`. If the people there can't solve your problem and you absolutely need to use a specific piece of "Windows-only" wireless hardware with your Linux system, a company called Linuxant (`www.linuxant.com`) provides an excellent piece of software called DriverLoader that is very similar to the `ndiswrapper` package. The Linuxant folks test their product on a huge selection of wireless hardware. They also offer Linux drivers for selected softmodem cards (modem cards that do everything in software, a traditional pain for Linux users). You can download a 30-day trial of the DriverLoader software to test it with your specific hardware, and also have the benefit of Linuxant's support personnel and extensive user community when diagnosing and resolving problems.

Summary

This chapter explored one of the most liberating and empowering features of computing today, wireless networking. Wireless networking is not only convenient from the standpoint of having fewer cables strewn around your house, but also enables people to do real work from their laptops, moving from conference room to conference room, office to office, and even city to city without having to plug their machines in and laboriously reconnect to and synchronize with a given network.

Chapter 26 begins the more server-oriented portions of this book, discussing how to set up the Apache 2 Web server on your Ubuntu system. Chapter 26 begins by providing a bit of background information about the Web and Web servers, and then explains the details of installing, configuring, and monitoring Apache 2, the latest and greatest Web server from the legendary Apache project.

Part IV

Configuring Servers on Ubuntu

Chapter 26

Setting Up a Web Server

Most of the significant advances in computing technology have what is known as a *killer app* (killer application) — one significantly unique, powerful, and compelling type of application that draws people to that technology in droves and makes it a part of the computing landscape for the foreseeable future. For personal computers in general, that application was the spreadsheet. For the Apple Macintosh, that application was desktop publishing. And for the Internet, that application was the World Wide Web. Sure, everyone loved e-mail, but the World Wide Web has turned the Internet into a seething pool of e-commerce, personal and technical information, social networking, and who knows what else in the future.

Chapter 9 explained how to use Firefox, the world's best Web browser, to surf the Web. This section explains the flip side of surfing the Web, which is how to set up a Web server so that you can deliver Web pages and other content over the Web to anyone who has access to your server. Most businesses and academic environments today have both externally available and internal-only Web servers. Many people even set up Web servers on their home networks to facilitate Web-based scheduling, document sharing, a central repository for photos, and just about anything else that you can think of.

This chapter begins with a bit of background on the Web, how Web servers work, and a history of Apache, the most popular Web server in existence. Subsequent sections explain how to install Apache, how to configure it, where Web content lives in an Apache server, how to extend and customize the Apache Web server, and how to troubleshoot connectivity or permissions problems.

World Wide Web 101

There are many excellent books about the World Wide Web and HTML, and this book isn't designed to be one of them. However, if you are new to the Web, this section provides some quick history and a sampling of Web buzzwords so that I won't surprise you by using new terms at random.

You Say URL, I Say URI...

As you may have noticed in the other chapters of this book, different Web-aware applications often use different terms to what you and I might simply think of as "Web addresses." URL (Uniform Resource Locator) is the traditional acronym and term for a Web address, but the acronym and term URI (Uniform Resource Identifier) is actually more technically correct. Another acronym and term that you may come across is URN (Universal Resource Name).

The relationship between these acronyms is the following: a URI is any way to identify a Web resource. A URL is a URI that explicitly provides the location of a resource and the protocol used to retrieve it. A URN is a URI that simply provides the name of a resource, and may or may not tell you how to retrieve it or where it is located.

The bottom line is that most people think of and use the terms URI, URL, and "Web address" interchangeably. If you want to pick one to use, URI is the right term to use.

In 1989, what has become the World Wide Web first entered the world in the mind of Tim Berners-Lee at CERN (Conseil Européenne pour la Recherche Nucleaire), the European Laboratory for Particle Physics near Geneva, Switzerland. The term *World Wide Web* wasn't actually coined until 1990, when Tim Berners-Lee and Robert Cailliau submitted an official project proposal for developing the World Wide Web. They suggested a new way of sharing information between researchers at CERN who used different types of terminals and workstations. The unique aspect of their information sharing model was that the servers would host information and deliver it to clients in a device-independent form, and it would be the responsibility of each client to display (officially known as *render*) that information. Web clients and servers would communicate using a language (protocol) known as *HTTP*, which stands for the HyperText Transfer Protocol.

> **NOTE**   Hypertext is just text with embedded links to other text in it. The most common examples of hypertext outside of the World Wide Web are various types of online help files, where you navigate from one help topic to another by clicking on keywords or other highlighted text. The most basic form of hypertext used on the Web is HTML, the HyperText Markup Language, which is a structured hypertext format that I'll talk about a little later in this section.

On the World Wide Web, the servers are Web servers and the clients are typically browsers, such as Firefox, Opera, SeaMonkey, Netscape, Microsoft Internet Explorer, Apple's Safari, and many others, running on your machine. To retrieve a Web page or other Web resource, you enter its address as a Uniform Resource Identifier (URI) in your browser by either typing it in or clicking on a link that contains a reference to that URI. Your browser contacts the appropriate Web server, which uses that URI to locate the resource that you requested and returns that resource as a stream of hypertext information that your browser displays appropriately, and you're off and running!

Today's browsers can understand many protocols beyond HTTP, including FTP (File Transfer Protocol, used to send and receive files), file (used to deliver plain-text files), POP (Post Office Protocol, used to send and receive electronic mail), and NNTP (Network News Transfer Protocol, used to send and receive Usenet News postings). Which protocol you use to retrieve a specific Web resource is encoded into the URI, and is referred to as a scheme in Web nerd terms. A URI specifies three basic things:

```
scheme://host/pathname
```

The `scheme` is one of http, ftp, file, and many more, and specifies how to contact the server running on `host`, which the Web server then uses to determine how to act on your request. The `pathname` is an optional part of the URI that identifies a location used by the server to locate or generate information to return to you.

Web pages consist of a static or dynamically generated text document that can contain text, links to other Web pages or sites, embedded graphics in a variety of formats, references to included documents such as style sheets, and much more. These text documents are created using a structured markup language called HTML, the HyperText Markup Language. (Markup languages were introduced and discussed in Chapter 10.) A structured markup language is a markup language that enforces a certain hierarchy where different elements of the document can appear only in certain contexts. Using a structured markup language can be useful to guarantee that, for example, a heading can never appear in the middle of a paragraph. Like documents in other modern markup languages, HTML documents consist of logical elements that identify the type of each element — it is the browser's responsibility to identify each element and determine how to display (render) it. Using a device-independent markup language simplifies developing tools that render Web pages in different ways, convert the information in Web pages to other structured formats (and vice versa), and so on.

Introduction to Web Servers and Apache

As mentioned in the previous section, the flip side of a Web browser is the Web server, the application that actually locates and delivers content from a specified URI to the browser. What does a Web server have to do? At the most basic level, it simply has to deliver HTML and other content in response to incoming requests. However, to be useful in a modern Web-oriented environment, a Web server has to do several things. The most important of these are the following:

- Be flexible and configurable to make it easy to add new capabilities, Web sites, and support increasing demand without recompilation and/or reinstallation.
- Support authentication to limit users who can access specific pages and Web sites.
- Support applications that dynamically generate Web pages, such as Perl and PHP, to support a customizable and personal user experience.
- Maintain logs that can track requests for various pages so that you can both identify problems and figure out the popularity of various pages and Web sites.
- Support encrypted communications between the browser and server, to guarantee and validate the security of those communications.

The order of importance of these various requirements depends on whether you are a systems administrator or e-commerce merchant, but all modern Web servers must provide at least these capabilities.

Many different Web servers are available today, depending on your hardware platform, the software requirements of third-party software that a Web site depends on, your fealty to a particular operating system vendor, and whether or not you are willing to run open source software, get additional power, and save money.

As you might expect, the first Web server in the world went online at CERN, along with the first Web browser. These were written and ran on NeXT workstations, not exactly the world's most popular platform (sadly enough). The first test of a Web server outside of Europe was made using a server running at the Stanford Linear Accelerator Center (SLAC) in the United States.

The development focus of Web servers that ran on more popular machines was initially the NCSA (National Center for Supercomputing Applications) Web server, known *NCSA httpd* (HTTP Daemon). Their development of a freely available Web server paralleled their development of the NCSA browser, known as Mosaic. (See Chapter 9 for information about Mosaic and its place in Web browser history.) When one of the primary developers of NCSA httpd (Rob McCool) left the NCSA, a group of NCSA httpd fans, maintainers, and developers formed to maintain and support a set of patches for NCSA httpd. This patched server eventually came to be known as the *Apache* Web server. Though the official Apache Web site used to claim that the name "Apache" was chosen because of their respect for the endurance and fighting skills of the Apache

Indians, most people (myself included) think that this was a joke, and that the name was chosen because the Web server initially consisted of many patches — in other words, it was "a patchy Web server."

Two Apache servers are available, contained in the packages `apache` and `apache2`. The primary differences between these two versions of the Apache Web server are their code base, their vintage, and how you install and maintain them. The `apache` package is the latest and greatest version of the Apache 1.x family of Web servers, which was excellent in its day, is still extremely popular, and is still in use in many Web sites across the Net. However, the `apache2` package contains the latest and greatest version of the Apache 2.x Web server, which is essentially "Apache, the Next Generation." Though things work differently in Apache 2.x, especially from a system administrator's point of view, Apache 2.x is a far superior Web server and where future Apache extension development is going to take place. This chapter therefore focuses on explaining how to install and configure the Apache 2 Web server. Any references to Apache in this chapter should be taken to refer to the Apache 2.x Web server.

Today, Apache Web servers installed at sites across the Internet deliver more Web content than any other Web server. I forget the name of the second most popular Web server, but it only runs on a single operating system (which is not Linux) and therefore loses conceptually as well as numerically.

Installing Apache

Apache is installed in different ways depending on whether you are running a system installed from an Ubuntu Server CD, an Ubuntu Alternate CD, or an Ubuntu Desktop CD. The differences boil down to whether or not your system has a GUI as follows:

- If you installed your system from an Ubuntu server CD and chose the Install to hard disk option, your system does not have a GUI unless you subsequently installed one. You will probably want to install the Apache 2 Web server using `aptitude`, as explained in the section entitled "Installing Apache from the Command Line," because this will also install some recommended packages that you will find useful, such as the Apache documentation.

- If you installed your system from an Ubuntu server CD and chose the Install a LAMP server option, your system does not have a GUI unless you subsequently installed one. However, the Apache 2 Web server was installed as part of your LAMP (Linux, Apache, MySQL, and Perl) server installation. You can skip this installation section and move on to the rest of the chapter.

- If you installed your system from an Ubuntu Alternate CD, you have even more options:

  - If you selected the Install in text mode option, your system has a GUI and you will probably want to install Apache using Synaptic, as explained in the section entitled "Installing Apache Using Synaptic."

  - If you selected the Install in OEM mode option, your system has a GUI and you will probably want to install Apache using Synaptic, as explained in the section entitled "Installing Apache Using Synaptic."

  - If you selected the Install a server option, your system does not have a GUI unless you subsequently installed one. You will probably want to install the Apache 2 Web server using `aptitude`, as explained in the section entitled "Installing Apache from the Command Line," because this will also install some recommended packages that you will find useful, such as the Apache documentation.

- If you installed your system from an Ubuntu Desktop CD, your system has a GUI and you will probably want to install Apache using Synaptic, as explained in the section entitled "Installing Apache Using Synaptic."

Installing Apache from the Command Line

It is easiest to install the Apache Web server from the command line using either `apt-get` or `aptitude`. Of these two, I suggest that you use `aptitude` to take advantage of its ability to install recommended packages as well as the basic packages required to run and monitor an Apache Web server on your Ubuntu system.

> **NOTE** As mentioned previously, two versions of the Apache Web server are available in different packages, which have different dependencies and recommended packages. This section focuses on installing the Apache 2 Web server. To install the older, Apache 1.3.x Web server, you must have the universe repositories enabled, and you would specify the `apache` package on the command line rather than the `apache2` package. I strongly suggest that you use the Apache 2 Web server unless you must use the Apache 1.3.x Web server because you need to use libraries or modules that are not yet available for Apache 2.

To install the Apache 2 Web server from the command line using `aptitude`, execute the following command:

```
$ sudo aptitude -r install apache2
```

You will be prompted for your password, and then again to confirm that you want to install the `apache2` packages, required packages for `apache2`, and recommended packages for use with the `apache2` package. Press return or type Y and press return to accept these packages, and the Apache 2 Web server and friends will be installed, added to your system's startup sequence, and started for you. You're now ready to configure your Web server and add content. Skip to the section entitled "Configuring Apache" for more information.

See Chapter 20 for more detailed information on installing applications using `apt-get` or `aptitude`.

Installing Apache Using Synaptic

To install the packages required to run and monitor an Apache Web server on your Ubuntu system, start the Synaptic Package Manager from the System ➪ Administration menu, and click Search to display the search dialog. Make sure that Names and Descriptions are the selected items to look in, enter **apache** as the string to search for, and click Search.

> **NOTE** After the search completes and, depending on how your repositories are configured, you will see that two Apache servers are available, contained in the packages `apache` and `apache2`. The primary differences between these two versions of the Apache Web server are their code base, their vintage, and how you install and maintain them. The `apache` package is the latest and greatest version of the Apache 1.x family of Web servers, which was great in its day and is still extremely popular and in use in a zillion Web sites across the Net. However, the `apache2` package contains the latest and greatest version of the Apache 2.x Web server, which is essentially "Apache, the Next Generation." Though things works differently in Apache2, especially from a system administrator's point of view, Apache 2.x is a far superior Web server and where future Apache extension development is going to take place. Telling you to install anything else would be doing you a disservice.

Right-click on the `apache2` package and select Mark for Installation to select that package for installation from the pop-up menu. You may also want to select the `apache-doc` package, which provides all of the official Apache project documentation for Apache 2. Figure 26.1 shows the basic `apache2` packages being selected for installation.

A dialog will display that lists other packages that must also be installed and asks for confirmation. When you see this dialog, click Mark to accept these related (and required) packages.

FIGURE 26.1

Installing the Apache 2 Web server and related packages

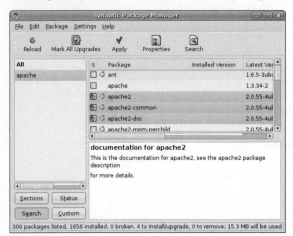

Next, click Apply in the Synaptic toolbar to install the Apache 2 server and friends on your system. Once the installation completes, you're already running an Apache 2 Web server, though it is somewhat limited in its initial capabilities. See the next few sections for information on how to configure it, install Web pages, and generally make your Apache 2 Web server more useful.

See Chapter 20 for more detailed information on installing applications using the Synaptic Package Manager.

Apache 2 File Locations

This section provides a quick overview of the default locations of the configuration files, binaries, and content associated with the Apache 2 Web server on your Ubuntu system:

- `/etc/apache2`: A directory containing the configuration files for the Apache 2 Web server. The primary configuration file in this directory is the file `apache2.conf`.

- `/etc/apache2/conf.d`: A directory containing local configuration directives for Apache 2, such as those associated with third-party or locally installed packages.

- `/etc/apache2/envvars`: A file containing environment variables that you want to set in the environment used by the `apache2ctl` script to manage an Apache 2 Web server.

- `/etc/apache2/mods-available`: A directory containing available Apache 2 modules and their configuration files.

- `/etc/apache2/mods-enabled`: A directory containing symbolic links to actively enable Apache 2 modules and their configuration files, located in the `/etc/apache2/mods-available` directory. This is analogous to the use of symbolic links to start various processes from the scripts in `/etc/init.d` at different run levels.

- `/etc/apache2/sites-available`: A directory containing files that define the Web sites supported by this server.

- `/etc/apache2/mods-enabled`: A directory containing symbolic links to actively enabled Web sites for this server, located in the `/etc/apache2/mods-available` directory. This is analogous to the use of symbolic links to start various processes from the scripts in `/etc/init.d` at different run levels.

- `/etc/default/apache2`: A configuration file that determines whether the Apache 2 should automatically start at boot time.

- `/etc/init.d/apache2`: A shell script that uses the `apache2ctl` utility to start and stop an Apache 2 Web server.

- `/etc/mime.types`: The default MIME (Multipurpose Internet Mail Extensions) file types and the extensions that they are associated with.

- `/usr/lib/cgi-bin`: The location in which any CGI-BIN (Common Gateway Interface scripts) for a default Apache 2 Web server will be installed.

- `/usr/sbin/apache2`: The actual executable for the Apache 2 Web server.

- `/usr/sbin/apache2ctl`: An administrative shell script that simplifies starting, stopping, restarting, and monitoring the status of a running Apache 2 Web server.

- `/usr/share/apache2-doc`: A directory that contains the actual Apache 2 manual (in the `manual` subdirectory). This directory is present only if you've installed the `apache2-doc` package (as suggested earlier).

- `/usr/share/apache2/error`: A directory containing the default error responses delivered.

- `/usr/share/apache2/icons`: A directory containing the default set of icons used by an Apache 2 Web server. This directory is mapped to the directory `/icons` in your Apache server's primary configuration file.

- `/var/log/apache2/access.log`: The default access log file for an Apache 2 Web server. This log file tracks any attempts to access this Web site, the hosts that they came from, and so on.

- `/var/log/apache2/error.log`: The default error log file for an Apache 2 Web server. This log file tracks internal Web server problems, attempts to retrieve nonexistent files, and so on.

- `/var/run/apache2/apache2.pid`: A text file used by Apache 2 to record its process ID when it starts. This file is used when terminating or restarting the Apache 2 server using the `/etc/init.d/apache2` script.

- `/var/www/apache2-default`: A directory containing the default home page for this Web server. Note that the default Apache 2 Web server does not display the content of this directory correctly — I'll use that as an example of configuring a Web site in the next section.

Some of these directories, most specifically the `/etc/apache2` configuration directory, contain other files that are included or referenced by other files in that same directory.

Configuring Apache

As mentioned in the previous section, the configuration files for the Apache 2 Web server are located in the directory `/etc/apache2`. Configuration files for Web sites that are available in an Apache 2 Web server are located in the directory `/etc/apache2/sites-available`. To actually support a site from your

Web server, you must create a configuration file for that Web server in `/etc/apache2/site-available`, and then create symbolic links to that configuration file in the `/etc/apache2/sites-available` directory.

The only Web site that is provided out of the box with a standard Apache 2 installation is its default Web site, which you would expect to be able to access at `http://hostname`. Unfortunately, attempting to access this URI on a newly installed Ubuntu Web server often displays the Web page shown in Figure 26.2.

FIGURE 26.2

The default page for a newly installed Apache 2 Web server

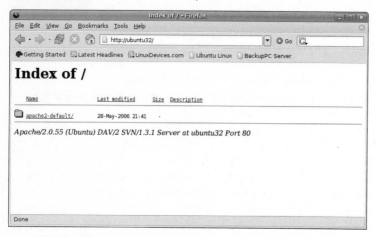

NOTE If you are creating a new Web site and want it to be your Web server's default page, you can simply put your content in the `/var/www` directory, where things would work fine immediately. I'm using the vagaries of Ubuntu's default Web page to demonstrate some of the statements in a server configuration file.

Let's use that as an opportunity to explore the configuration file for this Web site, explore its syntax, and change anything that we need to change to see a standard default Apache Web site. The following is a listing of the file `/etc/apache2/sites-available/default`, to which `/etc/apache2/sites-available/000-default` is a symbolic link to activate the site on this server. (I've added line numbers to make it easier to refer to different entries — they do not actually appear in the file!)

```
1. NameVirtualHost *
2. <VirtualHost *>
3.     ServerAdmin webmaster@localhost
4.     DocumentRoot /var/www
5.     <Directory />
6.         Options FollowSymLinks
7.         AllowOverride None
8.     </Directory>
```

```
 9.   <Directory /var/www/>
10.        Options Indexes FollowSymLinks MultiViews
11.        AllowOverride None
12.        Order allow,deny
13.        allow from all
14.        # Uncomment this directive is you want to see apache2's
15.        # default start page (in /apache2-default) when you go to /
16.        #RedirectMatch ^/$ /apache2-default/
17.   </Directory>
18.   ScriptAlias /cgi-bin/ /usr/lib/cgi-bin/
19.   <Directory "/usr/lib/cgi-bin">
20.        AllowOverride None
21.        Options +ExecCGI -MultiViews +SymLinksIfOwnerMatch
22.        Order allow,deny
23.        Allow from all
24.   </Directory>
25.   ErrorLog /var/log/apache2/error.log
26.   # Possible values include: debug, info, notice, warn, error, crit,
27.   # alert, emerg.
28.   LogLevel warn
29.   CustomLog /var/log/apache2/access.log combined
30.   ServerSignature On
31.   Alias /doc/ "/usr/share/doc/"
32.   <Directory "/usr/share/doc/">
33.        Options Indexes MultiViews FollowSymLinks
34.        AllowOverride None
35.        Order deny,allow
36.        Deny from all
37.        Allow from 127.0.0.0/255.0.0.0 ::1/128
38.   </Directory>
39. </VirtualHost>
```

The first thing that I want to change here is line 3, which sends any mail directed to the Webmaster for this site to webmaster@localhost, which probably doesn't exist on your machine. You can either set up a local alias for Webmaster in your mail server configuration (see Chapter 27, "Setting Up a Mail Server," for more information) or simply change this to an explicit site-wide address that you've already assigned somewhere. I would change this to webmaster@vonhagen.org.

The next thing to fix is line 16, which maps the top-level URI (i.e., anything that begins with a slash, followed immediately by the end of the line) for the site to the DocRoot's /apache2-default directory. To fix this, simply remove the hash mark at the beginning of the line.

Now, let's restart the Web server to see if this has changed things:

```
$ sudo /etc/init.d/apache2 restart
```

Visiting the same URI as before now shows the page shown in Figure 26.3, which is more like what you expect to see from a vanilla Apache Web server.

FIGURE 26.3

A better default page for a newly installed Apache 2 Web server

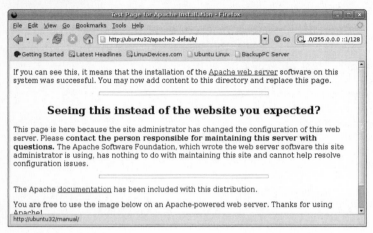

Poking around on this page, you can see that the author of the page created a hyperlink called documentation that points to /manual/. However, there is no such directory or an entry in the server's configuration file defining a redirect to some other directory. So let's make one. Create something like the entry for the /doc/ directory that's shown in lines 31 through 38, but simplify it a bit:

```
1. Alias /manual/ "/usr/share/doc/apache2-doc/manual/"
2. <Directory "/usr/share/doc/apache2-doc/manual/">
3.   Order deny,allow
4.   Deny from all
5.   Allow from 192.168.6 127.0.0.1
6. </Directory>
```

 Again, the line numbers are not actually present in the file — I'm just using them in the example to make it easier to refer to specific lines.

The first line defines an alias called /manual/ that actually points to the directory /usr/share/doc/apache2-doc/manual/, which is where Apache's online manual lives. The rest of the lines define who has access to that directory and under what circumstances. Line 2 defines the beginning of directives related to the directory /usr/share/doc/apache2-doc/manual/, and line 6 identifies the end of a block of directives for a specific directory. Lines 3, 4, and 5 specify how authentication works. Line 3 says that any statements denying access to the directory are processed before any that allow access to the directory. Line 4 denies all access to that directory, while line 5 allows access to that directory from any host whose first three octets are 192.168.6 (the subnet on which this Web server is running), and from the loopback address for the host. After adding these changes to the file (they must come before the </VirtualHost> directive shown in line 39 of the previous example because they are part of the definition for this host on this Web server) you can restart the Web server using the same command as before:

```
$ sudo /etc/init.d/apache2 restart
```

Visiting the same URI as before and trying to access the Apache documentation hyperlink now shows the page shown in Figure 26.4, which is more like documentation.

FIGURE 26.4

The apache documentation after updating the default server's config file

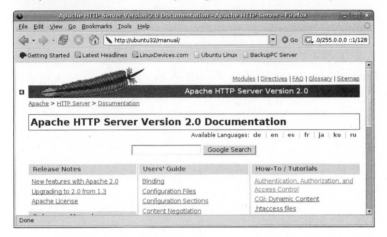

You may note that there was no equivalent to line 33 of the original server configuration file. This is because there was no need to provide these directory browsing options because I knew that the directory contained HTML files, so that the following options were not necessary:

- **Indexes:** Shows an index of the directory if no `index.html` file is present.
- **MultiViews:** Enables content negotiation, where the browser tries to find the best match for a request. In my case, I only want to see the docs in my default language, locale, and character set, so no negotiation is necessary.
- **FollowSymlinks:** I know that there are no symbolic links in this directory, so there's not need to specify that they should be followed.

The Apache documentation is really quite good and explains all of the site configuration directives that I don't have space to describe here.

Troubleshooting

As in any debugging or troubleshooting exercise, log files are your friends. Lines 25, 28, and 29 in the original server configuration file shown earlier in this chapter identify the log files used by this server, and the level of logging that occurs. Line 25 identifies the name of the error log file as `/var/log/apache2/error.log`. Line 28 sets the logging level to `warn` (warnings), which is slightly more useful than only logging errors, but is not as useful as `debug` when actually debugging a new site or server. Line 29 tells the server to create a single log file named `/var/log/apache2/access.log` that will log all access requests to the server in NCSA combined log format.

The following Apache log files are exceptionally useful for debugging purposes:

- `access.log`: Shows all attempts to access the server, listing the IP address of the host that attempted access, a timestamp, the actual request that was made, and information about the browser that the request was received from.

- `error.log`: Shows all errors of level warning or above (i.e., more serious) that the server encountered when trying to process an access request. This includes pages that can't be found, directories to which access was denied, and so on.

Apache 2's logging levels are very useful in controlling the amount and type of information that appears in the Apache logs. These levels are the following:

- **emerg:** only reports emergency conditions that make the Web server unstable.

- **alert:** logs situations requiring immediate action, and which may identify problems in the host system

- **crit:** logs critical errors that may indicate security, server, or system problems

- **error:** reports noncritical errors that indicate missing pages, bad server configuration directives, and general error conditions

- **warn:** logs messages that warn of noncritical problems or internal conditions that should be investigated

- **notice:** reports normal but significant conditions that should still be looked into

- **info:** logs informational messages that may help you identify potential problems or suggest possible reconfigurations

- **debug:** logs pretty much every state change on the system, such as every file open, every server activity during initialization and operation, and so on

You should never set the log levels lower than `crit` on any production Web server. I generally find that `warn` is the best choice for production servers, only using `notice`, `info`, or `debug` when a server is actually having performance or responsiveness problems. Also, don't forget that you actually have to look at the log files for them to be useful.

More Information

You can find many excellent sources of information about Apache 2 on the Internet and in books in which the sole focus is Apache 2. Some of my favorite resources are the following:

- `http://httpd.apache.org/docs/2.0/` — it doesn't get much more definitive than the actual Apache 2 docs. However, in addition to reference material, the Apache 2 docs include several tutorials and how-to style articles that provide practical, hands-on information.

- *Apache Server 2 Bible*, 2nd Edition by Mohammed J. Kabir (Wiley, 2002, ISBN: 0-7645-4821-2).

- *Hardening Apache* by Tony Mobily (Apress, 2004; ISBN: 1590593782).

Your favorite search engine, such as Google or Clusty, can help you find information about specific error conditions, warning messages, specific server configurations, and so on.

Summary

This chapter discussed how to install and configure the Apache 2 Web server, one of the most commonly used applications on any networked Linux system. A Web server is not only useful for delivering Web pages, but also provides the foundation of Web-oriented applications that are often used for system administration and monitoring tasks.

The next chapter continues the server-oriented theme of this chapter by discussing the mail servers that are available for Linux systems. The majority of the chapter discusses how to install and configure the Postfix mail server, a powerful, flexible, and easy-to-configure mail server that is a popular alternative to the traditional Linux sendmail server. This chapter also explains how to install and integrate related software, such as anti-SPAM and virus-scanning software.

Chapter 27

Setting Up a Mail Server

As discussed in the introduction to Chapter 26, most of the significant advances in computing technology have what is known as a killer app (killer application) — one significantly unique, powerful, and compelling type of application that draws people to that technology in droves and makes it a part of the computing landscape for the foreseeable future. For the Internet, this application was the World Wide Web, but for networking in general, this application is probably e-mail. I can't deny that the Internet is the world's biggest and most powerful network, but many businesses already depended on e-mail long before they had access to the Internet.

E-mail can be a tremendous time sink, but it is the lifeblood of much business and personal communication nowadays. Some of the many advantages of e-mail for business communication are the fact that it is asynchronous (you can send mail to anyone at your company at any time, and they can read it as soon as they have the chance) and location-independent (you can send mail to anyone at any location where your company has an office). Personal e-mail allows us to stay in touch with friends and family regardless of where they are. However, all of this requires a reliable transport mechanism (the Internet or your corporate network) and reliable software that handles mail transfer between computers, mail delivery into your mailbox, and provides the ability to read, store, and reply to e-mail.

Chapter 8 discussed the e-mail capabilities of Evolution, a powerful piece of personal information management software that is installed as part of every non-server Ubuntu installation. This chapter explains how to install and configure Postfix, an equally powerful piece of software that handles mail transfer; how to integrate Postfix with various mail delivery packages; and how to extend its capabilities to filter out the SPAM that drives many people crazy nowadays. However, before I get into the details, the first section discusses how e-mail works, defines some basic terminology and required software components, provides an overview of available Linux mail servers, and discusses some good reasons for running your own mail server. If you're an experienced sysadmin or are feeling lucky, feel free to skip ahead to the installation, configuration, and antivirus and SPAM filtering sections.

Introduction to Mail Servers

The components of an e-mail system can be confusing, so I usually generalize them as the difference between receiving and retrieving — my mail server receives e-mail for me, and my e-mail client (Evolution) lets me retrieve my e-mail from there to read it, archive or delete it, and so on. However, in official mailer-speak, there are actually three components involved in a mail system:

- **Mail Transfer Agent (MTA):** A program that handles transferring e-mail from one computer to another, using the Simple Mail Transfer Protocol (SMTP). Well-known examples of MTAs are Microsoft Exchange, Sendmail, Postfix, qmail, and exim. MTAs are often referred to as mail servers, which can be confusing because this is also the term commonly used to identify the host on which an MTA runs.

- **Mail Delivery Agent (MDA):** A program that actually delivers the e-mail received by an MTA into my personal mailbox and can often do both preprocessing, such as SPAM filtering and virus detection, and auto-responder tasks, such as sending "I'm on vacation" mail. The MDA also often handles the presentation of mail from the mailbox to the user, supporting protocols such as the Post Office Protocol (POP and POP3) and the Internet Message Access Protocol (IMAP) on the host where mail is stored. Common examples of MDAs on Linux systems are procmail, Qpopper, Cyrus, pop3d, Courier IMAP, and /bin/mail. MDAs can be directly integrated into an MTA, as is the case with Microsoft Exchange and often with Linux MTAs when mail is read directly from a traditional Unix-style mail file.

- **Mail User Agent (MUA):** A program that lets you send mail and read the messages in you personal mailbox using protocols such as POP, POP3, and IMAP. Most MUAs also provide support for composing and managing mail messages. Common examples of MUAs are Evolution, Microsoft Outlook, mutt, kmail, pine, and Thunderbird.

In most cases, users never see the MDA because it is integrated with the MTA, either by the software vendor or by the system administrator. Similarly, most users could care less about the MTA and use the term "mail server" to identify the host on which whatever MTA they are using runs. Although the MUA is the most important component of a mail system from the user point of view, the MTA is the most important component from a mail system's and system administrator's point of view because it both performs the actual transfer of mail from one computer to another and identifies the MDA and any other applications involved in preprocessing mail on its way to the user's mailbox.

Popular Linux Mail Transfer Agents

As you might expect, several MTAs are available for Linux systems. Though this chapter focuses on installing and configuring Postfix, other Linux MTAs all have their devotees. For this reason, it's nice to know a bit about each of the most popular ones so that you can feel that you made an informed decision by following the suggestions in this chapter and going with Postfix. The next few sections provide an overview of the most popular Linux MTAs and some of the features, benefits, and downsides of each.

Exim

Exim is a popular, fast, and flexible MTA written by Philip Hazel at the University of Cambridge, and was originally written as a replacement for a popular, older MTA known as smail. Exim is very popular with system administrators who also run mailing lists such as mailman, because it can be configured to automatically look for mailing lists before users. It supports an extensive set of features for checking incoming mail for problems without the external applications that most other MTAs require. Exim is the default MTA used on Linux distributions such as Debian.

For more information about Exim, see:

- Exim Home Page: `www.exim.org`
- Exim Documentation and FAQs: `www.exim.org/docs.html`

Postfix

Postfix is a popular, scalable, and secure MTA written by Witse Venema while working at IBM. Postfix was originally known as VMailer and was even marketed by IBM as Secure Mailer. In 1999, its name became Postfix, and the rest is history.

Postfix is reliable, fast, and easy-to-administer. Its configuration file is easy to read and edit, though of course you still have to know the many options that you can set and all of their possible values. It is a drop-in replacement for sendmail, with the exception that it requires tasks to run as a special Postfix user and group for security reasons.

For more information about Postfix, see:

- Postfix home page: `www.postfix.org`
- Postfix Resources and FAQ: `www.seaglass.com/postfix`
- Postfix Shrine: `www.stahl.bau.tu-bs.de/~hildeb/postfix`

Qmail

Qmail is an extremely fast, secure, and scalable MTA written by Dan Bernstein, a Computer Science professor at the University of Illinois at Chicago who is well known for his interest in cryptography and security. This focus manifests itself in qmail — since 1997, there has been a standing reward of $500 for anyone who finds a verifiable security hole in the latest version of qmail. It has never been claimed.

Qmail is extremely fast, secure, and scalable. Unfortunately, it is also encumbered by strange licensing requirements (for example, you cannot redistribute modified qmail source code without the direct approval of your changes by the author), it is not compatible with the Linux Filesystem Hierarchy Standard (it lives under `/var`), and its initial configuration and the irritations associated with adding new users is responsible for at least some portion of my grey hair. However, the licensing issues have primarily been responsible for its lack of widespread adoption by the Open Source community, because it isn't open source. As such, several qmail patches are available to add various capabilities, but it is simply tedious to always have to apply a variety of patches.

For more information about qmail, see:

- Dan Bernstein's qmail page: `http://cr.yp.to/qmail.html`
- Life with qmail: `www.lifewithqmail.org`
- qmail home page: `www.qmail.org`

Sendmail

As mentioned earlier in this chapter, sendmail is the most common mail transfer agent in use on Linux and Unix systems today. Note that I did not say "the most popular" — sendmail comes as the default MTA for most Unix and many Linux distributions, and therefore is often used "because it's there." If sendmail is used on many existing systems in your organization, it's also difficult to argue for using a different MTA on any new box, based on the "don't fix it if it's not broken" approach to system administration.

Sendmail was written by Eric Allman, whose delivermail program was the original ARPANET mail delivery system provided with 4.0 BSD Unix and early versions of 4.1 BSD. However, as the ARPANET grew, and then eventually became the Internet, delivermail proved to be too inflexible, largely because it used compiled-in configuration information. Sendmail was developed to use an external configuration file, and was first delivered with later versions of BSD 4.1. Sendmail's configuration syntax is both tremendously rich and fiendishly arcane, and is the biggest argument against sendmail. The configuration files actually used by sendmail are generated from the configuration file maintained by a system administrator using the m4 macro processor, which makes them tremendously painful to debug and maintain. Sendmail configuration questions are tremendously popular during the interview process for system administrators.

On the positive side, no Internet mailer is more mature than sendmail, because it has been in active use for over twenty years. It scales well, and can be integrated with most of the popular anti-SPAM and antivirus packages that are available. Sendmail has a somewhat undeserved reputation for security problems, which IMHO largely is because of the fact that is the biggest and oldest target.

For more information about sendmail, see:

- Open Source Sendmail Home Page: `www.sendmail.org`
- Sendmail, Inc.: `www.sendmail.com` (where Eric Allman is CTO)

Why Run Your Own Mail Server?

There are a number of good reasons to run your own mail server, but doing so also introduces both additional responsibilities and internal costs. All domain hosting companies and ISPs will manage a mail server for a domain, giving you some amount of control over its configuration. For example, you are usually given access to a Web-based control panel that enables you to create some number of e-mail accounts and mail aliases. However, this does not give you any control over the internals of the mail server. Some of the best reasons for wanting to run and manage your own mail server are the following:

- No limitation on the number of users or aliases. Most ISPs and domain hosting companies provide a certain number of each, and then impose additional charges for higher numbers.
- No limitation on the number of domains that can be served by a single mail server. Most ISPs and hosting companies charge for each domain and require that you administer each domain separately. You can configure a single mailer to support all of your domains, sharing a central configuration across multiple domains.
- The ability to use a different mail server than the one that is provided by your ISP or domain hosting company. You can select the MTA and MDA combination that best suits your requirements, not the convenience of your ISP or domain hosting company.
- The ability to integrate centralized SPAM and antivirus checking that is under your control and which you can fine-tune at no cost.
- Easy integration of additional capabilities such as mailing lists that may not be supported by your ISP or domain hosting company.

Although deciding to run your own mail server provides several benefits, it introduces several costs and responsibilities that you must be prepared for. Some of the more important of these are the following:

- Security becomes your concern and responsibility. When an ISP or domain hosting firm manages your mail server, its security is their responsibility. When you manage your own mail server, you are directly responsible for its security, which is especially important if you run an IMAP mail server, where all of your personal, SMB, or enterprise mail is permanently stored on the mail server.

- You will need to make sure that any host on the Internet can always contact your mail server. Beyond being responsible for the uptime of the machine that hosts the mail server, you will need to make sure that the MX records for all domains that it supports correctly identify the mail server. It will either have to have a fixed IP address it or will need to be correctly identified by a dynamic DNS system that is always available.

- You will become responsible for all of your mail server's system administration. Beyond ensuring that it is configured correctly (no open relays, please), you will be responsible for ensuring that a mail server is always available at the location identified by your domain's MX record, that backups are done, that the system and all of the software that you depend on is always kept up-to-date, and that SPAM filtering and antivirus checking are always up-to-date and correctly configured, and much more.

It's easy to overlook incidental costs when setting up your own mail server. When everything works correctly, as it does most of the time, things are great. But when something breaks, you are the one on the hot seat.

Installing Postfix and Friends

This section explains how to install the packages necessary for a simple Postfix mail server that automatically scans messages for SPAM and viruses and which users can access via the POP3 protocol. Postfix and related packages are installed in different ways depending on whether you are running a system installed from an Ubuntu Server CD, an Ubuntu Alternate CD, or an Ubuntu Desktop CD. The differences boil down to whether or not your system has a GUI:

- If your system does not have a GUI, follow the instructions in the section entitled "Installing Postfix and Friends from the Command Line."

- If your system has a GUI, follow the instructions in the section entitled "Installing Postfix and Friends Using Synaptic."

Of course, you can always use the command-line installation instructions on a system with a GUI by executing them within a GNOME Terminal or xterm window. Ubuntu enables you to do things your way.

In alphabetical order, the packages that you'll be installing are the following:

- clamav: An antivirus package that scans incoming mail for attachments that contain a virus and quarantines those messages so that people don't accidentally invoke the problematic attachment.

- mailx: A package that contains a simple command-line tool for sending mail, which is used by many system utilities, but (in our case) is extremely useful for quick mail server tests.

- mailscanner: A package that scans incoming mail using a variety of SPAM detection techniques and discards any matching mail.

- postfix: The Postfix mailer and all related utilities and configuration files.

- postfix-doc: Documentation for the Postfix mailer, installed in /usr/share/doc/postfix and /usr/share/doc/postfix-doc.

- postgrey: A greylisting implementation for use with Postfix. Greylisting causes incoming mail requests to be rejected the first time that they arrive, but accepted when the remote mail system tries to deliver them a second time. Many spammers only try to deliver mail once, so this simple utility can significantly reduce the amount of SPAM that your site receives.

- qpopper: A package that enables users to read their mail remotely, using the POP/POP3 protocol that is supported by most MUAs.

You don't have to install all of these now, of course, but I'm going to assume that these are all installed in subsequent sections of this chapter. I know what they say about what "assume" means, but in this case that won't include me.

Built-in Postfix Configuration Models

Regardless of whether you are installing Postfix and friends from the command-line or graphically, you will be required to select a default configuration model during the installation process. Five different configuration models are built into the Postfix package, each of which sets up the Postfix configuration files in a certain basic way. These configuration models are the following:

- **Internet site:** Mail will be sent and received directly from this machine via SMTP using Postfix. This is the default choice, and is probably the right choice if you are configuring an incoming and outgoing mail server for your domain and you have a direct connection to the Internet.

- **Internet site using smarthost:** This machine either receives mail directly from the Internet or from another machine using a utility such as fetchmail, but sends mail through another mail server. This is probably the right choice if you want to run a home, SOHO, or SMB network with its own mail server but want to leverage your ISP or domain hosting company's existing mail server.

- **Local delivery only:** The machine only delivers mail locally, and does not send mail over any network. This is the right choice if you are setting up a system on which you want system status messages to be delivered by local e-mail, or a system shared by multiple users who need to exchange mail only between themselves.

- **No configuration:** The installation process will not modify the generic Postfix configuration files. You will have to make extensive manual modifications to them to get Postfix to work correctly on your system.

- **Satellite system:** This machine does not receive mail and forwards all outgoing mail to another mail server for actual delivery.

If you are setting up a system that doesn't match any of the presupplied configurations, it's probably best to select the default value, Internet Site, because this will provide a reasonable template that you can then customize to match your exact requirements.

Installing Postfix and Friends from the Command Line

It is easy to install Postfix and related packages from the command line using either apt-get or aptitude. I suggest that you use aptitude to take advantage of its ability to install recommended packages as well as the basic packages required to run and support the Postfix mail server and related applications on your Ubuntu system.

To install the Postfix mail server and related applications from the command line using aptitude, execute the following command:

```
$ sudo aptitude -r install postfix postfix-doc postgrey mailscanner \
        mailx qpopper clamav
```

You will be prompted for your password (by sudo), and then again to confirm that you want to install the specified packages, any packages that they require, and any patches that they recommend. This will look like the following (though the exact list will differ depending on what you already have installed on your machine):

```
$ sudo aptitude -r install postfix postfix-doc postgrey mailscanner \
        maillx qpopper clamav
```

```
Password:
Reading package lists... Done
Building dependency tree... Done
Reading extended state information...
Initializing package states... Done
Building tag database... Done
The following NEW packages will be automatically installed:
  arj ca-certificates clamav-base clamav-freshclam debconf-utils
emacs21
    emacs21-bin-common emacs21-common emacsen-common laptop-detect
    libarchive-zip-perl libberkeleydb-perl libclamav1 libcompress-zlib-
perl
    libconvert-binhex-perl libconvert-tnef-perl libcurl3 libdigest-hmac-
perl
    libdigest-sha1-perl libgmp3c2 libhtml-parser-perl libhtml-tagset-perl
    libice6 libidn11 libio-multiplex-perl libio-stringy-perl libjpeg62
    liblockfile1 libmail-spf-query-perl libmailtools-perl libmime-perl
    libnet-cidr-lite-perl libnet-cidr-perl libnet-dns-perl libnet-ip-perl
    libnet-server-perl libpng12-0 libsm6 libsocket6-perl libssl0.9.7
libtiff4
    libtimedate-perl libungif4g liburi-perl libx11-6 libxau6 libxext6
libxmu6
    libxpm4 libxt6 mew-beta mew-beta-bin openssl perl perl-doc perl-
modules
    resolvconf spamassassin spamc ssl-cert tnef ucf unzip unzoo x11-
common
    xaw3dg
The following NEW packages will be installed:
  arj ca-certificates clamav clamav-base clamav-freshclam debconf-utils
    emacs21 emacs21-bin-common emacs21-common emacsen-common laptop-
detect
    libarchive-zip-perl libberkeleydb-perl libclamav1 libcompress-zlib-
perl
    libconvert-binhex-perl libconvert-tnef-perl libcurl3 libdigest-hmac-
perl
    libdigest-sha1-perl libgmp3c2 libhtml-parser-perl libhtml-tagset-perl
    libice6 libidn11 libio-multiplex-perl libio-stringy-perl libjpeg62
    liblockfile1 libmail-spf-query-perl libmailtools-perl libmime-perl
    libnet-cidr-lite-perl libnet-cidr-perl libnet-dns-perl libnet-ip-perl
    libnet-server-perl libpng12-0 libsm6 libsocket6-perl libssl0.9.7
libtiff4
    libtimedate-perl libungif4g liburi-perl libx11-6 libxau6 libxext6
libxmu6
    libxpm4 libxt6 mailscanner mailx mew-beta mew-beta-bin openssl perl
    perl-doc perl-modules postfix postfix-doc postgrey qpopper resolvconf
    spamassassin spamc ssl-cert tnef ucf unzip unzoo x11-common xaw3dg
0 packages upgraded, 73 newly installed, 0 to remove and 0 not
upgraded.
Need to get 5028kB/45.3MB of archives. After unpacking 129MB will be
used.
Do you want to continue? [Y/n/?]
```

Press Return or type **Y** and press Return to accept these packages, and the Postfix mail server and friends will be installed, added to your system's startup sequence, and started for you. When the Postfix server is configured, you will then see the screen shown in Figure 27.1.

FIGURE 27.1

Available Postfix configuration models

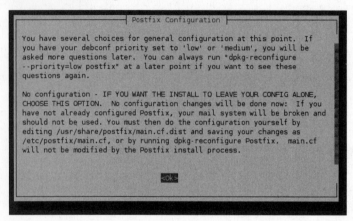

This screen describes the different configuration models that are built into the Postfix package, which were described earlier in the section entitled "Built-In Postfix Configuration Models." Press Return to display the screen shown in Figure 27.2.

FIGURE 27.2

Selecting your Postfix configuration model in text mode

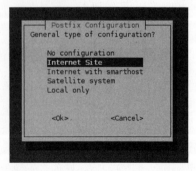

In most cases, you will want to select the default configuration model, Internet Site, by pressing Return. You can also use the up/down arrows to select another configuration and press Return to accept the highlighted choice. The screen shown in Figure 27.3 displays.

FIGURE 27.3

FIGURE 27.3

Specifying the name of your mail host in text mode

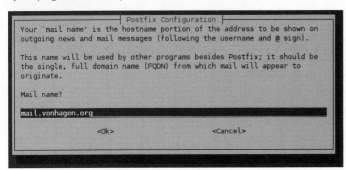

This screen enables you to specify the name of this host as any external hosts will look for it. By default, the actual name of the system is displayed. Use the left/right arrow and delete keys if you need to make any changes to the name of this host. Press Return to accept the name on this screen. The remainder of the configuration process will continue with no further questions.

You're now ready to configure your Postfix server and related applications. Skip to the section entitled "Configuring Postfix" for more information.

See Chapter 20 for more detailed information on installing applications using `apt-get` or `aptitude`.

Installing Postfix and Friends Using Synaptic

To install Postfix and related packages graphically, start the Synaptic Package Manager from the System ⇨ Administration menu, and click Search to display the search dialog. Make sure that Description and Name are the selected items to search through, enter **postfix** as the string to search for, and click Search. Right-click on the `postfix`, `postfix-doc`, and `postgrey` packages, and select Mark for Installation from the pop-up menu to select each of those packages for installation.

> **NOTE** After some of these selections, a dialog will display that lists other packages that must also be installed, and asks for confirmation. When you see this dialog, click Mark to accept these related (and required) packages.

Next, search for **mail** and right-click on each of the `mailx` and `mailscanner` packages and select Mark for Installation from the pop-up menu to select each of those packages for installation.

Then search for `qpopper`, right-click on that package, and select Mark for Installation from the pop-up menu to select that package for installation.

Finally, search for `clamav`, right-click on that package, and select Mark for Installation from the pop-up menu to select that package for installation.

Figure 27.4 shows the `postfix` and `postfix-doc` packages as selected for installation.

FIGURE 27.4

Installing the Postfix mail server and related packages

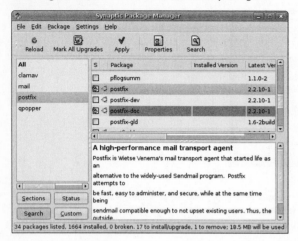

Click Apply in the Synaptic toolbar to install the Postfix mail server and friends on your system. When the Postfix server is configured, you will then see the dialog shown in Figure 27.5.

FIGURE 27.5

Selecting your Postfix configuration model graphically

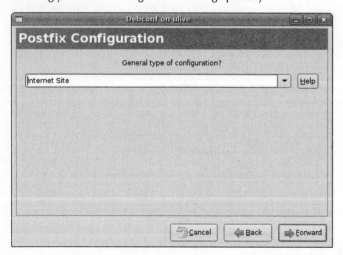

This dialog enables you to select one of the different configuration models that are built into the Postfix package, which were described earlier in the section entitled "Built-In Postfix Configuration Models." In most cases, you will want to accept the default configuration model, Internet Site, but you can also click the drop-down menu to select another configuration model. Once you have selected the appropriate configuration model for your mail server, click Forward to proceed. The dialog shown in Figure 27.6 displays.

FIGURE 27.6

Specifying the name of your mail host graphically

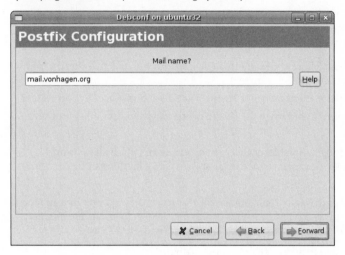

This dialog enables you to specify the name of this host as any external hosts will look for it. By default, the actual name of the system is displayed. Modify the name shown or click Forward to proceed. The remainder of the configuration process will continue with no further questions.

You're now ready to configure your Postfix server and related applications. The following section entitled "Configuring Postfix" provides more information.

See Chapter 20 for more detailed information on installing applications using the Synaptic Package Manager.

Configuring Postfix

As installed by default, your Postfix mail server is almost ready for prime time. It will already work fine locally, which you can test by using the command-line mail utility (which is provided by the mailx package that you installed on the previous section). To make your mail server able to accept incoming requests from and send mail to other hosts on a network, you will need to extend its capabilities somewhat. Similarly, the Postfix server by itself does local mail delivery, which is fine if all of your users want to log in on your mail server and read their mail there. Unfortunately, that is both poor security practice and a hassle for everyone. So you'll need to do a bit of fine-tuning to make our new Postfix mail server more usable for and by everyone.

The next section explores the default Postfix configuration file that was installed and configured in the previous section. The two sections following that address how to make your Postfix server work on your network and how to configure your mail server so that it accepts incoming POP mail requests.

As discussed in Chapter 8 and mentioned earlier in this chapter, POP and IMAP are the primary protocols used for remote systems to read e-mail on a mail server. The key difference between them is that POP is designed to store e-mail on the client, while IMAP is designed to store e-mail on the server. Each model has its advantages, but I believe that most people are more familiar with the POP model, so I'm going to focus on that in this chapter.

Postfix Configuration Files

The Ubuntu Postfix mail server uses three configuration files, all of which are installed in the directory /etc/postfix. These files are the following:

- dynamicmaps.cf: identifies additional capabilities to be loaded at run time based on the type of operation that is being performed

- main.cf: contains configuration information for Postfix that is used during message processing

- master.cf: contains parameters used when the Postfix master programs runs other programs from /usr/lib/postfix

Postfix can also use standard mailer configuration files such as /etc/aliases (which allows e-mail addressed to one user to be automatically delivered to another), but this is not a Postfix-specific configuration file.

The main.cf configuration file is the only Postfix configuration file that most users will ever have to modify. As installed on an Ubuntu system, the main.cf configuration file for a system following the Internet site model looks like the following (I've removed some irrelevant comments and white space):

```
smtpd_banner = $myhostname ESMTP $mail_name (Ubuntu)
biff = no
append_dot_mydomain = no
#delay_warning_time = 4h
smtpd_tls_cert_file=/etc/ssl/certs/ssl-cert-snakeoil.pem
smtpd_tls_key_file=/etc/ssl/private/ssl-cert-snakeoil.key
smtpd_use_tls=yes
smtpd_tls_session_cache_database =
btree:${queue_directory}/smtpd_scache
smtp_tls_session_cache_database = btree:${queue_directory}/smtp_scache
myhostname = ubuntu32.vonhagen.org
alias_maps = hash:/etc/aliases
alias_database = hash:/etc/aliases
myorigin = /etc/mailname
mydestination = mail.vonhagen.org, ubuntu32.vonhagen.org,
                localhost.vonhagen.org, localhost
relayhost =
mynetworks = 127.0.0.0/8
mailbox_size_limit = 0
recipient_delimiter = +
inet_interfaces = all
```

In order, these configuration variables do the following:

- smtpd_banner: Sets the value of the banner that is displayed when an SMTP connection is established. In this case, the banner is constructed by using the value of other variables set in the configuration file.

- biff: Determines whether the local e-mail notification service (biff) should be used for each user with new mail each time Postfix process the incoming mail queue. In this case, it is disabled because biff notifications can cause a performance drain, and are relevant only on the machine that houses the mail files. Users who use local mail files can enable this for themselves.

- append_dot_mydomain: Determines whether Postfix should append a domain name to mail sent to user@host. Nowadays, this is usually handled by the MUA, so this is disabled.

- delay_warning_time: Uncommenting this parameter would specify the period of time after which users would be notified if mail that they had sent had not yet been delivered. After all, the remote site could be using Microsoft Exchange, and might be down.

- smtpd_tls_cert_file: Identifies the full pathname of the file on this system that holds the certificate used by this machine when sending messages using TLS (Transport Layer Security).

- smtpd_tls_key_file: Identifies the full pathname of the file on this system that holds the RSA private key for the Postfix SMTP client when sending messages using TLS (Transport Layer Security).

- smtpd_use_tls: Determines whether this Postfix server should use TLS when a remote SMTP server announces STARTTLS support. If the remote server does not announce STARTTLS support, the message is sent in the clear.

- smtpd_tls_session_cache_database: Identifies the organization and location of the SMTP server TLS session cache used by the tlsmgr daemon.

- smtp_tls_session_cache_database: Identifies the organization and location of the SMTP client TLS session cache used by the tlsmgr daemon.

- myhostname: Identifies the actual Internet hostname of this system. By default, this value is the value returned by gethostname().

- alias_maps: Identifies the organization and full pathname of the aliases file used for local mail delivery.

- alias_database: Identifies the organization and full pathname of the aliases file used for local mail delivery, and which is updated using the traditional newaliases command. This is often the same file as that identified by the alias_maps parameter, but need not be.

- myorigin: Identifies the name of the host or domain that local mail is assumed to come from and is sent to. On Ubuntu systems, it is the name of a file containing whatever I specified as the mail name when installing Postfix. This is suitable for single-domain installations, but insufficient for Postfix mail servers that support multiple domains.

- mydestination: A list of domains for which mail is delivered via local mail delivery.

- relayhost: If outgoing must be sent to another mail server for delivery, this parameter identifies that mail server; otherwise, it is empty.

- mynetworks: Identifies the networks or specific hosts from which this mail server will send mail. In this case, the mail server will only send mail from the loopback network, which is a problem. This is discussed in the subsequent section entitled "Identifying Trusted Hosts and Domains."

- `mailbox_size_limit`: Identifies the maximum size of any mailbox on the system. In this case, 0 means that there is no limit.

- `recipient_delimiter`: Identifies the separator used internally by the Postfix server between user names and addresses

- `inet_interfaces`: Identifies the network interfaces on which the machine can receive mail. In this case, the postfix server will listen on all network interfaces.

A complete list of Postfix configuration parameters and possible values is available in the files section of the online reference information for the `postconf` command (`man 5 postconf`) or online at locations such as `www.postfix.org/postconf.5.html`.

Identifying Trusted Hosts and Domains

The `main.cf` configuration file in the previous section requires only one change to be a fully functional network mail server—the `mynetworks` parameter must be adjusted to add at least the local network. As installed by default, an Ubuntu Postfix server will listen for incoming requests on all network interfaces, but will only allow hosts on its loopback network to send e-mail through it.

The value of the `mynetworks` parameter can be a single host, an IP address and netmask to indicate a range of hosts or a subnet, or any number of comma-separated hosts or IP address and associated netmasks. The value of the `mynetworks` parameter in the `main.cf` file sets what is known as the *relay policy* for the host. A value must be present, or your mail server becomes what is known as an *open relay*, a mail server through which anyone can send e-mail. Open relays are favorite targets for spammers, because they can abuse them indefinitely.

In this case, my mail server handles mail for all of the systems on my SOHO office, all of which are in the 192.168.6.* address family, so I would change the value of the `mynetworks` parameter to be the following:

```
mynetworks = 127.0.0.0/8, 192.168.6.0/8
```

I then either restart the Postfix server (using `sudo /etc/init.d/postfix restart`) or use the `sudo postfix reload` command to cause the active Postfix daemon to pick up my changes to the configuration file. All hosts on my network can now send mail through the Postfix mail server.

Rewriting Addresses in Outgoing Mail

Though all hosts on the local network can now send mail through the mail server, many MUAs send mail using the fully qualified domain name of the host from which the mail was sent. This means that mail from me (wvh) on the host `64bit.vonhagen.org` goes out with an e-mail address of `wvh@64bit.vonhagen.org`. Though I don't particularly care about this, I probably don't have a mailbox there, and therefore people can't reply to such mail.

To correct this problem, we can use the Postfix configuration parameter `masquerade_domains` to identify domains for which Postfix should rewrite outgoing mail addresses so that they simply appear to be from `user@domain`. In this case, mail from `wvh@64bit.vonhagen.org` would go out simply as `wvh@vonhagen.org`, which is my actual e-mail address. In this case, I would add the `masquerade_domains` setting to my `main.cf` file:

```
masquerade_domains = vonhagen.org
```

I then either restart the Postfix server (using `sudo /etc/init.d/postfix restart`) or use the `sudo postfix reload` command to cause the active Postfix daemon to pick up my changes to the configuration file. All hosts on my network can now send mail through the Postfix mail server without identifying the specific host from which the mail originated.

Accepting Mail for an Entire Domain

As mentioned earlier, the mydestination parameter identifies what mail the host will deliver locally. The default Postfix configuration file accepts mail for localhost.localdomain, localhost, the actual hostname of the machine, and whatever you specified as the mail name of the machine on the configuration screens shown in Figures 27.3 or 27.6 (if that differs from the actual hostname of your machine). To make your new Postfix mail server a valid final destination for all mail for your domain, you must add the name of your domain to the list of destinations in your main.cf file. Because I specified mail.vonhagen.org as my mail name, my mydestination parameter currently looks like the following:

```
mydestination = mail.vonhagen.org, ubuntu32.vonhagen.org,
                localhost.vonhagen.org, localhost
```

I can either add my domain name to this list or set Postfix's mydomain parameter to the name of my domain and then leverage the value of that parameter to provide this information. I would add the mydomain parameter setting and then update the value of the mydestination parameter, which together would look like the following:

```
mydomain = vonhagen.org
mydestination = mail.vonhagen.org, ubuntu32.vonhagen.org,
                localhost.vonhagen.org, localhost, $mydomain
```

As with other configuration file changes, I would then either restart the Postfix server (using sudo /etc/init.d/postfix restart) or use the sudo postfix reload command to cause the active Postfix daemon to pick up my changes to the configuration file.

> **TIP** When you make the changes suggested in this section, you may also want to change the value of the myorigin parameter so that it is set to $mydomain. During installation, myorigin was set to whatever you specified as the mail name of the machine, which is useful because that value was also used in the values for your mydestination parameter, which in this case is useful if someone sends mail root@mail.vonhagen.org. However, after installation, it is more useful to have myorigin be the same as the value of mydomain.

Activating Qpopper for POP/POP3 Support

Qpopper (www.eudora.com/products/unsupported/qpopper/index.html) is a popular, free POP/POP3 server from the folks at Qualcomm, who sell the popular PC and Macintosh MUA, Eudora. I like Qpopper because it supports the vanilla Linux/Unix mbox format that Postfix uses by default on Ubuntu. (When using the mbox mailbox format, all messages are stored in a single file, and each message begins with the string "From user@domain", followed by the timestamp for the message.) I suggested that you install Qpopper in the section on installing Postfix — if you didn't and want to activate POP3 support on your new mail server, please install it now and then proceed with this section.

> **NOTE** As mentioned before, POP/POP3 and IMAP are alternate protocols for accessing your e-mail, and both can be used with Postfix as long as you install an appropriate server for that protocol on your mail server. Qpopper is fast, lightweight, and well-supported. However, if you want to support both POP/POP3 and IMAP, the Cyrus IMAP (http://asg.Web.cmu.edu/cyrus/) and Courier IMAP (www.courier-mta.org/imap/) packages are popular and are both available in the Ubuntu repositories. However, configuring the Cyrus IMAP server can be tricky, and the Courier IMAP server supports only the Linux/Unix maildir mailbox format, where each message is stored in a separate file, which is not the default behavior of Postfix on Ubuntu. Hence Qpopper, which is fast, easy, and "just works."

Ubuntu's Qpopper package provides a ready-to-run Qpopper daemon that is suitable for use with the `inetd` or `xinetd` Internet services daemons that were discussed in the section of Chapter 18 entitled "Configuring the svnserve Server." Both of these start various network services in response to specific types of incoming requests. If you have not already installed one of these, I suggest that you install the `xinetd` services daemon. You can then integrate Qpopper with `xinetd` by creating the following file with your favorite text editor and saving it as `/etc/xinetd.d/pop3`:

```
service pop3
{
    port             = 110
    socket_type      = stream
    protocol         = tcp
    wait             = no
    user             = root
    server           = /usr/sbin/in.qpopper
}
```

You can then restart the `xinetd` Internet services daemon using the command `sudo /etc/init.d/xinetd restart`, and Qpopper will be working correctly on your system. You can test that Qpopper is responding correctly to incoming POP/POP3 requests by configuring your MUA to point at your new mail server using the POP/POP3 protocol and checking your mail, or you can do so from the command line by using the `telnet` command to connect to port 100 (the POP/POP3 port) and seeing if you can login, as in the following example:

```
$ telnet mail.vonhagen.org 110
Trying 192.168.6.182...
Connected to 192.168.6.182.
Escape character is '^]'.
+OK Qpopper (version 4.0.5) at mail starting. <28861.1153954154@ulive>
user wvh
+OK Password required for wvh.
pass *********************
+OK wvh has 1 visible message (0 hidden) in 696 octets.
quit
+OK Pop server at ulive signing off.
Connection closed by foreign host.
```

As you can see, Qpopper responded correctly to my request on the POP/POP3 port, accepted my username and password, and listed the amount of pending mail that I have. Success!

Adding SPAM Filtering and Virus Scanning to Postfix

Now that you have a running mail server and are receiving incoming connections from other mail servers, you will quickly find that an incredible amount of the mail that you receive is SPAM (also known as *UCE, Unsolicited Commercial E-mail*). Some of that mail is going to contain virus-laden attachments. You may also, unfortunately, receive a virus from a friend who forwards you something that they thought was cute, but which actually contains a virus payload. If you're lucky, whoever was hosting your mail before you switched to your own mail server was filtering much of this out, and you may not even have known how bad things are in e-mail-land. Now that you're hosting your own mail server, you will quickly see that SPAM and virus-laden mail is an epidemic. No wonder it takes so long for me to connect to Amazon.com from the office some days...

Aside from the fact that you're now aware of the SPAM/virus epidemic, it is also now your responsibility to do something about it because you're responsible for your mail server. Luckily, there are some great ways to configure Postfix to automatically handle much of this for you. If you installed all of the packages that I suggested back in the section on "Installing Postfix and Friends," you've already installed the postgrey greylisting service and MailScanner. MailScanner scans incoming mail and rejects the SPAM that it can identify, and then can invoke other packages, such as SpamAssassin (`http://spamassassin.apache.org`), another package that does an even better job of SPAM detection, and ClamAV (`www.clamav.net`), which is an excellent open source antivirus package. All that remains to do now is to integrate these packages and Postfix.

At this point, you may be wondering why you should bother with an antivirus package on Linux, because Linux systems are essentially virus-free. I suggest that you integrate an antivirus package as a matter of course because some of the users of your mail server may also want to read mail on the Microsoft Windows machines that they otherwise use for playing games. More seriously, you may be setting up a mail server in a SOHO, SMB, or enterprise environment in which many of your users need to use Microsoft Windows systems. Either way, installing an antivirus package when you configure your mail server is preventative medicine. It costs you nothing, and if it saves one person the agony of getting a virus on their system and having to try to remove it, you're way ahead.

The next three sections discuss various levels of SPAM and antivirus protection. The first discusses greylisting as implemented by the `postgrey` package. The second discusses some simple Postfix parameters that you can add to your `main.cf` configuration file that will reject much incoming SPAM immediately, saving MailScanner the trouble of checking it. The third section then explains how to integrate MailScanner with Postfix and ClamAV with MailScanner to identify as much SPAM as possible that comes from correctly configured mail servers, and to check for viruses at the same time.

Greylisting via postgrey

In the section on "Installing Postfix and Friends," I suggested that you install `postgrey`, which is a greylisting application that was designed to work with Postfix. That package is set up and started automatically and requires no other mandatory configuration — if you installed it when you installed and started Postfix, it's already working for you.

As mentioned in the installation section, greylisting is a cool technique wherein your mail server rejects all incoming mail the first time that a remote mail server tries to deliver it to you. Most spammers only try once and then move on — they can't afford to endlessly retry sending mail to hosts that have already rejected it once. All real mail servers that are sending real mail will try to deliver the mail again, at which point your Postfix server will actually talk to them. At that point, the other techniques described in this section kick in.

> **NOTE** If you're interested, the term *greylisting* is related to two other techniques for avoiding SPAM. The term *blacklisting* refers to the practice of refusing to accept mail from hosts that are on a list of known or suspicious hosts. The term *whitelisting* refers to the practice of accepting mail only from a short list of known hosts, specific people, and so on. It's a shame that we all have to resort to these sorts of techniques to protect ourselves from idiot spammers, but that's the reality of the Internet today.

Though `postgrey` requires no specific manual configuration, there are several command-line options that are not active by default but which you may want to take advantage of. The `postgrey` service also has several features that you may want to take advantage of to customize how greylisting is done on your system. You can whitelist specific sites by adding them to the various whitelist files in /etc/postgrey. For example, the file /etc/postgrey/whitelist_clients identifies sites for which no greylisting will be done — all incoming mail from these sites will be accepted immediately. Similarly, the file /etc/postgrey/whitelist_recipients identifies users of your mail server that do not want greylisting — in other words, users for whom incoming mail will be accepted immediately, regardless of the site from which it originates. You should read the online man page for postgrey using the man postgrey command to see if there are options that you want to take advantage of to fine-tune how the postgrey service works on your system.

Adding Postfix Parameters to Reject Bogus Mail

As mentioned in the section entitled "Postfix Configuration Files," a tremendous number of Postfix configuration parameters are available, relatively few of which are actually set in the default main.cf configuration file installed with the Ubuntu Postfix package. In general, that's a good sign, letting you know that the defaults are typically correct. However, several of these parameters provide additional capabilities that can help your Postfix mail server reject SPAM out of hand by checking for things that do not conform to Internet electronic mail standards (as defined in the RFCs). Though the next section, "Integrating MailScanner, SpamAssassin, and ClamAV with Postfix," explains how to scan the content of incoming e-mail for SPAM, scanning incoming mail takes some amount of time, which reduces the overall performance of your system slightly. Any mail that you can reject before you even have to scan it is therefore a win for everyone.

Adding the following block of commands to your Postfix main.cf configuration file can be very effective in reducing SPAM (the line numbers are present to make it easy for me to refer to different lines — they should not be present in your main.cf file!):

```
 1  smtpd_delay_reject = yes
 2  smtpd_helo_required = yes
 3  smtpd_helo_restrictions =
 4      permit_mynetworks,
 5      reject_invalid_hostname,
 6      reject_non_fqdn_hostname,
 7      permit
 8  smtpd_data_restrictions =
 9      reject_unauth_pipelining,
10      permit
11   smtpd_sender_restrictions =
12      permit_mynetworks,
13      reject_non_fqdn_sender,
14      reject_unknown_sender_domain,
15      permit
16  smtpd_recipient_restrictions =
17      permit_mynetworks,
18      reject_unknown_recipient_domain,
19      reject_unauth_destination,
20      permit
```

Line 1 is required to use any of the subsequent blocks of restrictions, telling your Postfix server to wait until it receives certain commands from the remote mail server (i.e. a remote SMTP daemon that is a client of your mail server) before rejecting mail based on the rule chains that follow. The `smtpd_delay_reject` phrase is required because some SMTP servers misbehave if you reject mail before they've had the chance to waste at least some of your time. Line 2 rejects mail from any mail server that fails to correctly identify itself using the HELO or EHLO phrases required by the SMTP RFC. This saves you from having to check any of the subsequent rules.

Lines 3 through 7, 8 through 10, 11 through 15, and 16 through 20 are chains of rules that are applied to different portions of your mail server's interaction with a remote mail server:

- Lines 3 through 7 identify restrictions on the HELO or EHLO commands which are used by a remote mail server to identify itself to your Postfix mail server. Line 4 immediately permits connections from any mail server listed in the Postfix `mynetworks` parameter. Line 5 rejects connections from remote mail servers that identify themselves using a malformed hostname. Line 6 rejects connections from remote mail servers that do not identify themselves using a fully qualified hostname. Line 7 says that your mail server will accept HELO or EHLO commands from mail servers that have not failed the previous tests, and allows you to move on to the next set of tests.

- Lines 8 through 10 identify restrictions on the way in which the remote mail servers sends commands to your mail server. Line 9 tells your server to reject connections that send commands to your mail server too quickly, or at least before your mailer has told the remote mail servers that it can accept a fast stream of SMTP messages. Many bulk e-mailers automatically do this to try to speed up deliveries — after all, they have a zillion targets to send mail to, so they can't afford to waste time (except for yours). Line 10 says that your mail server will accept additional data from mail servers that have not failed the previous tests, and allows you to move on to the next set of tests.

- Lines 11 through 15 identify restrictions on the sender of the e-mail that your server is receiving (identified using the SMTP MAIL FROM command). Line 12 immediately permits connections from any mail server listed in the Postfix `mynetworks` parameter. Line 13 rejects mail from any sender whose name is not identified using a fully qualified host name. (Note that mail from your local network may use a short hostname, but we've already permitted mail from them.) Line 14 rejects mail from senders with unknown domains. Line 15 says that your mail server will accept mail from senders that have not failed the previous tests, and allows you to move on to the next set of tests.

- Lines 16 through 20 identify restrictions on the recipient of the e-mail your server is receiving (identified using the SMTP RCPT TO command). Line 17 immediately permits connections from any mail server listed in the Postfix `mynetworks` parameter. Line 18 rejects mail where the current mail server is not the final target of the mail and that target is not a valid domain. Line 19 rejects incoming mail if the recipient is not in the domains serviced by the current mail server (identified in the `mynetworks` parameter) or is not in the domains that your mail server will relay mail to (identified in the `relayhost` parameter). This prevents your mail server from being used as an open relay. Line 20 says that your mail server will accept mail for recipients that have not failed the previous tests, and allows your mail server to move on to actually processing and delivering the incoming mail.

Postfix provides many other checks that I haven't used here, such as checks that test whether the incoming mail is from a mail server that is known to be a source of SPAM (i.e., is on a blacklist). In my experience, this type of lookup is slow and these lists are often wrong. For example, some sites that support these blacklists identify any IP addresses that are dynamically assigned by providers such as Comcast as sources of SPAM. Though this may sometimes be the case, it often is not — for example, Comcast is my ISP, and I promise that I don't send SPAM.

The sample commands shown in this section should significantly reduce the amount of incoming SPAM that you receive. Once you've had the chance to experiment with this, you may want to try adding other, similar commands. For a complete list of other checks that you can do to reject incoming SPAM, see the files section of the online reference information for `postconf` command (`man 5 postconf`) for more information, which is also available online at locations such as `www.postfix.org/postconf.5.html`.

Integrating MailScanner, SpamAssassin, and ClamAV with Postfix

MailScanner is a fast, powerful tool that scans incoming mail for SPAM and can optionally be configured to scan incoming mail for viruses. The Ubuntu MailScanner package requires that the SpamAssassin package (discussed in the section of Chapter 8 entitled "Automatically Checking for Junk Mail") be installed on your system so that it can invoke the SpamAssassin package after performing its own SPAM checks, to maximize the chances that it will catch and flag incoming SPAM.

> **NOTE** The MailScanner package always claims that it is scanning for viruses even if it is not. This is because its configuration file contains a setting for the virus scanner that you want to use, which by default is set to none. Don't worry; I'll explain how to fix that.

I suggested that you install MailScanner and the ClamAV virus-scanning package in the section of this chapter entitled "Installing Postfix and Friends." If you didn't, please go back and see that section for information on how to install those packages.

Once installed, it is remarkably easy to add MailScanner to the Postfix food chain:

1. Add the following line to the end of your Postfix `main.cf` configuration file (`/etc/postfix/main.cf`):

   ```
   header_checks = regexp:/etc/postfix/header_checks
   ```

2. Use your favorite text editor to create the file `/etc/postfix/header_checks` with the following contents:

   ```
   /^Received:/ HOLD
   ```

   This line tells Postfix to scan every incoming message for instances of the string "Received:" at the beginning of a line and to move any matching messages (which will be all of them) to a HOLD queue. The HOLD queue is a temporary staging area that you'll use for scanning the incoming mail. Save this file and proceed to the next step.

3. Using your favorite text editor, bring up the MailScanner configuration file (`/etc/MailScanner/MailScanner.conf`) so that you can configure MailScanner to work correctly with Postfix as installed on your Ubuntu system. (By default, the Ubuntu MailScanner package is configured as it would be on a Debian system and is therefore configured for use with the exim mail server.)

4. Find the Run As User entries, remove the hash mark at the beginning of the line that says `Run As User = postfix`, and make sure that there is a hash mark at the beginning of any other line that begins with `Run As User`. These entries should now look something like the following:

   ```
   # Run As User = mail
   Run As User = postfix
   # Run As User = Debian-exim
   ```

5. Find the Run As Group entries, remove the hash mark at the beginning of the line that says Run As Group = postfix, and make sure that there is a hash mark at the beginning of any other line that begins with Run As Group. These entries should now look something like the following:

```
# Run As Group = mail
Run As Group = postfix
# Run As Group = Debian-exim
```

6. Find the Incoming Queue Dir entry and change its value to /var/spool/postfix/hold. This entry should now look like the following:

```
Incoming Queue Dir = /var/spool/postfix/hold
```

7. Find the Outgoing Queue Dir entry and change its value to /var/spool/postfix/incoming. This entry should now look like the following:

```
Outgoing Queue Dir = /var/spool/postfix/incoming
```

8. Find the MTA entry and change its value to postfix. This entry should now look like the following:

```
MTA = postfix
```

9. Find the Virus Scanners entry and set its value to clamav. This entry should now look like the following:

```
Virus Scanners = clamav
```

10. Save the /etc/MailScanner/MailScanner.conf file and proceed to the next step.

11. Use the following commands to ensure that the Postfix user and group owns MailScanner's working directory and the directory where it stores (quarantines) files that are suspected of containing viruses, so that the Postfix mail server can write to these directories:

```
sudo chown -R postfix:postfix /var/spool/MailScanner
```

12. Using your favorite text editor, modify the file /etc/default/mailscanner and remove the hash mark at the beginning of the line containing the run_mailscanner variable. This line should look like the following:

```
run_mailscanner=1
```

Enabling this variable will cause your system to automatically start MailScanner the next time you boot your system. Save the file and exit from the text editor.

Now, start MailScanner for the first time by using the following command:

```
sudo check_mailscanner
```

Now either restart the Postfix server (using sudo /etc/init.d/postfix restart) or use the sudo postfix reload command to cause the active Postfix daemon to pick up your changes to the configuration file.

To test that MailScanner is correctly integrated with your mail server, send yourself a piece of mail through your mail server. If MailScanner is working correctly (and the mail was not SPAM and did not contain a virus, you should see the following banner at the bottom of the message:

```
This message has been scanned for viruses and
dangerous content by MailScanner, and is
believed to be clean.
```

Congratulations! You are now doing a decent amount of SPAM filtering and are also checking for viruses in any mail received by your mail server!

> **TIP**   As mentioned previously, SpamAssassin is preconfigured for use with MailScanner and comes with several rules that it uses to test whether incoming messages should be marked as SPAM. You can obtain many other sets of rules for use with SpamAssassin that extend the basic capabilities that it provides. After you're comfortable with the fact that things are actually working correctly, you may want to add some of these other rule sets. See sites such as the Exit0.us SpamAssassin wiki (www.exit0.us/), and the SpamAssassin Rules Emporium forums (www.rulesemporium.com/forums/) or mailing list (http://lists.maddoc.net/mailman/listinfo/sare-users) are great sources for additional rules that you may find useful. However, remember that every additional rule that you add increases the amount of time that it takes to check each piece of incoming mail. Don't get carried away, or your mail server may be able to process only one or two incoming messages per day.

More Information

This chapter provides a thorough explanation of setting up a simple Postfix mail server on your Ubuntu system. If you are going to run your own mail server, you should purchase one of the various Postfix books that are available so that you have an exhaustive, dedicated resource at your fingertips if anything ever goes wrong. The ones that I am familiar with, all of which are great, are the following:

- *Postfix* by Richard Blum (Sams, 2001, ISBN: 0672321149): I have used this book for years, and it has always been an excellent basic reference for me, though it is the oldest and therefore is missing all of the configuration parameters that have been added since 2001.

- *Postfix: The Definitive Guide* by Kyle D. Dent, Wietse Venema (O'Reilly Media, 2003, ISBN: 0596002122): Things don't get much more definitive than the O'Reilly book, because Witse Venema is one of its authors.

- *The Book of Postfix: State-of-the-Art Message Transport* by Ralf Hildebrandt, Patrick Koetter (No Starch Press, 2005, ISBN: 1593270011): Ralf Hildebrandt is a well-known Postfix expert and advocate — his Postfix Shrine Web site was mentioned as an excellent Postfix resource (more useful if you happen to speak German, because parts of it are in that language). Don't worry monolinguals: the book is even better, and it's in English.

As with all hi-tech topics nowadays, your favorite search engine is your best friend when looking for immediate help with a specific configuration problem, error message, or general Postfix problem.

Summary

E-mail is one of the killer applications of today's Internet, and running your own mail server is standard operating procedure in many enterprise and academic environments, and is getting more and more common for home users. The complete control that running your own mail server provides can be a valuable asset in almost any environment, reducing if not eliminating SPAM and malicious system attacks through e-mail viruses and Trojans.

This chapter provided background information about the most popular Linux mail systems in use today, and then focused on installing and configuring the Postfix mail server. This chapter also explained how to integrate add-on services such as SPAM filtering and virus detection into a standard Postfix installation. Postifx is a powerful and easily configured mail server, with which a variety of additional open source services can be easily but tightly integrated.

Chapter 28 discusses how to install and configure a Dynamic Host Control Protocol Server (DHCP), which enables you to manage and monitor the distribution of IP addresses to client computer systems on your network. Dynamically assigning e-mail addresses enables you to serve a large pool of client systems with a relatively small set of IP addresses, and also simplifies ensuring that all client computer systems share the same network configuration data. Using DHCP also simplifies updating basic network information on client systems, because this information is stored and updated centrally and can easily be pushed to all clients by the DHCP server.

Chapter 28

Setting Up a DHCP Server

long time ago when even I was young, the Internet (or the ARPANET as it was called in those days) was a small place with a limited number of hosts, all of which had fixed IP addresses and names that were maintained in a file that everyone shared with everyone else, and then added their own local modifications for any private, local hosts and networks. However, as the ARPANET grew and more and more hosts became networked, maintaining all of this information in a single file became not only impractical, but also silly. This led to a flexible, software-based service known as DNS (the Domain Name System), which provided a flexible mechanism for identifying the hostname associated with an IP address, and vice versa. (For more information about DNS, see Chapter 29, "Setting Up a DNS Server.")

Why begin a chapter on DHCP (Dynamic Host Configuration Protocol) by discussing DNS? Because DHCP and its predecessors were largely developed to address similar sorts of scalability and flexibility by providing a similarly flexible service that could dynamically provide various types of network-related information. When few hosts at a site are networked and those hosts are all located on the same subnet, assigning them static IP addresses and statically maintaining other IP-related information such as name-server identities is reasonable. However, as the number of hosts on a network grows and hosts are added more and more frequently, requiring that someone from IT manually install and configure each host's networking quickly becomes impractical. Similarly, networked laptops are frequently used in multiple locations, each of which may require a different network configuration.

This chapter provides a bit of background information on DHCP and its predecessors, the types of problems that they were developed to solve, and then explains how to set up your own DHCP server and some of the issues to consider when doing so. This chapter focuses on DHCP servers for traditional IPv4 networks, but also provides occasional IPv6-related tips.

IN THIS CHAPTER

DHCP overview

Configuring a DHCP server from the command line

Configuring a DHCP server graphically

Troubleshooting DHCP

Overview of DHCP

DHCP stands for Dynamic Host Configuration Protocol. But what does that mean for the users of a network? It means that when everything is working correctly, you should be able to connect your computer to the data jack on the wall with an Ethernet cable, and the University's computer will recognize your computer and allow it to join the network.

DHCP is used to provide network configuration information to the computer systems on a network that are configured to retrieve information dynamically. These systems, known as DHCP clients, locate a system running a software service known as a DHCP server and obtain network configuration information from that system.

DHCP was created by the Dynamic Host Configuration Working Group of the Internet Engineering Task Force (IETF). It was originally created to satisfy the requirements of Internet Request for Comments (RFC) document 1531, which begat RFC 1533 (which begat RFC 2132), which begat RFC 1534, which begat RFC 1541, which begat RFC 2131, and so on. As with all Internet RFCs, reading these documents can provide some fascinating insights into the thought processes that led to the development of many of the concepts and services that we all take for granted on today's networks and the Internet in general. You can access the IETF's RFC archive through the URL `www.ietf.org/rfc.html`, or find those same RFCs at a somewhat easier-to-browse site at `www.faqs.org/rfcs`. Some of these are true classics, such as RFCs 1149, 2549, and so on.

DHCP is based on an earlier protocol for retrieving the information required to boot specific hosts known as BOOTP, and maintains some backward compatibility with BOOTP — hosts that require BOOTP (such as some embedded systems) can retrieve the required information from a correctly-configured DHCP server. The key difference between the two is that BOOTP was designed to provide specific responses to requests from specific hosts, whereas DHCP is a much more flexible system that responds to requests from essentially random clients. DHCP also provides a configurable mechanism for reallocating IP addresses to hosts that already have them and recovering network addresses that are no longer in use through its concept of limited-duration leases.

A DHCP client locates and retrieves network configuration information from a DHCP server through the following series of events (For simplicity's sake, this example ignores routing DHCP requests through relay agents.):

1. A client broadcasts a DHCP discover message to the address `255.255.255.255`. This broadcast includes information that uniquely identifies the client, such as its Media Access Control (MAC) address.

2. Any DHCP servers that receive the offer return an appropriate IP address by broadcasting a DHCP offer message. The IP address that is offered is based on the network interface and subnet from which the request was received, and is either a preallocated IP address that is associated with a specific MAC address, or one from the set of available addresses that this server can offer on the designated subnet. (The set of IP addresses that a specific DHCP server can provide is typically known as the pool of addresses for that server.) IP addresses that cannot be issued by a DHCP server are those that are already in use or those that are reserved for use by clients with specific MAC addresses.

   When broadcasting an offer message, the server temporarily reserves this address so that it does not offer it twice. The information returned to the client also includes information about any other configuration services that the DHCP server can provide for the client.

Picking the Right Lease Period

The lease time for your server's DHCP clients is a delicate balance between usability and serviceability. You want clients that have been configured via DHCP to keep that configuration as long as they need that information, but you also want to maximize the availability of DHCP configuration to other clients on your network. This is especially (and primarily) important on networks where the number of potential users exceeds the number of available IP addresses.

Identifying any conceivable patterns in how users access and use your DHCP server will help determine a usable lease period. For example, if you know that the number of possible clients exceeds the number of available IP addresses, it's in your best interest to keep the lease period as short as possible, On the other hand, you want to minimize network traffic and the load on your DHCP server. If you have many more users than IP addresses and mobile users frequently connect to your network, you will want to keep the lease time as short as possible. However, if systems typically appear on your network for a certain period of time (30 minutes, an hour, and so on), you will want to set the lease time to that period to minimize lease refresh requests.

Another consideration is the amount of time required to recover from network problems or hardware failures on the DHCP server. For example, if your DHCP server were to crash and burn, the lease period would define the maximum amount of time that DHCP clients would maintain their current network configuration.

Finally, consider the "silly user" factor. If clients of your DHCP server are setting up network services that they expect others to be able to access for a significant amount of time, you may need to make sure that your DHCP leases are valid for at least that period of time. Even though DHCP leases are supposed to be renewed when they are actively in use, this may not happen for one reason or another. As we all learned in Cub Scouts, Brownies, or similar groups, "Be prepared." If users report problems, you can always fix things and report a success story, but sometimes no comments are the best comments of all.

3. The DHCP client selects the best offer that it has received based on the type and number of services offered and broadcasts a request that identifies the IP address of the server whose offer it wants to accept. This broadcast enables all "also-ran" DHCP servers to drop any addresses that they may have temporarily reserved and move on.

4. The DHCP server identified in the second broadcast message allocates the IP address that it has reserved for the client and enters that IP address into its database of allocated IP addresses, along with a timestamp identifying when it was allocated and an identifier for the time period for which assigned IP addresses are valid (the lease period). The DHCP server then sends an ACK response back to the client that contains all of the network configuration information that it can provide.

5. The DHCP client uses the configuration information sent to it by the DHCP server to configure its network interfaces, DNS servers, and so on, and continues booting. The client also notes the duration of the lease period, and begins a countdown timer that will notify the DHCP server when the lease expires, asking for an extension. When this occurs, and if the extension request adheres to the DHCP server's lease policy, the DHCP server extends the lease.

When a DHCP server issues a lease for an IP address, it either begins a timer or simply polls to verify that the lease period for a specific IP address has not expired. Most DHCP clients notify a DHCP server that they no longer need an IP address as part of their orderly shutdown process. DHCP clients that "terminate abnormally" (i.e., crash) don't have time to do this, but any IP address that they allocated will automatically be freed for reuse by the DHCP server some period of time after the lease expires.

Alternate DHCP Servers for Ubuntu Systems

The Ubuntu repositories provide several DHCP servers in addition to the one that I suggested installing. One or the other of these may be better suited to your network configuration. Also, thanks to the fact that DHCP is indeed a standard, all DHCP servers use the same configuration commands. They may use different configuration files, but the commands that these files contain are the same across all DHCP servers. Optional DHCP servers available for Ubuntu are the following:

- `dhcp`: Version 2 of the ISC DHCP server. You may want to install this DHCP server if you want to use the `autodns-dhcp` package, which automatically updates a DNS server with information about hosts whose IP information was newly assigned via DHCP.

- `dnsmasq`: A small-footprint DNS server (and proxy) that also provides DHCP support. I don't recommend this package unless you have a specific reason not to use BIND, which is the standard, and most popular, DNS server. See Chapter 29, "Setting Up a DNS Server," for more information about BIND.

- `udhcpd`: A very small-footprint DHCP server designed primarily for use in embedded systems. You may want to install this DHCP server if memory or storage resource minimization is critical.

- `wide-dhcpv6-server`: A DHCP server for IPv6 hosts, this DHCP server requires that you use an IPv6 DHCP client such as `wide-dhcpv6-client` on any IPv6 systems that you want to configure using DHCP.

The DHCP server that you want to use is up to you. I suggest the `dhcpd3-server` package because it corresponds to the latest and greatest DHCP server available from the ISC. Your mileage may vary (or your environment may suggest or mandate a different DHCP server).

As you can see from this explanation, DHCP is an extremely clever and powerful mechanism that serves both the needs of hosts that need specific configuration settings (and which are therefore identified in the DHCP server's configuration information) and the requirements of random clients that just happen to appear on the subnet that a DHCP server is monitoring.

NOTE The flip side of flexibility is the ease with which the wrong thing can happen. For example, DHCP servers that are misconfigured or started by accident may provide DHCP clients with completely incorrect information. In my experience, the most common cause of DHCP problems is "randoms" starting invalid DHCP servers on networks that already have official DHCP server. In enterprise environments, nothing makes a sysadmin happier than someone starting a misconfigured DHCP server on their network(s). This is easy enough to do, especially on multi-homed systems (systems with multiple Ethernet interfaces) where I might have forgotten to identify the Ethernet interface that I wanted my DHCP server to listen on. Did I say "I"? I meant "someone."

Now that we're all one with the concept of DHCP servers and the types of information that they provide, let's install and configure one.

Installing a DHCP Server

Most server processes aren't installed as part of a default Ubuntu installation because, let's face it, not everybody needs (or wants) to run servers. However, as with all software packages on Ubuntu, the Synaptic Package Manager makes it easy to install a DHCP server. The one that I suggest installing is the Institutional Service Component's (ISC) v3 server, which is found in the package dhcp3-server. This is the latest and greatest DHCP server available, and is certainly the one that provides the most functionality. I also suggest that you install the gdhcpd package, which provides an easy-to-use graphical interface that simplifies configuring and customizing a DHCP server.

To install this package using apt-get or aptitude (without the graphical configuration tool), use the commands sudo apt-get install dhcpd3-server or sudo aptitude -r install dhcp3-server.

To install these packages graphically, start the Synaptic Package Manager from the System ➪ Administration menu and supply your password to start Synaptic. Once the Synaptic application starts, click Search to display the search dialog. Make sure that "Description and Name" are the selected items to search through, enter **DHCP** as the string to search for, and click Search. After the search completes, scroll down in the search results until you see the dhcpd3-server package, right-click its name, and select Mark for Installation to select that package for installation from the pop-up menu. Figure 28.1 shows the dhcp3-server package being selected for installation.

After you have selected the dhcpd3-server package, scroll down further in the search results until you see the gdhcpd package, which is a graphical utility for configuring and customizing a DHCP server. Right-click its name and select Mark for Installation to select that package for installation from the pop-up menu.

After selecting these packages for installation, click Apply in the Synaptic toolbar to install the DHCP server and its graphical configuration utility. When the installation completes, you can exit Synaptic Package Manager. Almost ready to serve!

FIGURE 28.1

Installing the DHCP server and friends in Synaptic

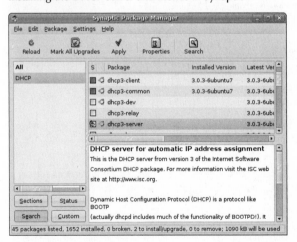

Managing a DHCP Server from the Command Line

There are always a few people who would rather fight than switch, which in this case means that they would rather create a DHCP server configuration file with a text editor than use a whizzy graphical tool. That's fine — using a text editor is probably faster if you know what you're doing (or are willing to accept the consequences). The next few sections explain how to manually create DHCP server's configuration file and discusses some of the more important options that you may need to add to a DHCP server's configuration file to maximize its usability in your environment.

Creating DHCP Configuration Files Using a Text Editor

This section explains the basics of a DHCP configuration file and the most common set of entries that you will need to put in your configuration file to serve a specific range of IP addresses via a shiny new DHCP server.

TIP The file `/etc/dhcp3/dhcpd.conf` is the configuration file used by the dhcpd3 server that I suggested installing in the previous section. If you installed another DHCP server, shame on you but I'm sure that you had your reasons, and its configuration file is probably the file `/etc/dhcpd.conf`, which is the traditional location for a DHCP server's configuration file. An easy way to verify the configuration file used by your DHCP server is the following command, where `server-name` is the name of the executable for your DHCP server:

```
$ strings `which server-name` | grep dhcpd.conf
```

This will display several strings, one of which will be the full pathname of your DHCP server's configuration file. This works for all of the DHCP servers that I've used — you may find that you need to be slightly more creative with the arguments to the `grep` command, but you'll certainly find your config file with some similar command.

To configure DHCP for your network, you need to add at least the following section (referred to by DHCP config file fans as a stanza) to your DHCP server's configuration file:

```
1: option domain-name "your.domain.name";
2: option domain-name-servers nameserver1-address, nameserver2-
address,... ;
3: option routers router-address;
4. option subnet-mask 255.255.255.0;
5: subnet subnet-address netmask netmask-for-that_subnet  {
6:   range full-start-address full-end-address;
7: }
```

NOTE The actual configuration file used by your DHCP server does not include line numbers (and cannot). I've added the line numbers to make it easier to match up entries in this sample file with the explanations that follow.

This example provides an extremely minimal DHCP server configuration file that is useful, but which leverages many of the default values provided by the DHCP server. Each line of this stanza has the following meaning:

1. The name of the domain to which any host that receives an IP address from this server should belong. On Linux systems, this domain is written to the file `/etc/resolv.conf` without preserving any existing entries. See Chapter 29, "Setting Up a DNS Server," for more information

about the /etc/resolv.conf file. This is a global setting for the DHCP server, and will apply to all subnet entries that it contains (unless they specifically override this value).

2. The name(s) of any DNS servers that any host that receives an IP address from this server should use to do DNS lookups. On Linux systems, these name servers are added to the file /etc/resolv.conf without preserving any existing entries. See Chapter 29 for more information about the /etc/resolv.conf file. This is a global setting for the DHCP server, and will apply to all subnet entries that it contains (unless they specifically override this value).

3. The third line identifies the IP address of the system through which requests for any host that is not found on the local network should be sent. This is a global setting for the DHCP server, and will apply to all subnet entries that it contains (unless they specifically override this value).

4. The fourth line specifies the default subnet mask to use on computers that get their IP addresses from this DHCP server. This is typically 255.255.255.0, but may differ depending upon the configuration of your network. This is a global setting for the DHCP server, and will apply to all subnet entries that it contains (unless they specifically override this value).

> **NOTE** Each global setting in the host section ends with a semicolon.

5. The fifth line identifies the subnet on which the DHCP server should hand out IP addresses. This is expressed by identifying the base address of a network, using zeroes for IP address fields that the DNS server can provide, and by specifying the subnet mask used to derive IP addresses on that network.

6. The sixth line identifies the range of IP addresses that the DHCP server can issue to clients.

7. The final line terminates the entry for the specified subnet.

After making these changes to your DHCP server's configuration file, you must start (or restart) the DHCP server. If the DHCP server is running and you installed the DHCP server that I recommended, you can kill and restart it by using the following command:

```
$ sudo /etc/rc.d/init.d/dhcp3-server restart
```

All other DHCP servers provide similar start/restart configuration scripts — if you installed another DHCP server, check its control files in /etc/init.d for the name of the script that you need to execute and any additional arguments that you may need to supply.

Specifying Additional DHCP Server Configuration File Entries

In addition to the DHCP configuration statements discussed in the previous section, you can specify several other options in your DHCP server's configuration file. Using these other options can provide your DHCP server with additional configuration information, which enables it to forward this information to any of its clients.

Additional global dhcpd.conf statements that you may find useful are the following. An example of a dhcpd.conf file that uses these statements is given following the list, to clarify the context in which each statement can be used:

- **default-lease-time**: This DHCP server configuration option enables you to specify the default period of time for which a lease will be valid. The time period is specified as an integer number of seconds.

- **ddns_update-style**: This declaration is used if your site uses a DNS (Domain Name Server) server that can be automatically updated as addresses are assigned by the DHCP server. If your site does not use a DNS server that accepts updates from a DHCP server, you should specify the ddns_update-style none command in your DHCP server's configuration file.

- `ip-forwarding`: If, for example, you don't want a DHCP client to be able to forward IP requests to other networks, you may want to set this parameter to `off`. This option is sometimes used on local-only IP networks.

- `max-lease-time`: This DHCP server configuration option enables you to specify the maximum period of time for which a lease will be valid. The time period is specified as an integer number of seconds.

You can also use DHCP to provide specific IP addresses to specific hosts within a subnet group, where each host is identified by MAC address. This is done using the `host` declaration within a subnet group. An example of this, an associated, host-specific command, is the following:

```
option ddns-update-style interim;
option default-lease-time 28800;
option max-lease-time 86400;
option ip-forwarding off;
 subnet 192.168.6.0 netmask 255.255.255.0  {
    range 192.168.6.160  192.168.6.190
    host dorothy {
        hardware ethernet 00:!E:0C:1D:75:1D;
        fixed_address 192.168.6.69;
        server_name "192.168.6.64" ;
        option routers 192.168.6.1;
        option host_name "dorothy" ;
    }
}
```

Note that the example for the specific host named `dorothy` overrides any default values specified earlier in the file.

Managing a DHCP Server Graphically

As you might expect, the Ubuntu repository provides an excellent GNOME utility for graphically configuring a DHCP server. You should have installed this package (`gdhcpd`) as part of the instructions for installing a DHCP server in the section of this chapter entitled "Installing a DHCP Server."

Installing the `gdhcpd` package creates a GDHCPD entry on the Applications ⇨ Internet menu, which you can select to start Ubuntu's graphical DHCP server configuration tool. Unfortunately, this menu item may not start the `gdhcpd` utility using `sudo`, which would mean that it can't write to the configuration file for your DHCP server (which is the file `/etc/dhcp3/dhcpd.conf` if you installed the ISC v3 DHCP server that I suggested earlier). To eliminate problems related to file protection issues, start the `gdhcpd` command from a GNOME terminal, `xterm`, or other Ubuntu command-line interface using the following command:

```
$ gksudo gdhcpd
```

After you supply your password, the `gdhcpd` utility starts, as shown in Figure 28.2.

FIGURE 28.2

Starting the GNOME DHCP configuration utility

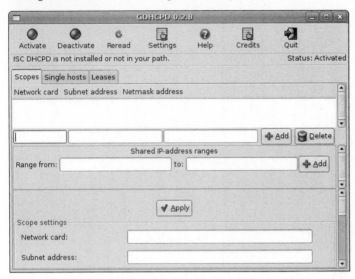

Don't worry if the gdhcpd application displays a message about not being able to find the DHCP server in your path, because (by default) it looks for a DHCP server executable named dhcpd, while the name of the ISC v3 DHCP server that I suggested installing is dhcp3.

The first thing to do is to identify the scope for this DHCP server, which is the Ethernet interface that this DHCP will listen on, the possible range of IP addresses that it will deliver, and the subnet mask that it will use. To do this, enter these values in the fields shown in Figure 28.3, which identify a DHCP server running on Ethernet interface eth0 of the host that will hand out IP addresses on the 192.168.6.0 subnet using a subnet mask of 255.255.255.0.

> **NOTE**   A *scope* is a way of identifying the complete range of possible IP addresses for a network. A scope typically defines a single physical subnet on your network to which DHCP services are offered. Scopes provide the primary way for a DHCP server to manage distributing and managing a specific range of IP addresses and delivering them (and other network configuration parameters) to clients on that subnet.

Once you have entered this information, click Add to define that interface/server/netmask combination. An entry for that server displays on the Scopes tab, as shown in Figure 28.4.

FIGURE 28.3

Identifying the DHCP server's Ethernet information

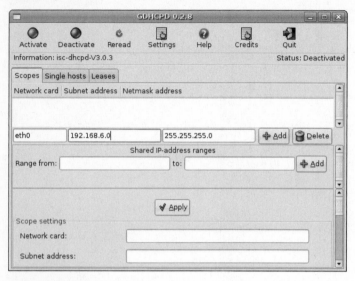

FIGURE 28.4

Successful addition of a DHCP server scope

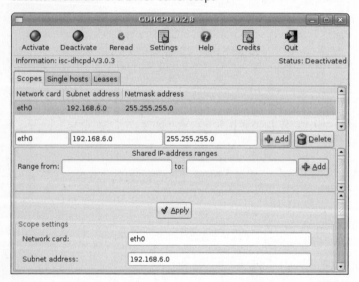

Next, enter the range of IP addresses that you want this DHCP server to offer to clients, as shown in Figure 28.5.

After entering these values, click Add to define this range. The defined range displays in the primary gdhcpd dialog, as shown in Figure 28.6.

FIGURE 28.5

Identifying a range of DHCP addresses to serve

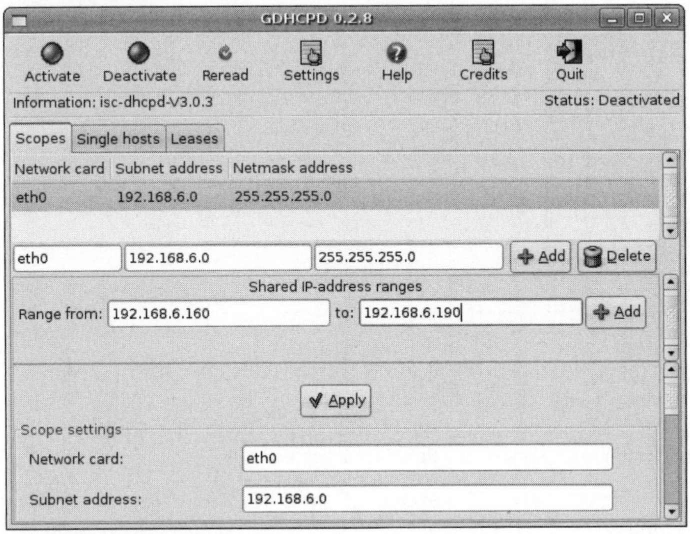

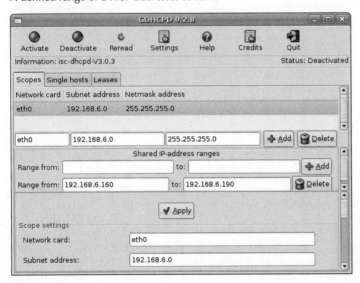

FIGURE 28.6

A defined range of DHCP addresses to serve

Finally, click Settings to examine the default settings associated with your DHCP server. The dialog shown in Figure 28.7 displays.

FIGURE 28.7

General DHCP server settings

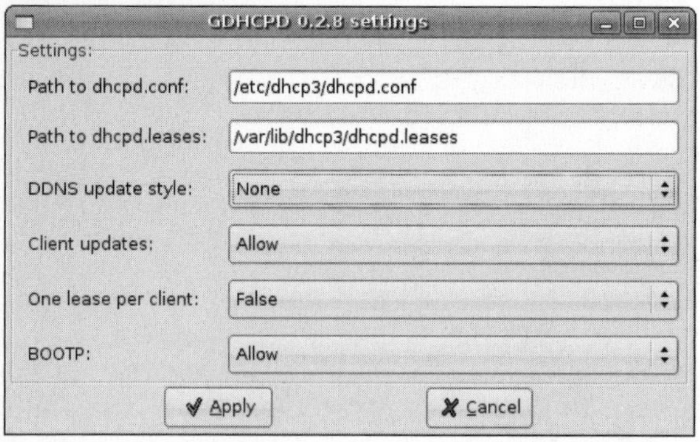

Change any of the values on this screen that reflect how your DHCP server should behave. If you are configuring a DHCP server other than the dhcp3 server that I suggested installing earlier in this chapter, you may need to change the name of the DHCP server's configuration file and the path to the file in which DHCP leases are stored to reflect the appropriate locations for that DHCP server.

You may also want to change general configuration items. For example, if the DHCP server that you are configuring can automatically update your DNS server, you should change the value of the DDNS update style parameter to either ad-hoc or interim (ad hoc has been deprecated and should not be used; interim allows your DHCP server to update a DNS server whenever it hands out a lease).

Once you have verified any global values that you want to set for your DHCP server, click Apply to close this dialog and return to the primary gdhcpd dialog.

If you are finished defining ranges of DHCP addresses that you want your DHCP server to offer to clients, click Quit to exit the gdhcpd configuration utility. Your DHCP server is configured—all that remains is to start it!

> **TIP** Before starting your DHCP server, you may want to check the section of this chapter entitled "Specifying Additional DHCP Server Configuration File Entries" to see if there are any other entries that you want to add to your DHCP server's configuration file.

To start your DHCP server using the new configuration file, execute the following command:

```
$ sudo /etc/init.d/dhcpd3-server restart
```

This terminates any version of the dhcpd3-server application that may be running and forces the process to restart, which reads your new configuration file. Congratulations—you're running a DHCP server.

At this point, you should check the file /var/log/messages to verify that your DHCP server started correctly. You can do this using a command like the following, which shows the last 100 lines in this file (just in case):

```
$ sudo tail -100 /var/.log/messages
```

If the DHCP server did not start correctly or clients cannot successfully connect to the DHCP server, see the following section for some debugging and troubleshooting tips.

Troubleshooting DHCP

The most common cause of DHCP problems is that the server did not start correctly or has already handed out all of the leases that are available to it. By default, any startup, status, and error messages from a DHCP server are written to the log file /var/log/messages. If your DHCP server does not start correctly, this file is the first place to look. If you have manually created your DHCP server's configuration file, missing semicolons or other syntax errors will cause the DHCP server to exit or, worst-case, start up in some mode other than the one that you intended.

If a client computer is unable to contact a DHCP server, it usually assigns itself an IP address like 169.x.x.x, which traditionally means that your computer can't connect to the network. If any client system gets an address in this range, the first things to check are the obvious ones — is the client computer actually connected to a port on your local network, and is the Ethernet interface that is connected configured as a DHCP client? On Ubuntu systems, you can check the configuration of your Ethernet interface(s) by selecting the System ➪ Administration ➪ Networking menu item and supplying your password. You should also check the /var/log/messages file on your DHCP server to see if the DHCP request from that client was received but rejected for some reason.

On multi-homed systems, a very common problem is that a DHCP server is listening on the wrong Ethernet interface, and is therefore not receiving DHCP client requests on that subnet. Starting a DHCP server on a specific Ethernet interface is done by identifying the name of that Ethernet interface on the command line that starts the DHCP server, which is typically in a file with a name like /etc/init.d/dhcpd. The name of this file may be different depending on the DHCP server that you are using.

A final suggestion is to explicitly force the client to release any lease that it may believe it currently has. The dhclient3 -r command (or dhclient -r command, if you are running a v2 DHCP client) forces the client to explicitly release any leases that it believes that it has. The DHCP client then exits — you can restart it by executing a command like the following:

```
$ sudo /etc/init.d/networking restart
```

This restarts all of the networking-related processes on your system, starting the DHCP client as part of that sequence if your system is indeed configured as a DHCP client.

Summary

Being able to dynamically assign and centrally manage client IP address and network configuration information dramatically simplifies life for many system administrators. This chapter explained how to install a Dynamic Host Configuration Protocol (DHCP) server on your Ubuntu system, using either command-line or graphical software management tools. It then explained how to configure your DHCP server either from the command line or user-friendly graphical tools. The chapter concluded by discussing potential problems that you may encounter when using and configuring DHCP, and provided ways to diagnose and correct them.

Chapter 29 discusses how to set up your own Domain Name System (DNS) server. A DNS server maps hostnames to IP addresses (and vice versa), and is often a necessity on corporate or academic networks where you must manage your own hostnames and internal IP addresses.

Chapter 29

Setting Up a DNS Server

As I mentioned in the DHCP chapter, a long time ago when even I was young, the Internet (or the ARPANET as it was called in those days) was a small place with a limited number of hosts, all of which had fixed IP addresses. The mappings between those IP addresses and the actual names of those hosts were maintained in a central text file. Yes, that's right, a single text file. Everyone shared this text file (HOSTS.TXT) with everyone else by retrieving it from the Stanford Research Institute's Network Information Center (the one true NIC) every so often, and then adding their own modifications for any private local hosts and networks. However, as the ARPANET grew and more and more hosts became networked, maintaining all of this information in a single file became not only impractical, but silly.

Not only was this file long (and getting longer), but its format was only specified by convention rather than explicit decree. Luckily, the Internet/ARPANET was created by smart people, so many improvements to this model occurred in the early 1980s. For example, in March of 1982, the hosts table definition was updated with DoD Internet Host Table Specification (RFC 810). Shortly thereafter, a server function to provide individual hostname/address translations was described in RFC 811, which introduced the idea of dynamically providing and maintaining host information. RFC 819, "The Domain Naming Convention for Internet User Applications", woke everyone up, and RFC 830, "A Distributed System for Internet Name Service" suggested the one true concept of a distributed system of name servers, each serving its local domain. 1982/3 was a busy year for the fundamental concepts that we all take for granted today (and may not even be aware of).

TIP Once the appropriate RFCs came out and people had the chance to think about them, implementation was the next step. By November, 1983, the concept and schedule for actually implementing DNS were developed and published in RFC 881, "The Domain Names Plan and Schedule," RFC 882, "Domain Names — Concepts And Facilities," and RFC 883, "Domain Names — Implementation And Specification."

In response to these RFCs, the clever folks at the University of California at Berkeley (UCB) created a software package called BIND, for Berkeley Internet Name Daemon. Amusingly enough, this was first written as a graduate student project. BIND was eventually taken over and maintained first by the university's Computer Systems Research Group (CSRG), and then by Digital Equipment Corporation (DEC) for a while, and then eventually by the Internet Systems Consortium (www.isc.org/), who still maintains BIND today. Many other DNS-related RFCs (973, 1035, etc.) have been published on DNS since the original flurry, some enhancing existing RFCs and some replacing them with newer, more modern and more specific, content. As mentioned in Chapter 28, "Setting Up a DHCP Server," you can find Internet RFCs at sites such as www.ietf.org/rfc.html or the somewhat easier-to-browse site at www.faqs.org/rfcs.

> **NOTE** References to BIND throughout the rest of this chapter should be taken to mean BIND version 9, which is the version that I suggest (and describe) installing and using.

DNS was primarily designed to address the scalability problems that prompted the migration of hostname/IP address mappings from a central file to a flexible mechanism that can be queried and which returns results. This has some great additional benefits for local subnets in today's ubiquitous networking universe, where private networks can support their own DNS servers that satisfy local, private requests while forwarding requests for external host information to higher-level name servers. These local name servers can also cache retrieved requests, reducing the amount of external network requests your name servers have to issue over time. Many sites run name servers that only serve to cache external requests, and are therefore known as "caching-only name servers."

The remainder of this chapter provides an overview of how DNS works, how to install the latest version of the BIND name server on your Ubuntu system, how to create the text files required for a basic BIND installation and integrate them into your BIND server, how to restart and test a BIND server, and how to diagnose many common DNS problems.

> **NOTE** BIND and DNS are rich, complex topics about which many entire books have been written. I can't afford to embed another one of those in this book. The section at the end of this chapter provides pointers to some more detailed, dedicated DNS and BIND resources that you can find online. If you are going to be setting up and managing complex or commercial DNS servers, I'd suggest that you pay a quick visit to any brick-and-mortar or online bookseller for dedicated DNS and BIND reference material that you will always have at your fingertips regardless of the state of your network. Two of my favorites are *DNS and BIND* by Paul Albitz and Cricket Liu (O'Reilly — make sure you get the latest edition!), and *Pro DNS and BIND* by Ron Aitchison (Apress). You can find the latter online at www.netwidget.net/books/apress/dns, but you should still buy a copy.

Overview of DNS and BIND

DNS gives your network an entry point into a hierarchical collection of hostname and IP address servers on an intranet or the Internet itself. All of the hosts on your network can query one or more local DNS servers for local hostname and IP address information. Requests for hostname and IP address information outside the administrative domain of your DNS servers are automatically passed up the DNS food chain until some DNS server can authoritatively give you the information you're looking for.

A common DNS misconception is that a system needs to run a DNS server to participate in DNS. This is not the case. Systems can be pure DNS clients without running a name server process. The client-side portion of the DNS system is known as a *resolver*, which is configured through the file /etc/resolv.conf (which I'll discuss later in this section). Whether a system participates in DNS at all is configured through your system's Name Service Switch file, /etc/nsswitch.conf, which is also discussed in detail later in this section.

Most hosts have traditional sources of hostname/IP address information, such as /etc/hosts files, as well as DNS servers. When an application needs to contact a specific host by name, your system goes through the following process:

1. It first checks the /etc/nsswitch.conf file's hosts entry to determine how your system is configured to resolve hostnames and IP addresses. The /etc/nsswitch (Name Service Switch) identifies the sequence in which files and network resources should be consulted to find a variety of information, including hostname/IP address information. The hosts entry generally looks something like the following:

   ```
   hosts:    files dns [NOTFOUND=return] nis nisplus
   ```

   The system on which this entry is used first looks in the /etc/hosts file for host information, and then consults DNS. If the host is not found after querying DNS servers, the hostname/IP address lookup fails. Items in a hosts entry after [NOTFOUND=return] are not consulted, but are often left on this line as a reminder that they are valid values for hostname/IP address information. In this example, the NIS and NIS+ information services would not be consulted.

> **TIP** Some older applications still consult another configuration file called /etc/host.conf. This file provides similar information to that provided in /etc/nssiwtch.conf files about the order in which an /etc/hosts file and DNS should be consulted using the following entry:
>
> ```
> order hosts,bind
> ```
>
> The resolver functions in most recent versions of glibc use /etc/nsswitch.conf. However, if you have changed your /etc/nsswitch.conf file and some specific application is consulting /etc/hosts and DNS in the wrong order, check your /etc/host.conf file. You may also want to report the problem to the current maintainer of the program that you were running.

2. Assuming the hostname or IP address of a specific host is not found in the /etc/hosts file, a system that is configured to consult DNS checks the contents of the text file /etc/resolv.conf to identify the DNS name servers that it should consult, in order. This file also often contains information such as the default domain that should be supplied when looking up non-fully-qualified hostnames. For example, the /etc/resolv.conf file on one of my Ubuntu systems looks like the following:

   ```
   domain vonhagen.org
   nameserver 0.0.0.0
   nameserver 68.87.75.194
   nameserver 68.87.64.146
   nameserver 207.44.142.94
   ```

   In this example, non-fully-qualified hostnames such as 64bit are assumed to be within the domain vonhagen.org. The name servers are queried in order until one responds or a maximum number of connection failures and associated retries have elapsed, in which case the query fails.

> **TIP** A nameserver specification of 0.0.0.0 is actually a shortcut for querying a local name server using the first IP address that was assigned to the local system. This is the loopback address, which is usually 127.0.0.1, but is not guaranteed to be. Using the shortcut 0.0.0.0 causes your request to be sent to an IP address that is known to be valid for the current host, whatever it may be.

3. When a DNS server responds, it first tries to resolve the query itself. DNS servers are configured through many specially formatted text files that are discussed in the next section. These files identify any DNS zones, which are essentially analogous to a domain or subdomain that the server can provide authoritative information for. If the hostname or IP address request is in a zone that the DNS server is authoritative for or is already present in the server's cache of previously-answered

requests, the DNS server will reply directly to the request. If the request is in a subdomain that the DNS server knows an authoritative source of information for, it will forward the request to that DNS server for resolution. That DNS server will then reply to the client.

4. If the first DNS server that responds cannot resolve the request in one way or another, it queries one of the Internet's top-level name servers (known as *root servers*) to identify the name server that it believes is responsible for the domain or the range of IP addresses that contains the IP address for which the application is looking for hostname information.

5. The root name server returns a pointer to the appropriate name server, which your system then queries for hostname or IP address information. If this name server is not actually authoritative for the domain or IP address that you are querying, it may forward the query to other name servers — this hierarchy continues until a name server is found that is actually authoritative for the domain or IP address that you are querying. This forwarding is generally invisible to you, and most often occurs when querying hosts on subdomains rather than top-level domains.

This combination of local, root, and hierarchical name servers is elegant in its simplicity. When your host finally receives the hostname or IP address that it is looking for, it typically caches that value so that subsequent requests for the same information won't have to go any further than the local name server.

BIND is generally configured in one of four ways:

- As a master server that is an authoritative source of DNS information for one or more zones, which generally map to a domain or subdomain.

- As a slave server that is an authoritative source of DNS information for one or more zones, but periodically retrieves and synchronizes this information from a master server rather being the actual repository for that information.

- As a caching-only server that is not authoritative for any zone, but which caches the results from DNS queries to minimize network traffic and expedite answering multiple requests for the same DNS information. Most Ubuntu server systems will run at least a caching-only name server for these reasons.

- As a resolver-only client that does not run a DNS server but whose DNS resolver is configured to consult name servers through its `/etc/resolv.conf` file.

Most desktop systems do not need to actually run a name server and will work fine as resolver-only clients. However, if you spend a vast amount of time surfing the Web or work on a heavily loaded network, you may want to upgrade your system to running a caching-only client. DNS servers do not consume a vast amount of system resources, but they do require memory, process slots, and so on. If a system that you are configuring or using does not need to provide host information for a zone (which would mandate running a DNS server), only the user(s) as a system can determine which of the caching-only or resolver-only configurations works best for that host.

Installing a DNS Server Using Synaptic

Though every Ubuntu system provides the basic client-side commands for querying and dynamically mapping hostnames to IP addresses, an actual DNS server is not installed as part of a default Ubuntu installation. Let's face it — not everybody needs to run a DNS server, and for small, home networks, maintaining your `/etc/hosts` files isn't that big of an issue if you only have a few machines. However, as with all software packages on Ubuntu, the Synaptic Package Manager makes it easy to install the BIND DNS server. To install this package, start the Synaptic Package Manager from the System ➪ Administration menu and supply your password to start Synaptic. Once the Synaptic application starts, click Search to display the search dialog. Make sure that Description and Name are the selected items to search through, enter **Domain Name Server** as the string to search for, and click Search. After the search completes, scroll down in the search results until you see the `bind9` package, right-click its name, and select Mark for Installation to select that package for installation from the pop-up menu. Figure 29.1 shows the `bind9` package being selected for installation.

FIGURE 29.1

Installing the BIND 9 DNS Server in Synaptic

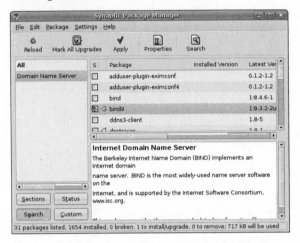

After selecting `bind9` for installation, click Apply in the Synaptic toolbar to install the BIND DNS server. When the installation completes, you can exit from Synaptic. Almost there!

Overview of BIND Configuration Files

The `/etc/nsswitch.conf` and `/etc/resolv.conf` files reflect your system's general approach to resolving hostname and IP address queries. The primary configuration file for the BIND name server, `named.conf`, is found in the directory `/etc/bind` on Ubuntu systems.

As delivered on Ubuntu systems, the `/etc/bind/named.conf` file primarily consists of statements that load other BIND configuration files, providing a simple, hierarchical structure for your BIND configuration files. The files that a BIND server on Ubuntu systems loads fall into several categories:

- Configuration files for the BIND server process, named. BIND installations on Ubuntu load a general, site-independent configuration file and a separate, site-specific configuration file. This simplifies future updates by making it easier to identify files that may have changed in the BIND installation on a specific system.

- Zone files that define the mapping of hostnames in that DNS zone to IP addresses.

- Reverse lookup files that define the mapping of IP addresses in a numeric DNS zone to hostnames.

As a specific example, the default `/etc/bind/named.conf` file on a BIND server on Ubuntu systems loads the following files. These are listed in alphabetical order, to simplify finding a file in this list rather than in the order that they are actually loaded:

- `/etc/bind/db.0`: Contains reverse lookup information that resolves the broadcast addresses `0.*`.

- `/etc/bind/db.127`: Contains reverse lookup information that resolves the loopback addresses `127.*`.

- `/etc/bind/db.255`: Contains reverse lookup information that resolves the broadcast addresses `255.*`.

- `/etc/bind/db.empty`: Contains a shared file that is used for each of the nonroutable IP address families specified by RFC 1918, "Address Allocation for Private Internets" (`www.faqs.org/rfcs/rfc1918.html`).

- `/etc/bind/db.local`: Contains hostname to IP address information for the local loopback interface, `127.0.0.1`.

- `/etc/bind/db.root`: Contains hostname to IP address information for the root name servers.

- `/etc/bind/named.conf.local`: Contains zone entries that identify any zones and IP addresses for which this BIND server is a source of authoritative information. This file is a local, host-specific supplement to the file `/etc/named.conf`.

- `/etc/bind/named.conf.options`: Defines the basic options with which the local BIND server has been configured.

- `/etc/bind/zones.rfc1918`: Provides reverse lookup information for each of the nonroutable IP families specified by RFC 1918, "Address Allocation for Private Internets" (`www.faqs.org/rfcs/rfc1918.html`). This file is not loaded by Ubuntu BIND servers by default, but can be loaded in your `/etc/bind/named.conf.local` file to reduce the time spent trying to resolve IP addresses in nonroutable networks.

In most cases, you will modify only the `/etc/bin/named.conf.local` file for your BIND server. In this file, you will add entries for files that define the zones and IP address ranges for which your BIND server can provide authoritative DNS information.

TIP The `/etc/bin/named.conf.options` file for BIND servers running on Ubuntu systems configures those servers to use `/var/cache/bind` as their default working directory. All temporary DNS data is stored in that directory. For this reason, all pathnames in the `/etc/bin/named.conf.local` file either should be the full pathnames of files located in nontransient directories in your filesystem, such as `/etc/bind`, or will be interpreted as files that are to be found in `/var/cache/bin`.

A sample `/etc/bin/named.conf.local.` file from one of my DNS servers looks like the following:

```
zone "vonhagen.org" {
  type master;
  file "/etc/bind/vonhagen.zone";
  check-names warn;
};

zone "168.192.in-addr.arpa" {
  type master;
  file "/etc/bind/168.192.in-addr.arpa";
};

include "/etc/bind/zones.rfc1918.local";
```

As you can see, this DNS server is a master server for the zone `vonhagen.org`, which uses IP addresses in the `192.168.*` family. Information about the zone `vonhagen.org` is provided in the file `/etc/bind/vonhagen.zone`. Reverse lookup information for IP addresses in the `192.168.*` family is provided in the file `/etc/bin/168.192.in-addr.arpa`. As discussed previously, full pathnames must be provided for any files not found in `/var/cache/bind`, which is the default BIND server's default directory. This file also loads a local copy of the default `/etc/bin/zones.rfc1918` file, which I have edited to remove null responses for the zone `"168.192.in-addr.arpa"` that I use locally.

The next section explains how to create the zone and reverse lookup files for any local systems for which your BIND server will provide authoritative information.

Creating DNS Zone and Reverse Lookup Files

As installed on Ubuntu systems, BIND is a caching-only name server that is appropriate for use on local servers or heavily network-dependent systems to help minimize the amount of external DNS traffic by caching DNS lookups so that subsequent requests for that same information can be provided from the cache rather than by repeating an external DNS request.

Many people want to run their own DNS servers to provide DNS information for the hosts that they are responsible for on their home, enterprise, or academic networks. As discussed earlier in this chapter, DNS information for each set of hosts and associated range of IP addresses is specified in a zone file, one that identifies the IP address associated with a specific hostname (known as name to IP address lookups), and one for reverse lookups that identifies the hostname that corresponds to a specific IP addresses. The next few sections discuss mandatory entries that are commonly used in both types of files, the format and content of a zone file, and the format and content of reverse lookup files.

> **NOTE** The files that I am calling *zone* and *reverse lookup* share the same format, and are both examples of zone files. I refer to them separately because it's convenient to think of them that way. They contain different types of records and serve different logical purposes in the context of a DNS server.

Using Common Entries for Zone and Reverse Lookup Files: SOA and $TTL

The beginning of both zone and reverse lookup files contain variable settings for the BIND name server process (`/usr/sbin/named`) and an entry that sets basic variables for each zone or range of IP addresses for which your name server provides authoritative information.

A zone file typically begins with a TTL (Time To Live) entry that provides a default value for any record in the zone file. A TTL value determines how long remote DNS servers can cache any information about that resource that they have retrieved from your DNS server. The default TTL value is preceded with a dollar sign to indicate that you are setting a BIND server variable, and takes a time value expressed in seconds (the default), minutes, hours, or days. The sample TTL value that I generally use is one day (`1d`), because I frequently add, rename, or change hosts on my networks. This setting therefore looks like the following:

```
$TTL 1d
```

The most important entry in a zone or reverse lookup file is the Start Of Authority (SOA) record, which defines global parameters for a zone or range of IP addresses. The format of an SOA record is defined in RFC 1035 (`www.faqs.org/rfcs/rfc1035.html`). A sample SOA record looks like the following:

```
@ 1d IN SOA ubuntu32.vonhagen.org. wvh.vonhagen.org. (
     2006070102 ; Serial
     21600      ; Refresh
     1800       ; Retry
     604800     ; Expiration
     900        ; Negative Cache TTL
)
```

> **TIP** One confusing thing about the SOA record (and, frankly, about many other DNS configuration file entries) is that many of the fields have default values and are therefore often omitted if the values that you specify are the same as the defaults. Personally, I find the practice of omitting values to be both lazy and the most common cause of DNS problems. The parser for DNS files is quite finicky (to use the technical term), and you will eventually burn yourself or one of your fellow sysadmins by leaving fields out. It's not as if any of the values in an SOA or other records in a zone or reverse lookup file are all that long or require all that much typing. Do everybody a favor—specify all of them.

The fields in an SOA record are the following:

- The first field identifies the root name of the zone associated with this SOA record. The @ symbol is a shortcut for this name, which is specified in the zone declaration in the BIND configuration file (in this case, the file /etc/bind/named.conf.local). You may occasionally see people put an actual zone name here—I prefer to use the @ symbol because it more clearly differentiates the SOA record from other records in a zone or reverse lookup file.

- The second field is the TTL value to this record. Even though I always put a default value at the beginning of a zone file, I simply repeat that value here to be more precise. This field is technically optional—if it is not specified, the default TTL for the server or an internal default value will be used.

- The third field identifies the record class of the SOA record. An IN entry identifies this as a DNS resource of the "Internet" class. This field is technically optional because IN is the default class type for any resource record in a zone or reverse lookup file, but I prefer to explicitly provide a class value for readability and clarity purposes. Other possible record classes are HS (Hesiod) and CH (Chaos), which are types of records that only MIT staff or Lisp machine fans will recognize.

- The fourth field identifies the name of the name server that provides authoritative information for this zone or IP address range. This name looks like a standard hostname, but usually ends with a period, which is the way in which the DNS configuration file parser identifies fully-qualified Internet information. Names that do not end with a period are assumed to be local names to which the root name for the zone or IP range should be appended. For example, if the name of your name server is ns1, the root name for this domain is vonhagen.org, and the IP address of your name server is identified in the zone or reverse lookup file, then either the entries "ns1" or ""ns1.vonhagen.org." are acceptable in this field. However, the entry "ns.vonhagen.org" is completely wrong because it does not end with a period, and the DNS parser therefore replaces it with ns1.vonhagen.org.vonhagen.org", which probably doesn't exist in your domain. Forgetting the period here is a common problem when creating zone or reverse lookup files.

- The fifth field is the e-mail address of someone that is responsible for this zone or IP address range. As with other Internet names in a hosts or zone file, this entry usually ends with a period to indicate that it is a fully qualified Internet name. The @ sign that is traditionally used in an e-mail address is invalid here because the DNS parser uses that as a shortcut for the root name of the zone or reverse lookup range, and is replaced with a period. Again, forgetting the period here is a common problem when creating zone or reverse lookup files. However, it's harder to see this problem because you simply don't get mail sent from the BIND user. If you see several e-mail failures for this user, check the syntax of the SOA records for your BIND server.

- The sixth field is actually a set of five parameters, separated by whitespace and enclosed within one set of parentheses. Many people, including myself, use semicolons (a comment character) to append text descriptions of each field that make it easier to see what each value means during future updates. The five values that you must supply are the following:

  - **serial number:** This is an unsigned integer that should be changed each time you modify a zone or reverse lookup file. This value is usually constructed by concatenating the four digits for the current year, two digits for the current month, two digits for the current day, and two final digits for a version number between 01 and 99. This makes it easy to decipher when the file was last modified and allows up to 99 revisions per day, which should hold just about anyone.

  - **refresh interval:** Identifies the amount of time in seconds after which a slave DNS server will update its zone and reverse lookup information from the master server for that zone.

  - **retry:** Identifies the time interval in seconds after which a slave DNS server whose refresh interval has expired but has failed to contact its master server will try to recontact that master server. This value should obviously be much smaller than the refresh interval.

  - **expiration:** Identifies the time interval between successful refreshes after which the zone data maintained by a slave server is no longer considered authoritative. Slave servers stop responding to DNS requests if this time period has passed and the master server still cannot be contacted.

  - **negative cache TTL:** The amount of time that a negative response, such as a nonexistent domain response, will be cached by the DNS server. Versions of BIND prior to version 9 used this value to represent the default TTL for a zone or reverse lookup file, which is now specified using $TTL (as described earlier).

The next sections describe how to create zone and reverse lookup files that use these common features.

Creating Zone Files

A basic zone file consists of four blocks of information:

- The $TTL and SOA statements described in the previous section.
- An entry that defines the name server for that zone.
- An entry that defines the mail server for that zone.
- Entries for all of the hosts in that zone that map hostnames to their associated IP addresses and that identify any aliases (CNAMEs) that are associated with those hosts.

A name server entry looks like the following:

```
@            . IN   NS    ubuntu32.vonhagen.org.
```

This entry identifies the root name of the zone using the same @ symbol shortcut as was used in the SOA record, the fact that this is an Internet class record (IN), the specific type (NS, for name server), and the hostname of the name server. The IP address of the name server is typically provided later in the zone file if it is in the same domain or subdomain. As with other Internet name entries in this file, the name of the name server must end with a period or the zone name will be appended to it. I use the @ shortcut to refer to the root domain in NS records because, frankly, this makes it easier for me to use a generic template for all of my zone files.

A mail server entry is very similar to a name server entry except that it uses the MX (Mail Exchanger) record type to identify a mail server, and you can optionally precede the name of the name server with a numeric weight that allows you to identify higher-priority mail servers. Lower values have higher priority. This is meaningless when you have only one mail server, but providing a value makes it easier for you to remember that this feature is available as your network and number of mail servers expand. A sample mail server entry looks like the following:

```
@                   IN   MX    10 mail.vonhagen.org.
```

The IP address of the mail server is typically provided later in the zone file if it is in the same domain or subdomain. As with other Internet name entries in this file, the name of the mail server must end with a period or the zone name will be appended to it. I also use the @ shortcut to refer to the root domain in MX records because, again, this makes it easier for me to use a generic template for all of my zone files.

After the name server and mail server records, the rest of a simple zone file typically consists of address (A) and canonical name (CNAME) records for hosts in the zone. Address records look like the following:

```
64bit         IN   A    192.168.6.64
64x2          IN   A    192.168.6.80
ubuntu32      IN   A    192.168.6.90
```

Note that no period follows the short names, because I want the root name of the zone to be appended to them. No trailing period is necessary after the IP address.

Canonical name records look like the following, and identify aliases for a host:

```
dualcore      IN   CNAME 64x2
```

No period follows the canonical name or the name of the host that this record provides an alias for. CNAME records require two DNS lookups, one for the name of the alias and a second to find out the IP address of the host that this is an alias for, and so should be used sparingly. CNAME records are most commonly used to map generic server names such as www, ftp, and so on to a specific machine.

A sample, complete zone file for the domain vonhagen.org on one of my local name servers looks like the following:

```
$TTL 1d

@ 1d IN SOA ubuntu32.vonhagen.org. wvh.vonhagen.org. (
        2006070108 ; Serial
        21600      ; Refresh
        1800       ; Retry
        604800     ; Expire
        900        ; Negative Cache TTL
)

@             IN   NS    ubuntu32.vonhagen.org.
@             IN   MX    10 mail.vonhagen.org.

64bit         IN   A     192.168.6.64
64x2          IN   A     192.168.6.80
ubuntu32      IN   A     192.168.6.90
mail          IN   A     207.44.142.34

dualcore      IN   CNAME 64x2.vonhagen.org.
www           IN   CNAME mail.vonhagen.org.
ftp           IN   CNAME:mail.vonhagen.org.
```

The entries for the `mail`, `www`, and `ftp` hosts are somewhat unique in this file, and merit some additional explanation and an associated apology. Because I use an ISP that already provides a public name server that is authoritative for the domain `vonhagen.org`, I added entries for the IP addresses of specific external hosts to my zone file so that I could find them internally while using this server as an authoritative source for my domain. People on external systems would still use the public authoritative name server for my domain, while internally, I could still find the right hosts for a few external systems. There are other, more complex but standard ways of doing this via delegation, but this hack let me keep my zone file simple while still doing the right thing.

Creating a zone file is half the DNS battle. Once you've created a zone file, you have to create a parallel file that identifies how a name server can deduce the hostname from an IP address, which is known as a reverse lookup file. These files are discussed in the next section.

Creating Reverse Lookup Files

A basic reverse lookup file, sometimes also referred to as a reverse map file, consists of three blocks of information:

- The $TTL and SOA statements described earlier in this chapter.
- An entry that defines the name server for that zone.
- Entries for all of the IP addresses in that zone and the hostnames that they point to.

A name server entry looks exactly the same in a reverse lookup file as it does in a standard zone file:

```
@          . IN    NS     ubuntu32.vonhagen.org.
```

This entry identifies the root name of the zone using the same @ symbol shortcut as was used in the SOA record, the fact that this is an Internet class record (IN), the specific type (NS, for name server), and the hostname of the name server. The IP address of the name server is typically provided later in the zone file if it is in the same domain or subdomain. As with other Internet name entries in this file, the name of the name server must end with a period or the zone name will be appended to it. I use the @ shortcut to refer to the root domain in NS records because, frankly, this makes it easier for me to use a generic template for all of my zone files.

After the name server record, the rest of a simple reverse lookup file typically consists of pointer (PTR) records, each of which identifies the hostname associated with a specific IP address in the range that this file describes. Completely qualified PTR records for IP addresses of the form *AAA.BBB.CCC.DDD* have the following format:

```
DDD.CCC.BBB.AAA.in-addr.arpa. IN   PTR    hostname.domain.tld.
```

The entries in the first field that correspond to an IP address are backward from the actual IP address because this file tells how to map IP addresses back to hostnames, and you therefore want to start with the least significant portion of the IP address, which most easily and uniquely identifies a specific PTR record. All PTR records must include the extension `.in-addr.arpa.`, either explicitly or by having it appended to the entry in the first field.

Sample pointer records from one of my reverse lookup files look like the following:

```
64.6    IN   PTR     64bit.vonhagen.org.
80.6    IN   PTR     64x2.vonhagen.org.
90.6    IN   PTR     ubuntu32.vonhagen.org.
```

Though the entries in the first field represent portions of an IP address, these entries are handled just like names, in the sense that because they are not terminated with a period, the root name of the zone (in this case, `168.192.in-addr.arpa`) is appended to them. The hostnames are terminated with a period to identify them as fully-qualified domain names.

A sample, complete reverse lookup file for IP addresses in the family below `192.168`, which are defined in the file `168.192.in-addr.arpa` on one of my local name servers, looks like the following:

```
$TTL 1d

@ 1d IN SOA ubuntu32.vonhagen.org. wvh.vonhagen.org. (
     2006070108 ; Serial
     21600      ; Refresh
     1800       ; Retry
     604800     ; Expire
     900        ; Negative Cache TTL
)


@       IN  NS    ubuntu32.vonhagen.org.

64.6    IN  PTR    64bit.vonhagen.org.
80.6    IN  PTR    64x2.vonhagen.org.
90.6    IN  PTR    ubuntu32.vonhagen.org.
```

Creating a reverse lookup file is the second half of the DNS battle. All that remains is to incorporate them into the BIND configuration for your name server, as described in the next section.

Incorporating Zone and Reverse Lookup Files with BIND

The previous two sections explained how to create zone and reverse lookup files. The files created in the previous two sections are the files `vonhagen.zone`, the zone file for the domain `vonhagen.org`, and the reverse lookup file `168.192.in-addr.arpa`, which maps IP addresses under `192.168` to the host-names in the `vonhagen.org` domain that they are associated with. To actually use the files you've created, you simply need to add them to the file `/etc/bin/named.conf.local` file for the name server that you want to serve as an authoritative source for this information. The `/etc/bin/named.conf.local` file on this server looks like the following:

```
zone "vonhagen.org" {
  type master;
  file "/etc/bind/vonhagen.zone";
  check-names warn;
};

zone "168.192.in-addr.arpa" {
  type master;
  file "/etc/bind/168.192.in-addr.arpa";
};

include "/etc/bind/zones.rfc1918.local";
```

These entries include each of these files and identify this server as the master server for the zone `vonhagen.org`, which uses IP addresses in the `192.168.*` family. Information about the zone `vonhagen.org` is provided in the file `/etc/bind/vonhagen.zone`. Reverse lookup information for IP addresses in the

192.168.* family is provided in the file /etc/bin/168.192.in-addr.arpa. The entries that identify these files use full pathnames because these files are stored in /etc/bind, not the server's default directory of /var/cache/bind as defined in the server's /etc/bin/named.options file. As mentioned previously, this /etc/bind/named.conf.local file also loads a local copy of the default /etc/bin/zones.rfc1918 file, which I have edited to remove null responses for the zone "168.192.in-addr.arpa", because valid values for this range of nonroutable IP addresses are explicitly provided in the file /etc/bin/168.192.in-addr.arpa.

After updating your /etc/bin/named.conf.local file, all that remains is to reload this information into the name server and test the name server, as described in the next section.

Restarting and Testing Your Name Server

The DNS server startup file for BIND 9 is the file /etc/init.d/bind9. Though this startup script provides reload and force-reload options, these options use a name server control utility (rndc) that may not be correctly configured (yet) on your system. For this reason, I tend to simply restart the BIND daemon using a familiar command like the following:

```
$ sudo /etc/init.d/bind9 restart
```

After supplying your password, you will see the familiar shutdown and startup messages from the script. You should then verify that the name server started correctly by checking for it in a process listing, using a command like the following:

```
$ ps alxww | grep named
```

If your configuration and zone files are valid, you will see a named process running on your system. Congratulations — you're running a DNS server. If not, proceed to the next section for some debugging tips, and then return to this section to complete your testing.

Next, add an entry for your new DNS server to the file /etc/resolv.conf. On the system where you are actually running the DNS server, you can add an entry like the following as the first name server entry in that system's /etc/resolv.conf file:

```
nameserver 0.0.0.0
```

As mentioned previously, a name server specification of 0.0.0.0 is just a shortcut for querying a local name server using the first IP address that was assigned to the local system. This is the loopback address, which is usually 127.0.0.1, but is not guaranteed to be. Using the shortcut 0.0.0.0 causes your request to be sent to an IP address that is known to be valid for the current host, whatever it may be.

Once you're sure that your name server is working correctly, you add the actual IP address of the host on which the name server is running to the /etc/resolv.conf file on all of your other systems.

Now it's time to test the DNS server. You can use several commands for testing a DNS server. The most common of these are the following:

- dig: The recommended tool for DNS testing nowadays, its output takes a bit of getting used to because of the richness of the information that it returns.

- host: The simplest tool for initial DNS testing.

- nslookup: Officially deprecated, this command is still found everywhere and is quite useful. Unfortunately, one of these days, the nslookup command will stop displaying a warning that it is deprecated, and will simply go away.

All of these commands are easy to use to test your new name server. The following is some sample output from each of these commands on the sample name server that I've configured in this chapter:

```
$ host 64bit
64bit.vonhagen.org has address 192.168.6.64

$ nslookup 64bit
Server:         127.0.0.1
Address:        127.0.0.1#53

Name:   64bit.vonhagen.org
Address: 192.168.6.64


$ dig 64bit.vonhagen.org
; <<>> DiG 9.3.2 <<>> 64bit.vonhagen.org
;; global options:  printcmd
;; Got answer:
;; ->>HEADER<<- opcode: QUERY, status: NOERROR, id: 47870
;; flags: qr aa rd ra; QUERY: 1, ANSWER: 1, AUTHORITY: 1, ADDITIONAL: 1

;; QUESTION SECTION:
;64bit.vonhagen.org.             IN      A

;; ANSWER SECTION:
64bit.vonhagen.org.     86400   IN      A       192.168.6.64

;; AUTHORITY SECTION:
vonhagen.org.           86400   IN      NS      ubuntu32.vonhagen.org.

;; ADDITIONAL SECTION:
ubuntu32.vonhagen.org.  86400   IN      A       192.168.6.90

;; Query time: 1 msec
;; SERVER: 127.0.0.1#53(127.0.0.1)
;; WHEN: Wed Jul  5 01:18:21 2006
;; MSG SIZE  rcvd: 91
```

The output of the host and nslookup commands is straightforward. The output of the dig command is the most verbose and useful for debugging purposes because it actually identifies the query that was sent to DNS, identifies the answer that it received, and lists the name server that was identified as being authoritative for the domain in which a host is located. For complete information on the dig command and its many options, see the online reference information for this command (man dig).

Troubleshooting DNS

One nice feature of BIND 9 is that the named process will not start if there are fatal errors in any of your configuration files. This can be quite irritating until you resolve them, but it does help prevent you from accidentally starting a mangled BIND server. Also, the definition of a fatal error is somewhat flexible. Syntax and parser errors that prevent all of your configuration files from being read correctly are fatal errors, while others that seem equally important, like missing files or missing or mangled records in a configuration file are not.

If your BIND server does not start correctly, the first place to look for information is the system log file on your Ubuntu system, `/var/log/syslog`. By default, BIND logs a variety of events to this file when you start or stop the named process, when events such as file reloads occur while the named process is running, and so on. A sample section of the `/var/log/syslog` file showing BIND messages are the following (I've removed the timestamp and host identification information that would normally begin each line):

```
named[19897]: starting BIND 9.3.2 -u bind
named[19897]: found 1 CPU, using 1 worker thread
named[19897]: loading configuration from '/etc/bind/named.conf'
named[19897]: /etc/bind/named.conf:60: missing ';' before end of file
named[19897]: loading configuration: failure
named[19897]: exiting (due to fatal error)
```

In this case, you can see that there is a missing semicolon on line 60 of my `named.conf` file. After correcting one error in a configuration file, you usually want to check the configuration file again, to make sure that you've eliminated all of the errors, not just one. The Ubuntu `bind` package includes a utility called `named-checkconf` that does just this. Running this utility provides an easy way of checking the syntax of a BIND configuration file without restarting the named process over and over, checking the log each time, fixing one problem or the other, and so on.

Another common message that you may see in `/var/log/syslog` is the following:

```
named[20222]: zone vonhagen.org/IN: loading master file: file not found
```

Oddly enough, the fact that the zone file `vonhagen.zone` could not be found is not a fatal error, so the BIND server is running — it just isn't providing any name information for the `vonhagen.org` domain. Aside from syntax errors in the filename, the most common cause of this error message is forgetting to provide the full pathname for an included file. As mentioned previously, BIND on Ubuntu systems is configured to use the directory `/var/cache/bind` as its working directory. It will look for any files without full pathnames in this directory instead of looking in `/etc/bind`.

The `named-checkconf` file checks the syntax of your `/etc/bind/named.conf` file and other configuration files that it includes — it does not validate the contents or syntax of your zone files. Luckily, Ubuntu's `bind` package includes another utility, `named-checkzone`, that does just that. Though it provides several options, the most common way of using the `named-checkzone` utility is by simply providing its two mandatory arguments: the name of the zone that a file describes, and the name of the file that describes that zone. This can be either a standard zone file or a reverse lookup file, because both of these are different types of zone files that have different logical purposes and contents. Some sample error output from running this utility follows:

```
$ named-checkzone vonhagen.org vonhagen.zone
dns_rdata_fromtext: vonhagen.zone:8: near '@': extra input text
zone vonhagen.org/IN: loading master file vonhagen.zone: extra input
text

 # named-checkzone 168.192.in-addr.arpa  168.192.in-addr.arpa
168.192.in-addr.arpa:11: unknown RR type 'ubuntu32.vonhagen.org.'
zone 168.192.in-addr.arpa/IN: loading master file: unknown class/type
```

Don't worry, I mangled copies of these files to illustrate common errors! The ones shown earlier in this chapter are still valid.

The first error, "extra input text" indicates a parser error when trying to read one of the records in this file — in this case, the SOA record. To generate this error message, I removed the closing parenthesis from the SOA record, which causes the parser to continue on to the next line and report that it found extra, unexpected text in the next line, which began with an @ symbol.

The second errors, "unknown RR type 'ubuntu32.vonhagen.org'" and "unknown class/type," are somewhat more insidious. These also indicate parser errors in reading one of the resource records, in this case on line 11. This is the name server declaration in my reverse lookup file. As I mentioned earlier in this chapter, the DNS file parser is very finicky. Though it is clever about using default values whenever possible, you still have to be very careful about how you use whitespace in the file. In this case, I had removed the leading @ symbol and deleted all of the whitespace at the beginning of this record, so that the IN declaration was at the beginning of the line. Because it appeared at the beginning of the lines, without any whitespace preceding it, this was interpreted as the root name of my name server entry, the NS entry was used as the record class, and the name of my name server, ubuntu32.vonhagen.org. was interpreted as a record type specification. Attempting to resolve this problem also displayed the message "zone 168.192.in-addr.arpa/IN: has no NS records" in the file /var/log/syslog, which was due to a similar parser error that I stumbled over en route to a valid name server entry.

Trying to resolve parser errors in zone files can be frustrating. Worst-case, you can fall back to providing an explicit value for every possible field, verifying that the file works correctly, and then simplifying the file until it looks the way that you want it to. Examples, such as those provided earlier in this chapter, are always useful for the purposes of comparison.

Parser and syntax errors can prevent your configuration files from being read at all or from being interpreted correctly. However, once these files are read and interpreted correctly, they may still not work correctly. The most common problem with any zone file is forgetting to append a period to what you intended to be a fully-qualified domain name, or putting a superfluous period at the end of a name that you meant to be concatenated with the root name for a zone. Names that do not end with a period are assumed to be local names to which the root name for the zone or IP range should be appended. For example, if the name of your name server is ns1, the root name for this domain is vonhagen.org, and the IP address of your name server is identified in the zone or reverse lookup file, then either the entries "ns1" or "ns1.vonhagen.org." are acceptable as the name of the name server. The first is a short name that does not end with a period, which means that the root name of the zone will be appended to it. The second is a fully-qualified domain name that ends with a period, so nothing will be appended to it. However, the entry "ns.vonhagen.org" is completely wrong because it does not end with a period, and the DNS parser therefore replaces it with "ns1.vonhagen.org.vonhagen.org", which probably doesn't exist in your domain.

This section has presented some of my "favorite" errors in BIND configuration and zone files, and some ways to identify and resolve them. You will undoubtedly see other error messages — unfortunately, this is part of the baptismal process of configuring and starting a BIND DNS server. Be prepared: First, don't panic, and second, have a browser open with your favorite search engine preloaded.

TIP If you are running a DNS server on a host whose IP address is assigned by a DHCP server (usually through a reserved MAC Address to IP Address mapping), the /etc/dhcp3/dhclient-script will overwrite your existing resolv.conf entries with the list that is maintained by the DHCP server each time that it checks or renews your lease. The best solution is to add your new DNS server to the official list maintained by the DHCP server. If you don't want to do this for some reason, you can add a line like the following to the file /etc/dhcp3/dhclient.conf:

```
prepend domain-name-servers 0.0.0.0;
```

This would put the name for the local host's DNS server as the first entry in your `/etc/resolv.config` file. Alternately, you can simply comment out the `make_resolv_conf()` function in the script file `/etc/dhcp3/dhclient-script` to prevent your system's `/etc/resolv.conf` file from being updated in the first place, but this cancels out some of the dynamic aspects of DHCP.

Getting More Information about DNS and BIND

As mentioned previously, DNS and BIND are rich, complex topics about which many entire books have been written. This chapter provided an overview of DNS and BIND and explained simple BIND configuration and troubleshooting. For additional information, see one of the books mentioned earlier or consult one of the following online resources:

- BIND 9 Administrator Reference Manual (`www.net.cmu.edu/groups/netdev/docs/bind9/Bv9ARM.html`): This is a copy of the official BIND 9 Administrator's manual, done by the BIND folks.

- Pro DNS and BIND (`www.netwidget.net/books/apress/dns`): This is an online copy of one of the DNS/BIND books mentioned earlier in this chapter.

- DNS Resources Directory (`www.dns.net/dnsrd`): This is a directory site that provides links to a huge collection of other BIND resources.

If you'll pardon the expression, these resources can help you resolve almost any DNS problem.

Summary

This chapter explained how a name server maps hostnames to IP addresses in a flexible, distributed fashion, and explained how to set up your own name server for the hosts on your local network, while still leveraging the other zillion name servers on the Internet. In real life, you would want to set up more than one name server on a local network of any significant size, to protect against the failure of any single system, but this chapter focused on setting up a single name server for smaller networks.

Chapter 30 continues our exploration of important system servers by explaining how to install and configure a print server. Unless you have more money and surface area than most people, you will want to attach printers to a small number of systems on your network and point your other systems to those print servers for printing purposes. Not only does this save money and simplify administration, but it also helps minimize the number of places that you have to explore to find missing printouts.

## Chapter 30

Setting Up a Print Server

I f you have a single system and a single printer, setting up and configuring printing is quite straightforward, and was explained in the section of Chapter 23 entitled "Adding a Printer." However, in today's more complex networked environments, the chances are that you want to access a printer on one system from many other systems, including machines that may run operating systems other than Ubuntu Linux for some legacy software or game-playing reason.

This chapter explains how to set up and tweak connectivity from other computer systems so that your printer is available to everyone else. For your convenience, this chapter also highlights the steps necessary to connect to shared Ubuntu printers from Microsoft Windows and Mac OS X systems. It concludes by providing some troubleshooting tips and discussions of common problems, as well as additional sources of information.

> **TIP**
>
> Hacking the Ubuntu printing system's configuration files and using unauthenticated printing as described in this chapter is really suitable only for home, SOHO, or SMB environments that are firewalled from the outside world, and in which you hopefully trust everyone. If you have Microsoft Windows systems in your network environment, you may simply want to set up a Samba server on the system to which your printer is attached. This will leverage your existing Windows authentication mechanisms (depending on how you configure Samba), and will also work with Apple's Mac OS X systems because of its built-in support for Windows printing and SMB. Setting up a Samba Server is discussed in Chapter 32, "Setting Up a Samba Server."

Linux and Unix Printing History

Today's printers are typically high-quality laser or inkjet printers, often capable of color printing and near photographic quality. The original Unix printing system, known as *Line Printer Daemon (LPD)* was designed to queue and print jobs that were intended for huge, text-only line printers. As more sophisticated printers were developed that were capable of higher-quality printouts (such as the original Xerox x9700, Canon-CX, and Imagen-300 laser printers), the original LPD print system continued to be used, but required that the jobs that you were printing be preprocessed so that they contained the special commands that the printer used internally to produce higher-quality printouts. This quickly became tedious, because it required users to know to which printer they wanted to print to to use the appropriate preformatting commands. Eventually, the LPD system was updated and a similar printing system known as LP was developed which encapsulated the knowledge about the formats required by specific printers, implementing the necessary preformatting commands internally by automatically executing them as filters (also known as print drivers) that performed the right formatting and other printer-specific commands before sending the jobs to the target printer. Other updated printing systems, such as lprng (lpr, Next Generation, based on the name of the print command used by the LPD system) have also flourished — both LPD and lprng are available in the Ubuntu repositories if you need them for compatibility reasons (or because they are the devil that you already know).

The evolution of multiple printing systems for Unix systems led to incompatibilities between the different print systems, requiring recompilation of the filters for specific printers on different Unix systems (if you could get the source code at all) and so on. Eventually, a company known as Easy Software Products began developing a more generalized printing system for Unix, Linux, and other Unix-like systems known as Common Unix Printing System (CUPS). The original version of CUPS used the standard networked LPD protocol, but quickly switched to using a new standard, the Internet Printing Protocol (IPP), which non-Unix/Linux systems such as Windows can use to print to CUPS printers. Easy Software Products also had the foresight to make the CUPS source code freely available under the GPL so that it could be compiled for multiple operating systems and thus become a true, cross-system standard popularized by zillions of users and system administrators. And this strategy has worked — today, CUPS is used in every major Linux distribution and most other Unix-like systems.

Most Linux distributions, including Ubuntu, provide their own utilities for setting up printers and doing some basic configuration of the printing subsystem. Ubuntu uses the GNOME printer configuration tool, which was described in the section of Chapter 23 entitled "Adding a Printer." However, in addition to standardizing how printing works across many Linux systems, CUPS added one especially nice gift for system administrators: a built-in administrative tool for CUPS configuration that is easily accessed through any Web browser via port 631. In this chapter, however, I am focusing on using the standard Ubuntu/GNOME printer configuration tools as much as possible.

Enabling Remote Hosts to Access Your CUPS Print Server

As distributed with most Linux distributions (including Ubuntu releases before this book was written), CUPS servers listen for incoming requests on port 631 of your host's external IP address. For some reason, this was changed with Ubuntu 6.06 so that the CUPS server only listens for requests on your host's loopback interface, 127.0.0.1, which effectively eliminates any hope of network printing. Luckily, this is easy enough to correct.

NOTE   To keep this chapter from containing the complete documentation for the CUPS configuration file, the print server described in this chapter is a simple print server without any special authentication requirements. This may be unsuitable for WAN enterprise or academic environments.

To enable network printing on your Ubuntu system, you must add your host's external IP address to the list of ports that your CUPS server listens on as follows:

1. Use the sudo command and your favorite text editor (hopefully emacs) to edit the file /etc/cups/cups.d/ports.conf with a command like the following:

```
$ sudo emacs /etc/cups/cups.d/ports.conf
```

After supplying your password, the specified file appears in your text editor, and should look like the following:

```
Listen localhost:631
Listen /var/run/cups/cups.sock
```

2. Add a line that tells the server to also listen on port 631 of your host's external Ethernet interface. For example, the host on which I'm running a test server has the hostname ubuntu32.vonhagen .org with the IP address 192.168.6.90, so I could add either of the following entries after the first line in the file:

```
Listen ubuntu32.vonhagen.org:631
Listen 192.168.6.90:631
```

The completed file would then look like the following:

```
Listen localhost:631
Listen ubuntu32.vonhagen.org:631
Listen /var/run/cups/cups.sock
```

Save the updated file, and exit the editor.

3. Restart the CUPS daemon on your system using the following command:

```
$ sudo /etc/init.d/cupsys restart
```

You should now be able to access the CUPS server from other hosts. As a quick test, you could attempt to display the CUPS administration in a browser from one of the other systems on your network. This would be a URL of the form http://hostname:631, because the CUPS server is still only listening on port 631. If the CUPS server is indeed listening on that port on your print server's external Ethernet interface, you will see a page like the one shown in Figure 30.1.

FIGURE 30.1

The CUPS server's Web interface

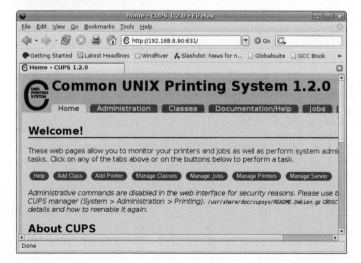

You should now be able to go to any of the other hosts on your network and create printer entries there. (Adding a printer on an Ubuntu system was discussed in Chapter 23. If you are creating network printer entries for this printer on Microsoft Windows or Apple Mac OS X systems, see the subsequent sections of this chapter for tips on how to define network printers on these operating systems.)

 When configuring remote printing from another Linux system to your Ubuntu print server, you need to use an Internet Printing Protocol URI of the following form:

```
ipp://hostname/printers/queuename
```

For example, if I were setting up a connection to the CUPS printer named SuperScript-660i running on the host `ubuntu32.vonhagen.org`, I would supply the URI `ipp://ubuntu32.vonhagen.org/printers/SuperScript-660i`. Depending on the type of other Linux systems that you are using, you may have to specify the IP address and queue name separately. In that case, the queue name would be `printers/queuename`.

Enabling Administrative Operations via the CUPS Web Interface

Performing administrative tasks through the Web-based CUPS interface is disabled by default on Ubuntu systems, though you can reenable Web-based support for these capabilities easily enough. The easiest way to do this is to add the `cupsys` user to the shadow group in `/etc/group` by using a command like the following:

```
$ sudo adduser cupsys shadow
```

After executing this command, you should restart CUPS so that it picks up the new membership information, by using a command like the following:

```
$ sudo /etc/init.d/cupsys restart
```

You should now be able to perform administrative operations such as creating printers using the Web interface (even though the warning message shown in Figure 30.1 will still be displayed). When prompted for a username and password, you can use any member of the `lpadmin` group (of which you should already be a member). Depending on your system's configuration and the version of CUPS that it is running, this may not be sufficient to enable access to all administrative pages of your CUPS server. See the section entitled "Access Controls for Portions of the CUPS Web Interface" later in this chapter for more information.

Integrating Windows Printing with an Ubuntu Print Server

Configuring a Microsoft Windows 2000 or XP system to print to a remote Ubuntu printer is as simple as setting up access to any other shared network printer. The following example provides screen shots from a sample Windows XP system, but the process is very similar on earlier versions of Microsoft Windows:

1. Select Start ➪ Settings ➪ Printers and Faxes.
2. Click the Add a Printer task. A hand waving dialog displays that does nothing. Click Next to proceed.
3. Specify that you want to create a remote printer, and click Next. The dialog shown in Figure 30.2 displays.

FIGURE 30.2

Providing the URL of your Ubuntu printer

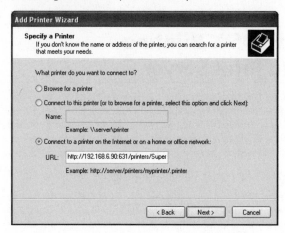

4. Enter a URL of the form `http://host:631/printers/queuename`. For example, to define a connection to a remote printer named SuperScript-660i that is attached to the host `ubuntu32.vonhagen.org`, I would enter the URL `http://ubuntu32.vonhagen.org:631/printers/SuperScript-660i`. Click Next to proceed. The dialog shown in Figure 30.3 displays.

FIGURE 30.3

Identifying your printer's manufacturer and model

5. Select the manufacturer and model of your printer so that Windows knows how to format documents before sending them to the printer. If the manufacturer or model of the remote printer isn't available in this dialog, you can either select a similar or compatible model or locate a Windows driver for your printer on the Web or on the CD that fell out of the box when you unpacked your printer. Click OK once you've made your selection.

6. A final hand waving dialog displays. Click Finish to close that dialog and return to the Printers and Faxes dialog.

That's all there is to it! If you want to verify that you printer works correctly, right-click on the icon for the new printer, select Properties, and click Print Test Page. A standard Microsoft Windows printer test page should emerge from your printer shortly.

Integrating Mac OS X Printing with an Ubuntu Print Server

Apple's Mac OS X has come a long way from previous versions of the Mac OS. Mac OS X is a true Unix-like system that provides an easy-to-use interface. Because Mac OS X includes and uses a huge collection of open source software, integrating your Mac OS X system with a remote Ubuntu print server is easily done with the familiar Mac OS X Printer Setup and Printer Browser tools. The screen shots in this section were taken from a sample Mac OS X 10.4 system, but the process is very similar on earlier versions of Mac OS X.

To create a Mac OS X definition for your remote Ubuntu printer, do the following:

1. Start the Printer Browser. You can do this several ways. I typically go to the Applications folder in a Finder window, select the Utilities folder, double-click the Printer Setup Utility, and click Add in its menu bar to start the Printer Browser. Regardless of how you get there, Figure 30.4 shows the Printer Browser with no printers defined.

FIGURE 30.4

Starting the OS X 10.4 Printer Browser

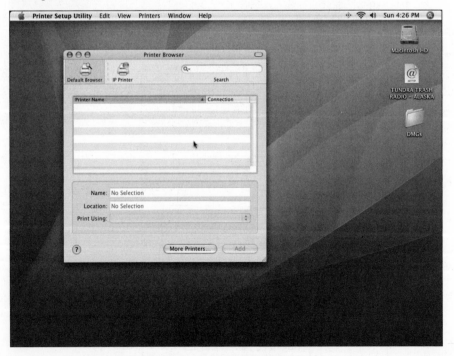

 If you are using Mac OS X 10.3 or earlier, hold down either Option key while clicking Add, and skip to Step 3 of this procedure to end up at the equivalent dialog.

2. Hold down either Option key and click the More Printers Button.

3. Click the drop-down menu at the top of this dialog and select Advanced, as shown in Figure 30.5.

FIGURE 30.5

Specifying advanced printer configuration

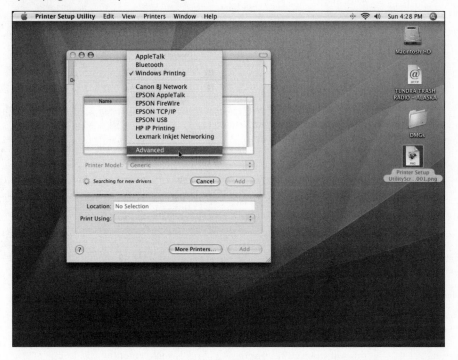

4. Click the Device drop-down menu and select Internet Printing Protocol using IPP. This displays a dialog like the one shown in Figure 30.6.

FIGURE 30.6

Specifying a name and the URI for your remote printer

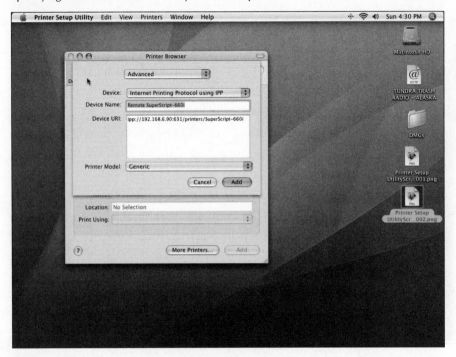

5. Enter anything that you'd like as the Device Name, and enter the Device URI (Universal Resource Indicator) for your Ubuntu printer in the following form:

   `ipp://host:631/printers/queuename`

   For example, to define a connection to a remote printer named SuperScript-660i that is attached to the host `ubuntu32.vonhagen.org`, I would enter the URI `http://ubuntu32.vonhagen.org:631/printers/SuperScript-660i`.

6. If you are using anything other than a generic PostScript printer, click Printer Model, and select the manufacturer and model of your printer. Figure 30.7 shows a driver being selected for an HP LaserJet 4 compatible printer being selected.

7. Click Add to proceed.

That's all there is to it! Your Ubuntu printer is now available for use from your Mac OS X system. Because Mac OS X doesn't provide an easy way of generating a printer test page, you can fire up your favorite application and print a sample page from there. Your print job should emerge from your printer shortly.

FIGURE 30.7

FIGURE 30.7

Identifying the manufacturer and model of your printer

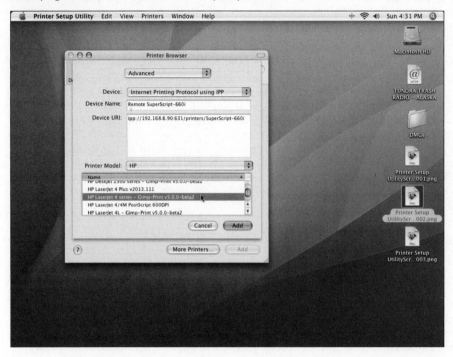

Troubleshooting Remote Printing

This section summarizes a few common sources of diagnostic information and potential problems that you may need to try, depending on the version of CUPS that you are running and whether or not you have typed every URI correctly.

Checking the CUPS Log Files

CUPS print servers maintain three log files that provide a variety of information about attempts to access or use them. These log files, stored in the directory /var/log/cups, are the following:

- access_log: Contains log messages for each remote host that attempts to access the CUPS print server.
- error_log: Contains log messages that record any errors encountered or produced by the CUPS print server.
- page_log: Contains log messages for every page printed by a CUPS server. These log messages also summarize information about the host from which the print job was received, the name of the printer being used, and so on.

Of these, the `access_log` and `error_log` files are the most useful for diagnostic purposes. Examining the end of these files after encountering a print failure usually shows useful, meaningful error messages. The `access_log` file will identify the IP address of the systems that have connected to your print server. This can help you verify that the remote system is actually connecting to the print server. Once you've established this, check the `error_log` file for tips about why the job may not have printed.

Accessing Controls for Portions of the CUPS Web Interface

The default CUPS configuration on Ubuntu systems tends to change with different releases, reflecting both enhancements and current security concerns. It's almost certain that the CUPS print server will be updated at some point while you are using this and subsequent releases of Ubuntu. If remote printing works fine but then ceases to work, you may need to add your remote hosts (or your entire network) to the list of acceptable locations in the CUPS daemon's primary configuration file, `/etc/cups/cupsd.conf`. The list of valid locations for incoming print jobs is stored inside the `<Location /> </Location>` stanza. If printing suddenly stops working, make sure that this stanza contains an entry that either enables access by default or explicitly allows access from the printer from all hosts on the local network. For example, a restrictive version of this stanza that denies access from anywhere other than `localhost` or any hosts on the `192.168.6.*` network would be the following:

```
<Location />
  Order Deny,Allow
  Deny From All
  Allow From localhost
  Allow From 192.168.6.*
</Location>
```

The CUPS configuration file that is provided as part of a standard Ubuntu installation at the time this book was written allows access from anywhere (once you've changed CUPS to actually listen on your print server's external Ethernet interface, as described earlier in this chapter. However, changes to the default configuration file are common, and it's pretty depressing to have printing cease to function after a system "update." For example, different portions of the CUPS administrative interface each have their own `<Location>` entries. If you cannot access them from your system, try adding an `Allow` entry for a specific host (rather than from an entire subnet, as described previously).

Handling Preformatted print Jobs

Another common update-related problem may arise if you receive an update that changes how CUPS handles different types of incoming print jobs. If you are printing from a remote system, such as a Microsoft Windows or Apple Mac OS X system, that system preformats the print jobs before sending them to the print server. If print suddenly stops working after an update and you see error messages in the `error_log` file about enabling raw input, make sure that the following entry is present in the file `/etc/cups/mime.types` and is not preceded by a hash mark:

```
application/octet-stream
```

The hash mark is a comment character in CUPS configuration files. This entry must be present for preformatted print jobs to be received via the HTTP protocol and sent to the printer.

After making any changes to any CUPS configuration file, you need to restart the CUPS daemon on your system using the following command:

```
$ sudo /etc/init.d/cupsys restart
```

Getting More Information About CUPS

As you have probably guessed, CUPS configuration is either extremely rich and powerful or extremely irritating—and usually both. The CUPS configuration file `/etc/cups/cupsd.conf` has so many possible options that it makes even the command-line `gcc`, `ls`, and `tar` commands jealous. If you try to do anything serious with CUPS beyond the simple print server described in this chapter, you will want more information. Some excellent sources of additional information about CUPS are the following:

- `www.cups.org/documentation.php`: The online documentation for CUPS that is available from Easy Software, Inc.

- `www.linuxprinting.org`: A site specializing in help with printing on GNU/Linux systems, this site features a very useful database of printers that are known to work with Linux (`www.linuxprinting.org/printer_list.cgi`) and a good deal of useful information about CUPS including a great CUPS troubleshooting tutorial. (I left out the URL for the latter intentionally because it would line-wrap into the next chapter.)

- *CUPS: Common Unix Printing System* (Michael R. Sweet, SAMS, 2002, ISBN: 0672321963)— Michael Sweet is one of the owners of Easy Software, Inc., and this is thus a pretty definitive book, not just for CUPS, but also for the Internet printing protocol. Unfortunately, the book is a bit old now, but it is still an excellent resource and my copy is a valuable asset.

As with other Ubuntu topics, you should also be able to get a significant amount of useful information from the online Ubuntu Forums discussed in Chapter 1 of this book.

Summary

Centralizing print services on one or a small number of computer systems is a good idea for almost any network. This chapter provided a bit of background about printing on Unix and Linux systems, and then discussed how to install and configure CUPS, the Common Unix Printing System. This chapter also provided specific information about enabling any Microsoft Windows or Mac OS X systems that you may still have lying around to print to your Ubuntu print server.

Chapter 31 explains how to share directories over a network using NFS, the Network File System, which is the standard distributed file system mechanism for all Unix and Linux systems. Sharing a central repository of project files, documents, and code over a network in a work environment is important from many standpoints, including increasing efficiency, minimizing confusion, and minimizing the size of your backups. Today, it is just as important in many home environments, enabling everyone on your home network to share access to your household's music collection, vacation photos, and any other files that you want your house mates, spouse, or children to be able to see.

Chapter 31

Setting Up an NFS Server

S haring groups of files that multiple people need access to is standard operating procedure in business today and, thanks to home networking, is getting to be SOP for home use as well. Providing centralized access to a collection of audio materials that you've extracted from your CD collection or the vacation photos from your most recent trips is just as important to the home user as providing centralized access to your procedure manuals and software source repository is to the business user or SOHO developer. Luckily, Linux systems provide several ways of sharing directories over a network, some oriented primarily toward Linux and other Unix-like systems, including Apple's Mac OS X, and others oriented more toward Microsoft Windows systems (which Linux and Mac OS X systems can also access, of course). This chapter discusses how to set up one of your Ubuntu Linux systems so that other systems can access its directories over the network using NFS, the Network File System, which is popularly used on all Linux and Unix-like systems. (For information on setting up your Ubuntu system to share directories with Microsoft Windows systems, see Chapter 32, "Setting Up a Samba Server."

Sun Microsystems' Network File System, better known simply as NFS, is the most common networked filesystem in use today, largely because it comes preinstalled and for free with almost every Unix and Unix-like system. NFS clients and servers are also available for almost every type of modern computer system, including those running Microsoft Windows and Apple's Mac OS X.

This chapter provides an overview of NFS, discusses different versions of NFS and their capabilities, and discusses the various applications associated with NFS. Beyond this background material, this chapter focuses on explaining how to set up your Ubuntu system to be an NFS file server — how to access NFS file servers from other systems was explained in Chapter 16. This chapter concludes by discussing NIS, the Network Information System, a distributed authentication mechanism that is commonly used in conjunction with NFS.

IN THIS CHAPTER

Overview of NFS

Installing an NFS server

Exporting directories using graphical tools

Examining the NFS configuration file

835

Overview of the Network File System

NFS is a network filesystem that provides transparent access to files residing on remote disks. Network filesystems are often commonly referred to as *distributed filesystems*, because the files and directories that they provide access to may be physically located on many different computer systems that are distributed throughout your home, academic environment, or business. Developed at Sun Microsystems in the early 1980s, the NFS protocol has been revised and enhanced several times between then and now, and is available on all Linux, Unix, and Unix-like systems and even for Windows systems from many third-party software vendors. The specifications for NFS have been publicly available since shortly after it was first released, making NFS a de facto standard for distributed filesystems.

NFS is the most common distributed filesystem in use today, largely because it is free and available for almost every type of modern computer system. NFS enables file servers to export centralized sets of files and directories to multiple client systems. Good examples of files and directories that you may want to store in a centralized location but make simultaneously available to multiple computer systems are users' home directories, site-wide sets of software development tools, and centralized data resources such as mail queues and the directories used to store Internet news bulletin boards.

The following are some common usage scenarios for using NFS:

- Sharing common sets of data files: Sharing files that everyone on your network wants to access, whether they are audio files, business data, or the source code for tomorrow's killer app, is the most common use of any type of networked filesystem.

- Explicitly sharing home directories: Suppose that the home directories for all of your users are stored in the directory /export on your NFS file server, which is automatically mounted on all of your computer systems at boot time. The password file for each of your systems would list your user's home directories as /export/user-name. Users can then log in on any NFS client system and instantly see their home directory, which would be transparently made available to them over the network.

> **TIP**   An alternative to the previous bullet is to automatically mount networked home directories using an exported NFS directory that is managed by an NFS automount daemon. Whenever access to a directory managed by an automount daemon is requested by a client, the daemon automatically mounts that directory on the client system. Automounting simplifies the contents of your server's /etc/exports file by enabling you to export only the parent directory of all home directories on the server, and letting the automounter manage that directory (and therefore its subdirectories) on each client. See the sidebar at the end of this chapter for general information on automounting, a complete discussion of which is outside the scope of this chapter.

- Sharing specific sets of binaries across systems: Suppose that you want to make a specific set of GNU tools available on all of the systems in your computing environment, but also wanted to centralize them on an NFS server for ease of maintenance and updating. To ensure that configuration files were portable across all of your systems, you might want to make these binaries available in the directory /usr/gnu regardless of the type of system that you were using. You could simply build binaries for each type of system that you support, configuring them to be found as /usr/gnu but actually storing them in directories with names such as /export/gnu/ubuntu, /export/gnu/solaris8, and so on. You would then configure each client of a specified type to mount the appropriate exported directory for that system type as /usr/gnu. For example, /export/gnu/ubuntu would be mounted as /usr/gnu on Ubuntu systems, /export/gnu/solaris8 would be mounted as /usr/gnu on Solaris systems, and so on. You could then simply put /usr/gnu/bin in your path and the legendary "right thing" would happen regardless of the type of system that you logged in on.

As you'll see in this chapter, NFS is easy to install, easy to configure, and provides a flexible networked filesystem that any Ubuntu, other Linux, Unix, or Unix-like system can quickly and easily access. In some cases, it's easy to trip over a few administrative gotchas, but Ubuntu provides powerful and easy-to-use tools that simplify configuring NFS file servers to "do the right thing."

Understanding how NFS Works

If you simply want to use NFS and aren't too concerned about what's going on under the hood, you can skip this section. However, this section provides the details of many internal NFS operations because some enquiring minds do indeed want to know and because, frankly, it's just plain interesting to see some of the hoops that NFS clients and servers have to use to successfully communicate between different types of computer systems, often with different types of processors. So, if you're interested, read on, McDuff!

The underlying network communication method used by NFS is known as *Remote Procedure Calls* (*RPCs*), which can use either the lower level Universal Datagram Protocol (UDP) as their network transport mechanism (NFS version 2) or TCP (NFS version 3). For this reason, both UDP and TCP entries for port 2049, the port used by the NFS daemon, are present in the Linux /etc/services file. UDP minimizes transmission delays because it does not attempt to do sequencing or flow control, and does not provide delivery guarantees — it simply sends packets to a specific port on a given host, where some other process is waiting for input.

The design and implementation of RPCs make NFS platform-independent, interoperable between different computer systems, and easily ported to many computing architectures and operating systems. RPCs are a client/server communication method that involves issuing RPC calls with various parameters on client systems, which are actually executed on the server. The client doesn't need to know whether the procedure call is being executed locally or remotely — it receives the results of an RPC in exactly the same way that it would receive the results of a local procedure call.

The way in which RPCs are implemented is extremely clever. RPCs work by using a technique known as *marshalling*, which essentially means packaging up all of the arguments to the remote procedure call on the client into a mutually agreed-upon format. This mutually agreed-upon format is known as eXternal Data Representation (XDR), and provides a sort of computer Esperanto that enables systems with different architectures and byte-orders to safely exchange data with each other. The client's RPC subsystem then ships the resulting, system-independent packet to the appropriate server. The server's RPC subsystem receives the packet, and unmarshalls it to extract the arguments to the procedure call in its native format. The RPC subsystem executes the procedure call locally, marshalls the results into a return packet, and sends this packet back to the client. When this packet is received by the client, its RPC subsystem unmarshalls the packet and sends the results to the program that invoked the RPC, returning this data in exactly the same fashion as any local procedure call. Marshalling and unmarshalling, plus the use of the common XDR data representation, make it possible for different types of systems to transparently communicate and execute functions on each other.

RPC communications are used for all NFS-related communications, including communications related to the authentication services used by NFS (NIS or NIS+), managing file locks, managing NFS mount requests, providing status information, and requests made to the NFS automount daemon. To enable applications to contact so many different services without requiring that each communicate through a specific, well-known port, NFS lets those services dynamically bind to any available port as long as they register with its central coordination service, the portmapper daemon. The portmapper always runs on port 111 of any host that supports RPC communications, and serves as an electronic version of directory assistance. Servers register RPC-related services with the portmapper, identifying the port that the service is actually listening on. Clients then contact the portmapper at its well-known port to determine the port that is actually being used by the service that they are looking for.

Communication failures occur with any networked communication mechanism, and RPCs are no exception. As mentioned at the beginning of this section, UDP does not provide delivery guarantees or packet sequencing. Therefore, when a response to an RPC call is not received within a specific period of time, systems will resend RPC packets. This introduces the possibility that a remote system may execute a specific function twice, based on the same input data. Because this can happen, all NFS operations are *idempotent*, which means that they can be executed any number of times and still return the same result—an NFS operation cannot change any of the data that it depends upon. Even though NFS version 3 uses TCP as its network transport mechanism, the idea of idempotent requests is still part of the NFS protocol to guarantee compatibility with NFS version 2 implementations.

As another way of dealing with potential communication and system failures, NFS servers are stateless, meaning that they do not retain information about each other across system restarts. If a server crashes while a client is attempting to make an RPC to it, the client continues to retry the RPC until the server comes back up or until the number of retries exceeds its configured limit, at which time the operation aborts. Stateless operation makes the NFS protocol much simpler, because it does not have to worry about maintaining consistency between client and server data. The client is always right, even after rebooting, because it does not maintain any data at that point.

Although stateless operation simplifies things, it is also extremely noisy, inefficient, and slow. When data from a client is saved back to a server, the server must write it synchronously, not returning control to the client until all of the data has been saved to the server's disk. As described in the next section, "Comparing Different Versions of NFS," newer versions of NFS do some limited write caching on clients to return control to the client applications as quickly as possible. This caching is done by the client's `rpciod` process (RPC IO Daemon), which stores pending writes to NFS servers in the hopes that it can bundle groups of them together and thus optimize the client's use of the network. In the current standard version of NFS (NFS version 3), cached client writes are still essentially dangerous because they are only stored in memory, and will therefore be lost if the client crashes before the write completes.

In a totally stateless environment, a server crash would make it difficult to save data that was being modified on a client back to the server once it is available again. The server would have no way of knowing what file the modified data belonged to because it had no persistent information about its clients. To resolve the problem, NFS clients obtain file handles from a server whenever they open a file. *File handles* are data structures that identify both the server and the file that they are associated with. If a server crashes, clients retry their write operations until the server is available again or their timeout periods are exceeded. If the server comes back up in time, it receives the modified data and the file handle from the client, and can use the file handle to figure out which file the modified data should be written to.

The lack of client-side caching also has a long-term operational impact because it limits the type of dependencies that NFS clients can have on NFS servers. Because clients do not cache data from the server, they must re-retrieve any information that they need after any reboot. This can definitely slow the reboot process for any client that must execute binaries located on an NFS server as part of the reboot process. If the server is unavailable, the client cannot boot. For this reason, most NFS clients must contain a full set of system binaries, and typically only share user-oriented binaries and data via NFS.

Comparing Different Versions of NFS

NFS has been around almost since the beginning of Unix workstation time, appearing on early Sun Microsystems workstations in the early 1980s. This section provides an overview of the differences between the four different versions of NFS, both for historical reasons, and to illustrate that NFS is by no means a done deal. NFS 4 resolves the biggest limitations of NFS 3, most notably adding real client-side data caching that survives reboots. The most common version of NFS used on systems today is NFS version 3, which is the version that I focus on in this chapter.

The following list identifies the four versions of NFS and highlights the primary features of each:

- **Version 1:** The original NFS protocol specification was used only internally at Sun during the development of NFS, and I have never been able to find any documentation on the original specification. This would only be of historical interest.

- **Version 2:** NFS version 2 was the first version of the NFS protocol that was released for public consumption. Version 2 used UDP exclusively as its transport mechanism, and defined the 18 basic RPCs that made up the original public NFS protocol. Version 2 was a 32-bit implementation of the protocol, and therefore imposed a maximum file size limitation of 2GB on files in NFS and used a 32-byte file handle. NFS version 2 also limited data transfer sizes to 8KB,

- **Version 3:** NFS version 3 addressed many of the shortcomings and ambiguities present in the NFS version 2 specification, and took advantage of many of the technological advances in the 10+ years between the version 2 and 3 specifications. Version 3 added TCP as a network transport mechanism, making it the default if both the client and server support it; increased the maximum data transfer size between client and server to 64KB; and was a full 64-bit implementation, thereby effectively removing file size limitations. All of these were made possible by improvements in networking technology and system architecture because the NFS version 2 was released. Version 3 also added a few new RPCs to those in the original version 2 specification, and removed two that had never been used (or implemented in any NFS version that I've ever seen). To improve performance by decreasing network traffic, version 3 introduced the notion of bundling writes from the client to the server, and also automatically returned file attributes with each RPC call, rather than requiring a separate request for this information as version 2 NFS had done.

- **Version 4:** Much of the NFS version 4 protocol is designed to position NFS for use in Internet and World Wide Web environments by increasing persistence, performance, and security. Version 4 adds persistent, client-side caching to aid in recovery from system reboots with minimal network traffic, and adds support for ACLs and extended file attributes in NFS filesystems. Version 4 also adds an improved, standard API for increased security through a general RPC security mechanism known as Remote Procedure Call Security - Generic Security Services (RPCSEC_GSS). This mandates the use of the Generic Security Services Application Programming Interface (GSS-API, specified in RFC 2203) to select between available security mechanisms provided by clients and servers.

Installing an NFS Server and Related Packages

To install the packages required to run and monitor an NFS server on your Ubuntu system, start the Synaptic Package Manager from the System ⇨ Administration menu, and click Search to display the search dialog. Make sure that Names and Descriptions are the selected items to look in, enter **nfs** as the string to search for, and click Search. After the search completes, scroll down until you see the `nfs-common` and `nfs-kernel-server` packages, right-click each of these packages and select Mark for Installation to select that package for installation from the pop-up menu. Figure 31.1 shows these packages being selected for installation.

NOTE As you can see in Figure 31.1, the Ubuntu repositories provide two NFS servers: one that runs in the Linux kernel and another that runs in user space. The kernel-based NFS server is slightly faster, though the user-space NFS server is slightly easier to debug and control manually. However, the kernel NFS server package provides some command-line utilities, such as the `exportfs` utility, that you may want to use to explicitly share directories via NFS (known as *exporting directories* in NFS-speak) and monitor the status of directories that you share using NFS. This chapter therefore explains how to install and use the kernel-based NFS server — if you have problems sharing directories using NFS, you may want to subsequently install the user-space NFS server to help with debugging those problems.

FIGURE 31.1

Installing the kernel NFS server package

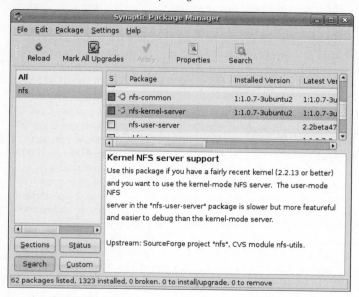

Depending on what software you have previously installed on your Ubuntu system and what you select in Synaptic, a dialog may display that lists other packages that must also be installed, and ask for confirmation. When you see this dialog, click Mark to accept these related (and required) packages.

Next, click Apply in the Synaptic toolbar to install the kernel-space NFS server and friends on your system. Once the installation completes, you're ready to share data on your system with any system that supports NFS.

See Chapter 20 for more detailed information on installing applications using the Synaptic Package Manager.

Using the Shared Folder Tool to Export Directories

At this point in this book, it should come as no surprise that Ubuntu Linux provides an easy-to-use graphical tool (`shares-admin`) that simplifies the process of defining and configuring the directories that you want to export via NFS from your Ubuntu system. To start this tool, select System ⇨ Administration ⇨ Shared Folders. After supplying your password in the administrative authentication dialog that displays, the Shared Folder tool starts, as shown in Figure 31.2.

Starting the Shared Folder administration tool

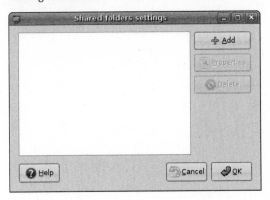

To define a directory that you want to share via NFS, click Add to display the dialog shown in Figure 31.3.

Defining a shared directory in the Shared Folder tool

As you can see from Figure 31.3, the default settings on this dialog are for sharing SMB filesystems via Samba, which is discussed in Chapter 32. To export a directory using NFS, click the Share with item and select NFS as the sharing protocol that you are working with. This displays the settings that are relevant for NFS, as shown in Figure 31.4.

FIGURE 31.4

Sharing settings for NFS directories

That's more like it. As you can see from Figure 31.4, the default exported/shared directory that is initially selected when you start the Shared Folder admin tool is your home directory. In this example, I'm going to share the directory that contains my online audio collection, which I should point out was either legally ripped from CDs that I own or consists of freely-downloadable live recordings. To specify another directory for sharing, click the Path item and select Other from the drop-down menu to display the directory selection dialog shown in Figure 31.5.

FIGURE 31.5

Selecting the directory that you want to export

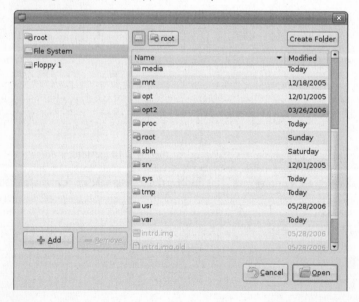

To select a directory somewhere on your system, click root and navigate through the directory tree on your system to select the directory that you want to export, which in this example is my /opt2 directory. Click Open to select that directory (or whatever directory you want to export) and return to the dialog shown in Figure 31.4, which now displays the name of the newly selected directory in the Path field.

Next, you'll need to identify the hosts that you want to be able to access (i.e., mount) this directory over the network. To define these, click the Add host button to display the dialog shown in Figure 31.6.

FIGURE 31.6

Defining who can access a shared directory

This dialog provides several ways to identify the hosts that can mount and access the directory that you are sharing. The Allowed hosts drop-down menu shown in Figure 31.6 provides four choices:

- **Hosts in the eth0 network:** Enables anyone who can reach your machine via your system's eth0 network interface to mount and access the shared directory.

- **Specify hostname:** Enables you to identify the name of a specific host that can mount and access the shared directory. Selecting this item displays an additional field on the basic dialog shown in Figure 31.6, in which you can enter the fully-qualified or local hostname of a machine that you want to be able to mount and access the shared directory.

- **Specify IP address:** Enables you to identify the IP address of a specific host that can mount and access the shared directory. Selecting this item displays an additional field on the basic dialog shown in Figure 31.6, in which you can enter the IP address of a machine that you want to be able to mount and access the shared directory.

- **Specify network:** Enables you to identify the IP specification for a subnet that can mount and access the shared directory. All hosts with IP addresses that are on this subnet will be able to mount and access the shared directory. Selecting this item displays two additional fields on the basic dialog shown in Figure 31.6, in which you can enter the subnet and netmask of the network whose hosts that you want to be able to mount and access the shared directory.

> **TIP** If you are identifying authorized hosts who can mount and access your shared directory by hostname, IP address, or subnet, you can always explicitly allow multiple hosts to mount and access the shared directory by using Figure 31.4's Add hosts button multiple times to define a specific set of hosts.

In this example, I'll enable access to all hosts on the 192.168.0.0 subnet to my shared directory, as shown in Figure 31.7. Note that this dialog enables you to grant read-only access to a shared directory by selecting the Read only checkbox. This provides a convenient way to give others access to shared data but prevents them from modifying anything in the shared directory. There is also slightly less overhead in exporting a directory to other systems as a read-only directory, so you may want to consider doing this if others need access to the shared data but you're sure that they'll never want to change anything there (or you don't want them to change anything there).

FIGURE 31.7

Enabling access to a shared directory for a specific network

Clicking OK in the dialog shown in Figure 31.7 returns you to the dialog shown in Figure 31.4, which is now updated to show the /opt2 directory that I am sharing in this example, as shown in Figure 31.8.

FIGURE 31.8

Network access settings for a directory shared via NFS

To continue, click OK to redisplay the dialog originally shown in Figure 31.2, which now contains the settings for our newly defined NFS shared directory, as shown in Figure 31.9.

Almost done! To subsequently modify or update the settings for any shared directory, you can right-click its name in the Shared Folder tool and click Properties to display the specific settings for that shared folder. To begin sharing the folder, click OK to start the specified type of file sharing and close the Shared Folder tool.

FIGURE 31.9

A shared directory in the Shared Folder tool

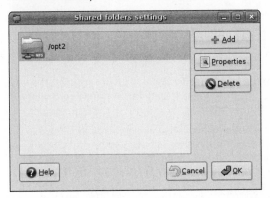

Verifying NFS Operations

The kernel NFS server package includes a utility called `exportfs` that you can use to list the directories that an NFS server is currently exporting from your system and reexport any new directories that you have just added to your system's NFS configuration, which is stored in the file `/etc/exports`. After you follow the instructions in the previous section, the contents of the `/etc/exports` file on your Ubuntu system are the following:

```
# /etc/exports: the access control list for filesystems which may
#               be exported to NFS clients. See exports(5).
/opt2          192.168.0.0/255.255.0.0(rw)
```

Any line in this file that does not begin with a hash mark is an entry that defines a directory that is being exported by NFS, and is commonly referred to as an *export specification*. To verify that the `/opt2` directory is being exported from your system (and to reexport it if necessary), you can use the `exportfs -av` command, which exports all available directories in a verbose fashion as shown in the following example:

```
$ sudo exportfs -a
exportfs: /etc/exports [3]: No 'sync' or 'async' option specified \
  for export "192.168.0.0/255.255.0.0:/opt2".
  Assuming default behavior ('sync').
  NOTE: this default has changed from previous versions
exporting 192.168.0.0/255.255.0.0:/opt2
```

This output demonstrates that the directory `/opt2` is being exported to all hosts whose IP addresses match 192.168.0.0.

NFS Users and Authentication

NFS uses the user ID (UID) and group ID (GID) of each user from a system's password file (/etc/passwd) to determine who can write to and access exported files and directories, based on the UID and GID that owns those directories on the file server. This means that all of your users should have the same user ID and group ID on all systems to which NFS directories such as home directories are exported.

In small networks, it is often sufficient to make sure that you create the same user and groups on all of your systems, or to make sure that the password and group files on your file server contain the correct entries for all of the user and groups who will access any directory that it exports.

In larger networks, this is impractical, so you may want to consider network-oriented authentication mechanisms, such as the Network Information System (NIS), which was developed by Sun Microsystems specifically for use with NFS. Unfortunately, discussing NIS installation and setup is outside of the scope of this chapter, but you can find a variety of excellent information about it online in documents such as the NIS HOWTO (www.linux-nis.org/nis-howto/). This document is available in Brazilian, English, French, and Polish, which works for me.

You'll not that the exportfs also complains about a missing option in the export specification for the /opt2 directory. In the /etc/exports file shown earlier in this section, you'll notice that the last entry in the /opt2 export specification ends with "(rw)". This final section of an export specification specifies any options associated with a specific exported directory. In this case, the only option specified is rw, which means that the directory is being exported as read/write so that authorized users can write to that directory, as well as read from it. (See the sidebar later in this section entitled "NFS Users and Authentication" for more information about how NFS identifies users.)

The warning message displayed by the exportfs command has to do with whether changes to files in a read/write directory are immediately written to the remote file server (sync, for synchronous operation), or are written lazily, whenever possible (async, for asynchronous operation). Synchronous operation is slower, because your system has to wait for writes to the remote file server to complete, but is safer because you know that your changes have been written to the file server (unless the network connection goes down, in which case all bets are off). Older versions of NFS simply assumed synchronous operation, but nowadays, NFS likes you to explicitly specify which option you want to use. To eliminate this error message, you can therefore edit the /etc/exports file directly to change rw to rw, async, which I generally recommend because it is faster than synchronous operation. After you make this change, the /etc/exports file looks like the following:

```
# /etc/exports: the access control list for filesystems which may be
exported
#               to NFS clients. See exports(5).
/opt2           192.168.0.0/255.255.0.0(rw,async)
```

You can now reexport this directory for asynchronous updates, and the exportfs utility is much happier, as in the following example:

```
$ sudo exportfs -av
exporting 192.168.0.0/255.255.0.0:/opt2
```

The nfs-common package provides a utility called showmount, which you can also run on an NFS server to display the list of directories exported by that file server, but which will not reexport them or change them in any way. Using the `showmount` command with its `-e` option (to show the list of exported directories on the test system used in this chapter) provides output like the following:

```
$ sudo showmount -e
Export list for ulaptop:
/opt2 192.168.0.0/255.255.0.0
```

For complete information about the `exportfs` and `showmount` utilities, see their online reference information, which is available by typing `man exportfs` or `man showmount` from any Ubuntu command line, such as an xterm or the GNOME Terminal application.

Manually Exporting Directories in /etc/exports

Although everyone loves graphical tools, it's sometimes nice to simply edit the underlying files that these tools manipulate — it can be much faster, and can be done from any device on which you can start a text editor.

As mentioned in the previous section, the file that contains exported directory information for NFS file servers is `/etc/exports`. Entries in this file have the following form:

full-path-name-of-exported-directory hosts(mount-options)

Each such entry in the `/etc/exports` file is referred to as an export specification. Hosts can be listed by IP address, hostname, or subnet to state that only those hosts can access a specific directory exported by NFS. Entries such as `192.168.6.61` would limit access to a specific NFS directory from that host, while entries such as `192.168.6.*` or `192.168.6.0` would limit access to a specific NFS directory to hosts on that subnet. By default, all hosts that can reach an NFS server have access to all exported directories (which is represented by a `*` preceding the mount options).

As you'd expect, many mount options are available. Some of the more commonly used mount options are the following:

- `all_squash`: Maps all NFS read or write requests to a specific user, usually "anonymous." This option is often used for public resources such as directories of USENET news, public FTP and download areas, and so on. All files written to an NFS directory that is exported with the `all_squash` mount option will be assigned the UID and GID of the user anonymous or some other UID and GID specified using the `anonuid` and `anongid` mount options. The default is `no_all_squash`, which preserves all UIDs and GIDs.

- `insecure`: Enables access to NFS directories by NFS clients that are running on nonstandard NFS network ports. By default, this option is off, and NFS requests must originate from ports where the port number is less than 1024. The insecure option may be necessary to enable access from random PC and Macintosh NFS clients. If you need to use this option, you should limit machines using the NFS option to a home network or secure corporate Intranet. You should not use this option on any machines that are accessible from over the Internet, because it introduces potential security problems.

- `no_root_squash`: Lets root users on client workstations have the same privileges as the root user on the NFS file server. This option is off by default.

- `ro`: Exports directories that you don't want users to be able to write to because it is read-only. The default is `rw`, which enables read/write access.

- `sync`: Forces writes to the NFS server to be done synchronously, where the client waits for the writes to complete before returning control to the user. This is the default — as explained in the previous section, you can also specify asynchronous operation (`async`), which is slightly faster.

Automounting NFS Home Directories

Automounting is the process of automatically mounting NFS filesystems in response to requests for access to those filesystems. Automounting is controlled by an automount daemon that runs on the client system. In addition to automatically mounting filesystems in response to requests for access to them, an automount daemon can also automatically unmount volumes once they have not been used for a specified period of time.

Using an automount daemon prevents you from having to mount shared NFS directories that you are not actually using at the moment. Mounting all NFS directories on all clients at all times causes a reasonable amount of network traffic, much of which is extraneous if those directories are not actually being used. Using the NFS automount daemon helps keep NFS-related network traffic to a minimum.

At the moment, two different automount daemons are available for Linux. The amd automount daemon runs in user space on client workstations and works much like the original SunOS automounter. The amd automounter is configured through the file /etc/amd.conf. For more information about amd, see the home page for the Automount Utilities at www.am-utils.org. The other automount daemon is called autofs and is implemented in Linux kernel versions 2.2 and greater. The kernel automounter starts one user-space automount process for each top-level automounted directory. The autofs automounter daemon is configured through the file /etc/auto.master or through NIS maps with the same name. Because the autofs daemon is part of the kernel, it is faster and the automounter of choice for many Linux distributions (such as Ubuntu). Both of these packages are available in the Ubuntu repositories, but discussing all of the nuances of automounting is outside the scope of this chapter.

See the man page for /etc/exports (by using the man 5 exports command) for complete information on the options that are available in this file.

Once you have created an entry for a new exported directory in your /etc/exports file, you can export that directory by rerunning the exportfs command with the -r option, which tells the NFS server to reread the /etc/exports file and make any necessary changes to the list of directories that are exported by that NFS server.

Getting More Information About NFS and Related Software

Not surprisingly, the Web provides an excellent source of additional information about NFS and NIS. For more information, consult any of the following:

- NFS FAQ (http://nfs.sourceforge.net)
- NFS HOWTO (http://nfs.sourceforge.net/nfs-howto)
- NIS HOWTO (www.linux-nis.org/nis-howto/)
- NFS Automount HOWTO (www.tldp/HOWTO/Automount.html)

Summary

This chapter explained NFS, the Network File System that is the de facto standard for sharing directories between Unix-like systems over a network. NFS is simple, lightweight, and fast — and its implementation has been freely available for any Unix-like system since the early 1980s. After a bit of background, this chapter explained how to install and configure NFS on your Ubuntu system(s) using both graphical and command-line tools.

Though NFS implementations for Microsoft Windows systems exist, most of them cost money, and thus they aren't an out-of-the-box alternative for people who have heterogeneous networks that host systems running Ubuntu, Mac OS X, and Microsoft Windows systems. (Mac OS X systems, with their Mach and BSD underpinnings, natively support NFS.) Interestingly enough, the most "standard" way of sharing files between these types of systems is by using a package known as Samba, which allows Ubuntu and other Unix-like systems to share directories and filesystems over a network using the proprietary Server Message Block (SMB) protocol used by Microsoft Windows systems (and from which Samba takes its name). Chapter 32 explains how to quickly and easily set up Samba so that everyone on your home network can access files stored on your Ubuntu systems, regardless of what operating system they are running, and at no cost.

Chapter 32

Setting Up a Samba Server

ike it or not, the planet is infested with Windows machines. As you can see
from statements like that, I'm probably as guilty as anyone of propagating
the "us vs. them" mentality when it comes to Windows vs. Linux. How I
personally feel about Windows and Microsoft really doesn't matter — the important thing in this chapter is to discuss the various ways in which software available on Linux systems makes it easy to integrate Linux and Windows filesystems
in both directions, getting features such as automatic printer sharing as freebies
along the way.

You'd have to have been living in a cave for the last five or so years not to have
heard of Samba, arguably one of the most popular applications ever written for
Linux and Unix-like systems. In a nutshell, Samba is a set of applications that
was originally developed to provide support for Microsoft's networking protocols
on Linux systems, but which has been ported to just about every other network-
aware operating system.

A huge number of books are available that are dedicated to discussing Samba,
explaining every nuance of its configuration files, installation, and use. My goal
in this chapter is not to embed another one inside a book on Ubuntu, but rather
to provide some interesting background information about Windows networking
and Samba, and then to explain how to use Samba to share directories and printers on your Ubuntu system so that Microsoft Windows users in your home, academic, or business computing environment can access them.

Overview of Microsoft Windows File Sharing

Networking and related technologies such as routing are probably responsible for
more acronyms than any other aspect of the computer industry. MS-DOS and
Microsoft Windows networking have contributed their share, largely because of

the ubiquity of these operating systems in modern computing environments. Because of the popularity of DOS systems (yesterday) and Windows systems (today), today's Windows systems provide support for almost everyone's networking protocols. Frankly, Windows does an admirable job of continuing to make forward progress while still maintaining backward compatibility with almost every ancient DOS application and networking protocol. Windows systems still support the Internet Packet Exchange (IPX) and Sequenced Packet Exchange (SPX) networking protocols used by Novell to provide the first PC file servers. However, more relevant for our discussion here are the networking protocols and attendant acronyms that were developed by Microsoft and used to provide file and resource sharing over PC networks without requiring the involvement of any third parties, thank you very much.

The *Basic Input and Output System* used by PCs to interact with local devices is best known by its initials as the PC's *BIOS*. As networks began to appear, Microsoft extended the capabilities of the BIOS to support accessing and sharing information over a network, naming the related protocols the network BIOS, or as it's more popularly known, *NetBIOS*. Just as the BIOS provides the basic functions that support all system input and output, the NetBIOS provides the basic functions that let you use and administer network services. NetBIOS commands and functions must be exchanged between networked systems and therefore require a lower-level network transport mechanism to move network packets from one host to another. The lower-level transport protocols that are still in common use in PC networking today are IPX, NetBEUI (Network Basic Extended User Interface), and TCP/IP (Transmission Control Protocol/Internet Protocol). Interestingly, the "Internet" in the full names of both IPX and TCP/IP refers to inter-network communications, not the Internet as we know it today.

Modern Windows systems send their NetBIOS requests by using TCP/IP as a transport protocol. On top of the NetBIOS level, Windows networking provides a higher-level interface for network services known as the Server Message Block (SMB) protocol, which is a networking protocol that can be easily used by applications. SMB is a connection-oriented protocol rather than a broadcast protocol, meaning that it depends on establishing connections to specific networked services provided by other networked hosts rather than simply broadcasting its availability. Once a connection is established, SMB provides four basic types of functions:

- Session functions that negotiate and establish networked connections between machines (often referred to as virtual circuits), authenticate, and verify the access privileges that each party has with the other.
- File functions that enable applications to open, close, read, and write remote files, shared directories, and so on.
- Printer functions that enable applications to spool output to remote output devices.
- Message functions that enable applications to send and receive control, status, and informational messages between different systems on the network.

SMB became an Open Group standard for networking interoperability in the early 1990s. Samba takes its name from SMB, the addition of two vowels making it easily pronounced and somewhat softer than simply being YAA (Yet Another Acronym).

In recent developments, an enhanced version of the SMB protocol called CIFS (Common Internet File System) was submitted by Microsoft to the IETF (Internet Engineering Task Force), an open association of people that are interested in the architecture of Internet communication and the smooth operation of the Internet. CIFS has been approved as a standard, and extends the capabilities of SMB by expanding its focus to sharing resources using even more open, cross-platform standards such as HTTP URLs (HyperText Transfer Protocol Uniform Resource Locators) and DNS (the Domain Name System used to map hostnames to IP addresses and vice versa).

Introducing Samba

When you get right down to it, more data is probably stored on Windows systems than on any other type of computer system. All of those 10GB home and office systems add up to a tremendous number of Windows filesystems holding a staggering amount of data. Samba gives Linux users transparent access to Windows filesystems, but is more commonly used to give Windows users transparent access to Linux, Unix, and Unix-like systems. Samba does this by providing a network interface that is compatible with the networked file and printer-sharing protocols used between Windows systems. To a Windows system, a Linux system running Samba looks exactly like a random Windows system that is sharing filesystems across the network. This enables Windows users to take advantage of the speed, power, and capacity of Linux systems without even realizing that they are accessing Linux filesystems.

Samba is a free and impressive interface for Linux, Unix, and other types of systems to any other networked device that can communicate using the SMB protocol, most notably Windows systems that provide networked access to files, directories, and printers. Samba enables Windows users to access Linux file systems and resources just like any other Windows shared file system or networked resource. For example, with Samba running on a Linux system on your network, Windows users can mount their Linux home directories as networked Windows drives and automatically print to Linux printers just like any other networking Windows printer. Samba, which was originally authored by Andrew Tridgell, is one of the most impressive pieces of interoperability software ever developed.

Samba includes both client and server software — in other words, client software that enables users to communicate from Linux machines to SMB hosts on your network, and server software that provides an SMB interface for your Linux machine. Using the Samba client software is discussed in Chapter 16. This chapter focuses on explaining how to install and set up a Samba server.

A Samba server actually consists of two processes, both of which can be started from the command line or automatically by integrating them into your system's startup procedure. These processes are smbd, the Samba daemon that provides file sharing and print services to Windows clients, and nmbd, the NetBIOS name server that maps the NetBIOS names used by Windows SMB requests to the IP addresses used by Linux systems. The Samba daemon is configured by modifying its configuration file, /etc/samba/smb .conf. On Ubuntu systems, you can either configure specific directories that you want to export via Samba using graphical tools, as explained in the section of this chapter entitled "Using the Shared Folder Tool to Share Directories," or you can manually modifying the Samba configuration file, as discussed later in the section entitled " Samba Server Configuration Essentials."

Interoperability between Linux and Windows systems is much more than just Samba. The Linux kernel provides built-in support for the protocols used to access Windows filesystems, enabling Linux users to mount Windows filesystems via entries in /etc/fstab, just like any other filesystem resource.

Installing the Samba Server and Friends

To install the packages required to run and monitor a Samba server on your Ubuntu system, start the Synaptic Package Manager from the System ⇨ Administration menu, and click Search to display the search dialog. Make sure that Names and Descriptions are the selected items to look in, enter **samba** as the string to search for, and click Search. After the search completes, scroll down until you see the samba-common and samba-server packages, right-click each of these packages and select Mark for Installation from the pop-up menu. You may also want to select the samba-doc and samba-doc-pdf packages, which respectively provide HTML and PDF versions of all of the official Samba project documentation, plus an online copy of a book entitled *Samba 3 By Example* by one of the leaders of the Samba project, John Terpstra. Figure 32.1 shows these packages being selected for installation.

Installing the Samba Server and related packages

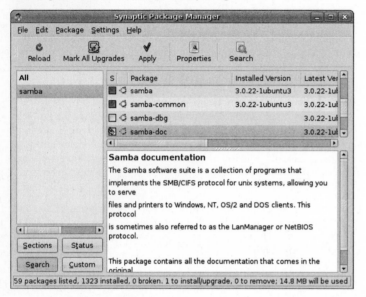

Depending on what software you have previously installed on your Ubuntu system and what you select in Synaptic, a dialog may display that lists other packages that must also be installed, and ask for confirmation. When you see this dialog, click Mark to accept these related (and required) packages.

Next, click Apply in the Synaptic toolbar to install the Samba server and friends on your system. Once the installation completes, you're ready to share data with any system that supports NFS.

See Chapter 20 for more detailed information on installing applications using the Synaptic Package Manager.

Samba Server Configuration Essentials

At the moment, the absence of a graphical tool for setting up and configuring Samba on Ubuntu systems is a rather glaring omission to the standard user-friendliness that Ubuntu users have come to expect. I'm not the only person to have noticed this, and there are active discussions on various Ubuntu lists and forums about developing such a tool. However, for the time being, you must do your initial Samba configuration in the aging but tried-and-true Linux way — by editing configuration files using a text editor. Samba's configuration file is /etc/samba/smb.conf. The Samba configuration file contains many helpful comments, which are lines beginning with a hash mark. It also contains many sample, inactive configuration commands, which are lines beginning with a semicolon. These indicate configuration commands that you may want to activate by removing the leading semicolon.

As you'll see in the next few sections, editing the file /etc/samba/smb.conf to configure Samba is actually quite simple, but is also somewhat inelegant when compared to the rest of the system administrative environment provided by Ubuntu Linux.

> **NOTE** Web-based system administration tools such as swat (Samba Web Administration Tool) and webmin (a more generalized Web-based administrative environment) are available from the Ubuntu repositories, but require special configuration before they'll work correctly in the Ubuntu environment. Rather than taking the conceptual detour of explaining how to use these tools, I'll continue to wait for a desktop GNOME/Ubuntu solution for Samba setup and configuration. After all, KDE already has such a tool in its Control Center — and GNOME can't (or shouldn't be) far behind.

Regardless of whether a graphical tool for Samba setup and configuration is available by the time that you read this (check the System ➪ Administration menu), the information in this section still applies, and it's actually quite useful to have some insights into where Samba configuration information is stored, and how the primary Samba configuration file is organized.

The next few sections focus on specific entries in the Samba configuration file that you may need to update to use Samba in your environment, instead of discussing the Samba configuration file in its entirety. Between the official Samba documentation, the online documentation that is provided as part of the samba-doc and samba-doc-pdf packages, and the many books available on Samba, there's no shortage of detailed information about every nuance of Samba — the rest of this chapter focuses on getting things to work, as quickly and as easily as possible.

Identifying Your Workgroup or Domain

The Samba configuration file is divided into several sections, each identified by a section name enclosed within square brackets. The entries related to the network identity of your Samba server and how you authenticate to it are located in the [global] section of the Samba configuration file /etc/samba/smb.conf.

The key entry that you must set to define how your Ubuntu server interacts with Windows systems is the workgroup entry, which identifies the workgroup or Windows domain to which your Samba server belongs. On a sample system of mine, this entry looks like the following:

```
[global]
    workgroup = WVH
```

This entry identifies my machine as belonging to the Windows workgroup or domain named WVH. In this SOHO example, it's a workgroup, but that is essentially transparent — the key thing here is that your Samba server is either a member of the workgroup/domain that you are already using at your site, or a primary domain controller that defines the domain that you want it to host.

> **NOTE** If you want your Samba server to function as the primary domain controller (PDC) for a Windows domain, you must also change the domain master setting in the Samba configuration file to yes, and make sure that the entry is not commented out. In this case, the entry would look something like the following:
>
> ```
> domain master = auto
> ```

This means that the Samba server will serve as a primary domain controller for your domain if no other domain controller can be located, which will be the case if your Samba server is hosting the domain.

This chapter explains how to use Samba as part of a workgroup, which is the typical way that Samba is used on a home or SOHO network. For information about setting up a complete Windows domain, make sure that you installed the samba-doc as suggested in the section of this chapter entitled "Installing the Samba Server and Friends," and consult the online copy of *Samba 3 By Example* that is provided in the directory /usr/share/doc/samba-doc/htmldocs/Samba3-ByExample.

Because this example shows a small workgroup, you will probably also want to activate the entries that tell Samba not to function as a WINS (the Windows NetBIOS name service, discussed earlier in this chapter), but to instead use your system's Domain Name Server to look up Windows hostnames, which should look like the following:

```
wins support = no
dns proxy = yes
name resolve order = lmhosts host wins bcast
```

The last entry tells Samba that clients will first look in their local `lmhosts` file for name information, will then check information in the file `/etc/hosts` on the Samba server, will then check WINS (which, in this case, is proxied to the local DNS server), and will finally use a broadcast to search for the right host. This combination covers the hostname lookup bases for every Samba server configuration that I've ever set up or used.

This completes the core modifications to the Samba configuration file that are necessary for Samba to be able to share files with the specified workgroup or domain. That wasn't so bad, was it?

Configuring Samba Authentication

In the workgroup configuration that we are using as an example in this chapter, Samba comes preconfigured to perform the type of authentication required by workgroup members. However, to be able to access shared resources, you must be able to authenticate to the Samba server. Samba maintains its own authentication information — to add login and password information about a user, you must use the `smbpasswd` command. When adding information about a user, you must use the `-a` option, followed by the name of the user that you want to add. The `smbpasswd` command will prompt you for a password and will then prompt you for that password again to ensure that you have typed the password correctly. A sample transcript of adding the user wvh is the following:

```
$ sudo smbpasswd -a wvh
Password:
New SMB password:
Retype new SMB password:
```

The first password prompt is from the `sudo` application, asking for my Ubuntu password so that I can perform this privileged operation. The second two are for entering and verifying the Samba password for the user wvh.

> **NOTE** The default security level in the Samba configuration file, `security = user`, requires that Samba users must also exist in the password file on the Ubuntu system, or you will receive an error message and the `smbpasswd` command will fail. For information about other security models and their implications, see the file `/usr/share/doc/samba-doc/htmldocs/ServerType.html` from the `samba-doc` package.

Sharing Printers and Home Directories Using Samba

After setting up the workgroup and creating a user, the next thing to consider is the general resources on the Ubuntu system that you want to make available to all users of Windows systems that connect to your Samba server. The most common examples of these are printers and users' home directories.

The entries in the [global] section of a Samba configuration file that are relevant to printers and printing on Ubuntu are the following, which you should make sure are not commented out (i.e., preceded by a semicolon):

```
load printers = yes
printing = cups
printcap name = cups
```

Later in the Samba configuration file, the [printers] and [print$] sections provide information about how your Windows system will interact with the Samba server. You won't need to change any of these, but for your reference, these entries are the following:

```
[printers]
   comment = All Printers
   browseable = no
   path = /tmp
   printable = yes
   public = no
   writable = no
   create mode = 0700
[print$]
   comment = Printer Drivers
   path = /var/lib/samba/printers
   browseable = yes
   read only = yes
   guest ok = no
```

The [printers] section identifies how the Samba server will handle requests for printer identification and incoming print requests from Windows clients, while the [print$] section maps the traditional Windows print$ share name to a directory on your Linux system where you can put the print drivers for specific printers so that your Windows clients can locate and load them if they are not already available on a client system.

Aside from printers, the most natural resource for users to want to access from their Windows systems is their Ubuntu home directories. This provides an easy way to use your home directory on a Samba server as a centralized place to store files, but also enables you to automatically back up files from your Windows system to the Samba server and enables you to leverage any standard backups that you are doing on the Samba server. (See Chapter 22 for more information about backing up files on your Ubuntu system.)

Happily, Samba's configuration file is already set up to support sharing home directories by default, as long as your Linux and Windows user names match. The section of the Samba configuration file that supports this is the following:

```
[homes]
   comment = Home Directories
   browseable = no
   writable = no
   create mask = 0700
   directory mask = 0700
```

As you can see from this configuration file excerpt, home directories are shared by default but are not writable from Windows clients. This is pretty inconvenient, so you will want to change the writable entry in this section of the configuration file to yes, as in the following example:

```
writable = yes
```

This enables users to both read and write files in their home directories.

> **TIP** If your Windows and Ubuntu users happen to have different logins, you can associate the two by creating appropriate entries in the file /etc/samba/smbusers. Entries in this file have the form UnixLogin = WindowsLogin. For example, to map the Ubuntu user wvh to the Windows user bill.vonhagen, I would create the following entry in the /etc/samba/smbusers file:
>
> ```
> wvh = bill.vonhagen
> ```
>
> If your Windows login names contain one or more spaces, you must enclose them within quotation marks in this file.
>
> In practice, I suggest keeping logins the same across Ubuntu and Samba systems, but this file can be used if you have different naming conventions for the users of different types of systems.

Verifying the Samba Configuration File

After making any changes to your Samba configuration file, you should verify that you haven't accidentally violated the syntax of the file. If a Samba configuration file contains any invalid entries, Samba displays an error message and will not load. This could be extremely discouraging, were it not for the fact that the Samba server package also provides a utility that tests the validity of a Samba configuration file and identifies the exact location of any errors that it finds. This utility is testparm, which you can run with no arguments to test the default Samba configuration file /etc/samba/smb.conf. The output from a run of the testparm utility looks like the following:

```
$ testparm
Load smb config files from /etc/samba/smb.conf
Processing section "[homes]"
Processing section "[printers]"
Processing section "[print$]"
Loaded services file OK.
WARNING: passdb expand explicit = yes is deprecated
Server role: ROLE_STANDALONE
Press enter to see a dump of your service definitions
```

As shown in the preceding example, after displaying some general information, the testparm utility prompts you to press Enter on your keyboard to see detailed information about the services that your Samba server has been configured to provide. An example of this detailed information is the following:

```
[global]
        workgroup = WVH
        server string = %h server (Samba, Ubuntu)
        obey pam restrictions = Yes
        passdb backend = tdbsam, guest
        syslog = 0
        log file = /var/log/samba/log.%m
        max log size = 1000
        name resolve order = lmhosts host wins bcast
```

```
        printcap name = cups
        panic action = /usr/share/samba/panic-action %d
        invalid users = root
        printing = cups
        print command =
        lpq command = %p
        lprm command =

[homes]
        comment = Home Directories
        read only = No
        create mask = 0700
        directory mask = 0700
        browseable = No

[printers]
        comment = All Printers
        path = /tmp
        create mask = 0700
        printable = Yes
        browseable = No

[print$]
        comment = Printer Drivers
        path = /var/lib/samba/printers
```

Depending on the version of Samba installed on your Ubuntu system and the changes that you have made to your Samba configuration file, your output may differ slightly.

The testparm utility only checks the Samba configuration file — it does not consult the running Samba service for information about how it is configured and the services that it provides. To do this, you can use the smbclient utility, as described in the next section.

Testing Samba Availability and Services

The Samba applications suite includes an application called smbclient, which is a command-line client for contacting and browsing Samba servers. You can also use this utility to test if your Samba server is up and running, and to list the services that it is providing.

If you have made any changes to your Samba configuration file, you should restart your Samba server before attempting to verify the services that it provides. To do this, execute the following command:

```
/etc/init.d/samba restart
```

This command shuts down any instance of the Samba server that is currently running, and then starts the Samba server again, which forces it to read your updated configuration file.

Once you have done this, you can query your Samba server by using the smbclient application; the -L option to list available resources; the name of the host that you want to contact; and the -U% option to show what a default, non-authenticated user would see. An example of this command and its output is the following:

```
$ smbclient -L ulaptop -U%
Domain=[WVH] OS=[Unix] Server=[Samba 3.0.22]
```

859

```
            Sharename        Type        Comment
            ---------        ----        -------
            ADMIN$           IPC         IPC Service (ulaptop server (Samba,
Ubuntu))
            IPC$             IPC         IPC Service (ulaptop server (Samba,
Ubuntu))
            print$           Disk        Printer Drivers

Domain=[WVH] OS=[Unix] Server=[Samba 3.0.22]

            Server                       Comment
            ---------                    -------
            ULAPTOP                      ulaptop server (Samba, Ubuntu)

            Workgroup                    Master
            ---------                    -------
            WVH                          ULAPTOP
```

The first portion of this output lists the shares available to the current user, which is an unauthenticated user. The second provides information about the name of the Samba server that you have contacted and the workgroup or domain that it is a member of.

Looking good! The next step is to see what an authenticated user would see. I'll use the sample user wvh, which I created earlier in this chapter. This time, the command and its output look like the following:

```
wvh@ulaptop:~$ smbclient -L ulaptop -Uwvh
Password:
Domain=[ULAPTOP] OS=[Unix] Server=[Samba 3.0.22]

            Sharename        Type        Comment
            ---------        ----        -------
            ADMIN$           IPC         IPC Service (ulaptop server (Samba,
Ubuntu))
            IPC$             IPC         IPC Service (ulaptop server (Samba,
Ubuntu))
            print$           Disk        Printer Drivers
            wvh              Disk        Home Directories

Domain=[ULAPTOP] OS=[Unix] Server=[Samba 3.0.22]

            Server                       Comment
            ---------                    -------

            Workgroup                    Master
            ---------                    -------
            WVH                          ULAPTOP
```

Note that because I specified an actual username, the smbclient utility first prompted me for my password on the Samba server, and then displayed slightly different information. The only real difference is that an authenticated user has access to his or her home directory on the Samba server, as you can see in the Home Directories entry in the Sharename section of the first portion of the smbclient output.

Congratulations! Now that it's clear that the Samba server is working and is correctly configured to allow users to access user-specific resources, it's time to add some system-wide resources that all authenticated users will be able to take advantage of. Luckily, as explained in the next section, you can even do this with a graphical tool.

Using the Shared Folder Tool to Share Directories

Though Ubuntu Linux doesn't provide a graphical tool for setting up and configuring Samba itself, it does provide an easy-to-use graphical tool (`shares-admin`) that simplifies identifying and configuring specific directories that you want to export via Samba from your Ubuntu system. If you have already exported shared directories using NFS, this tool should already be familiar to you — the Ubuntu and GNOME folks were clever enough to use the same tool for identifying and configuring both Samba shares and NFS exports.

To start this tool, select System ➪ Administration ➪ Shared Folders. After supplying your password in the administrative authentication dialog that displays, the Shared Folder tool starts, as shown in Figure 32.2. This dialog shows any shares that you have already defined, which in this case shows the /opt2 directory that I am sharing with NFS users.

Starting the Shared Folder administration tool

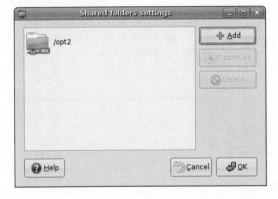

To define a directory that you want to share via Samba, click Add to display the dialog shown in Figure 32.3.

As you can see in Figure 32.3, this dialog is already set up with the basic information required for defining an SMB share. The default exported/shared directory that is initially selected when you start the Shared Folder tool is your home directory. This isn't all that exciting because Samba shares these automatically, so in this example, I'm going to share the directory that contains my online audio collection, which I should point out was either legally ripped from CDs that I own or consists of freely-downloadable live recordings.

FIGURE 32.3

Defining a shared directory in the Shared Folder tool

To specify another directory for sharing, click the Path item and select Other from the drop-down menu to display the directory selection dialog shown in Figure 32.4.

To select a directory somewhere on your system, click root and navigate through the directory tree on your system to select the directory that you want to export, which in this example is my /opt2 directory. Click Open to select that directory (or whatever directory you want to export) and return to the dialog shown in Figure 32.3, which now displays the name of the newly selected directory in the Path field.

FIGURE 32.4

Selecting the directory that you want to share

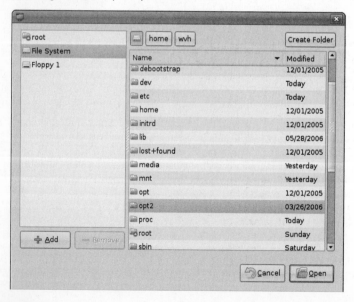

Next, you'll need to identify the sharing settings and name resolution mechanism to access (i.e., mount) this directory over the network. To verify these, click the General Windows sharing settings button to display the dialog shown in Figure 32.5.

FIGURE 32.5

Windows sharing settings for a shared directory

This dialog shows that this directory will be shared from your Samba server using the WVH workgroup, and that WINS need not be used to locate the server — hosts file or DNS information will suffice. Click OK to return to the dialog shown in Figure 32.3. You may want to enter some general information about the share that you are defining in Name and Comment fields, for future reference. This dialog also enables you to use the "Read only" checkbox to specify that you want the directory to be shared in read-only fashion. If this box is not selected, properly authenticated users can create and modify files in directories that they have access to. Similarly, you can select the Allow browsing folder checkbox to enable unauthenticated users to browse the shared directory without being able to examine any of the files that it contains. Figure 32.6 shows this dialog after specifying some general information.

FIGURE 32.6

Adding general information about a Samba share

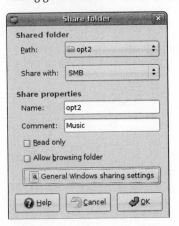

To continue, click OK to redisplay the dialog originally shown in Figure 32.2, which now contains the settings for your newly defined NFS shared directory, as shown in Figure 32.7.

FIGURE 32.7

Shared NFS and Samba directories in the Shared Folder tool

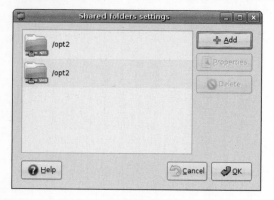

Almost done! To subsequently modify or update the settings for any shared directory, you can highlight its name in the Shared Folder tool and click Properties to display the specific settings for that shared folder. To begin sharing the folder, click OK to start the specified type of file sharing and close the Shared Folder tool.

As you might suspect, defining SMB shared in the Shared Folder tool actually just creates the correct entries for those shares in your Samba configuration file, just as creating NFS exports in this tool adds the correct entries to the `/etc/exports` file used by NFS. The entries that were added to the `/etc/samba/smb.conf` file for the share that you just defined are the following:

```
[opt2]
path = /opt2
comment = Music
available = yes
browseable = no
public = yes
writable = yes
```

Adding these entries to the standard Samba configuration file ensures that the newly defined shares will always be available as soon as the Samba daemon is started on the Ubuntu system that is acting as a Samba server.

Getting More Information About Samba

Not surprisingly, the Web provides an excellent source of additional information about Samba. Somewhat surprisingly, the Samba project itself provides some excellent documentation, as well as an online version of a great book about the current version of Samba, which is Samba version 3. As suggested earlier, you can install your own copies of the Samba documentation by installing the `samba-doc` and `samba-doc-pdf` packages when you install the Samba server. For more information, consult any of the following:

- `www.samba.org`: The main site for the Samba project, at which you can find the latest tips, tricks, and source code.

- `/usr/share/doc/samba-doc/htmldocs/Samba3-HOWTO`: A directory containing a HOWTO file in HTML format that explains how to install and configure Samba version 3, and answers many common questions. (You'll want to open the file `index.html` in this directory from your Web browser.) The HTML version of this document is provided in the `samba-doc` package.

- `/usr/share/doc/samba-doc/htmldocs/Samba3-ByExample`: A directory containing an HTML version of an excellent, hands-on book about Samba 3. This book was written by John Terpstra, one of the leaders of the Samba project, and explains how to install and configure Samba 3 for a complete spectrum of networked environments, from smaller SOHO environments (as discussed in this chapter) to enterprise environments with thousands of users. (You'll want to open the file `index.html` in this directory from your Web browser.) The HTML version of this document is provided in the `samba-doc` package. You'll probably also want to buy a paper copy of John's book — it's definitive, complete, and battery-free.

Summary

This chapter explained how to install and set up a Samba server to enable your Ubuntu system to access data shared on Microsoft Windows systems and vice versa. Samba is probably the best example of the value that open source software can bring to modern computing, enabling seamless data sharing between Unix-like and Microsoft Windows systems thanks to a fantastic combination of reverse engineering and insightful development.

Appendix

What's on the CD-ROM?

This appendix provides you with information on the contents of the CD that accompanies this book. Here is what you will find:

- System requirements
- Using the CD with Windows, Linux, and Macintosh Systems
- What's on the CD
- Troubleshooting

System Requirements

Make sure that your computer meets the minimum system requirements listed in this section. If your computer doesn't match up to most of these requirements, you may have a problem using the contents of the CD.

For Windows 9x, Windows 2000, Windows NT4 (with SP 4 or later), Windows Me, or Windows XP:

- PC with a Pentium processor running at 120 Mhz or faster
- At least 96MB of total RAM installed on your computer; for best performance, we recommend at least 128MB
- Ethernet network interface card (NIC) or modem with a speed of at least 28,800 bps
- A CD-ROM drive

> **NOTE** The Windows requirements for using this CD differ from the Linux requirements because the Windows requirements apply only to installing and using selected Open Source applications found on the CD, while the Linux requirements apply to running the entire Linux operating system.

For Linux:

- PC with a Pentium processor running at 90 Mhz or faster; for best performance, we recommend a Pentium III, Pentium 4, or AMD equivalent running at 700 Mhz or better
- At least 96MB of total RAM installed on your computer; for best performance, we recommend at least 256MB
- Ethernet network interface card (NIC) or modem with a speed of at least 28,800 bps
- A CD-ROM drive
- At least 3GB of available disk space if installing Ubuntu Linux

For Macintosh:

- Apple computer with a G3 or faster processor running Mac OS 9.0 or later
- At least 96MB of total RAM installed on your computer; for best performance, we recommend at least 256MB
- At least 3GB of available disk space if installing Ubuntu Linux

 **If you are a Macintosh user, see the instructions later in this appendix to determine if you can use the CD provided with this book with your Macintosh, or if you need to obtain and burn a different CD.**

Using the CD with Windows

To install the items from the CD to your hard drive, follow these steps:

1. Insert the CD into your computer's CD-ROM drive.
2. A window will appear, listing the Open Source software that you can install on your Windows system.
3. To install any of these packages, click the Install now button beside its entry. For more information about installing any of the software packages, see Chapter 2.

If you do not have autorun enabled or if the autorun window does not appear, follow the steps below to access the CD.

1. Click Start ➪ Run.
2. In the dialog box that appears, type *d:\start.exe*, where *d* is the letter of your CD-ROM drive. This will bring up the autorun window described above.
3. Choose the software that you want to install as described in Chapter 2.

Using the CD with Linux

The CD that is included with this book is for 32-bit x86 systems and will not work on 64-bit systems. To install or test-drive Ubuntu Linux on a 64-bit x86 system, you must obtain and burn a copy of the Ubuntu CD for 64-bit systems. See the instructions in Chapter 2 for information on obtaining and burning a CD that contains a bootable version of Ubuntu Linux that has been compiled for 64-bit systems.

To install or test-drive Ubuntu Linux from the CD to your hard drive, follow these steps:

1. Insert the CD into your computer's CD-ROM drive.

2. Reboot your computer system, booting from the CD-ROM. If your system is not already configured to boot from a CD before booting from the hard drive, you may need to modify your computer's BIOS settings in order to give precedence to booting from the CD-ROM drive.

3. Press Return or wait 30 seconds to boot into Ubuntu Linux.

4. Experiment with Ubuntu Linux or follow the instructions in Chapter 2 to permanently install Ubuntu Linux on your computer system.

5. To remove the CD from your CD-ROM drive, select System ⇨ Quit, and select Shut Down from the menu that displays. Remove the CD-ROM from your computer's CD-ROM drive when prompted to do so.

Using the CD with Mac OS

You can install Linux as the only operating system on an Intel-based Macintosh system by following the instructions in Chapter 2. Installing Linux as an alternate boot option to Mac OS X on Intel-based Macs requires use of Apple's Boot Camp software, which is not described in this book.

The CD that is included with this book is for 32-bit x86 systems and will not work on Mac OS systems based on the PPC architecture. To install or test-drive Ubuntu Linux on these systems, you must obtain and burn a copy of the Ubuntu CD for PPC systems. See the instructions in Chapter 2 for information on obtaining and burning a CD that contains a bootable version of Ubuntu Linux that has been compiled for PPC systems.

NOTE While you can easily run Ubuntu Linux on your Mac using the instructions in Chapter 2, installing Ubuntu to your Mac OS system so that you can run either Ubuntu Linux or the Mac OS requires that you have a free partition available that is at least 3GB in size. If you want to install Ubuntu on your Mac, want to preserve your installed version of the Mac OS, and do not have a free partition available, follow the instructions in Chapter 3 on repartitioning a Mac OS disk before attempting to install Ubuntu Linux.

What's on the CD

The following sections provide a summary of the software and other materials you'll find on the CD.

Applications

The CD provides a version of Ubuntu Linux from Canonical, Ltd., that you can either test-drive or install on a 32-bit, x86-compatible computer system. It also includes selected Open Source applications that have been compiled for use on Microsoft Windows systems. The following Open Source applications for Microsoft Windows systems are on the CD:

- AbiWord is a popular word processor that is part of the GNOME office suite and provides a free, Open Source alternative to expensive, proprietary word processors such as Microsoft Word.

- Gaim is an Open Source alternative to most instant messenger software that can exchange messages in all of the formats used by popular instant messaging packages from AOL, Yahoo, and so on.

- Gimp is a popular image creation and manipulation package that provides a free, Open Source alternative to expensive, proprietary software packages such as Adobe Photoshop. Using Gimp is discussed in the section of Chapter 12 entitled "Using the GIMP."

- Mozilla Firefox is an Open Source Web browser that provides a popular and secure alternative to Microsoft's Internet Explorer on Windows systems. The core capabilities provided by Firefox are easily extended using hundreds of plugins that are freely available over the Internet. Using Firefox is discussed in Chapter 9.

- Mozilla Thunderbird is an Open Source email client (MUA) that provides a popular and secure mechanism for reading email from POP/POP3 and IMAP mail servers.

Shareware programs are fully functional, trial versions of copyrighted programs. If you like particular programs, register with their authors for a nominal fee and receive licenses, enhanced versions, and technical support.

Freeware programs are copyrighted games, applications, and utilities that are free for personal use. Unlike shareware, these programs do not require a fee or provide technical support.

GNU software is governed by its own license, which is included inside the folder of the GNU product. See the GNU license for more details.

Trial, demo, or evaluation versions are usually limited either by time or functionality (such as being unable to save projects). Some trial versions are very sensitive to system date changes. If you alter your computer's date, the programs will "time out" and will no longer be functional.

Troubleshooting

The CD that is included with this book contains a complete version of Ubuntu Linux that you can either test-drive or install on your computer system. If you have problems installing or running Ubuntu Linux on a particular computer system, consult the Ubuntu Forums at http://www.ubuntuforums.org/.

If you are simply installing one or more of the Open Source applications found on this CD on a Microsoft Windows system and have difficulty installing or using any of these applications, try the following solutions:

- **Turn off any anti-virus software that you may have running.** Installers sometimes mimic virus activity and can make your computer incorrectly believe that it is being infected by a virus. (Be sure to turn the anti-virus software back on later.)

- **Close all running programs.** The more programs you're running, the less memory is available to other programs. Installers also typically update files and programs; if you keep other programs running, installation may not work properly.

Customer Care

If you have trouble with the CD-ROM, please call the Wiley Product Technical Support phone number at (800) 762-2974. Outside the United States, call 1(317) 572-3994. You can also contact Wiley Product Technical Support at **http://support.wiley.com**. John Wiley & Sons will provide technical support only for installation and other general quality control items. For technical support on the applications themselves, consult the program's vendor or author.

To place additional orders or to request information about other Wiley products, please call (877) 762-2974.

Index

SYMBOLS AND NUMBERS

A

U

GNU General Public License

Version 2, June 1991

Copyright © 1989, 1991 Free Software Foundation, Inc.

675 Mass Ave., Cambridge, MA 02139, USA

Everyone is permitted to copy and distribute verbatim copies of this license document, but changing it is not allowed.

Preamble

The licenses for most software are designed to take away your freedom to share and change it. By contrast, the GNU General Public License is intended to guarantee your freedom to share and change free software—to make sure the software is free for all its users. This General Public License applies to most of the Free Software Foundation's software and to any other program whose authors commit to using it. (Some other Free Software Foundation software is covered by the GNU Library General Public License instead.) You can apply it to your programs, too.

When we speak of free software, we are referring to freedom, not price. Our General Public Licenses are designed to make sure that you have the freedom to distribute copies of free software (and charge for this service if you wish), that you receive source code or can get it if you want it, that you can change the software or use pieces of it in new free programs; and that you know you can do these things.

To protect your rights, we need to make restrictions that forbid anyone to deny you these rights or to ask you to surrender the rights. These restrictions translate to certain responsibilities for you if you distribute copies of the software, or if you modify it.

For example, if you distribute copies of such a program, whether gratis or for a fee, you must give the recipients all the rights that you have. You must make sure that they, too, receive or can get the source code. And you must show them these terms so they know their rights.

We protect your rights with two steps: (1) copyright the software, and (2) offer you this license which gives you legal permission to copy, distribute and/or modify the software.

Also, for each author's protection and ours, we want to make certain that everyone understands that there is no warranty for this free software. If the software is modified by someone else and passed on, we want its recipients to know that what they have is not the original, so that any problems introduced by others will not reflect on the original authors' reputations.

Finally, any free program is threatened constantly by software patents. We wish to avoid the danger that redistributors of a free program will individually obtain patent licenses, in effect making the program proprietary. To prevent this, we have made it clear that any patent must be licensed for everyone's free use or not licensed at all.

The precise terms and conditions for copying, distribution and modification follow.

TERMS AND CONDITIONS FOR COPYING, DISTRIBUTION AND MODIFICATION

0. This License applies to any program or other work which contains a notice placed by the copyright holder saying it may be distributed under the terms of this General Public License. The "Program", below, refers to any such program or work, and a "work based on the Program" means either the Program or any derivative work under copyright law: that is to say, a work containing the Program or a portion of it, either verbatim or with modifications and/or translated into another language. (Hereinafter, translation is included without limitation in the term "modification".) Each licensee is addressed as "you".

    Activities other than copying, distribution and modification are not covered by this License; they are outside its scope. The act of running the Program is not restricted, and the output from the Program is covered only if its contents constitute a work based on the Program (independent of having been made by running the Program). Whether that is true depends on what the Program does.

1. You may copy and distribute verbatim copies of the Program's source code as you receive it, in any medium, provided that you conspicuously and appropriately publish on each copy an appropriate copyright notice and disclaimer of warranty; keep intact all the notices that refer to this License and to the absence of any warranty; and give any other recipients of the Program a copy of this License along with the Program.

    You may charge a fee for the physical act of transferring a copy, and you may at your option offer warranty protection in exchange for a fee.

2. You may modify your copy or copies of the Program or any portion of it, thus forming a work based on the Program, and copy and distribute such modifications or work under the terms of Section 1 above, provided that you also meet all of these conditions:

    a) You must cause the modified files to carry prominent notice stating that you changed the files and the date of any change.

    b) You must cause any work that you distribute or publish, that in whole or in part contains or is derived from the Program or any part thereof, to be licensed as a whole at no charge to all third parties under the terms of this License.

    c) If the modified program normally reads commands interactively when run, you must cause it, when started running for such interactive use in the most ordinary way, to print or display an announcement including an appropriate copyright notice and a notice that there is no warranty (or else, saying that you provide a warranty) and that users may redistribute the program under these conditions, and telling the user how to view a copy of this License. (Exception: if the Program itself is interactive but does not normally print such an announcement, your work based on the Program is not required to print an announcement.)

    These requirements apply to the modified work as a whole. If identifiable sections of that work are not derived from the Program, and can be reasonably considered independent and separate works in themselves, then this License, and its terms, do not apply to those sections when you distribute them as separate works. But when you distribute the same sections as part of a whole which is a work based on the Program, the distribution of the whole must be on the terms of this License, whose permissions for other licensees extend to the entire whole, and thus to each and every part regardless of who wrote it.

    Thus, it is not the intent of this section to claim rights or contest your rights to work written entirely by you; rather, the intent is to exercise the right to control the distribution of derivative or collective works based on the Program.

    In addition, mere aggregation of another work not based on the Program with the Program (or with a work based on the Program) on a volume of a storage or distribution medium does not bring the other work under the scope of this License.

3. You may copy and distribute the Program (or a work based on it, under Section 2) in object code or executable form under the terms of Sections 1 and 2 above provided that you also do one of the following:

a) Accompany it with the complete corresponding machine-readable source code, which must be distributed under the terms of Sections 1 and 2 above on a medium customarily used for software interchange; or,

b) Accompany it with a written offer, valid for at least three years, to give any third party, for a charge no more than your cost of physically performing source distribution, a complete machine-readable copy of the corresponding source code, to be distributed under the terms of Sections 1 and 2 above on a medium customarily used for software interchange; or,

c) Accompany it with the information you received as to the offer to distribute corresponding source code. (This alternative is allowed only for noncommercial distribution and only if you received the program in object code or executable form with such an offer, in accord with Subsection b above.)

The source code for a work means the preferred form of the work for making modifications to it. For an executable work, complete source code means all the source code for all modules it contains, plus any associated interface definition files, plus the scripts used to control compilation and installation of the executable. However, as a special exception, the source code distributed need not include anything that is normally distributed (in either source or binary form) with the major components (compiler, kernel, and so on) of the operating system on which the executable runs, unless that component itself accompanies the executable.

If distribution of executable or object code is made by offering access to copy from a designated place, then offering equivalent access to copy the source code from the same place counts as distribution of the source code, even though third parties are not compelled to copy the source along with the object code.

4. You may not copy, modify, sublicense, or distribute the Program except as expressly provided under this License. Any attempt otherwise to copy, modify, sublicense or distribute the Program is void, and will automatically terminate your rights under this License. However, parties who have received copies, or rights, from you under this License will not have their licenses terminated so long as such parties remain in full compliance.

5. You are not required to accept this License, since you have not signed it. However, nothing else grants you permission to modify or distribute the Program or its derivative works. These actions are prohibited by law if you do not accept this License. Therefore, by modifying or distributing the Program (or any work based on the Program), you indicate your acceptance of this License to do so, and all its terms and conditions for copying, distributing or modifying the Program or works based on it.

6. Each time you redistribute the Program (or any work based on the Program), the recipient automatically receives a license from the original licensor to copy, distribute or modify the Program subject to these terms and conditions. You may not impose any further restrictions on the recipients' exercise of the rights granted herein. You are not responsible for enforcing compliance by third parties to this License.

7. If, as a consequence of a court judgment or allegation of patent infringement or for any other reason (not limited to patent issues), conditions are imposed on you (whether by court order, agreement or otherwise) that contradict the conditions of this License, they do not excuse you from the conditions of this License. If you cannot distribute so as to satisfy simultaneously your obligations under this License and any other pertinent obligations, then as a consequence you may not distribute the Program at all. For example, if a patent license would not permit royalty-free redistribution of the Program by all those who receive copies directly or indirectly through you, then the only way you could satisfy both it and this License would be to refrain entirely from distribution of the Program.

If any portion of this section is held invalid or unenforceable under any particular circumstance, the balance of the section is intended to apply and the section as a whole is intended to apply in other circumstances.

It is not the purpose of this section to induce you to infringe any patents or other property right claims or to contest validity of any such claims; this section has the sole purpose of protecting the integrity of the free software distribution system, which is implemented by public license practices. Many people have made generous contributions to the wide range of software distributed through that system in reliance on consistent application of that system; it is up to the author/donor to decide if he or she is willing to distribute software through any other system and a licensee cannot impose that choice.

This section is intended to make thoroughly clear what is believed to be a consequence of the rest of this License.

8. If the distribution and/or use of the Program is restricted in certain countries either by patents or by copyrighted interfaces, the original copyright holder who places the Program under this License may add an explicit geographical distribution limitation excluding those countries, so that distribution is permitted only in or among countries not thus excluded. In such case, this License incorporates the limitation as if written in the body of this License.

9. The Free Software Foundation may publish revised and/or new versions of the General Public License from time to time. Such new versions will be similar in spirit to the present version, but may differ in detail to address new problems or concerns.

Each version is given a distinguishing version number. If the Program specifies a version number of this License which applies to it and "any later version", you have the option of following the terms and conditions either of that version or of any later version published by the Free Software Foundation. If the Program does not specify a version number of this License, you may choose any version ever published by the Free Software Foundation.

10. If you wish to incorporate parts of the Program into other free programs whose distribution conditions are different, write to the author to ask for permission. For software which is copyrighted by the Free Software Foundation, write to the Free Software Foundation; we sometimes make exceptions for this. Our decision will be guided by the two goals of preserving the free status of all derivatives of our free software and of promoting the sharing and reuse of software generally.

NO WARRANTY

11. BECAUSE THE PROGRAM IS LICENSED FREE OF CHARGE, THERE IS NO WARRANTY FOR THE PROGRAM, TO THE EXTENT PERMITTED BY APPLICABLE LAW. EXCEPT WHEN OTHERWISE STATED IN WRITING THE COPYRIGHT HOLDERS AND/OR OTHER PARTIES PROVIDE THE PROGRAM "AS IS" WITHOUT WARRANTY OF ANY KIND, EITHER EXPRESSED OR IMPLIED, INCLUDING, BUT NOT LIMITED TO, THE IMPLIED WARRANTIES OF MERCHANTABILITY AND FITNESS FOR A PARTICULAR PURPOSE. THE ENTIRE RISK AS TO THE QUALITY AND PERFORMANCE OF THE PROGRAM IS WITH YOU. SHOULD THE PROGRAM PROVE DEFECTIVE, YOU ASSUME THE COST OF ALL NECESSARY SERVICING, REPAIR OR CORRECTION.

12. IN NO EVENT UNLESS REQUIRED BY APPLICABLE LAW OR AGREED TO IN WRITING WILL ANY COPYRIGHT HOLDER, OR ANY OTHER PARTY WHO MAY MODIFY AND/OR REDISTRIBUTE THE PROGRAM AS PERMITTED ABOVE, BE LIABLE TO YOU FOR DAMAGES, INCLUDING ANY GENERAL, SPECIAL, INCIDENTAL OR CONSEQUENTIAL DAMAGES ARISING OUT OF THE USE OR INABILITY TO USE THE PROGRAM (INCLUDING BUT NOT LIMITED TO LOSS OF DATA OR DATA BEING RENDERED INACCURATE OR LOSSES SUSTAINED BY YOU OR THIRD PARTIES OR A FAILURE OF THE PROGRAM TO OPERATE WITH ANY OTHER PROGRAMS), EVEN IF SUCH HOLDER OR OTHER PARTY HAS BEEN ADVISED OF THE POSSIBILITY OF SUCH DAMAGES.

END OF TERMS AND CONDITIONS